Wakefield Press

Murder in the Colony

Paul Tucker was born into a military service family, and in his younger years lived in England, Europe and South-East Asia. His family settled in South Australia in 1973. In 1990 he joined the South Australia Police.

In January 2000 Paul was seconded to the Major Crime Investigation Branch (MCIB) to assist in the investigation into the murder of Robert Sabeckis in Maslin Beach. In June 2003 Paul obtained a permanent position at MCIB. During his time there he has attended over 100 suspicious death and murder scenes and has reviewed several cold cases, including the Family Murders.

Paul has been awarded the National Police Service Medal, the National Medal, the Australian Defence Medal and the South Australia Police Service Medal.

Paul lives with his wife and two adult children in Adelaide, and enjoys four-wheel driving, gardening and South Australian wine.

Murder in the Colony

South Australian Homicides, 1836–1886

PAUL TUCKER

Wakefield
Press

Wakefield Press
16 Rose Street
Mile End
South Australia 5031
www.wakefieldpress.com.au

First published 2022

Cover designed by Stacey Zass
Edited by Maddy Sexton, Wakefield Press
Typeset by Michael Deves, Wakefield Press

ISBN 978 1 74305 903 6

A catalogue record for this
book is available from the
National Library of Australia

Wakefield Press thanks
Coriole Vineyards for
continued support

Aboriginal and Torres Strait Islanders are warned that this publication contains names and images of deceased persons.

Contents

List of homicides in chronological order

Foreword

Chris Kourakis

It is a common misconception that judges are isolated and out of touch with their community. The reality is that through the cases they hear, particularly in the criminal jurisdiction, judges have a wider and deeper understanding of the struggles and dysfunction on the one hand, and the aspirations and common humanity on the other, of the people amongst whom they live. That is why Paul Tucker's chronicle of murders committed in South Australia, from the founding of the colony in 1836 and for the next 50 years, taps a rich source of information about the nascent South Australian community.

In this preface, I can do little more than sketch some broad themes about the early history of South Australia which Mr Tucker's painstakingly careful compilation reveals. The first is the establishment of British rule over the Aboriginal inhabitants of the colony through the enforcement of criminal law. The British Crown's declaration of sovereignty, and the recognition of Aboriginal people as British subjects governed by its laws, resulted in colonisation, not by military force, but by police and justice agencies. That process can be traced through the newspaper reports and court records of the arrest, charging and trial of Aboriginal defendants which are the primary sources for Mr Tucker's work.

Historical records do manifest some early intentions to apply British laws fairly to the indigenous inhabitants of the land over which the colony was established. So much is evident from the first known murder proceedings in the colony. The accused was an indigenous resident of Kangaroo Island, Reppindjeri, who was charged with the murder of a whaler who coveted Reppindjeri's wives. The only witnesses to the killing of the whaler were Aboriginals, who were not then recognised by the common law as competent to give evidence because they were not Christians. The only Justice of the

Supreme Court, Sir John Jeffcott, thought that he should first consult with Tasmanian judges on how to manage the 'first case in which any of the Aboriginal natives will be rendered amenable to our law' and about the 'many serious questions which will arise out of such a case'. However, on 12 December 1837, before he could reach Tasmania, Sir John Jeffcott drowned when the whale boat by which he was attempting to reach his ship overturned. Governor Hindmarsh himself reviewed Reppindjeri's case and decided that it was not murder but justifiable homicide. In the meantime, Reppindjeri managed to escape and no attempt was made to re-arrest him.

Just four years later the ship *Maria* was wrecked along the Coorong coast after leaving Port Adelaide on 26 June 1840. Between 20 and 30 passengers were helped ashore by local Ngarrindjeri, who had given similar assistance to other shipwrecked passages just two years earlier. However, as the passengers were passed from one Ngarrindjeri tribal group to another, a violent altercation broke out and all of the survivors were killed. In contrast to the approach of Governor Hindmarsh in the Reppindjeri case, Governor Gawler sent a band of police officers and sailors headed by the Commissioner of Police to exact retribution. They took over 60 prisoners, and on 22 August 1840 in a bush trial, sentenced two of them to death by hanging on hastily constructed gallows. The hangings caused much controversy and played a part in Governor Gawler's subsequent recall to England.

On 5 October 1840 Frank Hawson, a 10-year-old child, was left in a station hut at Kirton Point adjacent to the Port Lincoln township. He was speared when he confronted a group of Aboriginal men with a sword and a gun. His death so inflamed tempers that Governor Gawler, acting more prudently than he had in the case of the *Maria*, issued the following proclamation and warning:

Whereas an aggravated outrage has recently been committed by natives in the neighbourhood of Port Lincoln … I … do give notice and warning that the colonial government is ready to use all proper precautions for the protection of the colonists … and further that any persons who may use violent retaliatory measures against the natives, except in the most urgently necessary actual defence of life and property, will render themselves liable to be dealt with according to the extreme rigour of the law.

The harsh treatment of workers in the early days of the Colony is also illustrated by the charging of John Dutton, the 'chief head-man' of a whaling enterprise conducted on Granite Island, with the manslaughter of one of his workers. The worker drowned whilst escaping from Granite Island, where he had been chained and beaten.

There is also mention of an Aboriginal man who is referred to as a native mounted constable, possibly the first to be referred by that title. The officer, Melicka, was from the Mount Remarkable region and therefore possibly a Nukunu or Ngadjuri man. Melicka was attacked and stabbed in revenge for his part in apprehending an Aboriginal accused of murder some weeks earlier.

Perhaps most alarming is the statistical analysis of the data which reveals that of the 391 murder victims in that period, 116 were children and most of them were newborns. The high rate of infanticide reflected the abuse of young women and the harsh conditions of life in 50 years after the colony was founded.

I first met Paul Tucker when I defended a person who was on trial for a double murder. Some years later, as Solicitor General, I prosecuted a drug trafficking related murder, and Mr Tucker was one of the investigating officers. The prosecution case owed much to his careful, patient and diligent work in producing schedules and charts, which tracked the movements of the accused on the night of the murder by reference to positional data emitted by his mobile telephone, security footage from the premises he visited, and electronic records of his purchases. Those same skills are evident in this publication.

I commend Mr Tucker's text to anyone with an interest in the early history of South Australia, or in the frailties of the human condition generally. Its index, which includes the names not only of the accused but of the victims and known witnesses, makes the book a useful reference source for those who may wish to trace their family histories. The book is also a comprehensive data set which will provide a rich source of material to be mined by historians and sociologists in the study of the life of the settlers, and the peoples they dispossessed, in the 50 years following the establishment of South Australia.

The Honourable Chris Kourakis
Chief Justice of the Supreme Court of South Australia

Foreword

Michael David QC

'When I entered the legal profession in 1969, I had the impression that there was about one murder trial in the Supreme Court per year.

When I reached the statutory age of judicial retirement, the impression I have is that there is one per week.

Murder trials, despite their tragedy and sadness, have captivated people's interest and imagination for centuries. One can hardly see a film, read a book or watch television without a murder trial playing some part in the story.

South Australia has a reputation for the number of its murder trials which involve macabre factual situations and unresolved mystery.

This book is a fascinating and detailed anthology of virtually all recorded murder trials from the date of the proclamation of South Australia as a colony on 28 December 1836 for the next fifty years. Not only will it enthral those interested in the criminal law and the early history of South Australia, but also general readers of mystery and crime.

As I have already mentioned, it deals with the first fifty years of colonial life in South Australia. I hope there is more to come.'

The Honourable Michael David QC

Acknowledgements

The information used to compile this book has been obtained from various areas, including the National Library of Australia, the State Library of South Australia, the South Australian Supreme Court, the Records Management Unit of the South Australian Police, the South Australia Police Historical Society, the Australian Institute of Criminology and State Records of South Australia.

During the course of writing this book, I have had the valued assistance of Roger Byard, Mike Eichner, Paul Fallon, Nigel Hunt, Greg Hutchins, Peter Lines, Sandi McDonald, Michael Newbury and Tim Przibilla who read the manuscript and provided constructive comments.

I would like to thank Craig Rowley and Zenjo Babij from the Records Management Unit of SAPOL for going out of their way to find and retrieve historical documents for me.

Dorothy Pyatt OAM and Kathryn Woodcock from the South Australia Police Historical Society greatly assisted me in locating photographs, many of which have been used in this book. I thank them for their help.

I thank The Honourable Chief Justice Christopher Kourakis, The Honourable Michael David and Professor Roger Byard AO for their comments.

Glossary

Affidavit	A written statement confirmed by oath or affirmation, for use as evidence in court
Apoplexy	A stroke resulting from a brain haemorrhage
Approver	A person who confesses to a crime and accuses another of being involved
Articulo mortis	A Latin phrase meaning 'at the point of death' (see also: *extremis*)
Asphyxia	A condition arising when the body is deprived of oxygen, causing unconsciousness or death
Belaying pin	A solid metal or wooden device used on traditionally rigged sailing vessels to secure lines of running rigging. Largely replaced on most modern vessels by cleats, they are still used, particularly on square-rigged ships
Blackguard	A person, usually a man, who is not honest or fair and has no moral principles
Brigantine	A two-masted sailing ship with a square-rigged foremast and a mainmast rigged fore and aft
Chaff	Chopped hay and straw used as fodder
Chaff house	A subsidiary building used on a farm to store fodder
Chaffing	To mock, tease or jest in a good-natured way
Commuted sentence	The shortening of a term of punishment or lowering of the level of punishment; for example, a sentence of death may be commuted to life in prison
Confinement	Concluding state of pregnancy, from the onset of contractions to the birth of a child
Corroboree	An assembly of Aboriginal people typified by singing and dancing, sometimes associated with traditional sacred rites
Cutta	An Aboriginal weapon

Dog-cart	A light, two-wheeled, horse-drawn vehicle for ordinary driving, with two transverse seats back to back, and originally having a box under the rear seat for carrying a dog
Dray	A vehicle used to haul goods, especially one used to carry heavy loads
Dropsy	An old term for the swelling of soft tissues due to the accumulation of excess water
Dying Declaration	An oral or written statement by a person on the point of death concerning the cause of their death
Effusion	The escape of a fluid from its natural vessels into a body cavity
Extremis	A Latin phrase meaning 'at the point of death' (see also: *articulo mortis*)
Fowling piece	A shotgun for shooting wild fowl
Full Court	A court of law with a greater than normal number of judges
Growling	Aboriginal colloquialism for an argument or fight
Gunwale	The upper edge or planking of the side of a boat or ship
Hearsay evidence	Evidence based on what has been reported to a witness by others rather that what he or she has observed or experienced (not generally admissible as evidence)
Kirra	Boomerang
Laudanum	An alcoholic solution containing morphine, prepared from opium and formerly used as a narcotic painkiller
Laying/ laid/ to lay an information	Giving a magistrate a concise statement (an information), verbally or in writing, of an alleged offence and the suspected offender, so that he can take steps to obtain the appearance of the suspect in court
Lascar	A sailor or militiaman from the Indian Subcontinent or other countries east of the Cape of Good Hope, employed on European ships from the 16th century until the middle of the 20th century

Liniment	An embrocation for rubbing on the body to relieve pain, especially one made with oil
Lubra/s	An Aboriginal woman
Lucifers	Friction matches
Marpaung	An Aboriginal weapon
Miami	Hut or shelter
Milk fever	A fever in women caused by infection after childbirth, formerly supposed to be due to the swelling of the breasts with milk
Mustard plaster	A poultice made with mustard
Necrosis	The death of most or all of the cells in an organ or tissue due to disease, injury, or failure of the blood supply
Nolle prosequi	A Latin phrase meaning 'will no longer prosecute' or a variation on the same; it amounts to a dismissal of charges by the prosecution
Open verdict	A legal decision that records a death but does not state its cause
Orange-man	An international Protestant fraternal order based in Northern Ireland
Ostler	A man employed to look after the horses of people staying at an inn
Parley	A conference between opposing sides in a dispute, especially a discussion of terms for an armistice
Peritoneum	The serous membrane lining the cavity of the abdomen and covering the abdominal organs
Peritonitis	Inflammation of the peritoneum, typically caused by bacterial infection either via the blood or after rupture of an abdominal organ
Phthisis	A progressively wasting or consumptive condition, especially pulmonary tuberculosis
Picaninny gun	A small gun or pistol
Ponta	An Aboriginal word meaning stone

Poultice	A soft, moist mass of material, typically consisting of bran, flour, herbs etc., applied to the body to relieve soreness and inflammation
Protector of Aborigines	A government appointed position to watch over the rights of Indigenous Australians
Provocation	When a person is considered to have committed a criminal act partly because of a preceding set of events that might cause a reasonable person to lose self-control. This makes them less morally culpable than if the act was premeditated and done out of pure malice.
Recognisance	A bond by which a person undertakes before a court or magistrate to observe some condition, especially to appear when summoned
Roadstead	A place outside of a harbour where a ship can lie at anchor
Suffusion	A spreading out of a body fluid from a vessel into the surrounding tissues.
Surety, sureties	A person who is obligated by a contract under which one person agrees to pay a debt or perform a duty if the other person who is bound to pay the debt or perform the duty fails to do so
Waddy	An Aboriginal weapon
Wurley	An Aboriginal hut
Yamstick	A hardwood stick three or four feet in length with edged or pointed ends used by Aboriginal women for digging (as roots or bulbs)

Introduction

In the 50 years following the Proclamation of South Australia on 28 December 1836, 391 settlers and Aboriginal people were murdered. The data from these murders shows that of the 391 victims, 275 were adults, 116 (29.7%) were children and over half of those (58.6%) were newborns.

This book details those murders, committed between 28 December 1836 and 30 June 1886, including the worst recorded massacre in South Australia's history where 25 shipwreck survivors were killed.

On 26 June 1840 the *Maria* left Port Adelaide bound for Tasmania, but became shipwrecked off the Coorong. The survivors made it ashore and were assisted by a tribe of local inhabitants. While they were being guided back to Adelaide, all the survivors, including women and children, were killed. A party including 12 police and 11 sailors were sent from Adelaide to investigate. This resulted in the hanging of two Aboriginal men without a proper trial.

This was not the only massacre. In March 1849 James Brown was accused of shooting nine Aboriginal people, and in the following month, Patrick Dwyer was accused of poisoning five Aboriginal people. In 1877, William McGowan was charged with the murder of nine Europeans, after they drowned at Port Wakefield. These events were investigated but the prosecution against Brown fell apart due to no European witnesses. Dwyer escaped to California and McGowan was found not guilty.

The investigation of a death in colonial South Australia differed significantly to the current process of public prosecution. When the body of a deceased person was found, a coronial inquest was held as soon as possible. The body was either left in situ or taken to the nearest public house or hospital. A jury would be formed and at the start of the inquest they would view the body.

The coroner would authorise a post-mortem to be carried out, and the inquest would be adjourned. At the completion of the post-mortem, the inquest resumed and evidence was given. If the death was considered suspicious, the suspect would also be present.

During the inquest, the jury and the suspect all had the opportunity to ask a witness any question. At the completion of an inquest, the jury could find the suspect not guilty or guilty of murder or manslaughter. If the suspect was found guilty they were committed to trial at the Supreme Court.

Up until 1852, the evidence was sent to a grand jury in the Supreme Court. The grand jury, after reviewing the evidence, could accept or reject the case for trial. If the evidence was accepted, the trial would then commence before another jury. After 1852 the process of presenting evidence before the grand jury was abolished.

This process was certainly quick, as seen in the murder of William Duffield on 21 April 1839. The accused were located, sent to trial in the Supreme Court, sentenced to death and executed on 31 May 1839.

There have been many publications and academic papers written on the 'frontier wars' detailing the conflict between the European settlers and local Aboriginal people. The analysis of the data used to compile *South Australian Homicides* indicated that:

- Europeans were accused of murdering of 237 Europeans and 31 Aboriginal people
- Aboriginal people were accused of murdering 73 Europeans and 46 Aboriginal people.

For the offences of murder and manslaughter, sentences ranged from a few weeks imprisonment to the death penalty. The data from the 391 murders shows that 66 offenders were sentenced to death. Of those, 26 were commuted to a term of imprisonment and 40 were executed. Of those executions, 24 were Aboriginal, 15 were European and 1 was Asian. No Aboriginal people were executed for the murder of another Aboriginal person, and the only European executed for the murder of an Aboriginal person was Thomas Donelly in 1846.

A total of four women were sentenced to death. Three were commuted to a term of imprisonment while Elizabeth Woolcock, who was found guilty of poisoning her husband, is the only woman to have been executed in South Australia.

South Australian records do not contain a definitive list of murders committed in the early years. During the first 50 years of colonisation, 391 murders were reported. Although that does appear to be a long list, it is by no means conclusive. It is almost certain that additional murders occurred which were not reported to the authorities, or reported on in the newspapers at the time.

This book sets out, where the information is available, the circumstances of each of the reported murders, including details of the victims, offenders, their relationships, locations and the cause of death.

Some of the language used in the 1800s may by current standards be deemed to be offensive; it has been included to provide an accurate representation of the records.

Early reports of murders and court proceedings are mainly taken from newspaper articles. The information regarding the murder and subsequent court appearance differed between the newspapers, even those which were printed on the same day. The spelling of names, especially Aboriginal names, was sometimes different, even when printed in the same article in the same newspaper.

There are some occasions where a murder has not been counted or included. These include cases where a person kills another and it was found in a court to be a justifiable homicide, or where evidence presented at trial showed that the act of murder did not occur and that the death was otherwise explained. All other recorded murders are included.

The history of South Australia

The accounts of Matthew Flinders, Charles Sturt and other early explorers had shown the new province to be occupied by Aboriginal people, but their numbers, disposition and ways of life were almost entirely unknown in England. The British Colonial Office, keen to avoid the bloodshed that had accompanied the settlement of New South Wales and Tasmania, inserted in the Letters Patent a clause intended to secure the protection of the Aboriginal peoples' rights to land, and forced the colonisation commissioners to make other concessions, including the appointment of a Protector to safeguard Aboriginal interests in the new province.

Aboriginal people had occupied the land for at least 40,000 years. At the time the province was established, there were about 40 tribes across the state, each with its own distinct dialect and territory, but linked to its neighbours by intermarriage and ceremonial and trading links. The Aboriginal people who occupied the eastern shores of Gulf St Vincent lived in extended family groups or clans, each linked to a certain tract of country. The early settlers referred to these clans as the Adelaide tribe, the Willunga tribe, the Rapid Bay tribe, the Gawler tribe and the Para tribe.

Even before the establishment of the province, Aboriginal people in the south-east of the state had had contacts with outsiders. Sealing crews based on Kangaroo Island and other offshore islands since the 1820s had made occasional raids on coastal Aboriginal camps on the Fleurieu, Yorke and Eyre Peninsulas to kidnap women, who were taken back to the islands by the sealers.

In about 1830, smallpox spread down the River Murray from the colonies in eastern Australia and caused great loss of life among Aboriginal people all along the river to its mouth. The disease also spread to the Aboriginal tribes of the Adelaide Plains, the mid-north, and Yorke and Eyre Peninsulas. Early settlers in those regions recorded Aboriginal survivors of the epidemic who bore the distinctive pockmarked scars.

Estimates at the time of colonisation of the total Aboriginal population of the area that became South Australia range from about 10,000 to 20,000 people. Approximately two-thirds of these people lived in the more fertile south-eastern part of the state, including the Adelaide Plains and nearby ranges, the River Murray, and the Coorong and the south-east.

South Australia was an unusual settlement within the British Empire. Unlike the older colonies on Australia's eastern seaboard there were to be no convicts, and this commitment to a 'free' settlement was fiercely maintained. Historians are divided about the lasting impact of the absence of the 'convict taint' on the province's society and culture, but an awareness of difference distinguishes South Australians to this day.

South Australia was also created initially as a commercial and administrative partnership between the British Government (represented in the office of the Governor) and the South Australian Colonization Commission. The precise distribution of administrative powers between these two groups was never adequately defined, and constant conflict between them marked the early years of settlement. To further complicate matters, some members of the Colonization Commission had formed a joint stock company in 1835 to raise sufficient funds in land sales to satisfy the British Government that the new settlement was viable. The South Australian Company became, in effect, the financial basis of the new settlement, building much of the early infrastructure and providing banking and other financial services. In 1836 the first three vessels to leave Britain for the Province, the *John Pirie, Duke of York* and *Cygnet,* were either purchased or chartered by the Company for the voyage.

On 22 February 1836, the first of nine ships, the *John Pirie,* departed for South Australia. On 28 December 1836, Governor John Hindmarsh, accompanied by other officials from the *Buffalo,* came ashore at Holdfast Bay. In the heat of the summer afternoon, under an old gum tree, George Stevenson read the words of the Proclamation of the Province of South Australia:

PROCLAMATION
By His EXCELLENCY JOHN HINDMARSH,
Knight of the Royal Hanoverian Guelphic
Order, Governor and Commander-in-Chief
Of
HIS MAJESTY'S PROVINCE
Of
South Australia.

In announcing to the colonists of His Majesty's Province of South Australia, the establishment of the Government, I hereby call upon them to conduct themselves on all occasions with order and quietness, duly to respect the laws, and by a course of industry and sobriety, by the practice of sound morality, and a strict observance of the Ordinances of Religion, to prove themselves worthy to be the Founders of a great and free Colony.

It is also, at this time especially, my duty to apprize the Colonists of my resolution, to take every lawful means of extending the same protection to the NATIVE POPULATION as to the rest of His Majesty's Subjects, and of my firm determination to punish with exemplary severity, all acts of violence or injustice which may in any manner be practiced or attempted against the NATIVES, who are to be considered as much under the Safeguard of the law as the Colonists themselves, and equally entitled to the privileges of British Subjects. I trust therefore, with confidence to the exercise of moderation and forbearance by all Classes, in their intercourse with the NATIVE INHABITANTS, and that they will omit no opportunity of assisting me to fulfil His Majesty's most gracious and benevolent intentions towards them, by promoting their advancement in civilisation, and ultimately, under the blessing of Divine Providence, the conversion to the Christian Faith.

By his Excellency's command
ROBERT GOUGER,
Colonial Secretary
Glenelg, 28th December, 1836.
GOD SAVE THE KING.

The estimated European population in South Australia grew from 546 in 1836 to 3273 in 1837. As the number of European settlers grew and spread out over South Australia, it was inevitable that contact with Aboriginal tribes increased. After six months of colonisation, the first reported murder in South Australia since Proclamation Day occurred.

Homicide Records

Date	Victim	Accused
June 1837	**John Driscoll**	**Reppindjeri (Alick)**
Cause of death:	Spear wound	
Outcome:	Escaped custody	
Location:	Hindmarsh Valley	

Whaling in South Australia began around the mid to late 1700s when whalers and sealers hunted around the Southern Fleurieu Peninsula. One location where a lookout was set up was at The Bluff in Victor Harbor. This site was chosen as it was 150 metres above sea level, and whales could be seen far from the shore. The whalers and sealers were left there for a period of up to five months to hunt for their prey. When whales were spotted offshore, the whalers would row out to harpoon them, attach a rope to the animals and tow them back to shore.

John Driscoll was one of the whalers working at the Encounter Bay station. One of the local Aboriginal men was called Reppindjeri, who was also known as Black Alick or Elick. Around the time, there was friendly interaction between the whalers and the local Aboriginal population, and some of the whalers had taken Aboriginal wives. In late June 1837, Reppindjeri killed Driscoll somewhere between Hindmarsh Valley and Encounter Bay.

There are several variations on how Driscoll was killed. One is that Reppindjeri, his two wives and Driscoll were travelling together. Reppindjeri offered one of his wives to Driscoll, but Driscoll attempted to take the other wife, offending Reppindjerri. A fight broke out between them during which Reppindjeri stabbed Driscoll. Another theory is that Driscoll had kidnapped and tortured Reppindjeri and then attacked one of his wives, and in the ensuing fight, Driscoll was stabbed. Yet another theory is that there was a quarrel over Driscoll's apparent refusal to pay for sex with one of Reppindjeri's wives, and that during the quarrel Driscoll was stabbed. Either way, the only witnesses to the event were Reppindjeri and his wives. The death was kept quiet within the Aboriginal community until the details of the murder were revealed by a local Aboriginal woman who was the wife of a whaler.

When the whalers heard of the murder, they took Reppindjeri into custody and sent news to Adelaide for the authorities to attend. News of the murder reached Adelaide in late July, and Governor Hindmarsh immediately sent an investigative party to Encounter Bay. The group included Charles Mann, the Advocate General, William Wyatt, the recently appointed 'Protector of Aborigines', Onkaparinga Jack, who acted as a guide, and Cooper, who was an interpreter. On their arrival at Encounter Bay, they found Reppindjeri chained to the deck of Driscoll's ship, the *South Australia*.

Reppindjeri in chains, Police Historical Society, Photograph 9228

The difficulty was that the only witnesses to the crime were Aboriginal. According to British Law at the time, witnesses must have been able to articulate a clear belief in the Christian afterlife before their testimony was legally acceptable in court, and they must be able to swear fidelity before the Christian God. The issue of the legal status of the Aboriginal people was also tested, as the proclamation insisted that the Aboriginal population would receive 'the privileges of British subjects'. The whalers demanded that Reppindjeri was charged with murder and, as the law stated at that time, executed for that crime. However, Mann could not legally execute Reppindjeri.

The party left Encounter Bay and returned to Adelaide with Reppindjeri in custody. On 16 November 1837, Sir John Jeffcott, the first judge of South Australia, wrote a letter to Governor Hindmarsh outlining the failings of the current legal system in the colony. Jeffcott requested permission to travel to Van Diemen's Land and the city of Sydney to consult with the judges there. Jeffcott wrote:

> I am desirous of postponing the holding of a Court of Gaol Delivery until I have an opportunity of consulting with my legal brethren in Van Diemen's Land as to the course which, in the event of such a contingency happening, I ought myself to follow or advise your Excellency to pursue. Besides the cases of Stephens and Wright there is another case about to be brought before me at the approaching sessions about which I feel equal if not greater interest.

Sir John Jeffcott, State Library of South Australian, B 464

It is that of the native accused of murdering a white man, with whom there had been some quarrel about the native's wife, the deceased being a whaler; and, as this will be the first case in which any of the Aboriginal natives will be rendered amenable to our laws, you will readily believe that many serious questions will arise out of such a case upon which I should also wish to have the benefit of the opinion and practical experience of my brother judges at Van Diemen's.

Jeffcott left Adelaide for Van Diemen's Land on 19 November 1837. In early December, while waiting for a ship at Encounter Bay to take him to Van Diemen's Land, Jeffcott joined an expedition to explore the Murray Mouth. On 12 December 1837, Jeffcott was a passenger in an overloaded whaleboat that capsized in rough seas. Jeffcott fell into the water and drowned.

In May 1839, a public meeting concerning the Indigenous population in Adelaide was held. During the meeting, the *South Australian Gazette and Colonial Register*, 11 May 1839, reported:

The black who committed the murder, so frequently alluded to, was brought up to Adelaide by my advice and lodged in the gaol, (I will not say a place of security) on a charge of murder. This man was allowed to wander from that gaol, to go down alone and unaccompanied to the river to draw water for the marines, and one fine morning, thinking the other side of the river preferable, he makes his escape.

On 30 December 1889, Mr A Lindsay wrote a letter to the *South Australian Register*. In the letter he states that he recalled the murder in 1837, which was the first instance of an Aboriginal person killing a European after the foundation of the colony. He stated that it was thought at the time that to spare the life of 'the poor wretch' would be dangerous to the white man. Lindsay went on to say that Reppindjeri was of the large Encounter Bay tribe and had two wives, and that he very liberally made a present of one of them to a whaler named John Driscoll. Everything went on amicably for some time, till Driscoll, Reppindjeri, and the two women started for a trip to Adelaide. Driscoll began taking liberties with the woman who had not been given to him, to which Reppindjeri objected. The men quarrelled, and eventually the pair came to blows, until finally Driscoll was killed.

Reppindjeri was taken prisoner by the whalers, coopered up in an oil cask, and fed through the bunghole until he could be sent by sea to Adelaide for his trial. There was no gaol in Adelaide at that time, and Reppindjeri was kept chained up pending his trial at the marine's tents. Governor Hindmarsh had taken 22 marines out of HMS *Buffalo* to act as a police force. Before the trial could begin, the Governor himself investigated the case and came to the conclusion that the killing of Driscoll was not murder but justifiable homicide. One morning, around the same time that Jeffcott drowned, Reppindjeri escaped and no attempt was made to re-arrest him. Reppindjeri was well known at Encounter Bay for many years afterwards as the black fellow who had killed Driscoll.

Date	*Victim*	*Accused*
5 July 1837	**Aboriginal Woman**	**Aboriginal Man**
Cause of death:	Stab wounds, strangulation	
Outcome:	No action taken	
Location:	Adelaide	

It did not take long for the settlers in Adelaide to have firsthand knowledge of a murder. On 8 July 1837, in the *South Australian Gazette and Colonial Register*, under the heading 'Murder of a Native Woman' the following information was printed:

Temporary accommodation erected near the site chosen for the city of Adelaide, 1837, reproduction of a sketch by Colonel William Light.
State Library of South Australia, PRG 280/1/5/213.

A few days ago, a native woman was murdered by a chief, under circumstances which we are at a loss to describe, as being warranted by certain laws of their own, or the result of private revenge. There are two stories regarding this murder. One is that the woman belonged to a different tribe, and repudiated by her husband, was taken as a wife by a man of another tribe. The former husband followed her to Adelaide, accompanied by another, first stabbed her in the side, and then strangled her. The other version of the affair is; that the son of a chief refused to fight with a man of another tribe, and the chief decided that if his son would not fight, he should give up one of his wives. This was done, and the woman immediately murdered by the party to whom she was given up, as we have described. The body was buried by the Natives near the river.

No other record of this murder could be found.

Date	*Victim*	*Accused*
8 March 1838	**Enoch Pegler**	**William and George**
Cause of death:	Spear wound (kangaroo bone spear)	
Outcome:	Both escaped custody	
Location:	Port Adelaide	

On 6 December 1837, Enoch Pegler, a 24-year-old labourer, arrived in South Australia on board the *Navarino* from Gravesend. On Thursday 8 March 1838, Pegler was in the Port Adelaide area, near the Port River. Pegler had been drinking during the day and was under the influence of alcohol as he was seen staggering when trying to walk. That night as Pegler approached the river, he saw a group of Aboriginal people who were conducting a traditional ceremony. Pegler went to the group and tried to sit down between a man and a woman. Pegler was drunk and became a nuisance to all those in the group. Pegler's actions had interrupted the ceremony, which the group took great offence to. A number of Aboriginal men surrounded Pegler and one plunged a sharpened kangaroo bone into his heart. Pegler fell to the ground and died.

Pegler was found at around 6.30 the following morning by John Cavanagh, lying on a path about 30 metres from the Port River. When found, the body was cold to touch and there was a wound to his chest, which Cavanagh thought was caused by a spear of some type. When Cavanagh called out to two men who were thatching, he noticed several Aboriginal

Port Adelaide in 1844, from G.F Gregory's sketch.
State Library of South Australia, B7207

people on the south side of the river who shouted and held up their spears.

William Williams was working at the Commissioner's store when he was told that a man had been found dead. Williams spoke to several Indigenous people and found out that two men named William and George had committed the murder.

James Cronk, the assistant to the Protector, went in pursuit of the suspects upon hearing that a man had been killed. Cronk had been told that Pegler had been stabbed while asleep, drunk, reportedly because Europeans had killed four dogs belonging to local Aboriginal people. An Aboriginal boy corroborated Cronk's story that William and George had committed the murder. The boy was promised ten loaves of bread when he pointed out the two men.

On Friday 9 March, at Mr Lillyman's brewery, Mr George Stevenson Esq was specially appointed as a coroner to conduct an inquest into Pegler's death. The jury visited the spot where the body was found, and then returned to the brewery where the inquest resumed. Pegler's body was inspected by Dr Cotter, Dr Woodforde and Dr Gill, who found a spear wound in the chest that had pierced the heart. There were no other injuries and, due to the thought that death would have been instantaneous, it was thought there was no struggle. The inquest was adjourned for further investigation and resumed the following day.

William Williams testified that he had been told William and George were the murderers, but that they could not be found. Williams also presented two instruments to the coroner, one made of wood and another made from kangaroo bone. Williams told the coroner that these items were used as spears and that one was the murder weapon.

No further information on the identity of the offenders was obtained and the coroner handed down the verdict that 'the deceased, Enoch Pegler, was wilfully murdered by a native or natives unknown'. After further investigation, William and George, who were brothers, were captured and placed in irons. They were held in one of the tents, under the guard of one of the marines. During the night they both escaped with their irons on. The following year, George was caught, tried and executed for the murder of William Duffield (see 1 April 1839).

Date	Victim	Accused
August 1838	**Roach and Delve**	**Pilgarie**
Cause of death:	Assault (with a waddy)	
Outcome:	Found guilty of murder	
	Sentenced to death, executed 22 August 1840	
Location:	Cape Jaffa	

On 22 June 1838, the schooner *Fanny* was travelling between Hobart and King George Sound in Western Australia. The boat ran ashore in a squall near Cape Jaffa. A line was fastened to the shore and the passengers and crew all made it to dry land. Local Aboriginal people helped the survivors light fires and showed them the location of permanent waterholes.

Later, in early August, two men named Roach and Delve belonging to a fishery company in Encounter Bay went to the wreck of the *Fanny*, but were never heard from again. Three men went in search of them, finding only their clothes. Everything belonging to the wreck that was on shore was ransacked. It was suspected that local Aboriginal people had murdered Roach and Delve.

It was not until the *Maria* massacre (see July 1840) that the fate of Roach and Delve was confirmed. During the investigation into the *Maria*, local Aboriginal people identified a man from their tribe called Pilgarie as being one of those responsible for the murders of Roach and Delve. They stated that both were killed while they were sitting down by a blow of a waddy from behind. Pilgarie and another Aboriginal man named Mongarawata were both executed for the *Maria* massacre.

Date	*Victim*	*Accused*
21 April 1839	**William Duffield**	**Yerr-i-cha (George), Monichi Yumbena (Peter), and Parloobooka (Williamy)**
Cause of death:	Spear wound	
Outcome:	Yerr-i-cha found guilty of murder	
	Sentenced to death, executed 31 May 1839	
	Monichi Yumbena and Parloobooka found not guilty	
Location:	Torrens River	

Hearsay evidence is defined as second-hand evidence. It is not what a witness knows personally, but what someone else had told them. One exception to hearsay evidence is a dying declaration. The earliest incident of the admission of a dying declaration by a Court was in 1202. The medieval English courts adopted the principle of *Nemo moriturus praesumitur mentiri*: 'A dying person is not presumed to lie'. During the 12th century reign of Richard the Lionheart, when Christianity infused daily life, the courts assumed that murder victims would be afraid to risk God's wrath by uttering false last words.

The first time a dying declaration was accepted during a murder trial in South Australia was on Wednesday 22 May 1839 at the Supreme Court where three Aboriginal men were on trial for the murder of William Duffield.

On the morning of 21 April 1839, 46-year-old William Duffield was tending his sheep on the Torrens River, about seven miles out of Adelaide, when he saw a large group of Aboriginal people. Three of them left the main group and approached Duffield. The three men tried to draw Duffield's attention to the sheep, pointing at them and saying, 'plenty sheepy over there'. While Duffield was distracted, one of the three hit him with a waddy. Duffield fell to the ground and was held down while one of the men thrust a spear into his belly. The three left Duffield on the ground, taking some sheep with them.

Duffield was found alive and was attended to by Dr Nash. He was transported back to Adelaide, and was able to describe what had happened during the journey. Duffield provided Dr Nash with a description of the Aboriginal men and of the two dogs with them. Duffield considered himself in great danger of dying and said, 'The black rascals have done for me'. Duffield also told Mr Wigley, the resident magistrate, what had happened. Duffield later died from his injuries.

Three Aboriginal men, known as Parloobooka, Yerr-i-cha and Monichi Yumbena, were apprehended at the Para River by Captain Walker, who had recognised them after reading their descriptions in the newspaper. They were transported to Adelaide and kept in custody. While in custody they were visited by William Oldham, a teacher, and were shown a spear, which had traces of blood on it. Parloobooka stated the spear was his but said that the blood belonged to a possum or kangaroo. Yerr-i-cha was asked where he was when Duffield was murdered, and he stated that he was at the Para River but was not involved in the murder. Yerr-i-cha confessed to killing some sheep, and admitted to another witness that he was present with his two dogs when the white man was knocked down, but got frightened and ran away.

On Wednesday 22 May, Yerr-i-cha, Monichi Yumbena and Parloobooka appeared before the Supreme Court charged with the murder of William Duffield. The indictment was read and explained to them by James Cronk, who was sworn in as the interpreter. The advocate general, in opening the case, said:

> It has hitherto been the wide and benevolent practice of the inhabitants of this colony to treat the Aborigines with kindness and tolerance. The page of history is sullied with many and great atrocities committed by Europeans on the Aborigines in the West, but we may proudly boast that no South Australian has yet imbrued his hands in the blood of a native – they have invariably been treated with kindness. If we have encroached upon their hunting grounds, and scared away their game, we have given them food in return. We have conferred upon them recompense in granting them the glorious rights and privileges of British subjects.

He further stated,

> I am sure we all long to make them Christians, useful members of society, and valuable inhabitants of the colony, but in order to this, it must be impressed on their minds to pay respect to the proper

authorities. They have already seen many Englishmen punished for various offences, and one execution, I allude to the unhappy affair of Magee. If they want equal justice administered to them as well as to ourselves, if they find we treat them as we treat each other, they will soon learn to respect our laws ... When a murder is committed amongst themselves, I am led to understand they require blood for blood, but amongst them as amongst all other uncivilized nations, the friends of the deceased are the parties who administer justice. They, therefore, cannot wonder if we should punish them for committing that crime upon us.

The trial commenced and Mr Wigley gave evidence about what Duffield had told him before his death. In answer to a question from the judge, Wigley said that Duffield considered himself in imminent danger, but hoped that he should get better at the time he described the attack. Mr Mann, for the defence, contended that it was absolutely necessary for the admission of evidence, if not having been taken in the presence of the prisoners, that it should not only be in *extremis*, but in *articulo mortis*. The advocate general argued that his expressing himself to be in 'imminent danger was sufficient to admit the evidence'. His Honour ruled that the evidence was inadmissible.

Dr Nash, in his evidence, stated what Duffield had told him before his death. Mr Mann contended that this evidence was also not admissible, for he did not think that the deceased could be said to have made these statements in *articulo mortis*. His Honour ruled the evidence to be admissible, as he considered that the deceased imagined that he was about to die at the time he made the statements to Nash.

Nash also gave evidence that the spear shown to him was similar to the instrument that caused the fatal injury to Duffield, and that it entered the body to a depth of about eight inches.

At the completion of the one-day trial, the jury retired then returned after a considerable time, finding Yerr-i-cha guilty of the murder, and Monichi Yumbena and Parloobooka not guilty. The following day, on Thursday 23 May, Yerr-i-cha was sentenced to death. He was executed eight days later on 31 May 1839.

Date	Victim	Accused
26 April 1839	**James Thompson**	**Picta CulNaena (Tam O'Shanter), Wang Nucha (Tommy Round Head), and Tippa-Wair-i-Cha (Bob)**

Cause of death:	Assault (unknown weapon)
Outcome:	Wang Nucha found guilty of murder
	Sentenced to death, executed 31 May 1839
	Picta CulNaena and Tippa-Wair-i-Cha found not guilty
Location:	Gilles Plains

James Thompson was last seen alive when he took his flock out on the morning of 26 April 1839. Thompson took his gun and his two dogs with him. When Thompson did not return for breakfast, Cox, the hutkeeper, went looking for him. Cox located Thompson's 200 head of sheep, which were scattered and 'looked terrified'. Cox took them home and returned to the paddock where he saw 120 sheep with three Aboriginal men beside them, one of whom was called Bob. Bob threw a spear at Cox, and Cox fired a shot in return. Cox fired another shot and Bob ran off. Cox searched the area, and eventually located Thompson's body.

During the search for the three men responsible for the murder of William Duffield, which occurred five days before Thompson's, the search party, who had been tracking the men for several days, were near the Para River when they came across Mr Jacobs who informed them of Thompson's murder. Jacobs told the party that he had seen two Aboriginal men with two dogs the day before. The search party continued when they came across two Aboriginal people who told them of another group, including a man called Picta CulNaena, camped by the river. The search party continued and located a campsite and spoke to Picta CulNaena, who had not seen any other Aboriginal people.

The search party continued, and later that day it met with Mr Kerville. While they were talking to him a young Aboriginal boy arrived and told them that Picta CulNaena was Thompson's killer. The search party returned to Picta CulNaena's camp and took him and others into custody.

Picta-CulNaena (Tam O'Shanter), Wang Nucha (Tommy Round Head) and Tippa-Wair-i-Cha (Bob) were all charged with Thompson's murder and appeared before the Supreme Court on Thursday 23 May. During the trial evidence was given by Mr Cotter, who stated he had examined Thompson's body and found the skull fractured, apparently caused by a blow or a succession of blows, and he thought that due to the state of the skull, death must have been instant.

At the completion of the trial, Picta-CulNaena and Tippa-Wair-i-Cha were found not guilty. Wang Nucha was found guilty of the murder and was sentenced to death.

On Monday 27 May, Picta-CulNaena and Tippa-Wair-i-Cha were charged with killing and stealing sheep. The advocate general did not have sufficient evidence to proceed, so Picta-CulNaena was released. Tippa-Wair-i-Cha was then charged with throwing spears at Mr Cox with intent to murder. Tippa-Wair-i-Cha was found guilty and sentenced to 12 months imprisonment with hard labour.

On Friday 31 May 1839, Wang Nucha and Yerr-i-Cha (Duffield's murderer) were hung in the Parklands in North Adelaide. The executions were reported in the newspaper the following day, along with the following passage:

> One circumstance connected with this execution we must not neglect to notice. It seemed quite evident, from the remarks and conversation of the other natives, many of whom witnessed the execution, that they were aware of the cause of the death of the criminals, and most of them seemed to agree in the justness of the sentence; and we have no doubt but the example thus shown them will act as a terror to them, and will be a means of deterring them in future from interfering in any way with the property or lives of the settlers.

Date	*Victim*	*Accused*
August 1839	**Alexander Riches**	**John Dutton**
Cause of death:	Drowned	
Outcome:	Acquitted	
Location:	Encounter Bay	

John Dutton and Alexander Riches worked together at the whaling station on Granite Island at Encounter Bay. In early August 1839, Dutton, who was the chief Head Man, received information that a group of men were determined to abscond, taking with them some whale oil. Dutton organised for a watch to be stationed at night. That night, the men on the watch took into custody two men who had entered the area where the whale oil was kept, without being able to explain why they were there.

Dutton went to the huts where all of the whalers were sleeping. He ordered them out of bed, and, after tying their hands behind their back, fastened them all to a chain. While detaining them, he struck some of the men with his fist. A group of the men, including Alexander Riches, broke free from their chains, and went down to the reef, which was used as a crossing to the mainland at low tide. Riches attempted to cross first, as he had crossed frequently before. The water proved too deep, and Riches slipped into a hole and was not seen again. It was presumed that he drowned.

Soon after that, two men managed to get across to the mainland and went to Mr Strangways, a magistrate, to ask him to take action. Strangways refused so the men travelled to Adelaide and made a deposition against Dutton before Mr Wigley, the resident magistrate, who sent them to the advocate general. The advocate general stated that he must either have the case investigated before a magistrate who could go to Granite Island, or issue a warrant to apprehend Dutton.

The law at that time was that if anyone placed a man in confinement, with threats of violence towards him, and the man, in escaping from that confinement and threat, met with his death accidentally, the party who confined him would be guilty of manslaughter.

Mr Morphett, a magistrate, attended and obtained evidence in the presence of the police sergeant and other unknown gentlemen. They discovered that it seemed doubtful whether Riches was drowned at all, as his body had not been found, although a search had been made for it. Also, a man who was with Riches in the water swore that he would not have any fear of violence if he had returned to work. The case was dropped.

Riches' body was later found and buried. This information was sent to the government, and the coroner ordered to have the body disinterred for the purpose of holding an inquest. After a lengthy examination, a verdict of manslaughter against Dutton was returned. Dutton was taken into custody and refused bail.

On Wednesday 6 November 1839, Dutton appeared before the Supreme Court charged with inflicting several mortal wounds on Riches' body by kicking and striking him, and manslaughter. Dutton pleaded not guilty. The advocate general said that in the absence of all the witnesses except one, he was unable to go on with the case. He did, however, state that Dutton's conduct had been most reprehensible. The jury found Dutton not guilty of manslaughter and he was released.

Encounter Bay. The view is taken from the road leading to Mr Strangway's station, looking southwards over Victor Harbour, towards Granite Island, and Wright Island, with the conical bluff of Rosetta Head stretching out to the west.
George French Angas. State Library of South Australia, B 15276/16 Plate 16

Date	*Victim*	*Accused*
November 1839	**Thomas Young**	**Aboriginal people**
Cause of death:	Spear wounds, assault	
Outcome:	Offenders not located	
Location:	River Murray	

In November 1839, at an unspecified location near the River Murray, Thomas Young was tending to a flock of sheep. Young was employed by Mr Mackinnon as a sub-overseer. In early November, Young was returning to the camp from tending his flock when he was approached by a group of Aboriginal people who spoke to Young in their own language. While they were talking, Young was attacked and beaten to the ground. He was stuck with waddies and was speared many times. His attackers left him on the ground and stole some sheep.

As Young did not return to the camp, some co-workers went looking for him. Young was found lying on the ground and barely alive. He was taken back to the camp where he explained what had happened. Young died two days later from his injuries. The offenders were never located.

Around that time there were several attacks on sheep farmers, and on occasions the number of Aboriginal attackers numbered around 300. The attacks were usually quelled by firing a few shots at them, and in some cases, several Aboriginal people were injured.

Date	*Victim*	*Accused*
11 May 1840	**Sydney child**	**Dr Richard Manifold**
Cause of death:	Medical procedure	
Outcome:	Discharged	
Location:	Port Lincoln	

On 11 May 1840 in Port Lincoln, Mrs Sydney was approaching her full term of pregnancy and was close to giving birth. Mrs Sydney was assisted by a nurse and two other women, who ended up calling for assistance from 28-year-old Dr Richard Manifold. The birth became very difficult for Sydney, and although Manifold managed to deliver the child, it died within five minutes. The nurse and the other two women remained and assisted Manifold.

A coroner's inquest was held into the death of the child. Dr Manifold, the nurse and the two other women all gave evidence. Dr Harvey and Dr Watkins examined the body, finding that the child had injuries to the left thigh, the left leg, which was fractured in two places, and other injuries around the leg area. The doctors concluded that the injuries to the child were sufficient to cause death.

At the completion of the inquest, the coroner summed up the evidence in the case, and the jury returned the verdict that 'the child met his death by violence, but by whom inflicted, there is no evidence to prove'.

The following morning, Manifold was brought up before the resident magistrate to hear the evidence. During the hearing, the nurse, the two assisting women, and the two doctors were questioned at great length as to what happened during the birth. The investigation lasted several hours, and the resident magistrate postponed the adjudication for several hours, until after he had taken the dispositions of Sydney, who was too ill to attend the examination. Two days later, Sydney's statement was taken, and as a consequence, Manifold was committed to trial for manslaughter.

Manifold was transported to Adelaide. On 11 July 1840, in the Adelaide Supreme Court, Dr Manifold was discharged.

BOSTON BAY, PORT LINCOLN.
FROM A SKETCH IN OCTOBER, 1840.

Boston Bay, Port Lincoln. From a sketch in October 1840. Unknown artist.
State Library of South Australia, B 9483/3

Date	*Victim*	*Accused*
16 June 1840	**Rau child**	**Eleonara Rau**
Cause of death:	Neck/ throat wound	
Outcome:	Found guilty of concealment of birth	
	Sentenced to 12 months imprisonment with hard labour	
Location:	Klemzig	

On 18 November 1838, a group of 21 Lutherans arrived in South Australia on the *Bengalee*. George Fife Angas, who was interested in the emigration of German Lutheran settlers, assisted them in their travel. More Lutherans arrived over the following days. They hired several bullock drays and made their way inland. Angas owned sections 491 and 492 of land, which were situated on the northern bank of the River Torrens to the north-east of Adelaide. When the settlers arrived, they established the village of Klemzig, named after their hometown in Prussia. The village grew and the first Lutheran church and school in Australia were built. By 1840 there were 209 inhabitants living in 34 houses. 268 acres had been fenced into paddocks planted with wheat, barley and potatoes.

Klemzig, German village on the Torrens.
State Library of South Australia, PRG 280/1/40/72

On 16 June 1840, a young woman named Eleonara Rau gave birth to a son. Rau was a single woman who lived with her family. On 2 July 1840 the body of a male infant was found floating in the River Torrens. On 3 and 4 July 1840, an inquest was held at the village into the death of the child. Police Constable William Moore attended the inquest and attempted to find the mother of the child. Evidence was given which indicated that the child had been born alive and must have been killed almost immediately after the birth. The baby's throat had been injured by a sharp, unknown instrument that had separated the arteries.

While at the inquest Constable Moore spoke to the German interpreter and some of the jury, who were also German. Constable Moore was directed to a house in the village where he saw a young woman called Eleonara Rau. Constable Moore apprehended Rau and took her before the resident magistrate, Mr Wigley, for a medical examination. Dr Nash conducted the medical examination and testified that Rau had given birth within the last fortnight. Rau had stated to Dr Nash that she had given birth, wrapped the child in an apron, and put it into a kangaroo hole about a mile from Klemzig. Rau was remanded in custody for a week.

During subsequent hearings, Rau was charged with child murder and concealment of birth. Rau provided a statement in which she admitted giving birth to the child, but said that after a few breaths, the child died. She said the child would not have lived more than 15 minutes, and she did not report the birth, as she wanted to escape the disgrace of having the child. She attested that she did not cut the child's throat and that the injury must have happened while in the water.

In the Supreme Court in early September, the charge of concealment of birth proceeded, but the bill charging Rau with child murder was ignored. Rau pleaded guilty to concealment of birth and was sentenced to 12 months hard labour.

Reproduction of a coloured sketch of the Supreme Court, probably made in the 1840s. The Court stood in Whitmore Square on acre 614 at the south-east corner of the Square, and faced north.
State Library of South Australia, B2132.

Date	*Victim*	*Accused*
July 1840	**Passengers and crew of the *Maria***	**Mongarawata and Pilgarie**
Victims	*Crew*	*Passengers*
	William Smith (Master)	Mrs Smith
	John Tegg (Seaman)	Samuel Denham
	John Griffiths (Seaman)	Ann Denham
	John Durgan (Seaman)	Thomas Denham (12 years)
	James Biggins (Seaman)	Andrew Denham (10 years)
	John Cowley (Seaman)	Fanny Denham (8 years)
	Thomas Rea (Seaman)	Walter Denham (6 years)
	George Leigh (Boy)	Anna Denham (4 years)
	James Parsons (Cook)	James Strutt (Denham's servant)
	George Green	
	Mrs Green	
	Thomas Daniel	
	Kitty Daniel	
	Mrs York and baby*	
	Alec Murray	
Cause of death:	Spear wounds and/ or beaten	
Outcome:	Mongarawata and Pilgarie found guilty of murder	
	Sentenced to death, executed at the Coorong	
Location:	Coorong	

The wreck of the *Maria*, and subsequent massacre of 15 passengers and 10 crew members by members of a Ngarrindjeri clan, remains the largest massacre in South Australian history. Many details of the massacre remain unknown.

The *Maria* was a 136-ton, two-masted brigantine, built in Dublin in 1823, and at the time of her wreck was trading the southern waters of Australia with passengers and goods. The *Maria* left Adelaide on Saturday 20 June 1840, bound for Hobart Town, with no cargo and only the passengers and crew on board. About two days into their 15-day voyage, they hit a notorious submerged reef at Cape Jaffa during a storm. All the passengers and crew made it safely to shore in *Maria's* lifeboat, and even had time to rescue gold sovereigns, letters, muskets and a large bible. The lifeboat, hopelessly overloaded and unable to get back to the nearest civilisation at Encounter Bay, was abandoned at Kingston leaving the survivors to walk 190 kilometres back to Encounter Bay across the Coorong dunes. They initially tried to mark their distressed location to passing ships by erecting planks of timber upright at one-mile intervals along the shoreline.

The party was probably first met by Aboriginal people from the local Boandik tribe, who assisted them as far as their tribal boundary at Salt Creek. Here they were handed to the neighbouring Ngarrindjeri tribe, who took them along the Coorong showing them waterholes, fishing for them and even carrying their children. The survivors were handed from clan to clan as they progressed north-west, with two elderly Aboriginal men acting as guides for the journey. As they neared Lake Albert they came into the custody of the Milmenrura clan. The Milmenrura initially assisted the survivors, but were suspicious that they would not return with clothing and blankets as promised, and feared that the neighbouring Ramindjeri clan would claim the reward for themselves. The Milmenrura split the survivors into five smaller parties, spread them out, and then attacked and murdered them with spears and waddies. Some of the male survivors put up resistance, but it was futile and all were killed. The attackers then stripped clothing from the victims, along with some of their other possessions.

When news of a massacre on the Coorong first reached Encounter Bay on 23 July 1840, the *Maria* had not yet been listed as missing. Lieutenant Pullen and Doctor Penny from Encounter Bay, along with Aboriginal interpreters and other helpers, set out to determine the truth of the rumours. One week later, Pullen's expedition found a grave containing eight white people, some of whom had been dismembered and others cannibalised. He reported this to Governor Gawler in Adelaide, who was facing public outrage now that the massacre had been identified as the *Maria*. There was a risk that colonists would take matters into their own hands and seek revenge. Gawler summonsed the Police Commissioner, Major O'Halloran, and on 14 August 1840 gave him instructions – controversially – to take an expeditionary force to the Coorong with the mission 'to apprehend, and bring to summary justice, the ringleaders in the murder, or any of the murderers (in all not to exceed three)'.

O'Halloran's mounted expedition began on 22 August 1840. The following day they located and captured 45 men, women and children. On 24 August even more were captured, along with two Aboriginal men shot at while trying to escape by swimming away (they apparently survived). A search of nearby

Major O'Halloran's expedition to the Coorong, August 1840, unknown artist. Image obtained from; https://commons.wikimedia.org/wiki/File:Major_O%27Halloran%27s_ expedition_to_the_Coorong,_August_1840_-_Google_Art_Project.jpg
Original artwork at the Art Gallery of South Australia, Adelaide.

wurlies found newspapers, receipts, mail, pages of a bible, and even the *Maria's* ship's log. The captured Aboriginal people identified the ringleader of the massacre, Mongarawata, and assisted the expeditionary force to capture him. They also handed up Pilgarie, who they said had murdered a sailor named Roach while he was trying to recover the shipwrecked *Fanny* years earlier (see August 1838).

A brief court martial of the two prisoners was held in front of their tribe on the afternoon of 24 August 1840, and interpreted for them. The following day Mongarawata and Pilgarie were hung at the site where the survivor's bodies had been discovered, and their bodies were left hanging as a warning to others. After a day of rest, the expedition set about burning wurlies that contained bloodied clothing and other items from the survivors.

After the executions, the expedition continued searching for any sign of the Maria's passengers. Five bodies were discovered on 2 September 1840, also showing signs of having been beaten and speared. Although this brought the expedition to a close, the use of summary justice caused a political crisis for Governor Gawler, leading to suggestions he should be charged with murder. This scandal was compounded by his economic woes, and contributed to his recall to England and replacement by Governor Grey.

On 22 November 1840, Captain Nixon located another four bodies while surveying Lake Albert's shore. Dr Penny located four more bodies on 10 April 1841 at Noongong on the Coorong, opposite the execution site. Four bodies were never located. Gold sovereigns from the *Maria* washed up along the Coorong for years afterwards.

* There are reports that Mrs York was travelling with her baby. However, the baby is not listed on a letter sent to Major O'Halloran, the Commissioner of Police, from Custom House at Port Adelaide, listing all passengers and crew aboard the *Maria*. The letter states '24 in all'. The *Maria* incident is referred to in many publications and the exact passenger list ranges from 24 to the low 30s. In this record, I have included the York baby as being one of the passengers, making a total of 25 passengers and crew.

Date	*Victim*	*Accused*
26 July 1840	**John Gofton**	**Joseph Stagg**
Cause of death:	Gunshot wound	
Outcome:	Found guilty of murder	
	Sentenced to death, executed 18 November 1840	
Location:	Port Gawler	

In early 1839, John Gofton, a 36-year-old gardener, arrived in South Australia from Port Phillip in the employment of Mr Hawdon. Gofton was employed to look after cattle that Hawdon owned. In late May 1840, Gofton was sentenced to a term of imprisonment for cattle stealing and was taken to the Adelaide Goal. On Saturday 13 June, a prison guard was patrolling outside the gaol when he saw Gofton climbing over the fence. The guard fired at Gofton, without effect. Gofton ran from the gaol with the guard in pursuit. The alarm was raised, and many police and prison guards searched the area but failed to locate Gofton.

Gofton made his way north where he apparently met up with two associates named Best and Fenton, who were both implicated in the same offence Gofton was originally arrested for. Around 20 July, Mrs Robinson, who resided in the neighbourhood of the Para River, was at home when a man came to her house and said that he and his two friends were lost and had not eaten for several days. Robinson gave him a loaf of bread, for which the man insisted that she take half a sovereign in return. Robinson became suspicious of the man and later informed the police.

On Monday 27 July, Inspector Alex Tolmer, of the Mounted Police, was tracking Gofton in the Para River area with others, when they came across Gofton's body in the mangroves. Gofton had been shot in the head, just behind his ear. A large quantity of blood was located about five or six yards from the body, and it was suspected that the body had been moved after being shot. No firearm was located. Two sets of footprints were in the mud around the area. One belonged to Gofton and the other Tolmer thought belonged to a person he knew as Joseph Stagg. Tolmer knew that Stagg 'turned out his feet in a peculiar manner' and Tolmer also recognised the tracks of Stagg's horse, which were close by. Stagg, who was a runaway convict from Van Diemen's Land, was subsequently apprehended in Adelaide. A search of his property revealed some shoes that closely matched the shoeprints at the scene. Best and Fenton were not found, and there were no footprints located which placed them at the scene.

Gofton's body was transported to Adelaide, and on Tuesday 28 July, an inquest was held before Mr Nichols, the coroner, at the Australian Arms in Hindley Street. The jury first viewed the body, which was instantly recognised by several members as John Gofton. The inquest heard from Stagg, who stated that he knew Gofton, but had not seen him in several weeks. Stagg also stated that he had not been in that area for a long time, but eyewitnesses put Stagg riding his horse close to the scene around the time of the murder. The inquest continued until Thursday, when the jury retired for two hours before returning with a verdict of wilful murder.

On Wednesday 11 November 1840, Stagg appeared before His Honour Justice Cooper at the Adelaide Supreme Court, charged with the murder of John Gofton. The trial concluded on Friday 13 November when the jury found Stagg guilty of murder. Stagg was sentenced to death, still proclaiming his innocence. Before the court adjourned, His Honour called on Mr Tolmer, Inspector of Mounted Police, and stated that the jury had requested him to convey to Mr Tolmer their thanks for the manner in which his duty had been performed. His Honour thought Mr Tolmer was well entitled to the thanks of the jury, and the whole community. Stagg was executed on Wednesday 18 November 1840, still protesting his innocence.

Twelve years later, in 1852, John Benedict Lomas, who resided in England, sent a letter to the South Australian Government. In 1840, Lomas was a member of the South Australia Police and was the officer who arrested Stagg for Gofton's murder. Lomas provided a sworn statement in which he stated that he was the person who shot and killed Gofton.

In 1840 I belonged to the mounted police in Adelaide, South Australia. On Friday the 24th day of July, 1840, I was sent by Inspector Tolmer to look after a man who had broken out of gaol … I was despatched from Port Gawler to fetch some provisions for the remainder of the party. I was out during all the Sunday night and what occurred during that time is the principal thing I want to state. During that period I saw the prisoner John Gofton and knowing that he had a quantity of money by him (by hearsay) I shot him and left him where he was. I returned back to my own camp next morning by daylight.

The statement was sworn before Mr Whitaker, a magistrate, and sent by Lomas, via official channels, to Sir Charles Cooper, the Secretary of State. The details of the letter were investigated and Lomas was written off as a lunatic. It was reported in the *South Australian Register*, Friday 23 January 1852:

Mistaken Verdict, it is confidently stated that an official intimation has been received from the Secretary of State that an ex-policeman named Lomas, now confined in a lunatic asylum in England, has made certain revelations which go far to prove that he was the perpetrator of the murder for which Joseph Stagg was executed about 12 years ago in Adelaide. His Honour, Mr Justice Cooper and the Police Commissioner have the affair under investigation. Such of our readers as are old colonists will recollect that this alleged confession confirms suspicions pretty generally entertained at the time, and gives a mournful force to the declaration of innocence made by Stagg on the scaffold.

The *South Australian Register* reported on 19 February 1874 that John Lomas walked into the office of the newspaper to clear his name. Lomas stated that he remained in South Australia for 10 years after the execution but had to return to England to settle an estate. Lomas remained there for some time, due to the dispute over the estate and the proceedings in the Court of Chancery. While in England he saw a report in a newspaper stating that he had died as a lunatic, and that he had confessed to the murder of Gofton. Lomas denied that he was responsible for Gofton's murder and stated that he had several witnesses to confirm where he was at the time of the offence. Lomas had returned from England and had resided in Western Australia since 1857, where he owned a considerable property. Lomas stated that he had returned to South Australia to clear his name, as the authorities in Western Australia objected to him continuing in the service there, as Inspector of Mines, while such an accusation remained against him uncontradicted.

Date	*Victim*	*Accused*
5 October 1840	**Frank Hawson**	**Aboriginal people**
Cause of death:	Spear wounds	
Outcome:	Offenders not located	
Location:	Kirton Point	

Early in the morning on 5 October 1840, Frank Hawson, a 10-year-old child, was left in the station hut at Kirton Point, near Port Lincoln, while Edward, his older brother, went into town. At about 10 am that morning, a group of about 10 Aboriginal people surrounded the hut wanting something to eat. Frank gave them some bread as they were trying to break into the hut. Frank opened the door and stood there, holding a sword and a gun to frighten them away. Frank was then struck by one spear in the chest, and another in his thigh. Frank fired at the thieves, who ran off. They later returned and threw another spear, and Frank fired his gun again, scaring his attackers off once more. Frank tried to remove the spears, but as they were barbed, the pain was too great. He tried to saw them off, but had to stop because of the pain. Frank tried to burn the spears, but that did not work either.

When Edward returned, he saw the two spears, which were about seven feet long and still buried in his brother. Edward used a saw to cut the ends of the spears off and took him into town where he saw Dr Harvey. On the way, Frank was murmuring, 'I'm not afraid to die'. Frank later died from his injuries.

The remains of Frank Hawson, exhumed for honoured re-burial at Port Lincoln.
Dr. E. Kinmont kneeling, Dr. W. Ramsay Smith standing behind the remains.
State Library of South Australia, B 54013

Because of Frank's death, George Gawler, the Governor and Commander
in Chief of the Provence of South Australia, made the following proclamation:

By His Excellency Lieutenant-Colonel George Gawler, Knight of the
Royal Hanoverian Guelphic Order, Governor and Commander in
Chief of the Province of South Australia.

WHEREAS an aggravated outrage has recently been committed by
the Natives in the neighbourhood of Port Lincoln, in the murder of a
boy about ten years of age: Whereas similar atrocities on their part may
occur, and, whereas inconsiderate persons may thereby be provoked to
use violent measures against the Aborigines:

Now, therefore, I George Gawler, Governor and Commander In
Chief of South Australia, by these presents do give notice and warning,
that the Colonial Government is ready to use all proper precautions for
the protection of the colonists against the aggressions of the Aborigines,

and to apprehend, identify, and bring to punishment all offenders of this class. And further, that any persons who may use violent retaliatory measures against the natives, except in the most urgently necessary actual defence of life and property, will render themselves liable to be dealt with according to the extreme rigour of the law.

Given under my hand and seal of the province, at Government house, Adelaide, this Seventh day of October One thousand eight hundred and forty.

George Gawler

In 1911 the remains of Frank Hawson were exhumed and on 30 March 1911, the residents of Port Lincoln erected a monument over the reinterred remains. The monument bears the following inscription:

Erected by public subscription through the Port Lincoln Progress Committee in memory of Frank Hawson, aged 10, who was speared by the blacks, October 5, 1840. Re-interred under the monument, March 30, 1911. Although only a lad, he dies a hero. Gone, but not forgotten. At rest.

Date	*Victim*	*Accused*
4 November 1840	**Betty**	**Tom**
Cause of death:	Assault (whale bone)	
Outcome:	Unknown	
Location:	Encounter Bay	

On 14 November 1840, the following letter was published in the *South Australian Register*, regarding the murder of an 18-year-old Aboriginal woman called Betty by her husband Tom. No other reference to this murder could be found.

Gentlemen, – Permit me, through the medium of your valuable publication, to lay before you a brief account of a most atrocious murder, committed here on the evening of the 4th instant. About 5 o'clock P.M. of the above date, a policeman stationed at the point had occasion to come on board the *Lalla Rookh*, for some medicine for his wife, whom I had been attending for some days; this man informed me that a native woman, named Betty, had been shockingly cut on the head by a native man, known here by the name of Tom, belonging to the Big Murray Tribe; the policeman stated that he was sure she must be dead. I immediately went on shore, having taken dressings, &c., for the occasion. I found the poor young woman, who was not more than 17 or 18 years of age, laying close to the fishery, surrounded by a few female natives. I examined the wounds (five in number), three of which were two and a half inches long, and laid the skull bare; the other two on the top of the head were of less extent, but so deadly must the weapon have been, that the skull was fractured in the course of the sagittal suture. With the assistance of Captain Kenney, the commander of the *Lalla Rookh*, who kindly accompanied me on shore, I succeeded in shaving the head and applying the usual dressings; but when I found I could pass the probe into the brain from either of the wounds in the top of the head, I was confident there could not be a chance of recovery, more particularly as she was in a state of asphyxia, from loss of blood, when I saw her.

After her head was dressed she was removed to a native hut a short distance; but nature then was nearly exhausted. She passed a restless night, and death put a period to her sufferings at 10 o'clock this morning; the injuries she received being the cause of her untimely end. I am informed, by those that witnessed the affair, that the ruffian committed this barbarous murder with a piece of the bone of a whale, which are plentiful all over the beach at Encounter Bay, and for what cause I am quite unacquainted. The police authorities are on the alert for him, and I trust when this reaches you he will be brought to justice.

Date	*Victim*	*Accused*
2 August 1841	**Kudnurtya (Worta)**	**William Roach**
Cause of death:	Gunshot wound	
Outcome:	Discharged	
Location:	Between Light and Adelaide	

On 2 August 1841, William Roach, a 40-year-old stockkeeper, Edward Cross, a surveyor, and William Wilson were returning to Adelaide from near the 'Light' with several cattle when they came across Kudnurtya and his

two-year-old daughter near a fire. The remains of a calf, which belonged to the herd, were burning on the fire.

Roach told them to go, but Kudnurtya stepped towards Roach and struck him on the side with his spear. Roach discharged his musket at Kudnurtya who fell to the ground. Roach staggered back and said he had been speared.

When they returned to Adelaide, Cross and Wilson made a voluntary confession at the Police Barracks concerning the death. On Monday 30 August, Cross and Wilson were placed at the bar of the Resident Magistrate's Court, Adelaide, charged with murder. Roach was not in custody and the police were actively looking for him. The magistrate, Mr Wigley, put the matter off until Roach was found. On Wednesday 1 September, Roach, Cross and Wilson all appeared before the Court. Roach was charged with murder, and Cross and Wilson were charged with being accessory to the fact.

During the proceedings, Kalta Murianna, the two-year-old daughter of Kudnurtya, was put into the witness box, with her evidence translated by Mr Teichleman. Mr Smith, who appeared for Roach, took objection to the evidence, stating, 'it is not being competent for a magistrate to take any evidence, except on oath, on so serious a charge as the present'. Mr Wigley told Smith that he could take any information he liked. Kalta stated:

> I saw the three prisoners at the encampment of my father, on the evening of the eclipse of the moon. Wilson and Cross said to my father, 'now you go to Adelaide lest you be shot,' my father replied, 'shall I go to Adelaide?' Wilson and Cross then said to Roach, 'do not shoot him, they came from Adelaide to hunt Opossums.' Roach then shot my father with a long firearm, the prisoners, Wilson and Cross, were close to him at the time, my father dropped down dead. I left the body and ran away, there were no other natives in the neighbourhood, my father had no spear but a stick for throwing and another for fighting, he used neither of the offensive weapons against the prisoners, my father was cooking nothing but kangaroo bones when they came up. My father's name is Kudnurtya, when I went out afterwards with Mr Teichleman, I saw him pick up a piece of brass, that was the spot where my father had been lying dead.

Christian Teichleman gave evidence of attending the scene and finding the brass and an amount of blood on the ground. He could not say, however, if the blood was human, kangaroo or cattle. Teichleman tracked around the area but was unable to locate a body. The matter was adjourned for further evidence.

On Saturday 4 September, Cross, Wilson and Roach appeared once again before Mr Wigley. As there was no evidence to incriminate Wilson and Cross, they were discharged, then put in the witness box to give evidence. The matter was once again adjourned to Friday 10 September, when Roach was committed to take trial in the Supreme Court.

On Tuesday 8 March 1842, Roach appeared in the Supreme Court. The judge summed up the charges relative to Roach to the Grand Jury.

I have one or two remarks, too, to make in the case of William Roach, who was indicted last sessions for three different crimes, for murder, for shooting at a person with the intent of doing him some bodily harm, and for manslaughter. Now, the gentlemen of the jury threw out the bill on the two first points, that is, for murder, and for shooting with the intent of doing some bodily harm, but they found a bill for manslaughter. Now, it is impossible for me, gentlemen, to distinguish between finding in one case, and throwing out in the other. It left the prosecutor in a very difficult and critical position, because the depositions showed that the body of the deceased could not be found, and it was very difficult therefore to convict him of murder. Supposing the Grand Jury to have brought in a bill, the same would apply to manslaughter. When I look into the depositions, I cannot find anything to justify a bill being brought in for manslaughter, for though I find that the gun was fired by the prisoner Roach, I cannot find that the native man was struck by him.

The prisoner has had an opportunity of giving some account of this transaction, but he gives none, in fact, says nothing. If he had shown any probable cause for firing this gun, if he had shown it to be accidental or declared it to be so or had said anything about it, it would have enabled us to have formed some favourable opinion about the matter. Nor do the witnesses on behalf of the prisoner say anything on this point either. The evidence is, that the gun was fired, and that the native man was struck, but nothing is said of what has become of the body; and we are to infer from these circumstances, that, if he really was guilty, he was not guilty of murder. Now, as I understand, the whole matter was investigated before the Resident Magistrate, and, on the occasion of that investigation, Roach objected to give any explanation. In making these remarks, I consider the Grand Jury as merely putting the case in a proper train to pronounce sentence upon it, and if, upon you hearing the evidence brought before you, believe that he fired no gun, or that, if fired, it was fired by accident, or anything in point of fact below the crime of murder, you will not be justified in bringing in a bill against him for shooting with an intent to kill, or do some bodily harm.

The following day Roach appeared before the Supreme Court charged with the wilful murder of Kudnurtya. Roach was discharged.

Date	Victim	Accused
23 September 1841	John Williams	William Sturgess
Cause of death:	Assault (with a spade)	
Outcome:	Found guilty of manslaughter	
	Sentenced to transportation for life	
Location:	South Park Lands	

John Williams, 18, and William Sturgess, 27, were both employed as labourers on the Government works in the parklands. On Thursday 23 September, Sturgess' dog was violently attacking the younger brother of Williams. Williams saw this and ran towards them to rescue his brother. As Williams was running after the dog, he said to Sturgess, 'I would not keep that dog if I were you', to which Sturgess replied, 'he has not hurt the boy'. Williams followed the dog with a stick, but then took up a shovel and aimed a blow at the dog to drive the dog away. Sturgess saw what was happening and walked about 10 paces to where Williams was, carrying a spade. Williams had his back to Sturgess, and without saying a word, Sturgess struck Williams on the back of the neck with the spade. Williams then fell to the ground. Nick Bull, the Superintendent of the working men, saw what happened and took Sturgess into custody. Medical assistance was obtained for Williams, but he was dead. Corporal Moulton of the Mounted Police was riding past at the time and also saw Sturgess strike Williams. Bull took Williams to Moulton, who took Sturgess into custody. Sturgess was a married man whose wife was close to giving birth.

The following day, a coroner's inquest was held at the Red House Tavern, Thebarton, where evidence was given. At the completion of the inquest, the jury returned a verdict of wilful murder against William Sturgess, who was committed to trial.

The trial in the Supreme Court commenced on Thursday 4 November 1841. Sturgess was found guilty of manslaughter and sentenced to transportation for life.

Date	Victim	Accused
2 March 1842	John Brown and Francis Lovelock	Aboriginal people
Cause of death:	Spear wounds	
Outcome:	Unknown	
Location:	Near Port Lincoln	

John Brown had a large quantity of sheep and resided near the settlement of Port Lincoln. Brown employed a 12-year-old boy called Francis Lovelock as a hutkeeper.

On 2 March 1842, Brown was at the hut with Lovelock when Brown left to go to town. The hut was under observation by several Aboriginal people, and when they saw Brown leave, they attacked the hut and killed Lovelock. Brown returned to the hut and fought the attackers using his rifle. During the fight, Brown received fatal wounds and fell to the floor of the hut.

As news of the murders reached Adelaide, Mr C Dutton wrote to the newspapers with further details. This letter was printed in the *South Australian Register* on Saturday 2 April:

Gentlemen – No account having as yet appeared of the outrage committed at Port Lincoln by the natives, I beg to hand you a statement of what had occurred previous to my departure, to cause the whole of this small settlement to be thrown into a state of commotion. About two months before the melancholy deaths of Mr John Brown and his hut-keeper, Lovelock, the natives had become exceedingly troublesome to the settlers—stealing everything they could get at, spearing sheep and cattle, burning fences, and committing various acts of aggression. The great forbearance of the settlers towards them in overlooking repeated outrages is, I imagine, the cause of their becoming so daring, as a general impression had arisen amongst them that we were afraid to retaliate. One man (Mopa) now in the jail at Port Lincoln, I took in custody at my station, for firing the fence, and there are other charges against him. The day previous to the murder, Mr White's hut-keeper, Cartwright, at the Gawler Pond station, was attacked by the natives, but he avoided their spears by dodging amongst the trees and having the presence of mind to break them as fast as they threw them at him; their supply became exhausted, and he fortunately escaped.

Two days after the murders, two Aboriginal people came into town and gave information to Mr Schurmann, the missionary. The statement made by them is as follows:

The tribe had watched Mr Brown away from the hut, and had then murdered the hutkeeper, for the purpose of robbing the place, and that Mr Brown, returning immediately after they had effected their barbarous purpose, fell a victim also to these ruthless savages, in spite of a desperate resistance against numbers, for having discharged his rifle without effect, he had used the butt end, one of the murderers having been taken away for dead. Mr Brown had evidently struggled for his life like a brave man; he was found lying on his back, with the stock and barrel of his rifle shattered to pieces, lying by his side. The state of both victims when found was shocking in the extreme. Mr Brown had seven spear wounds; one had passed through a thick leather belt which he wove round his waist; the back part of his head was knocked in, and his hands were cut to pieces. Lovelock was also awfully mutilated, and they had both evidently struggled to the last. Some days after the melancholy occurrence the same tribe also attempted to attack my station, at Pilliwerter, about sixteen miles above Mr Brown's; and I took one of the suspected murderers (Namdeloa) in the act of pointing a spear at me and he is now keeping Mopa company in the jail. I am, Gentlemen. Your obedient servant, C. C. Dutton.

[Since receiving the above we have seen two letters from Port Lincoln, stating that the station of Mr McElliston, two miles from the town, had been attacked by about forty natives, and after driving off two masons who were building a house, with the hut-keeper from the hut, robbed it of pork, flour, tea, sugar, and other articles.]

By the *Governor Gawler* there have arrived in Adelaide from Port Lincoln Mr Macdonald, Mr Barnard, and four natives. Two of the latter are prisoners, one supposed to be of the tribe that murdered Mr Brown, the other for firing Mr Dutton's fence and trying to spear him. Mr Macdonald has brought up the other two to let them see how friendly the blacks and whites live together in Adelaide – Editors

A coronial inquest was later held into the deaths of John Brown and Francis Lovelock. A verdict was given as, 'wilful murder against some native or natives unknown'. There is no reference of court action taken against any person for the murders.

Date	Victim	Accused
29 March 1842	Rolles Biddle, Elizabeth Stubbs, and James Fastings	Nultia, Moullia, and Ngarbi (Little Jemmy)
Cause of death:	Spear and blade wounds	
Outcome:	Nultia and Moullia found guilty of murder Sentenced to death, executed 4 April 1843 Ngarbi found guilty of murder Sentenced to death, executed 1 August 1843	
Location:	Near Port Lincoln	

On Tuesday 29 March 1842, about four weeks after the murders of Brown and Lovelock, Rolles Biddle, a 32-year-old landowner, his 69-year-old housekeeper, Elizabeth Stubbs, her husband Charles Stubbs, and a shepherd called James Fastings were on Biddle's station near Port Lincoln when about 40 or 50 Aboriginal people surrounded the house. Fastings went outside to the hen house where he had spears thrown at him, one of which hit his leg, so he returned to the house. The group came closer to the property and began to destroy the fence. Fastings went outside and released the dogs onto the attackers, but he received a spear in the arm. Biddle fired his gun at the attackers, killing one and wounding another. Then a volley of spears came at them, one hitting Mrs Stubbs, who fell to the ground, and the other killing

Fastings. The group were overrun by their attackers and hacked to death. Mr Stubbs ended up with a spear in his eye, but as he was underneath Fastings he managed to survive the ordeal. When the attackers eventually left, Mr Stubbs was able to leave the property and get help.

Because of this incident, and the earlier murders of John Brown and Francis Lovelock, police and soldiers were sent to Port Lincoln from Adelaide to search for the offenders. In November that year, Utilta, a chief who was known in the Port Lincoln community as being well disposed and faithful to the European settlers, told Mr Driver, the Government Resident and Major O'Halloran, that the people who had murdered Biddle were in the neighbourhood. Utilta told them that the murderers had made war upon his tribe and killed two of his people, and he offered to accompany a party to show them where they were. Major O'Halloran and a party of volunteers immediately set out, and following the directions of Utilta, they succeeded in capturing seven men. Charles Stubbs identified two of the captives, known as Nultia and Moullia, as the murderers of his wife and Biddle.

Nultia, 37, and Moullia, 19, were subsequently transported to Adelaide for trial. On Thursday 23 March 1843, Nultia and Moullia appeared before His Honour Judge Cooper at the Supreme Court in Adelaide charged with murder. Both were found guilty of the murders and sentenced to death. They were returned to Port Lincoln where they were executed on 4 April 1843.

Later that year, an Aboriginal man named Ngarbi (Little Jemmy) was also identified as being involved in the murders. He was arrested and charged with the murder of Elizabeth Stubbs. On Thursday 20 July, Ngarbi appeared in the Supreme Court before Judge Cooper. Charles Stubbs again gave evidence and identified Ngarbi as being one of the attackers who murdered his wife. Ngarbi was found guilty and sentenced to death. Ngarbi was executed on 1 August 1843.

Date	*Victim*	*Accused*
2 June 1842	George McGrath	Wira Maldera (Peter),
		Wekweki (Jack), and
		Kooeykowminney (Billy/Jimmy)

Cause of death:	Assault (stick of oak)
Outcome:	Wira Maldera found guilty of murder
	Sentenced to death, executed 29 March 1845
	Wekweki found guilty of murder
	Sentenced to death, sentence reprieved 1 June 1848
Location:	McGrath Flat, Coorong

William Chase came to South Australia in 1838 and worked in various locations around the state. When Chase was working near the Murray, at Bonney's Water Holes, he knew a man called Wira Maldera. Chase crossed paths with Wira Maldera on several occasions over the next few years. On 1 June 1842, Chase was with George McGrath and William Pugh at Mr McLeod's station where they were making plans to travel to Portland Bay. Wira Maldera volunteered his services to travel with them. Wira Maldera was in the company of three other Aboriginal men, and Chase accepted their offer.

The group left and started their journey to Portland Bay, heading to Lake Alexandrina. On 2 June, they were camping at the Coorong and in the early hours of the morning, Chase, McGrath and Pugh were attacked as they were sleeping. The attack was sudden and unexpected, and the three tried to load their rifles, but they had no time. Chase and Pugh were injured and managed to run from the campsite. McGrath was fatally injured.

Chase and Pugh made their way back to McLeod's station, which was at the junction of the Murray and the Lake, where they told the station owner what had happened. When they left the campsite, they left their rifles, ammunition and blankets, but no one returned to the site to look for McGrath.

Several years later, Wira Maldera told another Aboriginal man called Pantowny that he had killed three white men. Wira Maldera told him that had struck all three men with a stick of oak and left them for dead. Wira Maldera was unaware that two of the men had survived. The information made its way to the police and Wira Maldera was located and arrested for McGrath's murder. Maldera appeared before the Police Commissioner's Court on Monday 20 January 1845, where Chase gave evidence. The magistrate adjourned the hearing and directed Mr Tolmer to send a police officer with Chase to identify where they were camped. During the later search, a skeleton, from which dogs had torn the flesh, was found near the site of the attack.

Wira Maldera later appeared before the Supreme Court where he was found guilty of murder. Wira Maldera was sentenced to death, and was executed on 29 March 1845.

On Monday 9 June, Wekweki (Jack) and Kooeykowminne (Billy/ Jimmy) appeared before the Supreme Court charged with McGrath's murder. The following day, Kooeykowminne gave evidence against Wekweki, who was found not guilty of murder but guilty of aiding and abetting the murder. Wekweki was sentenced to death, but on 24 June 1845 his Excellency the Governor reprieved the sentence, and he was released.

The area where McGrath was murdered is now called McGrath Flat, which is situated 23 kilometres south-west of Meningie.

Date	*Victim*	*Accused*
28 September 1842	**George Jefferay**	**John William Spicer**
Cause of death:	Assault (with tongs)	
Outcome:	Acquitted	
Location:	Rosina Street, Adelaide	

John William Spicer, a well-respected 38-year-old lawyer, had a 40-year-old servant named George Jefferay. On the evening of 28 September 1842, the police were called to a disturbance at Spicer's home in Rosina Street, Adelaide. When the police arrived, they looked through the window and saw Spicer hitting Jefferay on the head with some tongs. When Spicer saw the police, he threw the tongs away. Jefferay left the house by the front door, and fell to the ground. Medical attention was sought for Jefferay, but he subsequently died from his injuries.

Spicer was arrested and charged with assault, but as he was appearing in court, word was received that Jefferay had died, so the charge was upgraded to murder.

On Thursday 17 November, Spicer appeared before the Supreme Court charged with Jefferay's murder. Evidence was given that Spicer, Jefferay and another person had consumed five bottles of wine during the evening, and that Spicer was drunk when he assaulted Jefferay after a quarrel between them.

Dr O'Hea gave evidence of treating Jefferay for his injuries and sending him to the Adelaide Hospital for further treatment. Jefferay had several head injuries, and on his arrival at the hospital, was seen by a doctor who was unaware of the full circumstances of the incident. The doctor examined Jefferay, who only complained of soreness in the abdomen. The doctor thought that Jefferay did not need to be admitted, so he organised for the police to take him away. Jefferay was taken outside the hospital where he lay on the ground. Due to the low outside temperature and his head injuries, Jefferay died. Dr O'Hea stated that if Jefferay were given the treatment he had ordered, he would have survived his injuries.

Dr O'Hea also stated that he had been frequently called upon to sacrifice his time and attention to his professional duties to attend court, but had never received any remuneration, and asked His Honour whether there was a fund out of which payment could be made. His Honour replied that he knew of no fund for that purpose at present, but he promised to bring the matter under notice of His Excellence Captain Grey.

At the completion of the trial on Saturday 19 November, the jury retired for a period of four hours and returned a verdict of not guilty. On hearing the verdict, the countenance of the prisoner changed; he appeared very grateful for the verdict, bowed to the court, then fell into a chair and fainted. At the time it was reported that no trial since the establishment of the province had occupied so large a share of time, from nine am on Thursday morning to seven pm on Saturday evening, due to the amount of evidence given.

Date	*Victim*	*Accused*
25 January 1843	**Maria**	**George Gregory**
Cause of death:	Gunshot wound	
Outcome:	Acquitted	
Location:	Emu Flat, near Clare	

Henry Gale was the hutkeeper for Mr Hughes of Emu Flat. During the night around 25 January 1843, a number of sheep were taken from the property. The next morning Gale went over to the ranges to look for them, where he found one dead. When he returned to his hut, an Aboriginal man and woman came to the hut, but Gale told them to leave. Gale went to the head station where he saw Hugh Gordon and 19-year-old George Gregory, and told them about the two visitors.

Gregory and Gale located the pair, a male and a 23-year-old woman named Maria. Gale asked them if there were other Aboriginal people nearby, with the Aboriginal man saying there were more over the hill. Gale asked the pair to go with him to his hut, which they did.

As they came into a piece of scrub the male knocked Gale down and bolted. Gale chased him for about three-quarters of a mile, but lost him. Gregory was left with Maria. When Gale returned, Gregory was standing near Maria, who was lying on the ground. Gale saw that Maria had been shot.

At a later coronial inquest into Maria's death, Gregory was found guilty of murder and committed to trial at the Supreme Court.

Gregory appeared before the Supreme Court on Thursday 23 March charged with murder. During the trial, Gregory stated that when Gale and the Aboriginal man ran off, Maria started to walk away in a different direction. Gregory took hold of the woman, who was armed with a stick. Maria struck Gregory with the stick on the shoulder, and then started to attack him with it. Gregory fired his rifle at her, hitting her in the stomach. Gregory stated that he was in fear when he fired, as the woman was hitting him so hard he thought a blow on the bead with such a stick would kill him. At the completion of the trial, the jury acquitted Gregory.

Date	Victim	Accused
18 March 1843	**John Murdock**	**Charles Hedditch**
Cause of death:	Assault (with a stick)	
Outcome:	Found guilty of murder, found to be insane	
	Sentenced to be kept in gaol at Her Majesty's pleasure	
Location:	Craigdarroch, near Mount Barker	

John and Margaret Murdock came to South Australia on the *Indus* in 1839 and settled in the Mount Barker district. John died shortly thereafter. In 1841 Margaret Murdock lived on her property at Craigdarroch, near Mount Barker with her children, 10-year-old John and Andrew.

On Saturday 18 March 1843, young John left the house to go to a close waterhole to mind some cattle. Francis Kelly, who lived nearby, saw John and a man lying on the ground on the opposite side of the waterhole. Francis saw the man sit up and beat the ground with a stick. Later that evening, when John failed to return home, Andrew, along with Margaret and Thomas McCoull, a neighbour, went looking for him. When Margaret reached the waterhole, she found John lying face down. John was dead, and she noticed that he had a wound behind his right ear. She also saw a stick close by. Andrew and McCoull carried John back to their house and the police were called.

Around a week later, Charles Hedditch, a 27-year-old lunatic, confessed to the murder. Hedditch stated that he thought the boy was an evil spirit and had attacked him with a stick until blood had come out of both ears.

Hedditch appeared in the Supreme Court before His Honour Judge Cooper on Wednesday 19 July. Dr Innes gave evidence of attending at Mount Barker on the day of the murder to treat his patient, Charles Hedditch, who was suffering from delirium tremens. After further evidence was given, the jury, after a brief deliberation, found Hedditch guilty of the murder, but also found that he was insane at the time. Hedditch was sentenced to remain in gaol 'until her Majesty's pleasure is known'.

Thirteen years later, a letter was published in September 1856:

A letter was received from the Colonial Secretary, enclosing the report of the Acting Colonial Surgeon in reference to the case of Charles Hedditch, in the following terms;

'Charles Hedditch was for some time under my observation in gaol. He conducted himself orderly and quietly, and I am of opinion that it would be an act of great cruelty to have him placed under restraint. Mr Rankine is well aware of the facts of his case, and would take care to have proper steps taken should any symptoms of a serious nature manifest themselves.' W. M. Gosse, Acting Colonial Surgeon.

Charles Hedditch was released back into the community, and later died at Mount Crawford on 17 March 1865, aged 49.

Date	*Victim*	*Accused*
21 June 1843	**Aboriginal man**	**William Skelton**
Cause of death:	Gunshot wound	
Outcome:	Unknown	
Location:	Reedy Creek, near Kingston SE	

William Skelton was in charge of a number of sheep on a property at Reedy Creek, near Kingston SE, which belonged to Mr Hughes. During the night Skelton heard the sheep rush, so he got out of bed and went to the sheep pen.

Skelton called out but got no answer, and then saw a shape, which he thought was a native dog going over the fence. Skelton called out again and got no reply, so he fired his rifle towards the figure. Skelton investigated and found that he had shot an Aboriginal man who was about 20 years old. Skelton picked the body up and took it to his employer, Mr Hughes. The man died the next day, and Skelton and Hughes buried the body.

The police were later advised, and Skelton was charged with murder. Skelton appeared before the Supreme Court on a charge of 'feloniously and wilfully killing a native man'. He appeared several times between July and November 1843. On Tuesday 18 July, His Honour Judge Cooper referred to the murder:

> I cannot help observing, that cases of this kind were much more frequent, than was creditable to the reputation of the Colony. Last sessions a man was tried, and acquitted of the charge of killing a native woman. That verdict was a very merciful one, but not so merciful, I trust, as to countenance the idea that the lives of the natives are held too cheaply. The only observation I would make upon this case was, that it was one of great suspicion. I will not go into the general bearings of the case, but would leave it to the consideration of the Grand Jury with that solitary observation.

On his last appearance, on 7 November, it mentions the matter is for trial. No further reference could be found.

Date	*Victim*	*Accused*
June 1844	**Ngunnirra Bourka and Maryann**	**William Smith, Charles Pitt, and Charles Spratt**
Cause of death:	Gunshot wounds	
Outcome:	Discharged	
Location:	Mount Bryan	

In June 1844, William Smith, Charles Pitt and Charles Spratt were employed on a sheep station owned by Mr Hallett near Mount Bryan. Around that time, several sheep had been stolen. Smith, Pitt and Spratt were out looking for the sheep when they saw and approached a group of Aboriginal people, which included Ngunnirra Bourka, Maryann and Pari Kudmitya. Smith, Pitt and Spratt went up to Pari Kudmitya and asked him what he had done with the sheep. At the same time, Spratt struck Ngunnirra Bourka with a sword and then shot him. Another Aboriginal man, Big William, was struck with a sword by Smith, and Pitt fired his gun at Maryann, striking her in the abdomen. Two other people were shot, but their injuries were not fatal. The group of Aboriginal people ran off into the bush. Within two days, Ngunnirra Bourka and Maryann had died from their injuries.

The details of the murders were conveyed to the police, and after an investigation, on Tuesday 24 December 1844, William Smith, Charles Pitt and Charles Spratt were brought before the commissioner, charged with the murders of Ngunnirra Bourka and Maryann. The only witness was Pari Kudmitya, who testified that he and the other victims were running away at the time they were shot. At the completion of the evidence, all three men were committed to trial.

On Tuesday 11 March 1845, Pitt, Spratt and Smith appeared before the Supreme Court. The judge addressed the grand jury, saying

The next case is Charles Edmund Pitt, Charles Spratt and William Smith, who are charged with the wilful murder of a native man named Ngunnirra Bourka, and a native woman named Maryann, in July last. As I understand the learned Advocate General has not yet determined what course it will be proper for him to take in this case, I will defer my observations upon it until I learn that an indictment is ready to be submitted to you.

On 18 March 1845, the following was printed in the *South Australian*:

The Grand Jury having found no bill against Charles Edmund Pitt, Charles Spratt and William Smith, were brought before the Court this morning. The Court ordered that they should enter into personal recognizances to appear to answer any indictment that might be brought by the Advocate General against them, for the murder of two natives. They entered into recognizances accordingly, and their bail was discharged.

Date	*Victim*	*Accused*
12 June 1844	**Hyrdess child**	**Rosa, Julia, and Merlina Hyrdess**
Cause of death:	Knife wound	
Outcome:	Rosa acquitted of murder, found guilty of concealment of birth Sentenced to 15 months imprisonment Julia and Merlina acquitted	
Location:	Syleham, on the River Torrens	

Rosa Ann Dew Hyrdess, 19, resided at Syleham, near Adelaide, with her family, including her sisters Julia, 15, and Merlina, 14. On 12 June 1844, Samuel Taylor was by the River Torrens near where the Hyrdess family lived, when he saw Julia and Merlina close to the bank of the river. Merlina was carrying a small package, which Taylor saw her place in a hole near the river.

On 19 June, Rosa went to the hospital where she saw Nurse Mary Cantailion. Rosa told Mary that she had given birth and that she was very sorry for what she had done. She also said that a young man called John Ball had promised her marriage, but when she told him that she was pregnant, he said he would do away with it.

Later, a woman was walking her dog near the river where Rosa and Merlina were seen, when the dog located a package containing the body of a newborn female.

A doctor examined the child and found that it appeared to be in perfect health and would have arrived at its full term. The child was perfectly fresh, and no decomposition had taken place. A severe injury to the throat was found. The doctor located and examined Rosa, in her father's house. While he was examining her, she asked him what it was for, and he told her it was to ascertain whether she had recently delivered. Rosa said that he shouldn't have taken the trouble, as she would have told him that she had recently given birth. The doctor asked her what she had done with the child, and Rosa said she had destroyed it, that she was in a great deal of agony and pain at the time, and that she did it with a carving knife. The doctor asked Rosa what she had done with the knife, and Rosa said it was thrown into the river.

On Thursday 19 September, Rosa, Julia and Merlina Hyrdess all appeared before the Supreme Court charged with wilful murder. At the completion of the trial, Mr Fisher, for Rosa, addressed His Honour and the jury, objecting to the indictment, as there was no name stated in it. He cited Biss's case, which he considered conclusive, showing that the indictment must either state the name of the party killed, or that the party was unknown to the jurors. The advocate general argued that the case of Biss was totally different. His Honour adjourned the case for half an hour, to enable him to refer to the authorities on the subject. On his return, His Honour said he could not find an authority to guide him. The advocate general believed that it would be best if the prisoner was acquitted, but only on the condition that he would prepare another indictment. His Honour discharged Julia and Merlina, as no evidence was found against them, and he asked the jury to return a verdict of acquittal against Rosa, which they did. Rosa appeared the following day and was detained in custody until the next sessions.

Rosa appeared once more in the Supreme Court on 28 November, where she was acquitted of murder, but found guilty of concealment of birth. Rosa was sentenced to 15 months imprisonment.

Date	*Victim*	*Accused*
22 October 1844	**John Charles Darke**	**Aboriginal people**
Cause of death:	Spear wounds	
Outcome:	Offenders not located	
Location:	Darke's Peake	

John Darke, a 36-year-old explorer, set out from Port Lincoln with his expedition to explore the centre of the peninsula to the north-west of Port Lincoln on 29 August 1844. Darke kept a journal of the expedition, which was published on 15 November in the *South Australian*. A portion of that journal has been reproduced below:

August 29th—I left Port Lincoln accompanied by Mr John Henry. Theakston and two men, for the purpose of exploring the interior of the peninsula.

Oct. 22nd.—Accompanied by the blacks, who were joined by nine others, I proceeded on to the water hole, about three miles, but more easterly than our course; and came about two o'clock to a large grindstone rock where I found abundance of feed and water on a plain about 200 yards wide by half a mile long, surrounded by a thick scrub.

Continued by Mr Theakston.

Wednesday, Oct. 23rd—It is with sorrow I am competed to continue the journal of Mr Darke, he having been speared by three natives, whom he had treated in the most kind manner the day previous. About twenty of them made their appearance at eight o'clock. Mr Darke and myself went and made signs to them to keep from the camp, when some of them sat down, and we returned to breakfast shortly after, Mr Darke left me in the tent and went towards the scrub in an opposite direction to where he had seen the natives; when within two yards of a bush, he saw a man's eyes glaring at him, and in the act of throwing a spear; there were others behind another bush—and they all delivered their spears with too sure aim—one entered his stomach, and came out of his back—the other passed through his knee. I heard him call out and immediately ran towards him and fired at one of the natives, whom I saw in the act of throwing the spear which he had drawn out of Mr Darke's stomach. I did not hit him, but it had the effect of frightening them away. At the moment of my firing, other natives made their appearance around us in every direction; and made off. I had Mr Darke carried to the tent, and I cut out the barbed spear from his hip, and bled and did all I could for him, but found it was not possible to remove him on account of the dreadful nature of his wounds. He suffered very much, but was perfectly sensible, and spoke of the expedition, and his having accomplished much more than he had expected, and expressed great anxiety to be able to reach Port Lincoln. He appeared to be better in the evening.

Oct. 24.—I resolved to remove from this spot early in the morning, which I did, and after travelling over a very sandy, scrubby country, made a small patch of grass, about ten miles from the Table Topped Peaks of Mt Eyre; I here dressed the wounds of Mr Darke, and bled him, but found his extremities getting cold, and I informed him I feared the event. About ten o'clock he told me he was dying, that mortification had taken place, for he was out of pain; he gave me his last commands, and died at five minutes to twelve, quite calm to the last moment.

Oct. 25th.—I carried the body of Mr Darke to the Table Topped Peaks, and buried him on a small grassy plain at the foot of them, in a grave five feet deep.

On Saturday 12 February 1910, on page 12 of the *Advertiser*, an article titled 'Darke's Grave, The Monument Finished' was printed:

> Some time ago the Government surveyor on Eyre Peninsula was instructed to try and locate the grave of Mr J. C. Darke, who surveyed portion of the peninsula before being speared to death by natives. The surroundings were searched, and a plan sent of the open patch where the grave was supposed to be, but no sign could be found of the place where the remains of the late explorer were buried. While searching they came upon some wheel marks and bullock tracks, evidently those of a good many years ago. They followed these and came to an open area

Darke's monument at Darke's Peak (1935)
State Library of South Australia, B 9273

in the scrub to the west of Darke's Peak trigonometrical station. They noticed a mound about 40 yards away. Not far off was a hollow in the ground, which had seemingly been dug out to make the mound. That area was excavated and a skeleton was found.

A monument was erected bearing the following inscription, 'Sacred to the memory of John Charles Darke, surveyor, who was mortally wounded by Natives when exploring in this locality, October 23, 1844, and died the following day.' [Erected by the South Australian Government 1910]

Date	*Victim*	*Accused*
8 February 1845	Lygoe child	**Sarah Lygoe and Thomas James**
Cause of death:	Unknown	
Outcome:	Unknown	
Location:	Adelaide	

On 18 February 1845, an inquest was held at the Edinburgh Castle Hotel into the death of a newborn female, reportedly the child of Thomas James and Sarah Lygoe. James and Lygoe were in custody on suspicion of murder charges. Both stated that the child was stillborn, but evidence from several witnesses tended to contradict them. Both were remanded in custody until Wednesday 19 February when the inquest resumed. At the inquest's completion, James and Lygoe were found guilty of manslaughter and were committed on the Coroner's Warrant for trial.

On 10 March 1845, Jones and Lygoe appeared before the Adelaide Supreme Court. Both were charged with killing a newborn female child. Evidence was received that both Lygoe and Jones had for some time been living together as man and wife, and on 8 February, Lygoe gave birth to a child, which was seen dead the same day. The body was later found in the cemetery. The judge addressed the jury:

> If the child was born alive, then how did it come by its death[?] And if a verdict of murder or manslaughter is reached against the prisoners, you must be satisfied that the child came to its death by the means stated in the indictment, and if the means which caused the death of the child were wilfully used by the prisoners, or either of them, with that purpose, the crime committed will be murder; if the means were used carelessly and negligently, the crime will be manslaughter, but it is also possible that the death of the child may have been caused without any crime at all.

The court was adjourned. No further details located.

Date	Victim	Accused
23 June 1845	Salteye	**Terralia**
Cause of death:	Hanging	
Outcome:	Dismissed for want of evidence	
Location:	Near Kapunda	

PC Dennis Kenney was investigating the death of an Aboriginal woman called Salteye, who was found hanging on 23 June 1845. During the evening of Sunday 16 November, PC Kenney attended Mr Dutton's station, where he found Terralia at an Aboriginal campsite. PC Kenney approached Terralia and told him that he had a warrant. Kenney took hold of him, but Terralia's campmates also grabbed him, and a scuffle ensued. One of Mr Dutton's men came to PC Kenney's assistance and Terralia was taken into custody. As they were leaving, 20 armed Aboriginal people pursued them. One man approached PC Kenney and told him that they intended to put him into a water hole. PC Kenney placed Terralia on the back of his horse and they both rode into town.

On 19 November 1845, Terralia was placed before the Police Commissioners Court charged with murder. Terralia appeared several times before the Police Commissioner's Court, until a final appearance on Monday 15 December 1845, when Terralia was discharged for want of evidence.

No other details of the circumstances of the murder were found.

Date	Victim	Accused
1 July 1845	**William Brown**	**Aboriginal people**
Cause of death:	Assault (unknown weapon)	
Outcome:	Unknown	
Location:	Broadmeadows, near Hynam	

William Brown, 30, John Oliver and Adam Smith were friends in Melbourne who decided to go into partnership and set up grazing land in South Australia. Oliver and Brown went first and selected about 60 square miles of grazing land at Broadmeadows, where they intended to set up a large station. This was in an isolated part of the south-east and relations with the local Aboriginal people were good for the most part.

On 1 July 1845, Brown was splitting timber on the property, and then took a stroll to an area where a 'small tribe of strange blacks' were camped. Brown had been kind to the group of four men and five lubras who had been loitering about the station for several days. Brown was smoking his pipe alone when the group surrounded him, with one taking the opportunity to give him a stunning blow on the back of the head. Another snatched his gun from under his arm, and the rest of the men and women fell on him and killed him. They stripped his clothes and left his body where it fell. The group later came upon a shepherd with 1000 sheep a mile off. One of the group members pointed the gun at the shepherd, who managed to escape. The group took about 500 sheep from the flock and left the area.

A search was later conducted and most of the sheep were recovered, but the group was not found. The station of Messrs Brown and Oliver was about fifty miles west of the Glenelg, and fifty miles north of Mount Gambier.

William Brown was buried near the homestead at Broadmeadows. This was the beginning of the Hynam private cemetery.

Date	*Victim*	*Accused*
26 February 1846	**Donald Scott and**	**Nakhunda Bidden**
	Charles Whitney	**and Meiya Makarta**
Cause of death:	Speared and beaten	
Outcome:	Both prisoners discharged	
Location:	Near Mount Arden	

On 26 February 1846, Donald Scott and Charles Whitney (known as The Yankee) were tending to their sheep near Mount Arden. A group of Aboriginal people, including Nakhunda Bidden and Meiya Makarta, approached the flock, intending to steal some of the sheep. Scott and Whitney walked around to protect the sheep. Meiya Makarta threw a spear at one of the men, which hit him in the stomach. When he fell, Meiya Makarta, along with the rest of his group, beat him with waddies until he was dead. Nakhunda Bidden then beat the other man to death with his waddy. The sheep were driven away.

On 10 July that year, acting on information he received, Lance Corporal Kenney, accompanied by a local Aboriginal child and a policeman, went to an area near Mount Arden, towards the gulf. There he found the remains of Scott and Whitney, which were in a creek. The remains were covered with grass and sand, and Kenney found part of their clothes along with the bones.

The local Aboriginal child told Kenney that he recalled the two white-fellows some time ago in his country, and now they were dead. As a result, Kenney located and arrested Nakhunda Bidden and Meiya Makarta. On 22 July 1846, both accused appeared in the Police Commissioner's Court, charged with the murders of Scott and Whitney.

The 11-year-old boy testified that he was present when Scott and Whitney died, and that the two prisoners beat them with their waddies. One of the white men managed to fire his weapon, but it did not hit anyone.

The skulls and bones of the victims were produced in court, along with the clothing that they were wearing at the time they died. The 11-year-old witness recognised the clothing and the belt that the shorter man was wearing. Mr Tennent, who knew Scott and Whitney, stated that the belt produced in court was the one he had previously given to Scott. There was a spear hole and blood on the belt.

Dr James George Nash, colonial surgeon, stated that he had examined the bones and they were those of two humans, one of which must have been much taller than the other. He had examined the pelvic bones and he could say they were males. The distinctive marks, namely incisive teeth, which would have allowed him to say whether they were Aboriginal or European, were gone. It was impossible to say what the cause of death was as the bones had been so exposed to the weather, and appeared to have been gnawed by wild dogs. Both prisoners were committed to trial.

On Tuesday 17 March 1847, Nakhunda Bidden and Meiya Makarta appeared before the Supreme Court charged with murder. Both were discharged as the court found it impossible to communicate with them.

Date	Victim	Accused
1 September 1846	**Kingberri (Billy)**	**Thomas Donelly**
Cause of death:	Gunshot wound	
Outcome:	Donelly found guilty of murder	
	Sentenced to death, executed 29 March 1847	
Location:	Rivoli Bay	

Kingberri, who was also known as Billy, worked at a station owned by Mr Davenport, which was about 17 miles from Rivoli Bay. Thomas Donelly, 27, had also worked at the station, but had left in mid-August in 1846. On 1 September 1846, Kingberri was at the station along with other workers who were constructing a wash-pen. The men returned to the hut for lunch, where they saw Donelly sitting outside with a pistol in his belt. Donelly argued with several of the workers before he walked away. A 10-year-old Aboriginal boy called Jemmy was with Donelly, and he walked away with him. Kingberri also left, as he wanted to spend some time with his family. A short time later, the sound of a pistol shot was heard. The men followed the sound of the shot and located Kingberri on the ground. Kingberri had been shot in his side, and was bleeding profusely. The men attended to Kingberri's wounds, but he died the following day.

Jemmy was a witness to the shooting, and later gave an account of what he saw during Donelly's trial. Jemmy said that he had been with Donelly for about two months and had travelled in the bush with him. They went to the Davenport property and he saw Donelly shoot 'the black fellow' with a piccaninny gun. Jemmy said that 'the black fellow' was sitting down in his miami and that he was hurt badly. The man later ran into the bush.

Donelly fled and a warrant was later issued for his arrest. Donelly was later arrested about 150 miles from the Davenport property.

On Saturday 12 March 1847, Donelly appeared before the Supreme Court charged with wilful murder. He pleaded not guilty. Evidence was taken from the workers from Davenport's station and from the police. Jemmy was placed in the box to give evidence, where a difficulty arose. The Act required that a witness should declare that he would speak the truth, but Jemmy did not understand the abstract word truth. He could say however that he would tell no lies. His Honour was about to administer some substitute form of oath, when Mr Fisher, for Donelly, strongly urged the legal necessity of adhering strictly to the words of the Act. His Honour felt there was a difficulty, at the same time it was for the court to decide on the fitness of a witness to give evidence. In this case the boy had gone through the words of the Act, and he was made to understand that he was to honestly tell all he knew. It was the same thing only expressed in another language. After swearing the oath, Jemmy gave evidence.

At the completion of the trial, Mr Fisher addressed the jury asking them to throw aside Jemmy's evidence altogether. To the rest of the evidence, he attached no great weight, as it was entirely circumstantial.

His Honour commenced his charge to the jury, but finding there was no chance of the verdict being returned by noon, adjourned the court until Monday. The jury was left in the charge of the sheriff.

On Monday 15 March, the court resumed and His Honour summed up the evidence for three hours. The jury retired for two hours before returning a guilty verdict. When asked if he had anything to say, Donelly replied, 'I have got nothing to say, but that I am an innocent man'. Donelly was sentenced to death.

On 29 March 1847, Donelly was executed at the Adelaide Gaol. Donelly remains the only person to be executed for the murder of an Aboriginal person.

Date	*Victim*	*Accused*
3 November 1846	**Ronkurri (Jemmy McLean)**	**Rallooloolyoo (Larry)**
Cause of death:	Assault (with a waddy)	
Outcome:	Discharged	
Location:	Bremer River, near Strathalbyn	

In November 1846, Corporal John Alfred Burgon, of the mounted police, in company with Constable Mulberan, went to Mr Harriott's station on the Bremer River, near Strathalbyn. At the station, Burgon saw a deceased Aboriginal male, known as Ronkurri, lying on the ground with a fire burning around him. On examining the body, he found that his forehead and part of his face had been knocked in. The skin of his head was burnt and he was lying on his back as if he had died quickly, and had been killed while sleeping. Burgon obtained information that an Aboriginal man named Rallooloolyoo was responsible for the murder, and that he was at the Murray. Burgon travelled there with Constable Mulberan, where four Aboriginal men brought Rallooloolyoo to Burgon, who took him into custody. Rallooloolyoo's waddy, which had a split at the end, was located.

On Friday 13 November 1846, Rallooloolyoo, who was reported to be a very ferocious looking man, was placed at the bar charged with wilful murder. Kaldingyerap (Louise), Ronkurri's wife, testified that Rallooloolyoo was a 'Tatiara black'. She said that her husband was asleep by her side, and that the prisoner killed him with a waddy. She said that Ronkurri died before the sun was up, and that Rallooloolyoo was alone, and he had plenty of spears with him when he attacked. Kaldingyerap was woken after being hit upon the back. She saw Rallooloolyoo strike her husband three times, once near the right eye, once on the forehead and once on the side of the head. After her husband was dead, Rallooloolyoo told her to come on and follow him. They went through the scrub carrying the spears and a firestick. She had not seen her husband since his death, but she had been shown where he was buried. His Worship committed the prisoner for trial on Thursday 24th November.

On Wednesday 25 November 1846, Rallooloolyoo appeared before the Supreme Court. Mr Bartley, Rallooloolyoo's solicitor, moved that Rallooloolyoo should be discharged, as he could only speak a few words of English, which was insufficient for explaining to him what was taking place in court. It was feared it would be a hopeless task to acquire the prisoner's language, as not a word of it was intelligible. Rallooloolyoo could not even be arraigned. The judge ruled that he could not consider the plea from the prisoner who could not even communicate with the court. If the judge did accept the plea, he could try him, but it would be the same as in the case of an insane man, who could not be bound by a plea that he could not understand. Rallooloolyoo was remanded in custody.

On Monday 15 March 1847, Rallooloolyoo appeared before the Supreme Court, where he was discharged, with the crown declining to prosecute, as it had been found impossible to communicate with him.

Date	*Victim*	*Accused*
8 November 1846	**Melicka (Charley)**	**Manooka Bidea (Billy)**
Cause of death:	Spear wound	
Outcome:	Discharged	
Location:	Stoney Creek, near Mount Remarkable	

On 8 November 1846, PC Kenney arrived at his police station at White's Creek. About an hour after he arrived, a local Aboriginal person came to the station with information that Native Mounted Constable Melicka, also known as Charley, had been speared. Kenney rode to Stoney Creek where he spoke to some local Aboriginal people, and then rode to Wild Dog Creek, where he found Charley with a spear wound to his side.

Charley had been stabbed while he was asleep. He was still alive and when Kenney asked him who stabbed him, Charley replied, 'Black fellow Billy'. Kenney asked why, and Charley said, 'Long time ago, me take him, Peter, another one black fellow'. Charley died the following day. It appears that Charley was speared as he had previously apprehended an Aboriginal man called Peter for the murder of Mr Tennant's shepherds.

When the report of Charley's murder reached Adelaide, the following was reported:

> Charley, the native policeman, has, we hear, been murdered by some of the Mount Remarkable tribe, in revenge for his exertions in the recent captures. This is a most unfortunate occurrence, as he was one of the most civilized blacks we had, and had, as yet, shown no inclination to return to native habits.

Stoney Creek, Mt Remarkable, 1846.
State Library of South Australia, B 43319

A year later, in early September 1847, Manooka Bidea (also known as Billy), a Mount Remarkable man, was charged with the murder of Melicka.

On Tuesday 26 October 1847, Manooka Bidea appeared before the Supreme Court charged with Melicka's murder. Manooka Bidea was discharged for want of the necessary Aboriginal evidence to support the testimony of the police.

Date	Victim	Accused
11 November 1846	**Richard Carney**	**Tatty Wambourneen**
Cause of death:	Spear wound	
Outcome:	Discharged	
Location:	Rivoli Bay	

On 16 November 1846, Corporal McCullock received information about a man named Richard Carney, who had been murdered by local Aboriginal people close to the North Avenue, near Lake Munday. McCullock was told that while Carney was in friendly conversation with an Aboriginal man called Tatty Wambourneen and his lubra, he was pierced through the side with a barbed spear. While Tatty Wambourneen was spearing Carney, his lubra began beating him over the head with a waddy.

McCullock went in search of the victim and the offender. On 28 November, McCullock arrived back at Guichen Bay having apprehended Tatty on suspicion of murder. Tatty Wambourneen had been found with some of Carney's belongings in his possession, including some of his clothes.

Tatty Wambourneen appeared before the Supreme Court on Monday 8 March 1847, however, the court was unable to communicate with him, as his tribe was a distant one and its dialect was unknown. His Honour indicated that as the colony became more settled, the difficulty would no doubt be removed as the extension of sheep runs brought distant settlers in contact with fresh Aboriginal tribes. His Honour believed it would be his duty to remand the prisoner, against whom there was every reasonable presumption of guilt, and so prevent at least the bad example that might be occasioned by his going free, and carrying abroad among the other members of Tatty Wambourneen's tribe the idea that crime might be committed with impunity.

On 17 March 1847, in the Supreme Court, it was ordered that Tatty Wambourneen be detained until the September sessions, so further efforts could be made to communicate with him. A young boy from the same tribe as Tatty Wambourneen was being taught English, and it was thought that the adjournment would be enough time for the boy to learn English and to be able to interpret. The witnesses were informed that they were bound by law to appear in court again when called.

A year later, on Friday 17 March 1848, Tatty Wambourneen once more appeared before the Supreme Court, charged with Carney's murder. The advocate general said that notices had been served upon all witnesses who could be found, and they were in attendance in court, but two of the witnesses had left the colony, and one could not be found. Under these circumstances he would be obliged to consent to the prisoner's discharge. His Honour said the reason why the prisoner had been detained so long in gaol was that the court might be able to have the interpretation of the boy, and now that he could interpret, the witnesses could not be found. The prisoner was discharged.

Date	Victim	Accused
17 October 1847	**Mulianolo**	**Rambalta**
Cause of death:	Spear wound	
Outcome:	Found guilty, imprisoned for one to two years	
Location:	Port Lincoln	

There are few details regarding this murder, which occurred around Port Lincoln in 1847. The details of the offence are first mentioned in March 1849, where Rambalta appeared before the Supreme Court on a charge of murdering Mulianolo. Rambalta is later mentioned on page three of the *South Australian Register*, 26 June 1852, where he is in custody for one count of attempted murder after he had speared William Light. He was also charged with stealing at the police station house at Salt Creek. In that account, it is mentioned that Rambalta was tried for the murder of his wife, whom he speared, and was imprisoned in Adelaide for one or two years.

In the different reports in the newspapers, Rambalta is referred to as both Rambalta and Kambalta. No further information could be located.

Date	Victim	Accused
22 March 1848	**Mary**	**Milaitya (Bobbo)**
Cause of death:	Spear wounds	
Outcome:	Found guilty of murder	
	Sentenced to death, commuted to 12 months hard labour	
Location:	Near Burra	

Milaitya and his lubra, Mary, lived with other family members near Burra. On 22 March 1848, Jackey, Mary's brother, was in a wurley near a shepherd's hut with his father. In the middle of the night his father woke Jackey and said, 'Look out, someone has been spearing your sister'. Jackey got up and saw wounds on his sister's left arm and side.

Mary and Milaitya had been sleeping close to where Jackey and his father slept. After Mary was attacked, Milaitya said he was going into the bush, as Jackey's father would spear him in return. Mary told Jackey before she died that 'Bobbo has speared me'. Milaitya said the reason he had speared her was because she had no right to sleep in his wurley. Mary died before sunrise, and her father took her body and buried it nearby.

On Friday 16 June 1848, Milaitya appeared before the Supreme Court on the charge of murdering Mary. Jackey gave evidence, after which the jury retired, finding Milaitya guilty of murder on their return. Milaitya was sentenced to death, but the sentence was later commuted to 12 months hard labour.

General view of the Burra Mine, looking N.N.E.
State Library of South Australia, B 6820

Date	Victim	Accused
27 May 1848	**Edward Olliver**	**James Snow**
Cause of death:	Assault (with a stick)	
Outcome:	Acquitted of murder, found guilty of assault	
	Sentenced to six months imprisonment with hard labour	
Location:	Glen Osmond	

On 27 May 1848, 33-year-old Edward Olliver, James Snow and William Colton were drinking with other patrons at the Miners' Arms Hotel at Glen Osmond. Olliver had been drinking for some time and was intoxicated. Later that evening, Colton, in company with Snow and another person called Edwards, left the hotel and walked towards his home, which was about 600 yards away. Olliver, whose house was in the other direction, also left the hotel. About three minutes after they had left, Olliver approached Snow, Colton and Edwards, and said he would kick the three of them. Snow asked Olliver why he was following them, and to leave them alone. Olliver then got hold of Colton by the collar and kicked him. Snow asked Olliver what he was kicking Colton for, to which Olliver responded, 'I will give you a slap in the mouth too'. Olliver then let go of Colton's collar, and began to assault Snow. Colton saw Snow beat Olliver with a stick. Colton and Snow ran off, as there were several men coming to Olliver's aid. Olliver later died from head injuries.

Snow appeared in the Supreme Court on Saturday 17 June charged with Olliver's murder. Colton gave evidence and stated that he had known Snow for six months and had lodged with him for between four and five months. Snow frequently carried a stick, as his leg had once been broken, and sometimes failed him in walking. Snow was described as a kind-hearted young man, and generally bore a respectable character as a humane and sober man.

At the completion of the evidence, the jury retired and returned with a verdict of not guilty of murder or manslaughter, but guilty of assault. Snow received a sentence of six months hard labour, with one fortnight in solitary confinement.

Date	Victim	Accused
June 1848	**Hart**	**Aboriginal person**
Cause of death:	Unknown	
Outcome:	Accused died in police custody	
Location:	Mount Remarkable	

On 25 July 1848, on page two of the *South Australian*, the following was reported:

A boy, named Hart, who had deserted his employment at the North, that of a shepherd, a month or so back, has been found dead in a wallaby hole. His remains are too far decomposed to afford any clue to the cause of his death, which may possibly have been starvation. Suspicion also falls on the natives, though it would be difficult to assign any reason for their murdering a helpless lad, who had nothing with him to excite their avarice.

The next mention of this murder is two years later on 25 January 1850, on page four of the *South Australian Register*, where in a report on the status of the police force, it is reported that:

A native, in custody of the police for sheep stealing at Yorke's Peninsula, died on the 2nd December. And a native, charged with the murder of a boy named Hart, at Mount Remarkable, in June 1848, was apprehended on the 8th December, and killed by a fall from a horse on the way to Adelaide. Strict investigation has been made respecting the causes of their deaths, and from it there is every reason to believe, that they resulted from no improper treatment or want of attention of the part of the police.

Mount Remarkable, name by Edward Eyre in 1840, is now a national park, situated 238 kilometres north of Adelaide and 25 kilometres east of Port Augusta. It is also the name of the highest peak in the park, with a height of 960 metres. The Nukunu people, who called Mount Remarkable 'Wangyarra', ('arra' meaning running water) inhabited the area before the arrival of European settlers in 1844.

Date	Victim	Accused
23 June 1848	**John Chipp Hamp**	**Mingalta and Malgalta**
Cause of death:	Spear wound, laceration	
Outcome:	Both offenders found guilty of murder, sentenced to death	
	Pardoned by His Excellency on 14 February 1850	
Location:	Lake Newland	

On 23 June 1848, George Stewart went to Stony Point station at Lake Newland with two constables. The station belonged to Mr Pinkerton and was situated about 120 miles from Port Lincoln. When they arrived, they found the body of a 49-year-old shepherd called John Chipp Hamp. Hamp had sailed from England in the *Duke of Roxburgh* and landed at Holdfast Bay in 1838. After spending several years near Henley Beach, he took up land at Lake Newland in 1844.

Stewart saw that Hamp had severe head injuries and one very deep cut near the left ear, which appeared to have come from a saw. He also saw Hamp had a spear wound to his body. Everything had been carried away from the hut, including the stores, dishes, knives, blankets and several tin pots. Stewart walked around the area, and about 140 yards from the hut he saw some footprints in the ground. Stewart recognised one of the prints as belonging to Mingalta, as his big toe was injured. Stewart had last seen Mingalta in the area on 18 June.

The inhabitants of that part of the district had already asked for a police station in their neighbourhood, which had been refused, and it was feared they would be driven to take the law into their own hands, as attacks from the local Aboriginal tribes were frequent. Police Constable Geherty followed the tracks for about 20 miles until they faded out and were lost. Geherty also thought that the footprints around the hut belonged to Mingalta.

Sergeant Geherty, an early police officer in the Port Lincoln district.
State Library of South Australia,
B 46048

In 1849 Geherty saw Mingalta in Port Lincoln and took him into custody. Malgalta was also apprehended and on 26 September 1849, Mingalta and Malgalta were placed on trial in the Supreme Court for Hamp's murder.

At the completion of the trial, the jury, after a short consultation, returned a verdict of guilty against both prisoners. Both were remanded in custody until the following day. On Thursday 27 September, Mingalta and Malgalta were sentenced to death for the murder of John Hamp. Neither prisoner seemed to have the least idea of what was said. Malgalta nodded and grinned, as if to say, 'very good, very good'. Mingalta and Malgalta both received a pardon by His Excellency and on 14 February 1850 they were discharged.

Date	*Victim*	*Accused*
24 January 1849	**John Lester**	**Michael Callaghan**
Cause of death:	Assault	
Outcome:	Discharged	
Location:	Tapleys Hill	

On 24 January 1849, John Lester was in Greig's Public House at Tapleys Hill. Lester was acting in a violent manner towards others, setting his dog onto a child, and later onto a cat. The landlord put the dog outside, and Lester became angrier and said that he wanted to fight any man in South Australia who was his own weight or size. On several occasions, Lester was aggressive towards Michael Callaghan, who was also at the public house.

A fight broke out between Lester and Callaghan, during which Lester received several injuries. Later that day, Lester attended the Emu Public House at Willunga, where he met a friend called William Phillips. Phillips did not recognise Lester due to his injuries. The next day Phillips conveyed Lester to the nearest doctor, but Lester died on the trip. Just before he died, Phillips asked Lester who injured him, to which Lester replied, 'Callaghan has been my ruin, he has murdered me, and …' Lester did not finish his sentence, dying shortly afterwards. Callaghan was subsequently taken into custody on a charge of feloniously killing John Lester.

During evidence given at various hearings, it was stated that the injuries Lester received were apparently not sufficient to cause death in a healthy person, and in the opinion of a medical practitioner, Lester would have survived the injuries if he had been properly treated. Lester had been drinking for 10 or 12 days prior to the incident and had spent more than £40 on alcohol. On hearing the evidence, His Worship was of the opinion that at its worst aspect, it was not a case of aggravated manslaughter, but it was clear that the deceased died from the injuries received from Callaghan, who was committed for trial in the Supreme Court.

Callaghan appeared before the Supreme Court on Monday 12 March 1849, where the judge summed up the evidence to the grand jury.

> It is unhappily apparent that the deceased was the aggressor, and that the affray, which was the alleged cause of his death, was provoked by his intemperate language and behaviour of the prisoner ... and you will have to satisfy yourselves that the death of Lester is attributable to the affray with Callaghan, and not to continued intoxication and the neglect of the prescribed means for his recovery.

At Callaghan's next appearance, he was discharged on bail 'to answer any bill or indictment that may be preferred against him, for the manslaughter of John Lester'. No further appearance is noted.

Date	*Victim*	*Accused*
March 1849	**Nine Aboriginal people**	**James Brown**
	One man, three women,	
	Five girls (aged 15, 12, 2 years, 18 months and one infant).	
Cause of death:	Gunshot wounds	
Outcome:	Case dismissed	
Location:	Tatiara, near Guichen Bay	

In March 1849, James Brown, from Tatiara, a prisoner in the charge of Police Constable Farrell from Guichen Bay, arrived in Adelaide. Brown was fully committed by Captain Butler, on a charge of murdering five Aboriginal people. The evidence was chiefly Aboriginal, but it was said to be 'fearfully conclusive'. The bodies were burnt after the murders and a box full of the bones was brought to Adelaide to be produced in evidence. Brown was not tried during those sittings, as the necessary witnesses had not been brought in.

It was reported in the newspapers that:

So far from being fearfully conclusive, we understand the only evidence is that of one native, who states that he was not present when the alleged murders took place; who at first stated he was unable to recognise the prisoner as one of the parties seen by him near the place where the bodies were found, and afterwards gave very contradictory evidence. The prisoner is an old colonist and highly respectable, and any attempt to prejudice public opinion against him is to be deprecated. The prisoner will be brought up this day on a habeas corpus, and will probably be discharged on the ground of informalities in the warrant of commitment.

In the Supreme Court there was legal discussion regarding the lack of information on the warrant, and an application was made for a discharge on the ground of numerous irregularities in the warrant of commitment for the murder. Brown appeared before the Supreme Court on 28 March 1849, where he was granted bail. Evidence later revealed there to be a total of nine victims, all of whom had been shot by Brown.

Around the middle of June, an affidavit was received in the court from Mr Moorehouse, stating that on 23 February, five graves containing a number of bones belonging to both adults and children had been located. An affidavit from police corporal Burgon stated that he had endeavoured to procure the attendance of a female witness, but he could not find her. It was believed that she was removed or deterred from testifying against the prisoner.

The case against Brown was eventually dropped due to the failure to locate the female witness and the lack of European witnesses.

Date	Victim	Accused
April 1849	Five Aboriginal people	Patrick Dwyer
Cause of death:	Poisoned	
Outcome:	Dwyer arrested and released, then fled to California	
Location:	Thirty miles from Port Lincoln	

In April 1849, Patrick Dwyer was employed in the service of Mr Mortlock as a shepherd and hutkeeper on a property situated about 30 miles from Port Lincoln. It was not unusual for one person to perform these two duties, and as a result his wages were increased. Dwyer had, for about eight weeks, been in the habit of leaving his hut in the morning, going out with the sheep and returning at sunset. Day after day he left his provisions under the insufficient protection of a padlock. The local Aboriginal people soon became acquainted with the unprotected state of his provisions, and had twice broken open the door of the hut and stolen its contents. Dwyer appeared to have prepared for a third ransacking of the hut by mixing arsenic into a bag of flour. After Dwyer left the hut, thieves broke in and stole the contaminated flour. About a mile away, the flour was made into damper. Eight of the Aboriginal people ate the damper and five died. Dwyer was apprehended, but as the police were in possession of no facts that bore directly against him, he was released and told that he must appear in court when called upon. Police found arsenic inside the hut, but Mr Mortlock and others testified before the magistrate that arsenic had been used at that station for dressing sheep.

When at Port Lincoln, Mr Tolmer, the Acting Commissioner of Police, collected a portion of sacking he had found lying near the remains of the victims, which was later examined and found to contain arsenic. The presumption was that Dwyer had mixed the arsenic with the flour, and left the mixture in the hut, purposely to be taken and eaten by Aboriginal thieves.

Later that year, a report from the Police Commissioner's office dated 13 October 1849 stated:

It may not probably be out of place for me here to revert to the apprehension of Patrick Dwyer, on suspicion of poisoning five natives, which circumstance was reported in the preceding quarter. It is to be regretted, considering the seriousness of the case, that this individual was discharged by the Government Resident. Had he been remanded, to allow time for the production of further evidence, the police are now possessed of such material matter as would doubtless have ensured a conviction. He has since sailed for California, which precludes the possibility of him being re-apprehended.

Date	*Victim*	*Accused*
3 May 1849	James Beevor	Neentulta, Kulgulta, Yabmanna, Pullurunyu, Pakilti, Pullarpinye, and Maltalta

Cause of death:	Spear wound
Outcome:	Neentulta and Kulgulta found guilty of murder
	Sentenced to death, executed 9 November 1849
	All others acquitted
Location:	Fifty miles from Port Lincoln

On the morning of 3 May 1849, four Aboriginal people, including Neentulta and his lubra Yabmanna, had slept near the house of James Rigby Beevor, 38. Beevor's property was about 50 miles from Port Lincoln. A young Aboriginal boy called Pedilta or Pedtalta also slept there. In the morning, Pedilta left the property and when he returned in the evening, he found that Beevor had been murdered. The house had been ransacked and the flour, blankets and numerous other articles had been removed. The four campers were also gone. The police, with the assistance of Pedilta, followed the tracks and in a hole they located some of the property and a blanket and rug belonging to Neentulta and Yabmanna.

Those thought to be responsible for the murder were taken into custody, and on Monday 10 September they first appeared before the Supreme Court in Adelaide.

On Monday 24 September, only Kulgulta, Neentulta and Yabmanna appeared before the court. Kulgulta was charged with the murder and Neentulta and Yabmanna were charged with being an accessory before the fact.

On Tuesday 25 September, Neentulta, Kulgulta and Yabmanna appeared once more before the Supreme Court. This time all three were charged with Beevor's murder. Evidence was heard from Mr Ludwig and Mr Rigby, both of whom were living with Beevor at the time, but were away from the house on the day of the murder. The court heard that tobacco and clothing were traced to the prisoners and that there was no positive evidence that the two men actually inflicted the deadly wounds. Upon hearing this, Mr Bartley, for the defence, objected, since the indictment was explicit in saying that the prisoners had indeed inflicted the wounds that caused Beevor's death, and that therefore the question of stealing the property had nothing to do with the case before the jury. His Honour addressed the jury:

If there was sufficient connection between the time of the murder and the abstraction of the property from the hut, they were bound to make those circumstances lead their supposition, that the prisoners, if not the actual murderers, were there aiding and abetting, which in law was as bad as if theirs were the hands that did the deed.

At the conclusion of the trial, the jury retired before returning a guilty verdict against Neentulta and Kulgulta, and acquittal for the women (the article mentions 'females', but only names Yabmanna).

On 27 September, Neentulta and Kulgulta appeared before the Supreme Court where they were both sentenced to death. The sentence was interpreted to them, but they seemed scarcely to know what was meant.

On 9 November 1849, both prisoners were executed at the station where Beevor was murdered.

A year later, on 15 November 1850, another suspect called Maltalta, against whom a warrant had been issued by Mr W Peter, J.P. for Beevor's murder, was taken into custody and committed at Port Lincoln to take trial in Adelaide. Maltalta was transported to Adelaide where he stood trial in the Supreme Court and was subsequently acquitted. While Maltalta was making his way back to Port Lincoln, he was murdered by Aboriginal people from another tribe (see 11 February 1851).

Date	*Victim*	*Accused*
7 May 1849	**Ann Easton**	**Malpita, Pakilta, and Puturpynter**
Cause of death:	Spear wounds	
Outcome:	Pakilta and Puturpynter discharged	
	Malpita not located	
Location:	Near Port Lincoln	

During the search for the offenders in the murder of James Beevor (3 May 1849), word was received regarding the murder of 30-year-old Ann Easton. Police went to her residence and found her body on a bed, with a child of about six weeks next to her. The child was unharmed. It appeared that Easton was in the process of dressing the child when she was attacked. Easton died from multiple spear injuries. The search party continued on, now also looking for Easton's murderers.

The search party later came across a group of Aboriginal people. The encounter led to a confrontation, during which two Aboriginal people were shot and five taken into custody. The group had items belonging to both Beevor and Easton.

On Tuesday 25 September 1849, Pakilta and Puturpynter were put on trial for Easton's murder. The trial was proceeding well until the last witness, a local boy, stated that it was Malpita, who was not in custody, who was the culprit. The judge recommended that both prisoners be discharged, which they were. There is no reference to the apprehension of Malpita.

Two days later, on 27 September, James Easton, Ann's husband, wrote the following letter to the *South Australian Register*:

Gentlemen, I beg to call your attention to the incompetency shown by the interpreter, Mr Schurmann, during the late trials of the Port Lincoln blacks for murder. During the trial of Pakilte for the murder of my wife, when told to give the usual warning to the witness, to tell the truth, the form in which he put it was, 'Be careful of what you say, or the white men will be angry with you,' in consequence of which the old man became frightened, and did not tell all he knew respecting the murder. The black, on being questioned as to the names of the murderers, distinctly stated, three times, that the prisoner Pakilte, then in the dock, was one of the murderers, and he also named four more natives, amongst whom was one called Mabilte. However, owing to the interruptions of the prisoners' counsel, and the number of questions put to him in consequence, the black became confused, and the name of Mabilte, was confounded with that of Pakilte, who was, very fortunately for him, stated by Mr Schurmann, in his interpretation, to have been cutting grass at the time of the murder. Any person acquainted with the habits of the blacks will see in a moment how improbable it is that a black, the leader of the tribe, and noted for his coolness and daring, should be quietly cutting grass at a short distance from the hut, while his friends were murdering my unfortunate wife.

In such serious cases as have been before the Court this session, the most correct interpretation ought to be procured, in order that strict justice might be done between us and the blacks, and then such villains as Pakilte is well known to be, would not be allowed to go at large, to again pursue a career of crime. Mr Schurmann, unfortunately for the ends of justice, has proved himself in my case utterly unfit for the responsible situation he holds, by his ignorance of the particular dialect used by the natives of the western coast of Port Lincoln, which differs greatly from that spoken by the natives of the northern coast, and which was that used by him in speaking to the witness Eelgulta, who often misunderstood him. In the cases against the natives for the murders of Mr Beevor and Mr Hamp, the native witnesses, having often been in Port Lincoln, were better able to understand Mr Schurmann, and the blacks were in consequence convicted, which would also have been the case with Pakilte, had there been a competent person to interpret, and who could have been procured from Port Lincoln. There were persons in Court who could understand the witness Eelgulta better than Mr Schurmann, and to whom the black admitted, on leaving the witness box, having seen Pakilte, in conjunction with several others, murder my unfortunate wife. I trust that the feelings natural to a husband, on having a much-loved wife brutally murdered, and then seeing the murderer acquitted, owing to the ignorance or prejudice of a public servant, will be considered an excuse for troubling you with this long letter.

I beg to remain, Gentlemen, Yours, &c James Easton. Adelaide, September 27, 1849.

Date	Victim	Accused
3 July 1849	**Nantariltarra**	**George Field**
Cause of death:	Gunshot wound	
Outcome:	Discharged	
Location:	Hardwicke Bay	

George Field was an overseer on a property near Hardwicke Bay on Yorke's Peninsula. On 2 July 1849, a cook from the property went to the head station and told Mr Penton that some sheep had been taken by a group of Aboriginal people. The following morning, a group of men from the station, including Field, went to the area where the sheep were taken from and tracked the animals to an outstation near the sea. When the group were on the sandhills near the water, they saw a number of Aboriginal people with the sheep on the beach. The group of Aboriginal people ran away, and some of them entered the water to escape. Nantariltarra, who was also known as William, was one of those who entered the water, but when he was a short distance from the shore, he turned back as he heard the screams of a young girl who was still on the beach.

The shepherds started shooting at the group as they fled. Field took aim at Nantariltarra and fired, hitting Nantariltarra in the head, killing him instantly. The girl that Nantariltarra had returned for had entered the water and was swimming towards him. With Nantariltarra killed, the girl was without aid and drowned.

The others managed to escape, so the shepherds burnt the sheep carcases and rounded up the live sheep and left.

Kookonea saw Field shoot and kill Nantariltarra, and was one of those who managed to escape. Several weeks later, Kookonea took Sergeant Major McCulloch to the place where Nantariltarra and the young girl were buried. McCulloch examined the bodies and saw that the male had a bullet wound to the head.

On Monday 3 September 1849, George Field appeared in the police court charged with Nantariltarra's murder. Murra, a local boy who had witnessed the murder, gave a statement. As Murra could not speak English, Jim Crack acted as an interpreter. Murra stated that he was employed as shepherd by George Penton, but not at the station where Scott was killed (2 August 1849). Murra described a gathering of settlers, and a pursuit of the thieves, who were discovered at an encampment near the sea with several stolen sheep. At the approach of the search party, the fleeing Aboriginal people took to the water. Murra's father, Nantariltarra, was one of them. Nantariltarra heard a little girl cry on the beach, so he returned for her. Just as he reached her, Field shot him through the head. Nantariltarra fell back with his head under the water, and never moved again. The pursuing party consisted of Field, George Penton, a person named Palfrey, a shepherd named William Scott, a cook called William, a shepherd called Johnny, a gentleman whose name Murra did not know, and another shepherd. All were mounted except Scott.

Kookonea also gave evidence of the shooting. At the completion of the evidence, Field was committed to the Supreme Court.

On Friday 14 September, in the Supreme Court, the grand jury ignored the bill against George Field, charged with the 'murder of a native' at Yorke's Peninsula, and Field was discharged.

Date	*Victim*	*Accused*
12 July 1849	**Tom Armstrong**	**Thulta**
Cause of death:	Spear wounds	
Outcome:	Discharged	
Location:	Yorke's Peninsula	

On Saturday 14 July 1849, in the *South Australian Register*, it was reported on page three that 'the Aborigines on Yorke's Peninsula are becoming more troublesome than before as a Shepherd named Armstrong has been killed by a spear'. Armstrong died 18 hours after the wounds were inflicted.

The quarterly report of the Aboriginal Department states:

On the Peninsula, two shepherds have died from spear wounds, received at the hands of the natives. The first person, named Armstrong, was in Mr Milner Stephens' service as a shepherd, whilst, according to the statement made a few hours before his death, he was in the yard with his flock, he heard a dog barking in the scrub, about 200 yards away. He went to see what was the matter, when he suddenly came upon a group of about thirty natives, they were not encamped, but standing amongst the trees and bushes. One of them threw a spear, which knocked his hat off, and, turning round to go home, a second spear was thrown, which pierced him in the back. He did not admit having given any provocation. I met with a native boy, who was present with Armstrong on this occasion, but his narrative does not agree with the above. He states that he was shepherding for Armstrong, and Armstrong had requested him to bring a native woman to the station, if he should meet with any on the run. On the morning of the 11th July, the boy saw a native, named Thulta, with his wife, a little from the station, and told Armstrong where they were. Armstrong immediately went to them, seized the woman for sensual purposes, and after accomplishing all that he desired, liberated the woman to return to her husband. The passions of the husband were naturally aroused, and, whilst under their influence, avenged the insult upon Armstrong by spearing him.

A 39-year-old Aboriginal man named Thulta was eventually taken into custody, charged with the murders of Armstrong and William Scott (2 August 1849). Thulta was eventually discharged.

Date	*Victim*	*Accused*
2 August 1849	**William Scott**	**Wilcumramalap and Thulta**
Cause of death:	Spear wound	
Outcome:	Both discharged	
Location:	Hardwicke Bay	

On 2 August 1849, Sergeant Major McCulloch of the mounted police was informed that a shepherd named William Scott had not returned with his sheep to his hut, situated at Hardwicke Bay. The following day a search was undertaken, and about a mile from the hut they came upon the tracks of both humans and sheep. These were followed, and about a mile later a broken ramrod was found with fresh blood marks on it. Around five miles from the track, in dense forest, they came across an Aboriginal encampment, which had about 150 sheep in it. The search party rushed the camp, but they only located one man and some women and children. The women and children were released and a 23-year-old man called Wilcumramalap was taken into custody. Inside the camp the search party located a gun-barrel, a pistol, a book with Scott's name in it, and a cap that Scott used to wear. The prisoner, through an interpreter named Jimmy Crack, was asked where the white man was, and, without any hesitation, took the party to Scott's body. Scott was lying on his back with an incision from the breast to the navel, and part of the intestinal fat had been removed. His throat had been cut and he had two spear wounds in his back. Wilcumramalap was taken to a port to await a vessel sailing to Adelaide. When apprehended, Wilcumramalap told Jimmy Crack that he had killed the white fellow with 39-year-old Thulta.

On Tuesday 27 November, Wilcumramalap and Thulta appeared before the Supreme Court, charged with the murders of Scott and Tom Armstrong (12 July 1849). His Honour commenced his address to the grand jury, reminding the gentlemen that it was customary in South Australia for the grand jury to stand while the judge delivered his charge. The grand jury took the hint, and one or two members muttered an apology as they stood. His Honour continued, and spoke of the evidence against Wilcumramalap and Thulta, stating that with regard to the evidence against them, he could say nothing satisfactory, as the evidence came solely from Aboriginal witnesses, and that he could not say from the manner in which the depositions were taken, whether it was intended to charge Thulta with the murder of Scott or Armstrong or both. At the end of his address, His Honour left the evidence with the grand jury for their consideration, to see if there was a *prima facie* case against the prisoners.

On 11 March 1850, both Wilcumramalap and Thulta appeared before the Supreme Court where they were further remanded in custody.

On Saturday 20 April 1850, the 'Report of the Protector of Aborigines' was published, stating that 'Wilcumramalap and Thulta, charged with murder, were liberated, as there was not sufficient evidence to put them upon their trial'.

Date	*Victim*	*Accused*
2 August 1849	**James Stone**	**James Johnson**
Cause of death:	Gunshot wound	
Outcome:	Case dismissed	
Location:	Lake Bonney	

The Police Commissioner's report, dated 13 October 1849, reporting for the quarter ending 30 September 1849, contains the following passage relating to the murder of James Stone:

I regret, however, that some are of the most serious kind, and beg most particularly to advert to the case of J. Stone, near Lake Bonney. I had the honour of making a special report to you, at the time, on the subject, therein stating that I had taken every means which I could devise to bring the perpetrator of this cold blooded deed to justice. Corporal Howell, a young man of great zeal and perseverance, pursued a man answering the description of the party suspected over the River Murray, into the district of Mount Gambier, and succeeded in over taking him. Mr Sturt, however, before whom he was taken, discharged him, as there was not sufficient evidence to justify his sending him to Adelaide. I fear, from the length of time that has elapsed since the murder, there is very little chance of apprehending the guilty party.

On Tuesday 4 June 1850, James Johnson (also known as James Williams, William Cooper, and William Hamilton) appeared before the police court charged with Stone's murder. After several witnesses gave evidence, one of them testified that Johnson had a different appearance to the murderer. The magistrate dismissed the charge.

Date	Victim	Accused
12 August 1849	Milartyappa (Malappa)	Harry Valetta Jones and Henry Thomas Morris
Cause of death:	Gunshot wound	
Outcome:	Both acquitted	
Location:	Yorke's Peninsula	

On Wednesday 29 August 1849, Harry Valetta Jones and Henry Thomas Morris, 24, appeared in the Police Court on a charge of feloniously shooting at and wounding with intent to murder Milartyappa, an Aboriginal man, at Yorke's Peninsula on 12 August 1849. Morris was described as an early colonist, related to Governor Hindmarsh. Evidence was given by an Aboriginal boy, of about 10 years of age, through the interpreter Jim Crack. The boy stated that he knew Jones and Morris and that Jones shot first. Morris had a two-barrel gun and shot Milartyappa once in the arm and once in the foot. Jones shot Milartyappa in the body. On 1 September Milartyappa died from his wounds. The coroner held an inquest and the jury returned a verdict of wilful murder against Morris and Jones.

On 17 September 1849, Jones and Morris appeared before the Supreme Court charged with the wilful murder of Milartyappa. The trial proceeded before a jury. At the beginning of the trial, the advocate general stated that the prisoners were charged, one as the principal in the first degree and the other in the second degree. If the jury were to believe the evidence from Aboriginal witnesses, then no further testimony would be needed. During the opening address, he stated:

It might, certainly, be said their testimony was given without the sanction of an oath, but the police of the law of late years had been to let the court and jury deal with all evidence according to the circumstances before them. If these led to the belief that the truth came from the mouth of a witness, his evidence could not be thrown aside, savage and uncivilised though he might be.

During the trial, Mr Parker, for the defence, did not like the way the questions were being put to a witness. Parker submitted that if the law imposed on His Honour the necessity of taking 'native evidence', it did not impose the necessity or confer the privilege on the advocate general of putting leading or illegal questions. Parker stated that certainly was not the practice in England. The advocate general replied that 'the learned gentleman takes great pleasure in referring to his recent English experience, but, before long, he will find that many things that go smoothly in England do not work well here'.

At the conclusion of the trial, His Honour addressed the jury, expressing his regret that the evidence fell so short, and that there certainly seemed no course for him but to recommend that the jury acquit the prisoners. The jury, without leaving the box, returned a verdict of not guilty.

On the liberation of the prisoners, the silence, which had been rigidly preserved during the court's proceedings, gave way to a tumultuous expression of satisfaction. The long pent-up feelings of the audience found vent in a mighty volley of cheers, which completely put the efforts of the officers of the court at defiance. The cheers were repeated outside the court, and the traders of Hindley Street were startled occasionally by a sudden but simultaneous shout from a large body of people, who had not separated even at that distance from the courthouse.

Date	Victim	Accused
20 October 1849	Thomas Keorby	Francis Flynn
Cause of death:	Knife wounds	
Outcome:	Acquitted	
Location:	Strathalbyn	

On Saturday 20 October 1849, Francis Flynn and Thomas Keorby were drinking together at the Strathalbyn Hotel. When they left the hotel, they were both very drunk, but were on good terms with each other. They went to a house nearby in Strathalbyn, where Flynn fell asleep. Keorby woke Flynn up and asked him if he wanted a fight. Flynn stood up but Keorby knocked him down. A struggle followed and Flynn, feeling he was getting beaten, drew a knife and stabbed Keorby in the thigh, cutting his femoral artery. Flynn then stabbed Keorby in the abdomen. Keorby died from his injuries.

An Aboriginal man called Karkooanby witnessed the fight. During the autopsy a knife blade was recovered from the abdomen, which was identified as belonging to Flynn.

Flynn was arrested and charged with manslaughter. On Friday 30 November 1849, his trial in the Supreme Court concluded. Mr Gwynne conducted the defence, and in his summing up he stated that:

> The identity of the prisoner was not established, the only direct evidence being that of a native witness, whose testimony must be received with great jealousy, and now admitted that the night was dark when the deceased received the fatal wounds. But even if the jury were of opinion that the person spoken of by the witness was really the prisoner, the whole circumstances negated the idea of his intention to kill, it seemed far more probable that, contending with an assailant, when in the darkness he did not recognise, he acted in self-defence against a real or imaginary danger.

The judge then summed up and the jury, without retiring, acquitted the prisoner.

Date	Victim	Accused
25 December 1849	**John Smith**	**Carl Gottliet Keirnall**
Cause of death:	Assault (with an axe)	
Outcome:	Found guilty of manslaughter	
	Sentenced to seven years transportation	
Location:	Burra	

On Christmas Day 1849, 24-year-old John Smith went to the house of a German named Carl Gottliet Keirnall and asked for a light for his pipe. Keirnall obliged, and Smith left, but later returned again wanting another light. Some words were exchanged between Smith and Keirnall, during which

Smith said that he would burn down Keirnall's house, and put a candle up to the roof. Keirnall's wife attempted to snatch the candle from Smith and it fell to the ground. The argument escalated further and Keirnall struck Smith on the head with a stool, before retreating inside the house. Smith burst open the door and started to throw stones and the staves of a cask into the house. Keirnall came out the house and struck Smith on the back of his head with an axe, which caused him to bleed.

Smith went a short distance away then returned to Keirnall's house and burst through the door again. Keirnall came out with the axe and stuck Smith on the top of the head, completely splitting Smith's skull in two, with the heel of the axe coming in contact with the brain. Smith died from the injuries.

The following day, on 26 December, an inquest was held at Kooringa. The jury returned a verdict against Keirnall for the wilful murder of John Smith and he was committed under the coroner's warrant accordingly.

Keirnall appeared before the Supreme Count on Wednesday 13 March 1850, charged with the murder of John Smith. An interpreter was sworn in as Keirnall spoke only German. After hearing the evidence, the jury returned a verdict of manslaughter. During the sentencing on Friday 15 March, the judge stated that he was glad he had not been convicted of murder, as the case was a most aggravated one of manslaughter. Although there was some provocation, there was no excuse in the sight of God or man for the use of the axe. Keirnall was sentenced to seven years transportation.

Date	*Victim*	*Accused*
5 January 1850	**Amelia Fry**	**Robert Fry**
Cause of death:	Gunshot wound	
Outcome:	Robert Fry found deceased	
	Case treated as a murder-suicide	
Location:	Near Balaklava	

Robert Fry, 35, lived with his 34-year-old wife Amelia and their young children in Adelaide. Robert sold milk in Adelaide before the family moved to Yankalilla and then to the Wakefield River, near Port Wakefield. When they moved to the Wakefield River, they were described as a 'family of considerable means'.

In late 1849, Robert attempted suicide by cutting his throat while in the

Ladd's Inn at Gepps Cross. He was described as being in a 'disordered state of mind'. After medical treatment he returned to his station at Port Wakefield. In December, Robert wandered into the bush. Amelia became concerned for him, and a police search was undertaken, locating Robert soon afterward. Later, while at the homestead, Amelia entered their bedroom and surprised Robert, who had a pistol with him. Robert wandered into the bush once more, and when he returned after several days, he told Amelia that he had been dog shooting.

On Saturday 5 January, Robert took Amelia for a drive in his rig, leaving their three children, the youngest of whom was 10 months old, at the homestead. Later that evening, Mr Loveday, a surveyor who was engaged in that part of the country, located Amelia's body in the rig. She had been shot in the head. Her body had been rested on a pillow, and was carefully covered over. The Fry's horse was near the rig and had been non-fatally stabbed. Police from Clare were made aware of the murder and went to the area, looking for Robert in the bush.

It was reported that Robert, in a fit of madness, murdered his wife in the vicinity of their property near the top of the gulf, near the Wakefield. When Amelia was examined, she had a hammerhead whip firmly grasped in her hand. There were some marks of a scuffle on the ground, which indicated that Amelia had struggled for her life.

In February, some bullock drivers spotted Robert. He was nearly naked, and carried a rifle, a brace of pistols and a long knife. It was reported in Adelaide that:

> Fry, who recently murdered his wife, still lurks in the vicinity of his station, on the Wakefield. He continues to elude the police and possesses great cunning. It appears he has contrived to construct a hiding place upon an elevated position, by which he surveys, unseen, all that passes.

In June 1850, Mr Alexander McCulloch discovered Robert's bones, about half a mile from where Amelia was murdered. The bones had been scattered by wild dogs, but there was no doubt as to the identity, as the rifle, cutting knife, pistol and the pocket book belonging to Fry was by the bones. Also found was a bonnet which belonged to his wife.

FRYS CLUMP

It is alleged that Mr Robert Fry murdered his wife on this site early in 1850 and then took his own life in mid 1850 nearby. When the land was sold in the 1890's, the purchaser was instructed never to remove the clump of trees as they marked the spot where a man took his wife's life and near which he took his own life.
This clump of trees is shown on the original surveyor's map and along side it is printed "clump of trees where Fry's remains where found". Although regarded by many over the years with scepticism, the coroner's report in 1850 indicated amazing accuracy of the details handed down over the years. Heritage listed 19 May 1988.

At Section 151, Hundred of Dalkey, stands Fry's Clump, situated at Fry Flat, just south of Balaklava on the Balaklava to Mallala Road. This is reported as being the area where the murder suicide occurred.
Wikipedia Commons: Marionlad

Date	*Victim*	*Accused*
22 May 1850	**Alexander Wood**	**George Pyke**
Cause of death:	Assault	
Outcome:	Discharged	
Location:	The Dirty Light, near Saddleworth	

On Wednesday 22 May 1850, Alexander Wood, 60, and Philip Ross were in the stable of George Pyke's property. Pyke, who was 26 years old, owned a property at The Dirty Light near Saddleworth. Ross was killing a sheep and talking to Wood when Pyke came into the stable and said to Wood, 'This is a pretty work you have been at', before striking him over the eye. Wood staggered against Ross then walked out of the stable. Pyke followed Wood and hit him again, this time in the chest, knocking Wood to the ground. Wood managed to get up and ran off. Pyke attacked Wood because of a misunderstanding between Pyke's wife and Wood earlier in the day.

Wood later returned to the property, complaining of a sore chest. Wood went to the station owned by Mr James Rush, where his condition worsened. Rush told Wood that he would summon Dr Blood to treat him, but Wood said

Dr Matthew Blood,
approximately 1860.
State Library of
South Australia, B 9945

that he did not attribute his illness to the blows he received, and that he did not need to be treated. Wood said that all he needed was a mustard plaster on his chest. Wood eventually died on 1 June. No doctor was called to see Wood and he was buried without an inquest.

After authorities heard that no inquest had been held, one was convened. As a medical man could not be readily obtained, the jury felt satisfied with the evidence given. The body was not exhumed and the death was attributed to natural causes. The reason there was no exhumation was the nearest surgeon, Dr Blood, resided at Gawler, which was 34 miles away, and it would have occasioned a great delay to send for him.

On Thursday 4 July, Pyke appeared before the police court charged with feloniously killing and slaying Alexander Wood. The court heard that after the assault Wood complained of chest pains and general ill health. He refused medical treatment but requested a mustard plaster for his chest, however the station owner had no mustard. Wood had told a witness that the cause of the pains in his chest were occasioned by a blow by Pyke, but this was not taken into evidence as a dying declaration, since Wood was not aware that he was in a dangerous state. At the conclusion of the prosecution case, the defence stated that there was nothing in evidence to say that the assault could be the cause of Wood's death. His Honour stated that he still thought that it was a case that should go to a jury. Pyke was committed to trial for manslaughter, but was then bailed.

On Monday 12 August 1850, before the Supreme Court, the grand jury ignored the bill for George Pyke and he was discharged.

Date	*Victim*	*Accused*
27 May 1850	**Thomas Roberts**	**Patrick O'Connor**
Cause of death:	Gunshot and stab wounds	
Outcome:	Found not guilty	
Location:	Kooringa	

On a property near Kooringa, on 10 or 11 May 1850, 20-year-old Patrick O'Connor approached James White, the overseer, and asked for a job as a hutkeeper. White said that the owner of the property, Mr Bagot, had gone to town, but he could start work now until Bagot returned. O'Connor worked until Bagot returned, and was allowed to continue to be employed there. Later, O'Connor told White that he did not want to stay, as he did not like being a hutkeeper, so he rode off on his horse.

Thomas Roberts was also employed as a hutkeeper, and about three hours after O'Connor had left, rode to the head station to make a complaint against O'Connor.

On 28 May 1850, White, along with Bagot, received information from another hutkeeper that Roberts was missing. White and Bagot went to the hut to search for him. During the search they heard a dog bark, and recognised it as being Roberts' dog. They went to the dog and found Roberts' body on the side of a gully. After news of the murder became known, a witness came forward and said that he had seen O'Connor riding his horse near where the murder occurred, and that shortly after he heard two gunshots.

A post-mortem carried out by Dr Blood found that Roberts had a gunshot wound to the face, which shattered his chin, and a stab wound to the chest, which penetrated the heart. The weapon was a double-edged knife or dagger. There were also several stab wounds in his back that had penetrated the lungs.

When O'Connor was located, he had several items belonging to Roberts. O'Connor had also committed other offences, including highway robbery.

On Saturday 8 June, O'Connor appeared before the police court charged with wilful murder of Thomas Roberts, with firing at the passengers by the Northern Mail with intent to do grievous bodily harm, and with other stealing and fraud offences. O'Connor was committed to trial.

O'Connor appeared before the Supreme Court on Tuesday 20 August, charged with Roberts' murder. The trial went for two days, and at the completion of the evidence, the jury retired and returned with a verdict of not guilty.

Date	*Victim*	*Accused*
15 June 1850	**Male child**	**Unknown**
Cause of death:	Unknown	
Outcome:	Unknown	
Location:	Klemzig	

On Monday 17 June 1850, an inquest was held on the body of a newborn child found in the River Torrens at Klemzig on Sunday 15 June, at around three pm by Samuel Taylor. The water had risen overnight and the current was quite strong. James Nash, the Colonial Surgeon, had performed an examination of the body and believed that the child had been born at full term, but he was unable to say if he had been born alive. A verdict of wilful murder against some person or persons unknown was delivered.

Date	*Victim*	*Accused*
18 June 1850	**John Doyle**	**David Spears**
Cause of death:	Assault	
Outcome:	Case dismissed	
Location	Gawler	

On 18 June 1850, at Gawler, near the Gawler Arms Hotel, a fight took place between John Doyle and David Spears. Both men had been drinking. John Marsden and John Donnelly acted as a 'second' for Doyle and Spears. They fought for six rounds, and Doyle was seen to strike Spears twice before he retaliated. In one of the rounds, Spears was on the ground and Doyle would not let him get up, repeatedly hitting him in the head. In the last round, Spears hit Doyle in the head, and he fell to the ground and lay there until his second picked him up. Doyle was taken from the fight to his house, and died the following day.

Spears was arrested and charged with manslaughter, and Marsden and Donelly were charged with aiding and abetting. Spears appeared before the magistrate where his defence argued that Doyle's death could not be contributed to any of the blows during the fight, as Doyle had fallen during the day and evening due to him being drunk. It was also a cold night and a doctor stated that Doyle might have died from exposure.

The magistrate committed Spears to trial and was given bail, with two sureties of £50 each. Spears appeared on several occasions before the Supreme Court charged with murder, and on his final appearance on Monday 12 August 1850, the bills of David Spears, John Marsden and John Donelly were ignored.

Date	Victim	Accused
24 July 1850	**John Mansforth**	**John Yates**
Cause of death:	Knife wounds	
Outcome:	Yates found guilty of murder	
	Sentenced to death, executed 5 September 1850	
Location:	Skillogalee Creek, near Watervale	

John Mansforth and John Yates were in the service of a gentleman named Slater, and shared a hut near Watervale. Yates was employed as a shepherd and Mansforth as a hutkeeper. Mansforth was a military pensioner of steady and respectable habits, and was highly esteemed by his employer.

On Tuesday 23 July 1850, Mansforth received his wages from Slater, who told Mansforth to tell Yates to collect his wages. He also asked Mansforth to tell Yates that his job would be terminated, as there was another man to take his place. Later that evening, Mansforth and Yates met at the local hotel and had some drinks. After purchasing a bottle of whisky, Mansforth left and was later followed by Yates. Mansforth and Yates were seen quarrelling and a short time later, Yates was seen with a knife injury to his hand, and blood on his clothing. Mansforth was found dead not far from the hotel.

On Friday 26 July 1850, an inquest was held at Hailes' public house at Skillagolee Creek on the body of John Mansforth. Yates had been apprehended and was present at the inquest. Charles Hamilton Webb, surgeon, had made a post-mortem examination and found that Mansforth had severe head injuries including stab wounds. His throat had been cut and he had a stab wound in his abdomen. At the completion of the evidence, the jury returned a verdict of wilful murder against Yates, who was committed to trial.

Yates appeared in the Supreme Court on Monday 19 August 1850 before Mr Justice Crawford. At the completion of the trial, the jury found Yates guilty of wilful murder, and he was sentenced to death.

On Thursday 5 September 1850, James Yates was executed. Between four and six hundred adults were present to witness the hanging. Those that witnessed the execution, and who were present at previous ones, declared that there was a great mismanagement in the adjustment of the rope, the knot being at the back of the head as the body hung from the beam. But although convulsive motions were visible for a considerable time, it was thought that all sensation and consciousness departed with the fall. After hanging for the usual time, the body was cut down. A cast was taken from the murderer's head, and then he was buried within the precincts of the gaol.

Date	*Victim*	*Accused*
25 August 1850	**O'Brien child**	**Mary O'Brien**
Cause of death:	Asphyxiation	
Outcome:	Murder charge dismissed	
	Charged with concealment of birth	
Location:	Waymouth Street, Adelaide	

Mr O'Brien was a butcher who lived with his family on Waymouth Street in Adelaide. The O'Briens had a 17-year-old daughter called Mary, who gave birth to a baby boy on Sunday 25 August 1850. During the day, the child died, and Mary placed the body in a box in her bedroom. The box and body were found, and an inquest was held the following day at the Launceston Hotel in Waymouth Street. At the start of the inquest, the jury left the hotel and proceeded to O'Brien's house where they viewed the body. During the visit, Mary lay on the bed with her head uncovered, and was subject to the gaze of the jury.

The inquest returned to the hotel where it resumed. Dr Nash, the Colonial Surgeon, gave evidence and stated that he had examined the body of the male infant in question, and was of opinion that it had arrived at maturity. Its length was 19 inches and weighed five pounds. There had been haemorrhage from the nose, and a rag stuffed into its mouth. There were marks of violence in the throat, arising from compression of the windpipe. The lungs, with the heart attached, floated when placed in water. Nash was of opinion that the child was born alive, and had been suffocated by a combination of compression of the windpipe and the addition of the rag.

This being the whole of the evidence, the coroner asked the jury if they wished to hear any further medical testimony. They all expressed their conviction that Dr Nash's evidence was conclusive. The coroner then stated the facts of the case, and regretted that the accused party had not been present during the investigation. He added that their verdict would only put the girl on her trial, and not convict her. The jury, after a short deliberation, returned a verdict of wilful murder against Mary O'Brien.

On 25 November 1850, in the Supreme Court, before Mr Justice Cooper, the charge of murder against O'Brien was ignored and the bill for concealment of birth was adjourned. No further information located.

View of Adelaide looking north-west from the tower of the Adelaide General Post Office in 1870. Waymouth Street crosses diagonally through the image. State Library of South Australia, B 16004/9

Date	*Victim*	*Accused*
September 1850	**Budlaroo**	**Kutromee (Tommy Ross)**
Cause of death:	Suspected strangulation	
Outcome:	Discharged	
Location:	Black Springs, near Clare	

On Monday 9 September 1850, at Mr Dodd's hotel in Clare, an inquest was held regarding the remains of an Aboriginal boy named Budlaroo, whose bones were found buried in a tree hole on a sheep station at Black Springs. A post-mortem examination was conducted but due to decay, a cause of death could not be given. A piece of string with a peculiar twist was found, suggesting that the cause of death was strangulation.

Information was received that a person called Kutromee committed the murder, having told several other people that he had killed Budlaroo when he was drunk.

Kutromee, also known as Tommy Ross, was taken into custody by Clare Constables Gregg and Bell, and charged with the wilful murder of Budlaroo of the Broughton tribe. Kutromee was brought up before Edward Gleeson, JP, where he pleaded guilty to wilful murder and was committed for trial.

On 12 February 1851, in the Supreme Court criminal sittings before His Honour Justice Crawford, the bill against Kutromee was ignored, and Kutromee was discharged.

Date	Victim	Accused
2 November 1850	Henry Baird (Beard)	Pulgalta
Cause of death:	Spear wounds	
Outcome:	Discharged	
Location:	Streaky Bay	

The first European to explore the area around Streaky Bay was Dutch explorer Pieter Nuyts of the *Golden Zeepaard* in 1627. A monument stands on the median strip in Bay Road.

In 1802 Matthew Flinders named Streaky Bay whilst on his voyage in the *Investigator*. In his log on 5 February 1802, he wrote '... and the water was much discoloured in Streaks ... and I called it Streaky Bay'. It is now thought these streaks are caused by the release of oils by certain species of seaweed in the bay.

In 1839, Edward John Eyre, the renowned explorer, established a small base about three kilometres from the Streaky Bay township which he used as a store for his overland expeditions to Point Bell. This site, known as Eyre's Waterhole, can still be seen today just off the road to Port Kenny.

In 1848, 35-year-old Henry Baird, who was a single man, along with Mr and Mrs Sinclair, left Adelaide and went overland with his flocks of sheep to his station, which was situated on the west coast near Venus Bay.

In November 1850, information was received in Adelaide regarding the murder of Henry Baird, who had been killed by Aboriginal people near

Streaky Bay. The police had located Baird's body, which had been speared several times in the back. The bales in which Mr Baird's wool was packed were ripped open and the contents were scattered about the ground. It was thought that the bags were to be used as clothing by the murderers. It was reported that Baird had been pierced with 12 or 14 spears. The body had lain eight or nine days, and as it was so decomposed, it could only be recognised as a white man by the toes being closer together. The hut had been robbed and the police could only locate 1,350 sheep out of a flock of 2,600.

The police investigated the murder, and subsequently took Pulgalta into custody and conveyed him to Adelaide to face trial.

On Tuesday 20 May 1851, in the Supreme Court, before His Honour Justice Cooper, the court abandoned the charges against Pulgalta.

Date	*Victim*	*Accused*
1 February 1851	**Hadgee**	**Dumah**
Cause of death:	Assault	
Outcome:	Dumah found insane	
Location:	Adelaide Gaol	

On Saturday 1 February 1851, two Malayan men, Hadgee and Dumah, Dolah, a Chinese man, and an Aboriginal man named Pulgalta were in custody at the Adelaide Gaol. Hadgee and Dumah were in custody on a charge of committing a felonious assault on the high seas. A fight broke out between Hadgee and Dumah, where Hadgee received fatal wounds and later died.

On Monday 17 February 1851, a coroner's inquest on the body of Hadgee was held at the Adelaide Hospital. Evidence was received that Hadgee died because of five blows inflicted by Dumah.

During the inquest, Dolah was called to give evidence as he witnessed the murder. Dolah stated that he left China when he was a child, and had no clear notions of the religion taught there, nor had he acquired any other. He believed that when he died there would be an end of him. As Dolah had no belief in future reward or punishment, the coroner doubted the propriety of taking his statement as evidence. The foreman of the jury could not see why the man might not tell the truth notwithstanding, and added that 'much information might be shut out by refusing to take such evidence'. The coroner requested the interpreter to ascertain whether Dolah had any notion of an oath, or any mode by which he could be adjured to speak the truth. He replied that in China it was usual to cut off a cock's head, but he did not feel bound by that method. He had however seen men sworn in on some of the islands of the Indian Archipelago, by cutting their flesh, then giving their statement after sucking some of their own blood. He said by this method he must tell the truth, otherwise a God would pitch him from the masthead when next he went to sea. Dolah said another person must cut his flesh. Dr Moore pierced Dolah's hand, after which Dolah gave evidence, occasionally sucking at the wound.

Governor and staff at Adelaide Gaol, watercolour showing the courtyard with the Governor (W. B. Ashton), his son (A.G. Ashton) and staff, 1850.
State Library of South Australia, B 17790

Pulgalta, the Aboriginal man charged with the murder of Mr Baird near Streaky Bay (see 2 November 1850), also witnessed the murder. However, there were no means of obtaining his statement, as no one could be found who understood his language. Pulgalta was completely horrified at the barbarity he witnessed, and could not be prevailed to approach the cell where Hadgee had been murdered. At the completion of the inquest, the jury returned a verdict of manslaughter against Dumah.

On Saturday 17 May 1851, Dumah appeared in the Supreme Court. His Honour directed the jury to be sworn, but told them it was only for the purpose of enquiring into the sanity of Dumah, and not to decide upon the charge against him. It was reported that:

> Dumah's appearance was that of a complete idiot, his hair was closely cut and the conformation of his skull was thoroughly exposed to view, and exhibited in an exaggerated degree all those peculiarities which are observed in those of small intellectual power or absolute idiocy. All the animal propensities were largely indicated, and, judging from appearances, there did not seem to be room in his skull for more than an ounce of brains.

Dr Nash, who had examined Dumah, gave evidence. After hearing all of the evidence, the jury deliberated for a short time, before deciding that Dumah was insane, but they could not say how long he had been so. His Honour asked that Dumah be taken away, and intimated that he would make an order for him in the course of the day. No further information located.

Date	*Victim*	*Accused*
11 February 1851	**Maltalta (Maltalto)**	**Tuk Karin, Ngalta Wikkanni, and Konga Woilf**
Cause of death:	Spear wounds	
Outcome:	All three found guilty of murder, sentenced to death	
	Sentence commuted and all discharged	
Location:	Yorke's Peninsula	

On 11 February 1851, Kurra Wumba, Tuk Karin, Ngalta Wikkanni and Konga Woilf (also spelt Tukkurn, Nyalta Wikkanin and Kanger Worli) were camped at Wathkaure on Yorke's Peninsula when a man from a different tribe arrived. The visitor was asked his name and where his country was. He said his name was Maltalta and that he was a native of Port Lincoln and travelling from Adelaide to his home (see 3 May 1849). Maltalta took a firestick from the camp and went on his journey. Tuk Karin, Ngalta Wikkanni and Konga Woilf followed him, and as Maltalta made a fire around sundown, they attacked and

killed him with their spears. Kurra Wumba witnessed the murder. The police were advised, who took the three into custody.

The trial of Tuk Karin, Nyalta Wikkanin, and Konger Woilf commenced in the Supreme Court on Monday 19 May 1851. Kanyana, a 12-year-old boy, gave evidence that he saw the prisoners spear Maltalta, with each of them stabbing Maltalta once. Another Aboriginal witness stated that Maltalta was on his way to Port Lincoln and that the offenders followed him along the beach and speared him. They said they did not like a strange blackfellow to travel through their country. Three spears were thrown at him, and all entered his body. They covered him with bushes and left him to die. The prisoners gave evidence and stated that it was their custom to kill strangers when they came amongst them.

The jury, having retired for about 15 minutes, returned a guilty verdict against the three prisoners.

The judge directed the interpreter, Jim Crack, to inform the prisoners, and to ask them why they should not be condemned to be hanged. The prisoner Tuk Karin made some remarks, which Crack translated, that they 'did not like to be hanged'. The judge then proceeded, amidst almost breathless silence, to sentence the prisoners to be executed on 9 June 1851, and their bodies to be buried in the gaol. Their sentence was later commuted and they were pardoned and discharged from gaol on 16 June 1851.

Date	*Victim*	*Accused*
March 1851	**Marponin**	**Maramin (Doughboy),**
	(Salt Creek Paddy)	**Weepin (Billy), Parrot (Jemmy),**
		and Penchungy (Major)
Cause of death:	Assault (with sticks)	
Outcome:	Found not guilty	
Location:	Robe	

On Tuesday 20 May 1851, Maramin, Weepin, Parrot and Penchungy appeared before the Supreme Court indicted for the murder of an Aboriginal man named Marponin at Robe Town in March. The prisoners pleaded not guilty. A local boy named Warracherrie (Monkey) stated that he had seen two of the prisoners first knock Marponin down and then beat him with their waddies.

While giving his evidence, Warracherrie took ill and had to leave the court. The crown solicitor addressed the jury and left it for them to decide whether they thought the sole evidence of the boy sufficient to convict the prisoners. If they did not, it would be their duty to acquit them.

When Warracherrie was well again, he returned to the court, and the trial continued. Evidence was given that Marponin was a stranger of the Salt Creek tribe. Maramin, Weepin, Parrot and Penchungy were angry because Marponin made songs against them. The confrontation began with Weepin seizing Marponin, and Marponin biting Weepin's fingers and toes in return. The others then attacked him, beat him with sticks, and broke two of his ribs. Marponin died instantly, and the group buried him by moonlight in a wombat hole near the dray road leading to Haye's station.

Corporal Brooks, who found the body in an advanced state of decomposition in the wombat hole, gave evidence. Brooks saw evidence of injuries on the remains, including broken ribs on the right side. Warracherrie had previously stated the broken ribs were on the left side. Brooks could not say how long the body had been dead, or whether it was the skeleton of a man or woman. His Honour told the jury that he could not, in justice to the prisoners, say that the evidence was sufficient against them. The only evidence against them was Warracherrie's, and that was not consistent or distinct enough to fix the prisoners with the guilt of the crime charged on them. The jury, after a brief consultation, returned a not guilty verdict.

Date	*Victim*	*Accused*
5 March 1851	**Charles Crocker**	**Kumbilti and John Shepherd**
Cause of death:	Assault (with a spade)	
Outcome:	Kumbilti found guilty of manslaughter	
	Sentenced to two years imprisonment with hard labour	
	Shepherd released without charge	
Location:	Forty miles from Port Lincoln	

Charles Crocker, a 60-year-old shepherd, worked on a property owned by John Tennant, which was situated about 40 miles from Port Lincoln. On 5 March 1851, Crocker was found murdered in his hut and suspicion fell on John Shepherd, who was taken into custody but later released. After further examination of the scene, tracks belonging to an unknown person were found and followed. These tracks led to Kumbilti and Irtabidmi. Kumbilti had an amount of property belonging to Crocker with him. Kumbilti was arrested, along with Irtabidmi, who was arrested as an accessory to the murder. Irtabidmi provided the following statement and was subsequently used as a witness:

> I am the wife of Yulga. I was with my husband at the mine. Kumbilti forced me away from the mine. We went to Kulara, where the old man (Crocker) was the hutkeeper. We stopped outside of the door for some time. Kumbilti got up and went into the hut, and I went to the door. Kumbilti asked Crocker for 'mungy' [food]. Crocker said he would give him some if he would cut some wood. Kumbilti refused to do so. Crocker put his hand on Kumbilti to put him out the hut. Kumbilti resisted, and Crocker took up the spade, but did not strike Kumbilti with it. Crocker put down the spade and turned his back on Kumbilti. Kumbilti took up the spade and knocked Crocker down and while on the ground struck him several times on the head, which killed him. Kumbilti took some flour from a bag, and a rag and three hats, and went away, leaving Crocker dead in the hut.

On Friday 22 August 1851, Kumbilti appeared in the Supreme Court charged with the murder of Crocker. At the completion of the trial, the jury found Kumbilti guilty of manslaughter. Kumbilti was sentenced to two years with hard labour.

Date	*Victim*	*Accused*
14 April 1851	**George Jenks**	**Marialta, Ngamalta, and Cooleltie**
Cause of death:	Spear wounds	
Outcome:	Marialta and Ngamalta acquitted	
	Cooleltie found guilty of murder	
	Sentenced to death, commuted to two years imprisonment	
Location:	Lipson's Cove Station	

John Tennant arrived in South Australia with his wife and three children in 1839. Tennant found work as a shepherd and in 1844 he was in charge of moving sheep to Robe. In 1845 he purchased Tallala Station at Port Lincoln.

To claim the property, he led a party of 14 men and 8,000 sheep in what was the first successful attempt to overland sheep around Spencer's Gulf. Tennant's group set off from 'The Glen' near Williamstown on 3 November 1845 before their progress was stalled in the heat of the summer at Depot Creek near Mt Arden by a lack of water beyond Port Augusta. It was not until the beginning of July the following year that conditions were suitable to move the flocks down to Port Lincoln.

Tennant wanted more land and immediately took out an occupation licence on the select country he had just passed through to create Lipson's Cove Station. In surveying this new station, he engaged the services of a skilled draughtsman also new to the area, John McDougall Stuart. They became friends, and on 20 April 1860, during his fourth expedition into the north of Australia, Stuart named his discovery of Tennant Creek in John Tennant's honour.

On 14 April 1851, George Jenks was employed at Lipson's Cove Station as a shepherd. Jenks was cutting wood at his hut when he was attacked from behind by a group of Aboriginal people. During the attack Jenks received fatal spear wounds. As Jenks had not been seen for some days, a fellow shepherd named John Fuller went to the hut and found Jenks' body. The hut was ransacked and a 140-pound bag of flour, half a sheep, a double-barrelled shotgun, all of the bedding, and an amount of clothing had been stolen.

Two Aboriginal men named Marialta and Ngamalta were found and arrested for the murder. On Friday 22 August 1851, both appeared before the Supreme Court and were indicted for the murder of Jenks. However, the evidence was not sufficient to sustain the indictment, so both were acquitted.

Six years later, on Monday 18 May 1857, a third suspect called Cooleltie appeared before the Supreme Court on the charge of murdering Jenks. He was found guilty and sentenced to death. On 27 May 1857, BT Finnis, the Chief Secretary, commuted the death sentence to two years imprisonment with hard labour.

Date	*Victim*	*Accused*
11 May 1851	Wartpu Purti	Charles Jacques and
	(Jemmy Critchell)	Jeremiah Nicholls
Cause of death:	Gunshot wound	
Outcome:	Acquitted	
Location:	Kapunda	

On 11 May 1851, a group of men were drinking in the bar at the North Kapunda Arms. Just before midnight, about a dozen drunken Aboriginal people came to the door of the hotel for drink, which was refused. The group became angry, saying their money was as good as the white fellows'. They made a rush at the hotel and managed to enter. The owner, with the assistance of his customers, started to force the group from the hotel. As they were doing that, someone from outside threw a large stone, which struck a person in the bar on the forehead. After the door was closed, the group of Aboriginal people threw stones towards the hotel, breaking some of the windows. Most of the men from the hotel went out to drive them away. There were about a dozen men who went outside, including Jeremiah Nicholls and Charles Jacques. During the chaos, Wartpu Purti was fatally shot.

The police investigation revealed that when the men chased the group away, about six or seven shots were fired. There were even shots fired at the group from the houses near the hotel. Nicholls and Jacques were taken into custody and placed before a coroner's inquest. Further evidence was given, and at the completion of the inquest, the jury returned a verdict of wilful murder against Jacques and Nicholls, who were committed for trial on the Coroner's warrant.

Jacques and Nicholls appeared in the Supreme Court on 21 August 1851. At the completion of the trial, His Honour summed up the evidence and told the jury that they must find that one or other of the prisoners actually fired the gun, whilst the other was aiding and abetting. He thought the Crown had failed to sustain the charge against Nicholls, and the statement of Jacques, whether true or false, could not be taken against Nicholls, as he warned that evidence given by one accused against a co-accused could not be relied upon. As to the general evidence, the judge noted that in his experience, he never knew a case in which so much contradictory evidence had been offered.

The jury, after a deliberation of ten minutes, returned a verdict of not guilty, and the judge, in discharging the prisoners, trusted that they would take warning not to be spending their earnings drinking in public houses at late hours.

Date	Victim	Accused
15 May 1851	**William Bagnall**	**Murrepa**
Cause of death:	Assault (with a waddy)	
Outcome:	Found guilty, sentenced to six months imprisonment	
Location:	Yorke's Peninsula	

On 17 May 1850 William Bagnall was walking on his station on Yorke's Peninsula intending to burn some lime. Kerkarawilla was also on the station visiting a man called Jimmy, who was employed by Bagnall. Kerkarawilla saw Bagnall walking and threw a waddy and three spears at him. One of the spears pierced Bagnall's hip to the bone. Bagnall drew the spear out, and struck Kerkarawilla with it, breaking the spear on Kerkarawilla's head. Kerkarawilla ran off and Bagnall went to his hut, where he was confined to his bed from the effect of the wound for two days. Bagnall survived his injuries.

This watercolour, by Edward Snell, shows Bagnall (second from left) and Kerkarawilla (second from right), along with PC McCoy, Jimmy Crack and others, on the way to Adelaide for trial.

State Library of New South Wales, SV/88, by permission

Corporal McCoy was told of the assault and apprehended Kerkarawilla, who at first denied having thrown the spear, but afterwards claimed it as his own. Kerkarawilla was taken to Adelaide, where he appeared before the Police Court on Friday 2 June and was committed for trial.

Almost a year later, on 15 May 1851, Bagnall was back on his station on the Yorke's Peninsula when he was murdered. The offender was not located until a man named Witturri gave information to the police. Based on that information, Murrepa was arrested and taken to Adelaide. On Friday 26 September 1851, Murrepa was charged with the wilful murder of William Bagnall in the Police Court in Adelaide. Murrepa pleaded guilty.

Witturri stated that on 15 May he was present with some other Aboriginal people when Bagnall came and took away one of the women. Some of the group were lying in wait, ready to ambush Bagnall. When they saw him take the woman into the scrub, Murrepa rushed at Bagnall and struck him in the head with a waddy, knocking him to the ground. Murrepa then struck Bagnall on the head several times until the head was completely broken in. Murrepa was committed to trial.

Murrepa's trial began in the Supreme Court on Tuesday 10 February 1852. Murrepa now stated that he did not inflict the fatal blow, and that a white man was there, and that he did it. During the summing up of evidence, it was stated that the only evidence against Murrepa was the discovery of footprints near the body, which were identified as being Murrepa's by the police. The jury retired and after three-quarters of an hour, returned a verdict of manslaughter with a recommendation for mercy. Murrepa was sentenced to six months imprisonment with hard labour.

Date	Victim	Accused
15 October 1851	**Female child**	**Unknown**
Cause of death:	Exposure	
Outcome:	Unsolved	
Location:	Norwood	

On Monday 20 October 1851, an inquest was held at the Robin Hood Hotel, Kensington, into the discovery in the creek of the body of a female infant wrapped tightly in a shawl. A post-mortem revealed that the body had been in the creek for about four days. One witness stated that she had seen a person called Jane Condon with a similar shawl, and another witness stated that Jane's father was seen in the area carrying a small parcel. Timothy and Jane Condon were called to the inquest and stated that they lived in the family home at Norwood. Jane denied owning a shawl like the one the baby was wrapped in, and Timothy stated that he was carrying his lunch to work that day. Both denied any knowledge of the baby in the creek. Police Constable Mounsell stated that he attended at the creek and located the body of the baby. He tried to follow footprints from the scene, but the ground was too hard and did not leave enough prints. He returned the next day for a further search and located a Lucifer-box containing a small amount of cut tobacco.

At the end of the inquest the jury returned a verdict of 'wilful murder against some person or persons unknown'.

Date	Victim	Accused
26 October 1851	**John O'Dea**	**Sydney Glover, Charles Grosse**
Cause of death:	Gunshot wound	
Outcome:	Both acquitted	
Location:	Adelaide, near the Stagg Hotel	

Between eight and ten pm on 26 October 1851, John O'Dea was shot while he was in the parklands near the Stagg Hotel. Earlier, O'Dea had been a patron at the hotel when a disturbance broke out between some Irish patrons and the owners of the hotel. O'Dea was understood to be involved in the fight. After the Irish were locked out of the hotel, several stones and rocks were thrown at the windows. One rock hit the owner, Mr Glover, knocking him to the floor. A pistol was fired from the inside of the hotel towards the group outside, with the shot hitting O'Dea in the chest. O'Dea, who had a wife and nine children, died from his injuries. Dr Bayer attended at the Stagg Hotel and gave assistance to Glover, whose jaw had been broken by the rock. Charles Grosse and Glover's relative, Sydney Glover, were taken into custody. Sydney Glover also received medical treatment.

On Saturday 29 November, Charles Grosse and Sydney Glover appeared before the Supreme Court, charged with killing John O'Dea. At the completion of the evidence, His Honour pointed out to the jury that they must decide first, who it was that fired the pistol, and, second, the shooter's motive. If the pistol had been fired the moment after Mr Glover was struck, then the act would not only be excusable, but justifiable. Another view of the case might be whether Sydney Glover had any other intention in firing the pistol than to give an alarm. If indeed he acted with the knowledge that the pistol was loaded, and that there were persons in the direction in which he discharged it, he would undoubtedly be guilty of manslaughter. If Sydney's state of mind at the time must have been such that he would not be supposed to have acted calmly, then the jury would have to acquit. The worst view of the case was that the pistols had been brought downstairs with the intention of being used. His Honour also reminded the jury that at the time the pistol was fired, it was dark outside, and it should be remembered that the darkness outside would appear much greater than it really was to a person inside.

The jury retired for a few minutes, and then brought in a verdict of acquittal for both the prisoners. His Honour enquired if any attempt had been made to ascertain who it was that threw the large stone produced, and he was advised that there was evidence to prove that it was the unfortunate man O'Dea. The prisoners were immediately discharged.

Date	*Victim*	*Accused*
14 March 1852	**Robert Richardson**	**Billy and Jemmy**
Cause of death:	Spear wounds	
Outcome:	Unknown	
Location:	Younguna, near Burra	

Johnson Frederick Hayward was a sheep farmer in the Northern District. On Sunday 14 March 1852, he was called to see the body of a shepherd in his employ, named Robert Richardson, who had been murdered some few hours before near Younguna. The body was about a mile away from the hut. Richardson was lying on his back with spear wounds to the spine and loins, and his head was knocked to pieces. Two waddies were found near the body. Hayward looked about for the tracks of the murderers, and found the footprints of three bare-footed persons.

Hayward accompanied Sergeant Major Rose to search for the murderers. About 30 or 40 miles from the crime scene, they came on a camp of about 15 Aboriginal people. Billy and Jemmy were pointed out as being the murderers, and were taken into custody. Two of the footprints near the body corresponded exactly to the size of Billy and Jemmy's feet.

On Friday 16 April, at the Clare local court, Billy and Jemmy were charged with the wilful murder of Robert Richardson.

Sergeant Major Rose testified that he was present when Hayward measured the feet of Billy and Jemmy, and that they corresponded exactly with the size of the footprints found near where Richardson was murdered. Billy had a very peculiar foot, and Rose stated that he would be able to trace him anywhere. Billy and Jemmy were remanded for eight days to be brought up at Kooringa for re-examination.

In November 1852, Jemmy was still on remand for the murder. Billy was no longer mentioned in the court list. No further details could be found.

Date	*Victim*	*Accused*
26 June 1852	Jane McCaskill (McKascill)	Daniel Horgan
Cause of death:	Assault	
Outcome:	Found guilty of manslaughter	
	Sentenced to two years imprisonment with hard labour	
Location:	Magill	

Daniel Horgan married a widow called Ann McCaskill around April 1851. Ann had a young daughter called Jane by her first marriage. Horgan, an Irishman who was powerfully built man of about five foot eight inches tall, had been at sea before he arrived in South Australia.

In the evening of Friday 25 June 1852, Ann took Jane, who was two years and nine months old, to bed, where she slept all night. In the morning, Ann took Jane into an adjoining room where she laid her on some blankets, moving her outside into the yard a short while later.

Horgan went out of the house into the rear yard, and after a minute or two, Ann heard Jane scream. Ann went out and found Jane dying. She carried her to a neighbour called Mrs Ryan, who refused to help. She went to another neighbour and Dr Wark was sent for, but it was too late, as Jane had died.

After the incident, Horgan went off to the port. On hearing about the murder, and the fact that Horgan had ran off, Inspector Stuart sent detachments of the police force to different localities around Adelaide, looking for Horgan. Inspector Stuart searched the country between Adelaide and Mount Barker, but Horgan was not found. Horgan returned to the Magill area from the port, and was caught hovering about the village by Inspector Stuart, who would have passed him in the dark, had Horgan not startled Stuart's horse.

An inquest was held that day before Mr C Stuart at the World's End Inn at Magill. Dr Wark gave evidence of his examination of Jane. He stated that she had injuries on her head, and there was swelling or tumefaction on the upper part of the neck. He also found the head to be loose on the vertebral column. In Wark's opinion, the dislocation of the vertebral column close to the head had caused almost instant death, and such an injury could only have been occasioned by means of external violence. At the conclusion of the evidence, the jury returned a verdict of wilful murder against Horgan, who was committed to trial.

Horgan appeared before Mr Justice Crawford at the Supreme Court on Thursday 9 August 1852. Evidence was given that Horgan had frequently threatened the life of the child. The defence summed up by stating that the evidence of Dr Wark could not be relied upon, as he had first given the cause of death as dislocation of the neck, but the post-mortem found a different cause, which changed his evidence at trial. The credibility of Mrs McCaskill, the child's mother, was also challenged, as she was portrayed as a prostitute and a perjurer. She had stated to the coroner that she was married to the accused, but Horgan and other witnesses negated this.

The judge summed up by stating that if the jury believed that the accused had caused the injury with malice, then he would be guilty of murder, but if there were no malice, then he would be guilty of manslaughter. He advised them they had to believe the evidence of Mrs McCaskill that Horgan caused the injuries.

The jury retired, and after an hour and five minutes, returned a verdict of manslaughter. Horgan, who still strongly asserted his innocence, and insisted that he had not had a fair trial, was sentenced to two years hard labour.

Date	Victim	Accused
9 July 1852	**Warrin Yerriman**	**Crackingyounger**
	(Jimmy)	**(Mr Baker), Ballycrack (Charley),**
		and Pot Pouch (Teapot)

Cause of death:	Spear wounds
Outcome:	All found guilty of murder, sentenced to death
	All sentences commuted to transportation for life
	with hard labour
Location:	Binnum Binnum, near Naracoorte

Mr McLeod of Nallang had employed Warrin Yerriman on his property for about six years. On 8 July 1852, McLeod was in his hut when he heard his name called by Warrin Yerriman's lubra. McLeod spoke with the lubra who told him that her husband had been speared. McLeod went with her to Warrin Yerriman, whose dead body had 10 spears still lodged in him.

Another Aboriginal person told McLeod that the three responsible for the murder were Crackingyounger, Ballycrack and Pot Pouch. McLeod was told that they came and killed Warrin Yerriman then attempted to take his lubra. McLeod and others located and arrested the suspects and took them to the magistrate, where they were committed to trial.

Binnum Station, 1860.
State Library of South Australia, B 36872

The three prisoners appeared before Mr Justice Crawford in the Supreme Court on Friday 13 August 1852. During the trial, the defence stated that the indictment could not be sustained, as the prisoners, who were indicted as South Australian Aboriginal people, were proved to be from Port Phillip, and must therefore be treated as foreigners. His Honour said that they were still subjects of the Queen of England, but he would take note of the objection.

The prosecutor addressed the jury, urging that, as the prisoners were not engaged in an unlawful transaction (the stealing of a wife being a custom), the purposes of justice would be fully answered by a verdict of manslaughter. His Honour said that if the jury believed the prisoners were the persons who killed Warrin Yerriman, then it would amount to murder in the eyes of the law. It appeared that the deceased was asleep in his wurley, and that a member of the group had speared him in his sleep before making any attempt upon his wife.

The jury, after retiring for about a quarter of an hour, found the prisoners guilty. His Honour sentenced all three to be executed on September 16, and their bodies to be buried within the precincts of the gaol. The sentence was later commuted to transportation for life with hard labour. Crackingyounger, Ballycrack and Pot Pouch were delivered to the Superintendent of Convicts on 12 October 1852.

Date	*Victim*	*Accused*
30 September 1852	**Mr Brown**	**Aboriginal people**
Cause of death:	Spear wounds, mutilation	
Outcome:	Offenders not located	
Location:	Mount Arden	

In October 1852, the police constable stationed at Mount Remarkable received information about the murder of a shepherd known as Mr Brown, which occurred at Mount Arden. Information was also received that after the murder, about 500 sheep had been taken by a group of Aboriginal people. The constable started from his station to Mount Arden on 21 October with a party of settlers. When they arrived, they found Mr Brown's body, which had been speared and then mutilated. The party followed the tracks of the sheep for two days when, on the westward side of Lake Torrens, in the Port Lincoln District, they came across the sheep under the control of a group of Aboriginal people.

On attempting to retake possession of the sheep, the constable's party were assailed with spears and boomerangs. In retaliation, the group of settlers and the constable fired upon their attackers, shooting four Aboriginal people.

The rest retreated into an impenetrable scrub and although several attempts were made on the part of the pursuers to take some of them prisoner and to parley with them, their attempts were as often met by a spear. The constable's Aboriginal guide told him that the group of attackers were from Port Lincoln. After recovering between 400 and 500 sheep, the police and settlers returned to the station. No one was taken into custody for the murder of Mr Brown.

Date	*Victim*	*Accused*
9 December 1852	Henry Hiern, Dennis Wood Hiern, and Henry Holloway	Thomas Davies
Cause of death:	Drowned	
Outcome:	Acquitted	
Location:	Port Adelaide	

On 9 December 1852, Henry Hiern, Dennis Hiern and Henry Holloway were in Port Adelaide on the steamer *Cleopatra*. Henry Hiern arranged with Thomas Davies to take them from the *Cleopatra* and to land at the wharf, for a cost of £4.

Davies' boat was used as a water tank and was alongside the *Cleopatra* at the time. He was shown part of Holloway's and the Hierns' luggage on deck, the rest of which (about 30 packages weighing not less than three tons) was brought up afterwards. The arrangement made was that no other persons were to go in the boat. However, Davies loaded more luggage from six or seven other passengers who also boarded his boat. Some of the luggage was placed below deck, but some heavy objects were placed on the deck. The water tank was also nearly full.

When they left the *Cleopatra,* there was very little wind. The boat was within a quarter of a mile from Port Adelaide when it capsized. As a result, Henry Hiern, Dennis Hiern, and Henry Holloway drowned. Davies was arrested and charged with manslaughter and was committed to trial in the Supreme Court.

On Tuesday 15 February 1853, Davies appeared before the Supreme Court. Evidence taken showed that the boat was overloaded and sat low in the water. Davies stated that while the boat was tacking, the person who had charge of the main sail did not let it go, and as a result the boat overturned. At the completion of the trial, the jury retired for five minutes before they returned and acquitted Davies.

In 1853, William McKenzie named an area of Port Adelaide (the subdivision of Section 1107, Hundred of Port Adelaide) as Davis Town, after Thomas Davies. The area was also known as Staplehurst, and is now included in the suburb of Exeter.

Date	*Victim*	*Accused*
15 January 1853	**Robert Head**	**William Wright**
Cause of death:	Knife wound	
Outcome:	Found guilty of murder	
	Sentenced to death, executed 12 March 1853	
Location:	Wellington	

Robert Head was staying at McPherson's public house on the River Murray opposite the Wellington Ferry. He was travelling to the gold diggings. William Wright, a 49-year-old labourer who formally resided in one of the suburbs of Adelaide, arrived at McPherson's public house around 15 January. Wright had walked from Adelaide, and it was said that he had begged for food at various public houses on the way. Head, seeing the piteous condition of Wright, treated him to meat and drink, before setting himself down upon the sofa in the room where they were together, with the view of taking a nap.

Wright took 17 shillings in silver from Head's pocket thinking he was asleep. When Head felt Wright's hand in his pocket, he jumped up and accused him of robbing him, saying, 'Don't think I'm asleep, you've robbed me, give me my money'. Wright denied that he had taken anything and left the room and walked outside. Wright proceeded to sharpen his knife upon a grindstone, and sometime after returned to Head's room. On seeing Wright, Head called out to him to give him back his money. Wright cried, 'Take that', and stabbed Head in the left side of the throat, drawing the knife several inches along the wound. The jugular vein was severed, and Head fell to the ground and died.

Wright was subsequently arrested and a coronial inquest was held into Head's death. At the completion of the inquest, Head was found guilty of murder and committed to trial.

On Tuesday 22 February Wright appeared in the Supreme Court where a jury found him guilty of murder. He was sentenced to death, and was executed on 12 March 1853, and buried within the Adelaide Goal.

Date	*Victim*	*Accused*
19 February 1853	**George Arnold**	**Thomas Whitham, Henry Hunt (Fancy Harry), Sarah Kelly, and Ann Lynam**

Cause of death:	Assault
Outcome:	Found not guilty
Location:	Port Adelaide

On 19 February 1853, a disturbance took place at Port Adelaide, during which George Arnold was injured. Arnold was taken to his lodging house and in the morning he was found to have serious facial injuries. Arnold was taken to the Adelaide Hospital where he received treatment, but he died in early March.

At the coroner's inquest, evidence was given regarding the disturbance. Thomas Whitham, Henry Hunt (known as Fancy Harry), Sarah Kelly, and Ann Lynam were all implicated in being involved, but there was not enough evidence to commit anyone to trial. The inquest lasted four days, with the jury finding that Arnold was 'murdered by some person or persons unknown'.

After further police investigation, the four suspects were arrested and placed before Mr Newland, a special magistrate at Port Adelaide.

At the completion of the evidence, the prisoners were all committed for trial, but it was mentioned that 'the charge before the Supreme Court would be that they had created a riot, in the course of which murder was committed, and confederated to resist all persons interfering to prevent such riot'.

On Saturday 14 May, Whitham, Hunt, Kelly, and Lynam appeared before the Supreme Court. At the completion of the evidence, His Honour addressed the jury, stating:

> … in a charge of murder, the guilt or innocence of a prisoner must not depend upon speculation. It was not enough that there might appear a probability, however great, that death had been occasioned by the prisoners, the cause of death must be distinctly ascertained, and also the person by whom the injury was inflicted. Without a clear connection on both those points, the jury would not be justified in finding a verdict

of guilty. To him it appeared that there was no sufficient evidence of the cause of death, and that it would be very unsatisfactory to return a verdict against any of the prisoners. The jury, without retiring, returned a verdict of not guilty. As the prisoners had been in gaol for some time, and as the Crown Solicitor had not the least idea that they had any murderous intent, declined prosecuting the charges for assault and riot.

The prisoners were accordingly discharged.

Date	*Victim*	*Accused*
4 April 1853	**Watte Watte (Nancy)**	**Kanadla (Peter)**
Cause of death:	Assault (with a waddy)	
Outcome:	Found guilty of murder	
	Sentenced to death, commuted to two years imprisonment	
Location:	Lefevre Peninsula	

On Monday 4 April 1853, Maria, a young Aboriginal girl, saw 17-year-old Watte Watte alive and well. Watte Watte, who was known as Nancy, lived with her husband Kanadla, who was known as Peter, not far from where Maria lived on the Lefevre Peninsula. Around 11 pm, Maria heard Watte Watte screaming, so she went to her door and listened, but all was quiet. Maria then went to Kanadla and Watte Watte's wurley, but she did not hear Watte Watte at all. Maria heard Kanadla take his spear and waddy and leave.

Williamy, who was Watte Watte's father, lived close to Kanadla and Watte Watte's wurley. They all shared the same fire. Williamy saw Watte Watte alive on Monday during the evening, and later saw Kanadla strike Watte Watte with his waddy over her head and nose, after which she fell to the ground and died.

Kanadla fled and was later apprehended by Police Constable John Hegarty, with the assistance of Sergeant Gard, on the swamp near Mr Collinson's. Kanadla had a waddy in his possession that was stained with blood. He was told he was arrested for killing his lubra. Kanadla did not speak, but resisted arrest and tried to escape.

On Thursday 8 April 1853, an inquest was held at Calton's Hotel, Port Adelaide. An examination of the body revealed severe injuries to the face, as if from a violent blow from a blunt instrument such as a waddy.

Captain Jack, an Aboriginal man, identified the body as Watte Watte.

Captain Jack had seen her alive with Kanadla on the peninsula three days before, and had seen her lying dead in his wurley there the next day. There was much blood upon her head.

On 10 May 1853, Kanadla appeared before the Supreme Court on the charge of murder. At the conclusion of the trial, the jury retired for three quarters of an hour before finding Kanadla guilty of murder, with a recommendation for mercy on the grounds of the provocation he had received. The judge passed the death sentence but did say he would forward the recommendation of the jury to His Excellency for consideration. The sentence was later commuted to two years imprisonment.

Date	*Victim*	*Accused*
25 April 1853	**Selina Thomas**	**Elijah Thomas**
Cause of death:	Assault (with an axe)	
Outcome:	Found not guilty on the grounds of insanity	
	Kept in custody at the Lieutenant Governor's pleasure	
Location:	Fisher's Acre, Adelaide	

Elijah Thomas, 33, lived with his 30-year-old wife, Selina Thomas, and their two children in Fisher's Acre, which was a parcel of land near the corner of Wright Street and Morphett Street. On Monday 25 April 1853, Elijah murdered Selina with an axe. After murdering Selina, Elijah went to the local police station and said that he wanted a policeman, as two or three men had come into his house and beaten his wife. Elijah was questioned about the incident but he stuck to his story. The police attended the cottage on Fisher's acre, near Brown Street (now called Morphett Street) where they found Selina lying on the floor. The police could not see any footprints other than Elijah's in the mud around the door. Elijah was then taken into custody on suspicion of murder.

Later that day, an inquest was held at the Queen's Arms. Elijah was brought before the jury in the custody of police. He was a very good-looking man, and his black dress, though much disordered, had the appearance of respectability. There were several marks upon his nose, which appeared to be scratches received in a struggle. The body of his wife had severe injuries to the face, which were inflicted by an axe. The couple's two children were sleeping in the outer room at the time of the murder, and were not woken by the noise.

At the completion of the inquest, the jury found Elijah Thomas guilty of murder. Elijah was committed to trial.

On Wednesday 11 May 1853, Elijah appeared before the Supreme Court on the charge of murdering his wife. At the conclusion of the trial the jury returned with a verdict that Elijah was guilty of the murder, but he was insane at the time he committed it. The judge directed that the jury enter a verdict of not guilty on the ground of insanity, before ordering that Elijah be taken into custody and kept there until the Lieutenant Governor's pleasure was known.

Date	*Victim*	*Accused*
1 May 1853	**Port child**	**Fanny Port**
Cause of death:	Assault (unknown weapon)	
Outcome:	Found not guilty of murder	
	Found guilty of concealment of birth	
	Sentenced to two years imprisonment with hard labour	
Location:	Penwortham, near Clare	

Fanny Port worked for Mr Arthur Horrocks at Penwortham. Horrocks had suspected that Port was pregnant, but when he asked her if she was, she denied it. In May 1853, her appearance led him to believe that she must have delivered a child. He examined her room during her absence and found evidence of childbirth. Horrocks questioned Port, who confessed to delivering a child, but stated it was stillborn and that she had buried it. She showed him where the child was buried and Horrocks informed the nearest magistrate.

The coroner held an inquest, and Dr Stedman gave evidence of conducting a post-mortem. Dr Stedman stated that he had seldom seen a newborn child of a healthier appearance in every respect. He could not positively say how long it might have lived after its birth; it must have lived from five minutes to an hour, or perhaps longer. On examining the head he found some bruises, and on removing the scalp, he found the inner surface of the skull covered with effused blood. These bruises and the effusion of blood on the brain were sufficient to cause death, and might have been inflicted by any blunt instrument. At the completion of the inquest, the jury returned a verdict of wilful murder against Fanny Port.

On Tuesday 9 August, Fanny Port appeared before the Supreme Court on a charge of murder. At the conclusion of the trial, the jury retired for about 10 minutes before returning a verdict of not guilty of wilful murder, but guilty of concealment of birth. His Honour proceeded to pass sentence, saying:

> Fanny Port, you have been indicted for the wilful murder of your own child, the jury have acquitted you of that dreadful crime, but found you guilty of the lesser offence of concealment, and for that it is now my duty to pass the sentence of the law on you. Had the jury been compelled to have found you guilty of infanticide, it would have been incumbent on me to pronounce the sentence of death upon you, and having done so I would have no power to avert it. You would have been taken from where you now stand, and, in a few days, at the place of public execution, your life would have paid the penalty of the dreadful offence charged to you. Fortunately, the jury have been enabled to return a verdict that will only subject you to a lengthened term of imprisonment, and I trust you will so improve it as to return to society a reformed individual. I cannot but recollect that, suspecting your condition, your kind and considerate master told you that if you really were pregnant you should be taken care of. You did not avail yourself of that kind offer, and I cannot allow you to leave this place without sentencing you to the highest penalty which the law awards for the offence of which you have been convicted, which is that you be imprisoned in the common gaol of the province for the term of two years and be kept to hard labour.

Date	*Victim*	*Accused*
1 June 1853	**Ngallabann (Billy)**	**Worrungenna, (Diamond), Tengunnmoor (Charley), Tungkunnerramor (Jackey), and Crup-Crup Bonat (Cranky Jemmy)**
Cause of death:	Assault (with a waddy)	
Outcome:	Worrungenna, Tengunnmoor and Tungkunnerramor found guilty of manslaughter, sentenced to three years hard labour Crup-Crup Bonat dismissed	
Location:	Mosquito Plains	

In 1853, Ngallabann (Billy), an Aboriginal man who was reported to be 'partially civilised', worked as a shepherd for Mr Doughty on a property near

Naracoorte. On 1 June 1853, Worrungenna, Tengunnmoor, Crup-Crup Bonat and Tungkunnerramor forced Ngallabann to go with them. When Ngallabann did not return, fears for his safety arose, and after some time his body was found in a swamp at Mosquito Plains, fastened to the ground under the water by means of a waddy driven through the neck, with some sticks and logs placed on the body. On examination, the body was found to have several contused wounds on the head as if from waddies, which was pronounced as the cause of death.

The four suspects were apprehended in early September and were committed to trial. They arrived in Adelaide on Monday 6 September.

On Monday 12 December, Worrungenna, Tengunnmoor and Tungkunnerramor were indicted for the wilful murder of Ngallabann, in the Supreme Court. There is no reference to Crup-Crup Bonat appearing in court.

Mr Bartley appeared for the prisoners, who pleaded not guilty. Mr Bartley put in a plea denying the jurisdiction of the court, which was, after argument, overruled. When the prisoners were arrested and being duly cautioned, they made statements that the prosecutor wanted to admit into evidence. During the trial Mr Bartley opposed the reception of the prisoners' statements as evidence against them, and that being overruled, he addressed the jury, contending that the evidence could only warrant a verdict of manslaughter. His Honour summed up favourably to that view, and the jury returned a verdict of manslaughter. The prisoners were removed by order of His Honour. They each received three years imprisonment with hard labour.

Date	*Victim*	*Accused*
22 June 1853	**George Smith**	**James Searle**
Cause of death:	Assault (with a pitchfork)	
Outcome:	Found not guilty	
Location:	Port Adelaide area	

On 22 June 1853, James Searle was at a hotel in the Port Adelaide area. Searle sat down in the bar parlour and had a drink of gin. He was telling a friend about the business he had done in the Port that day. George Smith was also in the hotel, but he was asleep, as he had been drinking. Smith woke up and went into the parlour where Searle was drinking and started to interrupt

his conversation. Searle told him to hold his tongue, but Smith kept on badgering Searle.

Smith invited Searle to come outside and fight. Smith kept teasing and aggravating Searle, calling him a thief, a liar, and various other names. Searle said he would not be insulted like that, and left the hotel and got into his cart. Smith followed him outside. Searle stood up in the cart and told Smith that if he did not be quiet and go away, then he would hit him. Searle took up a pitchfork from the bottom of the cart, and struck Smith with it on the side of the head. Smith fell to the ground, bleeding from a wound below the right ear. All the time Smith was teasing Searle he appeared in good humour and jest. Searle seemed very angry and irritated just before he struck the blow. Smith saw the local doctor who treated the injury with leeches, and told Smith to rest in bed. Smith died a few days later.

The police apprehended Searle, who was described as an 'opulent farmer', residing at the Reedbeds, and was the father of 21 children. Police arrived at his house at four am, and, not even mentioning that Smith was dead, forced their way into the bedroom, where his wife had given birth to an infant during the night, and with drawn swords took Searle into custody for an assault.

At the coroner's inquest, the jury, after some consultation, returned a verdict of manslaughter against James Searle, who was committed to trial.

On 18 August 1853, James Searle appeared before the Supreme Court. At the conclusion of the trial, the jury retired for 20 minutes and returned with a verdict of not guilty. Searle was discharged.

Date	*Victim*	*Accused*
12 October 1853	David Broadfoot	Alexander Stephens and John Crawford
Cause of death:	Knife wound	
Outcome:	Stephens acquitted	
	Crawford escaped police custody, never located	
Location:	Cape Northumberland	

Captain David Broadfoot was the captain of the *Jane Lovett*, which was wrecked just off Cape Northumberland in September 1852. Broadfoot remained with the wreck to stop the cargo of gin, tea, cigars, cotton and soap from being plundered. Some months later, Broadfoot was found dead by Archy Taylor, who was delivering supplies to the wreck. Broadfoot was in his bunk with his throat cut, with a razor in his left hand. The razor was covered in blood but his hand was clean. John Crawford and Alexander Stephens, who were hutkeepers, became suspects, as they had often visited the vessel to plunder the cargo. A coroner's inquest was held, and the jury, having no evidence before them to incriminate any particular person, returned a verdict of 'found dead', but suspicion still rested upon Crawford and Stephens.

On 18 October 1853, Police Constables Olive and Dewhurst, and an Aboriginal guide, proceeded to Crawford's hut 12 miles from the wreck, and took Crawford and Stephens into custody. Crawford managed to escape. Stephens was brought before the magistrate, where he made a confession. He stated that he had been in the hold of the *Jane Lovett* to draw a jug of port wine, and just as he was entering the cabin with it, he heard Broadfoot ask Crawford, 'What are you sharpening that razor for?' to which Crawford replied, 'To cut your throat, and I would as soon cut your throat as I would a sheep's'. Stephens stated that Crawford cut Broadfoot's throat from ear to ear as he lay in his bunk. Stephens was committed to trial on a charge of wilful murder.

Crawford, who was still at large, and was frequently seen in the area, stated that there would be bloodshed before he was taken. He attempted to ride to Portland, but when near the punt at the Glenelg River he saw two gentlemen who knew him, so he went off the track into the bush.

On Friday 17 February 1854, Stephens appeared before the Supreme Court in Adelaide on the charge of murder. The defence moved to have Stephens discharged. The crown solicitor said the prisoner had been remanded to that session on consequence of the absence of witnesses. The advocate general had looked into the case, and agreed with him that they were not likely to get a verdict, and elected not to proceed. His Honour ordered that Stephens be discharged.

In the police commissioner's quarterly report, on 26 April 1854, Crawford's escape and the desertion of Constable Dewhurst was mentioned:

In my last report, I remarked upon the felony case No. 14, the murder of the master of the *Jane Lovett*. I regret being now obliged to inform you that John Crawford, who was charged with the crime, apprehended, but allowed to escape, has not been recaptured though every exertion has been made to retake him. I have reason to believe he has left this colony. Police Constable Dewhurst, from whose custody Crawford escaped, absconded to avoid the magisterial enquiry which was about to be made into his conduct. I have taken much pains to catch this man, but as yet, without success. He also has quitted this colony. The locality in which their crimes were committed favoured the escape of both Dewhurst and Crawford. I believe that Police Constable Dewhurst's offence stands almost unparalleled in the history of the South Australian Police, and I feel confident there is not another in the force who would disgrace himself.

On Friday 14 December 1945, the following article appeared in the *Advertiser*:

Cabin door for Museum

I hear that among the recent presentations made to the Nautical Museum at Port Adelaide is a historic cabin door from the schooner *Jane Lovett*, which went ashore near Cape Northumberland on September 19, 1852, while on a voyage from Melbourne to Port Adelaide. Passengers and crew landed safely and later made their way to Adelaide, but the unfortunate captain (deciding to remain) was murdered in his cabin by a couple of convicts from New South Wales who found their way on board. The cabin door, of Gothic design, has been presented by Mr. Ken Reed, of Whyalla, who formerly had it in his collection of museum pieces. It is remarkably well preserved, although naturally the worse for wear after knocking about the world for 100 years.

The cabin door is now located in the Port MacDonnell Maritime Museum.

Date	Victim	Accused
2 November 1853	**Joseph Taylor**	**Peter Fagan and Catherine Morris**
Cause of death:	Neglect	
Outcome:	Both found guilty of manslaughter	
	Morris sentenced to nine months imprisonment with hard labour	
	Fagan sentenced to four months imprisonment with hard labour	
Location:	Gray Street, Adelaide	

In October 1853, Mary Kenney left her son Joseph Taylor with Catherine Morris, 30, and Peter Fagan, 34, as she was going away to Melbourne. Kenny left £12 in advance towards keeping Joseph for six months. Morris had four children of her own, including a seven-month-old child, whom she would breastfeed along with Joseph. On 2 November, Morris breastfed Joseph and gave him some bread and milk. Morris found that Joseph would not eat as much as her child and that he was sickly. Around three o'clock in the afternoon, Fagan told Morris that Joseph looked like he was dying. Morris saw him in the cot and he had froth coming from his mouth. Morris told Fagan to get a doctor. Fagan left but returned alone, saying that he could not find one. Joseph, who was 12 weeks old, died.

During the coroner's inquest, Dr Nash, the Colonial Surgeon, gave evidence that apart from having no food in his system, Joseph was a healthy child. His opinion was that the probable cause of death was spasm of the glottis, which might have been brought on by violent crying for food. Evidence was also given that the money left to look after Joseph was spent on clothing and food, but not for Joseph. At the conclusion of the inquest, the jury found a verdict of wilful murder against Fagan and Morris.

On Thursday 7 December 1853, Fagan and Morris appeared before the Supreme Court in Adelaide on the charge of wilful murder. The judge summed up and reviewed the testimony of Fagan and Morris that the child was always sickly, compared with evidence from the medical men, who described the body as plump and healthy, and other witnesses who spoke of the child as being a fine and healthy infant. He then put it to the jury to decide whether the child died through want of food or not. He thought there could be no doubt the prisoners were either paid to take care of the child, or had voluntarily taken charge of it. In either case they were responsible for its safekeeping. Then came the important question: did either of them, knowingly and wilfully withhold food from the child, with the fixed intention to take its life. If so, the verdict should be for wilful murder. If, on the other hand, the jury were of the opinion that the child was kept without food, with no settled intention to kill it, but through criminal negligence, then the verdict must be manslaughter. The jury returned a verdict of guilty of manslaughter against both prisoners. Catherine Morris received a sentence of nine months hard labour, and Peter Fagan received a sentence of four months hard labour.

Date	*Victim*	*Accused*
1 March 1854	**Angus MacDonald**	**James Bryce and John Tippett**
Cause of death:	Assault (unknown weapon)	
Outcome:	Discharged, no evidence	
Location:	Near Gawler	

On 25 February 1854, Alexander Tweedie, a bullock driver, was at Salt Creek near Gawler when he saw Angus MacDonald. On 2 March 1854, Tweedie was in the area looking for his bullocks when he went back to the creek. On arriving, he saw MacDonald's body floating in the water. Tweedie was sure it was MacDonald, but he did not recognise a hat found near the body as belonging to MacDonald.

A post-mortem examination indicated that MacDonald had received several blows to this head and face prior to being put in the water. There were also marks on his chest and neck.

Suspicion fell upon James Bryce and John Tippett, as they were camping nearby. Both were arrested and brought before the police magistrate, charged with the wilful murder of Angus Macdonald. After evidence was given, His Worship said there was no evidence whatever to affect either of the prisoners, and therefore they would be discharged, but if they could do anything to assist the police by description of parties or otherwise, it would be all the better for them.

The Police Commissioner's quarterly report from 26 April 1854 states:

The murder of Angus Macdonald is a case involved in the deepest obscurity and I fear it is beyond the power of the police to bring the criminal to light. Every procurable clue has been carefully followed, and every effort has been made by the Police, but without the desired result. Inspector Hamilton has twice prosecuted enquiries on the spot, the water-hole in which the body was found has been dragged, as carefully as circumstances permitted, and four persons who were encamped near the spot some days previous to the discovery of the corpse, have been brought before the Magistrate for examination. One person alone remains unaccounted for, and owing to a variety of causes it cannot now be ascertained positively whether this person was the murdered man or the murderer. We must trust to time to clear up this mystery and though the murderer has escaped from the hands of human justice, he may yet be pursued to death by the cry of man's blood which he has shed upon the ground.

Date	*Victim*	*Accused*
28 July 1854	**Connell child**	**Mary Connell**
Cause of death:	Possible suffocation	
Outcome:	Fount not guilty	
Location:	Glenelg	

Mary Connell, 22, was a servant who worked for Richard Colley, a land agent who resided at Glenelg. On Friday 28 July 1854, one of Colley's other servants saw Mary walking from the watercloset on the neighbouring property, which belonged to Mr Hance. Mary reported that she had become ill and went to bed for several days. Another servant mentioned to Colley that she thought that Mary had given birth to a child. On the following Monday morning, Colley went to Mr Hance's watercloset with a candle, and found the body of a newborn child in the sink. Colley returned to his house and told his wife of his discovery, wrote a note to Dr Popham, and then went to town to advise the police.

Sergeant Major James Hall, from the mounted police, attended at the watercloset of Mr Hance. When he arrived, he found that Dr Popham had already attended the scene and had taken the child from the watercloset to his home for examination. Hall made his way to Dr Popham's house, encountering the doctor on the way. Hall told him that he had no authority to remove the body or examine the child at his house. Hall returned to Colley's house and arrested Mary for the murder of her child, but she was too ill to be removed, and remained at the house.

The law at that time ruled that dead bodies were to be conveyed to the nearest public house to wait for an inquest. The child was conveyed to the Glenelg Hotel at Holdfast Bay, where on Tuesday 1 August, an inquest was held into the death of the child. When the jury viewed the body, which had already been subjected to a post-mortem examination, the coroner expressed his great surprise that any surgeon should have ventured to make a post-mortem examination without proper authority.

Dr Popham was called and gave evidence that when he first saw the child it was lying on its left side. To the best of his judgment it had not moved, but lay there as it had fallen. He took the body to his surgery, opened it, and performed tests to the lungs to ascertain if the child had lived. Dr Popham concluded that the child was born alive. There were two bruises on the head arising from injuries inflicted before death. One was over the right side of the occipital bone, and the other on the scalp over the left parietal bone. Neither was of a character to cause death. He did not think that the fall would have killed the child, but believed it died from the effects of cold, and perhaps partial suffocation. There was some discussion between the coroner and Dr Popham regarding his authority to conduct a post-mortem. The coroner ordered Dr John Woodforde to conduct another post-mortem.

Dr Woodforde gave evidence, which contradicted that of Dr Popham. During Dr Woodforde's testimony, Dr Popham interrupted and wanted to ask questions, but the coroner refused. At the completion of Dr Woodforde's evidence, one of the jurors asked if the jury could hear further evidence of Dr Popham regarding the state of the body.

Portrait of Dr. Woodforde seated and resting an elbow on a small table. He wears a dark suit with frock coat and a chin strap beard. He was the ship's surgeon on the 'Rapid' and upon arrival in the colony was appointed by Colonel Light as surgeon to the Survey Department at Rapid Bay. He later established a private practice in Hindley Street. He was appointed Coroner for Adelaide in 1857. [On back of photograph] 'John Woodforde, M.D. / Medical advisor to Colonel Light. Arrived in South Australia on the 'Rapid' in 1836. State Library of South Australia, B 7008

The coroner said Dr Popham had no authority for making the post-mortem examination. He had interfered with the course of public justice, and he hoped such an occurrence would never happen again. He was not sure that Dr

Popham had not committed a misdemeanour, and he should consult the law officers of the Crown upon the subject.

Mr. Hitchcox, who was one of the jurors, begged that the opinion of the other jurors might be taken as to the propriety of examining Dr Popham. The coroner would not take his evidence at the time. The following conversation comes from the court's records:

Dr. Popham	'Will you allow me, Sir.'
Coroner	'Hold your tongue, Sir.'
Dr. Popham	'Will you.'
Coroner	'I will not allow any remark on what I say. If Dr Popham does not choose to hold his tongue, I believe that he has behaved in a most improper manner by interfering with the course of justice. But I do not say he did it intentionally.'
Mr. Hitchcox	'It seems unfair that Dr Popham should leave the court with an imputation on his character, without being allowed to speak.'
Coroner	'There is no imputation on his character. I do not say I shall not examine him when we meet again'.

After the court was adjourned, Dr Popham said he had been treated with 'more discourtesy, and in a more ungentlemanly manner, than he had ever been treated before'. The coroner asked the constable to 'Take that man away; I have a great mind to commit him for his insolence'. Dr Popham responded that the coroner knew better than to send him to gaol, and promptly left the room.

Mary Connell was eventually committed to the Supreme Court, charged with the manslaughter of her child. In the Supreme Court on Tuesday 22 August, Mary Connell appeared for trial, on the charge of manslaughter and concealment of birth. After the trial, the jury retired for a few minutes and returned with a general verdict of not guilty. Connell was discharged.

Date	*Victim*	*Accused*
9 November 1854	**Augusta Bell (Ulbrecht)**	**William Bell**
Cause of death:	Knife wounds	
Outcome:	Found guilty of murder	
	Sentenced to death, executed 27 December 1854	
Location:	Port Adelaide	

Augusta Bell, who was also known as Augusta Ulbrecht, lived with her husband, William Bell, at Port Adelaide. On Thursday 9 November 1854, an argument broke out between the two, with William accusing Augusta of becoming pregnant by a man called Alick.

Emma Johnson and her husband Frederick Johnson lived near the Bells' house. On Friday night, Augusta ran to the Johnson's house and told Emma of the argument, saying that William had cut her arm and taken such a strong hold of her that the gathers were torn out of her dress. A short time later, William arrived, taking hold of Augusta and starting to drag her home. Emma told William to let Augusta go, but William told her that Augusta was 'in the family way' by another man called Alick, and declared that he could not bear that. He also said that if he could not get his revenge on Alick that night, he could have his revenge on her, and he could soon have revenge on himself afterwards. William let go of Augusta and she asked if Emma could keep William talking until she had time to get home. Augusta left and Emma and William spoke for a while, then William left to go home.

The next morning Emma, fearing that something was wrong, requested two policemen to accompany her to the Bell house. They found Augusta on the bed, with her feet on the floor and the upper part of the body exposed. William had cut Augusta's throat and the bedclothes were saturated with blood. The police also saw cuts on Augusta's arms and hands. William was not in the house, and a search of the area commenced.

Police Constable George Smith located and arrested William on the following Thursday morning. William was hiding in the coalhole of the brig *Nonpareil*. After his capture, William admitted that he had cut Augusta's throat, and lay down in the bed next to her intending to die. When arrested, William had handkerchiefs tied around his neck, concealing a wound three inches in length.

In the Supreme Court, on Thursday 7 December 1854, William Bell was indicted for the wilful murder of Augusta. Bell expressed in a low tone his sorrow for having committed the offence. His Honour admonished Bell of the fearful position he placed himself in by pleading guilty to the dreadful charge laid against him. Mr Belt appeared for the defence, and, after a few words with Bell, in a subdued tone, said he was in a state of unconsciousness for some time before the deed was committed. His Honour said, 'Then you plead not guilty', after which Bell changed his plea.

At the completion of the trial, the jury retired for a few minutes, and returned with a guilty verdict. His Honour, who was occasionally inaudible through emotion, said, 'William Bell, you stand convicted on the clearest evidence of the most appalling crime that can be committed by any human being. It is now my duty, as the minister of the law, to pass upon you the sentence of the highest penalty which human laws can award. The sentence of the court is that, for the crime of which you stand convicted, you be brought back to the place you came from, and, on the 27th day of this present month of December, be taken to the place of execution, and hanged by the neck until you are dead, and may the Lord have mercy on your soul'.

The sentence was carried out on 27 December 1854.

Date	*Victim*	*Accused*
11 December 1854	Loorumumpoo (Billy)	Poowoolupe (Mr Bool) and Marielara (Jemmy Rankine)
Cause of death:	Assault (with a waddy)	
Outcome:	Marielara acquitted at trial	
	Poowoolupe escaped, never tried	
Location:	Wellington	

At an Aboriginal encampment near Cook's Station beyond Wellington, Poowoolupe (Mr Bool), a 30-year-old native policeman, struck Loorumumpoo (Billy) three times with a waddy. Marielara (Jemmy Rankin), who was also 30, then struck Loorumumpoo once with a waddy. Poowoolupe caught hold of Loorumumpoo by the neck, wanting to choke him. Loorumumpoo ran away, and Poowoolupe ran after him. Poowoolupe caught up with Loorumumpoo and dragged him away to the bush. Poowoolupe called out to Keemmin, who was standing close by. Keemmin kicked Loorumumpoo in the back twice, as he was afraid of Poowoolupe and had to do what he said. Loorumumpoo died from the beating, and Poowoolupe placed the body into a wombat hole.

Some time later, Poowoolupe showed Netterie, another native policeman, where the body was. Corporal Walton of the Mounted Police was advised, and attended at the wombat hole where he saw the body, which was so badly decomposed and eaten by ants that he was unable to recognise the remains. Poowoolupe and Marielara were taken into custody. On Monday 19 February they appeared before the Supreme Court, and were remanded until the next criminal sessions.

On Monday 13 August 1855, Marielara appeared before the Supreme Court charged with wilful murder. He pleaded not guilty. Poowoolupe was not in court, as it was reported during the trial that he had escaped custody. The crown solicitor warned the jury in his opening address that the case rested on the evidence of Aboriginal witnesses, who 'were, as they well knew, exceedingly ignorant of their duty as witnesses, and consequently their statements were to be taken with great caution'.

After the evidence was heard, Mr Hartley, for the defence, addressed the jury, contending that there was, so far as Marielara was concerned, no evidence of murder.

Mr Hartley stated that it appeared that the men were all together the evening before Loorumumpoo's death. They were playing marbles, and, except for Poowoolupe, all seemed on good terms with the deceased. Mr Hartley confessed he could not so confidently call for an acquittal had Poowoolupe been the person charged with the murder. It was in the power of the jury to return a verdict of manslaughter, but, looking at the evidence altogether, he submitted he was entitled to ask them to acquit the prisoner. The jury subsequently acquitted Marielara.

Date	Victim	Accused
26 December 1854	**Emily Bentley**	**Joseph Bentley**
Cause of death:	Assault	
Outcome:	Unknown	
Location:	Mount Remarkable	

Sometime in 1853, Joseph Bentley, 56, and Emily Bentley moved from Melbourne to Mount Remarkable where they resided in a hut on Mr White's station. On 26 December 1854, Emily was assaulted and later died.

On Tuesday 16 January 1855, Joseph was charged with Emily's murder. Joseph was taken to the local court at Kooringa. A coroner's inquest was held and an open verdict was given and Bentley was released. Further information pertaining to the murder was received a few days later, and as a result Joseph was again arrested.

On Friday 9 February 1855, Police Constable Moran lodged Joseph Bentley in the Adelaide Goal. When Bentley appeared before the court, he stated that there was no case against him, and complained about the police taking him into custody, because at the coroner's hearing the jury had virtually acquitted him.

Between the time of his wife's death, and his apprehension by police, Bentley had married a woman who was 29 years old.

Bentley was kept in custody and appeared before the Supreme Court. On one occasion there were no witnesses available, so the judge allowed Bentley to have bail.

Bentley was due to appear on 29 May 1855, but failed to attend. A bench warrant was issued for his arrest. It is unknown if Bentley was subsequently arrested on that warrant.

Date	*Victim*	*Accused*
24 January 1855	**William Thomas**	**John Smith**
Cause of death:	Knife wound	
Outcome:	Smith found guilty of manslaughter	
	Sentenced to life in prison	
Location:	Willunga area	

On 24 January 1855, a fight broke out between John Smith and William Thomas, with Thomas coming off second best. During the fight, Thomas managed to get hold of a gun, but it was taken from him. The fight broke up and Smith (who was also known as James Dixon) went into a shed, emerging with a bowie knife, which he used to stab Thomas in the back. Thomas, who now was armed, dropped his gun and fell down the moment he was stabbed. Smith was about to inflict another blow with the knife when a witness, Mr Chambers, threw a rock at Smith, which hit him. On recovering himself, Smith menaced Chambers with the knife, and went into the house. Smith soon emerged by the back door, bearing his clothes in a bundle, and still holding the knife in his hand. Chambers followed him with a stick for some distance towards the sea,

but Smith turned around, and brandishing the knife, swore he would give it to him if he approached. Chambers returned to Thomas, whom he placed in a bed, and dispatched messengers to the police and for medical aid. Doctors Jay, Knipe, and Mackintosh were called in, but Thomas subsequently died.

In February 1855, a coroner's inquest was held at Willunga. The jury returned a verdict of wilful murder against John Smith. Smith was said to be a runaway sailor and an escaped convict. Smith had not been taken into custody and was in hiding. A search of the area had failed to locate him.

Nine months later, on Thursday 18 October 1855, Smith was captured in the north of the state and taken before a special magistrate, where a remand was obtained, after which Smith was conveyed to the Adelaide Gaol.

On Wednesday 21 November 1855, Smith escaped from the Adelaide Gaol and proceeded north-east. When he was about two miles beyond Walkerville, members of the public spotted Smith, and alerted the police. Smith was captured and taken back to gaol.

On Monday 4 February 1856, Smith appeared before the Supreme Court on the charge of murdering William Thomas. However, the trial could not commence as Thomas' widow had remarried and was unable to attend court as a witness as she had recently given birth.

On Tuesday 4 March 1856, Smith appeared once more before the Supreme Court, where the trial commenced. At the conclusion, the jury retired and later returned with a verdict of manslaughter. The judge sentenced Smith to penal servitude for the term of his natural life.

Date	*Victim*	*Accused*
17 February 1855	**Thomas Lee**	**John Walker**
Cause of death:	Knife wound	
Outcome:	Found guilty of manslaughter	
	Sentenced to three years imprisonment with hard labour	
Location:	Adelaide	

On Saturday 17 February 1855, Thomas Lee was drinking with John and Jane Walker in the police paddock in Adelaide. During the evening an argument developed between John Walker and Lee, which resulted in Walker stabbing Lee. Thomas Lee made his way to the Adelaide Hospital where he received treatment. As the treating doctors thought Lee was close to death, they sent for Inspector George Hamilton, JP, to attend. Inspector Hamilton obtained a deposition from Lee. Walker was also present.

> Thomas Lee, believing he is about to die, states that on the evening of the 17th of February 1855, he was in company with John Walker, and Jane Walker, the wife of John Walker, in the Police Paddock, at Adelaide. Jane Walker was intoxicated. While they were talking in a friendly manner, John Walker turned around and stabbed him in the belly, and afterwards made a stab at Jane Walker. Taken before me this 17th day of February, 1855, in the presence of Joseph Carpenter Bompas, Esq. M.D. James Phillips, Esq., M.B., and John Walker.

Lee died from his injuries and Walker was taken into custody.

On Monday morning, 19 February 1855, Mr Stevenson attended at the Adelaide Hospital and swore in a jury, who immediately proceeded to view the body of Thomas Lee. The coroner directed the colonial surgeon and Dr Bompas, the resident hospital surgeon, to make a post-mortem examination, and adjourned the inquest to three o'clock that same day, at the Norfolk Arms Hotel, Rundle Street.

A painting of the Norfolk Arms Inn, Rundle Street, Adelaide, about 1854; reproduced from a water colour painting by H. Glover (in the possession of C.J.S. Harding).
State Library of South Australia, B 5852.

At three pm, the coroner and jury assembled, and Inspector Hamilton gave evidence regarding the deposition obtained from Lee. Hamilton stated that Lee was apparently in great pain and extremely faint but in his perfect senses when he saw him. Hamilton informed Lee that his statement would be evidence against John Walker. He distinctly stated that he believed he was about to die before he made his deposition. At the conclusion of the inquest, Walker was found guilty of murder and the coroner committed Walker for trial.

On Friday 25 May 1855, John Walker appeared before the Supreme Court on the charge of murder. At the completion of the trial, the jury retired and returned with a verdict of manslaughter. Walker was sentenced to three years hard labour.

Date	Victim	Accused
1 June 1855	Peter Brown	Wadniltie, Wenpalta, Pankalta and Ilyelta
Cause of death:	Spear wounds, assault	
Outcome:	All found guilty of murder	
	All sentenced to death, executed 14 January 1856	
Location:	Franklin Harbour, Cowell	

On 1 June 1855, 28-year-old Peter Brown was employed as a shepherd at the Middlecamp Station, near Franklin Harbour. Also at the station that day were four Aboriginal men, Wadniltie, Wenpalta, Pankalta and Ilyelta. They were at the station asking for tobacco, which Brown refused to give them. Brown left the station with his flock of 1,700 sheep. A short time after Brown left, Wadniltie, Wenpalta, Pankalta and Ilyelta also set off in the same direction.

In the evening, Brown's flock wandered back to the station, but Brown did not return with them. A search was conducted and Brown was found dead. It appeared that the group of men had followed him and attacked Brown while he was cutting a stick with his knife. Wadniltie had speared Brown, and Pankalta and the others beat him with waddies. They later dragged Brown's body away and threw it into a bush, with the intention of hiding it. The four left the area, taking about ten sheep from the flock with them.

The search party, which included some members of the same tribe as the four accused, followed their tracks. A few weeks later, on 23 July, Wadniltie,

Wenpalta, Pankalta and Ilyelta were located. They still had some of Brown's clothing with them. The four were arrested and taken to the Salt Creek (Arno Bay) Police Station, from which they managed to escape. About three months later they were recaptured and transported to the Adelaide Gaol.

On Tuesday 4 December 1855, in the Supreme Court, Wadniltie, Wenpalta, Pankalta and Ilyelta appeared and were charged with Brown's murder. The crown solicitor prosecuted and Mr Hartley defended. The crown solicitor stated that the evidence would show that the murder had been committed with malice and forethought, and with the express intention of stealing some sheep.

Mr Hartley submitted that the evidence was not of a sufficient character to incriminate the prisoner Ilyelta. He therefore asked for his acquittal under the direction of His Honour. The crown solicitor contended that the evidence showed Ilyelta was an accomplice and an approver.

His Honour then summed up the case, stating his desire for 'the jury to dismiss from their minds, in considering the case, the prejudice which might attach to birth and colour, and only to weigh the evidence as they would if they were trying one of their own countrymen'. He then carefully went over the case, and dismissed the jury to consider their verdict. The jury retired, and after a few moments returned into court and pronounced each of the prisoners guilty of murder.

On Friday 7 December, the four prisoners appeared again before the Supreme Court where they were sentenced to death. They were transported back to Port Lincoln on the government schooner *Yatala*, arriving at Franklin Harbour on 12 January 1856. The gallows were erected about 500 yards from the beach, where at eight am on 14 January, the prisoners were executed. Their bodies were taken down and buried by members of their tribe.

In 1881, it was reported that during the excavations for the Franklin Harbour Hotel, at Cowell, the remains of the four were discovered.

Date	*Victim*	*Accused*
1 September 1855	**Henry Nixon**	**Ogonoron (Black Billy)**
Cause of death:	Sword wounds	
Outcome:	Ogonoron charged with rape and attempted murder	
	Sentenced to death, commuted to life in prison	
Location:	Snapper's Point	

On Saturday 1 December 1855, Constable Henry Nixon had Ogonoron, also known as Black Billy, in custody. Nixon was taking Ogonoron to Adelaide as he had been arrested for 'ravishing' (raping) a young girl. At Snapper's Point (just above Glen Osmond) on the Eastern Road, Nixon took Ogonoron's irons off for a toilet break. Ogonoron snatched Nixon's sword and struck him with it, inflicting a wound on Nixon's forehead, the blood from which completely blinded him. During a struggle, Ogonoron inflicted several wounds on Nixon's head, face, and neck. Ogonoron escaped and Nixon was later found on one side of the road.

Dr John Woodforde attended to Nixon that evening. Nixon had many wounds about the face and neck, some of which were of a serious nature. One on the right side of the neck laid bare the carotid artery; had that artery been cut, death would have been instantaneous.

Ogonoron was located and on Wednesday 5 December 1855, in the Supreme Court, he was charged with raping Hannah Phillis on 1 August 1855 at the Source of the Torrens. Ogonoron pleaded guilty, but stated that he was intoxicated at the time he committed the offence. Ogonoron was then indicted for assaulting, with intent to kill, Constable Henry Nixon. The indictment contained the usual counts, varying the offence charged to cutting and wounding, with intent to maim, disfigure, disable, or to inflict grievous bodily harm. The prisoner denied the intent charged, but admitted that he committed the assault to make his escape from custody.

The judge left it to the jury to decide whether the wounds were inflicted with intent to murder, or merely to disable or inflict serious bodily harm. The jury, after some consideration, found Ogonoron guilty of attempted murder. Ogonoron was sentenced to penal servitude for the remainder of his life for the rape, and sentenced to death for the attempted murder. This sentence was later commuted to life imprisonment.

Nixon continued as a police officer and in 1861 he was promoted to Corporal in charge of the Port Elliot Police Station. On 15 October 1861, Nixon died. The cause of death was recorded as 'disease of the brain', but Nixon's treating doctor listed the injuries received six years earlier from Ogonoron as responsible for his death.

Henry Nixon's death has not been classified as a murder due to the 'Year and a Day Rule' which used to exist in Homicide. Historically, two different actions could be brought in respect of the same death. Usually an appeal for felony of death, a private prosecution by interested parties or relatives of the victim, would be followed by proceedings at the King's suit which was a public prosecution. Unlike the King's suit, private prosecutions, if not freshly pursued, would not be allowed. The Statute of Gloucester (1278), referring to the then normal action of the time of an appeal of felon for death, provided that if the relative of the victim brought the action within a year and a day after the 'deed' was done, the appeal could go forward. This provision was restrictively interpreted to mean there was a time limit on the actionability of the private prosecution. The rule evolved from being procedure to becoming a rule of substantive law, and in 1557 the rule was found in a legal textbook, which wrote, 'Also it is requisite to homicide, if one strikes another so that he dies, that death should be within a year and a day next following ...' The rule was then passed down through the centuries and was reflected in the definition of murder found in Chief Justice Coke's institutes: 'Murder is when a man of sound memory, and of the age of discretion, unlawfully killeth within any county of the realm any reasonable creature in rerum naturea under the King's peace, with malice aforethought, either expressed by the party or implied by law, so as the party wounded, or hurt, etc. die of the wound or hurt, etc. within a year and a day after the same'. The Year and a Day rule continued in South Australia until it was abolished in 1991.

In September 2008, Nixon's name was added to the National Police Memorial in Canberra, listed as having died from the injuries he received on duty six years before his death.

Date	*Victim*	*Accused*
September 1855	**Aboriginal woman**	**Aboriginal man**
Cause of death:	Assault	
Outcome:	Unknown	
Location:	Unknown	

A report from the 'Protector of Aborigines' appeared in the *South Australian Register* on Friday 21 September, page three:

I regret to inform you that a savage murder has been committed within my district. A young woman (native) was beaten about the head, her skull was fractured, and even her brains were made to gush out, for

134

refusing to become the partner of a man who desired her as his wife. All work here, therefore, is necessarily stopped, as I have undertaken to accompany the Native Police in search of the murderers.

No further information found.

Date	Victim	Accused
September 1855	Shepherd child	Jane Shepherd
Cause of death:	Neglect	
Outcome:	Found guilty of concealment of birth	
	Sentenced to nine months imprisonment with hard labour	
Location:	Port Lincoln	

There is little information regarding this matter, other than on Friday 7 December 1855, in the Supreme Court, Jane Shepherd appeared charged with feloniously causing the death of her infant daughter by culpable neglect at Port Lincoln in September 1855. Shepherd was also charged with concealing the birth of the child. Shepherd pleaded not guilty to the first charge, but guilty to the second. The prosecution withdrew the first count, stating that on examination, there was no evidence to support the charge. Shepherd was sentenced to nine months imprisonment with hard labour.

Date	Victim	Accused
21 September 1855	Mary	Waren-boor-inem (Mr Walker) and Parich-boor-imen (Blueskin Billy)
Cause of death:	Spear wounds, assault	
Outcome:	Both found guilty of manslaughter	
	Both sentenced to three years hard labour	
Location:	Glencoe, Spring Station	

Some Aboriginal families used to live all together on a certain tract of country, in territories that other families did not enter. A custom of the time was that when a woman belonging to one family died, the males belonging to that family immediately went to the closest family group and selected a woman who was then killed. The belief was that by killing the second woman, the family had gotten revenge on the evil eye that had bewitched her and caused her death.

On 21 September 1855, at Spring Station at Glencoe, Waren-boor-inem's lubra died. Waren-boor-inem, along with Tommy Taylor and Parich-boor-imen, went to the closest family group where he located a 28-year-old woman called Mary. Without any ill feeling against Mary, Waren-boor-inem, Tommy Taylor and Parich-boor-imen entered Mary's miami and killed her. The local police were notified and Waren-boor-inem and Parich-boor-imen were taken into custody.

On Tuesday 29 November 1855, in the Supreme Court, Waren-boor-inem and Parich-boor-imen were charged with murder. Tommy Taylor gave evidence and described how Warren-boor-inem and Parich-boor-imen had killed Mary, and that he had no hand in her death. The crown solicitor stated Mary was remarkably mild and inoffensive in her disposition, but had been apparently 'made a sufferer under a superstitious custom peculiar to the natives of the country'. Mr Hartley, the defence lawyer, argued that the evidence was not sufficient for the condemnation of the prisoners to suffer the sentence of the law. Tommy Taylor, who Hartley argued should be on trial along with Warren-boor-inem and Patrich-boor-imen, had provided the only direct evidence. He asked, therefore, for an acquittal under His Honour's ruling as to the insufficiency of the evidence. His Honour asked Waren-boor-inem through the interpreter, Mr Smith of Mount Gambier, whether it was the custom when a woman had been killed because of the death of another, to punish for the death of the second woman. His Honour was advised that it was not the custom.

His Honour then summed up, dwelling upon the effect Aboriginal customs might have upon the case and the fact that while the accused men held the act to be perfectly right and justifiable, the English law regarded it as murder. He also directed attention to the leniency that the law allowed, to find the prisoners guilty of manslaughter. The jury then retired, and after a brief interval returned a verdict of manslaughter. Waren-boor-inem and Parich-boor-imen were sentenced to three years imprisonment with hard labour.

Date	*Victim*	*Accused*
21 September 1855	**James Spencer**	**Unknown**
Cause of death:	Knife wounds	
Outcome:	Unknown	
Location:	Macclesfield	

James Spencer lived by himself in a hut at Macclesfield. On Friday 21 September 1855, Spencer voted in the South Australian election, and then went to the Macclesfield Hotel. He remained there for some time and around seven pm decided to return home. When Spencer left, he was sober and dressed in his best clothes. Spencer was a man of rather eccentric habits, and of a very 'reserved and retiring' manner. He had a friend called Crick who used to visit him each Sunday.

On Sunday 23 September, Crick went to Spencer's hut. When Crick arrived he saw the front door was open, so he went in, and found Spencer dead on the floor. Crick saw that Spencer had two wounds to the chest. A washbasin was standing on a bench close by the body, which had apparently been used by the murderer to wash his hands, as the water was bloody, and there were also stains of blood about the rim of the basin and on the bench.

An inquest was held on Monday 24 September 1855, at the Davenport Arms in Macclesfield, before Captain Davison, JP, and a highly respectable jury. After viewing the body and the hut, which remained in the same state as when the body was discovered, the jury retired, while Dr Chalmers, assisted by Dr Blue, conducted a post-mortem examination.

When the inquest resumed, the jury heard that Spencer had two stab wounds in the chest and three in the side. The fatal wound was in the chest, where the knife had penetrated to the heart and divided the large artery, causing instantaneous death. The wounds appeared to have been inflicted with a broad-pointed knife, probably a butcher's or sheath knife, similar to those sometimes worn by seamen.

Spencer may have been dead two or three days before being discovered. From this testimony, and the fact that Spencer was wearing the same clothes he wore on Friday 21 September, the day he was last seen alive, coupled with the fact that he was never known to wear those clothes (his best suit) except upon Sundays and on special occasions, it was surmised that he met his death on Friday night. Spencer's door was broken open, and there was no evidence of a struggle, so it appeared most probable that James had gone home and had found someone in his hut, and had been stabbed not long after returning home. The jury returned a verdict of wilful murder against some person or persons unknown.

Date	Victim	Accused
2 February 1856	Hocking child	Marianne Hocking and Martha Jones

Cause of death:	Neglect
Outcome:	Both found guilty of manslaughter
	Hocking sentenced to nine months imprisonment with hard labour
	Jones sentenced to 18 months imprisonment with hard labour
Location:	Auburn

Marianne Hocking was a cook at the Rising Sun Inn at Auburn, owned by Joseph Bleechmore. On Monday 4 February 1856, Bleechmore was told that Hocking had given birth, and that the infant was buried in the watercloset. Bleechmore told the police. Corporal Henry Peters attended and spoke to Hocking before inspecting the watercloset, where he found the body of a newborn child. Peters took Hocking into custody.

On Thursday 7 February, an inquest was held at the Rising Sun Inn before the coroner, Mr John Jacob. Evidence given implicated Martha Jones in assisting in the birth and the disposal of the body. Dr Foster Stedman, a surgeon, stated that in his opinion the child was born alive but had not gone full-term, suggesting that it was between six or seven months. He also thought that the child would have lived under any circumstances.

At the completion of the evidence, the jury returned the verdict 'that the said infant came to her death through neglect, and want of proper care required from the mother, Marianne Hocking, and Martha Jones, and that the said Marianne Hocking and Martha Jones are guilty of manslaughter and concealment of birth of the said infant'. Both women were committed for trial.

Hocking and Jones appeared in the Supreme Court on Friday 15 February, charged with the murder of a female child. At the completion of the trial, both were found guilty of manslaughter, and remanded until the following Monday for sentencing. On Monday 18 February, Hocking and Jones were placed in the dock to receive sentence. His Honour, addressing the prisoners, said, 'You have both been found guilty of killing a child born of Marianne Hocking'.

Hocking replied: 'I am guilty of concealing the birth, your Honour.'

His Honour: 'Yes, you are indeed guilty in that respect, and the jury have found you guilty of killing the child.'

Hocking: 'I never saw it, sir.'

His Honour: 'If you gave birth to the living child, and you left it exposed in a place where it died, that was killing the child. Unfortunately, the crime of which you stand convicted is very common in this colony, and I shall be glad if the punishment I am now about to inflict on you will act as a warning to others who may be led into temptation. I assure you it is most painful to pass sentence on you who, now while you are so young a woman, must be shut up in gaol for a considerable time, and when you come out you must come with the reputation of having destroyed your own child. Painful as is the duty, it must be performed, and I hope it will have the salutary effect it is intended to have. The sentence of the court is that you be imprisoned, for nine calendar months, with hard labour.'

His Honour then sentenced Jones:

With respect to you my feelings are very different. You are a person who, as you acknowledged to the girl Hocking, have been a mother of children yourself. I can only wonder how a woman who has reared children herself could be so lost to all proper sense of human feeling as to assist a young creature in destroying her infant babe. (The prisoner commenced crying bitterly). You may cry now, but I cannot but remember your conduct on another occasion, so very different to that you exhibit now. By the depositions, you appear to me to be a very heartless person, given to intemperate habits, and also addicted to the use of gross language, a woman who might have been supposed to have been an accessory to a crime of this kind. The jury found you guilty of manslaughter, and if the statement given against you were true, they might almost have been justified in finding you guilty of murder. I think it my duty to pass a heavy sentence upon you, and though it may not have the same effect upon you, it is to be hoped others exposed to temptation will be deterred from crime by a remembrance of your severe punishment. Your sentence is 18 calendar months imprisonment with hard labour.

Date	*Victim*	*Accused*
18 March 1856	**Hahn child**	**Bridget Hahn**
Cause of death:	Neglect	
Outcome:	Discharged	
Location:	Crafers	

Bridget Hahn lived with her family at Crafers when she became pregnant, giving birth in March 1856. Wilhelmina Preus, also of Crafers, assisted Hahn with the birth of a healthy son. When Preus placed the child by Hahn's side, she pushed it away from her, and said she did not want to have anything to do with it. Hahn had a plentiful supply of milk two days after the birth. On the third day, Preus noticed that the child was falling away, but she was told to mind her own business. Preus never saw Hahn give the child the breast, and the only food that was administered was goat's milk and oatmeal. After a short time, the child became ill and on 18 March, he died. After a coronial inquest, Hahn was committed to trial on a charge of manslaughter.

On Friday 16 May 1856, Bridget Hahn was placed in the dock of the Supreme Court charged with feloniously killing her infant son. Dr Alfred Bayer gave evidence that he had seen Hahn with the baby the day before he died, and that he had observed that the child was sinking and beyond hope of recovery. He had seen similar symptoms in cases where the mother had been attacked with the milk fever. The capabilities of mothers to afford sustenance to their children varied to a very considerable extent, and the milk might cease to come if the mother was not fed properly.

Mr Andrews addressed the jury for the defence. He called Mrs White, who stated that a week after the birth of the child, Hahn told her that she was starved, and must leave the house soon. A few days afterwards Hahn came to White's house. White told her to go home and fetch the baby, and Hahn replied that she dared not go there alone, as she was afraid her father would horsewhip her.

After hearing further evidence, His Honour said there was not sufficient evidence, in his judgment, to convict the prisoner. It was for the jury, however, to consider, and if they thought otherwise, then the evidence should be gone on with. The jury agreed, and returned a verdict of not guilty. His Honour, addressing the prisoner, said she was not without blame in reference to the death of her child, but there was not proof that its death was caused by her having wilfully neglected to provide it with proper sustenance. Hahn was discharged.

Date	*Victim*	*Accused*
September 1856	**Powang**	**Karende (Billy Goat)**
Cause of death:	Spear wound	
Outcome:	Found guilty of manslaughter	
	Sentenced to three months imprisonment	
Location:	Lake Albert or Yankalilla	

In September 1856, upwards of 70 men from the Lake Albert and Murray tribes engaged in a fight. Karende belonged to the Lake Albert tribe and Powang to the Murray tribe. During the fight, Karende threw a spear that pierced Powang's eye and killed him. The incident is reported to have occurred at Lake Albert and also at Yankalilla.

In the Supreme Court on Thursday 4 December 1856, Karende was charged with the manslaughter of Powang. George Mason, 'Sub-Protector of Aborigines', who resided at Wellington, acted as interpreter. Mason stated that the two tribes had been cautioned against fighting, and that battles were prevented wherever it was found possible, but in this case the preparations were conducted in secrecy and completed in such a short time that the event was not known to the police. Fights between tribes broke out frequently, often for reason that settlers found trivial. For instance, a young man taking away a young woman of another tribe without leave was grave cause for battle, as was an individual mentioning the name of a deceased person, which was considered most offensive. The fight in September 1856 had no clear motive.

Two Aboriginal people who had seen Karende throw the spear that killed Powang gave evidence. At the completion of the evidence, His Honour summed up, and the jury, after a brief retirement, returned a verdict of manslaughter. The jury recommended the prisoner to the merciful consideration of the court, on account of his long imprisonment, and because of the ignorance of Karende and his tribe to the operation of the English law. Karende, through the interpreter, in mitigation of sentence, said he threw the spear at random at the hostile tribe and not at Powang in particular.

His Honour, via the interpreter, informed Karende of the sentence that the law would sanction for his offence. Karende asked if he would be hanged, rejoicing and vowing never to fight again when His Honour told him that he would not be executed. His Honour, upon that promise and the recommendation of the jury, sentenced Karende to three months imprisonment.

Date	Victim	Accused
16 October 1856	Thomas Murriss (Layless)	Gregory Jordan, John Christoff, and Charles Forward
Cause of death:	Assault	
Outcome:	Jordan found guilty of manslaughter, sentenced to 12 months imprisonment with hard labour Christoff and Forward found guilty of aiding and abetting Christoff fined £10, Forward fined £20	
Location:	Watervale	

On the evening of 16 October 1856, Gregory Jordan, who was drunk, was at the Stanley Arms at Watervale. Jordan was in the taproom leaning his head on the bar when Thomas Murriss, who was also drunk, went up to Jordan and patted him on the shoulder. This started a fight between them. They fell upon the floor of the taproom struggling, and as they seemed determined to fight, the barman sent them outside. The fight continued in the yard and after a short time, Murriss declared he was 'ready to go on if anyone would pick him up'. John Christoff and Charles Forward volunteered to stand as 'seconds' to Jordan and Murriss. After each round, Jordan suggested that the fight should end on the condition that Murriss say that Jordan was the best man and Murriss should pay for Jordan's shirt, which had been torn.

Murriss would not agree and the fight continued with short intervals occurring between some of the rounds, during which the seconds proposed that they should discontinue the fight, as they had both proved good men. Jordan and Murriss separated and Jordan walked away. While putting his shirt on, Murriss said, 'I am as good a man as ever Jordan was', even though they had ceased fighting on the understanding that Jordan was to be considered as 'the best man'.

They fought again, until Murriss fell, unconscious, to the ground from a blow to the back of the ear. Christoff and another man took Murriss to the Stanley Arms and Dr Stedman was sent for. On his arrival he examined

Murriss, and bled him, which made him breathe freely, but after a short time he died. A post-mortem examination showed that Murriss had died from a suffusion of blood on the brain, caused by two severe blows behind the ear.

Jordan, Forward and Christoff appeared before Justice Boothby in the Supreme Court on Tuesday 2 December. At the completion of the evidence, His Honour summed up and the jury retired. After an absence of about 20 minutes, the jury returned, finding Jordan guilty of manslaughter and Forward and Christoff guilty of aiding and abetting. The jury accompanied their verdict with a strong recommendation that the mercy of the court be shown to Christoff. His Honour then passed sentence upon the prisoners. Jordan received 12 months imprisonment with hard labour. Forward was ordered to pay a fine of £20 and Christoff to pay a fine of £10. The fines were paid and Forward and Christoff left the court.

Date	*Victim*	*Accused*
17 October 1856	**James Mitchell**	**Three Aboriginal people**
Cause of death:	Assault (with a waddy)	
Outcome:	Two escaped, one died in police custody	
Location:	Angepena, near Mount Serle	

Photograph of a painting of Angepena, near Mount Searle, 1860, from the original in the Dixson Galleries, Art Gallery of New South Wales (permission obtained).
State Library of South Australia, B 16387/1

On Sunday 18 October 1856, an Aboriginal boy arrived at Mr Baker's head station at Mount Serle, with a piece of paper tied on a stick, which was the 'usual manner in which the natives carried letters'. The boy stated that James Mitchell, the hutkeeper at Angepena, an outstation about 13 miles off, wanted the dray sent with flour. The stockmen thought this to be strange, as it was understood that there was at least half a bag of flour in the hut. A stockman went to see Mitchell at his hut the following Tuesday with some tea and sugar, thinking it possible that it might be what was wanted.

On arriving at the hut, the stockman found Mitchell dead inside the door. Mitchell's head was covered to the chin with a neatly folded blanket. His face was so badly battered that his features were scarcely recognisable. Evidence of a severe scuffle existed in the shape of stones and waddies lying about, which the attackers had not removed. The voices of a group of Aboriginal people could be heard close by. A search was conducted in the hut and it was found stripped of all stores. The double-barrelled gun, with the stock shattered and bearing marks of blows, had one barrel discharged, the other loaded and at full cock. A search was conducted and about a quarter of a mile away a grave was found which contained the body of an Aboriginal person. The bodies appeared to have been dead for a few days. It was suspected that the attackers had sent the boy to the head station with the paper as a ruse to rob the dray of flour.

It was later reported in the *South Australian Register* on Saturday 23 May 1857, under the heading of 'Police Returns', that three Aboriginal people had been apprehended for Mitchell's murder. However, on their trip back to Adelaide, two of the prisoners escaped from the custody of the police, and the third died of his wounds.

Date	*Victim*	*Accused*
24 December 1856	**John Carthew**	**Stephen Ryan**
Cause of death:	Knife wound	
Outcome:	Ryan found guilty of manslaughter	
	Sentenced to two years imprisonment with hard labour	
Location:	North Kapunda	

On Wednesday 24 December 1856, Stephen Ryan and 21-year-old John Carthew were at the North Kapunda Inn. During the afternoon, Ryan was drinking in the taproom with some of his friends, before going into the bar where Carthew was. When Carthew saw Ryan enter the bar, Carthew wanted him to stand (buy) champagne, but Ryan said he wouldn't. Carthew continued to ask Ryan to stand champagne, and after a while Ryan became angry. The interaction between Ryan and Carthew caught the eye of Mary Ann Crace, the wife of the landlord, James Crace. Mary went and stood between Carthew and Ryan to prevent a quarrel. Carthew and Ryan had a fight, during which Ryan produced a knife and stabbed Carthew, who later died. During the autopsy, part of the knife blade was found in the heart. When Ryan was arrested, a broken knife which was stained with blood was found in his possession.

On Wednesday 18 February 1857, Stephen Ryan was indicted for the wilful murder of John Carthew before Acting Chief Justice Boothby in the Supreme Court. After the trial, His Honour said that, by English law, in order to find a person guilty of murder, the jury must be satisfied from the evidence that the accused had in his mind what the law called 'malice aforethought': the intent to kill. There could be no doubt as to the cause of Carthew's death, but the question was if Ryan had 'intentionally and with deliberate resolve' stabbed Carthew. It had been held that a man seizing a weapon close at hand, without previous intention to do so, and causing death, was only guilty of manslaughter. The fact that Ryan had the knife already in his hand held still stronger in his favour.

The jury, after eight minutes of consideration, found Ryan guilty of manslaughter. Fisher, for the defence, begged to remind His Honour that Ryan was an old man, the father of a family, and that a long imprisonment of their father would ruin his children's affairs. He hoped His Honour would see that justice would be satisfied by the infliction of a fine. His Honour, addressing Ryan, dwelt on the wickedness of entering into a quarrel with a knife in his hand, and sentenced him to two years imprisonment with hard labour.

Date	*Victim*	*Accused*
10 January 1857	**Michael Macnamara**	**Henry Kochne**
Cause of death:	Assault (with a pole)	
Outcome:	Found guilty of manslaughter, fined £20	
Location:	The South Road	

On Saturday 10 January 1857, Michael Macnamara was drinking at a public house on the South Road. As he was leaving, Henry Kochne passed with his dray along the road. Some insulting remark was made, after which Macnamara began to follow Kochne. Macnamara, armed with a bullock-whip, overtook

Kochne and began menacing him. In response, Kochne took up a pole which lay in his dray and struck Macnamara on the head, causing Macnamara to fall onto the road. Macnamara was unable to get up, so some witnesses assisted him and carried him to his house. He was attended to by Dr Henry Ayliffe for about a week, but died from his injuries. Dr Ayliffe thought that the blow to the head was the cause of death. Sergeant-Major Hall arrested Kochne, who expressed great sorrow for what had occurred and voluntarily pointed out the pole with which he had inflicted the injury.

On Tuesday 17 February 1857, Henry Kochne appeared before the Supreme Court where he was indicted for killing and slaying Michael Macnamara. At the completion of the evidence, Mr Gwynne, for the defence, addressed the jury. He dwelt on the admitted intoxication of Macnamara, the 'generally quarrelsome character of intoxicated Irish men of his class', the fact that Kochne retreated from the assault of Macnamara before he resorted to violence, and that he grasped the weapon to defend himself instinctively and without any predetermination to use it.

The jury, after considerable deliberation, found Kochne guilty of manslaughter, adding that the circumstances were of great provocation, and strongly recommended the prisoner to mercy. His Honour sentenced Kochne to pay a fine of £20, and to be imprisoned until the fine was paid. A person stepped forward, paid the fine, and Kochne was immediately discharged.

Sergeant Major James John Hall, Mounted Police, born 5 May 1821. He joined the Metropolitan Police 21 February 1842. He became a Lance Corporal 1 January 1847, Corporal 10 October 1847. He became a Sergeant 1 March 1852 and Sergeant Major 8 February 1853. He was made Inspector 12 June 1861 and finally left the Service 30 June 1861. At one stage he was living at the old Police Barracks on North Terrace, and whilst there a son was born to him; a volley of guns was fired to mark the occasion. This ambrotype photograph shows James John Hall in his ceremonial uniform holding a sword. State Library of South Australia, B 6028.

Date	*Victim*	*Accused*
15 May 1857	**Richard Moon**	**George Hobbs**
Cause of death:	Knife wound	
Outcome:	Discharged	
Location:	Port Augusta	

On Tuesday 18 August 1857, George Hobbs appeared in the Supreme Court charged with killing Richard Moon at Port Augusta. Mr Andrews appeared for the prisoner. The crown solicitor opened the case, stating that as a magistrate had handed the knife back to the prisoner, the chain of evidence had been broken, so there was no way of telling if the knife was the one used in the murder. His Honour suggested that the charge of murder should be abandoned, and that the prisoner should be charged with stabbing with intent to do bodily harm. This was because for a charge of intent, rather than murder, Moon's statement could be used as evidence. If the charge were murder, Moon's evidence could not be used. Mr Andrews asked that the prisoner should be acquitted on the charge of murder, as he had pleaded to that indictment. His Honour instructed the jury to acquit the prisoner on the present charge. The court adjourned till 10 am the next day.

Even though Hobbs was due to appear on a charge of wounding with intent, Hobbs was charged with manslaughter on Friday 21 August in the Supreme Court. After several witnesses had given evidence, Police Trooper William Jolliffe was recalled. Jolliffe said that when Moon was laying on his bed, he beckoned him to put his head down to hear what he had to say, and then said, 'I should not like that man to be committed as he did not do it'. Jolliffe asked him what he meant, and Moon replied, 'I did it myself'. Jolliffe asked him how, and Moon stated that he had used his own knife, and that he had buried it in the sand, motioning at the same time with his hand how he had scraped the sand over it. Jolliffe asked him where he buried the knife, but Moon was too weak to answer, becoming delirious before dying.

His Honour told the jury that this put an end to the case, for it would be highly wrong to convict the prisoner after the evidence of the last witness. His Honour stated:

Here was a sad instance of the evil influence of drink. Under the effects of drink the deceased had no doubt fallen into a state of *delirium tremors*, and then, it appeared, had inflicted a wound upon himself, which he afterwards said was done by the prisoner. The law of England was, that the evidence of a man uttered at his last moments should be regarded with the same solemnity as on oath and it must be so regarded in this case.

His Honour advised the prisoner to let this occasion be a warning to him, and said:

For although it was shown in the evidence that he was sober at the time, the whole affair had been produced by indulgence in intoxicating drink. This was the cause of the prisoner having been detained some months in gaol, and had been the means of putting the colony to the expense of at least £100. Those things should be enough to make society stand up and put an end to the evil, for the money spent by working men in drink would, if saved, be sufficient to buy them sections of land. This case was a deplorable example of the evil.

The crown solicitor said he was not aware of the evidence just given until the case was before the court. It was not the police constable's fault, since he tendered the evidence to the magistrate, and it was rejected. His Honour expressed his regret at this, as it had been the cause of great expense and loss of time. The prisoner was discharged.

This case has not been included in the statistics section, and is not regarded as a murder.

Date	Victim	Accused
19 June 1857	**Bullocky**	**Beerdea (Billy)**
Cause of death:	Unknown	
Outcome:	Pleaded guilty to manslaughter	
	Sentenced to six months imprisonment	
Location:	Tillowey, near Mount Remarkable	

On Monday 17 August 1857, in the Supreme Court, an Aboriginal man named Beerdea, alias Billy, was charged with killing Bullocky, another Aboriginal man, at Tillowey on 19 June 1857. The prisoner, after numerous questions, entered a plea to the charge of manslaughter, and was sentenced to six months imprisonment with hard labour.

No details of the incident were located.

Date	*Victim*	*Accused*
30 June 1857	**Cooekin**	**Goodoognaybrie (Timothy),**
	(Jimmy Adams)	**Toorapennie (Jemmy), and**
		Tommy

Cause of death:	Assault
Outcome:	Tommy died in custody
	Goodoognaybrie and Toorapennie pleaded guilty
	to manslaughter
	Sentenced to six months imprisonment with hard labour
Location:	Near Strathalbyn

On 28 June 1857, Cooekin (Jimmy Adams), Goodoognaybrie (Timothy), Toorapennie (Jemmy) and Tommy were at the Everly Inn near Strathalbyn where they purchased two bottles of brandy for 12 shillings. The publican, Mr Wells, broke the law, as it was an offence to sell alcohol to an Aboriginal person. The four took the alcohol to their camp where they all became drunk. On 30 June, a fight broke out between them, during which Cooekin was assaulted and died.

On the morning of Thursday 2 July, Cooekin's body was found in a waterhole, and Police Trooper Donnelly was advised. Donnelly received information about the fight, and apprehended Goodoognaybrie, Toorapennie and Tommy on suspicion of murder. All three told Donnelly that they had some knowledge of the death.

On Friday 3 July, an inquest on the body of Cooekin was held by special magistrate Dr Walker at the Everly Inn. At the completion of the evidence, the jury returned a verdict of wilful murder against Goodoognaybrie, Toorapennie and Tommy, who were committed for trial.

On Friday 17 July, Tommy died in the Adelaide Gaol from inflammation of the lungs.

The trial commenced in the Supreme Court on Monday 17 August. After the indictment was read and translated to the prisoners, they both pleaded guilty, and said that the man who was killed was drunk, and struck the first blow.

His Honour, in consideration of the circumstances which had been stated, imposed the term of punishment to six months imprisonment with hard labour. His Honour also stated:

I would at the same time have the prisoners to understand that if the natives entered into these fights and death ensued, they must be punished for the consequences. And, for the advantage of their own race, it is necessary that this should be the case, otherwise they would all become exterminated. I observe that the natives of New Zealand were arriving at the knowledge of this fact, and were expressing their regret that the laws which prevented Europeans from fighting were not also extended to themselves.

Date	*Victim*	*Accused*
11 August 1857	William Bereft (Beacroft)	Charles Gray and John Date
Cause of death:	Assault	
Outcome:	Discharged	
Location:	Coonatto, near Port Augusta	

On Tuesday 11 August 1857, William Bereft was at Mickies Public House at Coonatto. William Roberts, a draper from Port Augusta, and two of his friends, Charles Gray and John Date, were also there. Around 10 am, Mrs Holbkirk, who was also in Mickies Public House, approached Roberts and told him about an insult she had received from Bereft.

Coonatto Station homestead, 1860. Overseers' cottage on extreme left, homestead on extreme right. Situated about 4 miles northeast of Hammond in the hundred of Coonatto. State Library of South Australia, B 8015.

Date heard what Mrs Holbkirk had said, so he went to Bereft and asked why he had insulted her. Date told Bereft that it was a pity he should do this whilst her husband was away, and that he had better go back and apologise to her. Bereft started to walk out, then turned to come back and said, 'You bloody bastard, I would serve your sister the same way'. In response, Date struck Bereft twice over his left eye with the back of his hand, and Bereft fell to the ground. Gray went to Bereft and picked him up, then returned to his friends. Bereft left and went to a station owned by Mr Grant, which was about 50 miles from Port Augusta, where he died. At a subsequent coroner's inquest, Gray and Date were committed to trial.

In the Supreme Court on Wednesday 25 November 1857, Charles Gray and John Date were charged with the wilful murder of William Bereft. A police constable named Fox was present. His Honour, having ascertained that Fox was not in attendance as a witness, expressed his surprise that the case should have been 'got up' in such a careless manner, involving as it did such important consequences. He also remarked that there did not appear to be any evidence to incriminate the prisoner Gray. Mr. James Boucaut, for the defence, stated that if there were, it would deter many persons from acting the part of the good Samaritan.

His Honour stated that he was surprised that no evidence was given to prove the identity of the deceased, or that he had died as a result of the blows from Date. The crown solicitor stated that he had no evidence to prove the identity of the man whose death had occurred at Mr Grant's station, as he had written two or three times for further particulars, but he must say that he never knew a case sent to him so shamefully disorganised. The defence stated that Bereft 'might have been struck twenty times afterwards for aught they could tell to the contrary'. The crown solicitor expressed his intention not to press the charge any further. The jury, under the direction of His Honour, immediately acquitted the prisoners, and Date and Gray were accordingly discharged.

Date	Victim	Accused
October 1857	Wilddog	Warreah, Piulta, Goniah, and Moniah

Cause of death:	Knife wounds
Outcome:	Piulta found guilty of murder, sentenced to death
	Sentence commuted to six years imprisonment
	Warreah, Goniah and Moniah found guilty of accessory after the fact
Location:	Saltia Creek, near Port Augusta

On 15 November 1857, Police Trooper Thomas Clark, stationed at Mount Remarkable, sent a report to George Hamilton, the Senior Inspector of the mounted police, outlining the report of a murder:

Sir, I have the honor to report for the information of the Police Commissioner, that when I was taking agricultural and statistical returns, on the 3rd of this month, Mr Higgins overseer to the Wareowin Sheep Run, reported, that a native named Wilddog, who he had sent with wool drays, in company with two white men to Port Augusta, about the 8th of October, had left the drays at Pitchy Ritchey Pass, the drays going a second time to the Port, the Bullocks drivers were told by two natives, Mr Lounder Jemmy and Mr Ragless Jack, that three other natives had enticed Wilddog away from the drays to corroberry, but as soon as they had got him away, they had murdered him. Mr Higgins said he firmly believed he was dead, or he would have been back to his own country. I proceeded to Pitchy Ritchey, to gain information from the settlers in that neighbourhood, none of them had heard anything of it, after two days search, I found the two natives which had reported the case to the bullock drivers, they told me a native boy George had told them that he had seen three natives murder Wilddog, for stealing another blackfellows lubra, I caused one of them to come along with me, to search for the deceased remains, but was unsuccessful, not being able to find out where the boy was, I was unable to gain information the three reported murderers. I know them to be notorious bad ones, capable of doing anything that is bad, I shall visit that quarter soon, and hope to gain the required information, which will inable me to apprehend the Guilty.

On Thursday 11 February 1858, Warreah, Piulta, Goniah, and Moniah appeared before the Supreme Court where they were indicted for Wilddog's murder. Mr Andrews appeared for the prisoners. Evidence was given by an Aboriginal boy who, through an interpreter, stated that the man who was killed was from another tribe. He had a 'growl' with Piulta at a place called Saltia Creek. Piulta afterwards threatened to 'take the fat out' of the deceased, and then killed him with a knife. The others assisted, and one of them buried the body in a wombat hole. He stated that the group also took several shillings from Wilddog.

Trooper Clarke stated that he apprehended the prisoners at different places. They all spoke with some knowledge of the murder, and Piulta said that he (Clarke) was a 'bloody fool' for arresting him for killing a black fellow, saying that Wilddog had killed many white men and stolen their clothes, and that he had killed Piulta's brother. Piulta also said that the other three prisoners helped him.

Mr Andrews addressed the jury for the defence, and intended that the prisoners, if they committed the offence, might have done so on meritorious grounds, for the deed might have been a very praiseworthy one according to the institutions of their own customs. But, admitting them to have broken the English law, there was nothing to show that any other than Piulta had had anything to do with killing the man.

His Honour summed up, and instructed the jury that if they were satisfied that Piulta wilfully stabbed the deceased they must find him guilty of murder, and that his companions either assisted him in that murder, or that they were accessories after the fact. The jury retired, and upon returning found Piulta guilty of murder, and Warreah, Goniah, and Moniah guilty of being accessories after the fact. Piulta said, through the interpreter, that Wilddog had killed two men belonging to his tribe some time ago.

His Honour said that he had no discretion in passing sentence, before sentencing Piulta to death. The execution was ordered to take place in three weeks, but the sentence was commuted to six years imprisonment with hard labour.

Date	Victim	Accused
15 October 1857	**Willamy Warriah**	**Warreah**
Cause of death:	Assault	
Outcome:	Found guilty of manslaughter	
	Sentenced to three months imprisonment with hard labour	
Location:	Beltana	

On 15 October 1857, Warreah assaulted Willamy Warriah at Beltana. Willamy Warriah later died from his injuries. Police Trooper Richard Saunders, who was stationed at Mount Remarkable, located Warreah and took him into custody. Warreah was brought before the local magistrate where he was committed to trial at the Supreme Court in Adelaide. Warreah was held in custody in the cells at the Mount Remarkable police station, until Warreah managed to escape on Thursday 9 November.

On 11 November, Trooper Saunders wrote to Senior Inspector George Hamilton of the mounted police in Adelaide. In the letter, Saunders stated that Warreah had been kept in a cell, and due to the heat and confinement it was usual practice to wash the prisoner and the cell each day. The prisoner was allowed to stay out of the cell for a few hours each day. When the prisoner was out of the cell, he was chained and was watched by one of the troopers stationed there. On 9 November, Saunders was the only trooper at the station, and as the previous night had been very hot and sultry, the stench in the cell and on Warreah was as bad as it had been the day before. Saunders took Warreah out of the cell, placed handcuffs on him, and attached a large heavy bullock chain to him. Warreah was given soap and water and he washed himself. When finished, Saunders took the soap and water and washed out the cell. Saunders returned to where Warreah had been and saw that he had made his escape. Warreah had managed to keep a small part of the soap and while Saunders was fetching water, Warreah had used the soap on his wrists and managed to slide the handcuffs off.

Warreah was located some weeks later and was taken to Adelaide. On Thursday 11 February 1858, Warreah appeared before the Supreme Court where he pleaded guilty to manslaughter. He was sentenced to three months imprisonment with hard labour.

Trooper Saunders remained with the police, and rose to the rank of Inspector. Saunders retired to his residence at Norwood. On Saturday 14

October 1916, the following obituary appeared in the *Observer*:

Mr Richard Saunders, an ex-inspector of Police, died at his residence in Montrose Avenue, Norwood, on Tuesday, at the age of 85. He formerly held the position of officer in charge of the south-eastern division of the South Australian Police Force for many years, and retired from the service at the expiration of the period. The inspector was an able, experienced, and popular officer. He joined the force as a mounted constable in February, 1853, shortly after his arrival in this State from California. In those days the life of a mounted constable was by no means an easy one, especially when serving in the sparsely settled districts, and during the first few years that Mr. Saunders served in the force he experienced many hardships. On one occasion he was sent from Adelaide to Robe with important despatches for Governor Young, and as many parts of the south-east were flooded at the time the journey proved difficult and dangerous.

He was almost drowned while fording Reedy Creek, and was compelled to spend the night on a small hillock which rose a few feet above the flood waters. The return journey proved even more difficult than that to the south-east, for when crossing the Coorong Mr. Saunders lost his way, and wandered during 36 hours without food. About this time complaints began to come in from pastoralists who had taken up country in the far north and north-eastern parts of the province, and were considerably annoyed and inconvenienced by the blacks. Mr. Saunders was accordingly told off with other troopers to protect the settlers these outlying districts from the depredations of their troublesome neighbours. He remained in the north for a number of years, and experienced many changes of fortune.

He was a member of the party which accompanied Major Warburton on his exploring expedition from Port Augusta westward, but found the work so full of danger and difficulty that he made up his mind not to volunteer for such service again. Mr. Saunders attained the rank of first-class constable in February, 1857, and was raised to the rank of corporal in November of the same year.

In June, 1864, he was promoted to the rank of sergeant, and three years later, in consequence of having been advanced to the position of sergeant-major, he was recalled to Adelaide, where he spent six years of active service. On July 1, 1873, he received his commission as an inspector of mounted police. When he entered the force Commissioner Tolmer was head of the department, and he served under no fewer than five Commissioners.

Inspector Richard Saunders of the South Australian Mounted Police, 1903. State Library of South Australia, PRG 280/1/5/445.

Date	Victim	Accused
30 November 1857	**Keating child**	**Honora Keating**
Cause of death:	Neglect	
Outcome:	Found guilty of concealment of birth	
	Sentenced to 12 months imprisonment	
Location:	Kapunda	

On 30 November 1857, 21-year-old Honora Keating gave birth to a son. She concealed the child under a heap of stones and grass in a dry part of the bed of Allen's Creek in Kapunda. The child was located alive several days later and was suckled for two or three days by a Mrs Hays, until he died on 7 December. A police investigation revealed that Keating was the mother of the child, but the father was not identified.

On Thursday 11 February 1858, Honora Keating appeared before the Supreme Court where she pleaded guilty to aggravated assault.

His Honour stated that as Keating was previously indicted for feloniously concealing, and afterwards for murder, he must know why it had been altered to aggravated assault. The crown solicitor said that he found, after preparing the information for murder, that Dr Chambers, the coroner in Adelaide, had not identified the body of the infant. The crown solicitor said that he found it useless to proceed on the charge of murder.

Mr Bagot, who appeared for Keating, said he would call some witnesses to character. Mrs Haimes, the wife of John Haimes, a brewer, said Keating had lived with her for nine months as a domestic servant and was a very kind girl in general. Mr. Bagot said that Keating was 21 years of age and that the child must have been born at the place where it was found, and the natural shame of the girl would most likely have induced her to conceal the body, with the intention of taking it away as soon as the night came to a place of safety.

His Honour asked how long after the prisoner had delivered the baby before the child was found. Upon discovering the child had been alive for three days, His Honour asked if Keating might have visited the child in the meantime, with Mr Bagot responding that she could have. In sentencing Keating, His Honour said:

> There could be little doubt that the shame of giving birth to a child who had no legitimate father had induced her to treat the child as she had done. It could hardly be conceived, however, unless she had seen the child and paid some attention to it, that it could have been found in the state it was. Still, leaving it in an exposed state, from which it might have died, was a very serious offence, and most be marked by a suitable punishment.

Keating was sentenced to twelve months imprisonment.

Date	Victim	Accused
8 December 1857	**Coodnogee**	**Midluck and Tommy**
Cause of death:	Assault (with a waddy)	
Outcome:	Both found guilty of manslaughter	
	Sentenced to six months imprisonment with hard labour	
Location:	Dunns Bridge, Balaklava	

Since prehistoric times the Balaklava district has been near the boundaries of the Kaurna and Peramangk peoples. The first Europeans to traverse the district were John Hill and Thomas Burr on 29 April 1840. They discovered

Diamond Lake and camped near Owen. The first European settlers in the area were James and Mary Dunn, who opened a hotel to service bullock teamsters carting copper ore upon the Gulf Road between the Burra mine and the export port of Port Wakefield in 1850.

The Gulf Road copper ore traffic came to a sudden end in 1857 when a railway connected Burra and Gawler. The teamster's loads were then replaced by a flow of pastoral produce to the port, consisting mainly wool and grain.

Balaklava was laid out by Charles Fisher in 1869 and named after the Battle of Balaklava. He built large grain stores on the tramway from Hoyleton to the port at Port Wakefield, intending to encourage farmers to settle near the town.

In December 1857, information was received in Adelaide from Captain Jackson of Port Wakefield that a 'fatal outrage' had been committed on an Aboriginal man by other Aboriginal people at Dunn's Bridge, 18 miles from Port Wakefield, on the road to Burra. This location is on the outskirts of Balaklava on Dunn Road. It appeared that Coodnogee had forcibly taken a lubra from a hostile tribe, an act which some of its members were determined to avenge. Having waited for a favourable opportunity, one of them broke Coodnogee's skull with a waddy, and then forced the waddy through the fracture until the brains protruded from the mouth, while another assisted in the murder by violently squeezing his bowels upwards. Through the prompt and energetic conduct of Mr Woods, the head of the police at Port Wakefield, the murderers were secured and brought before the magistrate of that district.

On Thursday 11 February, the two offenders, Midluck and Tommy, appeared before the Supreme Court where they pleaded guilty to manslaughter. They were each sentenced to six months imprisonment with hard labour.

Date	*Victim*	*Accused*
May 1858	**Johnny Come**	**Eight Aboriginal people**
Cause of death:	Unknown	
Outcome:	Discharged	
Location:	Bakers Range near Naracoorte	

In 1858, John Matthews was employed at Baker's Range by Mr Taylor. On a Sunday morning, while Matthews was at breakfast, one of the Aboriginal people camped at the station came down to the home and asked him for the loan of a shovel. Mrs Butcher, who was also in the employ of Taylor, enquired why he wanted it. The man replied that one of the men was dead in the camp, so Matthews gave him a shovel.

After breakfast, Butcher, Miss Taylor and Matthews went to the camp. When they arrived, Matthews saw a bundle containing what he thought was the body rolled up in a rug. He heard a noise coming from inside bundle, but Matthews did not enquire about the noise and after remaining there for a short time, the three returned to the house. Neither Matthews nor anyone else advised the police about the death.

In May 1860, the authorities received information regarding the murder of an Aboriginal man called Johnny Come, which had occurred two years earlier. As a result of a police investigation, it was discovered that Johnny Come was the person Matthews saw wrapped in the carpet. The police arrested eight Aboriginal people and charged them with Come's murder.

The prisoners were brought up before Mr Henry Jones, JP, and Dr Gunning, JP, where it was found that there was insufficient evidence to commit them. The prisoners had suffered three weeks incarceration on a low diet, and after fully explaining to them the enormity of the offence they were charged with, and after cautioning them about their future conduct, Jones and Gunning ordered them to be discharged.

Date	*Victim*	*Accused*
15 September 1858	**Lennon child**	**Winnifred Lennon**
Cause of death:	Suffocation	
Outcome:	Pleaded guilty to concealing the birth of a child	
	Sentenced to four months imprisonment	
Location:	Lefevre Peninsula	

On Thursday 16 September 1858, a coroner's inquest was held at the Blackler's Hotel at Port Adelaide, regarding the body of a child found on Lefevre's Peninsula. Winnifred Lennon, who was thought to be the mother of the child, was present at the inquest. After hearing evidence that day, the inquest was adjourned.

On Friday 17 September, the inquest resumed and further evidence was heard. At the completion of the evidence, the coroner stated:

The evidence, although very strong and presumptive, was only circumstantial. The circumstances, however, led to the conclusion that the prisoner was the mother of the child. The second point was as to the cause of death, which was a subject of great difficulty to prove. I do not see, from a review of the evidence, that the jury could justly find a verdict of murder. Many circumstances rendered it possible that the child might have died immediately after, or in course of birth.

The jury, after a short consultation, returned a verdict that the child had died from suffocation, but by what means such suffocation had been caused there was not sufficient evidence to show.

Later that day, Lennon appeared before the police court at Port Adelaide, charged with concealing the birth of a child. Evidence was given by Dr Gething, who stated that he had examined the body of the child shown to him in the police station the day before. From that examination he was of the opinion that the child had breathed freely after birth. There were no external marks of violence, but great congestion of the face, the upper part of the chest and the scalp. The indications were such as would appear if the child had been suffocated or smothered. Death might have been caused by exposure and neglect, but the body did not show such symptoms. From the circumstances of the case, he should consider that the child had been born alive, and might have otherwise lived.

The magistrate considered the evidence of Dr Gething, the evidence of the police, and that of witnesses Mrs Turner and Mrs Montgomery, before ruling that Lennon be committed on the charge of wilful murder of her child, in addition to the crime of concealment.

On Monday 22 November 1858, Lennon appeared in the Supreme Court on the charge of wilful murder and concealing the birth of her child. After some discussion, the charge of murder was withdrawn, and Lennon entered a guilty plea to the concealment charge. His Honour, after addressing the prisoner on the sinfulness of the crime which she had committed to conceal her own shame, said that although she had already been in gaol for two months, which, no doubt, had been a punishment to her, it was not sufficient. The law 'required more to mark the gravity of the crime'. His Honour then sentenced her to a further imprisonment of four months.

On 22 September 1862, Winnifred Lennon appeared once more before the court, charged with a similar crime.

Date	Victim	Accused
October 1858	Aboriginal man	Aboriginal person
Cause of death:	Assault (with a tomahawk)	
Outcome:	Unknown	
Location:	Near Mount Gambier	

The *South Australian Register* reported on Wednesday 3 November 1858 that:

Some excitement has prevailed in this township for the last few days, in consequence of the intelligence of a fearful murder committed by the natives on one of their own countrymen. Information was given to the police that a blackfellow was buried at a certain spot in the bush, and on proceeding there a body was found most fearfully mutilated, it evidently having been hacked nearly to pieces with a tomahawk. It had been so carefully concealed at the root of a tree that no discovery would have been made without a minute search. It is understood that the perpetrators are known, and before long their capture is almost certain.

A search was undertaken to locate the offenders, but no further information could be found.

Date	Victim	Accused
2 December 1858	Unknown	Meenalta, Marguiltie, and Coonguiltie
Cause of death:	Unknown	
Outcome:	Discharged	
Location:	Port Lincoln	

On Thursday 17 February 1859, Meenalta, Marguiltie and Coonguiltie appeared in the Supreme Court charged with committing murder at Port Lincoln on 2 December 1858. The crown solicitor stated that upon looking over the depositions it would be impossible to sustain an indictment against the three prisoners. As there were several witnesses in town, he asked that they might at once be released from their obligation to appear in court, in order that they might return by the *Marion*, which would sail on Saturday, otherwise they might be detained in Adelaide for a considerable length of time without an opportunity of returning home. His Honour complied with the application, and the prisoners were ordered to be discharged.

Port Lincoln, circa 1860, viewed from Boston Bay,
showing the Pier Hotel and buildings along Tasman Terrace.
State Library of South Australia, B 16756.

Date	*Victim*	*Accused*
16 January 1859	**Kilmartin child**	**Bridget Kilmartin**
Cause of death:	Unknown	
Outcome:	Found guilty of manslaughter	
	Sentenced to four years imprisonment	
Location:	Glenelg	

On 17 January 1859, Thomas McMahon was walking on the beach at Glenelg when he saw a bundle on the sand. It was lying in such a place that it would be underwater at high tide. When he got closer to the bundle he noticed some hair sticking out. He continued on and met a man and told him what he had found, and then told the police. Police Constable David Davie attended and found two cards lying on the sand about two feet from the bundle. One of the cards read 'Mrs Mundy, Midwife, Sturt Street, Whitmore Square, near Rose Inn'.

The police went to Sturt Street where they spoke to Lucy Mundy, a midwife, who stated that she delivered a male child to Bridget Kilmartin at the Hindmarsh Hotel on the morning of the last day of December. Mundy saw Kilmartin again on Sunday 2 January, when she and her child were all well, but an attendant said that Kilmartin did not like to suckle her child. Mundy asked Kilmartin to take the child to her breast.

The police went to Kilmartin's house where she was taken into custody. On Tuesday 18 January, an inquest was held at the Glenelg Hotel. Mrs Mundy gave evidence that she believed that the body found on the beach was Kilmartin's child. She could not, from the state it was in, swear to the features (no one could), but it had the same long black hair, and was in other respects the same.

William Home Popham, a qualified medical practitioner, stated that he made a post-mortem examination. The body was in an advanced state of decomposition, had been dead several days, and had lived from four to five days. Popham could form no idea of the cause of death. He speculated that the cause could have been exposure, suffocation, or drowning. The body had evidently been under water for some time. At the completion of the evidence, the jury returned a verdict of wilful murder against Kilmartin, who was committed to trial.

On Monday 28 February, Kilmartin appeared in the Supreme Court. After hearing the evidence, the jury retired for almost two and a half hours before returning and finding Kilmartin guilty of manslaughter. His Honour then addressed the jury saying, 'I presume gentlemen that you find that the prisoner caused the death of the child by exposure?' A juror responded, 'We find that the child died through the neglect of the mother'. Mr Andrews, the defence solicitor, asked if the jury would state by what neglect the child had died. His Honour stated that the jury's verdict was neglect by the mother.

Kilmartin was sentenced to four years imprisonment.

Date	*Victim*	*Accused*
4 March 1859	**Baldanant** (**Cold Morning**)	**Wooloobully (Billy Glen)**
Cause of death:	Spear wound	
Outcome:	Acquitted	
Location:	Mount Burr	

At Mount Burr, near Glencoe, an Aboriginal man called King John died. A quarrel arose because not all of the Aboriginal people in the area assisted in the funeral ceremonies of the deceased chieftain. Jonny Doating was one who was reproached by Baldanant, as he neglected to pay proper respect to the King. A third man, Wooloobully, was standing near and observing the quarrel.

Wooloobully ran towards Baldanant and thrust a barbed spear into his body, killing him instantly. Wooloobully was later arrested, and on Monday 16 May 1859 he appeared in the Supreme Court charged with murder.

Evidence was given that the murder took place just after holding a corroboree. Baldanant at the time had a gun, which he fired twice in the direction of Wooloobully, who in retaliation threw his spear at Baldanant. As soon as Wooloobully saw the effects of his spear, he ran up to Baldanant and offered him his head to be waddied, and expressed his sorrow for the deed he had done.

Police Constable Dan, who arrested Wooloobully, stated that he told him he only threw the spear to frighten Baldanant, and that he never intended to kill him.

His Honour spoke at some length about the difference between murder and manslaughter, told the jury that given the evidence, the only charge could be manslaughter. He concluded by saying:

The conduct of the prisoner was not that of civilised men, but of savages. There was a total want of any motive in the case, and it could not be understood what was meant when the prisoner, after he threw the spear, went up to the deceased, and offered his head to be waddied. It would appear that he wished to do penance for the injury he had done. His whole demeanor throughout showed that he was sorry, and it appeared his character was good, and under the circumstances thought the jury might either bring him in guilty of manslaughter, or acquit him.

The jury, after a short retirement, acquitted Wooloobully.

Date	*Victim*	*Accused*
24 April 1859	**Male child**	**Unknown**
Cause of death:	Unknown	
Outcome:	Unknown	
Location:	Thebarton	

On Easter Sunday 1859, 14-year-old William Hall was walking with a friend and his dog near the River Torrens when they noticed a child floating in the water. Their Newfoundland went into the river and brought it back to the riverbank. They then told a lady walking nearby what they had found.

Constable Baker arrived and searched the area for any evidence of who may have left the child there. Baker then took the child to the New Market Inn where an inquest was held on Easter Monday.

Dr Moore, the colonial surgeon, gave evidence at the inquest about the post-mortem examination. He stated the child was born at its full term and the external appearances were those of a healthy child. There were no marks of external violence except on the left side of the head near the back, but he doubted if that caused death. The body was starting to decompose, but the chest appeared full, as that of a child which had breathed. He also found extravagated blood under the bone of the skull.

Dr Moore also said that from the evidence he had heard, he believed the effusion to have been caused by the fall from the bank of the river and that it was clearly the result of mechanical violence during life. He did not believe the effusion to have been the result of a protracted or difficult labour, because if it had been caused by protracted labour the chances were that the child would have been stillborn. In fact, the general appearance of the body would have been altogether different.

The coroner said he had no further evidence to offer. He was present at the post-mortem examination, which was very carefully performed, and had no hesitation in saying the child was born alive. The coroner thought that the jury could not bring in any other verdict than wilful murder against some person or persons unknown, but he would leave it to them to decide. The case appeared to him a most brutal one to have been bestowed upon the infant.

The jury ultimately returned a verdict of wilful murder against some unknown person or persons.

Date	Victim	Accused
27 July 1859	**Ann Gillen**	**Anton Sokolowski**
Cause of death:	Medical procedure	
Outcome:	Discharged	
Location:	Clare	

Around 20 July 1859, Ann Gillen delivered a stillborn child. Dr Sokolowski attended to Gillen, and in the days following the birth, she complained of being in pain and that Sokolowski had hurt her. Gillen's pain became worse and she later died.

On Wednesday 27 July, an inquest was held at the Shamrock and Thistle

Hotel in Clare. The inquest was held on account of a report in circulation that Gillen had been improperly treated by Sokolowski whilst attending to her in childbirth. Philip Gillen gave evidence, stating that Ann delivered a stillborn child and a week after the birth complained of being in pain.

Doctors Kay and Webb made a post-mortem examination of the body, and stated that they found the interior of the womb in a state of mortification and the peritoneum was inflamed.

Dr Webb stated that the mouth of the uterus was lacerated to the extent of one and a half inches, injuries caused, in his opinion, by some extraordinary violence. He also examined the powders left by Sokolowski. Four of these powders contained about two grains each of quinine. He stated that the primary cause of death, in his opinion, was the rupture of the mouth of the womb, combined with the mortification as a result of the rupture, and the use of improper medicines and remedies.

The coroner carefully went over the evidence, dwelling upon the fact that Sokolowski had not called any other 'medical man' to advise and consult with him. The jury retired, and after an absence of three hours returned a verdict of manslaughter against Sokolowski. The jury stated that 'the deceased in their opinion came to her death by the neglect of Sokolowski in him not using proper instruments during her confinement, and that further medical aid ought to have been called in'. Sokolowski was released on bail.

On Saturday 30 July, Sokolowski surrendered to his bail on a charge of manslaughter and appeared before Mr E B Gleeson, SM, at the Clare Court. After hearing from several witnesses, His Worship believed that the evidence was not sufficient to warrant his committing the prisoner for trial, and therefore discharged him from custody.

Edward Burton Gleeson, SM, 1865.
State Library of South Australia,
B 29501.

Date	*Victim*	*Accused*
August 1859	Pantwirri (Johnny)	Langarynga (George) and Eyungaree (Jerry)

Cause of death:	Stab wounds (unknown weapon)
Outcome:	Both found guilty of manslaughter
	Sentenced to six months imprisonment with hard labour
Location:	Lake Albert area

On Friday 19 August 1859, in the Supreme Court, Langarynga and Eyungaree of Lake Albert were indicted for feloniously killing and murdering Pantwirri, another member of their tribe.

Police Trooper Rickeby stated that based on information he received, he went to a spot where he exhumed a body. Rickeby found marks of a large wound on the head, and several other wounds about the body, apparently inflicted by a pointed instrument. Puteiri, another member of the Lake Albert tribe, testified that he witnessed the murder. This was all of the evidence.

His Honour summed up, and directed that the evidence would only support a charge of manslaughter. The jury retired and shortly returned a verdict of manslaughter.

His Honour addressed some remarks to the prisoners, explaining to them the gravity of their crime, and hoped that when they came out of confinement they would be 'careful to avoid quarrels with their brethren, and study habits of industry and peace'. He sentenced them to six months imprisonment with hard labour.

At the conclusion of the case, Mr Bartley drew His Honour's attention to a note written at the foot of the depositions written by Mr Laurie, the committing Magistrate at Goolwa, which read:

> I have reason to believe that the murder was committed under the influence of superstition, deceased being regarded as a wizard, and supposed to exercise an evil influence. Perhaps the Protector of Aborigines could ascertain this for certain. I have only rumor to go upon.

Mr Bartley continued that it struck him as being quite inconsistent with Mr Laurie's duties as a magistrate to attach such a note to the depositions, as it was to the prisoner's prejudice. The magistrate's duty was rather that he should favor the prisoner's innocence, than add anything to assist in proving him guilty.

His Honour said there was no doubt it was a proper communication to make to the crown solicitor, but it should be done by letter, and not be made a part of the depositions. The crown solicitor, no doubt, would instruct Mr. Laurie that it was improper to make his communication in that way.

Lake Albert.
'The view from this spot, which is situated on the South Eastern shore of Lake Albert upon the borders of the extensive scrub which is known as the "Desert", commands a prospect of the greatest portion of the Lake, with the distant country beyond, and Mount Barker visible above the horison. To the right, where the lake sweeps, round to the N.W., are situated Bonney's Wells ... The scrub forming the foreground of this illustration, stretches along inland from the Coorung for a distance of from forty to fifty miles, and consists of dwarf eucalypts, xantharaea, and a great variety of small shrubs and other plants that delight in a sandy soil'.
State Library of South Australia, B 15276/44

Date	Victim	Accused
12 December 1859	**William Rule**	**James Irvine**
Cause of death:	Assault (with saucepan handle)	
Outcome:	Found not guilty	
Location:	Clare	

On Monday 12 December 1859, William Rule and James Irvine were travelling on a dray from Bungaree to Clare when a dispute broke out between them. A third person called Earle was also travelling with them. All three men had been drinking. Rule was drunk and became unruly, throwing some things out of the dray, including a saucepan which broke when it fell to the ground. During the dispute, Irvine struck Rule with the handle of the saucepan.

When they reached Clare, Rule went home where he was later treated by Dr Kay. Rule at first told Kay that he had fallen from the dray, but as his condition worsened over the following days, he told Kay that he was stuck with a saucepan handle by James Irvine. Dr Kay told Rule that his wound had become dangerous. The following day, Dr Kay saw Rule once more, and his condition was deteriorating. Dr Kay asked Rule again how the injuries happened, and Rule replied again that Irvine had assaulted him. Dr Kay did not report that statement to the authorities, nor did he put him on oath or report it to a person who had the power to swear him and take a statement on oath. On 25 December Rule died from his injuries.

On Monday 26 December, a coroner's inquest was held at the Traveler's Rest Hotel in Clare. The inquest was adjourned for the production of an important witness. The inquest resumed on several occasions, but the witness could not be found. On Monday 2 January 1860, the inquest resumed but one of the jurors, Mr Frederick Stacey, was ill, so the matter was once again adjourned. The inquest resumed on 9 January and was informed that Mr Stacey had died, so a new juror was sworn and the evidence was gone over again. At the conclusion of the evidence, the jury, after an hour and a half's deliberation, returned a verdict of manslaughter against Irvine. The coroner committed Irvine to trial at the Supreme Court and released him on bail.

On Tuesday 16 February 1860, Irvine appeared in the Supreme Court charged with manslaughter. Irvine, who was on bail, surrendered himself and pleaded not guilty. During the trial, the evidence of Dr Kay was discussed. This evidence was admitted during the coroner's inquest, however during the

Supreme Court trial it was argued that some statements made by Rule were improperly received by the coroner at the inquest. His Honour stated that the testimony of a man in *articulo mortis* may be received. The crown solicitor stated that there was no evidence to prove that Rule was in *articulo mortis* when he made those statements. Moreover, the statements themselves were contradictory, and it was most unjust that they should prejudice Irvine's case.

Dr Kay, who was called and waited for, but did not appear, did not have his testimony heard. His Honour remarked that in the absence of Dr Kay and the third man who was in the cart, it would be impossible to convict the prisoner. The prisoner therefore must be discharged, or verdict taken of not guilty. His Honour addressed the jury, saying that Rule might have met with his death from drunkenness or a wound, or both, and the wound might have been the result of accident, for any evidence that appeared to the contrary. The jury at once delivered a verdict of not guilty and Irvine was discharged.

Date	*Victim*	*Accused*
13 May 1860	**John Jones**	**Manyalta and Kainmulta**
Cause of death:	Spear wound	
Outcome:	Manyalta found guilty of murder	
	Sentenced to death, executed 5 October 1860	
	Kainmulta acquitted	
Location:	Mount Joy	

In May 1860, Police Trooper O'Shanahan visited the hut John Jones worked from at Mount Joy. On entering the hut, O'Shanahan found Jones deceased on the floor. Jones had a spear wound under the left shoulder blade, as well as wounds on both arms (one above and the other below the elbow), and an incision under the left ear, with a piece of the ear taken off. O'Shanahan saw there were tracks about six or eight yards from the door. The hut had been pillaged of about 40 pounds of flour, some beef and tea, blankets and other small articles belonging to Jones. An investigation revealed that Jones was murdered by Manyalta and Kainmulta. O'Shanahan located Manyalta and charged him with Jones' murder.

On Friday 17 August, Manyalta appeared before the Supreme Court charged with murder. The chief witness against Manyalta was Poongany, an Aboriginal boy who was described as:

A remarkably intelligent little fellow, who, although very deficient in the knowledge of English, made up for that deficiency by figuring with his arms and body to show the particular parts of the tragedy which Manyalta and the absent murderer [Kainmulta] took in it.

Poongany stated that Kainmulta speared the white fellow, indicating on his own body to demonstrate where Jones' wounds were. He continued, saying that 'Kainmulta hit him crackaback,' pointing out the number of blows dealt upon Jones' head, finishing with a motion to represent his falling dead on the ground. The spear used by the prisoner, which O'Shanahan found in Kainmulta's wurley, was produced.

Mr Andrews for the defence made an address to the jury after the evidence was heard, suggesting that the real murderer was the man who could not be found. His Honour summed up at great length upon the conclusion of evidence. The jury retired for about half an hour, and returned with a guilty verdict.

His Honour told the prisoner that he had been found guilty of a wilful murder, in taking the life of an innocent man. He said, as he was not sure he should be understood, that it was 'useless for him to make any lengthened address to him, but his duty was to see the verdict of the jury carried out, and therefore would pronounce upon him at once the awful sentence of the law, and he hoped that his fate would be a warning to his people, that if they killed they also must die, and to know that they who take a life must lose life'. The judge added that although it was not part of the sentence, that the prisoner would be buried within the precincts of the gaol. Manyalta was executed on 5 October 1860.

Kainmulta was later located, and on Thursday 6 December 1860, he appeared in the Supreme Court charged with Jones' murder. At the trial, Poongany, who was examined at the former trial, was put in the box to give evidence in this case. It was reported that:

The intelligence and aptitude which he displayed in describing the manner of the murder on that occasion, seemed to have entirely deserted him, for when placed in the box, and the Crown Solicitor proceeded to examine him, instead of answering his questions, all that he did was to repeat, echo like, the questions put to him. However, by an enormous expenditure of patience on the part of the Crown

Solicitor, and a considerable knowledge of blackfellows 'talkee talkee,' he managed to extract from the youthful savage sufficient to prove that Jones was murdered, and that he was present at the murder, but his efforts to get from him the proper facts to sustain the indictment were fruitless.

At the conclusion of the trial Kainmulta was acquitted.

Date	*Victim*	*Accused*
4 September 1860	McCombe child	Mary McCombe
Cause of death:	Unknown	
Outcome:	Found guilty of concealing the birth of a child	
	Sentenced to 12 months imprisonment with hard labour	
Location:	Adelaide	

Mary McCombe was a 20-year-old servant at the Destitute School where John Pound was a teacher. On 4 November 1860, Pound saw McCombe in the bed of a nearby creek, about 200 yards from the school, digging underneath the bank. Pound asked McCombe what she was doing and she replied that the boys had found a baby, and she was going to bury it. Pound asked where it was, and McCombe held up the body of a male child by the leg or arm. The child was dead, and Pound told her not to bury it, as the police had better see it. She said it was better to bury it than to allow it to remain stinking. 'Besides,' she said, 'the dogs have been at it'. Pound then wrapped the body in a blanket, and took it to the dead house. He had noticed McCombe's state two weeks before 4 November, and thought that she was pregnant. The police were informed and with Dr K Moore, the colonial surgeon, spoke to Pound and McCombe.

Dr Moore knew McCombe and had thought for some weeks that she was pregnant. Moore examined McCombe and found there was clear evidence of her having given birth in the previous week. Moore also examined the body of the child, the lower part of which was in a good state of preservation, but whose head was decomposed. He made a post-mortem examination, and had no doubt it was born alive, but he could not say how many days it lived.

An inquest was held on Monday 5 November, before Dr Woodforde JP at the hospital. At the completion of the evidence, the jury found 'that the said child was found dead, but how it came by its death there is no evidence to prove'.

On Monday 26 November 1860, Mary McCombe appeared in the Supreme Court charged with the wilful murder of her son. McCombe pleaded guilty in ignorance of the nature of the indictment. On it being explained, she pleaded not guilty.

McCombe appeared again on Friday 30 November where her trial commenced. The crown solicitor drew the attention of the jury to the difference the law made in the punishment if there was evidence of the child breathing after being born and if it were born dead. In the one case it would be murder and in the other manslaughter. If the evidence proved that although the child had breathed, its death was caused by any act not prompted by malice, the charge would only be manslaughter.

His Honour addressed the jury, stating that a newborn infant required 'certain attentions to secure the continuance of its life'. He told the jury that the law recognised crimes of omission as well as commission, and that if the child died through the wilful neglect of its mother, it would be murder. If a mother exposed her infant to the elements, and the hardships of an exposed and unprotected state, it would be murder, but if she did it without malice, and merely to rid herself of a burden, and only with a wish to avoid the consequence of her own shame, then it would be competent for them, the jury, to find her only guilty of the concealment. According to the evidence there was no doubt she did conceal the child, because she confessed its birth to Mrs Redmond.

The jury retired, and in about a quarter of an hour found Mary guilty of concealing the birth of the child. Mary was sentenced to 12 months imprisonment with hard labour.

Date	*Victim*	*Accused*
October 1860	**Pinderrie**	**Popeltie and Padneltie**
Cause of death:	Assault (with a yam stick)	
Outcome:	Popeltie acquitted, Padneltie discharged	
Location:	Franklin Harbour area	

In the Supreme Court on Thursday 6 December 1860, Popeltie and Padneltie of the Port Lincoln district were indicted for the murder of Pinderrie, another member of their tribe.

Two Aboriginal men called Jemmy and Tommy were put under examination, but very little could be made of them. The crown solicitor tried for a long time, but he was unable to get any relevant information regarding the murder.

Police Trooper Bissett, who understood the language of the tribe to some extent, was put into the witness box, and stated that he arrested the two prisoners from Popeltie's confession to Bissett that he killed Pinderrie. There was no evidence against Padneltie, who was subsequently discharged. Bissett then resumed his evidence against Popeltie. The day before Bissett arrested Popeltie he asked where Pinderrie was, and who killed him. At first he could get no answer, but after persisting with his questions, Popeltie got frightened, 'trembled,' and then told him where Pinderrie was buried, and that he killed him with a yam stick in his wurley.

It came out in evidence that Pinderrie, before he was murdered, was ill, and Popeltie was seen to give him food and show him other attention. It also appeared that Pinderrie was considered amongst his tribe as being 'cranky'.

His Honour said while Aboriginal people were made amenable to British laws, and were made to submit to its punishments, it was once common justice to them that they should have the benefit of its protection and humanities, and that they should not be convicted except upon clear and unmistakable evidence.

His Honour directed the jury's attention to the circumstance that the prisoner was considered to be a madman, and that there was no evidence how the murder took place, only the prisoner's confession through the policeman. The jury subsequently acquitted Popeltie.

Date	*Victim*	*Accused*
11 January 1861	**Thomas Gustava Bergeest**	**Nelgerie (Billy) and Tilcherie (Harry)**
Cause of death:	Spear wound	
Outcome:	Both found guilty of murder	
	Sentenced to death, executed 7 September 1861	
Location:	Fowler's Bay	

On Friday 11 January 1861, Thomas Bergeest was sitting near his flock of sheep at Fowler's Bay, when he saw a party of Aboriginal people approaching him. Bergeest became alarmed, standing and beginning to walk slowly to his hut, keeping his eyes fixed on the party. Two spears were thrown at Bergeest, one inflicting a fatal wound in the body. Bergeest fell to the ground and was hit by some of the attackers. Some time later, Bergeest's body was found on the side of the road by Mr Tulloch, who informed the Port Lincoln magistrate.

A party of police and native trackers left from Port Lincoln in search of the murderers, whose tracks were found near the body. While in the area, Police Troopers Poynter and Madge, and Corporal Shannon received information that two men, 20-year-old Nelgerie and 17-year-old Tilcherie, were responsible for the murder, and could be found at Denial Bay. On reaching Denial Bay, the officers located Nelgerie with about a dozen others camped in the bush. Nelgerie was taken into custody without difficulty. While in custody, Nelgerie confessed his participation in the murder, saying that he only threw a piccaninny spear. Poynter took Nelgerie to Port Lincoln while Madge and Shannon, along with the trackers, followed the tracks of Tilcherie, who was located and taken into custody. Nelgerie, Tilcherie, along with Tulloch and two native trackers called Bobby and Monkey, were transported to Adelaide on the *Marion*. On the way, Tilcherie confessed to throwing a spear at Bergeest, but later changed his story that he was only present when he was murdered.

On Thursday 15 August 1851, Nelgerie and Tilcherie appeared in the Supreme Court on the charge of murder. At the completion of the trial, the jury returned a guilty verdict. Both were sentenced to death.

They were transported to Fowler's Bay where the execution was to take place. When they reached the Fowler's Bay, Nelgerie and Tilcherie acknowledged their guilt and pointed out the bush under which their victim was seated when they first saw him. They showed the spot where they speared Bergeest as he was retreating from them, and the place where they took him after the fatal wound. On Saturday 7 September, the gallows were erected upon the site of the murder, as indicated by the prisoners. It was reported:

At the execution were about 25 male adult natives of their tribe. Considerable impression was evidently produced upon the Aboriginal spectators. They were among the most uncivilized of Australian savages, and utterly without clothing. When the bodies of the criminals were taken down, an attempt was made to induce some of the blackfellows to assist in removing them, but they rushed away in evident terror. The interment was performed, in accordance with the warrant, at the place of execution, so that the remains of the murderers now rest beneath the spot where they speared the shepherd.

Date	Victim	Accused
28 January 1861	**Donk child**	**Anna Donk**
Cause of death:	Loss of blood, exposure	
Outcome:	Found guilty of concealment of birth	
	Sentenced to 18 months imprisonment with hard labour	
Location:	Tanunda	

Anna Donk was a 20-year-old servant who was in the service of the Fiedler family on their farm in Tanunda. During the evening of Monday 28 January 1861, Donk complained to Mrs Fiedler of being ill, and having a stomach-ache. Several times during the evening, Donk went outside the house and refused to come back inside. Mrs Fiedler saw Donk walking across the ploughed ground, where she sat down for some time, before she slowly returned to the place where she had been sitting previously.

Mrs Fiedler told her husband Frederick that she thought there was something wrong, so they both went to the place where Mrs Feidler had seen Donk sit. Frederick found the body of a newborn female child, which was still warm, in a furrow of the ploughed ground. When Frederick found the body, Mrs Feidler fainted.

Wilhelm Eberhard, a medical man who was not licensed under the act of the colony, but had been practicing as a doctor in Tanunda for eight years, arrived at the farm to see Donk.

At a later coronial inquest, evidence was given by Eberhard that he had examined Donk and found that she had recently given birth. Eberhard stated he had performed a post-mortem examination and thought that the child had been born alive, as he was certain that it had breathed. He considered that its death was the consequence of loss of blood from the umbilical cord, which had not been tied. He saw no marks of violence or any other cause of death. Exposure might have been a cause of death in addition to the loss of blood. Donk was found guilty of murder and was committed to trial.

On Thursday 14 February 1861, in the Supreme Court, Anna Donk was charged with the wilful murder of her daughter. Mr Boucaut defended the prisoner. The crown solicitor stated the facts, and remarked that it was competent to the jury to return a verdict of wilful murder, manslaughter, or of concealment of birth.

Mr Boucaut said it was necessary, in order to warrant a verdict of guilty of concealment, that the jury must be satisfied that the prisoner secretly buried or otherwise disposed of the body with intent to conceal the birth. The evidence was clear that Mrs Feidler saw the birth, and directed her husband where to find the body. It was therefore impossible, he submitted, to convict the prisoner of concealment.

His Honour said it was for the jury to say whether the pretence of stomachache by the prisoner, when she must have known the state she was in, was not intended to conceal the birth, and whether she had not afterwards placed the body in the ploughed ground so as to conceal the birth. The jury retired for several minutes then returned with a guilty verdict for concealment of birth.

His Honour stated that the case was in itself most serious, and it was one of a class of crime that seemed to be a 'growing evil' in the colony. So far as he remembered, there was scarcely a criminal sitting in which there was not a case of the kind, and if something was not done to repress it, they would have child murder practiced in every direction. Donk was sentenced to 18 months imprisonment with hard labour.

Date	Victim	Accused
11 March 1861	Mary Rainbird, Emma Rainbird, and Robert Rainbird	Warretya (Old Man Jack), Warretya (Kapunda Robert), Moanaitya (Jacky Pike), Warretya (Goggle-eyed Jemmy), Tankawortya (Jimmy Alick), and Pilti Miltinda (Bobby)
Cause of death:	Assault (Iron pole and sticks)	
Outcome:	Pilti Miltinda (Bobby), Tankawortya (Jimmy Alick), Warretya (Goggle-eyed Jimmy), and Warretya (Kapunda Robert) found guilty of murder, sentenced to death Executed 7 June 1861 Warretya (Old Man Jack) and Moanaitya (Jacky Pike) discharged	
Location:	Hamilton, near Kapunda	

Robert Rainbird, his wife Mary and a baby son called Allan arrived in South Australia on the *Anglia* in May 1852. The Rainbirds' first son, Henry, died on the voyage and was buried at sea. Allan died within weeks of arriving in the new colony. Robert and Mary spent some time living in

Hindley Street before they made their way to a new home near Hamilton.

By 1861, Robert and Mary had two children, Emma, six, and Robert, three. Mary and her children were seen alive by Robert at seven am on the morning of 11 March 1861. They were seen again at about one pm on the same day by a neighbour. When Robert returned in the evening he could not locate his family. A search was conducted and Mary's body was found in a wombat hole. Her head was fractured and her dress had been torn from her. Emma and Robert's bodies were also found.

After an investigation, six Aboriginal men were arrested for the three murders. On Friday 17 May 1861, Warretya (Old Man Jack), Warretya (Kapunda Robert), Moanaitya (Jacky Pike), Warretya (Goggle-eyed Jemmy), Tankawortya (Jemmy Alick), and Pilti Miltinda (Bobby) appeared before the Supreme Court and were indicted for feloniously, wilfully, and of malice aforethought, killing and murdering Mary Rainbird, Emma Rainbird and Robert Rainbird at Hamilton.

Pilti Miltinda (Bobby) State Library of South Australia, B 8386. Permission to publish obtained from the Chair of Ngadjuri Nation Aboriginal Corporation and the State Library of South Australia

At the trial, Moanaitya (Jacky Pike) gave evidence against the others. He stated that all of the prisoners were present at the time of the murders. Moanaitya stated that when they arrived at the Rainbirds' house, he asked Mary for some water, which she gave him. After drinking it, he walked off, then turned around and saw Tankawortya (Jimmy Alick) strike Mary with a cutta (a native weapon). He also saw Warretya (Goggle-eyed Jimmy) handling an iron bar. Jacky Pike said:

I was walking along the road, and I looked round and saw Jemmy Alick [Tankawortya] kill the woman, and I saw Goggle-eyed Jemmy [Warretya] kill the little girl, and then Kapunda Robert [another named Warretya] kill the little boy.

Jacky Pike also stated that Mary was taken into the house by Jimmy Alick, who tore her clothes off and raped her. That evidence would be confirmed by other witnesses who found Mary's body with her dress torn from it. After Mary was murdered, Jacky Pike saw Old Man Jack and Jimmy Alick bury Mary's body in the wombat hole.

At the conclusion of the trial, the jury retired for upwards of an hour. On their return, they delivered their verdicts. Warretya (Old Man Jack) was found not guilty. Warretya (Kapunda Robert), Warretya (Goggle-eyed Jemmy), Tankawortya (Jimmy Alick), and Pilti Miltinda (Bobby), were all found guilty of murder.

His Honour sentenced the men, and ordered their execution. All four were executed at the Adelaide Gaol on 7 June 1861.

Date	Victim	Accused
2 May 1861	**Margaret Impey**	**Mangeltie (Jimmy) and Karabidue (Willy)**

Cause of death:	Spear wound, assault
Outcome:	Both found guilty of murder
	Sentenced to death, executed 14 September 1861
Location:	Mount Wedge

On the morning of 2 May 1861, Mr Impey left his wife, 31-year-old Margaret, alone in their hut and went out with his sheep. When he returned later that day he found Margaret lying dead on the floor of the hut, covered with a blanket. On examination he found her throat speared and the back part of her head completely smashed in.

The next morning a search was conducted and the footprints of Aboriginal people were found outside the hut. Mr Impey noticed about half a bag of flour and some blankets had been taken from the hut. A tracker was procured from the head station, who identified the tracks as belonging to two men known as Mangeltie and Karabidue, who had been frequently employed by the settlers.

On Thursday 15 August 1861, Mangeltie and Karabidue appeared in the Supreme Court on a charge of murder. At the conclusion of the trial, the jury returned a guilty verdict and both were sentenced to death. They were conveyed on the *Yatala* and arrived at Venus Bay on Friday 13 September. The following day, at Cheraroo, they were executed.

Date	*Victim*	*Accused*
10 May 1861	**Williams child**	**Rachel Williams**
Cause of death:	Unknown	
Outcome:	Unknown	
Location:	Unknown	

In late June of 1860, Rachel Williams gave birth to a baby girl. On 2 July Williams and her child left the house where she was staying with the intention of going to the Destitute Asylum. Williams later went to a friend's house but she did not have the baby with her. The friend asked after the baby, and Williams said that she had sold it to a woman she met when she was travelling to Adelaide. She said the woman paid her five shillings to pay for her train fare. The woman lived somewhere between Adelaide and Kapunda. Williams told another person that she had killed the baby and had buried it on the road to Kapunda.

On Saturday 18 May 1861, in the Police Courts, Rachel Williams appeared charged with wilfully murdering her illegitimate child.

Acre 409, an early view of the Adelaide Police Court, 1860.
State Library of South Australia, B 58365

Williams appeared in court on several occasions and the matter was postponed. The prosecution had a number of witnesses, however the identity of the woman from the train, and the body of the child, were never located. Williams last appeared before the police court on June 29, where she was released on bail. No further information could be located.

Date	*Victim*	*Accused*
17 October 1861	**Nicholas James**	**George Burkby**
Cause of death:	Vehicle collision	
Outcome:	Acquitted	
Location:	Mount Barker	

On Thursday 17 October 1861, 19-year-old George Burkby was employed to drive Nicholas James and two others to Nairne, in a light dogcart which had a shaft-horse and outrigger. Burkby was travelling at a normal pace on the Mount Barker Road until he approached the hill near German Town. Burkby drove rapidly past the Mount Barker mail, where the guard noticed that the reins were loose and that Burkby was making no effort to restrain the speed of his horses. Soon after passing the mail, and going down the hill, Burkby's horses broke into a gallop. Witnesses saw Burkby trying to pull them in. The road being steep and sinuous, Burkby lost all control over the horses, and the vehicle was overturned. The horses were killed, the trap was broken to pieces, and James was seriously hurt, dying from his injuries five days later.

On Monday 9 December 1861, Burkby appeared before the police court in Adelaide, charged with the murder of James. Burkby was remanded for trial. On Thursday 13 February 1862, Burkby appeared before the Supreme Court on a charge of killing and slaying Nicholas James.

Burkby gave evidence stating that he endeavoured to restrain the horses when they started at a gallop and that he had not been regularly employed on that road, but had been casually engaged to drive on that occasion. When arrested on the charge of manslaughter he said it was only an accident and he could not help it. During the trial, it was stated (although it was not admitted in evidence) that before James died, he fully acquitted Burkby of all blame.

Mr Andrews, for the defence, made a long, earnest, and able speech, contending that there was no evidence of culpable negligence on the part of the prisoner, and that without such evidence it was impossible for Burkby to be convicted. His Honour left it to the jury to find whether the death of Nicholas James resulted from the accident, and whether the accident was occasioned by the negligence of the prisoner, with both conditions necessary to support the indictment. The jury retired and on their return, Burkby was acquitted.

Date	Victim	Accused
12 November 1861	**William Lawless**	**Peter Stars**
Cause of death:	Bayonet wound	
Outcome:	Found guilty of manslaughter	
	Sentenced to nine years imprisonment	
Location:	Springfield Farm, near Gawler	

Catherine Flanery and 24-year-old William Lawless were servants to 64-year-old Peter Stars, who resided at Springfield, near Gawler. On 12 November 1861, three men called Hamlin, Blencowe, and McMullen arrived at the property to see Stars, and during the afternoon the four men began to drink. Later that evening, Hamlin, Blencowe and McMullen left to go home.

At about nine pm that evening, Flanery heard a noise outside and went out to investigate it. When she came back to the house, Flanery went into the parlour where she saw Stars and Lawless lying on the floor. Lawless was lying on top of Stars. Lawless said, 'I am stabbed', but he did not say who did it. Flanery became frightened and noticed a bayonet lying on the ground. She picked up the bayonet and ran out of the house before throwing the bayonet down on the ground and running to get help.

Sergeant Benjamin Hunt and Trooper Blake arrived and found that Lawless was dead. They conducted a search, finding blood-stained clothing in Stars' bedroom. An old rusty bayonet was located about 150 yards from the house. Trooper Blake arrested Stars for the murder and conveyed him to Gawler.

A coroner's inquest was held at the Mill Inn, where it was heard that Stars and Lawless were the best of friends. Dr Popham conducted a post-mortem on Lawless and gave evidence as to the depth and breadth of the wound on the left side. The wound was five inches deep and three-quarters of an inch wide, and was caused by a bayonet. The jury, after deliberating for two hours, returned a verdict of wilful murder against Stars.

On Wednesday 4 December 1861, Stars appeared before the Supreme Court where he was indicted for feloniously, wilfully, and maliciously killing and murdering William Simpson Lawless. At the conclusion of the trial, the jury retired for about half an hour, and on their return found Stars guilty of manslaughter. His Honour sentenced Stars to nine years imprisonment.

Date	*Victim*	*Accused*
20 January 1862	**Hooper child**	**Annie Hooper**
Cause of death:	Strangulation	
Outcome:	Found guilty of manslaughter	
	Sentenced to four years imprisonment with hard labour	
Location:	Pirie Street, Adelaide	

On Monday 20 January 1862, acting on information received about a birth of a child, Police Constable Badman attended Mr Roundsevell's premises in Pirie Street where he saw evidence that a birth had recently taken place. Badman located 20-year-old Annie Hooper in the kitchen and arrested her on the charge of concealing the birth of a child. Hooper said, 'I did not mean to do it; I was frightened to tell my mistress. The child was dead, the child was dead'. Badman asked her where her child was, and Hooper told him that it was under the bedclothes at the foot of her bed. Badman returned to the room, and found the body of the child wrapped in a coloured cloth. He put the body, together with the afterbirth and several stained clothes, into a sack, and took both the sack and Hooper to the police station. At the station, he noticed that a cloth was tied around the child's head, and drawn tightly round the neck.

On Tuesday 8 February 1862, Annie Hooper appeared before the Supreme Court on the charge of murdering her newborn child.

Colonial surgeon Dr Robert Waters Moore gave evidence of making a post-mortem examination of the body of the child, which was at its full term. He saw a string tied twice round the neck, which was doubly knotted. There were no marks of violence on the body of any importance. The assistant colonial surgeon was present when the examination was made, and stated that the ligature around the child's neck was sufficiently tight to have stopped the breathing of a newborn child. He considered loss of blood and the ligature to be the cause of death.

At the completion of the trial, the jury retired for a quarter of an hour before returning with a verdict of manslaughter.

On 19 February 1862, Annie Hooper was placed in the dock. His Honour remarked on the mercy shown by the jury in light of the severity of the crime, before sentencing Hooper to four years hard labour.

King William Street, north east corner of North Terrace intersection, looking towards Government House. Horse drawn traffic can be seen including cabs for hire standing in the middle of the street. Circa 1863. State Library of South Australia, B 478.

Date	*Victim*	*Accused*
4 February 1862	**Richard Pettinger**	**John Seaver**

Cause of death: Gunshot wound

Outcome: Found guilty of murder, sentenced to death
    Executed 11 March 1862

Location: Government House, Adelaide

On 4 February 1862, Police Inspector Richard Pettinger was at Government House when a shot was fired. Pettinger was located on the floor in the hall with severe head injuries. There were many people at Government House that day as there was a sale of Sir Richard MacDonnell's furniture and effects. Police Constable Badman, along with several detectives, was amongst the visitors. Badman noticed that John Seaver, who had recently been discharged from the police force, was present. Badman saw Seaver leave by the back passage but did not at first suspect him, although he noticed he appeared agitated.

The first impression was that Pettinger had shot himself, but Badman soon detected evidence which led him to arrest Seaver.

Pettinger had been in the police force for nearly nine years. He was a 'most estimable' young man, and worked his way from the ranks first into the Commissioner's office as clerk, where he was promoted to the office of Inspector. He left a wife and three very young children.

Seaver was a man of 49 years of age, tall, athletic, and upright in his carriage. He has been in the army, and served many years in the West Indies. He was recommended for the post of constable by Captain Brinkley, but was dismissed at the insistence of Inspector Pettinger for drunkenness and neglect of duty.

On Tuesday 18 February 1862, Seaver appeared in the Supreme Court charged with murdering Richard Pettinger. At the completion of the trial, at seven pm, the jury retired, returning ten minutes later with a guilty verdict. Seaver, on being asked what he had to say, complained that he had not had the services of an experienced counsel. His Honour addressed Seaver:

> John Seaver, you have been found guilty of the wilful murder of Richard Palmer Pettinger on the clearest evidence. The jury have listened with the closest attention to the case, and would I am certain have been happy to have given you the benefit of any reasonable doubt did the circumstances disclose any such reasonable doubt. They have been unable to find any such doubt, and I must say that I should have been surprised if they had. It is now my duty to pass the awful sentence of the law upon you, which is that you be taken to the place from whence you came and from thence to the place of execution, where you shall be hanged by the neck until you are dead, and may the Lord have mercy upon your soul.

Seaver was executed on 11 March 1862.

Date	*Victim*	*Accused*
4 February 1862	**Jane Macmanamin**	**Malachi Martin and William Wilson**

Cause of death:	Strangulation
Outcome:	Martin found guilty of murder, sentenced to death
	Executed 24 December 1862
	Wilson found guilty of accessory after the fact
	Sentenced to four years imprisonment
Location:	Salt Creek, Coorong

Malachi Martin, 36, and his wife Catherine ran a small inn at Salt Creek. Jane Macmanamin was a woman in her late thirties who was employed at the inn as a servant. Catherine was previously married to William Robinson, who was friends with Martin. In 1856, Robinson and Martin went on a cattle search together and Robinson disappeared. His death was ruled a suicide. Several years later, Martin married Catherine.

While working at the inn, Macmanamin had become suspicious about Martin being involved in Robinson's death, and in other unsolved crimes that were taking place in the area. On 4 January, Macmanamin was alone with Martin at the inn, as Martin had arranged for his wife and another person to be away. Martin strangled Macmanamin and later buried her in a wombat hole about two miles from the inn. When his wife returned, Martin told her that Macmanamin had decided to go and visit her sister at Guichen Bay. A friend of the Martins visited the inn and saw that Macmanamin's belongings were still there. Martin told him and others a different story to account for Macmanamin's departure, arousing suspicion.

Over three months later, on 27 May 1862, Jane's body was found by an Aboriginal person in a wombat hole, and the local police were informed.

William Wilson, 34, was a friend of Martin's. After the body was located, Wilson was at the Wellington Hotel. He had been drinking and he told a friend that he had seen Macmanamin dead in the inn, and that Martin had killed her. This information was conveyed to the police.

On Wednesday 3 December, Martin and Wilson appeared before the Supreme Court charged with murder. At the completion of the trial, Martin was found guilty of murder and sentenced to death. Wilson was found guilty of being an accessory after the fact and sentenced to four years imprisonment. Martin was executed on 24 December 1862 at the Adelaide Gaol.

Date	*Victim*	*Accused*
24 February 1862	**Robert French**	**John McMahon**
Cause of death:	Assault	
Outcome:	Found not guilty	
Location:	Bulls Creek	

On 24 February 1862, Robert French and John McMahon, among others, were at work at Mr Stone's farm at Bulls Creek, using a thrashing machine.

After supper, McMahon went outside, followed a few minutes later by French and some of the other workers. As soon as French got outside, McMahon said to him: 'Now you have had your yarn out'. McMahon then punched French in the face. The two men fought for a while and fell to the ground. After a short time they both got up, but McMahon swore at French and wanted to keep fighting him. French declined, saying he did wish to make a blackguard of himself. Soon afterwards French started to complain of severe pains in his stomach, which rapidly disabled him, and the next day be died.

McMahon appeared before a coronial inquest where he was found guilty of murder and committed to trial. On Wednesday 14 May 1862, John McMahon appeared before the Supreme Court, indicted for feloniously killing and slaying Robert French. At the conclusion of the evidence, the jury retired for an hour. When they returned, the foreman said that they all agreed that the prisoner was not justified in doing what he did, but there were two or three who did not think him guilty. His Honour referred the case to the doctor's evidence, and if they believed that evidence, the prisoner was guilty, and if they believed the prisoner was not justified in what he did then he was guilty. The jury sat silent in the box for some minutes, when His Honour went over the ground again. The jury, however, could not agree, and again retired, and nearly an hour afterwards again returned to court with the same dilemma. His Honour, after again explaining the point for decision, said he would give them another quarter of an hour, and if they could not agree by that time he should adjourn the court till nine o'clock, when he would again be in attendance. The jury again retired, and after 20 minutes returned a verdict of not guilty.

Date	Victim	Accused
9 March 1862	William Walker	Magnultie (Meengulta, Magnulte, or Uringi)

Cause of death:	Spear wound
Outcome:	Found guilty of murder
	Sentenced to death, executed 8 September 1862
Location:	Kongarie, near Mount Wedge

William Walker, a 45-year-old hutkeeper, and Mr Tootill, a shepherd, were both employed at the same hut near Mount Wedge by Mr Love, who resided at the head station, The Wedge, near Talia. The hut was situated about twelve miles from Venus Bay and about eight miles from Mount Wedge. Tootill left in the morning of 9 March 1862 to tend to the sheep, leaving Walker alone in the hut.

When Tootill returned to the hut at around four pm, he found Walker lying on the ground, shaking. Tootill noticed Walker had a spear wound in his side, which was bleeding. Tootill went to get help and returned later with Mr Phillips and two Aboriginal people, Luyelta and Chalgulte. Tootill noticed that all the blankets and other supplies, including flour, tea and sugar, had been taken. Luyelta and Chalgulte searched the area around the hut and located about 30 pounds of flour and a broken spear. Walker died from his injuries the next morning.

Trooper Geharty was notified about the attack and went to the hut, arriving in time to see Walker before he died. After Walker's death, Geharty, with Luyelta and Chalgulte, followed some Aboriginal tracks for three days, when they came across some damper at an abandoned campsite. They continued following the tracks and found further campsites where damper had been made. Geharty thought they were getting closer to the attackers, so they tied up the horses and continued on foot.

Trooper O'Shannahan, who was also in the search party, arrested Magnultie at Lake Gardiner, about 150 miles from Talia. Magnultie (also known as Meengulta, Magnulte or Uringi) was caught as he was making his way through the bush to his camp. When asked about the murder, Magnultie said, 'Yes, me spear him, white fellow', and then, holding up his hand, said, 'Only coome spear'. 'Coome' meant one – Magnultie wished O'Shannahan to understand that he killed Walker with only one spear. After O'Shannahan arrested Magnultie, he showed him the spear, and Magnultie said, 'That my spear, me spear him, white fellow, with that spear'.

On Thursday 14 August 1862, Magnultie appeared in the Supreme Court charged with Walker's murder. Evidence was given about Magnultie's sister, who had clothing belonging to Walker in her possession.

At the conclusion of the trial, Magnultie was found guilty of murder and sentenced to death. He was transported to Venus Bay, where he was executed on 8 September 1862.

Date	Victim	Accused
10 May 1862	**Marianne Paulovitch**	**Eliza Paulovitch**
Cause of death:	Neglect	
Outcome:	Paulovitch found insane	
Location:	Morphett Vale	

Andrew and Eliza Paulovitch lived at Morphett Vale when in February 1862, 26-year-old Eliza gave birth to a daughter who they named Marianne. Several weeks after the birth, Eliza started to neglect Marianne and expressed an unwillingness to suckle her. Marianne died on 10 May. On 12 May 1862, Mr Peake, the coroner for the district, conducted an inquest at the courthouse at Morphett Vale. A post-mortem examination was conducted by Dr Montgomery, who stated that it appeared that Marianne, who was just three months old, had died from starvation.

Dr Montgomery stated that he had examined Eliza and found her to be a lunatic incapable of taking care of her family. All of the other witnesses agreed that Eliza was in an unsound state of mind.

Botanic Gardens, Adelaide, 1860, with the impressive Lunatic Asylum building provides a backdrop for a view of the recently planted Botanic Gardens, which were opened to the public in 1857.
State Library of South Australia, B 2773.

The coroner advised the jury that if they found Marianne had died by the malicious or wilful neglect of its mother, then the mother was guilty of murder. If, however, they found Marianne had died by simple neglect, without any malicious intention or malice aforethought, the crime would be manslaughter.

The coroner also pointed out that in a child of tender years sucking at the breast, the law held the mother responsible if that child perished from want, but later in life when the child was weaned, and came to be supported on ordinary food, the father would be held responsible in case of its death from starvation caused by his neglect.

The jury retired and returned and found that 'the deceased, Marianne Sarah Paulovitch, died at Morphett Vale, on the 10th day of May, of starvation, caused by the neglect of her mother, and that Eliza Paulovitch was guilty of manslaughter'. The jury also found that Eliza was of unsound mind.

On Friday 16 May 1863, before the Supreme Court, Eliza was brought from the Lunatic Asylum to plead to a charge of murdering her infant by neglecting to suckle it properly. After evidence was given about her mental ability, the jury at once agreed that she was insane. His Honour ordered the information be withdrawn and ordered that she be kept in safe custody in the asylum until His Excellency's pleasure should be known.

Date	Victim	Accused
4 August 1862	Yaditepunen (Black Jimmy)	Yeppungen (McKenzie's Jemmy), KingPullen (Little Johnny), and Linikkerperrup (Guichen Bay Jackey)
Cause of death:	Assault	
Outcome:	All found guilty of manslaughter	
	All sentenced to six months imprisonment with hard labour	
Location:	Guichen Bay	

During the afternoon of 4 August 1862, Linikkerperrup was alone in the yard at McQueen's Public House at Guichen Bay. He then walked to his camp where he went to bed. During the evening, he got up and became involved in an altercation with Yaditepunen, Yeppungen, Milkoomaday, Warrungmecunum, KingPullen, and Yiepelpunnan. Yaditepunen pulled out a knife to frighten them, as they had assaulted him. Most had been drinking and Yaditepunen was drunk. Linikkerperrup saw Yeppungen kill Yaditepunen. The body was carried away and buried.

Police Trooper Thomas Budd received information about the murder. Budd asked Native Policeman Billy about it, who confirmed that it was true. Billy had heard that the body was buried near McKenzie's, so the police went there and dug to a depth of about four feet, locating the body.

On Saturday 9 August 1862, an inquest was held in the courthouse at Guichen Bay, before Mr C Brewer and a jury, regarding the murder of Yaditepunen, who was better known as Black Jimmy. The police had apprehended Yeppungen, Milkoomaday, KingPullen, Warrungmecunum, Linikkerperrup and Yiepelpunnan on suspicion of committing the murder. Evidence was received from Dr J Mustarde, who had carried out a post-mortem examination. Dr Mustarde stated that the cause of death was the rupture of the liver, caused by violent pressure on the chest. He also found a broken rib caused by pressure and not a blow, and that the neck was dislocated, but that injury would not have caused immediate death.

At the conclusion of the inquest, the jury retired but were unable to come to a verdict. The foreman stated that it was unfair to only hear evidence from three of the accused, and not all of them. The coroner would not allow the inquest to resume and returned the jury to their deliberations. The jury refused to come to a verdict so the coroner locked them in a room for the night, without any heat, food or chairs, and in the morning he again asked if they had reached a verdict. The jury again refused to reach one, so the coroner dismissed them and another inquest was held the next day.

After the second inquest, which heard the same evidence, the jury returned a verdict of manslaughter against Yeppungen, KingPullen and Linikkerperrup. The others were acquitted. The three later appeared before the Supreme Court where they were found guilty of manslaughter and each sentenced to six months imprisonment with hard labour.

Date	*Victim*	*Accused*
17 September 1862	**Anne Bean**	**James McEnhill**
Cause of death:	Vehicle collision	
Outcome:	Acquitted	
Location:	Light Square, Adelaide	

Around four pm on Wednesday 17 September 1862, Anne Bean was in a dogcart with her son, Arthur, travelling through Light Square towards Currie Street. Around the same time, 33-year-old James McEnhill was unloading rubble from a dray with other labourers in Franklin Street. However, one of the wheels of the dray had sunk into a hole, and some men were trying to dig it out. McEnhill, who was in charge, used a whip to get the horses to move. Just as the men managed to free the dray from the hole, the horses bolted. McEnhill did not have hold of the horses when they were freed, and the horses, with the dray attached, ran towards the post office. The horses turned left on King William Street and left again on Currie Street, towards Light Square.

As Arthur drove the cart through Light Square near the corner of Currie Street, he noticed the two horses pulling a dray, which was without a driver, coming out of Currie Street towards him. The dray collided with their cart and Arthur and his mother were thrown onto the road. Arthur saw a wheel going over his mother. Anne was taken to the Prince Albert Hotel where she was attended to by Dr Mayo, but died from head injuries after about 10 minutes.

On Thursday 18 September an inquest was held at the Golden Fleece, Currie Street, into the death of Anne Bean. At the conclusion of the inquest, the jury found that 'Anne Bean came to her death by being thrown from a dogcart, and that she was thrown from the dogcart in consequence of two horses and a dray, the property of James McEnhill, violently coming into contact with the dogcart, and that the horse and dray caused the death of Anne Bean in consequence of the neglect of James McEnhill'. The coroner committed McEnhill for the manslaughter of Bean, and refused bail.

On Monday 24 November, McEnhill was placed on trial before the Supreme Court. At the conclusion of the trial, the jury retired for a quarter of an hour, and returned with a verdict of not guilty.

Date	*Victim*	*Accused*
22 September 1862	Lennon child	Winnifred Lennon and William Reylin
Cause of death:	Haemorrhage/ blood loss	
Outcome:	Lennon found guilty of manslaughter	
	Sentenced to four years imprisonment with hard labour	
	Reylin discharged	
Location:	Wakefield Street, Adelaide	

On Monday 22 September, 23-year-old Winifred Lennon gave birth to a son in a house in Wakefield Street. The police became aware of the birth and heard that the child was missing, so they visited the house. When they arrived they found evidence that a birth had recently taken place, but Lennon was not there. The police spoke to William Reylin, a photographic artist, who took them to his house in Rundle Street where Lennon was employed as his servant. Lennon was located at Reylin's house and was questioned about the birth. Lennon told the police that the body of her child was in the watercloset. When the police went to the watercloset, Lennon ran away. Reylin was arrested and a search was organised to find Lennon, who was located the following day in a bean field at Kensington. Lennon was arrested and charged with child murder.

On Wednesday 24 September, Lennon and Reylin appeared in the Adelaide Police Court where they were charged on suspicion of having murdered Lennon's newborn child. Both were committed for trial at the Supreme Court. Reylin was allowed bail but it was refused for Lennon.

On Thursday 27 November 1862, Lennon and Reylin appeared before the Supreme Court on the charge of murdering Lennon's newborn child. At the start of the trial, His Honour questioned the strength of the evidence against Reylin. The crown solicitor stated that the only evidence was that he was seen carrying a package from his house in Wakefield Street to his work premises at Rundle Street. The package was described as being the same size and shape as the one the child was found in the watercloset. His Honour stated that the jury would not be able to convict on that evidence, and as a result he was discharged.

Evidence was then heard against Lennon. At the conclusion of the trial the jury retired for about 20 minutes. They returned and found Lennon guilty of manslaughter.

On Thursday 4 December, Lennon appeared before the Supreme Court for sentencing. Lennon, in answer to the question of why the sentence of the court should not be pronounced, said that if His Honour would be merciful to her this time, she would never appear before him again. His Honour stated that it was not the first time she had been in a court of justice for a similar crime, so he could not pass a lenient sentence. Lennon was sentenced to four years imprisonment with hard labour.

This was the second time Lennon appeared before the Supreme Court for child murder. See 15 September 1858.

Date	*Victim*	*Accused*
1 December 1862	**Robert**	**Henry Hammond**
Cause of death:	Assault (with a bullock whip)	
Outcome:	Found guilty of manslaughter	
	Sentenced to 18 months imprisonment with hard labour	
Location:	Nuccaleena Mine, near Blinman	

On 1 December 1862, Elizabeth Falkner was at her house at the Nuccaleena Mines when 40-year-old Henry Hammond (also known as Yankee Harry) rode past with his bullock. After he had gone by, Falkner noticed a bag containing meat on the ground. She took the bag inside to look after it. Soon after she heard a cry from the direction of Hammond's tent. The next day Hammond came to her house to light his pipe, and Falkner gave him his meat back. Hammond stated that he had beaten an Aboriginal man, as he thought that he had stolen his meat. Falkner recalled that Hammond had a bullock whip in his hand when she saw Hammond the day before, just prior to hearing the crying.

Later, Corporal Wauhop was called to Blackfellow's Creek where he found the body of an Aboriginal man called Robert. He saw a cut to the back of Robert's head. Wauhop investigated the death and on 9 December 1862 he arrested Henry Hammond and charged him with Robert's murder. When arrested, Hammond stated that he was returning with his dray from the Nuccaleena Mine where he got some mutton, which was lost on the road. He did not notice it missing until after leaving Mrs Falkner. Hammond noticed Robert and his lubra walking in his tracks, and that he had suspected that they had stolen the meat, which they both denied. Hammond went back a short way with Robert to see if they could find the mutton but there were no signs of it. Hammond went to his tent where he again accused Robert of taking the meat, which he denied. Hammond struck Robert with his whip and knocked him down. Robert ran to the creek and fell into the water. Hammond went to him, but he appeared near dead. Hammond left the creek but returned later, finding that Robert and his lubra were gone.

On Monday 16 February 1863, Henry Hammond appeared in the Supreme Court charged with manslaughter. The judge summed up the evidence, and without retiring, the jury found Hammond guilty of manslaughter. Hammond was sentenced to 18 months imprisonment with hard labour.

Date	Victim	Accused
13 December 1862	**Joseph Ryder**	**Charles Harding**
Cause of death:	Vehicle collision	
Outcome:	Found guilty of manslaughter	
	Sentenced to 12 months imprisonment with hard labour	
Location:	Nairne	

On Saturday 13 December 1862, 16-year-old Joseph Ryder, his 18-year-old sister Amelia, and Elizabeth and Robert Gordon were walking on the road from Mr Milway's shop at Nairne. Amelia gave Joseph six pounds of sugar to carry. Just as they were opposite the old mill, Amelia heard a cart coming at a furious rate. She and Elizabeth went to one side of the road, and Robert and Joseph went to the other. Amelia said, 'It's Harding, he must be drunk'. Amelia thought that Harding was drunk because of the speed he was coming at, and the way he took a sharp turn. After the cart had passed, she saw Joseph on the ground. She went to him and lifted his head up, and felt that his head was bleeding. The cart did not stop.

Dr Octavius Weld attended and took Ryder to a nearby residence, where he died shortly afterwards. Police Constable Plunket, on hearing of the accident, attended Harding's house. 45-year-old Harding was intoxicated and claimed to know nothing of the accident. Harding was arrested and cautioned. While Plunket was removing Harding from his house, there was a slight struggle, but Plunket managed to restrain Harding.

Nairne township, approximately 1872, with the Millers Arms Hotel in the centre and the school to the right. State Library of South Australia, B 7800

On Monday 15 December 1862, an inquest was held at the Millers Arms Hotel, Nairne, on the body of Joseph Ryder Junior. At the conclusion of the inquest, the jury retired, returning after 30 minutes with the verdict that Joseph Ryder died through the furious and reckless driving of Charles Harding, who was then committed to trial at the Supreme Court.

Harding appeared in the Supreme Court on Friday 13 February 1863, where the jury found him guilty of manslaughter. Harding was sentenced to 12 months imprisonment with hard labour.

Date	Victim	Accused
27 January 1863	Casey child	Margaret Casey
Cause of death:	Suffocation	
Outcome:	Found guilty of manslaughter	
	Sentenced to five years imprisonment with hard labour	
Location:	Mount Gambier	

In January 1863, Margaret Casey was employed as a cook at the South Australian Hotel in Mount Gambier. Robert Long, the landlord of the hotel, employed Casey as a single woman. No one suspected that Casey was pregnant. Catherine Driscoll knew Casey as she was also employed as a servant in the hotel and they shared a room together. On Monday 27 January, Casey complained to Driscoll that she felt ill and had pains inside her. Casey went to bed at around 10 pm and Driscoll went to bed later that evening.

Around six the following morning, Elizabeth Nelson attended at the hotel and, from information she received from Driscoll, went to Casey's room. Casey was sitting on the floor and said she felt ill. Nelson gave Casey a glass of alcohol and went to get Elizabeth Long, who was Robert's wife. When Elizabeth went to Casey's room it was locked, but Casey opened it and let her in. On entering the room, Elizabeth saw a pool of blood in the chamber pot. Elizabeth sat next to Casey and heard a baby cry three times. Elizabeth searched the room but did not find the baby.

Dr Edward Weill attended and examined Casey and asked her where the baby was. Casey made an evasive reply and Weill stepped back to the end of the bed. Casey then threw the baby at Weill, who examined it and found it dead. The body was examined further, and it was found that the baby was born alive, and that the cause of death was suffocation from being smothered by blankets.

On 28 January 1863, an inquest was held at the South Australian Hotel into the death of the newborn son of Margaret Casey, who had been arrested on suspicion of murder and was present at the inquest.

Casey stated that she had rolled the baby up in a piece of carpet and it had fallen onto the floor. The jury retired and returned with a verdict that Casey was guilty of manslaughter. Casey was remanded to the next session of court at Mount Gambier.

Casey appeared in the Circuit Court at Mount Gambier on 24 April. She was found guilty of manslaughter and sentenced to five years imprisonment with hard labour.

South Australian Hotel, Mount Gambier, 1880.
State Library of South Australia, B 15843

Date	*Victim*	*Accused*
12 February 1863	**Nanangaleen**	**Tarryaka (Tom Tom)**
	(Manangatio, Billy)	**and Warrangarina (Copney)**
Cause of death:	Assault (with a marpaung)	
Outcome:	Both found guilty of manslaughter	
	Tarryaka sentenced to six months imprisonment	
	Warrangarina sentenced to three months imprisonment	
Location:	Wellington	

On Saturday 14 February 1863, around Wellington, a father and son named Tarryaka (Tom Tom) and Warrangarina (Copney), killed Nanangaleen (Manangatio, or Billy). Wullthalowrie (Buffalo) knew all three of the men, and witnessed the murder. Wullthalowrie saw Nanangaleen fight with Tarryaka. Their tribe's king had made a speech, after which Nanangaleen jumped up with his shield and jack spear, before throwing the spear at Tarryaka's wurley. The spear would have struck Tarryaka if he had not stooped down. The pair agreed to fight with waddies. While fighting, Nanangaleen knocked Tarryaka down. Warrangarina then struck Nanangaleen with his marpaung, hitting him on the head. Nanangaleen exclaimed, 'Who is that hitting me', before walking away towards the river with the assistance of Jemmy Giles, where he died about half an hour later.

Wellington Police Station, 1864.
State Library of South Australia, B 5684

An inquest was held the following day at the McPherson Inn in West Wellington. Wullthalowrie and Warpaulingerie, who had both witnessed the fight, gave evidence. Warpaulingerie stated that he knew all three men, and that he saw Warrangarina hit Nanangaleen on the head. He said that Nanangaleen struck Tarryaka, who fell to the ground. Nanangaleen continued to hit Tarryaka while he lay on the ground, so Warrangarina struck Nanangaleen to protect his father. A third witness, Counterowlingillie (Captain Death), also gave evidence and corroborated Warpaulingerie's evidence. At the conclusion of the inquest, Tarryaka and Warrangarina were committed on a charge of manslaughter.

On Wednesday 20 May, Tarryaka and Warrangarina appeared before the Supreme Court where they were both found guilty of manslaughter. Warrangarina was sentenced to three months imprisonment, and Tarryaka was sentenced to six months imprisonment.

Date	Victim	Accused
8 May 1863	**William Maylor**	**Jane Adwin**
Cause of death:	Knife wound	
Outcome:	Found guilty of manslaughter	
	Sentenced to two years imprisonment with hard labour	
Location:	Penola	

At about seven-thirty pm on Friday 8 May 1863, Lance Corporal John Morton was on duty in the township of Penola when he was told that Jane Adwin had stabbed William Maylor. Morton attended Maylor's hut and found him lying on the bed. Maylor had a wound to his abdomen, which was about an inch and a half in length. Maylor's intestines were protruding, and he was very weak from loss of blood. Adwin was sitting next to the bed. Maylor said to Morton, 'I hope you will not hurt a hair on Jane's head, it was my fault, she did it in self-defence'. Maylor also said that Adwin did it to save herself, but he did not mention what he was doing to her. Morton arrested Adwin on a charge of stabbing Maylor. Adwin stated that Maylor had been 'ill-using' her and that she had cut him with a knife. He had struck her twice and in the struggle she must have cut him. Morton seized Adwin's dress, which had blood on the sleeve, two butcher's knives, one of which had what appeared to be blood on it, and some shears. Maylor died from his injuries.

On Monday 18 May 1863, an inquest was held at Penola on the body of William Maylor. James Maylor, 15, stated that he was outside the hut when his father was stabbed. Adwin was the housekeeper and lived in the hut. He heard his father say to Adwin, 'You are never satisfied except when you're at the public house', to which Adwin replied, 'I'll drive this knife through your skull'. The next thing he heard was his father calling him, so he went inside and saw blood coming from his belly.

Dr Thomas Bayton stated that he was called to see William Maylor and found a punctured wound in the left side. He treated Maylor for several days but then the wound became infected and Maylor died from the injury on 16 May. Bayton stated that the butcher's knife would have caused the injury.

At the conclusion of the inquest, Jane Adwin was found guilty of manslaughter and was sent to the Robe Town Gaol to await her trial.

On Tuesday 27 October 1863, in the Circuit Court at Mount Gambier,

Jane Adwin appeared charged with the manslaughter of William Maylor. Adwin was found guilty of manslaughter, with a recommendation of mercy by the jury. Adwin was sentenced to two years imprisonment with hard labour.

Date	*Victim*	*Accused*
September 1863	Cusak	Morculta, Niccaltie, Kacuppia, and Poonbinga
Cause of death:	Unknown	
Outcome:	All discharged	
Location:	Gum Creek, near Port Lincoln	

On Thursday 12 May 1864, Morculta, Niccaltie, Kacuppia and Poonbinga appeared in the Supreme Court in Adelaide charged with murdering Cusak in September of 1863. Mr Bruce defended the accused. The crown solicitor said he noticed from the depositions that the magistrate had made one of the accused, Poonbinga, an approver, without any authority from the crown, and in his evidence he had implicated himself, so that some confirmation of his statements would be necessary to enable the jury to convict. His Honour stated that if there were no confirmatory evidence it would be folly to proceed. Mr Bruce asked that a verdict of not guilty should be taken. The crown solicitor objected, as it was possible that additional evidence might be obtained. He would, however, withdraw the information. His Honour then directed that the prisoners should be discharged.

Date	*Victim*	*Accused*
7 September 1863	Robins child	Emily Robins
Cause of death:	Neglect/ exposure	
Outcome:	Acquitted	
Location:	Tanunda	

At about nine am on Monday 7 September 1863, the body of a newborn female child was found in a paddock in Tanunda. Mr Keynes, who owned the paddock, was mowing the barley for green feed when he noticed the body. Dr Pablet examined the body before removing it from the paddock. Shortly afterwards, 20-year-old Emily Robins was arrested on suspicion of murder. Dr Millner, of Angaston, attended and made a post-mortem examination of the child, and an examination of Robins.

The following day, a jury of 14 was empanelled and viewed the body. Dr Millner, the principle witness, sent a note saying he could not attend as he had been delayed by a patient, so the inquest was put off until the following day.

The inquest reopened at two pm on Wednesday 9 September, and evidence was taken from many witnesses who stated there was no doubt that Robins was 'in the family way'. Dr Millner stated that the child was full-grown and had died from exposure to the air and the cold. He also stated that Robins had given birth within the last two or three days. Robins' parents were examined, who both denied all knowledge of the pregnancy. The jury deliberated for about half an hour and returned stating 'the verdict of the jury is that the female child found dead in Mr Keynes' paddock on Monday 9th, died through the neglect of the mother, and that Emily Robins is the mother of the said child'.

On the next day, being court day, the case was re-heard before J Browne, SM, and C Barton Esq, JP, after which Robins was committed for trial at the Supreme Court for wilful murder.

Robins appeared before the Supreme Court on Thursday 3 December 1863, where the same witnesses gave evidence. The land where the body was located was about 100 yards from where Robins lived. At the summing up, the judge told the jury that they could, if they thought that there was insufficient evidence for murder, convict her of concealing the birth of her child, provided they were satisfied that she had a child. The judge then stated that there was nothing directly connecting Robins to the child. There was evidence that she had given birth, but in a capital crime, the jury would have to decide whether the child in the paddock belonged to Robins. The paddock was accessible to anyone, and the neighbourhood was well populated, so another woman may have had a child and placed it in the field. The jury retired before returning and acquitting Robins.

Date	*Victim*	*Accused*
27 October 1863	**John Plunkett**	**John Smith and John Grant**
Cause of death:	Assault	
Outcome:	Smith found guilty of manslaughter	
	Sentenced to 18 months imprisonment with hard labour	
	Grant found guilty of manslaughter	
	Sentenced to 12 months imprisonment with hard labour	
Location:	Wallaroo	

On 27 October 1863, a fist fight occurred at the Wallaroo Hotel between John Plunkett and John Smith. During the fight, Smith struck Plunkett and both fell to the ground. Plunkett could not get up so Corporal Bentley was sent for. When Bentley arrived, he sent for Dr Sholl. Dr Sholl examined Plunkett and found that he had swelling and pain to the back of his neck, which was red. Plunkett told Sholl that there were no ill feelings between him and Smith, that he did not blame anyone else for his injury, and that he had been drinking that evening. Sholl believed that the injury was caused not by a blow to the head, but rather the fall to the ground. Plunkett subsequently died, and the cause of death was determined to be an extension of the spinal cord.

On 2 November 1863, an inquest was held at Bentley's Wallaroo Inn. John Smith and John Grant were present and in custody at the inquest.

Evidence was given regarding the fistfight, which implicated John Grant and his involvement in the fight. A verdict of manslaughter was returned against Smith and Grant at the conclusion of the inquest.

On Friday 27 November, Smith and Grant appeared before the Supreme Court. At the conclusion of the trial they were found guilty of manslaughter, but the jury recommended them to mercy. The judge said that he thought that was a pity, as in his opinion the judges were, as a rule, too merciful. He would, however, attend to their recommendation.

On Wednesday 9 December Smith and Grant were sentenced in the Supreme Court. Smith received 18 months imprisonment and Grant received 12 months imprisonment, both with hard labour.

Date	Victim	Accused
November 1863	Woolgaltie (Jemmy)	Koongiltie (Peter)
Cause of death:	Assault (with a waddy)	
Outcome:	Found to be justifiable homicide	
Location:	Mount Wedge	

This incident was found not to be a murder, but to be justifiable homicide. It has been included for interest only and has not been added to any statistics.

On Thursday 12 May 1863, 20-year-old Koongiltie, who was also known as Peter, appeared in the Supreme Court charged with the murder of Woolgaltie, who was also known as Jemmy. In his opening address, the crown solicitor abandoned the murder charge and continued with a charge of manslaughter. The evidence to be heard was to come solely from Aboriginal witnesses, and there were the usual difficulties with obtaining this evidence. His Honour found it difficult to explain to witnesses the importance of telling the truth.

Evidence was given that Koongiltie had returned to his wurley after a hunting expedition, carrying a prime wallaby, and Woolgaltie, suffering from the pangs of an empty stomach, demanded that Koongiltie give him the wallaby. Koongiltie refused to give up the wallaby and went into his wurley. Woolgaltie called out to Koongiltie to come out and fight, but Koongiltie did not want to. Woolgaltie threw three waddies at Koongiltie, so Koongiltie retaliated and threw a waddy at Woolgaltie, which hit him in the head. Woolgaltie fell to the ground, and died three days later from his injuries.

The judge summed up the evidence, stating that Woolgaltie had unlawfully demanded the wallaby from Koongiltie, who had the right to defend his property, and that Woolgaltie threw three waddies at Koongiltie, who only threw one back. The jury retired for a short time before returning to acquit Koongiltie, finding the case to be one of justifiable homicide.

Date	Victim	Accused
December 1863	Meenulta	Russell Barton and Alexander Miller
Cause of death:	Assault (with a whip)	
Outcome:	Both acquitted	
Location:	Chilulta, near Port Lincoln	

In December 1863, Meenulta was with his lubra, Choolebunga, near Chilulta when Russell Barton and Alexander Miller rode up. They all knew each other, and Barton had previously made threats against Meenulta. Miller held Meenulta by the arm as Barton hit Meenulta with a whip until he fell to the ground. Choolebunga ran off. Miller and Barton later saw Choolebunga, who asked them where Meenulta was. The men said that he had run away, and Miller told her not to tell the policeman.

On 6 March 1864, Trooper O'Shanahan was in company with Trooper Provis, Choolebunga and Pongulta (also known as Wangro), searching the area around Chilulta, near Mr Marchant's head station, for Meenulta. They located the remains of a person, but they could not tell if it was a male or female, as the remains were badly decomposed. Nothing but one of the feet could be recognised. They were unable to tell if the body was a black or white person.

After a police investigation into the death, on Monday 16 August 1864, Barton and Miller appeared before the Supreme Court charged with murder. Choolebunga gave evidence and stated that she knew Meenulta and that he was now dead. She said that she was once the lubra of Meenulta and that the last time she saw Meenulta alive was when she saw him with Miller, who was on horseback. She last saw Meenulta when she was with the Troopers, when a body was located. Choolebunga said that she recognised the toes of the body as the same as Meenulta's.

Pongulta gave evidence and stated that he was the present owner of Choolebunga. He stated that Barton had asked him, 'Where is that fellow Meenulta, him come back here and I'll kill him'. Pongulta warned Meenulta that Barton would kill him. He later saw Meenulta go to Mr. Marchant's station for tobacco. Later, Pongulta went with the police and Choolebunga where he saw the body, which he recognised as Meenulta.

The defence argued that the only evidence that Meenulta was the person whose remains were found was from testimony from two Aboriginal witnesses, and the identification was only by his toes. Other than that, there was no evidence that Meenulta had died. If it was accepted that Miller and Barton were involved in the assault of Meenulta, there was no evidence to say that the assault caused his death.

At the conclusion of the trial, the jury retired for 20 minutes before acquitting both Miller and Barton.

Date	*Victim*	*Accused*
8 January 1864	**Pompey**	**Samuel Stuckey**
Cause of death:	Gunshot wound	
Outcome:	Information dismissed	
Location:	Umberatana Station, near Beltana	

In early January 1864, an Aboriginal man called Pompey, who was regarded as a troublesome and dangerous character, headed a tribe of Aboriginal people of the Saltwater Creek Tribe around Beltana. On 8 January, Pompey led some of his tribe to a hut at an outstation with the intent to rob it. There was a woman in the hut and some threats were made to her. She managed to escape and reported the matter to Mr Stuckey at the Umberatana Station, who went to the Aboriginal camp with others with the intent to stop the violence and apprehend Pompey. Hoping to secure Pompey by merely disabling him, Stuckey fired at him, intending to only strike one of his legs, but the shot proved fatal, and Pompey died.

Later that month, information was received in Adelaide regarding Pompey's death. Mr Walker, who was the 'Protector of Aborigines', went to the north where an inquest was held on 16 February by order of the Attorney General. Mr G Smith, SM, held the inquest, where evidence was given about Pompey, the raid on the hut, and the subsequent shooting by Mr Stuckey. The jury returned a verdict of justifiable homicide.

Umberatana Station Homestead, 1865. State Library of South Australia, B 38777.

Stuckey was later arrested and charged with murder based on the information of Inspector Peterswald. On Saturday 12 March, Stuckey appeared in the police court in Adelaide. Evidence was given that Pompey was running away at the time he was shot. Stuckey stated that he wanted to arrest Pompey as he had killed one of his shepherds the night before. There was some argument as to shooting at a fleeing felon, but as the suspected murder of the shepherd the night before was not proven, there was no justification for Stuckey to shoot at him. The magistrate adjourned the matter and Stuckey was released on bail.

Stuckey appeared again in the police courts on Tuesday 3 May, where further evidence was received and more legal argument took place. At the conclusion, His Worship thought that no jury would convict him of manslaughter or even murder, and as a result the information was dismissed and Stuckey was released.

Date	*Victim*	*Accused*
5 September 1864	**Webb child**	**Annie Webb**
Cause of death:	Suffocation	
Outcome:	Found guilty of concealment of birth	
	Sentenced to four months imprisonment	
Location:	Kapunda	

Annie Webb was a 15-year-old girl who was in the service of Thomas Sabine, a priest in the Holy Orders at Kapunda. Annie had been working for the Sabines for several weeks, when on 5 September 1864, acting on information from his wife, Thomas Sabine went to the watercloset and found the body of an infant in the soil. The child was naked and appeared to be dead. Webb was questioned, and she stated that she was the mother of the child, but it had been born dead. At a later coroner's inquest, Webb was found guilty of murder and remanded to appear in the Supreme Court.

On Wednesday 30 November 1864, Annie Webb appeared before the Supreme Court charged with the murder of her newborn female child. Dr Tallis gave evidence that the child had breathed and died. There were no marks of violence and he explained that the child might have been suffocated accidentally through inexperience, and said that some women omitted to call in proper assistance. He also stated that he had examined Webb and found that she had recently given birth.

Sarah Webb, Annie's mother, stated that she saw her daughter at Mr Sabine's on the evening of 4 September, and that she was complaining of feeling ill. About two months previously, Sarah had spoken to Annie and told her that if she were pregnant, her husband would turn her out of doors, as Annie had just turned 15.

At the conclusion of the trial, the jury retired and returned with a verdict of guilty of concealment of birth, with a recommendation of mercy on account of the threat from her father. The crown solicitor considered it his duty, in justice to the prisoner, to mention that he was 'in possession of information to show that the prisoner, when seduced, was not a voluntary agent, but there was some violence on the part of the seducer'. His Honour took that into consideration and sentenced Webb to four months imprisonment.

Date	*Victim*	*Accused*
13 October 1864	**Bridget Ashley**	**Charles Ashley**
Cause of death:	Knife wounds	
Outcome:	Found guilty of manslaughter	
	Sentenced to life imprisonment with hard labour	
Location:	Hindley Street, Adelaide	

On Thursday 13 October 1864, Elizabeth Dixon was in Morphett Street when she saw her neighbours, Charles, a 44-year-old shoemaker, and his wife Bridget Ashley, walking with another man into their house. Bridget asked Dixon if she would like to join them, which she did about 15 minutes later. When Dixon arrived at the Ashley house, Bridget and Charles were arguing. After a short time Charles left the house, followed later by Bridget, Dixon and the young man. The three of them went to the Adelaide Hotel in Hindley Street to get a drink. While they were there, Charles came into the bar and asked Bridget for a glass of beer, which she refused to give him. Charles asked Bridget several times for a drink, but she would not get one for him.

Charles left the hotel and returned about five minutes later. Charles went to Bridget and again asked for a beer. Charles had his hand in his pocket and Dixon noticed he was holding a knife. Dixon grabbed hold of his hand and said, 'What in the name of God have you got there?' Charles said, 'I'll soon show you what it is'. Dixon then ran to the other end of the bar and hid her head in her dress. She looked up and saw that Bridget had blood on her. Charles had hold of Bridget's chin and in his other hand he had a knife, which was buried into Bridget's neck. Dixon ran to the door and called for the police, and Lance Corporal Sullivan came in at once and arrested Charles.

Hindley Street, looking west, approximately 1866.
State Library of South Australia, B 73320/3

Charles Carr, a labourer of Grenfell Street, was in the bar at the same time and saw Charles strike Bridget down. When Carr went to pick Bridget up he noticed the knife in her throat. He saw Corporal Sullivan come into the bar and arrest Charles. Bridget was taken to the Adelaide Hospital, where she died the next day from her injuries.

On Friday 14 October, an inquest was held at the Adelaide Hospital on the body of Bridget Ashley, who had died from multiple stab wounds in her neck and face. Evidence was received from Lance Corporal Robert Besley, who identified the body. He had known her to be a woman of 'intemperate habits' who had been frequently locked up for being drunk.

Lance Corporal Sullivan stated that on hearing a cry for the police, he entered the Adelaide Hotel where he arrested Charles Ashley for attempting to murder his wife. After being cautioned, Charles stated that he did it because he was jealous of her. At the conclusion of the inquest, the jury found Charles guilty of wilful murder.

Charles Ashley appeared before the Supreme Court on Friday 9 December. He was found guilty of manslaughter and sentenced to life imprisonment with hard labour.

Nearly two years later, on Tuesday 21 July 1868, Charles Ashley died in gaol from disease of the liver and dropsy. His conduct during his sentence was spoken of as very exemplary, and during his illness, he admitted the justice of his sentence, and expressed the 'sincerest contrition for his grievous offence'.

Date	*Victim*	*Accused*
10 November 1864	**John Torpey**	**Frederick Stafford**
Cause of death:	Gunshot wound	
Outcome:	Found guilty of manslaughter	
	Sentenced to two years imprisonment with hard labour	
Location:	Nuccaleena	

On 9 November 1864, John Torpey, 29-year-old Frederick Stafford, and Cornelius Kellard were in the Bushman Inn at Nuccaleena. All three stayed the night, and in the morning they had breakfast with other guests. After breakfast, Kellard, William George, William Cox and Torpey went back to Kellard's bedroom. After about half an hour, Stafford came in and sat opposite them to have a joke with them. Stafford said that he had some wine, and that he would treat them a nobbler (small serving) of it. Kellard said that he did not want any wine, or any intoxicating thing, and carried on joking with the others. Kellard joked that a dose of poison or arsenic would be more becoming to clear them out of the place. Stafford went to his swag, undid one strap, pulled out a double-barrelled pistol and said, 'If you want poison, here it is for you'. Stafford cocked the pistol and Torpey asked if it was loaded, which Stafford said it was. Torpey said, 'If it is, for God's sake leave down the hammer'. Stafford was sitting about two feet opposite Kellard and Torpey when the pistol went off. Kellard jumped up and seized the pistol, which went off again. Torpey cried out that he was shot, and Kellard saw blood on Torpey, who had been shot in the groin.

William Davis, a miner and a friend of Torpey's, was standing at the bar of the Bushmann's Inn when he was told his friend had been shot. David went to Torpey and pulled down his trousers to see the wound. Davies said, 'You are all right, I think you won't die yet'. Davies went out and found Stafford and gave him a few slaps, then went back to Torpey.

The ruins of the hotel at Nuccaleena, taken on September 29th, 1920. According to regulations, this hotel is situated half a mile from the mine. Until 'quite recently' [quote in 1920], the track between the mine and the Inn was, in places, literally covered with thousands of empty bottles. Mount Tamoshanter is in the background.
State Library of South Australia, B 669.

Davies remained with Torpey for the next few days but Torpey gradually got worse. Torpey told Davies that he thought that Stafford meant to shoot either Kellard or him, and that he did not think that Stafford had a grudge against them.

Dr Thomas Cotter attended to Torpey and found that he had 14 shots in the lower part of this body and 17 shots in his hand. Cotter passed a probe into one wound and found a solid body in it, which was too dangerous to remove. Torpey lived for about 14 days before he died from the injuries.

On 9 December, the coroner, Mr G Smith, held an inquest on the body of John Torpey. Dr Cotter conducted a post-mortem examination that revealed that the femoral vein had been cut by one of the bullets, which had then rested on the thighbone. Cotter also examined bullets shot from the pistol and found they were similar to what he recovered from Torpey.

At the conclusion of the inquest, the jury found that Stafford was responsible for Torpey's death. Safford was committed for manslaughter.

Stafford appeared before the Supreme Court on Friday 17 February 1865, where a jury found him guilty of manslaughter. Stafford was sentenced to two years imprisonment with hard labour.

Date	Victim	Accused
February 1865	**Oongiltie**	**Nielbury**
Cause of death:	Spear wound	
Outcome:	Found guilty of manslaughter	
	Sentenced to three years imprisonment with hard labour	
Location:	Wallanippie, near Smokey Bay	

Smokey Bay's coastline was first sighted and mapped by Captain Matthew Flinders in 1802, who named it after the amount of smoke from fires lit by the area's Aboriginal people. In the early 1860s pastoralists arrived in the district. Former Adelaide civil servant Charles Francis Heath (1832–1883) established a sheep grazing property which he named Wallanippie Station after the Aboriginal name of a waterhole near his homestead at the back of Point Brown Peninsula.

In February 1865, some local Aboriginal people, including one called Oongiltie, were working on Heath's property. Heath sent Oongiltie on an errand and while he was gone, Oongiltie's lubra ran off. Around the same time, Heath saw another man in the area, 18-year-old Nielbury. Heath was not sure if Oongiltie and Nielbury were from the same tribe. Heath never saw Oongiltie alive again.

In March that year Police Trooper White received information from Choonbeenya about Oongilite's death. As a result, White and Heath searched the property and located Oongiltie's body. White saw that Oongiltie had a broken spear in his body. Nielbury was later located and arrested by White for Oongiltie's murder.

On 16 August 1865, Nielbury appeared before the Supreme Court charged with murder. Police Trooper Provis acted as an interpreter for the court. After a few preliminary questions, suggested by His Honour, had been put to Nielbury, he stated that Nielbury admitted to having speared Oongiltie, but he said that Oongiltie did not die at the time. They had been 'growling' about a lubra and had resorted to their spears to settle the dispute.

Choonbeenya gave evidence and stated that it was about five moons since he had seen Nielbury. He was at a place called Murrumbinga, and he saw Oongiltie die at this place. Oongiltie died because Nielbury speared him, with the wound on the right side of the body. Nielbury speared Oongiltie because they had a 'growl' about a lubra named Jenny. When they growled, Oongiltie had one spear with him and Nielbury had four spears. Both Nielbury and Oongiltie threw one spear each, with Nielbury throwing his first. They had been growling a long time before they threw spears. Nielbury threw the spear at Oongiltie when the sun was very high, and at night Oongiltie died. Nielbury later took the lubra away to Wallannippy. The lubra was present during the growl, and saw the spear thrown. Choonbeenya covered up the body and afterwards showed it to Police Trooper White.

The jury, after a very brief consultation, and without retiring, found Nielbury guilty of manslaughter.

His Honour passed sentence during which he stated:

> … I am sorry I cannot explain to the prisoner what I would say to a white man placed in his position, but I must ask the police to explain to the blacks where the prisoner came from that when they engaged in fights with deadly weapons they are by the law of England, by which they were protected, guilty of a serious offence, and that the English law watched with jealous care the lives of Her Majesty's subjects all over the world. The sentence of the Court was that he be imprisoned and kept to hard labour for three years.

Police Trooper Provis said, 'I am afraid I shall not be able, your Honour, to make them understand all that', to which His Honour replied, 'But you can explain it in a general way. You can make it known to them that Nielbury was imprisoned because he killed a fellow'. The sentence was explained to Nielbury who was then taken to gaol.

Date	*Victim*	*Accused*
April 1865	**John Walter Jarrold**	**Parrallana Jacky**
Cause of death:	Unknown	
Outcome:	Unknown	
Location:	Blanchewater	

In the *South Australian Register*, the following letter was printed on Saturday 10 June 1865:

'Blanchewater'. A private letter, dated Blanchewater, May 15, just received, contains the following information about the murder committed by the natives in this quarter recently and the state of the country generally.

The blacks are getting very troublesome up here now. They have killed one of Mr Jacob's shepherds, a young man named Walter Gerald. There have been seven and sometimes eight of us out looking for the body for a month off and on, and at last I found it under a few dry sticks and some stones. The wild dogs had eaten the poor fellow's feet off. The only things they (the natives) left with him were his boots, and they were by his side. They have left there now and gone to give Mr. Stuckey's run a turn. They robbed one or two of his shepherds' huts, and then attacked one of his flocks, taking, I believe, about 500 of his sheep. The shepherd took to his heels, he having no firearms with him to protect himself with, the best thing he could do. If the police do not come up here, and put a stop to their goings on there will be more mischief done yet by them.

At last we have had a few nice showers of rain, which were wanted very much. They have made the grass spring a little, but not enough to do much good.

SSS Lubra, unknown date. State Library of South Australia, B 72784.

On Friday 30 June, a further letter was printed which gave the correct details of the victim as 25-year-old John Walter Jarrold, who had been found with severe head injuries. A local Aboriginal man was thought to be responsible. The police from Angepena rode to Blanchewater to investigate the murder.

In October 1865, Police Trooper Poynter arrived in Adelaide on the steamer *Lubra*, from Port Augusta, having in his custody Parrallana Jacky, on the charge of murdering John Jarrold. No further reference of Parrallana Jacky attending court could be found.

Date	*Victim*	*Accused*
5 August 1865	**Kelly child**	**Mary Kelly**
Cause of death:	Suffocation/ neglect	
Outcome:	Found guilty of manslaughter	
	Sentenced to 12 months imprisonment	
Location	Kapunda	

On Saturday 5 August 1865, Robert Hooper, the landlord of the Prince of Wales Hotel at Kapunda, was showing a man around the hotel when he was called by a guest called Joseph Barnden, who said he heard something crying in a box alongside his bed in his room. Hooper went to the room where he saw a box. He removed the lid and took some clothing out and found a child, who was alive and moving. Hooper called for his wife and told her to call for Dr Matthew Blood and the police to attend. Hooper knew of no one who was pregnant, and knew that any one of the servants had access to the room. Mrs Hooper took care of the child.

Dr Blood arrived and examined the female child. He saw that she was very weak and very black in the face. There was blood coming from the mouth and nostrils and she was near death. He believed that the child had been suffocated, and that was the cause of the blood from the nose and mouth. She was moaning weakly at intervals and he managed to partially restore the child. The child died the following day. The cause of death was given as improper management causing loss of blood and suffocation.

Dr Blood told Mrs Hooper that he would examine every female in the Hotel to find the mother. He asked 16-year-old Mary Kelly, who had been employed as a servant at the hotel for the past eight months, if she knew anything of the child. Kelly said that she was the mother, and that she had put the child in the box just after lunch. She said the father was a man named Hassett. Blood examined Kelly and found that she had recently given birth.

Prince of Wales Hotel, Kapunda, 1860.
State Library of South Australia, B 9952.

On 8 August 1865, an inquest was held at Kapunda. The suspect, Mary Kelly, appeared in custody. Dr Blood and the Hoopers gave evidence. At the completion of the inquest, the jury retired before delivering a verdict of manslaughter. Kelly was committed under the coroner's warrant for trial.

On Wednesday 23 August, Kelly appeared before the Supreme Court on a charge of murder. Evidence was given that the final cause of death was suffocation, but the suffocation could be attributed more to the neglectful placement of the child in the box, rather than Kelly physically suffocating it. The judge told the jury that the evidence did not support a charge of murder, but there was enough to support the charge of manslaughter. The jury, without retiring, found Kelly guilty of manslaughter, but recommended her to mercy. His Honour stated that the crime that Kelly had committed was so common in the province that he should be obliged to pass a severe sentence. Kelly was sentenced to 12 months imprisonment.

Date	*Victim*	*Accused*
23 October 1865	George Young	John Walker
Cause of death:	Shear blade wounds	
Outcome:	Found guilty of manslaughter	
	Sentenced to 10 years imprisonment with hard labour	
Location:	Pooginook Station, Waikerie	

John Walker, 37, and his wife lived at Pooginook, a station owned by his brother in law, Mr Taylor. Walker left the station in early October as a consequence of some unpleasantness with his wife. In the evening of Monday 23 October 1865, Walker returned to the station while Mr Taylor was absent. George Young, who was employed as the cook, was in bed. Walker gained entry to the house through a window and attacked Young with a shear blade, stabbing him in several places, including the abdomen. Walker then attacked his wife, piercing her through the wrist and the neck. Walker left the station and handed himself up to the police at Overland Corner. Young died the following day, but Mrs Walker survived the attack. Walker was taken to Angaston for an inquest.

On Friday 8 December, Walker appeared before the Supreme Court on a charge of murder. At the completion of the trial, the jury found Walker guilty of manslaughter. On Thursday 14 December, Walker appeared once more before the Supreme Court. His Honour stated that he had paid very careful consideration to the evidence and he had since then taken care in reading the depositions which were taken in another matter, for the purpose, if he could, to see if there was anything to lessen the offence. He stated that undoubtedly the jury took a very merciful view of his case, because he considered the evidence before them would well have warranted them in finding him guilty of murder, and in that case the utmost penalty of the law would have been carried into effect, and he must mark his sense of the seriousness of the matter by passing upon him a heavy sentence. Walker was sentenced to 10 years imprisonment with hard labour.

Date	*Victim*	*Accused*
24 October 1865	**George Smith**	**Robert Sutcliffe**
Cause of death:	Assault	
Outcome:	Found guilty of manslaughter	
	Sentenced to four years imprisonment with hard labour	
Location:	Portland Hotel, Portland	

Around seven-thirty pm on Tuesday 24 October 1865, Edward Parsons, the barman of Portland Hotel, was standing behind the bar when George Smith came in and asked for a pint of beer in a bottle. Robert Sutcliffe, who was 30 years old, was also in the bar with other patrons. Parsons went into the yard to get a bottle, and when he returned Sutcliffe was chaffing Smith about being an ex-policeman. Parsons told Sutcliffe to stop, but Sutcliffe said he did not care and that he was the best man in the house. The chaffing continued and Sutcliffe challenged Smith to a fight. Smith did not reply to Sutcliffe, but said to Parsons, 'Ted, I can't stand this'. Soon after, Sutcliffe's wife came to the door and called him away. Smith went out about a minute later and after a short time Parsons heard a child crying outside. Parsons went outside and saw Sutcliffe and Smith struggling on the ground, with Sutcliffe on top of Smith. A man named Henry Pudney got Sutcliffe off of Smith. When Sutcliffe was standing, he kicked Smith twice, while he was still on the ground. Smith said that his leg was broken and Sutcliffe replied 'A good job to you … I wish I had broken your neck'. Smith was helped up, but he could not stand on his leg as a bone was protruding from the skin.

Smith was taken to the Adelaide Hospital where Dr John Benson, the assistant colonial surgeon, treated him. Smith was suffering from a fracture of the fibula and compound dislocation of the tibia inwards. Doctors Benson and Moore treated the injuries, but the following morning they told Smith that he had to have his leg amputated. Smith refused. A few days later, Smith said that he wanted to have it amputated, but he was delirious, and gangrene of the foot had set in, so they were unable to operate. Smith later died from his injuries.

On Tuesday 31 October, an inquest was held by Dr Woodforde at the Adelaide Hospital on the body of George Smith, who had died at five am that morning.

Henry Pudney gave evidence and stated that he saw the fight outside the hotel, and that he saw Sutcliffe punching Smith while he was on the ground.

Adelaide Hospital, 1865. State Library of South Australia, B 21363.

After pulling Sutcliffe away, he saw Sutcliffe kicking Smith while he was on the ground. Dr Benson stated that the injury to Smith's leg was the cause of death. At the conclusion of the inquest, the jury retired for a short deliberation, and returned with a verdict of manslaughter against Sutcliffe.

On Thursday 7 December, Sutcliffe appeared before the Supreme Court on a charge of manslaughter. At the completion of the trial, the jury found Sutcliffe guilty. On Thursday 15 December, Sutcliffe again appeared before the Supreme Court where he was sentenced to four years imprisonment with hard labour.

Date	*Victim*	*Accused*
8 December 1865	**Carl Neumann**	**Moonabuckaneena (Frank) and Freddy**
Cause of death:	Spear wound	
Outcome:	Both acquitted	
Location:	Perrigundee, near Lake Hope, near Moomba	

The following article was printed in the *South Australian Advertiser* on Saturday 17 March 1866:

> We have been favored with the following extracts from a letter just received in Adelaide from Lake Hope, dated 21th [*sic*] February: —'One of the stock keepers of Mr. Dean's party has died from the wounds inflicted by the natives. An inquest was held on the body, and the verdict was wilful murder against 30 or 40 unknown. Some of the blacks implicated in the murder were followed up to Cooper's Creek, but without success. The party had a very bad trip of it. They did not take sufficient rations, and for eight days they lived on six ounces of bread per day, no meat, no sugar, nor any tea, nothing but flour. Dr. Walker and the Inspector of Mounted Police were with the party, which numbered 15. They all shared alike. The doctor went to protect the blacks. He will give a deplorable account of the country. It is no wonder that Burke and Wills died on account of the barren state of the country. The wonder is that King survived, he must have had a very strong constitution. An inquest has been held on the native shot by Trooper Gason while capturing him. The verdict was 'justifiable homicide" according to the direction of the Coroner to the jury. The same trooper apprehended another native here for murder, but there was not sufficient evidence against the black. We have had plenty of rain up here, and now there is any amount of feed for cattle and horses.

About six months later, on Tuesday 4 September 1866, 25-year-old Moonabuckaneena (Frank) and 28-year-old Freddy appeared before the Supreme Court in Adelaide charged with Neumann's murder. William Rook, a stockkeeper, stated that on the evening of 7 December, he and a number of others were camped at Perrigundee, when they retired at around nine pm. At about two am he was woken up by someone calling out, 'Here are the niggers [*sic*]'. Rook got up and saw a number of Aboriginal people with spears, waddies and boomerangs attacking the camp. He saw Neumann speared. He did not recognise Frank and Freddy in the attacking party, which numbered about 200. The fight lasted about 10 minutes.

At the conclusion of the trial, both were acquitted.

Date	Victim	Accused
20 January 1866	**Male child**	**Unknown**
Cause of death:	Assault	
Outcome:	Unsolved	
Location:	Port Adelaide	

On Monday 22 January 1866, Owen Williams was moving his barge near Fletcher's Slip, Port Adelaide, when he saw a bag in the water. He reached it with a boathook and pushed it to shallow water. The bag looked like a piece of a bran bag, tied with a white cord. He opened the bag and found that it contained the body of a newborn male child. At the time, the tide was ebbing, so Williams thought that the bag could not have been deposited in the water from the jetty near the slip; he thought that it more likely had floated from the bridge.

Fletcher's Slip, 1871.
State Library of South Australia, PRG 1373/2/19

On January 23, an inquest was held at the local court at Port Adelaide on the body of the newborn child. Dr Robert Gething made a post-mortem examination and stated that the umbilical cord was cut and tied clumsily, and that the child was fully developed and healthy. The skull was fractured and there were large clots of blood on the surface of the brain. Gething stated that the injuries had been inflicted while the child was alive, and they were quite sufficient to cause death. He believed the body had been in the water about 24 to 36 hours. The jury, without further consultation, returned a verdict of wilful murder against some person or persons unknown. In February, the government posted a reward of £50 for information regarding the murder, however, no information was received.

Date	*Victim*	*Accused*
8 February 1866	**William Forrester**	**Michael O'Donnell**
Cause of death:	Knife wound	
Outcome:	Found guilty of murder	
	Sentenced to death, commuted to life imprisonment	
Location:	Gilbert Town (now Tarlee)	

William Forrester was the publican of the Bow and Arrow Hotel at Gilbert Town. On Thursday 8 February 1866, Charles Brown, a farmer, was in the bar of the hotel with Forrester, Michael O'Donnell, and some others. O'Donnell left the hotel and Brown was invited into another room by Forrester. Shortly after, at around 10 pm, Forrester said he would not serve any more drinks and went to bolt the door. Brown heard someone outside who wanted to get inside, and then a glass window was broken. Forrester went outside and found O'Donnell there. O'Donnell grabbed Forrester by the shoulders and Brown, hearing the commotion outside, went to Forrester's aid. Forrester cried out and said he was stabbed. Brown saw that Forrester was bleeding and he and others carried him back into the hotel. Forrester died from his injuries about 20 minutes later.

On Friday 9 June, an inquest was held into the death of William Forrester. Evidence was given that O'Donnell wanted accommodation for the night but did not like the room. There was an argument between O'Donnell and Forrester during which Forrester told O'Donnell to leave. O'Donnell remained on the porch after the door was locked and broke a window. Forrester came out onto the porch, where O'Donnell attacked and eventually stabbed Forrester.

Police Corporal O'Brien took O'Donnell into custody. He saw blood on O'Donnell's hands and clothing. At the completion of the inquest, the jury returned a verdict of guilty of murder against O'Donnell, who was remanded in custody.

On Tuesday 28 August, O'Donnell appeared before the Supreme Court, charged with the murder of Forrester. The jury found him guilty of murder and the judge sentenced him to death. The sentence was later commuted to life imprisonment.

Date	*Victim*	*Accused*
29 March 1866	**Harriet Stone**	**Jane Green**
Cause of death:	Assault	
Outcome:	Found guilty of manslaughter	
	Sentenced to six months imprisonment	
Location:	Franklin Street, Adelaide	

On 29 March 1866, Harriet Stone was living in Franklin Street. Stone was heavily pregnant and was due to give birth to her first child within two or three weeks. Jane Green, who was 28 years old, and Ester Smith also resided in Franklin Street. On 29 March, Smith saw Green shouting at Stone. Smith told Green to leave Stone alone, but Green said she would not and started to hit Stone and pull her hair. Green knocked and punched Stone all over her body and could not be pulled away from her.

Franklin Street looking east, 1867.
State Library of South Australia, B 9780

After a while the fight ended. Later the same day Smith spoke to Stone who said that she was going to catch a cab to her father's house in Stephens Place, as she was so frightened of Green that she could not stay in her own house.

Later that day, Stone was seen by Dr Bayer, who was called to the house at four pm. When he arrived, Stone was unconscious and suffering from convulsions. As she was unable to swallow, an enema was given with medication. Bayer left, and returned at around 10 pm with Dr Phillips to induce labour. Phillips saw that the whole of Stone's body appeared swollen, so he prescribed leeches on her temples. Stone died at 11 pm that night.

On 30 March at the Globe Inn, Rundle Street, an inquest was formed to look into the circumstances of the death of Harriet Stone, who died from the alleged cruelty and ill treatment from Jane Green. Green was in police custody on suspicion of having caused the death by an assault or other means. The jury viewed the body, which was considerably discoloured with some scratches on the face.

Rundle Street, Adelaide, 1866 looking west from Gawler Place.
On the extreme right is the Globe Inn.
State Library of South Australia, B 2568

Elizabeth Beckwith, also of Franklin St, stated that she saw Green force her way into Smith's house and assault her. At the conclusion of the inquest, the jury could not come to a verdict, as they thought that a post-mortem would be necessary. The coroner ordered one and the inquest was adjourned.

The inquest resumed on Wednesday 4 April, with the post-mortem results showing that Stone's brain was congested on the right side and there was a large patch of blood under the tissue of the right breast, which was attributed to violence prior to death. The doctor who completed the post-mortem stated that if Stone had not been assaulted, she would have been alive. The jury retired and returned a verdict of manslaughter against Jane Green, who was committed to the Supreme Court.

On Thursday 30 August, Green appeared before the Supreme Court charged with murder. At the completion of the trial the jury retired for an hour, before returning and finding her guilty of manslaughter, with a recommendation for mercy. On Saturday 8 September, Green appeared once more before the Supreme Court. His Honour said that he entirely acquitted her of any intention of causing the death of the deceased, but he could not acquit her of a reckless disregard of the suffering and consequences that flowed from her violence. Green was sentenced to six months imprisonment.

Date	*Victim*	*Accused*
17 May 1866	**Bruder child**	**Henrietta Bruder/Binder**
Cause of death:	Neglect	
Outcome:	Found guilty of concealment of birth	
	Sentenced to two years imprisonment with hard labour	
Location:	Near Angaston	

Henrietta Bruder (also spelt Binder) was a 19-year-old servant living at Mr Ossey's property at Angaston. On 17 May 1866, she woke Ossey, saying that she wanted a doctor. Ossey called for Mrs Winter, but Bruder then said she did not want a doctor anymore. The next morning, Ossey went into the barn and saw a spade with blood on the handle. He searched the barn and saw a patch of ground that had been recently dug. He dug down himself and found the body of a newborn female child. He also saw a pool of blood nearby. Ossey called for the police, and Police Trooper Howe arrived and arrested Bruder, who denied any knowledge of the matter. Dr Horton examined Bruder and found that she had recently given birth. Horton also made a post-mortem examination and stated that in his opinion, death resulted from exposure to cold and want of proper treatment.

On 19 May, an inquest was held at Angaston. At the completion of the inquest, the jury, after a short retirement, found Bruder guilty of manslaughter.

On Tuesday 21 August Bruder appeared before the Supreme Court, charged with the murder of her illegitimate female child. At the conclusion of the trial, the jury found Bruder guilty of concealment of birth. Bruder was sentenced to two years imprisonment with hard labour.

Date	Victim	Accused
2 January 1867	**Cooelta**	**Pagulta**
Cause of death:	Stab wound	
Outcome:	Acquitted (*nolle prosequi*)	
Location:	Weedina, near Wudinna	

On Friday 17 May 1867, 25-year-old Pagulta appeared before the Supreme Court charged with feloniously killing and slaying Cooelta. The crown solicitor stated that there was not an interpreter present, and he was unable to proceed with the case. His Honour, Mr Justice Gwynne, supposed that the prisoner must be acquitted.

It appeared there had been a quarrel between Pagulta and Cooelta, who was stabbed in the side and later died from the wound. Pagulta, in depositions, said that he intended to wound Cooelta rather than kill him. Information from the arresting police trooper said that Pagulta's attack was in response to Cooelta beating his lubra.

The difficulty was that the court could not communicate with Pagulta, and without that the trial would be 'mere mummery,' which His Honour had no desire to participate in. The crown solicitor stated that the case might stand over to the next sittings, but His Honour stated that unless an application was made to let it stand over, the prisoner must be arraigned and discharged. The crown solicitor stated that Pagulta had been in gaol for three months, and he would now enter a *nolle prosequi*, as it was hardly worth swearing in a jury. Pagulta was arraigned and a plea of not guilty was entered for him. The crown solicitor tendered no evidence, so Pagulta was acquitted.

Date	Victim	Accused
February 1867	**Samuel Stubbs**	**Tommy Dutton**
Cause of death:	Stab wound (with a kangaroo bone)	
Outcome:	Discharged	
Location:	Anlaby, near Kapunda	

Five-year-old Samuel Stubbs was the son of Samuel and Marian Stubbs. They were an Aboriginal family who, in February 1867, lived around the Anlaby area near Kapunda. Sometime that month another Aboriginal boy called Tommy Dutton called Samuel into the woolshed at Anlaby and struck him on the head with a waddy. Dutton also pierced Samuel's hip joint with a kangaroo bone. Samuel did not die until two days after Easter, and had in the interim travelled over a considerable portion of the country.

Anlaby Station, approximately 1860.
State Library of South Australia, B 9948

On Monday 20 May 1867, Tommy Dutton was placed in the dock at the Police Court at Kapunda, charged with murdering Samuel Stubbs. Police Corporal O'Brien asked for a remand for the production of evidence, which was granted.

On Wednesday 22 May, Dutton appeared in court again. Evidence was taken from Wirrimee, an Aboriginal medicine man. Wirrimee, through an interpreter, stated that he had seen Stubbs prior to his death, which he attributed to the wound in the joint of the hip, causing inflammation, which had gone up into the stomach. The bench considered the evidence was not sufficient to justify them in committing the prisoner, who was subsequently discharged.

Date	Victim	Accused
5 June 1867	**Brown child**	**Margaret Brown**
Cause of death:	Haemorrhage	
Outcome:	Found not guilty	
Location:	Chatham Street, Adelaide	

Jane Hughes lived in a house in Chatham Street, Adelaide. In early May 1867, 27-year-old Margaret Brown arrived and stayed with her. After a few weeks, Hughes was told by some of her neighbours that Brown was pregnant. Hughes didn't believe them, but when she asked Brown she replied that 'time would tell'.

On Wednesday 5 June, Brown did not eat her breakfast and went into the yard to the privy where she stayed for about 20 minutes. After she had left, Hughes entered the privy and saw that the floor was covered with blood. Hughes called Brown back in and asked her what was wrong. Brown said that she had had a miscarriage and that she put the child in the privy.

At around 10.20 am, Corporal Sullivan arrived at the house, and saw Brown sitting on the kitchen floor. She was dressed and there was some blood on the floor. Sullivan then went into the privy and saw the blood on the floor there. He returned to the kitchen and arrested Margaret for concealing the birth of her child.

Sergeant Everdell attended the house and with the assistance of a night watchman, they removed the floor of the closet and recovered the body of a child, which was wrapped up and taken to the hospital. Dr Corbin examined the child and found that it had breathed, but that the lungs were not fully inflated. Corbin thought that haemorrhage from the umbilical cord might have been the cause of death.

On Thursday 6 June, an inquest was held at the Adelaide Hospital. The coroner remarked that he would be glad if the prisoner could have been present to ask some questions, but they all knew that she had just given birth the day before and was unable to attend, and the inquest must proceed in order that the child might be buried. At the conclusion of the inquest, the jury returned with a verdict of manslaughter against Brown.

On Tuesday 2 July, Brown appeared before the Police Court in Adelaide where she was charged with killing her newborn child. She was committed for trial in the Supreme Court, where she appeared on Friday 16 August, charged with the murder of her newborn child. At the conclusion of the trial, the jury, after a short retirement, returned a not guilty verdict. Brown was discharged.

Date	*Victim*	*Accused*
22 September 1867	**Eliza Goodridge**	**John Goodridge**
Cause of death:	Razor wounds	
Outcome:	Found guilty of murder, sentenced to death	
	Commuted to life imprisonment	
Location:	Evelyn Street, Mount Gambier	

On Sunday 22 September 1867, John and Eliza Goodridge were in their house at Evelyn Street with their children. John had been writing, and one of his children had either torn or displaced his papers. John struck the child on the head with a pair of shears, and Eliza chastised him. John stood up and approached Eliza with a knife in his hand. Eliza told one of her children to go to Dr Peel and tell him to come at once. After the child had left the house, John sent another child to her bedroom. John approached Eliza and stabbed her three times in the back and side. Eliza managed to get out of the house, but fearing for the safety of her children who were still inside the house, she went back in. John grabbed her head and drew a razor across her neck. Other people nearby heard crying and went into the house where they apprehended John and gave assistance to Eliza.

Eliza's injuries appeared severe and Dr Wehl, JP, attended to take her dying depositions, but as she seemed to be improving, it was not thought necessary to take them. Eliza stated that John had been intending to murder her for months, and that he had frequently threatened to do so. Eliza had recently found the knife that he stabbed her with under his pillow. Eliza's condition deteriorated and she died from her injuries the following Wednesday. At the coroner's inquest the following day, the jury, after 12 minutes, returned a unanimous verdict of wilful murder against John Goodridge, who was committed to trial.

On 8 November, John Goodridge appeared before the Mount Gambier Circuit Court where he was found guilty of the murder and sentenced to death. On Saturday 23 November, it was reported that 'the Executive had resolved to commute the sentence of death passed upon the murderer Goodridge onto one of imprisonment for life'.

An 1868 view north along Bay Rodd, Mount Gambier, the buildings on the left side of the road, are the Police Station, Church of England, Post Office and Methodist Church.
State Library of South Australia, B 36218

229

Date	*Victim*	*Accused*
13 October 1867	**Stephens child**	**Mary Stephens/Stevens**
Cause of death:	Suffocation	
Outcome:	Found guilty of manslaughter	
	Sentenced to nine months imprisonment	
Location:	Willunga	

In October 1867, Daniel and Mary Stephens (also spelt Stevens), who had been married for about five months, lived in Willunga. On 13 October, Mary, who was 32 years old, felt unwell and stayed in her bed. Mary sent for Catherine Hewettson, who lived nearby, to look after her. Hewettson attended and gave Mary some castor oil before leaving. Hewettson returned about an hour later and saw that Mary was still in her bed. Hewettson asked Stephens if she was in labour, which she denied. Hewettson looked around the room and noticed the body of a child in the chamber utensil.

Dr Mackintosh and the police were advised and attended at the Stephens' house. Dr Mackintosh spoke to Stephens about the child and she told him that the child was better off dead. Mackintosh later made a post-mortem examination of the child and found the cause of death to be suffocation.

A group of men in 1880, outside an early stone and timber house with a thatched roof which was the original 'Bush Inn' at Willunga.
State Library of South Australia, B 55417/74.

On Monday 21 October 1867, an inquest was held at the Bush Inn, Willunga, on the body of the newborn child. At the completion of the evidence, the jury returned a verdict of wilful murder against Stephens.

On 3 December, Stephens appeared before the Supreme Court on a charge of killing and murdering her newborn son. Stephens entered a plea of not guilty. The crown solicitor opened the case, but Stephens was undefended. At the request of His Honour, Mr Mundey and Mr Way watched the case on her behalf.

The judge summed up the evidence and told the jury that in order to find Stephens guilty of murder, they must be satisfied that the child was born alive, that the mother killed it, and that she did so with malice. If they found that she wilfully neglected the proper precautions that ought to have been taken with the child, they could convict her of manslaughter. The third possible verdict was concealment of birth. The jury, after an absence of an hour and a half, returned with a verdict of manslaughter, but recommended mercy on the ground of surrounding circumstances. His Honour commented on the enormity of the offence with which she had been charged, and said the jury had very wisely convicted her of the lesser crime, which was however, a most serious offence. Stephens was sentenced to nine months imprisonment.

Date	*Victim*	*Accused*
13 November 1867	Peter Franklin	Poolunta Yaria (Warrikimbo Reuben), Billybung (Billabong) and two unknown others

Cause of death:	Strangulation
Outcome:	Poolunta Yaria acquitted
	Billybung not charged
	Two unknown others not located
Location:	Beltana

On 13 November 1867, Peter Franklin, an Aboriginal man from Port Lincoln, was in the employment of Mr Frew at Moolooloo. Frew sent Franklin to look for a stray horse at Beltana. Franklin camped for the night with some other Aboriginal people at Beltana Creek, but was never seen alive again. Frew became concerned when Franklin had not returned to the station, so

he searched the area for 10 days, to no avail. Frew had some other Aboriginal people from Port Lincoln in his employment, including Frankin's brother, so he sent two of them to Beltana to look for him. When they arrived in Beltana, Peter's brother spoke to one of the local Aboriginal people, and as a result he was taken to the spot where Franklin was buried.

Police Trooper Gregory received information about Franklin's murder and travelled to Beltana and then to Mundowdna, where he located and arrested Billybung.

H.C. Swan, stipendiary magistrate (foreground) stipendiary magistrate, Besley, Bryan Charles, Police Inspector (extreme right) pictured in Northern Territory, 1880.
State Library of South Australia, B 11660

An inquest was later held before Mr H Swan. Four men were implicated, three from Stuart's Creek and one from the Warrakimbo tribe. Evidence was given that when Franklin was watering his horse at a well, the four men, including Billybung, approached him. One of the four took Franklin's horse and led him to a creek. Franklin followed with the other three and when they reached a secluded place, Billybung struck Peter with a heavy stone, and the others attacked him, during which Franklin was strangled. The body was hidden in a clump of trees and was partly covered with earth. Great credit was given to Police Trooper Gregory for the prompt manner in which he arrested the ringleader Billybung at Mundowdna, which was about a hundred miles north of Beltana.

On 22 August 1868, 26-year-old Poolunta Yaria (Warrikimbo Reuben), who was also implicated, was arrested at Mount James for Franklin's murder and also the murder of James Wade (see 5 August 1868). When arrested, Poolunta Yaria said that he knew why he was arrested, and that he was very sorry to have killed Franklin, as he was a countryman of his from Port Lincoln. He said that Billybung made him kill Franklin and that Warrikimbo Tommy tried to stop Billybung from killing him, but Billybung threatened to kill Warrikimbo Tommy if he interfered. Poolunta Yaria was committed for trial at the Supreme Court.

On Friday 27 November, Poolunta Yaria appeared before the Supreme Court in Adelaide charged with the murders of Peter Franklin and James Wade. Poolunta Yaria was the only one of the original four accused implicated in Franklin's murder. At the completion of the trial, Poolunta Yaria was acquitted.

Date	Victim	Accused
7 December 1867	Female child	Unknown
Cause of death:	Unknown	
Outcome:	Unsolved	
Location:	Athelstone	

On Tuesday 10 December 1867, James Hersey was walking in Athelstone when he found the body of a newborn female child wrapped in a calico petticoat, lying in the dry bed of the Fifth Creek. The road to the creek was a public road and the body was lying about eight feet from the usual wheel tracks. It had not been buried, but a few stones and some sand had been placed over it. No traces of any person having been near the creek had been found, and Hersey had not seen any unknown females in the village during the days before the discovery.

An inquest was held the following day at the Reservoir Hotel. Dr Benson of Kensington had made a post-mortem examination, but was unable to give a cause of death. He stated that due to the decomposition, he was unable to find any bruises. He thought that the child had been there for about three or four days. The jury, after a short deliberation, believing the infant to have been born alive, returned a verdict of wilful murder against some person or persons unknown.

Date	*Victim*	*Accused*
20 January 1868	**Pope child**	**Catherine Pope**
Cause of death:	Haemorrhage	
Outcome:	Found guilty of manslaughter	
	Sentenced to 12 months imprisonment	
Location:	Evanston	

On 20 January 1868, 25-year-old Catherine Pope, who was a servant to Mr Turner, SM, at Gawler, gave birth to a son. The following day, Jane Willman, who was a friend of Pope's, went into her room where she saw a pair of scissors wrapped in a tablecloth with bloodstains on it lying on top of a box. Willman thought nothing more of it. Later that day, Pope took the box from the room and asked John Shirer, a coach driver, to drive her with the box to an address. When they arrived, Pope told Shirer to take the box to an address she gave him in Adelaide. Shirer forgot to do so and took the box home. Shirer later opened the box and discovered the body of a child. Shirer advised the police and Corporal Birrell, who was stationed at Gawler, located and arrested Pope on a charge of concealing the birth of a child.

At a later coronial inquest, Pope was found guilty of murder and committed to the Supreme Court. On Wednesday 19 February, Pope appeared before the Supreme Court on a charge of feloniously killing and murdering her illegitimate newborn son. Pope was undefended. Jane Willman gave evidence on what she had seen in Pope's bedroom, and Dr Popham gave evidence of a post-mortem he had conducted. Dr Popham stated that the child was fully formed and had lived an external existence from the mother. The lungs were fully inflated and all of the organs were healthy. He had no doubt that the child had died from a loss of blood due to the umbilical cord not being tied.

His Honour summed up and told the jury that they must be decide that the neglect of Pope was wilful, in which case she was guilty of murder. If the neglect was not wilful, but nevertheless very culpable, she would be guilty of manslaughter. If they should not find either of these verdicts, they could bring in a third finding of concealment of birth. The jury found Pope guilty of manslaughter, and she was sentenced to 12 months imprisonment.

Date	Victim	Accused
30 January 1868	Jinny (Buckatoo)	Jacky (Tilty)
Cause of death:	Assault (with a yamstick)	
Outcome:	Acquitted	
Location:	Bimbowrie, near Olary	

On 30 January 1868, a group of Aboriginal people were staying at Boolkamatoo, near Olary. Among the group were Punch, Jacob, Tommy, Jacky (a 22-year-old also known as Tilty), and Jinny (Buckatoo), who was Jacky's lubra. Jinny ran away from Jacky and went to Bimbowrie, which was about four miles away. Jacky, in company with Punch, Jacob and Tommy, followed Jinny's tracks and found her in a wurley. When they arrived Jacky hit Jinny twice on the head with a yamstick. Jinny fell down and the next morning complained of a headache. By dinner, her condition had worsened. Jinny died the next morning and was wrapped in a blanket and buried.

Police Trooper O'Mahoney, acting on information he had received, found and exhumed Jinny's grave, finding her body wrapped in a blanket and wallaby skins. She had three wounds on the head, one on each side and one on the top of her head, which had penetrated to the brain. O'Mahoney thought that the wound on top of Jinny's head looked like a spear wound. He subsequently arrested Jacky, who said that he did not kill Jinny, saying she had died from 'some' disease.

On Wednesday 20 May 1868, Jacky appeared before the Supreme Court in Adelaide, charged with Jinny's murder. Mr Stow defended Jacky, who pleaded not guilty. After hearing the evidence, Mr Stow, in an address to the jury on behalf of Jacky, pointed out that it had been shown that only two wounds had been inflicted by Jacky, and that when the body was exhumed there were three wounds discovered on the head. His Honour, in summing up, told the jury that in his opinion there was no direct evidence to connect the prisoner with Jinny's murder. The jury, without retiring, found Jacky not guilty.

Date	*Victim*	*Accused*
5 August 1868	**James Wade/ Wald**	**Poolunta Yaria**
		(Warrikimbo Reuben)
Cause of death:	Assault (with a waddy)	
Outcome:	Acquitted of murder	
	Later found guilty of theft	
	Sentenced to one years imprisonment with hard labour	
Location:	Nilpena station, near Beltana	

On 5 August 1868, James Wade (also spelt Wald) left the Edeowie Public House, taking several bottles of alcohol with him. While Wade was walking on the road, he met an Aboriginal man called Poolunta Yaria (Warrikimbo Reuben). Wade asked him his name, and hearing the reply, Wade said, 'The police are looking for you, I'll take you to Port Augusta'. Poolunta Yaria then struck Wade with his waddy and killed him.

After a short time, Wade's body was found in the far north, at Nilpena Station. Mr H Swan, SM, held an inquest. About the time of the discovery of the body, Poolunta Yaria arrived at an Aboriginal camp at Beltana, where he told a young Aboriginal boy that he had killed a white man and covered him with his blanket. He also said that he had stolen his alcohol, which he had hidden. That information was conveyed to the inquest and after all the evidence was heard, the jury returned a verdict of wilful murder against Poolunta Yaria, who was still at large.

Around 22 August, Poolunta Yaria was apprehended by Police Troopers Gregory and Porter at Mount James for the murders of Wade and Peter Franklin (see 13 November 1867). On 1 September, Poolunta Yaria was committed to the Supreme Court on two charges of murder. Police Trooper Curnow conveyed him to Adelaide.

On Friday 27 November, Poolunta Yaria appeared before the Supreme Court charged with two murders. At the conclusion of the trial he was acquitted.

On Thursday 1 December, Poolunta Yaria appeared before the police courts in Adelaide charged on the information of Sergeant Major Saunders, who alleged that on 5 August, Poolunta Yaria, armed with a waddy, stole a pocket book and money from James Wade. At the conclusion of the trial, Poolunta Yaria was found guilty and sentenced to imprisonment with hard labour for one year.

Date	*Victim*	*Accused*
3 November 1868	**Demschke child**	**Mary Demschke**
Cause of death:	Assault/ neglect	
Outcome:	Found guilty of concealment of birth	
	Sentenced to six months imprisonment	
Location:	St Kitts (near Truro)	

In November 1868, 18-year-old Mary Demschke was in the service of the Steinert family at St Kitts. Demschke had been in their service for about six weeks. Caroline Steinert had asked her several times if she was pregnant, but Demschke always denied it. Demschke said that she was unwell on Monday evening, and went to bed early. On the morning of 3 November, Steinert noticed Demschke's appearance had changed, so when she went out to work in the field, Steinert searched her bedroom where she found several marks. Steinert and her husband both examined the bedroom as they both thought that Demschke had given birth. During the search they noticed some ashes on a shovel, and in the ash-pit they located a bag with the body of a female child in it. The police were called and Demschke was arrested.

Truro, approximately 1880.
State Library of South Australia, B 70616

On 6 November 1868, an inquest was held at the Crown Inn at Truro. Dr Ayliffe of Angaston conducted a post-mortem and stated that he believed that the child had been born alive, and gave a cause of death as a combination of an injury to the head, loss of blood and exposure to the cold. The jury retired and returned a verdict of guilty of manslaughter.

Demschke appeared before the Supreme Court on Tuesday 1 December, charged with feloniously killing and slaying her child. At the conclusion of the trial, the jury returned and found her guilty of concealing the birth of her child. His Honour addressed Demschke, saying that he hoped she would never be placed in her present position again, and sentenced her to be imprisoned for six months.

Date	*Victim*	*Accused*
5 December 1868	**Frederick Jackson**	**George Tyrrell**
Cause of death:	Assault	
Outcome:	Acquitted	
Location:	Adelaide	

William Simpson was an assistant in the publishing department of the *Advertiser*. On the afternoon of Wednesday 2 December 1868, Simpson was in the office when he heard a noise amongst four or five of the boys, including Frederick Jackson and George Tyrrell, who were employed as express runners. From his office, he told them to be quiet, before approaching the group and again telling them to be quiet. The boys ran away with the exception of Jackson and another boy called Shaw. Jackson, who was seven years old, started laughing and asked if he could remain in the office, but Simpson refused, and took him by the shoulder and led him out. As he let go of him, George Tyrell tried to get hold of Jackson, saying, 'Ah, did you do it?' Tyrell ran after Jackson, to frighten him, and playfully lifted his foot to kick him. At the same time, Jackson turned around, receiving the kick in the stomach. Jackson cried a little at the time, but continued to play for the rest of the day. Later, when Jackson was home, he became ill. As his condition worsened over two days, his mother called for a doctor.

On Saturday morning, Dr Frederick Spicer attended the Jackson house in Wright Street. Dr Spicer examined Jackson and found him to be cold and clammy and in a collapsed state. Spicer considered him to be dying and administered brandy as a stimulant. Later that day, Jackson died from his injuries.

On Monday 7 December, an inquest was held at the Rose Inn, Sturt Street.

The coroner, before taking evidence, informed Tyrell that if he had no counsel to appear for him, he might examine and cross-examine any witnesses called upon to give evidence.

Advertiser *buildings, approximately 1870, King William Street, Adelaide.*
State Library of South Australia, B 71005/16.

Dr Spicer advised the coroner that he did not know the cause of death, as he had not made a post-mortem examination because he had not been instructed to do so. The inquest was then adjourned to enable Dr Spicer to conduct a post-mortem. After the post-mortem, the inquest resumed. Dr Spicer stated that on opening the cavity of the abdomen he found the 'peritoneum one mass of inflammation'. He testified that a sudden cold or external violence might have been the cause, and that it might have been caused by a kick in the abdomen.

After all the evidence had been heard, the coroner informed the jury that if they thought that Tyrell had kicked Jackson with the intent to hurt him they would have to return a verdict of murder, but if they thought it had been done in order to frighten him, they must bring in a verdict of manslaughter. After retiring for 45 minutes, the jury returned a verdict of manslaughter against Tyrell.

On Thursday 11 February, Tyrell appeared before the Supreme Court charged with manslaughter. At the completion of the trial, the jury acquitted him.

Date	*Victim*	*Accused*
24 December 1868	Whycanning (Betsy)	Bookmark Jack
Cause of death:	Assault (with a waddy)	
Outcome:	Found guilty of manslaughter	
	Sentenced to life imprisonment with hard labour	
Location:	Weston's Flat, near Blanchetown	

On 24 December 1868, Bookmark Jack, a 30-year-old Aboriginal man, was with other Aboriginal people at Weston's Flat, near the North West Bend. Bookmark Jack, along with others, was drinking and 'in a glorious state of drunkenness, bordering on madness'. During the evening Bookmark Jack hit Whycanning (Betsy), his lubra, on her head and ribs with a waddy. Whycanning died from her injuries during the night. In the morning, when sober, Bookmark Jack saw what he had done and buried Whycanning, without making any noise, between the graves of two other Aboriginal people. The police were advised of the matter, and Bookmark Jack was apprehended. On Monday 4 January 1869, Police Trooper Hewens and Bookmark Jack left Blanchetown for Adelaide.

On Friday 12 February, Bookmark Jack appeared before the Supreme Court, charged with feloniously and wilfully killing and murdering Whycanning. William Smith, of the North West Bend, stated that on 24 December he was at Weston's Flat and during the evening he went to the camp of some Aboriginal people, one of them being Bookmark Jack. Whilst there he saw Bookmark Jack strike a woman named Whycanning across the right shoulder with a stick. The blow was given with so much force that he heard something crack. Bookmark Jack followed up the blow with other strikes across her body until she fell to the ground. He then kicked her several times in a 'very dangerous place' and dragged her about five yards by the hair, then put a blanket over her. Smith said that Whycanning was Bookmark Jack's wife.

Evidence was also given which revealed that prior to the assault, Whycanning complained to others about being unwell. Mr Stow, for the defence, stated that there was no case to answer as the evidence merely went to prove that Whycanning was ill on 24 December, and that she had received some blows from Bookmark Jack that evening and had since died. The cause of death could not be shown. His Honour disagreed and addressed the jury, pointing out the difference between murder and manslaughter, and intimating that in his opinion Bookmark Jack was guilty of manslaughter. The jury retired and after some consideration found Bookmark Jack guilty of manslaughter.

On Thursday 18 February, Bookmark Jack appeared before the Supreme Court where he was sentenced to life imprisonment with hard labour.

Three years later, on Thursday 13 July 1871, Bookmark Jack died in the Dry Creek Labour Prison. An inquest was held and it was determined that he died from disease of the lungs.

Date	*Victim*	*Accused*
5 January 1869	**Bottrill child**	**Elizabeth Bottrill**
Cause of death:	Haemorrhage/ blood loss	
Outcome:	Acquitted	
Location:	Kangarilla	

Between nine and ten pm on the night of Tuesday 5 January 1869, George Mutton, a farmer of Kangarilla, was going from his house to Mrs Sarah Hancock's property, when he saw Elizabeth Bottrill in a paddock belonging to her family. Bottrill said to him, 'Oh George, what people have been saying has come true'. Mutton took this to mean that Bottrill had given birth. Bottrill then asked him for a favour. Mutton said that he would do anything for her, after which Bottrill asked him to bury the child. Mutton went to Bottril and saw a bag on the ground, which contained the body of a male child. Mutton buried the child and then went to Mrs Hancock's, who he told what had just happened. They both returned to the paddock where Mutton had buried the child and retrieved it. Hancock opened the bag and saw that the child had a string tied around his neck.

Bottrill later appeared before a coroner's inquest where she was committed to take trial at the Supreme Court. On Friday 12 February, Bottrill appeared before the Supreme Court, charged with taking the life of her illegitimate infant child.

Dr Maurau stated that he had examined Bottrill and was certain that she had given birth. He conducted a post-mortem, where he found an indentation around the neck, which could have been caused by a piece of tape. He stated that the body was drained of nearly all blood, a result of the umbilical cord having been cut with a sharp instrument and not having been tied. Dr Maurau stated that the child had an external existence from his mother and was satisfied that it had died from loss of blood, and not strangulation. He also stated that some women were sometimes frantic, and even out of their minds, when giving birth to children.

Mr Way, for the defence, stated that no case had been made, as Dr Maurau had proved that the child died from haemorrhage and not strangulation, and the jury could not convict her in consequence of her ignorance. After a brief retirement, the jury acquitted Bottrill.

Date	Victim	Accused
13 June 1869	Mount Remarkable Tommy	Jimmy Yates and Bullocky Tommy
Cause of death:	Assault (with a waddy and tomahawk)	
Outcome:	Found not guilty	
Location:	Coonatto, Willochra Creek	

On 13 June 1869, Bullocky Tommy, who was 30, Jimmy Yates and Mount Remarkable Tommy were at Coonatto, at Willochra Creek. Jimmy Yates and Bullocky Tommy went to see Mount Remarkable Tommy in his hut. The three started arguing when Mount Remarkable Tommy asked Bullocky Tommy how Mount Brown Mary was. Mount Brown Mary was Bullocky Tommy's sister, and Mount Remarkable Tommy told him that he had slept with her. Bullocky Tommy struck Mount Remarkable Tommy with a tomahawk, breaking his wrist and collarbone and inflicting a number of severe flesh wounds upon other parts of the body. Jimmy Yates also struck Mount Remarkable Tommy.

Dr Charles Davis went to the camp where he found Mount Remarkable Tommy with several injuries, including a broken arm, a broken collarbone and a wound to the abdomen. Dr Davies thought that he would not recover from the abdomen wound. Mount Remarkable Tommy died from his injuries the next day.

On Monday 5 July 1869, an inquest was held. At the completion of the inquest, a verdict of manslaughter was given against Jimmy Yates and Bullocky Tommy, and apprehension warrants were issued for their arrest.

On 29 July, Bullocky Tommy, who had been arrested, was committed to trial for brutally beating to death Mount Remarkable Tommy. Jimmy Yates, who had been implicated in the affair, had been induced to turn Queen's evidence in order to clear himself.

On Friday 20 August, Bullocky Tommy appeared before the Supreme Court charged with feloniously killing and slaying Mount Remarkable Tommy at Willochra Creek. Jimmy Yates gave evidence against Bullocky Tommy. At the conclusion of the trial, the jury, after a brief consultation, found Bullocky Tommy not guilty.

Date	*Victim*	*Accused*
28 September 1869	**Scott child**	**Sarah Scott**
Cause of death:	Asphyxiation	
Outcome:	Discharged	
Location:	Mount Gambier	

In September 1869, Sarah Scott, who had been married for about three weeks, lived with her husband at Mount Gambier. Ann Learney lived next door to the Scotts. On Sunday 26 September, Sarah Scott went to Learney's house and asked to be let in. Scott said that she was in a very bad way and that she was in labour and about to have a child. Scott said that she did not want her husband to know about it and asked Learney if she could send for her sister. Learney asked if her husband was the father, and Scott said that the father was James O'Brien. Scott's condition worsened, so Learney went next door and told her husband. In the early hours of Monday 27 September, Scott gave birth to a boy. After the child was born, Scott made some comments about killing him.

The Farmer's Inn, Mount Gambier (later the Federal Hotel) 1860.
State Library of South Australia, B 38080

Scott told a neighbour called Mrs Baker that she didn't want the child, and that she refused to feed him. Scott offered the child to Baker and told her she would pay her if she kept it. Baker looked after the child in her house, but later visited Scott and left the child with her. Baker returned to the Scott's house later that day and saw Scott crying and saying said that her child was dead.

On Wednesday 29 September 1869, an inquest was held in the Farmer's Inn, Mount Gambier. The jury proceeded to the Scott's residence, and viewed the body of the infant. Scott, acting under the advice of her legal adviser, gave no evidence.

Dr James Jackson testified that he examined the child just after he was born, and had found him to be a strong and fully grown healthy child. He later performed a post-mortem on the baby and found extreme lividity around the neck and ears, which was unusual. He could find no wound or external injury and stated that the death was not natural and that the child had died from asphyxia. At the conclusion of the inquest, the jury found Scott guilty of wilful murder, after which she was taken into custody.

On Thursday 14 October, Scott appeared before the Circuit Court, Mount Gambier, charged with committing infanticide. At the conclusion of the trial, the jury retired but were unable to reach a decision. Scott was discharged.

Date	*Victim*	*Accused*
5 February 1870	**Yaltilta (Google Eye)**	**Bambenia (Ingelta)**
Cause of death:	Spear wound	
Outcome:	Found guilty of manslaughter	
	Sentenced to two years imprisonment with hard labour	
Location:	Bramfield, near Elliston	

On 5 February 1870, at Bramfield, Yaltilta, who was also known as Google Eye, and Teltilta told a woman named Polly to return to her rightful husband. Yaltilta was using a waddy to ensure that Polly did as she was told. Around the same time, an Aboriginal man named Bambenia, also known as Ingelta, who had eloped with Polly, snuck behind Yaltilta, and when he was about seven paces from him, speared him through the back. Yaltilta died the following Monday afternoon.

When hearing details of the murder, Sergeant Bentley, who was in charge of the Port Lincoln district, started off immediately with a local tracker.

Bambenia was apprehended near Gum Flat Station. It was reported in the newspaper at the time that:

> Perhaps it may not be out of place to remark that the unfortunate Google Eye might have been alive this day but for the mistaken leniency towards the blacks by the powers that be, as some years ago the same Bambenia stood his trial in Adelaide for the murder of Chuddahead*, alias Josey, at Mount Wedge. He makes boast that on that occasion of his killing Chuddahead he was let go, and presented with a new blanket and tomahawk, and looks forward with confidence to the same treatment on this occasion.

Gum Flat Station, 1870. State Library of South Australia, B 4956

On Friday 25 February, Bambenia appeared before the Supreme Court. Evidence was given that Bambenia was protecting his wife, who was being hit with a waddy on her back. At the conclusion of the trial, the jury found that Bambenia was guilty of manslaughter. He was sentenced to two years imprisonment with hard labour.

Author's note: Apart from this reference to the murder of Chuddahead, no other record could be found.

Date	*Victim*	*Accused*
5 March 1870	Lionel Edwards	William Sedgley and James Dunn

Cause of death:	Assault (with a stone)
Outcome:	Sedgley found guilty of manslaughter
	Sentenced to 12 months imprisonment
	Dunn acquitted
Location:	Auburn

On Saturday 5 March 1870, Lionel Edwards, a resident of Rhynie, attended a sale at Auburn. While he was there he went to Mr Jacka's eating-house to obtain some refreshment. While at the eating-house, an argument arose between Edwards, 29-year-old William Sedgley and 22-year-old James Dunn, regarding the merits of a racehorse named Creeping Jenny. Sedgley said he would draw a cheque and stake it against Edwards' money to run Creeping Jenny against any horse in the district. Edwards said, 'your cheque might be like mine', which Sedgley took offence to. A brawl broke out, during which Edwards was struck on the forehead with a stone. This injury brought on inflammation of the brain, which ultimately caused Edwards' death.

At the subsequent inquest, both Sedgley and Dunn were found guilty of manslaughter. A few days later, 43 vehicles and 93 horsemen attended the funeral of Lionel Edwards, as he was well respected in the neighbourhood.

Dunn appeared before the Supreme Court on Friday 20 May where he entered a plea of not guilty. The crown solicitor stated that the Crown did not offer any evidence against him, and as a result Dunn was acquitted and discharged.

On the same day Sedgley also appeared, charged with feloniously and with malice aforethought killing and murdering Lionel Edwards. At the conclusion of the trial, the jury retired and returned with a verdict of manslaughter, with a recommendation to mercy. Sedgley was sentenced to 12 months imprisonment without hard labour.

Date	Victim	Accused
21 March 1870	Mary Legge	William Legge
Cause of death:	Knife wound	
Outcome:	Found guilty of manslaughter	
	Sentenced to 10 years imprisonment with hard labour	
Location:	Hindley Street, Adelaide	

William and Mary Legge lived in Hindley Street, Adelaide. On Sunday 21 March 1870, William, who was 29 years old, had been out drinking all day and arrived home drunk. Shortly after, Mary returned home, also drunk. William told Mary to go to bed, but she refused to do so. The pair quarrelled, and William told Mary that if she did not go to bed, he would 'put an end' to her, but Mary still refused to go to bed. William went into a back room and took a table knife out of a drawer. As he returned to the room he said, 'I'll do you for now'. William caught Mary by the hair and stabbed her two or three times in the neck. Mr Roskelley witnessed the attack, and went to Mary's aid when she fell to the ground. William turned to Roskelley and said that he would stab him if he tried to help. Mary cried out, and then died. William threw the knife down and headed for the door, but he was prevented from leaving. The police and Dr Carey were sent for and William was taken into custody.

Hindley Street, approximately 1870, looking west from a point opposite Gilbert Place, on a wet day. On the left, a large model of an emu stands above the verandah of 'Emu House'. State Library of South Australia, B 1934

An inquest was held on Monday 21 March in the Phoenix Hotel, Hindley Street. At the conclusion of the inquest, the jury found that William was guilty of wilful murder.

On Tuesday 17 May, William appeared before the Supreme Court charged with the murder of his wife. The judge, in summing up, stated that there was a question of whether the prisoner knew he was doing wrong with the knife. The jury had been asked to believe that he was moved to the act by sudden provocation. His Honour stated that William and Mary went out together and that on their return she began using bad language towards him. William asked her to go to bed, and the language she used was of the 'most offensive and provoking character, and would have an irritating effect on any man'. The jury had to decide if the 'provocation' of refusing to go to bed, as well as the bad language used by Mary would justify the stabbing, and therefore reduce the charge from murder to manslaughter. His Honour also stated that it had been held that no language, even if it were of the most opprobrious and disgusting character, would justify the use of a deadly weapon. The jury retired to consider their verdict, and after 15 minutes returned and found William guilty of manslaughter. William was sentenced to 10 years imprisonment with hard labour.

Date	*Victim*	*Accused*
28 April 1870	**Alexander Barre**	**William Pomroy**
	(French Alick)	
Cause of death:	Assault	
Outcome:	Found not guilty	
Location:	Moonta	

On 28 April 1870, at Moonta, a fight occurred between Alexander Barre and William Pomroy during which Barre received serious facial injuries. Dr Lloyd Herbert treated Barre, who was unable to eat food properly and suffered severe pain to the left side of his head.

Barre saw Mr N Bennett, the clerk of the court, and laid an information outlining charges against Pomroy for assault. The information was filed and the case was heard before the magistrate on 6 May.

On Saturday 21 May 1870, Jane Allen found Barre covered up with sacks in a hut. She removed the sacks and saw that Barre was dead. Allen knew Barre as French Alick, and had last seen him 10 days before. An inquest was held before Mr Wyatt and a jury of 13, with evidence given by Jane Allen, Dr Herbert and others.

Dr Herbert stated that he had examined the body and found it to be that of Alexander Barre. He recognised the body due to the injury to the left side of the face, as it was sunken in. The inquest was adjourned until the next day.

Dr Herbert made a post-mortem examination of the body with the assistance of Dr Goyer. The body was very decomposed. The two doctors found that Barre had suffered a broken cheekbone and a fractured skull. Both wounds were extensive and were found to be sufficient to cause death. Dr Herbert stated that it would not have been possible for a person to live long after receiving such a blow. At the conclusion of the evidence, the jury, after a short consultation, returned a verdict of manslaughter against Pomroy.

On Thursday 11 August 1870, Pomroy appeared before the Supreme Court. At the conclusion of the trial, Pomroy was found not guilty and was released.

Date	*Victim*	*Accused*
17 June 1870	**Dumbledon child**	**Fanny Dumbledon**
Cause of death:	Haemorrhage	
Outcome:	Discharged	
Location:	Albion Hotel, Adelaide	

In June 1870, Jane Sinnott and 18-year-old Fanny Dumbledon both lived at the Albion Hotel in Morphett Street, Adelaide, where they were employed as servants. Around six am on Friday 17 June, Sinnott heard a baby crying, and thought that it sounded like a newborn infant. The crying lasted about three or four minutes. Sinnott thought that the crying was coming from Dumbledon's room next door. Sinnott saw Dumbledon at around quarter past nine later that morning sweeping the passage. She said good morning to her and Dumbledon took hold of her arm and told Sinnott that she had had a baby, but it was dead, and asked her not to tell Mrs Lamb, as she would look after it soon. Catherine Lamb was the wife of John Lamb, the landlord of the Albion Hotel, and had previously asked Dumbledon if she was pregnant, which Dumbledon had denied.

The police arrived and Dumbledon was taken to the destitute asylum. The body was located and Jonah Witcombe, the government undertaker, removed the infant from the Albion Hotel and took it to the cemetery.

On Saturday 9 July, Dumbledon appeared before the police courts on a charge of unlawfully, feloniously and of malice aforethought killing and murdering her illegitimate newborn daughter. Dr Logan, senior house surgeon of the Adelaide Hospital, stated that he made a post-mortem examination of the child and thought that the child had died from blood loss from the umbilical cord. At the conclusion of the inquest, Dumbledon was committed for trial at the Supreme Court.

On Friday 12 August, Dumbledon appeared before the Supreme Court charged with the murder of her infant child. His Honour remarked that the evidence did not seem to justify her being put upon her trial, and on his direction she was discharged.

Date	*Victim*	*Accused*
17 June 1870	**O'Neil child**	**Susannah O'Neil**
Cause of death:	Neglect	
Outcome:	Found not guilty on the grounds of insanity	
Location:	Silverton, near Cape Jervis	

In April 1870, 25-year-old Susannah O'Neil gave birth to a child at Silverton, near Cape Jervis. Mrs Jerome attended to O'Neil when she gave birth, and for four days afterwards. The child was doing very well during that time. About seven weeks later Jerome visited O'Neil and saw that the child was in a very dirty and neglected state. Jerome pressed O'Neil to feed the child, which she only did after a good deal of urging. Jerome knew that O'Neil was the wife of a labouring man who was only receiving about eight shillings a week. They lived in a one-roomed house with their three other children. Jerome did not consider that O'Neil was a person of sound mind.

On 17 June, the child died. At a subsequent coroner's inquest, O'Neil was committed to trial. On Thursday 1 December 1870, O'Neil appeared before the Supreme Court charged with murdering her eight-week-old daughter at Silverton. She pleaded not guilty and her lawyer indicated that he would produce evidence to show that O'Neil was insane at the time of the offence.

Dr Baruh stated that he saw the body of the child and judged the cause of death to be neglect and want of proper food. Dr Baruh never saw the child alive but he knew O'Neil and considered her 'nearly an idiot, but not quite'. He believed that at the time of the inquest she was suffering from milk fever.

Talisker Mine, Silverton, 1869. State Library of South Australia, B 27347

O'Neil was never capable of taking care of children, and he believed the child suffered greatly from poverty and neglect.

His Honour told the jury there was further evidence which might be called if it would be any satisfaction to them, but it was his duty to tell them a person was not liable for their acts when they were not in a sound state of mind. The jury found O'Neil not guilty on the ground of insanity. His Honour said that O'Neil would be detained until directions for her to be taken care of in the destitute asylum were received from the executive.

Date	*Victim*	*Accused*
5 August 1870	**Edward Gasgoine**	**Theresa Clarke**
Cause of death:	Poisoned	
Outcome:	Discharged	
Location:	Kooringa	

This case has been included because of a dying declaration made by Edward Gasgoine, who believed that Theresa Clarke had poisoned him. Gasgoine died and Clarke was charged with his murder and kept in custody. It was not until forensic examination of the content of Gasgoine's stomach revealed that he was

251

not poisoned, and had died from acute peritonitis. This death has not been included in the statistics.

In August 1870, a 52-year-old bushman Edward Gasgoine, in company with Henry Lindsay, his wife Sarah Lindsay, and Theresa Clarke, also known as Mrs Brown, arrived in Burra and went to Mrs Beal's lodging-house. Clarke's alias, Mrs Brown, was said to be a prostitute well known in Adelaide. Gasgoine and Clarke had been cohabitating for a few weeks and were looking for work in the bush. Gasgoine became ill and he thought that Clarke was poisoning him. He received medical assistance but his condition worsened. As Gasgoine believed he was dying, he made a dying declaration taken on oath by Dr Dashwood, JP:

> I Edward Gasgoine, do solemnly declare that I am 52 years of age, widower, no family, came out to the colonies in the year 1852. That I am a butcher, but have been acting for several years in the capacity of shepherd. That I believe I am dying from the effects of poison administered to me by one Theresa Clarke, at 9.00 am, on Monday the 3rd day of August of the present year, given me in tea; she also gave me more poison in tea on the same day, and a larger dose on the 4th day of August during the afternoon. I cohabitated with Theresa Clarke for a few weeks in Adelaide, and she is now travelling northward in company with a man and woman called Henry Lindsay and Sarah Lindsay. I make this statement voluntarily, believing it to be the truth, so help me, God, at the hour and data as above stated.

Gasgoine later died.

On Saturday 6 August, an inquest was held at the Miners' Arms at Burra. At the request of Dr Dashwood and the police, an adjournment was ordered by the coroner to permit an analysis of the contents of the stomach and kidneys of Gasgoine. Theresa Clarke was charged with murdering Gasgoine by administering poison and was kept in custody.

On Saturday 20 August, the inquest resumed. Dr Dashwod testified that the post-mortem examination had found that the deceased died from an attack of acute peritonitis. He stated that the symptoms of peritonitis very much resembled the symptoms of arsenic poisoning. Dashwood removed the stomach and other viscera for the purpose of analysis. Mr Ey, an analytical chemist of Adelaide, had examined the stomach content and found a small portion of white powder, which he found to consist of magnesia. He found no trace of either mineral or vegetable poison.

At the completion of the evidence, the jury returned a verdict of death by natural causes. Clarke was discharged from custody and at the request of the jury an order was given to her for the purpose of receiving rations.

Date	*Victim*	*Accused*
1 October 1870	**Poolpa (Jenny)**	**Mealie (Atiltie)**
Cause of death:	Assault (with a waddy)	
Outcome:	Found guilty of manslaughter	
	Sentenced to 12 months imprisonment with hard labour	
Location:	Corunna, Port Augusta West	

On 1 October 1870, on the Corunna Run at Port Augusta West, Mealie (Atiltie) assaulted Poolpa (Jenny), his lubra. Tilgerry, who knew Mealie and Poolpa very well, witnessed the attack. Tilgerry saw Mealie throw a waddy at Poolpa after which she fell to the ground. She had a good-sized hole in her head and died three days after the attack. Tilgerry later told a police constable about the attack, and took the constable to the grave.

On Saturday 15 October at Port Augusta West, an inquest was held by Mr Burgoyne on the body of an Aboriginal woman, which had been exhumed the previous day on the Corunna Run. After taking medical evidence, the jury returned a verdict of wilful murder against Mealie and a warrant was issued for his arrest.

Police Trooper O'Shanahan arrested Mealie on 28 October on the west coast, about 200 miles from Corunna. After being cautioned, Mealie said that on the day of the murder his leg was sore and that his lubra left the wurley, and when she came back he hit her with the waddy. Mealie said that he wanted some water and when Poolpa would not bring it, he struck her.

On Friday 2 December, Mealie appeared in the Supreme Court charged with Poolpa's murder. After some discussion between the prosecutor and the judge regarding if the charge would be murder or manslaughter, the judge said:

> I don't think the case is one of murder. I thought the way I should put it was this. Suppose a white man was unwell, and feeling his wife did not

pay proper attention, but ran away, and he threw a heavy walking stick at her, which struck her and caused death. That would not be murder. If he shot her with a pistol it would. I don't know whether a waddy in the hands of a black man is equal to a gun in the hands of a white. We don't know these things.

His Honour then briefly addressed the jury, pointing out that the evidence showed what amounted to manslaughter, and if they believed the evidence, it would be their duty to find a verdict accordingly. After considering the evidence, the jury found Mealie guilty of manslaughter.

On Friday 9 December, Mealie appeared before the Supreme Court where he was sentenced to 12 months imprisonment with hard labour. During his sentencing remarks, His Honour stated that he was ' … sorry to say white men beat their wives and threw sticks at them sometimes as well as the blacks, and I do not know that the contrast was much in favour of the whites, only that they do not strike so severely.'

Date	*Victim*	*Accused*
11 October 1870	**Partington child**	**Mary Partington**
Cause of death:	Assault	
Outcome:	Found guilty of murder, sentenced to death	
	Commuted to 10 years imprisonment with hard labour	
Location:	Port Lincoln	

On 17 October 1870, Port Lincoln police received a report that a child had been wilfully murdered and buried in the sand hills adjacent to the residence of a 28-year-old widow named Mary Partington. Sergeant Bentley went to her house and told her that he had heard a rumour that she had given birth. Partington admitted that she had indeed given birth around six days earlier and that she had buried the child but could not recall the exact place. Sergeant Bentley immediately arrested Partington on suspicion of having concealed the birth of her child.

A search was undertaken in the sand hills about ten yards from Partington's house. During the search the body of a newborn child was located, buried about 18 inches below the surface. Bentley examined the child and saw that the face was bruised and deformed and the right cheekbone was broken. On examining the hut where Partington resided, he found the wall was spattered with blood. Dr Stedman examined the blood and found one of the spots to contain some human hairs. Partington was brought before an inquest on 24 October where she was committed on the charge of murder.

On Wednesday 7 December 1870, Partington appeared before the Supreme Court charged with the murder of her daughter. Evidence was given that she was a widow with seven children, and made a living by washing and nursing. Her neighbours had noticed that there was a change in her appearance and asked her if she was pregnant, which she denied, saying that she would not disgrace her family. A month or two afterwards they noticed that she was much thinner.

Port Lincoln, view showing the sweep of Boston Bay with Boston Island in the distance. In the middle ground township buildings and the jetty can be seen with the John Watherstone, *a steamer with two masts, at anchor, 1870.*
State Library of South Australia, B 4944

Dr Foster Stedman stated that he had conducted a post-mortem examination of the child. He found extensive bruises on the head and a fractured cheekbone, and deduced that the child had breathed on its own after birth. There was no decomposition on 17 October, but the body was discoloured the next day. He could confidently state that the child was born alive and was rather above the average size and weight. He believed that death was caused by effusion of blood on the brain through violence.

At the conclusion of the evidence and summing up, the jury retired.

After an hour's consideration, they returned with a verdict of wilful murder against Partington, with a strong recommendation to mercy on account of her children. Partington, when asked if she had anything to say, complained that the witnesses had not spoken of a statement she made that the child fell from her arms during her confinement. His Honour directed that a sentence of death should be recorded against Partington, intimating that he would communicate the case to the executive, with the recommendation of the jury. His Honour said that the sentence could be recorded, but he would not go through the solemn form of the law.

Partington appeared the following day before Justice Gwynne who stated that he had no authority for his abstaining from passing the sentence of death upon the prisoner, who was placed in the dock. His Honour then sentenced Partington to death. Partington's sentence was later commuted to 10 years imprisonment with hard labour.

Date	*Victim*	*Accused*
14 November 1870	**Hugh Ward**	**John Edwards**
Cause of death:	Assault (with a stick)	
Outcome:	Acquitted	
Location:	Thebarton	

Hugh and Catherine Ward lived in Thebarton with their children, including their daughter Mary, who was married to 48-year-old John Edwards. On Monday 14 November 1870, Hugh returned home from work, leaving to go into town at around six-thirty pm. He returned home at around ten pm and went to bed where he had tea and bread and butter. Hugh started 'grumbling' about three-quarters of an hour later, but no one in the house took any notice of him. After a while, Mary thought Hugh was asleep, so she blew the candle out. Mary then heard Hugh moving about the bedroom.

Catherine also heard someone moving around in the bedroom, and saw that Hugh was holding a weapon that she could not identify. Hugh started to strike anything that was in his way, including his son-in-law, John Edwards. Hugh knocked his daughter down with the weapon, but Edwards prevented him from hurting her. Edwards opened the door and let the children out. Catherine managed to leave the room, but Hugh ran after her with a pitchfork, which Mary wrenched from him. Catherine ran towards the road but fell to the ground and Hugh went to her and kicked her. With Mary's assistance, Catherine managed to get up and go to a neighbour's house where she stayed. While Mary was helping Catherine to get away from Hugh, she saw Edwards come across a paddock with a stick in his hand, and on the way to their neighbour's house, Mary heard the sound of four or five blows, which sounded as though they were being dealt by a stick.

The following day, Hugh went into the chemist owned by William Allott. Hugh complained that he was suffering pain from bruises on his arms and side. He also said that Edwards had hurt him by striking him with a rail during a quarrel. Allott told him to go to the hospital and Hugh said that he had but they refused to do anything for him until the next morning.

On Wednesday 16 November, Hugh attended the Adelaide Hospital as an outpatient, where he was seen by Frederick Logan, the senior house surgeon. Logan examined Hugh and found that his right arm was out of the joint at the shoulder and that he had multiple bruises on his body. Hugh was in a weak state and was admitted, dying later the same day. A post-mortem examination was conducted. Logan thought that the cause of death was shock to the system, caused by the violent treatment Hugh had received.

On Thursday 17 November, an inquest was held at the Adelaide Hospital. After all of the evidence had been heard, the jury, after lengthy consideration, returned with the verdict that Hugh came to his death from blows inflicted by Edwards. The coroner committed Edwards to the Supreme Court.

On Thursday 8 December, Edwards appeared in the Supreme Court charged with feloniously killing and slaying one Hugh Ward. During his summing up, the judge said, 'There is no direct evidence to show that the prisoner even struck the deceased. It is highly probable he did, and the question for the judge is not whether the jury might give a leap in the dark, a sort of guess, but whether there is reasonable evidence, and such as would justify the jury in coming to a conclusion. I really do not think there is.' The jury, having consulted, thought they would have to acquit the prisoner. A verdict of acquittal was entered and Edwards was discharged.

Date	*Victim*	*Accused*
16 November 1870	**James Jeames**	**Richard Dewdney**
Cause of death:	Undetermined	
Outcome:	Acquitted	
Location:	Streaky Bay	

On 16 November 1870, Mary Feltos saw a person she knew called James Jeames lying on the beach at Streaky Bay. Jeames was with Richard Dwedney and a person called Snell. Feltos saw Dewdney and Snell take Jeames up by the arms, carry him to a boat and throw him in. Dewdney and Snell then got in and rowed the boat out to sea, before lifting Jeames up and throwing him into the water. When he came up, Feltos could just see the top of his cap. She saw them put the oars out, and when Jeames went to catch them, they pulled them away. They repeated this, and then someone called out that they should not drown the man. They lifted him up and down in the water several times, and then pulled him into the boat. This lasted about 15 to 20 minutes.

Distant view of the Streaky Bay township, 1880; the police station is identified as being in the left-hand corner.
State Library of South Australia, PRG 280/1/2/260.

James Mudge also saw Snell and Dewdney throw Jeames into the water and saw that the water was up to Jeames' shoulders. After being dragged back into the boat, all three came ashore and Jeames walked to the police station, but no one was there. Jeames had been drinking with Dewdney and Snell and none of them were sober. Over the next two days, Jeames complained of shortness of breath. He died on 16 November.

At a subsequent coroner's inquest, Dewdney was committed to trial at the Supreme Court on a charge of murder. On Thursday 23 February 1871, Richard Dewdney appeared before the Supreme Court charged with killing and murdering James Jeames. Foster Stedman, who had carried out a post-mortem examination 10 days after Jeames had been buried, gave evidence. Stedman said that the liver was large and very much congested. He further stated that for a person suffering from liver complaint, immersion in the water for three to ten minutes would be detrimental to their health, and could accelerate death.

The defence submitted that there was no case for the jury. He argued that the death was a result of Jeames' actions, saying that he might have lived had he removed his wet clothing earlier. The jury retired and after 45 minutes returned a verdict of not guilty.

Date	*Victim*	*Accused*
26 December 1870	**Adelaide Jemmy**	**Donald McPherson**
Cause of death:	Assault (with a sharp instrument)	
Outcome:	Acquitted	
Location:	Between Penola and Naracoorte	

On Monday 26 December 1876, the Boxing Day races were held at the Gate Hotel between Naracoorte and Penola. Willcaneraman and some friends, including Adelaide Jemmy and his lubra, were at the hotel. Adelaide Jemmy was not drinking and was sober. In the evening Willcaneraman went home to sleep. The next morning, Willcaneraman looked for Adelaide Jemmy but could not find him. Willcaneraman located Adelaide Jemmy's track on the road and followed it for nearly a mile when he found Adelaide Jemmy lying dead on the ground. Willcaneraman then went back to his camp and woke up the other campers, and also told Mr Kirby.

The following day, a coronial inquest was held. Adelaide Jemmy's face and head were covered with numerous wounds indicating that a savage assault must have taken place. Evidence was heard from Willcaneraman and other witnesses, who all testified that they had seen Adelaide Jemmy and his lubra at the hotel, but no one saw or heard anything that could assist in the investigation.

Dr Wilson of Penola conducted a post-mortem examination. Wilson found that the cause of death was head injuries caused by an assault. He found that the scalp was bruised and cut, and he thought that a sharp instrument had caused the wounds.

At the conclusion of the evidence, the jury returned a verdict 'that the deceased was found dead, having come to his death from the effects of wounds on the head, inflicted by person or persons unknown.'

Mount Gambier Hospital, approximately 1870.
State Library of South Australia, B 10031

On 22 February 1871, the following appeared in the *Border Watch*:

Death at the Hospital. On Sunday morning, a man named Donald McPherson died in the Mount Gambier Hospital. He was under treatment for epileptic fits, from which he had suffered for several years. He was buried on Monday. McPherson was recently charged by the police at Penola with being concerned in the murder of the blackfellow at the Gate Hotel some months ago, but was acquitted.

Apart from this reference, no further information about the trial or the circumstances of the incident could be found.

Date	*Victim*	*Accused*
2 January 1871	**James Smith**	**Daniel O'Leary**
Cause of death:	Assault	
Outcome:	Found guilty of manslaughter	
	Sentenced to imprisonment for one month	
Location:	Drop Drop, near Mount Gambier	

On 2 January 1871, a number of races were held in Mr Frew's paddock at Drop Drop, near Mount Gambier. Amongst the spectators were Daniel O'Leary and James Smith, both of whom were drinking. They were at the racecourse nearly the whole day and Smith became very quarrelsome, seeking arguments with several people. O'Leary had quarrelled with Smith during the day and at one time they wrestled on the ground. While they were on the ground, a witness heard O'Leary say that Smith had torn his coat. The two were separated by some of the bystanders and Smith walked off with some friends. One of those friends, William Frew, endeavoured for an hour or so to prevent Smith from quarrelling with others, but after failing to do so, he left him.

Just before sundown, after the last race had finished, Smith was in company with Thomas Pressey. Just as Pressey turned away from Smith, he heard a rustling noise and turned back and saw O'Leary punch Smith in the head. No words were spoken when O'Leary hit Smith with a heavy blow, knocking him to the ground. The ground where he fell was stony, and Smith landed near or on a flat stone. O'Leary jumped on his horse after striking Smith, and rode off.

Smith was assisted by witnesses, but he was insensible and unable to speak. After being attended to for a few minutes, he was conveyed home in a cart. Dr John Baird was called to see Smith about midnight and found him to be insensible and suffering from tetanus with opisthotonus (severe spasms). His condition worsened and he later died.

On Wednesday 19 April 1871, O'Leary appeared before the Circuit Court at Mount Gambier, charged with having feloniously, wilfully and without malice aforethought, murdered James Smith. In his post-mortem examination, Dr Baird found that Smith had head injuries including a fractured left temple and a fractured middle meningeal artery. He gave the cause of death as pressure of the blood on the brain. He stated that a man's fist could not cause such a fracture, but falling on a stone could.

At the completion of the evidence, the jury retired and later returned with a verdict of manslaughter, with a recommendation for mercy on account of the peculiar circumstances of the case and O'Leary's previous good character. His Honour sentenced O'Leary to one month of imprisonment.

Date	*Victim*	*Accused*
30 April 1871	**Eliza Douglas**	**Charles Douglas**
Cause of death:	Assault	
Outcome:	Found guilty of murder, sentenced to death	
	Commuted to life imprisonment with hard labour	
Location:	Nailsworth	

On Sunday 30 April 1871, the inhabitants of the quiet village of Nailsworth on main North Road were alarmed to hear that Charles Douglas had murdered Eliza Douglas, his wife. Both Charles and Eliza were 47 years old. Charles had called a neighbour, between four and four-thirty am, telling him that his wife was dangerously ill. The neighbour entered the cottage and found Eliza on the floor with serious head wounds. Charles went into his bedroom and found his gun, seemingly with the intention of putting an end to his life. The gun was not loaded and while Charles was searching a shelf for the power and shot, a witness manage to remove the gun from him. Eliza died from her injuries about 15 minutes later. The police attended and after making some enquiries, arrested Charles for the murder. Charles declared that on coming home early in the morning he found his wife on the floor and had then roused his neighbours.

Eliza was formally the widow of the late Mr Greig, the landlord and owner of the White Hart Hotel, who left her a considerable amount of property.

On Monday 1 May, an inquest was held at the Windmill Hotel. The jury, after being sworn in, proceeded to the residence of the deceased to view the body. Charles was present at the inquest, and still seemed to be under the influence of drink. Evidence was given which indicated that Charles had been picked up by a cab in King William Street at around one-thirty on the Sunday morning and taken home. The police, after examining the house, could find no evidence of a break-in, as the windows were secure. At the conclusion of the inquest, the jury returned a verdict of manslaughter against Charles, who was committed to trial.

Windmill Hotel, Prospect, approximately 1881.
State Library of South Australia, B 8488

On Wednesday 17 May, Charles appeared before the Supreme Court charged with murder. After the evidence was presented, His Honour summed up and pointed out the time difference from when Charles arrived home to the time when he raised the alarm by going to his neighbour's house. When the neighbour did arrive, there was no light on in the house as the lamp was broken on the floor, and Charles had to ask the neighbour to get a lamp and some matches. His Honour pointed out that if there was no light in the house, then Charles could not have seen his wife on the floor, as it was too dark. The jury retired and after about 20 minutes they returned and found Charles guilty of murder, but with a recommendation for mercy. His Honour addressed Charles, telling him that he had had a fair and patient investigation, and everything that could have been suggested to show that he was not guilty of murder, but of a lesser crime, had been put before the jury, but they had found him guilty of murder. Douglas was then sentenced to death. The sentence was later commuted to life imprisonment with hard labour.

Seven years later, on 15 March 1878, at the Yatala Labour Prison, an inquest was held on the body of Charles Douglas, who died the previous day aged 54. Evidence was given from Dr Way, who had been treating Charles since 1874 as he was suffering from epilepsy and general disability. Some weeks prior to his death, symptoms of inflammation of the liver started to appear, which gradually increased until his death.

Date	Victim	Accused
9 May 1871	Little child	Elizabeth Little
Cause of death:	Assault	
Outcome:	Found not guilty and discharged	
Location:	Langhorne Creek	

Edward Hector lived with his wife and family on a vineyard at Langhorne Creek. The Hector family employed a number of servants, one of whom was 18-year-old Elizabeth (Lizzie) Little. On 9 May 1871, when Hector arrived home, his wife told him that Little was ill. Hector sent someone to go to Little's mother's house to bring her to the vineyard. Mrs Little did not come, but Little's sister arrived. Hector had suspected that Little was pregnant. Later that night, at around 10.30 pm, he went outside where he thought he heard the sound of a baby crying in the paddock. He thought that the cry might have come from a nearby wurley so he waited for a short time and listened. He heard further noises and went to get someone else. He found John Moss, and both went to listen again. They heard a weaker scream and both felt satisfied it was from the direction of the wurley, so they returned to the house. About a minute later, Moss knocked on Hector's door and said that he had found a child. They both went to a watercloset and found a newborn child, who was still alive. The found a lever and a hammer, and with the assistance of another man, managed to get the child out. Hector wrapped the child in a flannel and took it to the wurley, where a lubra washed and dried it. Hector saw some bruising on the child and a cut over the eye. The fall in the water closet was about three feet into soft soil.

Moss told Hector that he had asked Little about two weeks previously if she was pregnant, but she told him to mind his own business. Hector again called for Little's mother, who came to the vineyard and took the child from the lubra. She kept it warm and tried to feed it, but it would not eat. She had no idea that the child belonged to her daughter until she asked her about it. Little told her that Moss was the father. Mrs Little kept the child warm, but it was very weak, and later died.

On 17 May, an inquest was held at Langhorne Creek into the death of the child. Dr Hugh Ferguson made a post-mortem examination and found that the baby was fully developed. There were marks on the left side of her head and two or three small dots on the front left side. He found that the right collarbone was fractured and the skull was extensively fractured. He found the brain ruptured and a small quantity of skull had pierced it. He gave the cause of death as great violence, adding that death would have been hastened by the cold and exposure. He did not think that the injuries could have been caused by the fall in the closet, or that they could have occurred during birth. He stated that the injuries were not received by accident. The jury, after a short deliberation, returned a verdict of manslaughter.

On Tuesday 15 August, Little appeared before the Supreme Court charged with feloniously and of malice aforethought killing and murdering her infant child. At the conclusion of the trial, the jury retired and returned with a verdict of not guilty. On the announcement of the verdict, signs of approval were manifested in the body of the court, but these were promptly repressed. Little was discharged.

Date	*Victim*	*Accused*
17 May 1871	**George Chisman**	**John Ramsay (Ramjee)**
Cause of death:	Assault	
Outcome:	Found not guilty and discharged	
Location:	Gray Street, Adelaide	

On 17 May 1871, Joseph Lucas of Gray Street, Adelaide, was standing on his porch when he saw a group of boys run past, followed by 60-year-old George Chisman. Chisman was being followed by man called John Ramsay (Ramjee), a 62-year-old Lascar. Lucas saw Ramsay grab Chisman on the shoulder and punch him in the head. Both Ramsay and Chisman went around the corner, so Lucas followed them. As Lucas turned the corner, he saw Chisman lying on his back and Ramsay rising up from stooping over him. Lucas called out 'murder', pushed Ramsay away from Chisman and stood between the two. Chisman said he could not move, but Lucas raised him up. Chisman said he could not move his leg. Ramsay came up and shook his fist in Chisman's face and told him to let him go. Lucas took Chisman away to his home and called for the doctor. Chisman told Lucas that he had never seen Ramsay before and did not know what he wanted.

Dr Samuel Elison, the junior house surgeon of the Adelaide Hospital, was at the hospital when Chisman arrived. Chisman was suffering from a fracture of the neck and of the right thighbone, and a contusion of the right hip. A few days after he was attacked, traumatic delirum and diarrhoea set in, and Chisman died from exhaustion. Dr Elison thought that the injuries Chisman had received were the cause of death.

On Tuesday 6 June an inquest was held at the Adelaide Hospital. Mr W Bundey attended to watch proceedings on behalf of Ramsay. After hearing the evidence, the coroner said that if the jury believed that the death was caused by the assault made upon Chisman by Ramsay, and caused through malice, they would find a verdict of wilful murder against him. If they believed that he caused the man's death without any intention of having done so, their verdict would be that of manslaughter. The jury, in a few minutes, returned a verdict of manslaughter.

On Wednesday 16 August, John Ramsay stood trial charged with unlawfully and with malice aforethought killing and murdering George Chisman. At the conclusion of the trial, the jury found Ramsay not guilty, after which he was discharged.

Date	*Victim*	*Accused*
5 June 1871	**William Howard**	**Sarah Howard**
Cause of death:	Neglect	
Outcome:	Charge withdrawn	
Location:	Adelaide	

In 1870, 18-year-old Sarah Howard, who had been working as a prostitute for two years, became pregnant to an unknown male. In May 1871 Howard went to the Destitute Asylum to have the baby, which she named William. Three or four weeks after the birth of the child she left the asylum and went to the Norwood Refuge, but she was refused admittance because she had a baby with her. Howard took William to live with Mrs Frances Lewis in Acland Street. William became ill and Howard took him to the hospital to get some medicine. Howard was told to administer it to the child occasionally, which she did. On Monday 5 June William died.

On Wednesday 7 June, an inquest was held at the National Hotel on Pirie Street, into the death of five-week-old William Howard. Samuel Ellison, junior house surgeon of the Adelaide Hospital, gave evidence that he had made a post-mortem examination on William's body. He stated that the child was emaciated, weighing only four pounds, one ounce, and that the stomach and intestinal canal were empty. There was no fat on the body and he could not detect any disease to account for the death. He believed that the child was starved to death.

National Hotel, Pirie Street, 1870.
State Library of South Australia, B 21369

Frances Lewis stated that Howard came to live with her about four weeks prior and that she had the baby with her. Lewis stated that Howard was very attentive to William and she was certain that the child was well nourished. She did not notice much change in the child from the time they arrived at her house to when he died.

The coroner summed up and the jury, having deliberated for a short time, returned with a verdict of guilty of manslaughter, upon which the coroner committed her for trial.

On Thursday 10 August, Howard appeared before the Supreme Court, where the crown solicitor presented a certificate from the attorney-general to the effect that there was no case against the prisoner. Howard was discharged.

Date	*Victim*	*Accused*
29 June 1871	Thomas Garraway	Carl Jung
Cause of death:	Gunshot wounds	
Outcome:	Found guilty of murder, sentenced to death	
	Executed 10 November 1871	
Location:	Blackwood Flat, near Mount Gambier	

Thomas Garraway occasionally acted as an assistant bailiff at Mount Gambier. Carl Jung was a German wineseller and shoemaker who settled at Blackwood Flat, near Mount Gambier. On Wednesday 28 June 1871, Garraway arrived at Jung's home and stayed the night. Garraway had a court order for possession of Jung's property. On Thursday morning Garraway proceeded to execute his commission, and took possession of Jung's horse and cart and a number of pigs, with which he set out for Mount Gambier. Garraway was not seen alive again.

On Friday, there was fear of foul play on the account of the mysterious disappearance of Garraway. A search had been organised and Jung was questioned as to the whereabouts of Garraway. Jung assured them that Garraway had left his house the day before and that he had settled with him. Jung remained at his property until midday on Saturday, before he fled. Prior to leaving, Jung sold all of his personal effects that he could find buyers for, and told his family that they would never see him again.

Garraway was still missing, so a larger search was conducted with the aid of some local Aboriginal men, during which Garraway's body was located about 30 yards off the road. Suspicion fell on Jung and the police discovered that he had fled his house.

Jung returned to his house on Monday night for food, and the police, who suspected he would do so, apprehended him. He was taken to Mount Gambier where he made a full confession. He stated he had followed Garraway and overtook him at the Deep Gully and asked for the return of his pigs. Garraway refused so Jung shot him, firing both barrels of the gun at once.

At the inquest, Dr John Baird stated that he conducted a post-mortem examination and found that Garraway received two gunshot wounds, one in his side and the other in his head. Police Constable Driscoll stated he was present when the body was found, and that he located a silver watch and chain, a distress warrant for £8, a memorandum book and a pair of spurs on Garraway's person. Driscoll stated that he had known Garraway for about five years, as he was formerly a police constable.

The jury, after a brief deliberation, returned with a verdict of wilful murder against Carl Jung.

Mount Gambier Court House 1880. State Library of South Australia, B 21766/8

On Friday 20 October, Jung appeared before the Circuit Court in Mount Gambier where he entered a plea of not guilty for the wilful murder of Garraway. At the completion of the trial, the jury retired, and after 17 minutes returned with a verdict of wilful murder with a recommendation for mercy. The judge sentenced Jung to death by hanging, and on Friday 10 November, Jung was executed within the precincts of the Mount Gambier gaol.

Date	*Victim*	*Accused*
21 December 1871	**John Guerin**	**Ernest Boehm**
Cause of death:	Gunshot wounds	
Outcome:	Found guilty of manslaughter	
	Sentenced to two years imprisonment with hard labour	
Location:	Athelstone	

John Guerin, who was 26, and his brother, James Guerin, lived at Bulls Creek. They both worked at the new reservoir at Athelstone. Around eight pm on Thursday 21 December 1871, they were walking home from work. James, who was walking ahead of John, came to the house where Ernest and Herman Boehm lived. Herman was sitting outside, and James asked him about a knife and a pipe that he had previously left there. Herman and James quarrelled about the knife and pipe before James walked away. John caught up with James, and James told him that he had quarrelled with Herman. John went to Herman and a started to fight him, but Herman ran off, with John giving chase.

James turned and saw 48-year-old Ernest, armed with a gun, run after John and Herman. Ernest stood and fired at John from about 15 yards away, hitting him in the chest. James ran at Ernest and wrestled the gun from him. James sent someone to fetch the doctor and the police, but John died after a few minutes.

Dr John Benson attended the scene and found that John had extensive gunshot wounds to the chest. A post-mortem examination was later conducted, in which about 50 or 60 gunshot wounds, extending from the chin to the last rib, were found.

On Friday 22 December, an inquest was held at the Reservoir Hotel near Payneham. At the conclusion of the inquest, the jury found Ernest, a market gardener, guilty of wilful murder. Ernest made no statement and was committed to trial.

Ernest August Boehm appeared before the Supreme Court on Friday 16 February 1872. At the conclusion of the trial, Boehm was found guilty of manslaughter and sentenced to two years imprisonment with hard labour. During the sentencing, the chief justice stated:

Dr John Benson, 1874.
State Library of South Australia, B 11314

I fully concur in the justice of the verdict. The law makes allowances for the circumstances under which an act of that kind may have been committed, and I feel that in this instance there was considerable provocation. This circumstance, however, does not justify, it only palliates the act. It must not in any way be understood that even under such circumstances a person is justified in doing any act that may result in death.

Date	Victim	Accused
10 January 1872	**McGillivray child**	**Christina McGillivray**
Cause of death:	Strangulation	
Outcome:	Found guilty of manslaughter	
	Sentenced to two years imprisonment	
Location:	Worrolong, near Mount Gambier	

Johann Schinckel was a farmer at Worrolong who had a number of servants at his property, including 21-year-old Christina McGillivray, who had been in his service since the previous October. When she started work, Johann thought that Christina was stout, but he did not notice any subsequent changes to her figure. McGillivray kept company with a man called James Callaghan, who frequently visited her.

Schinckel got up at around four-thirty am on 10 January 1872, when his daughter, who slept in the same room as McGillivray, told him that McGillivray was unwell. Johann went into the old washhouse where he noticed an amount of blood on the floor and the washing tub. He also saw a knife on the table that had blood on it. Schinckel went to see McGillivray who said that she was ill. Schinckel went to Mount Gambier and brought James Callaghan to the farm. Callaghan spoke to McGillivray and as a result a doctor was sent for.

Dr E Wehl arrived at the farm around one pm and spoke to McGillivray. After examining her, he discovered that she had recently given birth. McGillivray told Wehl that the body could be found in a shed, where it was recovered. A post-mortem examination showed that the child was fully grown and

Dr Edward Wehl of Mount Gambier, 1870. State Library of South Australia, B 3016

had a separate existence from the mother. A strip of calico or tape was tightly tied around the neck. Wehl stated that the umbilical cord had been cut or torn so short that he could not determine if the child had died from strangulation alone, as the cord having been cut that short would probably have caused the death of the child.

On Thursday 11 January, an inquest was held at Worrolong. After all of the evidence was given, the jury, after a few minutes of consultation, retuned with a verdict of wilful murder against McGillivray, who was committed to take trial on the charge of infanticide at the next sittings of the Circuit Court at Mount Gambier.

On Wednesday 17 April 1872, Christina McGillivray appeared before the Circuit Criminal Court in Mount Gambier where she was found guilty of manslaughter and sentenced to two years imprisonment.

Date	*Victim*	*Accused*
6 April 1872	**James Burke**	**Christopher Charlton**
Cause of death:	Assault	
Outcome:	Found guilty of manslaughter	
	Sentenced to 18 months imprisonment with hard labour	
Location:	Exchange Hotel, Kadina	

On Saturday 6 April 1872, 26-year-old James Burke was at the Exchange Hotel at Kadina having a drink. Christopher Charlton, a 50-year-old farmer from Green's Plains, was challenging any person in the hotel to a fight. Without the slightest provocation, Charlton seized Burke by the neck, and pushed him against the bar, kicking him at the same time. Burke fell to the ground and was picked up. Dr Robinson was called to see Burke around five pm that day. Burke had a lacerated wound on the scalp near the forehead that was about four inches long. Robinson cleaned the wound and left. Later that evening, Robinson was called back to see Burke and found that Burke's pupils were dilated and that he had lost about 20 to 25 ounces of blood. Robinson treated Burke, but he died from his injuries at seven-thirty that evening.

After the assault, Charlton left the hotel and retuned home. The police went to Charlton's house early on Sunday morning, arrested him and conveyed him to the Kadina lockup.

At two pm that day, the coroner, Mr G Birks, held an inquest at the

Royal Exchange Hotel, Kadina 1880.
State Library of South Australia, B 28698

Exchange Hotel. Evidence was given by Alexander Saunders of Kadina, who stated that he knew Burke, who he said was slightly given to drink, and used to reside in Adelaide where he worked for the *Advertiser*. James Oatrey gave evidence that he was in the bar at the same time as Burke and Charlton. Oatrey saw Burke sitting with Mr Curtis, and when Curtis got up and went to the bar, Burke followed him. When Burke got to the bar, Charlton, without saying anything to Burke, grabbed Burke by the collar and shoulder and threw him towards the counter, kicking him all the while. Burke did not say anything to Charlton before or during the assault.

Police Trooper O'Mahoney stated that he arrested Charlton at four in the morning. Charlton stated that he could not remember the assault, but his wife came into the room and said, 'Oh, yes you do Charlton. When you came home last night you said that you murdered [unknown] at Kadina'. Charlton did not contradict his wife.

At the completion of all the evidence, the jury found Charlton guilty of unlawfully killing and slaying Burke. Charlton was committed to trial at the Supreme Court.

On Tuesday 28 May, Charlton appeared in the Supreme Court charged with murder. At the conclusion of the evidence, His Honour summed up, and the jury, without retiring, returned a verdict of manslaughter. His Honour, in passing sentence, spoke strongly 'upon the deplorable fact of the inordinate indulgence in intoxicating liquor being so frequently the cause of crime, and so often advancing as a palliating circumstance'.

Charlton was sentenced to 18 months imprisonment with hard labour.

Date	*Victim*	*Accused*
6 April 1872	**Hayward child**	**Mary Hayward**
Cause of death:	Strangulation	
Outcome:	Found guilty of concealment of birth	
	Sentenced to six months imprisonment with hard labour	
Location:	Humphrey's Springs (Alma Plains), near Riverton	

On Saturday 6 April 1872, Mrs Smyth, who lived with her family on a property at Humphrey's Springs, saw one of her servants, 18-year-old Mary Hayward, walk over to the barn. Hayward had reported not feeling well, and Smyth told her to go inside and go to bed. Hayward refused and said that she had an internal pain that was not very serious. Later that day Smyth sent one of her children into the barn to check on Hayward. The child reported that they had seen blood in the barn. The next day, Smyth went into the barn and spoke to Hayward, who said that she had 'been bad once before and that time she thought she would die'. Hayward later left the barn and went into the house to bed. Smyth had a look in the barn, locating the body of a newborn girl behind some wheat bags. She left the barn, locking the door behind her, and went inside the house and spoke to Hayward, asking her why she did not say she was pregnant. Hayward said that she did not want anyone to know. She had wrapped the child in an old coat as she did not want the children outside to hear it. Smyth went to Riverton where she notified the police.

On Sunday 7 April, at Humphrey's Springs, an inquest was held before Mr Thomas Giles and a jury of 12 into the death of a newborn infant. A post-mortem was conducted which concluded that the child was fat and well nourished and had lived and breathed. There was discolouration on the neck from pressure, but there were no signs of a blow. There were patches of blood on the brain, but these might have been caused during the birth. The lungs were inflated and slightly diseased, but not sufficiently to have attributed to the death. The umbilical cord had not been tied. The cause of death was given as strangulation, but the haemorrhage from the umbilical cord might also have caused the death. The jury retired and returned with a verdict of wilful murder against Hayward, who was committed for trial.

On Thursday 16 May, Hayward appeared in the Supreme Court charged with killing and murdering her illegitimate daughter. At the conclusion of the trial, the jury retired for a period of 20 minutes and returned with a verdict of concealment of birth, with a recommendation of mercy due to her age. Hayward was sentenced to six months imprisonment with hard labour.

Date	*Victim*	*Accused*
30 April 1872	**William Mason**	**James Edwards**
Cause of death:	Assault	
Outcome:	Found not guilty	
Location:	Kenton Valley, near Gumeracha	

The first Europeans to explore the district around Blumberg were Dr George Imlay and John Hill in January 1838. In 1839–1840 the South Australian Company claimed several Special Surveys in the district, which were later subdivided to allow for closer settlement. Around 1848, migrants who had temporarily settled at Lobethal began looking for land of their own. Pastor Fritzsch recommended a spot beside the Torrens, where he camped on the way to Bethany. Blumberg grew with homes on land leased from George Fife Angas and a church some distance away. The town prospered by the 1850s, and the area was producing enough grain to justify the construction of the Blumberg Flour Mill (now the site of the motor museum). In 1865, during the local gold rush, the Blumberg Inn was built.

In 1917 Blumberg, along with many German towns in the district, had its name anglicised. Blumberg became Birdwood, named in honour of Sir William Birdwood, the Australian Imperial Force general who led the ANZACs at Gallipoli.

On Tuesday 30 April 1872, John Kinnane, the publican of the Travellers' Rest at Blumberg, was visited by Anderson, 45-year-old William Mason, John Hepworth and 37-year-old James Edwards, who all arrived for a drink. They stayed until around midday when they all left together in a bullock-dray. When they left they were not quite sober, but Mason was more under the influence than the others. They had no arguments while at the house, and they took three quarts of beer with them when they left.

When they got about a half a mile from the Traveller's Rest, Mason tried to quarrel with Anderson, who had not provoked him. Edwards told Mason to sit down and be quiet, saying, 'Don't let us quarrel old man, come along quietly'. Mason said he wanted to fight Edwards, but Edwards did not want to fight him. Mason persisted and they got off the dray and had a fight. Edwards struck Mason with his hand and Mason fell to the ground. Mason said, 'Well, I will be quiet and go on'. They all got back onto the dray and went to camp in Tyman's paddock at Kenton Valley. When at the camp Mason lay down on a bunk for about an hour. When he got up, he had some tea and again challenged Edwards to a fight. Mason and Edwards scuffled again, during which Edwards struck Mason on the chin, causing Mason to fall to the ground. Mason lay there and someone covered him with a blanket, thinking he was not hurt but suffering effects from the drink. Later, Mason was checked and found to be breathing heavily and foaming at the mouth. A doctor was called to attend but Mason died.

Gumeracha in the 1870s. State Library of South Australia, B 10608

On Wednesday 1 May an inquest was held at the District Hotel in Gumeracha, on the body of William Mason.

Dr John Gorse conducted a post-mortem examination and found swelling and several small abrasions near the left eye. The cause of death was given as a blood clot on the brain, caused by either the blow to the head or fall to the ground. The jury retired for about 20 minutes and returned with the verdict that 'the said William Mason came to his death by effusion of blood on the brain, caused by a blow and fall given by one James Edwards in a fair stand-up fight, and, therefore, that the said James Edwards is guilty of manslaughter under great provocation'. Edwards was committed to trial.

On Tuesday 28 May, Edwards appeared in the Supreme Court charged with the murder of Mason. At the conclusion of the trial, Edwards was found not guilty. His Honour said that he quite concurred in the finding of the jury and dismissed the prisoner.

Date	*Victim*	*Accused*
7 July 1872	**Cheepa**	**Morcutla**
Cause of death:	Assault	
Outcome:	Acquitted	
Location:	Coralbignie, Gawler Ranges	

On Friday 29 November 1872, 30-year-old Morcutla appeared before the Supreme Court charged with feloniously and with malice aforethought killing and murdering an Aboriginal person named Cheepa at Coralbignie in the Gawler Ranges.

Coralbignie, approximately 1870. State Library of South Australia, B 8061

Before the jury were sworn in, one (Mr S Stokes, a chemist from Norwood) asked if capital punishment was the penalty in this case. His Honour said the prisoner was liable to that punishment should he be found guilty. With this knowledge, Stokes expressed a disinclination to sit. The crown challenged him accordingly, and another gentleman was called to take his place. The case was then proceeded with, but it broke down almost immediately. The principal witness was an Aboriginal man named Multa, who detailed all circumstances of the quarrel between the prisoner and the deceased at the preliminary examination. As Multa gave his evidence in the Supreme Court, it was found that he knew nothing beyond what he had been told by others. Seeing this, the prosecution was abandoned, and the prisoner was acquitted and discharged.

Date	*Victim*	*Accused*
24 July 1872	**James McFarlane**	**John Tynan**
Cause of death:	Assault	
Outcome:	Found guilty of manslaughter	
	Sentenced to two years imprisonment with hard labour	
Location:	Fisher's Place, Adelaide	

On Wednesday 24 July 1872, Mary Connor, the wife of William Connor of Selby Street, Adelaide, heard some men fighting and quarrelling in her husband's cottages in Fisher's Place. In one of these cottages lived 64-year-old James McFarlane. Connor went to the door and asked them what they were arguing about. She saw a man named John Tynan holding McFarlane against the wall of the cottage, but he let McFarlane go when Connor was speaking to them. Connor heard Tynan ask McFarlane for money. McFarlane asked Connor to call a constable, and she saw that McFarlane's face was cut and bleeding. While McFarlane was speaking to Connor, Tynan jumped up and attempted to strike McFarlane. Connor went to her own house then returned about five minutes later finding Tynan sparring up to McFarlane. Tynan stopped when Connor called out to him. McFarlane walked off and Tynan ran after him, appearing as though he wanted to strike him. McFarlane went to Connor and spoke to her for a short time and Tynan walked off.

Around five-thirty pm that day, Police Constable Lynch found McFarlane lying on the footpath outside the Prince Albert Hotel in Wright Street. Lynch, who thought that McFarlane was intoxicated, took him to the police station in

Prince Albert Hotel, Wright St, 1890.
State Library of South Australia, B 10431

a cab. While there, McFarlane showed symptoms of suffering from a fit, so he was taken to the Adelaide Hospital. Lynch had known McFarlane for a long time as a fishmonger, and had frequently seen him intoxicated.

Dr Samuel Ellison, acting house surgeon at the Adelaide Hospital, treated McFarlane and found that the pupil of his left eye was contracted, that he was breathing heavily, and that he had abrasions on his face. McFarlane remained in that condition until he died the following Monday. Ellison could find no evidence that McFarlane had been drinking.

On Tuesday 30 July, an inquest was held at the Adelaide Hospital on the body of James McFarlane. W Carter, who resided with McFarlane, gave evidence. Carter stated he had known McFarlane for about six years and that McFarlane was also known as Hugh Morgan. Carter stated that he was in the house when McFarlane arrived home, and that Tynan was there with a woman called Dublin Kate. Tynan asked McFarlane for the money he owed, but McFarlane said he did not owe him anything. Tynan said he would beat it out of him if he wasn't paid. Carter saw Tynan strike McFarlane a number of times and when McFarlane was on the ground, Tynan knelt on him to get some money from his pocket.

Dr Ellison gave evidence of conducting a post-mortem and said that the cause of death was due to a blood clot between the membrane and the brain, which may have been caused by being knocked about.

At the conclusion of the inquest the jury retired, and after a short deliberation returned a verdict that McFarlane came to his death from injuries received from John Tynan. The coroner issued a warrant for Tynan, who was not present at the inquest. He was arrested that afternoon.

On Friday 16 August 1872, 36-year-old John Tynan appeared in the Supreme Court charged with the murder of James McFarlane. At the completion of the trial, the jury found Tynan guilty of manslaughter. Tynan was sentenced to two years imprisonment with hard labour.

Date	*Victim*	*Accused*
18 December 1872	**Thomas Holyoake**	**John Hope**
Cause of death:	Assault	
Outcome:	Found guilty of manslaughter	
	Sentenced to 12 months imprisonment with hard labour	
Location:	Kanyaka, near Quorn	

On 18 December 1872, Thomas Holyoake, a 31-year-old hawker, was drinking and gambling with John Hope at a camp at Kanyaka, near Quorn. They were both by the side of Holyoake's cart, and during the evening a quarrel broke out between them that turned into a fistfight. Hope wanted to get away, but as he was getting onto his horse, Holyoake struck him. Hope turned around and rushed at Holyoake and both fell to the ground. Holyoake fell heavily and was unable to move, subsequently dying from his injuries.

A coronial inquest was held and at the completion of the evidence, the jury found Hope guilty of murder.

On Friday 11 February 1873, John Hope appeared before the Supreme Court charged with the wilful murder of Thomas Holyoake. At the start of the trial, the crown stated that the indictment for murder could not be proceeded with as the evidence only supported the charge of manslaughter. His Honour concurred and said that death seemed to have been caused by a hasty blow in a drunken brawl, without any serious injury having been intended. Hope entered a guilty plea to manslaughter.

His Honour stated that he trusted that the slight sentence he would pass would be sufficient to induce the prisoner to keep from drinking, gambling and quarrelling in the future. Hope was sentenced to 12 months imprisonment with hard labour.

Date	*Victim*	*Accused*
28 December 1872	William Wyatt Jr	James Slape
Cause of death:	Assault (with a mattock)	
Outcome:	Slape committed suicide in Adelaide Gaol	
Location:	Burnside	

Dr William Wyatt, the son of Richard Wyatt, was born in Plymouth, Devon, England. He was apprenticed at 16 years of age to a Plymouth surgeon, Thomas Stewart. Wyatt continued to study medicine and obtained the qualification of MCRS (Membership of the Royal College of Surgeons) in February 1828.

Wyatt immigrated to South Australia as surgeon of the *John Renwick*. He arrived in Adelaide on 14 February 1837, and practised there for a short time. In August he was appointed city coroner and also served as the third part-time 'Protector of Aborigines' from 1837 until 1839.

In May 1838 he was on the committee of the South Australian School Society, amongst various other committees. On 28 February 1843 he was chairman of a meeting called to discuss the best means of 'civilising' the local Aboriginal people. In 1847 he was appointed as coroner for the province of South Australia, and in 1849 he was a member of the provisional committee of the South Australian Colonial Railway Company.

In his final years, though becoming infirm, Wyatt still attended to his many duties, and passed some hospital

William Wyatt, circa 1860.
State Library of South Australia, B 927

281

accounts for payment just a week before his death at 82 on 10 June 1886. He bought some town lots at the first land sale held at Adelaide on 27 May 1837, which laid the foundation of a considerable fortune. He performed many acts of philanthropy in a quiet way and showed much interest in the social life of Adelaide, but never entered politics. He was married and left a widow and his only child to have survived past infancy, William Wyatt Jr.

At about eight pm on Saturday 28 December 1872, William Wyatt Jr went to the house of James and Catherine Slape at Burnside to speak about some work. Wyatt had only been there for a few minutes when 48-year-old James came home and told Wyatt to get out. Wyatt did not reply and remained seated at the table. Catherine went into another room and could hear James and Wyatt talking, after which James left the house. Catherine told Wyatt that he should leave, as James was a madman when he had been drinking. Catherine thought that James had gone outside to get an axe, as he had a habit of chasing her with it. After a few minutes, James returned with a mattock and struck Wyatt in the head with it. Catherine ran out of the house to get help.

Frederick Waterhouse, curator of the museum, lived close to the Slape house. He was at home on the night of the murder when he heard a tapping at his kitchen door. His daughter answered it and then told him that something had happened at the Slape's house. Waterhouse went to the Slape house with another neighbour called James Young. Together they found Wyatt lying on the floor in a pool of blood. James was still in the room and Waterhouse said, 'Good God Slape, what have you done?' James replied in an 'idiotic tone', 'I am afraid I hit him too hard'.

Dr John Benson attended at the house and examined Wyatt. Benson found that he had severe head injuries and thought that death would have been instantaneous. Police Trooper Richard Fisher arrived and arrested James. Fisher located the mattock, which was covered in blood and hair.

On Sunday 29 December an inquest was held on the body of William Wyatt Jr at the Burnside Inn. After Catherine Slape gave an account of the murder, the coroner asked James about Catherine's evidence. James stated that he didn't recollect anything about the murder, and that he could not contradict what his wife had said.

At the conclusion of the evidence, the coroner summed up, telling the jury that it must be clear to them that they could not bring in a verdict of manslaughter, and that they must bring in one of murder. After a short retirement, the jury returned with a decision that William Wyatt Jr had been killed by the actions of James Slape, but they believed that Slape was too heavily affected by alcohol and not in his right mind at the time of the attack. The coroner refused to take the verdict in that form, and said the jury must bring it in a more definite form. The jury, after another short retirement, returned with the verdict of 'unpremeditated murder'. Slape was committed for trial and transferred to the Adelaide Gaol.

Slape never went to trial, as the following day he hung himself in his cell using the rope from his hammock.

Date	Victim	Accused
29 March 1873	**Ellen Hunt (Laycock)**	**Susan Appleby**
Cause of death:	Neglect	
Outcome:	Found not guilty	
Location:	Stirling North (near Port Augusta)	

In early January 1873, Ellen Hunt, a newborn baby, was taken to Susan Appleby's house at Stirling North. Ellen was brought by Appleby's mother, who would not tell Appleby who Ellen's parents were. Appleby was asked to look after Ellen for five shillings a week, which she accepted. Louisa Kite, a neighbour of Appleby's, saw Ellen when she arrived at the house and thought that she looked like a fine and healthy baby. Kite visited Appleby's house over the next few months and noticed that Ellen was not putting on weight and that she nearly always had an empty bottle with her. Kite did not think that Ellen was fairly dealt with by Appleby.

On 23 March, Appleby took Ellen to see Dr William Markham, who examined her and found that she was suffering from hunger and from a skin disease. Ellen died six days later.

On 29 March and 7 April, an inquest was held at Stirling North on the body of Ellen Hunt, or Laycock, aged three months. Evidence was given by Dr Markham, who stated that Ellen had died from Marasmus, a form of severe malnutrition where the body weight is reduced to less than 60% of the normal expected body weight for the age.

Appleby stated that when she received the child, it was delicate and thin and had to be fed with a spoon and that she fed and clothed the child, but she never seemed satisfied with the amount of food she was given. Robert Appleby agreed with the evidence of his wife, and stated that he thought that his wife was capable of nursing two children with the help of a bottle, but did not think that five shillings a week was sufficient.

Kite testified that if Appleby had looked after Ellen properly, she would still be alive. Evidence was received from other witnesses who stated that Appleby did not look after Ellen well, and that they thought Ellen was starving and always cold.

At the conclusion of the inquest, the jury ruled that Ellen had died of starvation, and that Appleby was therefore guilty of manslaughter.

On Monday 19 and Tuesday 20 May 1873, Appleby appeared before the Supreme Court charged with manslaughter. At the completion of the trial she was found not guilty and discharged.

Date	Victim	Accused
15 May 1873	**Mary**	**Narikonyary (Isaac)**
Cause of death:	Gunshot wound	
Outcome:	Found not guilty	
Location:	Seven miles out of Robe	

George and Harriet Sneyd were the landlords of the Telegraph Hotel, which was situated about seven miles from Robe. On Wednesday 14 May 1873, Harriet saw four Aboriginal people, Annie, Yet Plummy (Frank), Narikonyary (Isaac), and his lubra Mary, camped on a hill behind the hotel. They had arrived from the Dairy Range where they had been shooting kangaroos. When they made camp, Narikonyary went into the kitchen of the hotel and got some beer. The group drank three pots of beer before skinning a kangaroo and getting a fourth pot. After finishing the drinks, all four of them returned to the camp. Annie and Mary were sitting by the fire talking. Yet Plummy was on the opposite side of the fire and Narikonyary was sitting next to him. Narikonyary had a gun in his hand. Narikonyary and Mary had an argument during which Mary called him 'a … dog,' and Narikonyary called her 'a … bitch'. During the argument, Yet Plummy heard a gun go off and saw Mary drop to the ground. Yet Plummy took the gun from Narikonyary and went and told Harriet Sneyd what had happened. Harriet went to the camp and found the body wrapped up in a blanket. She had not heard a gunshot that evening.

Around eight-forty am, Police Trooper Allen was at the Robe Police Station when Yet Plummy arrived and told him that Narikonyary had shot his wife during an argument. Allen visited the Telegraph Hotel and found Narikonyary in the kitchen, where he arrested him. Narikonyary told Allen that he would 'speak truth Mr Allen. You can cut my ... throat. I was drunk Mr Allen. I will give myself up at once. I did it'.

On Thursday 15 May, an inquest was held at the Telegraph Hotel. Harriet gave evidence about the group arriving and camping on the hill. She stated that they were not sober when they arrived, but she could not say they were drunk.

Dr J Mustarde stated that he examined the body and found a gunshot wound on the right side of the head, between the ear and eye. The upper part of the skull was shattered, proving that the shot must have been fired from a very short distance. There was also the appearance of burnt powder around the wound. Death would have been instantaneous.

The jury, after consideration, returned a verdict of manslaughter aggravated by intoxication. The coroner declined to receive the verdict and on reconsideration a verdict of wilful murder was given, adding a recommendation that the police should make enquiry into the matter of supplying Aboriginal people with alcoholic drinks.

On Saturday 17 May, Harriet Sneyd and Annie Hunt, who also worked at the hotel, appeared before the police court in Robe charged with supplying the four Aboriginal people involved in the murder with intoxicating drink. Both pleaded guilty and were fined £5 each. George Sneyd also appeared before the court on the same charge, but he pleaded not guilty. After a short trial, he was found guilty and fined £10 plus court costs.

Narikonyary appeared before the Circuit Court at Robe on Friday 10 October charged with murder. During the trial, the crown solicitor abandoned the charge. His Honour, in summing up, stated that the issue was murder or misadventure, laying down the rule that though drunkenness was no extenuation of crime, it might be considered with regard to misadventure. The jury returned a verdict of not guilty.

The Sneyds appear again on 10 March 1875 after George murdered Harriet and later committed suicide.

Date	Victim	Accused
5 June 1873	Frederick Burt	William Ridgway
Cause of death:	Assault (unknown weapon)	
Outcome:	Found guilty of murder	
	Sentenced to death, executed 1 January 1874	
Location:	Coonatto Run	

Frederick Burt, 45, and William Ridgway, 20, were employed at the Coonatto Station in 1873. Francis Fowke, the overseer at the station, paid Burt and Ridgeway what they were owed on 5 June 1873, as they were both leaving to travel to Adelaide.

Thomas Williams, the cook at Coonatto, saw Burt leaving the station that day, along with Ridgway. Ridgway had a horse loaded with their swags, and both Ridgway and Burt were walking alongside it.

Michael Martin, a boundary-rider living at Pinda, saw Burt about two or three days before he left Coonatto. Burt told him that he expected to leave shortly, and that he and Ridgway were going to Adelaide together. Ridgway later visited Martin's house without Burt. Martin asked Ridgway where Burt was, and Ridgway said that he had left him to go with another person who had some sheep with him. Martin's wife noticed that Ridgway had spots of blood on his trousers, but she thought nothing of it at the time.

Reginald Leyfang, a farmer living on Willochra Creek, saw Ridgway in the beginning of June, without Burt. Leyfang noticed that Ridgway had a £10 note and a £1 note with him. Robert Veaitch, who was with Leyfang, saw the £10 note, and thought it looked like the one he paid Burt with during harvest-time.

In August that year, Robert Heron discovered Burt's body lying under a bush, covered with tree branches. Heron went to Coonatto and told Fowke. The police at Melrose were advised. On 14 August, Thomas Williams attended the Melrose Police Station where he identified Burt's body. He noticed that the body had a deformed finger, which he knew that Burt had. The size and general appearance of the body was similar to that of Burt.

On Thursday 21 August, William Ridgway was brought before the Melrose Court charged with murdering Frederick Burt on the Coonatto Run, by fracturing his skull with an unknown weapon. Dr Matthew Moorhouse stated that he examined the body and found that it had three wounds to the left side

Melrose Post office and Police Station, 1876–1877.
State Library of South Australia, B 58001/15

of the head, caused by a blunt instrument. The injuries were quite sufficient to cause death.

Police Trooper Richard Noble, stationed at Clare, arrested Ridgway at Sevenhills. Ridgway insisted that he did not kill Burt. Ridgway gave evidence that he and Burt had left Coonatto together but after four miles they met with a white man who was taking sheep to Umberatana and offered them a job. Burt accepted the offer and went with the man. At the completion of the hearing, Ridgway was committed to trial at the Supreme Court.

On Tuesday 9 December 1873, Ridgway appeared before the Supreme Court charged with wilful murder. The trial ended on Thursday 11 December. At the completion of the trial, the jury retired for a period of one hour, and returned with a guilty verdict, with the recommendation to mercy. His Honour sentenced Ridgway to death by hanging, and on 1 January 1874, the sentence was carried out.

Date	Victim	Accused
26 July 1873	Charles Withecombe (Wittacombe)	Joseph Adams, Thomas McLean, William Edgar, and Benjamin Rebbeck

Cause of death:	Assault (with a rolling pin)
Outcome:	Adams and McLean found guilty of murder
	Both sentenced to death, later commuted to life imprisonment
	Edgar and Rebbeck charged with accessory to murder
	Both found not guilty
Location:	Port Adelaide

On Saturday 26 July 1873, the *Tongay*, a barque, was anchored in the roadstead at Port Adelaide. That morning, 30-year-old Captain Charles Withecombe (also spelt Wittacombe) went ashore for some time and returned on board around five pm.

Joseph Adams, 18, Thomas McLean, 21, William Edgar, 25, and Benjamin Rebbeck, 22, belonged to the *Tongay*'s crew and were on board when Withecombe returned. Around seven pm that evening, Adams, McLean, Edgar and Rebbeck asked William Ferguson, the chief officer, to see Withecombe. Ferguson called for Withecombe to come up onto the deck, which he did. Withecombe went and spoke to the group about an incident earlier that week where the police had brought McLean and Adams on board as they had a warrant of deliverance. The four crewmen asked Withecombe what he was going to do with them, to which he replied, 'I will tell you on Monday morning'. While the four were talking to Withecombe, Ferguson saw Adams step out from the others and strike Withecombe across the face. Withecombe fell to the ground. Adams used a weapon, but Ferguson was not able to see it properly. Ferguson took Withecombe to his cabin and called for a doctor. Withecombe never recovered from the assault and died within two hours. The police were called and the four were taken into custody.

On Monday 28 July, an inquest was held at Port Adelaide on the body of Charles Withecombe. The accused were in custody and present during the inquest.

Evidence was given which indicated that Adams may have used a rolling pin to assault Withecombe, and that McLean had kicked Withecombe when he was on the ground. The cause of death was given as head injuries. At the conclusion of the inquest, the jury returned and found Adam and McLean guilty of wilful murder, and Edgar and Rebbeck of being accessories to the fact.

On Thursday 14 August, the four prisoners appeared before the Supreme Court. At the completion of the trial, Adams and McLean were found guilty of murder and Edgar and Rebbeck were found not guilty of being accessories, as the jury thought they were not aware of the unlawful intent of Adams and McLean. Adams and McLean were recommended to mercy on account of the provocation they had received and their youth.

The associate put the usual question to the prisoners as to whether they had anything to say why sentence of death should not be passed upon them. Adams replied that he was not guilty of wilful murder. McLean said:

> Not guilty either. In the evidence of Dr Gething he explains the cause of the captain's death, which he says was caused by blows from a blunt instrument. Death, he said, would not have been accelerated by a kick, and that if he had been kicked an external mark would be shown, and therefore, I do not think I am guilty. I am found guilty, but I didn't intend to do the man any harm, as God is my Judge. I am found guilty, however, and must suffer, I suppose.

Both Adams and McLean were sentenced to death. On Saturday 23 August, it was reported that the executive had commuted the sentence of death to imprisonment for life with hard labour.

On Saturday 11 October that year, the following appeared on page five of the *South Australian Register*:

> We understand that a draft for £70 was sent to the widow of the late Captain Withecombe by this mail, with the accompanying letter. Up to the present time the Treasurer has received about £100. A tombstone is to be placed over the grave in the Alberton Cemetery. Any person still holding a subscription-list is requested to forward it at once to the Secretary to the fund, Messrs. Levj & Co., Port Adelaide. The letter referred to is as follows:

> 'St. Paul's Parsonage, Port Adelaide, S. A. October 9 1873.

Dear Madam — Will you allow me, in the name of a large number of subscribers, to express our deep sympathy with you in the severe trial you have recently undergone. Shocked as you must have been by the unexpected tidings of your husband's death, I think you would have been somewhat comforted could you have known how deeply the feelings of the colonists were moved, and how much they grieved at the severe blow that had fallen upon you. It was immediately determined to erect a tombstone over your husband's grave, and send a photograph of it; but the subscriptions we have received so far exceed the estimated cost that we are able in addition to beg your acceptance of the enclosed draft for £70. We trust that this mode of expressing our sympathy will not be displeasing, and that you will find some consolation in the thought that though your husband died so suddenly is this distant land, he was not without friends, who gave him Christian burial and cared for the place of his rest. Believe me, my dear Madam, yours very truly. S. Green'.

Around seven years later, on Monday 16 August 1880, the following appeared in the *Advertiser*:

Some years back the master of a vessel named the *Tongay* was murdered in the Gulf and with characteristic liberality the residents of Port Adelaide initiated a subscription fund which amounted to a handsome sum. Portion of this was sent to the widow of the deceased in England, and the balance of about £30 was set aside to erect a monument. Through some oversight the monument has not yet been erected, and this is the more to be regretted inasmuch as the relative of the deceased have repeatedly written asking to be supplied with photos of the memorial stone. The matter should be at once looked into.

Date	*Victim*	*Accused*
9 August 1873	**Donnaller (George)**	**Johnny, Dick, and Billy**
Cause of death:	Assault (with a waddy)	
Outcome:	All three found guilty of murder	
	Sentenced to death, later commuted to two years hard labour	
Location:	Tilly's Swamp, near Kingston SE	

On 9 August 1873, Donnaller, who was also called George, his lubra Mary, and other Aboriginal people including Johnny, Dick and Billy were at Tilly's Swamp near Kingston. During the evening, Donnaller and Mary went to their wurley. Sometime after, Johnny, Dick and Billy entered the wurley and carried Donnaller out by the neck and legs. Two others called Betty and Jerry were also in the wurley, but they were too frightened to render any assistance. The next morning Donnaller had not returned so Mary went looking for him, later finding him dead. Dick threatened to kill Mary if she said anything, and offered her money not to tell anyone.

On 24 October 1873, PC Robert Morris, who was stationed at Kingston, was handing out rations when he saw Mary without Donnaller. Morris noticed that something was wrong with her, though she made no complaint. Morris questioned Mary and she told him about her husband being murdered in August. Morris, along with Police Trooper Shields, who was also stationed at Kingston, located and arrested Johnny on a charge of murder. When arrested, Johnny stated that Old Man Dick made him do it, and that he kept pushing him on. He also stated that he and Billy carried Donnaller out of the wurley and that Dick waddied him. Billy was later arrested and Dick was arrested near Salt Creek. When Dick was arrested, he confessed that he and Billy had killed Donnaller.

Donnaller's body was exhumed and on Saturday 1 November, an inquest was held at the Royal Mail Hotel, Kingston SE. Betty gave evidence and said that she remembered Johnny and Billy taking Donnaller out of the wurley. She later saw Donnaller dead, and said that Johnny and Billy were smoking him. Betty heard Johnny and Billy offer Mary money not to tell anyone what had happened.

Jerry stated that he saw Johnny and Billy take Donnaller out of the wurley, but Dick stayed outside. Dick had a waddy, while the other two were unarmed. He saw Donnaller dead the next day and saw that he had a mark of a waddy across his forehead and all over his body.

Dr Thomas Brittain stated that he examined the body of the deceased and had found he had received injuries to the upper part of the spine, causing a fracture, and severe head injuries caused by a blow, and a deep penetrating wound on the left hip, also caused by some blunt instrument. He considered the injuries to the upper part of the spine and head injuries sufficient to cause death, and that a waddy might have inflicted the injuries.

At the completion of the evidence, the jury found that Donnaller had died from wounds inflicted by Johnny, Billy and Dick. All three were committed to trial at the Supreme Court.

On Saturday 15 November, Johnny, Billy and Dick escaped from the Robe Gaol. All three were captured in April the following year, and on 24 April 1874, they appeared before the Supreme Court in Robe where they were all found guilty of murder and sentenced to death. There was a recommendation to mercy from the jury.

A later reference to Johnny, Billy and Dick was made in the House of Assembly on Wednesday 6 July 1874. It was reported that the sentence was commuted to two years imprisonment with hard labour. This was due to the crime having been committed in carrying out a tribal custom, and the court 'appeared impressed with a sense of difficulty in bringing a case of this nature under the operation of our Criminal Law, where the prisoners had doubtless acted under the belief that they were performing a sacred duty'.

Date	*Victim*	*Accused*
4 September 1873	**Thomas Woolcock**	**Elizabeth Woolcock**
Cause of death:	Poisoned	
Outcome:	Found guilty of murder, sentenced to death	
	Executed 30 December 1873	
Location:	Yelta	

Thomas Woolcock lived with his wife, Elizabeth and son, Tom, at Yelta, near Moonta. Tom was Thomas' child from his first marriage. Thomas became ill in July 1873, and was treated by Dr John Dickie on 27 July. Dickie thought that Thomas was suffering from a bilious attack. There was slight gastric irritation and he thought he saw symptoms of gastric fever setting in. As the symptoms were only premonitory, he thought he would wait a few days. After some time, Thomas appeared to be worse, so he sent for Dr Bull, who also treated him.

Dr Herbert also visited Thomas and had treated him by encouraging excessive salivation. Even after being treated, the gastric and intestinal irritation continued. Thomas was visited by the doctors every two or three days and in spite of all treatment, the condition continued. There were severe bowel complaints and vomiting, and Thomas was unable to keep any food down. Thomas passed a considerable quantity of blood and was vomiting nothing but blood and mucus. There were few head symptoms during the illness, which was thought to be very unusual in these cases. Thomas died from pure exhaustion, brought on by excessive purging and vomiting and want of proper nutriment. Dr Dickie thought that a great variety of poisons would give similar results, but that mercury was the likeliest culprit.

On Thursday 4 September 1873, an inquest began at Yelta, near Moonta, on the body of Thomas Woolcock. A post-mortem was conducted and evidence was given that the condition of the body might have arisen from natural causes, but the doctors considered some of the symptoms to be associated with mercurial poisoning. At the completion of the inquest, the jury

Thomas and Elizabeth Woolcock, with Thomas' son Tom.
State Library of South Australia, B 12311

retired for 28 minutes before returning. The foreman stated, 'We find that the deceased, Thomas Woolcock, came to his death through the effects of slow irritative poisoning, and that we are of opinion the poison was given him by his wife, Elizabeth Woolcock'. Elizabeth was committed to trial at the Supreme Court for the wilful murder of her husband.

Elizabeth Woolcock appeared before the Supreme Court on Tuesday 2 December. In his opening address, the crown solicitor outlined the case and stated that it showed the most deliberate intention of poisoning that he had ever known:

> The evidence of Dr Gosse and Mr Francis would show the presence of mercury in very large quantities. Poisoning by mercury might take place by very small doses, and this had been the case here. The kind of mercury used was known as precipitate powder, a highly irritant poison.

The prisoner and the deceased had a lived on very bad terms since their marriage. The prisoner had conducted herself in a highly improper way with a man named Pascoe, who was lodging with her husband, and this had led to quarrels between the deceased and Pascoe, and [the] deceased had ordered Pascoe out of the house. The prisoner had often talked to others about the effect of poison, which evidently showed that her mind was running on the subject. And it would be shown that she had purchased precipitate powder from a chemist in Moonta. It will be shown that the prisoner never allowed any one to assist her to prepare the meals of the deceased and that the murder could not have been committed by anyone but her.

The trial lasted for three days. At the conclusion of evidence, the jury retired for little less than half an hour and returned a guilty verdict, with a recommendation to mercy on account of the youth of the prisoner. The sentence of death was passed by His Honor, which was carried out on 30 December.

Elizabeth Woolcock remains the only woman to be executed for murder in South Australia.

Date	*Victim*	*Accused*
7 March 1874	**Thomas Hanlin**	**William Niblock**
Cause of death:	Assault	
Outcome:	Found guilty of manslaughter	
	Sentenced to 18 months hard labour	
Location:	Foote's Creek, near Truro	

On Sunday 8 March 1874, an inquest was held at Mrs Buxton's wine shop in Foote's Creek, on the body of Thomas Hanlin, a labourer from Foote's Creek. Edwin Byrne, a labourer from Murray Flats, gave evidence, stating that he had known Hanlin for about six years. Byrne said that he last saw Hanlin alive on the previous evening at around six pm outside Mrs Buxton's house, when his face was bleeding from the temple. Byrne bid him good evening and Hanlin said, 'Oh, look at my face'. Byrne never spoke to him again. About 10 minutes later Byrne saw Hanlin and 30-year-old William Niblock coming out of Hanlin's house together. Niblock went to Byrne and, pointing at Hanlin, said, 'Ted, don't you come here at all, that bloody old wretch called my missus a whore, and I'll kill him'. Byrne went away for about five minutes, and on returning he saw Niblock coming from Hanlin's house towards Mrs Buxton's. Byrne left and returned at around eight pm. Byrne was told that Hanlin was dead and that Niblock had killed him. Byrne saw Hanlin's body on the ground outside Mrs Buxton's.

Ann Buxton stated that she was a married woman and kept a wine shop. She had known Hanlin for about a year and she last saw him alive the afternoon before when he was sitting outside her shop. She said that Niblock came into the shop and said, 'Hanlin called my wife a bloody whore, and I won't have it'. Niblock went outside and told Hanlin that he would not have his wife called such names. Buxton stayed inside and a short time later James Boxall came in and said that Hanlin was dead.

Boxall stated that he last saw Hanlin the previous evening lying on the ground as Niblock was kicking him in the face. Hanlin was not speaking at all, and Boxall told Niblock to leave Hanlin alone. Niblock stopped and walked off. Boxall went to Hanlin and found that he was dead. Boxall sent for the police at Kapunda. Both Hanlin and Niblock had been drinking, but neither was drunk.

Dr Renner examined Hanlin and found the face and forehead showed signs of violence as the head was swollen. On the right temple was a cut over an inch long, and the left temple was fractured. Renner believed that either the blow to the temple, or the fracture of the skull was sufficient to cause death.

The jury, after retiring for two and a half hours, found Niblock guilty of manslaughter. Niblock was committed for trial.

On Wednesday 17 June, Niblock appeared before the Supreme Court. After a short retirement, the jury returned and found Niblock guilty of manslaughter. Niblock was sentenced to 10 months imprisonment with hard labour.

Date	Victim	Accused
19 March 1874	Susannah Moore	William Moore
Cause of death:	Assault	
Outcome:	Acquitted	
Location:	Fiddler's Green, near Truro	

On Wednesday 19 March 1874, James Snodgrass was on business in Truro when he saw William and Susannah Moore. Snodgrass paid Susannah for a cow he bought from them a month before. Susannah was wearing a yellow wincey dress and a jacket and skirt of the same colour. Snograss thought that William was under the influence of liquor. Snograss heard William say to Susannah, 'I will sell out and go home, you can stay here if you like'.

Later that day William, who was 43, and Susannah, who was 45, were at their home at Fiddler's Green, near Truro. Gottlieb Gregurke, who was a neighbour of the Moores, saw an intoxicated William acting in an excited state. Gregurke heard a lot of noise coming from the Moore's house around sundown, with William making most of the noise. Gregurke looked out of his window and saw William in the kitchen turning up buckets, cups and saucers, and throwing them outside. Gregurke heard William cursing and swearing before he saw him go down to the well. After a short time he heard Susannah scream once. It was nearly dark and Gregurke heard the well bucket go down into the well. Gregurke thought that something was wrong so he went to the well where William was standing. William said, 'She is gone'. Gregurke went for assistance and found Ernest Aldenhoffer. Both men went to the well. Aldenhoffer was lowered into the well, which was about 125 feet deep, and found Susannah's body floating in the water. They managed to retrieve Susannah from the well, but she was dead. The body was in the well for about three-quarters of an hour and during that time William did not assist in getting her out.

Dr Hermann Martens attended the scene and saw that Susannah had cuts to the right and left side of the head. There were some other light bruises and Dr Martens thought it was possible that the injuries were caused by her falling down the well. Dr Donald MacLachlan also examined the body and found a scalp wound and a triangular shaped cut on the left-back part of the head. He thought that her head wounds might have been the result of her falling on some hard and blunt object. There was also a blue mark on her chin, which he could not account for.

On Thursday 20 March, at the Moore's house, an inquest was held on the body of Susannah Moore. The jury viewed the body before evidence was given. Gregurke gave his account on the evening's events and added that he had heard William say many times that he was going to kill his wife, and that twice before he had taken a butcher's knife from him. Once he had seen William throw a knife at Susannah.

William stated that he saw his wife at the well the day before in the afternoon and he went to help her draw water. He did not say how she fell into the well, but he stated that she never screamed when she fell and he called out to her to catch the bucket but she never answered.

The jury, after deliberating for a considerable time, returned with a unanimous decision that Susannah had come to her death as a result of William's actions, and found him guilty of manslaughter. The jury also expressed their approbation at the courage of Mr Ernest Aldenhoffer in going down the well to bring up the body.

On Friday 12 June, William Moore appeared before the Supreme Court on the charge of murdering his wife. At the conclusion of the trial, the jury acquitted him.

Date	*Victim*	*Accused*
19 May 1874	**Townsend child**	**Mary Agnes Townsend and Mary Townsend**
Cause of death:	Undetermined	
Outcome:	Mary Agnes found guilty of concealment of birth Sentenced to 12 months imprisonment Mary discharged	
Location:	Adelaide	

Around 11 am on Friday 5 June 1874, Constable Michael Shanahan went to the Stag Inn on Rundle Street, Adelaide, as he had received information regarding some clothing that had been found in the watercloset. Shanahan went with Mr Pratt to the watercloset in the rear yard, which connected to a blacksmith's shop and was open to anyone. While searching, Shanahan found a bundle in the eastern corner, under the seat. Shanahan asked what the bundle was, but Pratt dismissed it as a bundle of rags. Pratt then said in a jocular tone, 'Another case of infanticide'. Shanahan moved the bundle and noticed it contained the body of an infant child. Shanahan picked it up and washed the dirt from it and remained there until other police arrived. The body was wrapped in what appeared to be part of a chemise.

Rundle Street, Adelaide, looking west from East Terrace, 1866.
State Library of South Australia, B 1876

After taking the body to the hospital, Shanahan went to the home of Mrs Townsend, in company with Sergeant Sullivan and Detective McLaughlin, where they made a search. A mattress was found which had a stained area on it.

Inspector William Peterswald sent for Mrs Townsend and her 18-year-old daughter Mary Agnes Townsend, to attend at the police station. Peterswald questioned Mrs Townsend alone, who denied any knowledge of Mary Agnes being pregnant. She stated that she had noticed a change in her appearance but gave no reason for it. She consented for Mary Agnes to be examined by the colonial surgeon, who found that Mary Agnes had recently given birth. Mrs Townsend and Mary Agnes were detained.

On Saturday 6 June an inquest was held at the Adelaide Hospital to ascertain the cause of death of the newborn girl.

Dr William Jay examined the child and found that the body was in an advanced state of decomposition. No bruises or injuries could be seen, and the umbilical cord had been torn off about an inch and a half from the abdomen and was unsecured. Inside the child's mouth he found a piece of wood. Due to the decomposition he was unable to tell if the child had been born alive, but if it had been alive, then the wood in the mouth would have been sufficient to cause the death. He thought that the child was born about a fortnight before being found.

The coroner summed up the evidence and the jury retired before they returned with the verdict of wilful murder against some person unknown.

The following day, in the Adelaide Police Court, Mary Agnes Townsend and her mother Mary Townsend were both charged with murdering the child and committed for trial in the Supreme Court.

On Thursday 18 June 1874, Mary Agnes appeared before the Supreme Court where she was found guilty of concealment of birth and sentenced to 12 months imprisonment. The charges against her mother, Mary Townsend, were not proceeded with and she was discharged.

Date	*Victim*	*Accused*
7 June 1874	**George Knight**	**James Cavendish**
		and Joseph Wilson
Cause of death:	Assault	
Outcome:	Acquitted	
Location:	Hindley Street, Adelaide	

On Saturday 6 June 1874, during the late evening, 34-year-old George Knight, James Cavendish, Joseph Wilson, and three other men, named George Whitington, Britcher, and Harry, were at a brothel in Hindley Street owned by Alice Rogers. Knight had arrived before the other men. Around two-thirty the following morning, they were all having a drink. Around three am, Knight asked if there was any beer, then said he was going. Cavendish offered some drink but Knight refused, as he did not have any money. Knight left then briefly before returning and saying something to Cavendish, then hitting him. A fight ensued and Cavendish hit Knight, knocking him through a door and onto the floor.

Amelia Smith was asleep in a bedroom of the brothel when she was woken by her bedroom door bursting open, followed by two men falling into her room. One man was face down and the other was on top of him, punching his neck and face. She saw that the man being hit was Knight, whom she had known for the past nine years, and the other man was Cavendish. A man pulled Cavendish off of Knight, so she helped him up and washed the blood from his face. Knight said that he felt bad and went to Amelia Williams' room. Smith saw him again later that day in Williams' bed. He said that he had a pain in his chest and a doctor was sent for. Knight died about 20 minutes later.

On Monday 8 June, an inquest was held at the Galatea Hotel, Hindley Street, on the body of George Knight. The two men, James Cavendish and Joseph Wilson, who were supposed to be implicated in the murder, were present. Dr Robert Peel had made a post-mortem examination of Knight and stated that both eyes were blackened and there was a wound on the right cheekbone, eyebrow, chin and temple. There was a small quantity of dried blood on the right ear. The cause of death was given as the blow on the temporal muscle.

At the completion of the inquest, the jury, after a short retirement, found James Cavendish to have caused George Knight's death, Joseph Wilson to be an accessory to the fact, and George Whitington highly culpable for not endeavouring to prevent the fight.

On Tuesday 16 June 1874, Cavendish appeared before the Supreme Court charged with manslaughter. The crown solicitor stated that he had withdrawn the charge against Wilson, as there was no evidence against him. At the conclusion of Cavendish's trial, the jury acquitted him.

Date	Victim	Accused
4 July 1874	**Stott child**	**Isabella Stott**
Cause of death:	Undetermined	
Outcome:	Discharged	
Location:	Alma Plains, near Riverton	

On 4 July 1874, 17-year-old Isabella Stott, a servant to Robert Laurie at Alma Plains, gave birth to an illegitimate son. Laurie had noticed a change in Stott's appearance, so he questioned her. Subsequently a search was made in her bedroom where the body of a male child was found hidden in a box.

Dr Giles of Riverton was sent for, along with the local constable. Stott was taken into custody and a coronial inquest was held, which heard evidence from Laurie and Dr Giles. At the completion of the evidence, the jury found Stott guilty of murder and she was committed to trial.

On Thursday 10 September, Stott appeared before the Supreme Court charged with murder. Dr Giles stated that he conducted a post-mortem on the body and found that the child had been born alive, but was unable to state the precise cause of death.

At the conclusion of the evidence, the defence argued that there was no evidence of a capital offence, and secondly, that no concealment of birth had been proved. His Honour upheld the first point for the defence, but decided there was sufficient evidence of concealment of birth to go to the jury.

His Honour summed up the evidence, and said it appeared to him that the facts did not lead to the conclusion that there had been any attempt whatever to conceal and dispose of the body of the infant. The jury, after a few minutes absence from the court, returned a verdict of acquittal, and Stott was discharged.

Date	*Victim*	*Accused*
31 August 1874	**Bridget Eliza White**	**Bridget White**
Cause of death:	Suffocation	
Outcome:	Discharged	
Location:	Currie Street West, Adelaide	

Bridget and John White resided in Currie Street, Adelaide, with their six-month-old daughter, Bridget Eliza. The Whites, along with Eliza Hyde, Olivia Demond and Mary King, all lived in a brothel in Currie Street. It was common for the four women to be intoxicated. On Monday 31 August 1874, Bridget lay with her child at two-thirty in the afternoon, but did not stay longer than 20 minutes. At four-thirty pm her older son looked at the baby and said it was asleep. At five-thirty pm she found her child cold so she sent for the doctor.

Police Constable Duncan attended at the house and saw Bridget holding the child in her arms. Bridget was worse for drink and seemed to be recovering from intoxication. The other women in the house were also drunk.

On Tuesday 1 September, an inquest was held at the Ship Inn, Currie Street, to ascertain the cause of the death of Bridget Eliza White.

Eliza Hyde, who lived with Mrs White, said she last saw the baby alive around four pm, in her mother's arms. She saw two pots of beer in the house during the day. Olivia Demond gave corroborative evidence.

John Lane, who lived next door but one to Mrs White, stated he heard that the child was dead around seven pm, and at once told the police. He saw a large quantity of beer go to the house during the Sunday and Monday. Another neighbour called Susan Viant corroborated the drinking at the house, and had once complained to the landlord because of the conduct within the house.

Dr Clindening stated he had at various times visited Mrs White's children, but had not lately seen the deceased. He attended the house on the Monday evening but was unable to give a certificate for burial. He stated that Mrs White was more or less excited with drink. He could not say that the mother was drunk, but seemed to be recovering from the influence of drink. Demond was also intoxicated. A post-mortem examination was made that morning, which found the child to be well nourished and healthy. There were no marks of external violence. On opening the head Clindening found a quantity of blood between the scalp and the skull. He could find no disease that could account for the death. He did not think the infant had died in a fit and, looking at all the circumstances of the case, his opinion was that death was caused through the child being overlain, or suffocated.

The coroner summed up the evidence before the jury found that Bridget Eliza White had died from suffocation by her mother, Bridget White, and that Mary King, Olivia Demond and Eliza Hyde were accessories. The coroner committed the four women to the Supreme Court for trial on a charge of manslaughter.

On Thursday 10 September, White, Hyde, Demond and King appeared before the Supreme Court, charged with manslaughter. His Honour said he confessed he did not understand the grounds on which the women had been committed. If, when a child was found dead without any marks of violence upon it, the onus was cast on prisoners who happened to be in the vicinity to show they were not implicated, the committal might be justified, but not otherwise. It appeared to the judge that there must 'of necessity be positive evidence in some way against such persons before they could be put upon their trial'. The crown solicitor said he had been making enquires, and found no other evidence was forthcoming. No indictment had yet been laid against the women. His Honour said to the crown solicitor, 'Then I think you will be exercising a wise discretion not to indict them'. The crown solicitor said that he would convey His Honour's opinion to the attorney-general. All four women were discharged.

Date	*Victim*	*Accused*
2 September 1874	**Ballard child**	**Sarah Ballard**
Cause of death:	Haemorrhage	
Outcome:	Found guilty of concealment of birth	
	Sentenced to four months imprisonment	
Location:	Goolwa	

Sarah Ballard, a single woman aged 18 years, lived with her parents at Goolwa. On the evening of 2 September 1874, Ballard was seen by a neighbour, Mrs Wright, coming from the vicinity of the watercloset. Wright noticed that Ballard's clothes were smothered with blood, so she asked Ballard what was the matter with her, and Ballard told her that she had had a baby. Ballard said that the child had been born when she was in her bedroom about an hour before. Mrs Wright asked her what she had done with it, and Ballard replied that she had buried it in the garden. A search was made and the child was found buried at the rear of the watercloset in about 11 inches of loose soil. A coronial inquest was convened and Ballard was committed to trial.

On Thursday 12 November, Sarah Ballard appeared before the Supreme Court charged with the murder of her illegitimate child at Goolwa. Evidence was given that a post-mortem examination supported the fact that the child was born alive and that death was caused by haemorrhage from the rupture of the umbilical cord.

In cross-examination, the medical office said that probably in a case of sudden birth, owing to pain, the mother might be rendered insensible, and the child might bleed to death. The crown solicitor abandoned the charge of murder and addressed the jury simply on the concealment. Evidence was received from the witnesses that Ballard was of weak intellect. At the completion of all the evidence, the jury retired and returned with a verdict of concealment of birth, with a recommendation to mercy. Ballard was sentenced to four months imprisonment.

Date	Victim	Accused
16 November 1874	**John Lewis**	**Evan Ellis**
Cause of death:	Assault	
Outcome:	Acquitted	
Location:	Blinman	

On 16 November 1874, John Snell, John Lewis and Evan Ellis were in the vicinity of Barnes' Hotel at Blinman. All three were intoxicated. Snell asked Ellis to come home with him and the two walked up the road. Lewis followed a short time later and on overtaking the two, said to Ellis, 'I was mistaken in you today. I thought you were a Cornishman. The next time I'll tommy-axe you'. In response, Ellis told him he was an 'old dad'.

Snell and Ellis went on a little further down the road. Lewis was following them, saying, 'We'll have it out here'. Lewis caught hold of both Ellis and Snell by the arms, and struck Ellis in the face. Snell got in between them, but Lewis struck at Ellis again. Ellis fell on his hands and knees and when he got up he said, 'No man can stand this' and struck Lewis with his fist. Lewis fell down and died almost immediately.

At a coronial inquest, Ellis was found guilty of murder and committed to trial. On Friday 12 March 1875, Ellis appeared before the Supreme Court in Adelaide, charged with feloniously killing and slaying John Lewis. The acting crown solicitor, in opening his case, stated that it was one in which the prisoner had received great provocation.

After hearing evidence, His Honour said, 'If a person be so persistently assaulted he may surely strike in return. It seems to me that the prisoner only struck the blow in self-defence'. The acting crown solicitor said he could not carry the case further. The jury acquitted Ellis, who was discharged.

Date	Victim	Accused
18 January 1875	**Edward McMahon**	**James Reilly**
Cause of death:	Assault	
Outcome:	Found guilty of manslaughter	
	Sentenced to 14 days imprisonment	
Location:	West Terrace, Adelaide	

On Monday 18 January 1875, James Patten, 39-year-old Edward McMahon and 43-year-old James Reilly were working as labourers in the paddock behind the West Terrace Cemetery. Around 11 that morning, a disturbance broke out between McMahon and Reilly. McMahon was helping to measure stones, and Reilly was there with some other men. McMahon said, 'You are troubling yourself too much', and Reilly called him a liar. After a few more angry words, Reilly again called McMahon a liar. McMahon and Reilly started to fight as Patten watched, but he did not see who struck the first blow. As the fight progressed, McMahon received a blow to his head and fell immediately to the ground. Patten went to McMahon and helped him up. Patten thought that McMahon was not hurt too much, so he decided to go home to Hilton for dinner. When Patten returned to the paddock about an hour later, he was told that McMahon was dead.

Later that day, an inquest was held on the body of Edward McMahon. Dr Phillips examined the body and stated that he found sufficient evidence to satisfy him as to the cause of death. McMahon was lying on his right side and had marks behind the left ear, bruises that could have come from a man's fist. He stated that McMahon appeared to have been in good health and that the bruise could not have occurred as a result of a fall. He did not think that a post-mortem was necessary and that death would have been instantaneous from the blow. Dr Phillips stated that death was caused by a profound and overwhelming shock to the nervous system. He said that McMahon might have received heavier blows before, but this one in particular was an unfortunate blow, which struck an important part of the head.

Catherine McMahon, Edward's wife, who lived on the Mile End Road, stated that she last saw her husband that morning. She said that he was not a bad-tempered man and was steady and industrious. He had lost the use of one arm to rheumatism and could not lift it above his shoulder. She had sent her child with her husband's dinner to him but he returned saying that he thought that his father was dead. She went to the paddock where he was working and found him lifeless.

At the conclusion of the inquest, the jury found that 'the deceased, Edward McMahon, came to his death from a blow inflicted by James Reilly in a fair stand-up fight'. Reilly was committed for trail to the Supreme Court for manslaughter.

On Monday 22 March, Reilly appeared in the Supreme Court charged with feloniously killing McMahon. At the completion of the trial, the jury found Reilly guilty of manslaughter, with a recommendation of mercy. Reilly was sentenced to 14 days imprisonment.

Date	*Victim*	*Accused*
20 January 1875	Timothy Maloney	Catherine Maloney, Charles Merritt, George Northover, and Duncan Waddle

Cause of death:	Assault
Outcome:	Maloney and Northover discharged prior to trial
	Waddle acquitted
	Merritt discharged (*nolle prosequi*)
Location:	Nantawarra, near Port Wakefield

On Wednesday 20 January 1875, Timothy Maloney was at the property of his employer Charles Merritt at Nantawarra. While there, a scuffle broke out between Merritt and some of his men, during which Maloney was punched, kicked and jumped on.

The following Saturday, Maloney was taken to the Terminus Hotel at Port Wakefield, with the intention of travelling to Adelaide for medical advice. Dr Marriott was in Port Wakefield and examined Maloney, and pronounced him unfit to travel. Maloney told Dr Marriott that he was suffering from some internal injury that had occurred on the previous Wednesday when he was at Nantawarra. Maloney's condition gradually worsened before he died on the Sunday. An inquest into his death commenced in the Port Wakefield Court House that night, which ended at four am on Monday. The jury assembled for a second time later in the morning.

Dr Henry Marriott conducted a post-mortem examination of Maloney and found a rupture of a portion of the small bowel and a rupture of the large intestine. He gave the cause of death as peritonitis from effusion of fluid into the cavity of the abdomen, caused by violence or a fall.

Investigations had revealed that Maloney's wife Catherine, along with Charles Merritt, George Northover and Duncan Waddle, were all implicated in assaulting Maloney. All four accused gave evidence at the inquest and stated that Maloney was the aggressor and was intoxicated. Catherine stated that Maloney tried to assault her and that the others were told to protect her. The disturbance lasted on and off from when Maloney arrived at the property on the Thursday to the following day.

At the completion of the evidence, the jury, after deliberating for two hours, returned the following verdict:

We consider that the cause of death of the deceased, Timothy Maloney, to be peritonitis, caused by violence or a fall, which caused a rupture of the intestines, and we consider that manslaughter has been committed, either by his wife Catherine Maloney, Charles Merritt Jr, Duncan Waddle or George Northover, there not being sufficient evidence to prove which of the said parties committed the said act. The jury wish to add as a rider that great provocation was given by the deceased Timothy Maloney.

The accused were committed for trial at the Supreme Court on a charge of manslaughter. On Wednesday 17 March, all four accused appeared before the Supreme Court. Prior to a trial commencing, the acting crown solicitor handed in the attorney-general's certificate that there was no case against Catherine Maloney and George Northover, so they were discharged. Duncan Waddell went to trial for the murder of Maloney and was acquitted. Charles Merritt was due to commence his trial when the acting crown solicitor entered a *nolle prosequi*, and Merritt was discharged.

Date	*Victim*	*Accused*
1 February 1875	**James Glassenbury**	**Mary Glassenbury**
Cause of death:	Neglect	
Outcome:	Acquitted	
Location:	Adelaide	

On 6 November 1874, 27-year-old Mary Ann Glassenbury gave birth to a child whom she named James. During the birth, Elizabeth Waite, who was not a midwife, but was a neighbour of Glassenbury's, assisted out of charity. When James was born, he was a healthy child. Four days after he was born, Waite heard James crying, so she and three other women managed to get into Glassenbury's house to see what was wrong. They found her on the floor, too drunk to get into bed. Waite attended to James as best she could before leaving. Glassenbury had three other children, and her husband was away with work. Waite offered to take James and look after him, but Glassenbury refused.

On 7 December, Dr Duncan attended at Glassenbury's house where he examined James and found him to be extremely emaciated. Glassenbury had no milk and was feeding James maizena, a cornstarch. Dr Duncan told her that she might as well feed James pounded stones, and that if she had no breastmilk then the best thing he could recommend was cow's milk mixed with a little limewater.

In January 1875, Dr Clindening visited Glassenbury and James and found that James was still emaciated. Glassenbury told Dr Clindening that James never had any breast milk and was nearly always crying. On 1 February, James, who was nearly three months old, died.

On Thursday 4 February, Mary Glassenbury appeared in the police court in Adelaide on a charge of murdering her infant son. A number of witnesses gave evidence, with some testifying that Glassenbury was a common drunkard and did not attend to her family properly. She was often drunk at eight in the morning. Philip Woolman stated that he had heard Glassenbury say, 'I hope the little thing will be stiff and a corpse between this and tomorrow night'. Woolman told Glassenbury that she deserved hanging, but she abused him. Glassenbury made no statement and was committed to take trial at the Supreme Court.

On Monday 22 March, Glassenbury appeared before the Supreme Court where she was acquitted. His Honour, in addressing her, stated that he regretted there was no power to place her in seclusion from 'that drink to which she was dreadfully addicted'. He said that if she continued drinking as she was, she would continue to fail in the performance of her duties as a mother and a wife. He trusted that the death of her infant, and the critical position she had just been in, would warn her to be sober for the future.

Date	*Victim*	*Accused*
6 February 1875	**Klopp child**	**Caroline Klopp**
Cause of death:	Neglect	
Outcome:	Found guilty of concealment of birth	
	Sentenced to 12 months imprisonment	
Location:	Port Pirie	

On 6 February 1875, Caroline Klopp, a domestic servant in the employ of Mrs Oliver at Port Pirie, confessed to Mrs Oliver that she had given birth to a child and hidden it amongst the cases at the back of Wood and Oliver's store.

A search was undertaken which resulted in the discovery of a baby girl with a cord tied around the neck. The face was black as if from strangulation, and there was dirt in the mouth.

Horse-drawn carts waiting outside the Wood and Oliver store
and the Port Pirie Hotel in Ellen Street, Port Pirie.
State Library of South Australia, PRG 280/1/38/52, 1876

An inquest was held the next day where Dr Comyn, of Georgetown, who had made the post-mortem examination, stated that the cord was not sufficiently tight to cause death or fully stop respiration, and that death probably resulted in exposure and neglect. He also stated that the child, in his opinion, could not have lived many hours with the cord on.

The jury found that the child died from wilful neglect on the part of the mother of the child. A rider of the jury censured Dr Comyn for the 'unsatisfactory manner' in which he gave evidence.

On Thursday 18 March, Klopp, who was indicted for infanticide, withdrew her plea of not guilty, and, by the advice of her solicitor and with the consent of the acting crown solicitor, pleaded guilty of concealing the birth of her child.

Klopp appeared once more before the Supreme Court on Wednesday 24 March, where she was sentenced to 12 months imprisonment.

Date	*Victim*	*Accused*
27 February 1875	**Sylvia Howard Ellis**	**Eliza Ellis (Dinton)**
Cause of death:	Neglect	
Outcome:	Discharged	
Location:	Adelaide Gaol	

On 1 February 1875, Eliza Ellis, also known as Eliza Dinton, gave birth to a daughter, who she named Sylvia Howard Ellis. Around three weeks after her birth, Ellis was not coping with Sylvia, and she left her at the gates of the Dominican Convent. Ellis was found and was charged with abandoning her child, receiving seven days imprisonment at the Adelaide Gaol.

Dr Alexander Paterson, medical officer of the gaol, examined Sylvia and found that she was suffering from convulsions. Susan Howell, matron of the gaol, examined Ellis when she first arrived and found that she had no milk for the child. Ellis also informed Howell that she had given birth on 1 February, and that she had been unable to feed Sylvia since the birth.

Sylvia died on 27 February, and an inquest was held at the Adelaide Gaol on the same day. Dr Paterson stated that the immediate cause of death was convulsions, but he believed death was accelerated by deprivation of food. When the child had been in the gaol, she had all care and suitable artificial food and medicines available, and if she had proper attention from its birth mother, Sylvia would have lived.

At the completion of the evidence, the coroner summed up and the jury retired, returning with the verdict that Sylvia had died from natural causes, accelerated by the lack of food. The jury added that they thought there was 'great blame attached to the mother for leaving her child exposed in the open air as she did'. The coroner said the jury had taken a lenient view of the case, and he regretted he could not agree with them. The verdict was such as one he could not commit the woman for trial.

On Monday 1 March, Ellis appeared before the Police Court in Adelaide, charged with the murder of her child. Further evidence was given on Ellis' neglect of her child and how she did not care for it. At the completion of the proceedings, Ellis was committed for trial in the Supreme Court.

On Monday 22 March, Ellis, appeared before the Supreme Court on a charge of murdering her infant child. The acting crown prosecutor handed in the attorney-general's certificate that there was not sufficient cause for putting her on trial, and Ellis was accordingly discharged.

Date	*Victim*	*Accused*
10 March 1875	**Harriet Sneyd**	**George Sneyd**
Cause of death:	Knife wounds	
Outcome:	Found guilty of murder	
	Sentenced to death, commuted to life imprisonment	
	Committed suicide six years later in October 1881	
Location:	Naracoorte	

On Wednesday 10 March 1875, George Sneyd went to the house of Mrs Marshall, who resided in the township of Naracoorte. He went there to see his wife, Harriet Sneyd, who had been staying at the Marshall's house for about a month. Harriet had moved out because she had been frightened of George, who had threatened to murder her on several occasions, for some time.

George spoke to Mrs Marshall and asked to see his wife. She refused, saying that his wife was too frightened to see him. George said that he would give her 24 hours to prepare for death. George had hidden a large carving knife up his sleeve, and waited at the house for about an hour. When George saw his wife go to an adjoining bedroom, he followed her and stabbed her. Harriet called out, 'He has stabbed me in the heart'. Mrs Marshall heard the scream and ran to the bedroom where she saw Harriet on the floor and George stooping over her in the act of stabbing her in the arm. Mrs Marshall approached them and wrestled the knife from George. She then sent a boy for the police, who arrived and took George into custody. Dr Gunning attended and treated Harriet.

On Monday 15 March, George was taken before the Stipendiary Magistrate charged with malicious wounding and was committed to trial at the Circuit Court in Robe. George was placed in the custody of Trooper Yates, and they left Naracoorte for Robe. Prior to their arrival, Harriet died from her injuries. This information was telegraphed to Robe, and Trooper Morris was dispatched from Robe to Naracoorte to meet up with Trooper Yates and George and tell them to return to Naracoorte for the inquest.

The inquest was held on Thursday 18 March with Mr Smith, the Stipendiary Magistrate, acting as the coroner. Trooper Yates gave evidence, stating that at around eight pm on 10 March, he received information that George Sneyd was stabbing his wife in Mrs Marshall's house. He immediately went to the house and found Harriet lying on the bedroom floor bleeding from multiple wounds. Yates secured George who he found sitting in an adjoining

311

room. When Yates gave George the usual caution, George said, 'I am not sorry for what I have done, I am only sorry for having been brought to it by her'.

At the completion of the inquest, the jury retired for about two minutes, and upon their return, the foreman reported that they had reached a unanimous verdict of wilful murder against the prisoner. George Sneyd, who preserved his composure during the inquest, and appeared rather indifferent to his position, was committed to trial at Robe.

On Friday 9 April, Sneyd appeared before the Robe Circuit Court where he was found guilty of murder and sentenced to death. On Thursday 29 April, the Executive Council met and decided to commute the sentence to imprisonment for life with hard labour.

Parkside Lunatic Asylum, 1880.
State Library of South Australia, B 62414/1/67

Over six years later, on 21 October 1881, an inquest was held at the Parkside Lunatic Asylum on the body of George Sneyd. The jury found that Sneyd had committed suicide by stabbing himself.

George and Harriet Sneyd had previously given evidence as witnesses in the trial of Narikonyary, an Aboriginal man who murdered his wife (see 15 May 1873).

Date	Victim	Accused
5 May 1875	**Unknown child**	**Unknown**
Cause of death:	Assault (with a rock)	
Outcome:	Unsolved	
Location:	Naracoorte	

On Wednesday 5 May 1875, the body of a newborn child was found in a paddock at Naracoorte. A large stone block was lying on the head, which was bruised. The body was removed to the local police station, where the following day, a post-mortem examination was conducted. An inquest into the death was held and the cause of death was given as a head injury, probably by the stone block. The jury returned a verdict of wilful murder against some person unknown.

Date	Victim	Accused
11 July 1875	**Mary Buchan**	**William Page**
Cause of death:	Strangulation	
Outcome:	Found guilty of murder	
	Sentenced to death, executed 27 October 1875	
Location:	Mount Gambier	

Around six-thirty pm on Sunday 11 July 1875, 20-year-old Mary Buchan met a man called William Page near the Church of England, and was convinced by him to go for a walk instead of going to church. That evening, at around eight pm, some people who were leaving the church heard screams coming from Mrs Mitchell's paddock. They stopped to listen more, but the screams stopped. They thought that the screams were from a 'well-known character' in the neighbourhood, and thought no more of it.

Buchan did not return home that evening and was reported as missing by her mother. The police took Page into custody, as he was the last person seen with her. Page told police that Buchan wanted to go to her father, who was in another colony, and that she had left on a horse. Page was kept in custody for a week so his story could be checked, and during that time some sort of confirmatory evidence arrived from Casterton in Victoria, where a young woman had passed through, matching Buchan's description. Page was about to be released when it was discovered he had a warrant for wife desertion at

Normanville, so he was taken before the Police Court. The case was proved, and in default of payment of the amount ordered, he was committed to gaol for four months.

Buchan's mother did not believe the supposed sighting of her daughter in Casterton, so she made her own enquiries. She received information from the Casterton Police, which revealed that the person who rode through the town the day after Buchan disappeared was wearing different clothing and was with a man. Buchan's disappearance became more suspicious when police considered the possibility that Buchan, a young girl ignorant of the country, would ride for over 50 miles on the worst road in the district in a pitch dark night, and turn up 'fresh and hearty in company with a new squire' in Casterton.

Mary Buchan, approximately 1870. State Library of South Australia, B 1674.

On Monday 2 August, Buchan's body was found in Mrs Mitchell's property, Hedley Park, buried about two feet in the ground. She was covered with a shawl and upon examination, it was found that she had been beaten and strangled. Her head had been battered and she had hand marks on her throat.

An inquest was held the following day, and adjourned until Friday 6 August for the production of Page. At the conclusion of the inquest, the jury found Page guilty of wilful murder.

On Wednesday 6 October, William Page appeared before the Mount Gambier Circuit Court, charged with murder. Page pleaded guilty, and the effect of the confession on the crowded court was 'electrical'. There was a hum of astonishment for several minutes, and the police had some difficulty in restoring order. After a few minutes pause, the following took place:

Judge's Associate: 'You have been found guilty on your own confession of the wilful murder of Mary Buchan. Have you anything to say?'
His Honour interrupted and said to Page: 'Do you, prisoner, persist in that plea?'
Page: 'Yes'
His Honour: 'How do you plead?'
Page: 'I plead guilty.'
His Honour: 'Do you understand the full effect of the plea?'
Page: 'Yes.'
His Honour: 'And you still plead guilty?'
Page: 'Yes'.

The judge then sentenced Page to death. On Wednesday 27 October, Page was executed. Page had written a confession regarding Buchan's murder, which was released after the execution. In part, he stated:

... I there met Mary J Buchan on the road and we walked together to the open ground opposite the hay stacks, where we sat down for about an hour. Afterwards we passed into the paddock with the intention of crossing to the MacDonnell Bay Road. As we stood for a short time I said something about her being too fond of another young man. I cannot remember the exact words. Mary took offence at this, and said she would have nothing to do with me, as she knew I was a married man, and that I was only making a fool of her. She then took off her finger the ring I gave her and offered it to me, which I refused. She let it fall, and in doing so she must have dropped the ring into the outside pocket of my coat, where I found it when I got home. On this she turned to go from me, and my anger being greatly excited, on the impulse of the moment, I took the whip-handle from my pocket and struck her on the side of the head with it. She staggered and screamed. I then struck her a second time, when the whip-handle broke. These were all the blows I struck. She fell with a moan. When I saw, as I believed, that she was beyond recovery, then I strangled her.

Page carried the body to the place where it was found and left it there. He returned later that night with a spade and buried the body.

Date	Victim	Accused
24 July 1875	**Unknown child**	**Unknown**
Cause of death:	Strangulation	
Outcome:	Unsolved	
Location:	River Torrens, Adelaide	

On Sunday 25 July 1875, between two and three in the afternoon, Albert Gottaschalck went to the Torrens with his sister and a friend. When they were near the old ford on the eastern side of the fence, he caught sight of a child's head on the ground. At the time, Gottaschalck was going up the bank towards the railway shed. The body was lightly covered over with grass. Gottaschalck saw Police Constable James Hammill nearby and told him what he had found. PC Hammill went down to the riverbank and examined the body of a newborn female. He noticed that the child had a piece of tape tied tightly around the neck, and it appeared so tight that the flesh was cut through. He thought that the body might have been there one or two days.

On Tuesday 27 July, an inquest was held at the Destitute Asylum on the body of the newborn female child. Dr Robert Peel gave evidence and stated that he had made a post-mortem examination of the child, and that she was well nourished and fully developed. There were a number of bruises on the body, including on the right leg, knee and heel, and the left arm, right shoulder and right breast. There was a fracture of the orbital bone and a large clot underneath the skullcap. The afterbirth was still attached to the body. It was his opinion that the child had had an existence independent of its mother, but did not think it lived more than a few minutes. He thought that the tape around the neck was sufficient to cause death by strangulation, and that the birth could have been from Friday night to Saturday morning.

The jury returned a verdict of wilful murder against some person or persons unknown.

Date	*Victim*	*Accused*
November 1875	Coolcawaninie	Milly Ingarlta, Coongulta, and Wongie
Cause of death:	Assault (with a waddy)	
Outcome:	Milly Ingarlta died in the Adelaide Gaol prior to trial	
	Coongulta and Wongie found not guilty	
Location:	The Wedge, Port Lincoln	

On a Saturday in late November 1875, Milly Ingarlta, Coongulta and Wongie left Gum Flat to visit their relatives at the Wedge. The next day, Coolcawaninie, who was 'rather prone to growling', quarrelled with them for drinking some water. The men, resenting the accusation as unjust, beat Coolcawaninie with their waddies so heavily that she died. Trooper Clode, who became aware of the death, arrested the three and brought them to Port Lincoln.

Court House and Police Station, Port Lincoln approximately 1870.
State Library of South Australia, B 7987

On Monday 20 December, the three men appeared before the magistrate. Giving evidence, Clode stated that the prisoners told him that they did not look upon their conduct as a crime. One assured the trooper that he was not only the first to strike her, but also the last. The three were committed for trial at the Supreme Court.

On Sunday 20 February 1876, Milly Ingarlta died in the Adelaide Gaol. An inquest was held on Monday 21 February where Dr Paterson, colonial surgeon, stated that Milly Ingarlta first came to his notice on 3 January when he complained of colic. On examination he was found to be suffering from disease of the heart and lungs. The cause of death was given as heart disease.

On Thursday 23 March, Coongulta and Wongie appeared before the Supreme Court charged with murdering Coolcawaninie. Maria Kierobie, Wangelta and Yangelta gave unsworn evidence. All of the witnesses testified that Coolcawaninie was alive one Sunday morning, and she was dead that evening. No one saw how she died, but they all stated that Coolcawaninie was sick and used to spit blood. There were no eyewitnesses to the assault and the only evidence was the conversation that the prisoners had had with the police trooper. At the conclusion of the trial, the jury retired for 45 minutes, before returning and finding the prisoners not guilty. Both were discharged. His Honour stated that he quite agreed with the verdict, as it would have been dangerous to convict on the evidence given.

Date	*Victim*	*Accused*
1 February 1876	**Hanchie**	**Chelengie (Peter)**
Cause of death:	Assault (with a boomerang)	
Outcome:	Acquitted	
Location:	Yardea, north of the Gawler Ranges	

On 1 February 1876, Chelengie, Hanchie, Coolbylti, and a large number of other Aboriginal people were at Yardea, north of the Gawler Ranges. A fight broke out amongst the group, during which a number of spears were thrown. The spears that were used were the same as those for spearing kangaroos, and if they had struck anyone, they would have been killed. During the fight Hanchie received a fatal wound. Chelengie was taken into custody, and was charged with Hanchie's murder.

On Thursday 23 March 1876, Chelengie appeared before the Supreme Court charged with murder. Coolbylti gave unsworn evidence and stated that Hanchie threw four spears at Chelengie, but the other Aboriginal people warded them off. Hanchie was going to throw another spear when Chelengie threw his boomerang, which struck Hanchie, who fell to the ground. The impact caused the boomerang to break in two. Chelengie did not throw anything else before the boomerang. At that stage of the evidence, His Honour stated that the conduct of the prisoner was most natural, and he had only acted in self-defence. The jury acquitted Chelengie.

Date	*Victim*	*Accused*
28 April 1876	**Cox child**	**Lavinia Cox**
Cause of death:	Haemorrhage	
Outcome:	Pleaded guilty to concealment of birth	
	Sentenced to three months imprisonment	
Location:	Caltowie, near Jamestown	

In March 1876, 17-year-old Lavinia Cox gained work as a servant for Robert and Emily Williams of Caltowie. Robert noticed that Cox had a 'peculiar' figure. At about 10 pm on Friday 28 April, Cox complained to Emily that she had violent pains, but said that she had had them before and asked for ground ginger in warm water. Emily spoke to Cox about her condition, and asked her if she was pregnant. Cox denied that she was and went to bed. Robert and Emily also went to bed. During the night, Robert heard Cox go out several times. When Robert called Cox the following morning, he found that she had already gone out. He saw her in the watercloset washing out a bowl. Robert looked in and he saw that there was blood on the seat and the floor, which he told his wife about. Robert went outside to a small hut in the yard, where he noticed a little mound of chaff heaped up. He moved the mound with his foot and found the body of a newborn infant. Robert removed the child and put it under lock and key and sent for the police. After being told of the blood in the watercloset, Emily questioned Cox, and searched her bedroom where she found Cox's skirt with blood on it.

Police Trooper O'Brien attended and took possession of the body and arrested Lavinia on a charge of killing her newborn infant. After being cautioned, Lavinia stated that the child was born in the watercloset around 11 pm on the Friday night and that she took it to her bedroom but it died during the night.

Globe Hotel, Jamestown, 1878.
State Library of South Australia, B 11520

On Sunday 30 April, an inquest was held at the Jamestown Hotel into the death of the child of Lavinia Cox. Dr Riddell, Master of Surgery, stated that he examined the body of a full-grown newborn. He conducted a post-mortem examination and stated that he found the lungs were healthy and floated in water. The stomach and brain were also healthy. He stated that the child had breathed and had a separate existence from the mother. The umbilical cord had been severed or cut with a blunt instrument and never tied. There were no marks of violence on the body, only a depression on the lips. Riddell was of the opinion that the child had bled to death from the umbilical cord not being tied. Riddell also examined Lavinia and stated that she had all the signs of having recently given birth.

The jury, after half an hour's consultation, returned with the verdict that the child had died as a result of the umbilical cord not being tied. As a rider, they added that they were of the opinion that it was done through ignorance. Cox was committed to trial at the Supreme Court.

On Friday 16 June, Cox appeared before the Supreme Court charged with murder. Mr Bundey, who appeared for Cox, stated that he had looked through the depositions, and found that they did not support the first charge of murder, but they did support the charge of concealment of birth. Bundey stated that he had advised his client to plead guilty to that charge. The crown solicitor stated that he would accept that plea and concurred with the view that Mr Bundey had taken as to the depositions.

On Monday 19 June, Cox appeared once more in the Supreme Court where she was sentenced to three months imprisonment.

Date	*Victim*	*Accused*
22 June 1876	**Mary James**	**John Harman Jr**
Cause of death:	Assault (with a weight)	
Outcome:	Found guilty of manslaughter	
	Sentenced to 12 months imprisonment with hard labour	
Location:	Third Street, Bowden	

Fanny Gapper was a servant to 21-year-old John Harman Jr, who had a shop at Third Street, Bowden. Around nine-thirty am on Thursday 22 June 1876, Gapper was at home when Harman arrived home in a state of intoxication. Mary James, who was Harman's 52-year-old mother in law, also lived in the house. When Harman arrived, James scolded him, calling him names. Harman had some fish in his pocket, one of which was a Tommy Ruff. He took the fish out and struck James across the face with it. James went outside and picked up a piece of brick and threw it towards Harman. In response, Harman picked up a chair and threw it at James, who had gone outside to the stockyard. James seemed to be very angry, but Harman was not. Harman went inside and into his bedroom and started to take off his boots. James went into his room and threw a brick at him. Harman picked up the brick and followed James outside. After about three minutes, Harman came back inside and said to his wife, 'Oh Kate, I have killed the old woman'. Gapper went outside and saw James lying on the footpath in front of the shop door. Harman and John Conway carried James inside and called for the doctor.

Dr Thomas Seabrooke of Hindmarsh was called to see James and found her comatose, with a contused laceration on the right temporal region, and comminuted fracture of the bones. Dr McIntyre was sent for, and on his arrival they performed an operation to remove some pieces of bone pressing on the brain. James died from her injuries at 10 pm that night.

On Friday 23 June, an inquest was held at the Tanner's Arms, Bowden, on the body of Mary James. John Conway, a butcher of North Adelaide, gave evidence, stating that he was in Harman's shop the morning before when Harman arrived home drunk. James was in the shop and started to abuse Harman when he arrived. She had called him a 'dirty low blackguard', before

Harman had said anything. After about 15 minutes, Harman chased James into the backyard, where Conway saw James throw a brick at Harman, hitting him on the shoulder. James went into the shop and picked up a chopper and threatened to split Harman's skull. Harman walked past her and went into his bedroom and James followed, carrying a brick. She said she would split Harman's skull with it. Conway later saw James on the ground outside the house.

Evidence was given that Harman had struck James with a four pound weight that he kept on the counter of his shop. James had picked up the weight as she went out into the yard. She threw the weight at Harman and he picked it up and threw it back, hitting her on the head. The jury, after a short deliberation, found Harman guilty of manslaughter under great provocation. Harman was committed to the Supreme Court.

On Wednesday 20 September, John Harman Jr appeared before the Supreme Court charged with murder, defended by Mr W Bundey. At the completion of the trial, the jury retired for 20 minutes, and on their return found Harman guilty of manslaughter, under very great provocation, and earnestly recommended him to the mercy of the court. Harman appeared before the Supreme Court the following week where he was sentenced to 12 months imprisonment with hard labour.

Date	*Victim*	*Accused*
10 September 1876	**Ellen Benjamin**	**Benjamin**
Cause of death:	Exposure	
Outcome:	Discharged	
Location:	Long Valley, near Strathalbyn	

On Sunday 10 September 1876, David Bews, an Aboriginal man, was at Long Valley. There were five or six other Aboriginal people there, including his wife Ellen Bews and their child, Eli. Benjamin and his lubra, Ellen Benjamin, were also there. They were drinking wine and all were drunk. Later that evening, David Bews saw Benjamin and Ellen Benjamin leave.

Two other Aboriginal men, James Jackson and Charley Redman, went from Strathalbyn to Long Valley and camped near Mr Kennedy's property. During the evening Benjamin came to their camp, but Ellen Benjamin was not with him. When they asked him where she was, he said that he had left her on the side of the road. Benjamin had been drinking and he stayed in the camp. The next day, on Monday morning, Jackson, Redman and Benjamin left around six am and walked on a road. Benjamin left them and about 100 yards later they found Ellen Benjamin's body.

On Tuesday 12 September 1876, an inquest was held at the Strathalbyn Court House regarding the death of Ellen Benjamin. Ellen Bews gave evidence, stating that they were all drinking wine, but Ellen Benjamin was drinking the most. Eli Bews stated that he saw Benjamin pushing Ellen Benjamin around. They had no sticks or waddies at the camp at Long Valley.

Dr Blue and family at Strathalbyn, 1880.
State Library of South Australia, B 28922

Dr W Blue made a post-mortem examination. He stated that the body was fairly nourished and there were no marks of external violence, except for a wound at the back of the head. It was an incised wound about three-quarters of an inch long, down to the skull, probably made by some sharp instrument. The wound was not sufficient to cause death. The lungs were in a highly congested state, and the heart was full of blood. His opinion was that Ellen had died from exposure after receiving the wound, which would probably have stunned her.

The jury, after consideration, returned with the verdict that the deceased came to her death from the infliction of a blow upon the head, which stupefied her, and from subsequent exposure to the very cold night. From the evidence, the jury were unable to say who inflicted the blow.

Benjamin was later arrested for Ellen Benjamin's murder. On Tuesday 19 September, Benjamin appeared before the Strathalbyn Magistrates' Court, where further evidence was obtained regarding the death of Ellen Benjamin. At the conclusion of the evidence, the magistrate discharged Benjamin due to lack of evidence.

August Dreachler was then charged with supplying Benjamin with two gallons of wine. Dreachler pleaded guilty and was fined £10. Eilen Andrews, Eilen Rankine, Ellen Bews, David Bews and Benjamin where then charged with being drunk and riotous on Sunday 10 September at Long Valley. They all pleaded guilty and were fined five shillings each, or in default seven days imprisonment. The fines were paid and all were set free.

Date	*Victim*	*Accused*
17 November 1876	**Lucy Capel**	**Alfred Dickinson**
Cause of death:	Poisoned	
Outcome:	Discharged	
Location:	Grote Street, Adelaide	

John Capel (also spelt Caple), a coachbuilder, lived with his 60-year-old wife Lucy at their house on Grote Street, Adelaide. Around midday on 9 November 1876, Lucy was taken ill and complained of a pain on her right side near her hip. Lucy went to bed, but the following morning she was still complaining about the pain in her hip. After breakfast, Dr Astles called to see Lucy, and suspected that she was suffering from an attack of sciatica. Dr Astles prescribed medicine that John filled at the chemist on King William Street. The medicine was filled in two bottles; the larger bottle was liniment, to be applied three times a day, and the other instructed that one tablespoon of the mixture was be taken every four hours.

Margaret Sutch, who was in the employ of the Capels, gave the medicine bottles to Lucy on Friday 10 November. Lucy took a tablespoon full of the medicine in the smaller bottle and immediately complained about the taste. Sutch applied a little of it to her tongue and washed her mouth out afterwards saying that the 'stuff was regular poison'.

After taking the medication for several days, Lucy's condition worsened. John saw that Lucy was 'nearly mad' and found her on the bed in a state of stupor, unconscious and scarcely moving. John called for Dr Astles again and when he arrived he found Lucy in an insensible and comatose condition. He thought that it was impossible to have an effect as this unless she had taken the wrong medication. On close examination of Lucy, he detected a strong smell of liniment on her breath and after examining the bottles he found that the labels had been put on the wrong bottles, and Lucy had taken the liniment instead of the medicine. Astles treated Lucy but she later died. A post-mortem examination was later conducted and the cause of death was given as pneumonia and bronchitis, accelerated by the poison taken the week before.

On Friday 17 November, an inquest was held at the Metropolitan Hotel in Grote Street, into the circumstances attending the death of Lucy Capel. Victor Dumas, a chemist, testified that the prescription was made up by one of his assistants named Alfred Dickinson, who had been in his employ for about 12 months. Dumas examined the bottles and said that the label on the bottle was wrong, as it should have had 'poison' and 'for outward use only' printed on it. Dumas had discharged Dickinson when he found out what had happened. At that stage, the inquest was adjourned for Dickinson to attend and give evidence.

The inquest resumed on Tuesday 21 November. Evidence was given by Dickinson, who was in custody on a charge of manslaughter. Dickinson gave a statement through his solicitor, in which he stated that he did recall the time he made up the prescription for Mrs Capel. He further stated that if he did wrongly label the bottles, he knew nothing about it, and if he did so, it was a misadventure and that he had no intention of doing any harm. He had been engaged for five years in dispensing medication and had never made a mistake before.

The coroner summed up the evidence, and stated that although Mrs Capel was in bad health and did not have long to live, the law was so strict that if a life were shortened by one single minute by the act of another person through carelessness, he was held liable. The jury retired for about an hour and a quarter and returned with the verdict that:

The cause of death was congestion of the lungs and bronchitis, accelerated by poison dispensed by Alfred Dickinson, who we find, consequent thereon, to be guilty of manslaughter. We add as a rider that we are of the opinion that Mr Dumas is exonerated from any blame.

The coroner then committed Dickinson for trial at the Supreme Court, but under the circumstances, he would accept bail.

On Wednesday 30 March 1877, Dickinson appeared before the Supreme Court where he pleaded not guilty to feloniously killing and slaying Lucy Capel. At the conclusion of the evidence, the judge pointed out that the evidence was of a very indefinite character. It was not sufficiently strong either one way or the other as to the cause of death, and under the circumstances he considered it foolish to continue the case. The crown prosecutor agreed and Dickinson was discharged.

Date	*Victim*	*Accused*
18 November 1876	**James Grant Walsh**	**Felix O'Neill**
Cause of death:	Assault (with a spade)	
Outcome:	Found guilty of manslaughter	
	Sentenced to seven years imprisonment with hard labour	
Location:	Paradise	

Richard Fullalove was a labourer who resided at Paradise. During the evening of Saturday 18 November 1876, he was drinking at the Paradise Bridge Hotel. At around 11 pm he left the hotel to go home, which was about 200 yards away. When he arrived home, he started to move his furniture to the house on the opposite side of the road. After removing some items, he returned to his house when he met a group of men, all of whom were armed with spades and sticks, in the middle of the road. Among them was 30-year-old Felix O'Neill and another called Fox. Fullalove went towards his house and the group followed him. Fullalove asked them what they wanted and one responded 'blood or money', and struck Fullalove in the chest with a stick, which knocked him backwards. Fullalove went through the house and out the back door where he saw O'Neill. Fullalove said, 'Mr O'Neill, what do you want here?' O'Neill responded, 'You bloody thief, I'll let you know what I want here'. O'Neill picked up a large stone and threw it at Fullalove, who ran back into the house and out of the front door.

A fight broke out, and Fullalove armed himself with a broom handle. Fullalove was knocked to the ground and four of the group were hitting him. Fullalove saw 18-year-old James Walsh standing on the road and he called for assistance. Walsh entered the property and pushed some of the men off

Fullalove and started to pick him up. At that time O'Neill struck Walsh on the back of the head with the blade of a spade. Walsh fell to the ground and managed to scramble to the roadway. Fullalove ran off and the others dispersed. Fullalove saw Walsh later that night and saw that his head was cut and this shirt was covered with blood. Fullalove was later told that Walsh had died.

Police Trooper Pascoe arrested O'Neill for Walsh's murder. When arrested, O'Neill said, 'I'll tell you the truth. I struck him to save another. When I came home last night I heard a row at Fullalove's house between Fox and Fullalove. I was looking on when I saw Fox was struck. I saw Walsh strike Fox. I picked a stick up from the ground and struck Walsh on the head. I was quite sober. I did not know who it was I struck the blow'.

On Monday 20 November, an inquest was held at the Paradise Bridge Hotel to ascertain the circumstances into the death of James Walsh. Felix O'Neill was present. Dr John Benson stated that he last saw Walsh on Sunday morning, and that Walsh died just five minutes after his arrival. Benson, with Dr Sprod, conducted a post-mortem examination and found a wound on the back of the head, which was about an inch-and-a-half long. There were no injuries to the outer cavern of the skull, but on opening it he found a large clot of blood caused by the rupture of a large artery. Benson stated that a blow from a spade or a heavy piece of wood could have caused the injury.

At the conclusion of the evidence, the jury retired then returned with a verdict of manslaughter against O'Neill, who was committed to trial.

On Wednesday 4 April, O'Neill appeared before the Supreme Court where he pleaded not guilty. At the conclusion of the trial, O'Neill was found guilty of manslaughter. On Saturday 7 April, O'Neill was sentenced to seven years imprisonment with hard labour.

Date	*Victim*	*Accused*
14 December 1876	**Frederick Went**	**William Hocking**
Cause of death:	Assault	
Outcome:	Case dismissed (*nolle prosequi*)	
Location:	Morphettville	

Henry Tothill was a horse trainer who lived with his family at a property at Morphettville, where he also had a number of stables. Tothill employed several boys to work at the stables, including Frederick (Fred) Went, who was 14 years old.

Early on Thursday 14 December 1876, Tothill left the property, leaving 28-year-old William Hocking in charge. Tothill gave orders to Hocking that he was to look after the boys and if they deserved it, he could give them a cut with the whip. Tothill knew that Hocking and Went had fallen out several times before.

Later that evening, after Tothill had returned home, Mrs Tothill called out for an axe, but none of the boys would fetch it for her. Hocking asked Went why he did not get it, and Went replied that he had not been asked. Hocking told Went to get the axe, but he refused. Hocking said that he would make him get it, taking hold of Went's arm and dragging him about 40 yards. Went lay down on the ground and Hocking took hold of his collar and one of his legs and lifted him up off the ground, to about chest level. There were five or six boys there at the time when the scuffle took place. Went fell to the ground and received serious injuries.

Mrs Tothill saw what was going on and called out to her husband saying that Went was 'down', meaning that he looked deceased. Tothill went outside and saw Went being held by two other boys. He took Went, who was in an insensible state, into his house. Tothill bathed Went's temples with water and vinegar and took him in a trap to the local doctor. The doctor told Tothill to take him back home and continue the treatment. Tothill took Went back home, but he died later that night.

On Saturday 16 December, an inquest was held at the Morphett Arms Hotel into the circumstances of the death of Frederick Went. At the completion of the evidence, the jury retired for about 20 minutes to consider their verdict. When they returned, the foreman informed the coroner that they were unable to come to a verdict, as there was not the slightest chance of their agreeing. The jury were then discharged. Hocking was later charged with manslaughter and committed to trial in the Supreme Court.

On Wednesday 28 March 1877, Hocking appeared before the Supreme Court charged with feloniously killing and slaying Frederick Went. At the conclusion of the trial, the jury retired but were unable to come to a verdict as some of the jury were in favour of a guilty verdict, whilst others could not decide either way. The point of contention was the lawfulness of the prisoner lifting the boy up before he sustained the injury. His Honour stated that if the prisoner took the lad up in a reasonable manner to correct him, the result of the fall might be regarded as misadventure, but if he took him up for the purpose of punishment or assault, the act was unlawful, and the charge could be sustained. The jury again retired, but were unable to come to a verdict, so they were discharged. Hocking was remanded until the following day.

On Thursday 29 March, Hocking appeared before the Supreme Court where the crown solicitor said that he had seen the witnesses, and found that he could bring forward no fresh evidence, and should therefore enter a *nolle prosequi*. Hocking was discharged.

Date	*Victim*	*Accused*
15 December 1876	**William Knox**	**Winginia (Sambo)**
Cause of death:	Assault (with a stone)	
Outcome:	Found guilty of manslaughter	
	Sentenced to 12 months imprisonment with hard labour	
Location:	Yantanabie	

On 19 December 1876, the body of William Knox was found at Yantanabie. As it was believed that he had died from want of water, an inquest was deemed unnecessary, and Knox was buried. In the latter part of August 1877, Police Trooper McCord heard a rumour among some local Aboriginal people in the Gawler Ranges that Winginia, also known as Sambo, had killed Knox. Police Trooper Clode, stationed at Kadina, located and arrested 38-year-old Winginia at Holverginia. Clode cautioned Winginia and they started to travel towards Yantanabie. On the road, Winginia told Clode, 'Me have been killing that white man, me kill him along ponta' (ponta, in this case, meaning stone). Further along the road, Winginia picked up a piece of sandstone and told Clode that it was the same type of stone that he had used to kill Knox. Winginia explained that he and Knox quarrelled over a lubra and that Knox was to give him four shillings, but afterwards refused to keep to his bargain, and gave him a drink instead. They then had a fight, and each knocked the other one down. After the fight, Knox sat down and Winginia threw a stone at him, hitting him on the head.

Knox's body was exhumed and an inquest was held on 4 October 1877, at Walpuppie, where other evidence was given that Knox had promised Winginia some money, but had neglected to give it to him, so Winginia threw a stone at Knox that hit him in the head and killed him. At the completion of the inquest, the jury found Winginia guilty of manslaughter. Winginia was committed to take trial at the next criminal sittings.

On Friday 16 November 1877, Winginia appeared before the Supreme Court charged with feloniously killing and murdering William Knox. At the completion of the trial, the judge ruled that the evidence given at trial by Winginia's two lubras was inadmissible, as they occupied the same position towards the prisoner that a married woman would to her husband. The consequence was that the crown case was so much weakened that the judge stated that he did not consider it possible to sustain the capital charge of murder. His Honour, in summing up the evidence, laid stress on the prisoner's own admission of his guilt. The jury retired before returning and finding Winginia guilty of manslaughter. Winginia appeared before the Supreme Court on Tuesday 20 November, where, through an interpreter, he stated that he had no objection to the court sentencing him. He did kill the whitefellow with the stone, but the whitefellow was the first to attack him. Winginia was sentenced to 12 months imprisonment with hard labour.

Date	*Victim*	*Accused*
25 December 1876	**Gertrude Dudley**	**John Dudley**
Cause of death:	Knife wounds	
Outcome:	Found guilty of manslaughter	
	Sentenced to life imprisonment with hard labour	
	Released after three years	
Location:	North Terrace, Adelaide	

Gertrude Dudley was a 19-year-old servant of Mr Edmeads, who resided on North Terrace in Adelaide. Gertrude was married to John Dudley, but in December 1876 she was residing at North Terrace, and her husband was living at Kadina. On 25 December 1876, Gertrude was at Edmeads' house when she noticed John outside. John was throwing small stones at her window. Gertrude went outside to see John, and while they were talking, John stabbed Gertrude multiple times. Gertrude staggered back into the house where the occupants tried to help her. John followed not long after Gertrude and said, 'That woman is my wife. She was false, and I have stabbed her'.

Police Constable Holzerland attended at the house, where he saw that Gertrude had been stabbed and was bleeding. Holzerland went into the backyard and found a bloodstained butcher's knife after a short search. Holzerland took the knife inside the house and John confirmed that it was the weapon he had used. Arrangements were made to take Gertrude Dudley to the Adelaide Hospital. Holzerland took John into custody.

Dr William Gardner was the senior house surgeon on duty when Gertrude was admitted. It was about 11 pm on Christmas night and Gertrude had multiple severe stab wounds to the upper part of her body. She was treated for the wounds but on the next day peritonitis had set in and she gradually got worse.

King William Street, Adelaide, east side, between Pirie and Grenfell Streets.
In the centre is the Clarence Hotel, and to the right is the Wesleyan Book Depot.
State Library of South Australia, B 1023, 1870

On Friday 29 December Gertrude was convinced she was going to die, so Gardner contacted the police. The city coroner attended and took a dying declaration from Gertrude:

> I believe I am going to die. On Monday 25th day of this month I went out with my husband, John Dudley. I went to the Clarence Hotel. The young man he was jealous of was there, named William Blackwell. Went with Blackwell to North Adelaide. My husband followed us. Blackwell went home. I went to my house. My husband pelted stones at the window. I went out to see him. He said why did I deceive him. He asked me to embrace him for the last time. I did so. He then began stabbing me. I fell down and got up again. I ran to the house. He

followed me. He said he was going to give himself to the police. It was between ten and eleven o'clock at night. He stabbed me seven times. Did not see the weapon he used. I am 19 years of age. I had connection with Blackwell once.

Gertrude died later that day.

On Wednesday 3 January, an inquest was held at the Adelaide Hospital on the body of Gertrude Dudley. Dr Gardner gave evidence of conducting a post-mortem where he found that Gertrude had six distinct stab wounds, one of which pierced the diaphragm and the liver. Gardner stated that the butcher's knife produced in court (which was found by Police Constable Holzerland) was capable of inflicting all of the wounds.

At the conclusion of the evidence, the jury returned a verdict of wilful murder, under the grossest provocation. The coroner said he should have to ask the jury to alter the verdict by striking out 'under the grossest provocation'. The jury responded by adding that '... the jury wish to express their opinion that the above deed was committed under the greatest provocation, and strongly censure the unmanly and sneaking conduct of the witness Blackwell'. Dudley said, 'I did not know my wife was untrue to me before the night of the 25th December, when I caught them together in the act of connection'. Dudley was committed to trial.

On Tuesday 27 March, Dudley appeared before the Supreme Court where he was found guilty of manslaughter. Dudley appeared once more on Wednesday 4 April where he was sentenced to life imprisonment with hard labour for the term of his natural life.

In April 1880, His Excellency the Governor remitted the sentence and Dudley was liberated. It was reported that:

The sentence of John Dudley, who was condemned to imprisonment for life for the manslaughter of his wife, Gertrude Dudley, on March 27, 1877 has been remitted by His Excellency the Governor. Shortly after Dudley was sentenced a movement was started in his favor, and the Government were memorialised to commute the sentence on the ground of extenuating circumstances connected with the case. At the trial it was shown that the prisoner committed the crime through the infidelity of his wife. The Executive refused to commute the sentence at the time, but it was believed that after the expiration of a part of the sentence they would again take the case into consideration.

Ten years later, on Tuesday 10 December 1889, Dudley appeared before the Adelaide Licensing Bench to have the Publican's Licence for the Henley Beach Hotel transferred to him. Inspector Sullivan opposed the application on the ground that Dudley was not a fit and proper person to hold a licence. Sullivan referred to Dudley's previous conviction, and also accused Dudley of drunkenness. Dudley's application was refused.

Date	*Victim*	*Accused*
6 January 1877	**Robert Rogers**	**Thomas Gale**
Cause of death:	Assault	
Outcome:	Case dismissed (*nolle prosequi*)	
Location:	Stony Creek	

On 6 January 1877, Robert Rogers, who was 40, John Orchard, and Thomas Gale were at Stony Creek when Gale asked Rogers for £15 that Rogers owed to him. Rogers said he did not have it, so Gale rushed him. Rogers, who was sitting on a log, fell backwards, hitting his head on some stones. Rogers got up and some words were exchanged before Gale again ran at Rogers, who tried to defend himself, but was knocked down once more. Rogers got up, but Gale knocked him down yet again. Rogers appeared to be stunned and there was blood coming from his face. Gale struck Rogers with his fist, but Rogers did not strike back.

A few months later, Rogers was living in the destitute boarding house at Port Augusta. Dr Cotter saw Rogers there, as he was suffering from decay of the lower jaw. Rogers had several bruises on his face, connected with an extensive surface of diseased bone. Cotter had known Rogers for two years and always considered him a man of sound mind. Cotter believed the wounds to be at least three months old. Due to Rogers' condition, he was examined by Dr William Markham, the hospital surgeon, who found Rogers in a state of low muttering delirium with a pulse of 130. Rogers was suffering from necrosis of the lower jaw.

Rogers was admitted into the hospital, where nurse Mary Martin placed Rogers in a bed in a padded room, and dressed his wounds. She gave Rogers some food before leaving him at around two pm, as Rogers was lying down singing a tune. Martin returned at five-thirty that afternoon and found that Rogers had died.

On 18 March, at Port Augusta, an inquest was held into the death of Robert Rogers, who died at the Port Augusta Hospital on 17 March from wounds supposed to have been inflicted by Thomas Gale at Stony Creek on 6 January. Dr Markham stated that he had not conducted a post-mortem so the inquest was adjourned.

When the inquest recommenced, Dr Markham stated that the head and face injuries found on Rogers were inflicted more than six weeks prior, and that the injury to the brain was most likely the cause of death. The inquest was again adjourned.

Circa 1885, view of the two storey brick hospital at Port Augusta, with a number of nurses on the first floor verandah, and a horse and buggy outside the front entrance.
State Library of South Australia, B 23913/A.

On 23 March, the inquest recommenced. Francis Whitby, JP, stated that he saw Rogers on 14 March and took a dying declaration from him, in which Rogers stated that he had a fight with Gale, during which he was knocked down several times. Rogers also stated that he was hit with fists, sticks and stones.

Thomas Gale agreed that they did fight, as Rogers had been singing rude songs about his wife. Gale stated that he punched Rogers in the face and struck him with the back of his hand. At one time, Rogers came at him with a stone, so Gale hit him between the eyes.

At the conclusion of the inquest, the jury found that Rogers had died as a result of injuries received from Gale, and that Gale was guilty of manslaughter. Gale was then committed for trial.

On Tuesday 19 June, Gale appeared before the Supreme Court charged with the manslaughter of Rogers. The crown solicitor entered a *nolle prosequi* and Gale was released.

Date	*Victim*	*Accused*
25 February 1877	**Female child**	**Unknown**
Cause of death:	Neglect	
Outcome:	Unknown	
Location:	Light Square, Adelaide	

On Sunday 25 February 1877, Colin Cowie was with two other boys in Light Square when they noticed a woman near a parcel, which was on the ground. The woman left and after a short time Cowie and the others went to the parcel, which was wrapped in brown paper and calico and tied with a string. Cowie opened the parcel and discovered a body of a female infant inside, so he contacted the police.

Dr Robert Peel made a post-mortem examination and found that the infant was fully grown and was well nourished. The brain was healthy but on opening the head he found a large quantity of effused blood under the skullcap. There were signs that the infant had had a separate existence from the mother. Peel also thought that the child had lingered in the birth, during which respiration was suspended. The umbilical cord was partially cut and torn. He thought that if a medical man had been present at the birth, then the child would have lived.

On Monday 26 February, an inquest was held at the Hamburg Hotel into the circumstances of the death of the female infant found in Light Square on Sunday morning. After hearing the evidence, the jury, after three-quarters of an hour of consideration, returned a verdict that the child had come to its death through the culpable neglect of some person or persons unknown.

Date	Victim	Accused
April 1877	Mary Myles	William Myles
Cause of death:	Assault	
Outcome:	Charges withdrawn	
Location:	Edwardstown	

William Myles, a 48-year-old labourer, and his wife Mary lived in Edwardstown. On Friday 13 April 1877, Dr John Foster, who resided at Sturt, was called to see Mary. Foster found Mary ill in bed, suffering from extreme pain. She had no use of her legs and was in a most exhausted state. Foster found marks of violence on various parts of her body, which he thought must have been caused by severe blows. Foster asked Mary how she got the marks, and she replied that her husband had kicked her. Foster thought that Mary would have been kicked two or three days before his visit. Mary was very exhausted, nearly pulseless, and the bed she lay in was in a 'filthy and wretched state'. Foster sent her to hospital and gave her an order of admission.

Sophia Turner was the nurse who took care of Mary in hospital. When she asked Mary how she received the bruises, Mary told her that 'the old man did it'.

Dr William Gardner treated Mary in hospital and found she was suffering from inflammation of the lungs. Her condition gradually worsened and she died on Sunday morning. On making a post-mortem investigation, Gardner found several bruises on her arms and legs, which would have been produced by kicks. Under the scalp he found an effusion of blood on the right side, probably caused by a blow or a fall. There was inflammation of both lungs and the liver and kidneys were large and fatty. The cause of death was given as inflammation of the lungs, and effusion of blood on the brain. He thought that if Mary had been ill treated or knocked down, such treatment would have accelerated her death.

On Tuesday 17 April, an inquest was held at the Adelaide Hospital on the body of Mary Myles. Evidence was received from several neighbours who stated that William Myles drank a great deal and was violent towards his wife. William and Mary frequently quarrelled and Mary often complained about her husband's ill treatment. On one occasion, William had chased Mary down the road with a stick.

The coroner summed up the evidence and said that although it was clear that Mary had died from diseased lungs, it was for the jury to consider whether the death had been hastened by her husband's violence. Even if her life were only shortened by a few moments, then he was guilty of manslaughter. The jury, after a short retirement, found that Mary's death had been accelerated by her husband's violence. William Myles was taken into custody on a charge of manslaughter.

Myles appeared before the Supreme Court on Tuesday 12 June 1877. The crown solicitor withdrew the prosecution and Myles was released.

Head and upper body portrait of William Edwards, 1851, the original proprietor of Edwardstown (from a portrait by Charles Rodius) in profile. Edwards laid out the suburb of Edwardstown in 1838.
State Library of South Australia, B 7006

Date	*Victim*	*Accused*
18 April 1877	**Robert Woodhead**	**Charles Streitman**
Cause of death:	Knife wounds	
Outcome:	Found guilty of murder	
	Sentenced to death, executed 24 July 1877	
Location:	Wallaroo	

On Wednesday 18 April 1877, Robert Woodhead and Lucas Sharples, who were both court bailiffs, visited the house of Charles Streitman, as they had a warrant to execute on him. At the house, Sharples told Streitman that he had a warrant for £11. Sharples left the house, leaving Woodhead there.

Bridget Quin, a young servant of Mrs Streitman, was in the house when Woodhead was there. She saw Woodhead sitting on the sofa and Streitman, who had a knife in his hand, approaching Woodhead. Quin ran out of the house and afterwards she saw Woodhead leave. Woodhead, who had just been stabbed by Streitman said, 'Oh Charlie, I did not know you was going to do that'.

Mr McPhillips was in his house when there was a knock at the door. He opened it to see Woodhead, who asked to come in as he had been stabbed. McPhillips sent for a doctor. Dr Richard Jay arrived at the house at around 11.30 pm and found Woodhead in a state of collapse. He found a large wound to the right side of his neck, which Jay stitched up. Woodhead had lost a large quantity of blood and subsequently died. Dr Jay thought that the wound to the neck was the cause of death, as it had cut the jugular vein.

Before Woodhead died, Mr Edmunds, the magistrate, took his dying declaration. Woodhead stated:

My name is Robert Woodhead. I know I am dying. I went to Streitman's house this evening with the bailiff as assistant. The prisoner said I was not to remain all night, but he must have inferred that I was going to do so. I thought he was going to raise the money. This was about 7 o'clock. Streitman asked if I wanted to take his jumper. I said, 'No, I only want the money, but not for myself.' He said, 'You are not going to stop all night.' Said I hoped not. He then went out. About quarter past 11 by his clock I saw him coming back. He said nothing and went into the bedroom. Shortly after he came out with a dagger or carving-knife, and seemed much excited. I was sitting on the sofa. He said, 'You shall not stay here in my house all night. What are you doing here?' He then stabbed me in the left arm. I said, 'What are you doing, Charlie?' I then jumped up and rushed to the door. Before I got there he stabbed me again in the right side of the neck, saying, 'Take that.' I bolted out of the door, leaving my hat. Made my way for the hospital, not to let my children see, but was so faint from the loss of blood that I stopped at Mr McPhillips'. Streitman made no previous threats, but inferred he was going to pay the money or forcibly eject me. He has never threatened me at any previous time, or was there any ill-feeling. I could not say if he was sober.

Commercial Hotel, Wallaroo, 1890.
State Library of South Australia, B 9706

On Thursday 19 April 1877, an inquest was held at the Commercial Hotel, Wallaroo, on the body of Robert Woodhead. After the jury were sworn in, they attended the house of Mr McPhillips to view the body. They returned to the hotel where evidence was given by Sharples, Quin and other witnesses. At the conclusion of the evidence, the jury retired and after a quarter of an hour's deliberation, returned a verdict that they were unanimously of the opinion that the deceased died from the effects of a wound on the neck, and that Charles Streitman was guilty of wilful murder. Streitman was committed to trial.

On Tuesday 26 June, Streitman appeared before the Supreme Court. On being asked whether he was guilty or not guilty, Streitman said, 'I don't know, I can't say I feel guilty. I saw the knife, and I saw the man, but I don't know anything about it'. His Honour said, 'He pleads not guilty', and the trial commenced. At the completion of the trial, the jury retired and in 12 minutes returned a verdict of wilful murder, recommending the prisoner to mercy on the grounds of his previous good character and the state of his wife's health. Streitman was sentenced to death. On 24 July Streitman was executed at the Adelaide Gaol.

Date	Victim	Accused
19 April 1877	**Margaret Hurley**	**Matthew Elsegood**
Cause of death:	Poisoned	
Outcome:	Found not guilty	
Location:	Marion	

Michael and Bridget Hurley lived at Marion with their two children. The eldest was twelve, and the younger, Margaret, was two-and-a-half. In April 1877, Margaret complained of sore lips, so on Wednesday 18 April, Bridget sent her eldest daughter to the store to get some worm powder, which was provided to her by Matthew Elsegood. The following morning she divided the powder up and gave a dose to Margaret, and some to another child. Directly after taking the powder, Margaret became ill and vomited for some time. Bridget sent for some brandy, which she mixed with a teaspoonful of water and gave to Margaret, who vomited it up but appeared to be getting better. The following day she sent for Dr Ferguson, who ordered some milk and brandy. Ferguson found Margaret to be very weak and low, and that she required care and attention. Margaret was nearly pulseless and her eyes were turned up and partially fixed. She was restless and cold and her tongue was brown and dry. Margaret died the following morning.

On Monday 23 April, at the Marion Inn, Marion, an inquest was held on the body of Margaret Hurley. Dr Ferguson gave evidence, stating that he had not made a post-mortem examination or analysed the powder. He thought that the powder was a horse powder and must contain a potent drug or chemical. At that stage the inquest was adjourned for the examination of the powder.

On 25 April, the inquest continued. George Francis, an analytical chemist of Adelaide, stated that the powder consisted of emetic tartar coloured with Armenian bole. He stated that emetic tartar was an irritant poison in large doses, but in small doses it acted as a depressant.

The coroner summed up stating that Margaret had been given 12 grains of tartar emetic when the ordinary dose for a child was the 12th part of a grain, and that there was no doubt that the taking of the powder caused her death. He further stated that there could be no doubt that Elsegood supplied the powder in a 'most careless manner' without asking any questions of the girl who fetched it. He thought it a pity that storekeepers and others ignorant of medicine should be allowed to sell medications.

Sturt Road, Marion approximately 1880.
State Library of South Australia, B 32143

The jury retired, and after half an hour of deliberation found Elsegood guilty of manslaughter, with a recommendation to mercy on account of Elsegood's character.

On Tuesday 19 June, Elsegood appeared before the Supreme Court where he pleaded not guilty on the charge of feloniously killing and slaying Margaret Hurley. The judge said that he had read over the depositions and could see no ground for the charge of manslaughter, as the most that could be said of it was that it was an unfortunate accident. He then directed the jury to find for the accused a verdict of not guilty, which they did. Before discharging Elsegood, the judge expressed his sympathy for the unfortunate position in which Elsegood had been placed, and cautioned him to be more careful in dispensing such medicines in the future.

Date	Victim	Accused
August 1877	**Henry Graham**	**Coochinna and Waragutty Pallina**
Cause of death:	Spear wounds	
Outcome:	Offenders not located	
Location:	Kallakoopah Creek, near Innamincka	

In August 1877, Henry Graham, a station-hand from Queensland, was travelling in the far north when he went missing. At the time it was thought he perished in the heat. In February 1879, Mr W Cornish of the Survey Office was surveying in the West Frome, via the Mundowadon area of the far north, when he was told that Aboriginal people had murdered Graham. The murder was supposed to have occurred north of Cowarie, and two Aboriginal men called Coochinna and Waragutty Pallina were reported as the murderers.

Cornish was told that Graham had reached Throowaduboorina, a dry clay pan or lake about 40 or 50 miles north of Cowarie, where he was met by the two men. Graham wanted them to guide him through their country, but they refused, so Graham struck one with his fist then drew his knife. Before he could do anything with it, one of the men drew his Kirra (boomerang) and struck Graham across the forehead, knocking him down. Coochinna and Waragutty Pallina then speared him several times. Once Graham was dead, the two men partly buried him with some of his property including his revolver, knife and some blankets.

Cornish ended up speaking to Coochinna, who gave his own account of the interaction. Graham, on leaving Cowarie, took the Aboriginal men with him to show him through the country, but as Graham had scarcely any rations they were continually quarrelling about what was caught during the day. Eventually Graham struck Coochinna on the head with a stick for stealing some of the damper, after which he ran away and went back to his own people. When he returned to his camp, he was berated for not killing the white fellow, so he and Waragutty Pallina left with the intention of doing so if they found him. Graham had become lost and was trying to make his way back to Cowarie when he was met by the Coochinna and Waragutty Pallina and killed.

Cornish was taken to where the body was buried at Kallakoopah Creek, where he put a cross above the grave. On 19 December 1877, Police Trooper Henry Quincey-Smith from the Mount Freeling police station sent a report to Sergeant Major Woodcock at Melrose, which stated:

Sir, I have the honour to inform you that I have been unsuccessful in finding the body of Henry Graham, I was told at the Mission Station that he had been killed for his blankets (by natives who had never seen a white man) on a creek above Salt Creek, seven days travel without water, at Cowarie I obtained a blackfellow who took me to Salt Lake, where he said the man had been killed, but all he knew was from what other blacks had told him, I was unable to find any native, but saw a very large camp on Salt Creek, recently deserted, the native did his best to find the body for me but I was compelled to give up the search for want of water, that in the lake being salty making me very ill.

On my return when at Reaglin's Camp at Coopers Creek, was aroused just before daylight by blacks running into camp crying Pinga, Pinga, (war party) they moved close to the hut for protection and two who Pinga wanted to kill were allowed inside, with the assistance of Messer's J Heaylon, G Jones and W Weston dispersed the Pinga Party. Afterwards went accompanied by J Heaylon to see that the Pinga had entirely gone, came across some of them sneaking back, on coming up with them, one gave me two blows, nearly breaking the middle finger of the left hand, another gave me a slight wound on the left breast, my horse was very restive trying to make him face the blacks, the saddle came right around and I fell, the blacks immediately came at me but Mr Heaylon galloped up to defend me or I must have been quickly killed. The natives all made off and we returned to camp, when I found that the Pinga had killed a blackfellow named Bobby about three miles from our camp, went to the place and saw the body, I counted 29 spear wounds and found three large two-handed kirra (weapons in the shape of a boomerang, but larger) broken and with blood on them, they had evidently been broken hitting the man on the head. The Pinga was comprised of Lake Hope, Perrigunde, Parrachana and Cutta Piarie blacks were from 100 to 150 strong. I was wearing a pith helmet, had I had on my uniform cap or a canvas hat, I must have been seriously injured as a boomerang was thrown and broke hitting the helmet just over the front peak. I have the Honour to be sir, your obedient servant, Henry Quincey-Smith

On 12 April 1879, a letter was published in the *South Australian Register*, which complained of the police investigation into Graham's murder:

> … shortly afterwards a police force was dispatched in that direction, who showed great zeal in 'taking things easily' so that they might lengthen out of the time for which they were paid extra pay, and also by going in any direction but the right one. The so-called search of the police has been the laughing-stock of the district.

There are no records of either offender being captured.

Date	*Victim*	*Accused*
20 October 1877	**Hannah Morgan**	**Walter Bucke**
Cause of death:	Assault	
Outcome:	Found not guilty	
Location:	Pirie Street, Adelaide	

Walter Bucke was a 36-year-old singing and music teacher who had an office above a shoemaker's shop in Pirie Street. Hannah Morgan, who was 17 years old and had left her family home at the age of 16, lived in Bucke's office, and was pregnant with Bucke's child. Bucke was at times violent to Morgan. On one occasion, when Morgan was pregnant, she was seen lying on the floor with Bucke kneeling on her chest. On a separate occasion, Bucke was seen standing behind Morgan, holding her arms and pulling them back while he placed his knee in her lower back, forcing her stomach out. Morgan was seen with bruises to her arms and ears and she complained that Bucke had assaulted her. Bucke, on occasion, used to take away Morgan's clothing and lock her in his office so that she could not escape.

Morgan gave birth to a stillborn female child on 15 October 1877. The next day, she was admitted to the Adelaide Hospital suffering from inflammation of the lining membrane of the abdomen. Morgan's condition deteriorated and became more serious as delirium and diarrhoea had set in. Morgan died on 20 October.

An inquest was held at the Hotel Europe on 8 November, where Dr William Gardner stated that the act of Morgan being pressed violently on the shoulders and being made to get on to her knees would be likely to produce a great strain on the muscles, which in turn could harm the unborn child.

The coroner stated that Bucke had behaved in a most disgraceful and disreputable manner towards Morgan, and there was evidence before him that showed violence by Bucke towards Morgan. The coroner stated that the evidence showed that Bucke was carrying out 'his wicked designs of getting rid of the child'. He stated that the law was that:

> If medicine be given to a woman to procure abortion, or if an instrument be used for the same purpose, and she died, this is murder, for though her death be not intended the act is deliberate and malicious, and attended with manifest danger to the person upon whom it is practised.

Pirie Street, looking east from Pultney Street, approximately 1868–1880.
State Library of South Australia, B 45002/64

The jury retired for 30 minutes and returned with a verdict of wilful murder against William Bucke. The coroner issued instructions for his immediate arrest.

By that time, Bucke had fled to Melbourne, but he was later arrested in Albury in New South Wales. Bucke had assumed the name of Ferdinand Burrars and had also altered his appearance. The police thought that they had the wrong man until they found one of Bucke's business cards in his luggage. Bucke was extradited back to South Australia and appeared in the police court charged with murder. Bucke was remanded in custody to take trial in the Supreme Court.

On Friday 15 March 1878, Bucke appeared in the Supreme Court. After receiving some evidence, the crown solicitor, at the suggestion of the judge, withdrew the prosecution on the grounds that there was no evidence against the prisoner. His Honour said that there had been a considerable amount of excitement over the case, which could have no influence on those sitting to try the prisoner. At the judge's direction the jury returned a verdict of not guilty.

Date	Victim	Accused
18 November 1877	Alexander Ness	James Day
Cause of death:	Assault	
Outcome:	Day not located	
Location:	Hansborough, near Kapunda	

On 18 November 1877, Alexander Ness had been living for about a week at John Canny's house at Hansborough Bridge, near Kapunda. Canny held a licence for a wine shop at his store and served wine and beer. It was not unusual for those who had had too much to drink to sleep it off in the chaff house. Around five in the evening, Ness was in the chaff house when James Day went in. Both Ness and Day were drunk, as they had been drinking in the wine shop that day.

Around the same time, Edward Murphy was in the wine shop when someone came in and said that there was row in the chaff house. Murphy went to the chaff house and saw Day kicking Ness, who was lying on the ground. Day was saying something, but Murphy could not make it out as Day was in a great rage. Murphy stopped Day kicking Ness, who got up after a while and walked about the yard. Ness complained to Murphy that his left side and chest hurt.

About a week later, on Saturday 24 November, Ness went to see Dr Frederick Renner. Ness complained of pain in his arms and across the region of his stomach. Ness' breathing was very short and quick. Renner saw that Ness had been drinking, and thought that the alcohol was aggravating his symptoms. Renner examined Ness and found marks of violence on both arms and torso and concluded that Ness was suffering from internal injuries. Renner ordered Ness to the Kapunda Hospital and prescribed a warm bath and a narcotic for his relief. When Ness heard of the warm bath he objected and left the hospital without taking any of the remedies prescribed.

Ness' condition worsened and, two months later, on 22 January, he was admitted to the Adelaide Hospital. He complained of a pain and swelling in the stomach and told the treating doctors that he had been kicked and beaten about nine weeks previous. Dr Austin Ward treated Ness for disease of the liver, but Ness' condition gradually worsened until he died on 27 January.

Just prior to his death, Ness gave the following dying declaration to the coroner:

> I believe that I am going to die. James Day jumped on me across my belly, nine weeks ago, between Kapunda and Eudunda at Canny's wineshop, on a Saturday. Day is a stone-breaker like myself. He was drunk when he injured me, and I also was a little 'on' and asleep. I never hit him nor have I ever had any quarrel with him. He did not assign any reason for jumping on me. Mr Kildae, a farmer, and Murty Dale, were present at the time. My belly has been sore ever since. I do not know where Day lives, but think he is working at Port Augusta. I am a rope maker by trade, and a native of Belfast, Ireland. It was before breakfast that Day jumped on me.

An inquest was held at the Adelaide Hospital on Friday 1 February 1878. Detective Borch stated that on Tuesday 29 January, he took a photograph of Ness. That photograph was taken into evidence and was shown to each witness. At the completion of the evidence, the coroner, in summing up, reflected on the character of Canny's wine shop, and said he hoped the police would take steps to prevent such scenes of drunkenness and riot as the evidence showed they were frequent occurrences. The jury, after retiring for two hours, found that Ness died from inflammation on the membrane of the lung, accelerated by drink and injuries inflicted on him by Day. The coroner issued a warrant of apprehension for Day for the manslaughter of Ness. It is unknown if Day was ever arrested.

Date	*Victim*	*Accused*
26 November 1877	**Patrick Bannan**	**Hugh Fagan (James Lynch)**
Cause of death:	Assault (with an axe)	
Outcome:	Fagan found guilty of murder	
	Sentenced to death, executed 16 April 1878	
Location:	Saltia	

Patrick Bannan, who was 45 years old, and Hugh Fagan, who was 58 years old, were both engaged on the Port Augusta railway works and were working near Saltia. On 26 November 1877, Fagan and Bannan were drinking when Fagan accused Bannan and his friend of burning his hut. Fagan attacked and stabbed one man in the face with a penknife. Fagan left, but returned shortly afterwards with an axe he had borrowed. Fagan found Bannan asleep and struck him twice in the head with the axe. Bannan died instantly from the injuries. When arrested, Fagan said what he had done would be 'a lesson from South Australians to Victorians'.

Saltia, entrance to Pichi Richi Pass, with the Saltia Inn in the centre, 1876–1877.
State Library of South Australia, B 370

An inquest was held on Tuesday 27 November at Port Augusta where a verdict of wilful murder was returned against Fagan. On Tuesday 19 March 1878, Fagan, who was also known as James Lynch, appeared before the Supreme Court charged with the murder of Patrick Bannan, to which he pleaded not guilty. At the conclusion of the trial, the judge pointed out that the evidence was not challenged. As to any provocation, there was no evidence that the deceased set fire to the prisoner's wurley; the prisoner only accused him of it. Further, it did not appear that Bannan gave any provocation whatsoever. Even if he had set fire to the wurley, or given provocation, that circumstance would form no justification of the prisoner's conduct. The jury, after deliberating for about 15 minutes, brought in a guilty verdict.

Fagan was sentenced to death, and on Tuesday 16 April he was executed within the walls of the Adelaide Gaol.

Date	Victim	Accused
December 1877	Chunkey	Woomatie (Paddy Parker), Koolma (Johnny), and Warpooka (Jacky Stinker)

Cause of death:	Assault (with a tomahawk)
Outcome:	Koolma acquitted
	Woomatie and Warpooka found guilty, sentenced to death
	Sentence commuted to life imprisonment
Location:	Manna Hill

As reported in the *Wallaroo Times and Mining Journal* on Saturday 15 December 1877:

A strange story of a crime and a successful vendetta reaches us from the Oleana run on Manna Hill (belonging to Mr J Duncan, M.P.) It appears that about two years ago a well to do blackfellow named Chunkey carried off three lubras from the Binbowrie tribe. In performing this feat Chunkey put one of the tribes under a spell from which he died. This was done, it is related, by pointing (a stick) at the victim, pointed at one end and a ball of fat and ochre at the other. Whether it was potent or not, the black died, and a vendetta was sworn against Chunkey, which the three blackfellows, Paddy, Jacky and Jackey

Tinker were told to carry out. They waited nearly two years to find the opportunity which but recently presented itself. Chunkey, who had accumulating wealth, and at the time of his death was possessed of a team of horses, a tent and a bank book showing a pretty round balance at the bank, was camped on the station. Paddy and the Jackeys came upon him, and tomahawked him, after which they set upon him with yam sticks and mutilated his body fearfully. They were tracked for fifty-two miles and arrested by Trooper Porter, and an inquest was held on the body, which resulted in a verdict of wilful murder being returned against the prisoners who are now in Redruth Gaol.

Author's note: The spelling of the offender's names in the newspaper differs from the court records.

Redruth Gaol, Burra, 1933. State Library of South Australia, B 8635

Redruth Gaol was erected in 1856 at a cost of nearly £3200. It was set back from the mine and the town, well outside any possible mining claims. Redruth Gaol was the first gaol erected in South Australia outside of Adelaide. Thomas Perry was Gaol keeper for 25 years and the gaol was often referred to as 'Perry's Hotel'.
The building was used in SA Film Corporation's 1979 film, Breaker Morant.

On Wednesday 20 March 1878, Woomatie (Paddy Parker), 30, Koolma (Johnny), 40, and Warpooka (Jacky Stinker), 35, appeared before the Supreme Court on a charge of murder. Evidence was given by Thomas Joyce, who stated that he heard the three men threatening to kill Chunkey and that he had warned them against doing so. Evidence was also given by Aboriginal women, who, not being considered citizens, were not sworn in, but simply desired by the court to tell all they knew of the affair. This evidence was not corroborated by sworn testimony and as a result, Koolma was acquitted, even though the judge remarked that the evidence appeared very conclusive. In his summing up, His Honour stated that in respect to the evidence against Woomatie and Warpooka, there seemed no reason why the finding of the jury should be for the lesser offence of manslaughter. The jury found Woomatie and Warpooka guilty of murder, with a recommendation of mercy, on the ground of the prisoners' ignorance of the laws and the difficulty they had of understanding them properly. Woomatie and Warpooka were sentenced them to be executed, after which they were removed from the court.

On Monday 8 April, the Executive Council held a meeting where it was decided to commute the sentences of Woomatie and Warpooka to life imprisonment.

Date	*Victim*	*Accused*
8 December 1877	**Marty Cullinan,**	**William McGowan**
	John McGillicuddy,	
	Michael Foley (Shea),	
	James Richardson,	
	Michael Cahill,	
	George Culhane,	
	Jeremiah Hannafin,	
	Edward Staunton, and	
	William Richards	
Cause of death:	Drowned	
Outcome:	Found not guilty	
Location:	Port Wakefield	

On 8 December 1877, the above were passengers on the steamer *Wakefield*, travelling from Port Adelaide to Port Wakefield. There were a total of 23

onboard the steamer, most of whom were Irish immigrants. The captain of the steamer was William McGowan. On approaching Port Wakefield, McGowan spoke to the captain of the *Morning Star*, who told him that he would be unable to get out of the port if he went in. McGowan stopped the *Wakefield* and lowered its small boat into the water. The passengers were ordered to get into the boat, so that they could be taken ashore. After disembarking the passengers, the *Wakefield* turned and steamed towards the *Morning Star*. After a few minutes, the small boat started to take on water and the passengers started to wave their hats as a signal of distress. At first, those who saw the passengers waving thought they were saying 'good night', but when it was realised what was happening McGowan immediately had the steamer turn around and return to the assistance of the boat. As the *Wakefield* approached, a rope was thrown to the boat, which was seized by a passenger, who jumped overboard from the boat. A second rope was thrown, which was seized by another passenger. The passengers became excited and some of them stood up. A ripple caused by the approaching steamer went over the gunwale, and the boat capsized. McGowan threw over a buoy and jumped into the water to try to save lives, but nine of the passengers, who were aged between 18 and 24, were drowned.

About 250 people attended a funeral held for the drowned men. The Reverend Mr Bogle conducted the service over the bodies of two who were Protestants, and a layman over those of the Roman Catholics. All were buried in one grave in the cemetery, with the Protestants being laid together apart from the Catholics. The bodies were at first placed in the coffins in their clothes, but the friends and countrymen of the deceased men had them washed and their clothing removed.

On 11 December Captain McGowan disappeared from Port Wakefield in a small boat with provisions and various stores. Two days later, he was picked up in an exhausted and mentally distressed condition by the master of the cutter *Sarah*. He was charged with manslaughter before the Police Magistrate in Adelaide and committed for trial.

On 22 and 23 March 1878, McGowan appeared before the Supreme Court charged with killing and slaying the deceased passengers. At the trial, Captain Blanch testified that the boat the passengers were in was originally built as a lifeboat and had cork and other buoyant material in it, but this had been removed prior to the accident. The boat was constructed to accommodate 13 passengers in the event of shipwreck, and to carry provisions and water for one month. On this occasion, there were at least 23 persons in the boat. There was also conflicting testimony from either side as to how much freeboard the boat had when she left the steamer with the people on board, with the defence saying it was nine inches and the prosecution witnesses saying six inches. At the completion of the evidence, the jury retired for half an hour before bringing in a unanimous verdict of not guilty. The crown solicitor said he would not proceed with other charges, and McGowan was discharged.

Date	*Victim*	*Accused*
25 December 1877	**Michael Doyle**	**William Webb**
Cause of death:	Assault	
Outcome:	Found not guilty	
Location:	Wellington Hotel, Waterloo	

Wellington Hotel, Waterloo 1936.
State Library of South Australia, B 31819

On Christmas Day 1877, between 9 and 10 pm, Michael Doyle and 24-year-old William Web quarrelled and fought outside the Wellington Hotel. An earlier altercation had occurred inside the hotel when Webb, who was under the influence of alcohol, threw some beer over Doyle. Doyle resented this, and both he and Webb went outside to settle the dispute. They fought for three rounds, with Webb falling under in the first two rounds, and Doyle falling in the third. Doyle was stunned by the fall, but soon recovered and the two shook hands and became friends. Doyle went home and went to sleep. The next morning, Doyle was found dead in his bed. There were other men in the same room, but they had heard nothing during the night. A warrant was issued for the arrest of Webb.

An inquest was held at the Wellington Hotel the following day. Several witnesses were examined, with the evidence falling in Webb's favour. At the completion of the inquest, the jury found that Doyle died from the effects of the fight and that Webb was guilty of manslaughter. They strongly recommended Webb to mercy given that Webb had been the one to end the fight, and that the men had shaken hands and become friends.

Doyle was said to have a cousin in Adelaide and a widowed mother and sister in Ireland. He was a sober steady man, and was also sober at the time of the quarrel, but Webb was said to have been half drunk.

On Friday 15 March, Webb appeared before the Supreme Court charged with unlawfully causing the death of Michael Doyle. At the conclusion of the trial, the jury found Webb not guilty.

Date	*Victim*	*Accused*
12 March 1878	**Mary Prest**	**Jonathan Prest**
Cause of death:	Assault (with metal tongs)	
Outcome:	Found guilty of murder	
	Sentenced to death, executed 16 July 1878	
Location:	Clare Street, Portland Estate (Port Adelaide)	

Mary and Jonathan Prest lived in Victoria for many years, and some of their children were born in Ballarat. Mary, who was 45, and Jonathan, who was 49, had eight children: six boys and two girls. The eldest daughter was married and lived in England. Around 1872 the Prest family moved to South Australia. In 1878, Jonathan was employed as a foreman of the carpenters working on the Marine Board buildings. The family lived in a five-roomed cottage, just at the rear of the Portland Hotel. Jonathan was always subject to fits of temper towards his family, but to those he worked with he was regarded as a quiet, well disposed person. During his outbursts he would tell their 16-year-old daughter Elizabeth that he would throw her out of the house and 'make her walk the streets'.

On Thursday 7 March 1878, Jonathan arrived home drunk and began to kill the fowls and ducks in his front garden. He then went into the front bedroom, took the family Bible out and left to go to the Exchange Hotel. Mary locked the door and when Jonathan returned he broke into the house and attacked Mary, who later reported him for assault. They both appeared in the Port Adelaide Police Court on Saturday 9 March, when the case was adjourned to 14 March.

On Tuesday 12 March, both Mary and Jonathan were home. Mary was ironing and Jonathan asked her not to appear against him in court. Mary told him that she must appear against him because he had already admitted to the assault when in court on Saturday. After some more conversation between them, Jonathan called Mary a 'bloody whore' and other names. Jonathan picked up a set of metal tongs and struck Mary on her forehead.

Elizabeth was in the room at the time and tried to get the tongs from her father. She was unable to, so she ran out into the street, calling 'murder'. A neighbour called Mrs Levack ran into the house and wrestled the tongs from Jonathan, who left the house. Levack assisted Mary, who was on the floor. Dr John Toll was sent for and soon arrived, but Mary was dead. Mary was bleeding from her right ear and had a lacerated wound over the right parietal bone. There was another head

Dr John Toll, approximately 1898. Dr Toll married Florence Margaret Mortlock, daughter of William Ranson Mortlock, at St Peters Cathedral, North Adelaide, on 29 December 1881. Dr Toll, Surgeon Major with 1st Mounted Rifles Contingent, died in 1900 aboard the SS Australasia *while being invalided home from the Boer War. He had been invalided for several weeks and in his weakened state he died due to an epileptic fit.*
State Library of South Australia, B 6526.

wound that was about two inches deep. Toll thought that the tongs could have inflicted the wounds.

Jonathan walked towards the Port and was soon apprehended by Sergeant Sullivan as he passed the police station. Sullivan had heard that Jonathan had been quarrelling with his wife again, but was unaware of the serious nature of the matter. Jonathan told Sullivan that he had assaulted his wife and that he thought she was dead.

An inquest was held at the Portland Hotel at five pm that afternoon until seven pm, when it was adjourned until the next morning. The inquest resumed the following day, and at the conclusion, the jury found Jonathan guilty of wilful murder. With it being known that Jonathan was to be taken to Adelaide, a crowd of about 200 gathered on the steps of the Police Station. Sergeant Sullivan prevented any disturbance by organising for Jonathan to be taken out of the back door through the court to the railway station, while in the company of a police constable in plain clothes.

On Monday 17 and Tuesday 18 June, Jonathan appeared before the Supreme Court charged with his wife's murder. At the completion of the trial, the jury retired for an hour and a half, and returned with a guilty verdict. Jonathan was sentenced to death. When asked if he had anything to say, Jonathan replied, 'At the time I knew nothing whatever about it, I was quite innocent'.

On Tuesday 16 July, Jonathan Prest was executed at the Adelaide Gaol.

Date	Victim	Accused
18 March 1878	**John Kennedy**	**John Sheehan**
Cause of death:	Assault	
Outcome:	Found not guilty	
Location:	Bogan Hotel, Mannum	

On 18 March 1878, John Kennedy went with John Fullick to the Bogan Hotel at Mannum where they had a drink with 30-year-old John Sheehan. While there, Sheehan asked Kennedy for some money he was owed. Kennedy stated that he had no money and they began to argue. Fullick said to Kennedy, 'Don't have any row about it Jack, let's go to dinner'. Fullick turned to go out when he heard Sheehan say, 'Kennedy, I would not take a drink from you'. Fullick heard a fall and turned to see Kennedy lying on his back on the floor.

Sheehan's hand was twisted around Kennedy's neckerchief, and his arm raised about to strike. Fullick told Sheehan not to strike a man while he was down, so Kennedy got up and said, 'Men, will you see me fair play?' Kennedy and Sheehan then squared up against each other. Sheehan caught Kennedy by the throat and bore him down, during which Kennedy struck his head. They fought for a short time before Kennedy said, 'Let me alone, I want no more of it'. Sheehan grabbed Kennedy's wrist and hit him above the eye. The fight then ended and they separated.

Bogan Hotel, Mannum 1877.
State Library of South Australia, PRG 1258/2/767

Later that afternoon, Elizabeth Schutze and Louisa Grosser, who were also in the Bogan Hotel, went to the watercloset, when they saw Kennedy with his head hanging down. Grosser threw some water over him, thinking he was drunk, but he did not move. They found that he was dead. Police Trooper Hurley later arrested Sheehan for Kennedy's murder.

Dr Francis Paoli made a post-mortem examination of Kennedy and found that he had a contusion of the external side of the left eye and a large contusion on the neck. On opening the skull he found blood between the ventricular artery and the brain. The left carotid artery was broken just above the collarbone. The cause of death was given as the rupture of the carotid artery.

An inquest was held on 19 March 1878 where the jury, after deliberating for 20 minutes, returned and found Sheehan guilty of manslaughter, but recommended him to mercy.

After being arrested, Sheehan 'went mad' over the affair and had to be confined in the Adelaide Lunatic Asylum. After treatment, Sheehan was discharged in time for his trial. On Friday 21 June, Sheehan appeared before the Supreme Court where he represented himself. In addressing the court, Sheehan stated that Kennedy and he were old schoolmates, that they had always been friends, and that there were no hard feelings between the two, either before or at the time of the occurrence. At the completion of the evidence, the jury returned a verdict of not guilty, and Sheehan was discharged.

Date	*Victim*	*Accused*
27 March 1878	**Cornelius Mulhall**	**Logic**
Cause of death:	Assault (with sticks and a knife)	
Outcome:	Found guilty of manslaughter	
	Sentenced to 14 years imprisonment with hard labour	
Location:	Tingatingatina Station (Tinga Tingana)	

Cornelius Mulhall worked as a stockman and boundary rider at the Tingatingatina Station, situated about 80 miles from the Queensland border. Each stockrider could choose his own 'blackboy' as an assistant and was charged with clothing him, while the station would cover the rations and a horse. Mulhall chose 30-year-old Logic as his assistant.

On 14 or 15 March 1878, Mulhall and Logic left the station to go around the run to look after the cattle. If the weather were fine then the ride would take two or three days, but if it were boggy it would take about five days. On the day that they left, the ground was boggy, so they were not expected back for at least five days. Logic had been at the station for a considerable time and was a member of the Dierie tribe, who were camped near the station. The day after Mulhall and Logic left the station, the tribe suddenly left the camp.

After five or six days Mulhall and Logic had not returned. The station manager, Thomas Bollard, accompanied by two white men and an Aboriginal man named George, started in pursuit of the Dierie tribe. They tracked them for about forty miles before coming across two lubras and an old man. Acting on what they were told, Bollard and his party turned off and picked up Mulhall's tracks. After following the tracks for about 25 miles they found Mulhall's body. Mulhall had three wounds on his left temple, which appeared to have been inflicted with a knife. The search party

Logic, 1881.
South Australian Police Historical Society, photograph 2410

rolled Mulhall in a blanket and buried him, then followed Logic's tracks.

Logic later told an Aboriginal man named Charley about Mulhall's murder. Logic said that Mulhall had growled at him for not coming on with the packhorse, and had struck him with a stockwhip. Logic ran away but later returned and caught Mulhall by the leg, threw him to the ground, and killed him with sticks and a knife.

Logic remained on the run for several years. In November 1880, Logic was arrested and taken to Port Augusta where he was brought before the local magistrate. Logic was committed to trial and on Tuesday 22 February 1881, he appeared in the Supreme Court in Adelaide, charged with murder. At the completion of the trial, Logic was found guilty of manslaughter and sentenced to 14 years imprisonment with hard labour.

Logic was an inmate of Yatala Labour Prison on Monday 12 October 1885, when he was sent with a prison gang to the quarries to break rocks. About an hour before the gang was due to return, Logic escaped and made a rush for liberty. Half of the guards in charge of the squad gave chase and fired their revolvers at him, but without effect. Logic stripped off his prison clothes and ran naked towards Modbury. Logic increased his distance between him and his pursuers, and in the undulating nature of the country, he doubled back towards the Levels, which were to the north of the prison. By this time the gap between Logic and the guards had increased, but they could still see him and kept pursuing him. In the meantime, the booming of the alarm gun, and the clanging of the gaol bell, notified the guards off duty that someone had got away, so, under the direction of the governor, a large posse was assembled, and joined in the hunt. Logic gradually outdistanced the guards, and getting into the saltbush country on the flats, he was eventually lost. Due to the fading light, the group returned to the gaol, with mounted constables taking up the search, but Logic was not found. An examination of his chains indicated that he had secured an old file and gradually severed his irons, which he slipped out of at an opportune moment. Logic was captured in early December that year and was returned to gaol.

Date	*Victim*	*Accused*
10 April 1878	**Mount Brown Charley**	**Murrayon (Ragless Jack/ Mount Arden Jemmy)**
Cause of death:	Gunshot wound	
Outcome:	Found guilty of murder	
	Sentenced to death, commuted to 14 years imprisonment	
Location:	Spear Creek, near Woolundunga	

The following information appeared in the *South Australian Chronicle and Weekly Mail* on Saturday 27 April 1878, regarding a murder at Spear Creek, near Woolundunga:

> The murdered man was an Aboriginal called Mount Brown Charley, and his murderer was an Aboriginal known as Ragless Jack. The latter is a very intelligent native, and being a handy fellow on a station, is often in the receipt of regular wages, and, having money at command, had invested in a gun and ammunition, with which (when he returned to a wild life, as he did occasionally) he used to kill his game. At the time of the murder Charley was sitting down in Spear Creek, there being only a lubra, Mount Arden Mary, with him, when Jack came up to the place and shot him in the back of the head, while standing within a yard or two of his victim. He then compelled the lubra to assist in hiding

away the body, and threatened that if she told the white men he would shoot her too. The lubra says they had no quarrel, but that they had quarrelled before because Charley would not let Jack have Mitchie, a young girl of his, for a lubra. After the deed was done Jack and the lubra washed the blood away from the stones where it took place. There was no other evidence of the murder except that of the lubra, but the body was seen and identified by Mr T.S. Smith and other witnesses, whom Mary conducted to the place where the body was laid, and the medical evidence of Dr Cotter was to the effect that death had been caused by a gunshot wound, inflicted in the manner described by the lubra. An inquest was held on Friday, the 12th inst., the verdict of the jury was that the deceased, Mount Brown Charley, was wilfully murdered by one Ragless Jack, by being shot with a gun. The murderer is at present hiding somewhere in the hills, but will, doubtless, be discovered before long and brought to justice.

On 18 May 1878, Police Trooper Cowie arrested 40-year-old Murrayon, also known as Ragless Jack or Mount Arden Jemmy, near Woolundunga. He was brought up before Mr Gower, SM at Port Augusta and remanded in custody.

On Friday 8 August 1878, Murrayon appeared before the Supreme Court where he was found guilty of wilful murder and sentenced to death. On Tuesday 2 September, the Executive Council commuted the sentence to 14 years imprisonment.

Police Troopers Cowie and Walters, 1880. State Library of South Australia, B 35179

Date	Victim	Accused
1 July 1878	**Female child**	**Unknown**
Cause of death:	Suffocation	
Outcome:	Offender not located	
Location:	Adelaide	

On Sunday 7 July 1878, William Hall, Robert Ashley and Richard Dyer, all aged 16, were walking near the Exhibition Buildings in the Botanic Park, when they went behind the bamboo near the breakwater of the creek. While there, Hall noticed a bag lying among the bamboo. He picked up the bag, which was not tied, and opened it, finding the body of a newborn female child. Hall saw Mr Whitehead nearby and told him what he had found. Whitehead notified a nearby police constable who removed the body to the deadhouse.

Dr William Talbot Clindening conducted a post-mortem examination. He found that the child was fully developed and had had a separate existence from the mother. The body was well nourished, but the lower part of the face, including the nose and the mouth, were flattened and pressed towards the right side. The body had not been washed and there were no marks of violence on it. Clindening thought that the child had been in the bag for six or seven days, and that the cause of death was suffocation.

On Tuesday 9 July, an inquest was held before city coroner Mr T Ward at the Destitute Asylum. After receiving evidence, the coroner, addressing the jury, pointed out that it was possible that the child might have been accidentally smothered, but it was plainly shown that the infant had had a separate existence, so they were led to conclude that the child had been destroyed by some person, and it was their duty to consider whether this had been a fact. The jury, after a short retirement, found that the child had been wilfully murdered by 'some person or persons unknown'.

Date	Victim	Accused
9 July 1878	**Henry Farrell Mansell**	**Henry Burke**
Cause of death	Assault (with an axe)	
Outcome:	Found not guilty due to unsound mind	
	Sentenced to imprisonment until His Excellency's pleasure was known	
Location:	Moralana Station, 70 miles from Blinman	

About 11 am on Tuesday 9 July 1878, Henry Mansell and William Budge were talking in the stockyard of Moralana Station. Mansell had been the manager of the station for 10 years. At that time Henry Burke, a 36-year-old blacksmith who was also known as Michael, came into the yard, carrying a tomahawk. Burke was laughing and said, 'Now I've got you'. Burke walked up to Mansell and struck him in the head with the axe, knocking Mansell's hat off. Burke struck Mansell again, knocking him to the ground. Burke ran towards the cart shed where he saw William Bradbury. Bradbury saw Burke with the axe and thought that Burke was committing suicide, but when Burke saw Bradbury he again said, 'Now I've got you'. Bradbury ran away and Burke chased after him. Bradbury ran around a hut but was eventually caught by Burke, who grabbed him by the shoulder and raised the axe. Bradbury told him not to be a fool, and Burke replied, 'You must die'. As the axe was descending, Bradbury tried to grab it from Burke's hand, but his grip was too tight. Bradbury pushed Burke and managed to get away.

Burke returned to Mansell, who was on the ground and being assisted by Budge. Burke called out, 'Now, Budge, I'll let you have it'. Budge ran off and Burke stood over Mansell and struck him twice more in the head. Burke then got onto his horse and rode off, taking the axe with him. After Burke had ridden off, Budge went back to Mansell and carried him out of the yard. Budge assisted Mansell, who had serious head injuries, but he died.

Burke rode to Hookina and went to the Hookina Hotel where he bragged about killing Mansell with a tomahawk. When asked why he did it, Burke said that Mansell had pulled him out of bed naked. Burke appeared to be 'quite insane and wandering in his mind'. While being spoken to, Burke knocked a man down without any provocation whatsoever, and seemed quite unconscious of having done so. No one at the hotel really believed Burke's claims, but he was strapped onto a sofa due to his behaviour. On the evening of Thursday 11 July, Trooper Daer arrested Burke at the Hookina Hotel and took him to the Blinman Police Station.

On the same day at Moralana, an inquest was held on the body of Mansell. Dr Clutterbuck of Blinman conducted a post-mortem examination, finding four external wounds on Mansell's head. On closer examination he found that the upper part of the nose and a large portion of the bone of the forehead had fractured into small fragments, a portion of which had penetrated the brain. Clutterbuck thought that either of the large wounds would be sufficient to cause death. At the completion of the evidence, the jury returned a verdict of wilful murder against Burke.

On Wednesday 18 September, Burke appeared before the Supreme Court charged with wilful murder. The defence put forward evidence that Burke was of unsound mind at the time of committing the murder. At the completion of the trial, the jury found that Burke did commit the murder but was of unsound mind at the time. His Honour sentenced Burke to be kept in strict custody at the Adelaide Gaol until 'His Excellency's pleasure is known'.

Date	*Victim*	*Accused*
8 August 1878	**McNeill child**	**Lucy McNeill**
Cause of death:	Suffocation	
Outcome:	Found guilty of concealment of birth	
	Sentenced to 12 months imprisonment with hard labour	
Location:	Hutt Street, Adelaide	

Lucy McNeill had been a domestic servant to Mr J Darling Jr in his house on Hutt Street for around six weeks. Prior to her engagement there, Darling's parents had employed McNeill. She was described as a person of an excellent character and her parents were very respectable people. On Thursday 8 August 1878, McNeill complained to Mrs Darling of being unwell, but as Mr Darling was away from home, not much notice was taken of her complaint. That afternoon McNeill gave birth and placed the child into a box in her bedroom.

The following day McNeill did her work as usual, but complained of being rather unwell. As nothing very unusual was noticed in her appearance, both Mr and Mrs Darling did not suspect anything. On the following Tuesday morning McNeill, who had become very ill, confessed to what had happened. She later said that the child was born alive and that she had placed her hand over its mouth until it was dead. Dr Gardner examined McNeill and found that she had a high fever. The police attended and were directed to the box in McNeill's bedroom where the body was found. Detective Doyle spoke to McNeill who said that she had given birth between three and four pm, and that she had put the baby in her box. She added: 'I don't care what's done with me, it's only my poor father I think about'.

At the inquest on Tuesday 20 August, Dr Gardner stated he conducted a post-mortem and found that the child was born alive and had a separate existence from the mother. He thought the cause of death was suffocation. At the completion of the inquest, the coroner summed up the evidence, noting the cause of death, and that the weight of evidence pointed to McNeill's guilt. The jury, after a deliberation of three-quarters of an hour, returned a verdict, with which they became dissatisfied. They retired again for fifteen minutes, before agreeing to the verdict that the child was born alive, and that McNeill had suffocated the child without premeditation. The coroner committed McNeill to take her trial at the next criminal sittings on a charge of manslaughter.

On Tuesday 1 October 1878, McNeill appeared before the Supreme Court charged with murder. At the conclusion of the evidence, the judge informed the jury that there was no case of child murder to go before them. The crown solicitor addressed the jury in support of a charge of concealment of birth. The jury retired before returning a verdict of concealment of birth. McNeill was sentenced to 12 months imprisonment with hard labour.

Date	*Victim*	*Accused*
11 August 1878	**Sarah Lowe (Keats)**	**Thomas Bascombe and Mary Bascombe**
Cause of death:	Assault	
Outcome:	Mary acquitted, Thomas found not guilty	
Location:	Little Swamp, six miles from Port Lincoln	

On 12 August 1878, the following information was sent from Port Lincoln and printed in the Adelaide papers regarding the supposed murder of Sarah Lowe:

> A supposed case of murder occurred yesterday at a place called 'The Swamp', about 6 miles from here, on the Western Road. The victim was an old woman named Sarah Lowe, and her son-in-law, Thomas Bascombe, was accused of being the cause of her death by throwing firewood at her. An inquest was held on the body today by Mr J S Browne, S.M., at the Sportsman's Arms. The evidence went to prove that the affair was the result of a drunken spree, which commenced on Friday last, and ended in the death of the unfortunate woman early on Sunday. Several witnesses were examined, but their evidence was too conflicting and unreliable to convict the accused, and the jury therefor

[*sic*] returned an open verdict, as follows, 'The deceased, Sarah Lowe, came to her death by blows inflicted on her head, but there is not sufficient evidence to prove by whom'.

A police investigation was conducted after further evidence was brought forward, and on 16 August, Thomas, 58, and Mary Bascombe, 40, were committed for trial for the wilful murder of 59-year-old Sarah Lowe (who was also known as Sarah Keats). The prisoners maintained the same stolid indifference throughout as they did before the coroner's jury. The proceedings lasted nearly five hours.

On Friday 20 September, Thomas and Mary Bascombe appeared before the Supreme Court charged with murder. Evidence was given that an argument occurred between all three during which Lowe received three wounds to her head, which were caused by a length of firewood. Dr Alfred Parker, of Port Lincoln, stated that the wounds were severe enough to cause death. All of the evidence was circumstantial, and at the end of the crown case, the judge directed the jury to acquit Mary, as there was no evidence against her. The judge then told the jury that they must be convinced that Thomas's actions were the cause of Lowe's death, in which case they would have to charge him either with murder or manslaughter. If there were any doubt however, they were directed to acquit him. The jury retired to consider their verdict against Thomas and after about a quarter of an hour, returned a verdict of not guilty.

Date	*Victim*	*Accused*
19 August 1878	**John Pells**	**Thomas Harrop**
Cause of death:	Assault	
Outcome:	Found not guilty	
Location:	Green's Plains, near Kadina	

On Monday 19 August 1878, John, 49, and Esther Pells were travelling in Thomas Harrop's wagon. John and Harrop had been drinking earlier that day at Kadina and were friends. They had left Kadina and John was a 'little the worse for liquor'. When they were near the Cornwall, Harrop, who was walking behind the wagon, started calling John names. John was sitting at the back of the wagon and had his feet hanging down. Harrop put a chain across

John's feet as a joke, and Esther told Harrop to stop teasing him and that they wanted to get off. Harrop then struck John on the head. John got off the wagon and Harrop struck him again, caught hold of him and threw him over his head onto the ground.

Richard Guy, a farmer, saw the fight between John and Harrop. Guy saw John tumble from the wagon onto the ground and then saw Harrop strike him. John and Harrop had a round or two and Harrop knocked John down. Harrop's horses started to run off, so Harrop ran after them. John got up and chased after Harrop, and they both struggled and fell to the ground. Harrop got up and went to the wagon, but John remained on the ground. Esther called out to the trap that was travelling in front of them, and two men came to her assistance. John was picked up and placed into the tray and taken to see Dr Robinson, but he was not available, so he was taken to the hospital, where he died.

Dr James Hamilton made a post-mortem examination of John and found that he had died from a rupture of the bladder. Hamilton stated that being thrown on a road would cause the injury, and, provided the bladder was full, the danger would be increased. Hamilton stated that the rupture of the bladder was generally caused by indirect violence and that all of the other organs were quite healthy.

An inquest was held on Monday 16 August with Mr Shepherdson, SM, acting as the coroner. At the completion of the evidence, Shepherdson said that there was no evidence to support a capital offence, as there was no malice shown, which constituted the difference between murder and manslaughter. The jury retired for a short time and returned with the verdict that the 'deceased came to his death through rupture of the bladder, but how that occurred there was not sufficient evidence to prove'. The coroner's opinion differed from the jury's and he took it upon himself to commit Harrop on a charge of manslaughter. Harrop was given bail.

On Wednesday 25 September 1878, Harrop appeared before the Supreme Court charged with killing and slaying John Pells. At the completion of the trial, the jury returned a verdict of not guilty after deliberating for three minutes.

Date	Victim	Accused
28 October 1878	**Benedict Suck**	**David Smith**
Cause of death:	Assault	
Outcome:	Acquitted	
Location:	Queenstown	

On Monday afternoon 28 October 1878, Benedict Suck, 10-year-old David Smith, who was part Aboriginal, John Hoey and 12-year-old George Ward were near Mr Leslie's School. Suck, Ward and Hoey were throwing stones at each other when Smith went up to Suck and grabbed him by the shoulders and shook him. Smith and Suck started to fight each other after Smith kicked Suck in the stomach. Suck said that he did not want to fight anymore but Smith continued fighting. The fight lasted about half an hour and after Suck was kicked he said, 'Oh, my head,' and lay down on the ground. Smith went on hitting him, kicking Suck as he was on the floor and kneeing him in the stomach. Ward and another youth called O'Halloran tried to stop the fighting. No one in the group threw stones at Smith and none of the other boys were fighting.

George Ward managed to pull Smith from Suck, after which Smith shaped up to Ward. Ward threw Smith on the ground where Smith bit Ward on the leg and ran off. After Smith ran off, Suck got up and walked home crying.

When Suck arrived home his mother, Ellen, found him leaning in a stooping position against the kitchen wall. Ellen asked him what was wrong, but could not get a reply so she sent for Dr Gething. The next morning, Dr Toll went to the house and examined Suck. Toll found Suck suffering from severe abdominal injury. He visited again that afternoon as his condition worsened. Suck died later that evening.

A post-mortem was carried out by Dr Toll, who found that Suck had a rupture of the diaphragm of the left side of the spine. There was also injury to the liver and the stomach, so much so that the contents of the stomach had passed into the cavity of the chest. He stated that the injuries could have been caused by a severe blow or pressure from a knee. The immediate cause of death was given as shock to the system from the injuries received.

An inquest was held at the Alberton Hotel on Thursday 31 October. At the completion of the evidence, the coroner addressed the jury, saying that they may believe that Smith was not liable to the charge of murder owing to his young age, but that the law provided that a person between the age of seven and fourteen years could be found guilty, unless they were very simple-minded. There were previous cases where children had been tried and sentenced for murder, but the sentences were usually reprieved and the children punished in another way.

Alberton Hotel and Shipwright's Arms, approximately 1889.
State Library of South Australia, B 31890

The jury, after a brief retirement, returned a verdict of manslaughter, but strongly recommending the prisoner to mercy on account of his youth. Smith, after being cautioned said, 'I am very sorry I did it. I never meant to kick the boy. I can't remember how I did it, or how I kicked him with my knee'.

On Friday 22 November, Smith appeared before the Supreme Court where the jury returned a verdict of not guilty, but recommended that the judge should reprimand Smith. The boy's stepfather was instructed to keep a tight rein on his son's exhibitions of temper.

Date	*Victim*	*Accused*
7 November 1878	**Walter Long Couzner**	**Catherine McCaffrey**
Cause of death:	Neglect	
Outcome:	Found guilty of manslaughter	
	Sentenced to six months imprisonment	
Location:	Adelaide	

In early 1878, Phoebe Louise Couzner, a single woman, was in the service of Mr and Mrs Flight in Gouger Street, Adelaide. While there, Couzner gave birth to a boy who she named Walter Long Couzner. Couzner nursed Walter for about three months before leaving him in the care of Mrs McCaffrey, who promised to look after and suckle him. Couzner knew that McCaffrey had a baby of her own, and she appeared to have plenty of milk. Couzner visited Walter once a week to pay McCaffrey for her services. On her visits, Couzner noticed that Walter was looking ill and she told McCaffrey that she did not think he was being fed properly.

McCaffrey looked after Walter for about five months, feeding him breast milk for the first week but then switching to bread and milk. Another wet-nurse took Walter for a week, but returned him saying that Walter was unwell. McCaffrey took Walter to the doctor at the hospital and was given some medicine for him.

Eliza Flight accompanied Couzner on several visits to Walter at McCaffrey's house. Flight saw that Walter was dirty and asked McCaffrey why she never washed him. McCaffrey replied that she had two or three other babies to attend to and could not be supposed to attend to it as if it was her own baby. Walter failed to put on any weight, and at two pm on Thursday 7 November he died.

A post-mortem was conducted by Dr Gardner who found that Walter, who was eight months old, was dirty and had an eruption on the head, the discharge from which had matted the hair. He could find no evidence of any abnormality to the organs and stated that the cause of death appeared to be gradual wasting from improper feeding.

On Friday 8 November, an inquest was held at the West Terrace Hotel, Waymouth Street, before the city coroner. The jury was much distressed after being shown McCaffrey's child, who was plump and healthy, compared with the mere skeleton that was Walter. During the inquest McCaffrey stated that she did not suckle the child, as she had not been asked to do so. She also stated that she kept the child clean. Couzner and Flight testified that she was paid seven shillings a week to suckle the child and look after him.

West Terrace Hotel, approximately 1888.
State Library of South Australia, B 9768

The coroner, in summing up, stated, 'The woman herself admitted that she had not given the breast because there was no agreement, but even if there was no bargain one would think that seeing the baby in a dying condition the common feeling of humanity would cause her to suckle it'. The jury, after 20 minutes, returned with the verdict that Walter had died as a result of McCaffrey's neglect. They also thought that when Couzner and Flight saw the state of the child they should have removed it. The Coroner committed McCaffrey for trial for manslaughter and stated that the other child in her custody should be removed to the Destitute Asylum.

On Friday 22 November, McCaffrey appeared before the Supreme Court where she was found guilty of manslaughter and sentenced to six months imprisonment without hard labour.

Date	Victim	Accused
14 November 1878	James Crabb, W Bennets, and Edward Quintrell	John Roberts
Cause of death:	Severe concussion/ shock	
Outcome:	Found guilty of manslaughter of James Crabb Sentenced to two years imprisonment with hard labour Case for the deaths of W Bennets and Edward Quintrell dismissed (*nolle prosequi*)	
Location:	Moonta Mines	

James Crabb, W Bennets, Edward Quintrell and John Roberts worked at the 85 fathoms level in the Hughes mineshaft at the Moonta Mines. On 14 November 1878, Roberts set the fuse of an explosive while working within the mine. He was with another person, and when the fuse was set, they both walked off in the same direction. Roberts called out 'fire' and set off the explosive. Crabb, Bennets and Quintrell were also in the mine, and approached the explosive from the other direction, not hearing Roberts's call. Crabb, Bennets and Quintrell were caught in the explosion and died.

The 27th Rule of the Moonta Mines was that 'Miners, when ready to blast, must shout fire before the fuse is ignited, and should there be any thoroughfare near, one of the pair must be stationed at each entrance, to prevent any person approaching before the explosion takes place'. The rule was posted within the mine, and was read out to the miners.

An inquest was held at the Moonta Mines Institute that day. Roberts stated that he set the fuse and called out 'fire' several times. He did not expect there to be anyone coming from the other direction, as it was too early for the next shift to start. Roberts said that if he thought that there was anyone in that area, he would have gone in that direction to prevent any entry.

Dr Edmond Archer stated that he had examined the bodies of the victims and found that two had skull fractures but one did not. He believed the cause of death was severe concussion and shock to the system, and that the explosion caused the injuries.

At the completion of the inquest, the jury retired before returning with the verdict that 'the deceased men came to their death through the explosion of a hole at the 85 fathom level north of Hughes shaft, Moonta Mines, and that the loss of life was caused by John Roberts neglecting his duty in not complying with the regulations of the mine'. Roberts was taken into custody on the charge of manslaughter.

On Tuesday 18 March 1879, Roberts appeared before the Supreme Court charged with the manslaughter of James Crabb. At the completion of the trial, His Honour, in addressing the jury, explained that there were two kinds of manslaughter, one voluntary and the other involuntary. Involuntary manslaughter regarded the death of a person or persons as a direct result of the negligence of someone performing a lawful act, or a neglect of duty.

The jury retired for a short time then returned a guilty verdict, with a strong recommendation for mercy. The crown solicitor entered a *nolle prosequi* in respect to the deaths of Bennets and Quintrell. Roberts appeared once more before the Supreme Court the following day where he was sentenced to two years imprisonment with hard labour.

Date	*Victim*	*Accused*
20 November 1878	**William Murnane**	**William Wilkinson**
Cause of death:	Bushfire	
Outcome:	Found not guilty	
Location:	Kalkabury, Yorke's Peninsula	

William Wilkinson owned about 500 acres between the townships of Maitland and Atherton. On the eastern side of his block the mallee had been cleared, but on the southern side it was still thick. Wilkinson had told those he knew that he would clear the southern side by burning it.

On 20 November 1878, two fires were started on the southern side of his property. After the fires had been burning for a while, the wind changed direction and the two fires became one and got out of control. The fire headed in the direction of the Murnane property.

William and his brother Michael Murnane were at their farm just prior to the wind change. William, who was 19 years old, told Michael that he was going to see where the fire was burning and asked Michael if he wanted to join him. Michael declined as he thought it was too dangerous. After the wind changed, the smoke around the Murnane farm became so thick that it was necessary to have lighting on inside the farmhouse to see clearly. After the fire had passed the farm, William's body was found near their boundary fence. William was considered to be a very quick runner, and it was thought that after the wind change he tried to outrun the fire front, but was overtaken by the flames.

Wilkinson was charged with manslaughter and on Wednesday 26 March 1879 he appeared before the chief justice in the Supreme Court. This was the first prosecution ever instituted in the colony of South Australia where a victim had been killed by an uncontrolled fire. The crown solicitor stated that if Wilkinson caused the fire, he either acted unlawfully by making a fire under the circumstances and at the time when he ignited the scrub on his land, or he performed a lawful act in an unlawful manner by not having a sufficient number of persons at hand to keep the fire under control. His Honour stated that if a man set fire to his house by negligence and a person was killed thereby, it would be manslaughter. But if while the house was burning a person jumped into the flames and was killed it would not be manslaughter. The defence argued that that there was no direct evidence that Wilkinson had lit the fire. The jury retired and retuned with a verdict of not guilty.

Date	Victim	Accused
12 December 1878	**Sarah Fergusson**	**David Fergusson**
Cause of death:	Assault	
Outcome:	Found not guilty	
Location:	High Street, Kensington	

Around midnight on 11 December 1878, Eliza Oaten was called by her daughter Eliza to the front yard of their house at High Street in Kensington. While in the yard they heard their 70-year-old neighbour David Fergusson repeatedly say to his wife, 'Sit up and come away'. Oaten got closer to the fence and heard Sarah say, 'I can't David'. David replied, 'I'll make you', and then there was silence. Oaten waited about 15 minutes but heard nothing more so she went back to bed. Oaten was aware that David used to mistreat 73-year-old Sarah. The younger Eliza heard some more shouting come from the Fergusson's house, so she looked out of the window and saw David exit the house before re-entering it, carrying a length of wood. Eliza heard Sarah scream once more, but heard nothing after this.

Around nine the next morning, the Oatens went to the Fergusson's house where they found Sarah lying on the floor. There was a piece of wood covered in blood and hair lying on the floor. Sarah had bruising on her face and neck, as if someone had squeezed it. Oaten accused David of beating her. David told her to mind her own business and to 'look after my wife, see the state she is in'.

Police Constable David Cormack arrived and arrested David for assaulting his wife, for which he was later committed to trial.

Sarah was admitted to the Adelaide Hospital that evening. Dr Ward examined Sarah and found severe bruising to her face and left arm. Owing to her age he considered the injuries serious. Sarah denied that she had been assaulted and said that she had fallen down. She remained at the hospital until 7 January, when she was removed to the Destitute Asylum. Sarah died from her injuries on 23 January 1879.

An inquest was held at the Destitute Asylum where David was brought from gaol, as he was still in custody awaiting trial for the assault on his wife. Dr Ward had conducted a post-mortem examination and gave the cause of death as inflammation of the lungs, accelerated by the injuries she had received. The coroner said that although there was no direct evidence to show who had mistreated Sarah, the evidence pointed strongly to her husband as having committed the assault. After about twenty minutes of deliberation the jury handed in verdict of manslaughter. David was committed to trial.

On Friday 28 March 1879, David appeared before the Supreme Court charged with the murder of his wife, Sarah Fergusson. During the trial, Dr Ward stated that the inflammation of the lungs that eventually killed Sarah set in three days before her death. He was still of the opinion that the beating Sarah had received had contributed to her death, but did state that this opinion was 'merely a matter of conjecture'. At the completion of the trial the jury found David not guilty.

Date	*Victim*	*Accused*
9 June 1879	**Annie Statton**	**Unknown**
Cause of death:	Apoplexy	
Outcome:	Offenders not located	
Location:	Kooringa	

Edward and Annie Statton were married on Thursday 5 June 1879, at Kooringa, near Burra. Later that day they travelled by train to Adelaide. On the train ride, Annie suffered from a headache, which was thought to be caused by the motion of the train. Edward and Annie returned to Burra on Monday 9 June and went to Annie's mother's house for a cup of tea. They returned to their own home and went to bed at around 10.30 pm. About a quarter of an hour later they were awoken by rocks being thrown on the tin roof of their house. In response, Annie jumped right off the bed, trembling with a racing heartbeat. Annie did not get much sleep that night and in the morning, at around seven am, Edward went to her mother's house and got some brandy for her, which was mixed with sugar and hot water. Edward went to work and Annie's mother went to their house to look after her. Edward returned home and found that Annie had gone to her mother's house and was lying on the sofa. Annie did not want to go home as she was frightened, and she seemed timid and nervous. The following day, on Wednesday morning, Annie said she was better and got up to get some breakfast, but during the day she got worse and the doctor was called for.

Dr Sangster attended and prescribed some medication for her, however over the next few days, Annie's condition became worse, and she died in the early hours of Monday morning.

An inquest was held at the Miners' Arms Hotel on Monday 16 June where Dr Sangster gave evidence that he was called to see Annie the previous Wednesday morning, where he found her suffering apparently from nervous headache. Sangster prescribed her medication, and visited her again on Thursday, when she was much in the same condition. He told her mother that he did not consider the case serious. Sangster visited her again on Saturday morning. There was no change in Annie's symptoms, but there had been some vomiting on the Friday afternoon.

When Sangster visited on Sunday morning, Annie was showing symptoms of hysteria for the first time. Dr Sangster altered the prescription and left. He heard nothing more until the next morning when her husband called and said that she was dead. Dr Sangster, with Dr Nesbitt and Dr Brummit, conducted a post-mortem examination where they found a clot in the substance of Annie's brain. They gave an opinion that death was caused by hemorrhage into the brain which was probably caused by a lesion that began around the same time as Annie's first fit of fright. They stated that the usual causes of hemorrhage were injury to or disease of the vessels. No signs of injury were found and it was thought that hemorrhage may be produced by severe shock to the nervous system and sudden and violent emotion. Sangster found there were no symptoms that pointed to apoplexy, but it was 'usual for violent emotions to produce hysteria in women'.

The jury, after a lengthy consideration returned a verdict that Annie had died from apoplexy caused by a sudden shock of fright, and that a person or persons unknown were responsible for her manslaughter. The jury also suggested that 'the attention of the authorities should be called to the annoyance to which newly married couples are subjected to in Burra, in order that the police may be instructed to put a stop to such a reprehensible and dangerous practice'.

Date	*Victim*	*Accused*
12 June 1879	**Mary Kain**	**Abigail Fitzgerald**
Cause of death:	Medical procedure	
Outcome:	Found guilty of manslaughter	
	Sentenced to three months imprisonment	
Location:	Waymouth Street, Adelaide	

Mary Kain, who was 24 years old, lived with her husband James and their 18-month-old daughter in Waymouth Street, Adelaide. Winifred Kelly, a single woman and a friend of Mary's, lodged in a room at their house. Mary was pregnant and close to giving birth.

Between seven and eight in the evening of Wednesday 11 June 1879, Mary started to feel unwell, so she told James to fetch Mrs Fitzgerald, an elderly woman who had worked as a nurse for a considerable amount of time. Fitzgerald arrived at the Kain's house and assisted Mary. Kelly also assisted when she was asked to do so. During the evening, James heard Mary cry out several times in great pain. Around 11.30 that night James went into Mary's bedroom. James asked Fitzgerald how his wife was getting on, and she replied that she would be alright. Mary said to James, 'Jimmy, good-bye, I am going'. James asked if he should call for a doctor, but Mary did not want one. In the early hours of the morning James called for a doctor and a priest, as Mary's condition was getting worse.

William Prendergast, a priest, arrived at the house at around three in the morning. He found that Mary was speechless and senseless and close to death. Prendergast asked Fitzgerald if there was a chance of Mary living, and she told him there was not. Prendergast was with Mary for about 10 minutes before she died. Fitzgerald told him that she had sent for a doctor and that the child was dead when born. Dr Mayo arrived at the house between three and four in the morning, after Mary had died.

An inquest was held at the West Terrace Hotel on Waymouth St, on Friday 13 June. During that inquest, Dr Mayo had performed a post-mortem and was of the opinion that Fitzgerald must have used extreme violence during the birth. He stated that in his extensive experience, he had never met with such a case. Mayo gave the cause of death as injuries received during labour, 'flooding' and great exhaustion. Mayo had known Fitzgerald for many years and found her to be a good nurse, but he could not remember her being a midwife. Dr Phillips assisted Mayo with the post-mortem and corroborated his opinion. Phillips also stated at the inquest that he did not think that Fitzgerald should have undertaken such an important case, and agreed that he had known Fitzgerald as a nurse, not a midwife.

At the completion of the inquest, the coroner reiterated to the jury the extent of the violence of the case, and its sad nature. He also noted that, from the evidence given, if Fitzgerald had called for medical assistance then Mrs Kain and the baby might be alive. The jury retired before returning a verdict of manslaughter. The coroner formally committed Fitzgerald to trial. In response, Fitzgerald said, 'I have nothing to say beyond that I have been treated unjustly by the doctors'.

On Wednesday 20 August, Fitzgerald appeared before the Supreme Court charged with wilfully killing and slaying Mary Kain. At the completion of the evidence, the jury retired and after a brief deliberation brought in a verdict of manslaughter. His Honour sentenced her to three months imprisonment without hard labour.

Date	*Victim*	*Accused*
21 June 1879	**James O'Leary**	**Herman Stubing**
Cause of death:	Assault	
Outcome:	Found not guilty	
Location:	Hamilton	

In the evening of Saturday 21 June 1879, Herman Stubing, his brother Albert Stubing and James O'Leary were at the public house at Hamilton. A row took place outside the bar, and O'Leary called Albert 'a thundering ...

liar'. Stubing said something in reply to O'Leary and both exchanged words before beginning to wrestle each other. Someone called out, 'Have it out', and both Stubing and O'Leary took off their coats and began to fight. There were about a dozen people at the public house watching the fight. Stubing and O'Leary ended up outside on the roadway and were striking blows at each other and wrestling, eventually falling to the ground. They both got up and began another round, the result being a second fall to the ground. There was a third round, but this time when they fell to the ground, O'Leary was unable to get up.

O'Leary was on the ground for about five minutes before he was removed to a shed and a tarpaulin was wrapped around him. He was then taken to a friend's house. On Monday morning, O'Leary's father came for him and took him away in a wagon to his own house between Hamilton and Marrabel, where a doctor was sent for.

Dr Wall attended and examined O'Leary and found that his lower limbs were completely paralysed. He considered the injuries could have been caused by a fall during the scuffle. On 24 June O'Leary was removed to the Kapunda Hospital where he died around three weeks later. The cause of death was concussion of the spine, producing paralysis.

Prior to his death, O'Leary made a dying declaration to a justice of the peace, in which he stated that he did not know who struck the first blow, and that there was no ill feeling between himself and Stubing before the fight took place.

Stubing was subsequently committed to trial, and on Friday 15 August he appeared before the Supreme Court charged with O'Leary's murder. At the completion of the trial, His Honour told the jury that if they were satisfied that the deceased died from injuries inflicted upon him by Stubing during an unlawful fight which arose out of angry feeling, they would return a verdict of guilty, but if they believed that Stubing only defended himself against an unlawful attack they would acquit him. The jury retired and returned with a verdict of not guilty.

Date	Victim	Accused
17 July 1879	**Sullivan child**	**Johanna Sullivan**
Cause of death:	Drowned	
Outcome:	Found guilty of murder	
	Sentenced to death, commuted to 14 years imprisonment	
Location:	Glenelg	

Johanna Sullivan, a single 23-year-old woman, gave birth to a son on 3 July 1879 in Adelaide. Anna Steehr, a midwife, assisted Sullivan in the birth and during the first few days after it was born. On 16 July, Steehr saw Sullivan and the child, who looked healthy.

On 17 July, Sullivan was seen with her two-week-old baby on the Adelaide to Glenelg tram. Sullivan was taking care of the child and had him wrapped up in a scarlet shawl. Agnes Stone was on the tram at the same time and noticed that the baby had its face covered and was making sounds as if it wanted it uncovered. Stone told Sullivan that she thought that the baby should be unwrapped slightly, to uncover the face. Sullivan opened the shawl and Stone saw the baby's face, which had some marks on the upper lip like pimples or small sores.

On 18 July, William Arnold was riding his horse on the Glenelg beach, about half a mile south of the jetty, when he noticed the body of a baby lying in the seaweed. Arnold rode to the police station where he reported his discovery.

Dr Fergusson attended at the beach with the police. He took the child to the deadhouse where he conducted a post-mortem examination. Fergusson found that the child was healthy and had no infection or diseases that would have caused death. He found there were some slight superficial abrasions on the right ear and the right side of the head, and there was a slight bruise on the left side of the back of the head. Fergusson stated that he considered the cause of death was suffocation by drowning and that he thought the child had received some shock to the system before it was drowned, such as a blow to the head. He believed that the child was alive when placed in the water. Agnes Stone, who had seen Sullivan and the child on the tram, later identified the body.

On Saturday 19 July, Steehr saw Sullivan without the child. Sullivan told Steehr that she had given the baby to a woman to keep for eight shillings a

*Glenelg Esplanade approximately 1880. The residence on the right is a pair of
semi-detached residences erected for Sir Henry Ayers (north portion) and
Sir Thomas Elder. The dividing wall breasts the Tower. The town Hall can be seen
at the end of the esplanade, the jetty is on the left.*
State Library of South Australia, B 62414/1/90.

week, and that she had gotten a job as a wet nurse. Steehr went with Sullivan
to Dr Campbell where she said that the woman who had her baby had gone
to Gawler.

On 22 July, Detective Hammill attended Mr McLean's house at Prospect
where Sullivan was employed as a wet nurse. Hammill arrested Sullivan for the
murder of her child and cautioned her. When arrested, Sullivan told Hammill
that the baby had taken a cold in a train and died, so she had 'put it away' on
the beach.

On 26 July an inquest was held before the City Coroner at the Pier Hotel,
Glenelg, where Sullivan was committed for trial.

On Wednesday 20 August, Sullivan appeared before the Supreme Court
charged with the murder of her illegitimate child. Evidence was heard from a
witness who saw Sullivan walking on the beach carrying a baby, and later alone
in the Pier Hotel, where she ordered a brandy. Mr Hamlin, the landlord of the

hotel, said that it was a rather unusual experience to have women calling at the bar for a brandy and as such he took particular notice of her. Johanna appeared to be 'under the influence of great agitation' at the hotel. At the completion of the evidence, the jury retired for 10 minutes, and returned with a verdict of murder, but with a recommendation for mercy. Sullivan was sentenced to death, however on Tuesday 2 September, the Executive Council commuted the sentence to 14 years imprisonment.

Date	*Victim*	*Accused*
24 July 1879	**Emma Wildy**	**Charles Harvey**
Cause of death:	Assault (with a poker)	
Outcome:	Harvey committed suicide	
Location:	Weller Street, Goodwood Park	

Twenty-year-old Emma Wildy had been a servant for five years to Mrs Weller, a respectable aged widow who resided at Weller Street at Goodwood Park. Emma was described as 'an intelligent and amiable young girl of prepossessing appearance'. Charles Harvey, the 22-year-old carpenter son of respectable parents living in Wright Street, was in a relationship with Wildy. Harvey had been paying attention to Wildy, and was intimately acquainted with the Weller family, having frequently stayed in the Weller house. In the days leading up to 24 July 1879, Mrs Weller noticed that there was some estrangement between Harvey and Wildy, but it was considered to be nothing beyond a slight coolness. Harvey was described as being:

> A young fellow of ordinary temperament, but subject at times to fits of gloominess, which, however, never amounted to ill-temper or even sulkiness, but were described as being more of the character of despondency.

At around one pm on Thursday 24 July, Mrs Weller left her home with her nephew to visit the city. She left her father, Richard Barker, an exceedingly deaf 90-year-old, in the house. Harvey was at the house repairing some fencing. Wildy was sitting at the kitchen table reading a book when Harvey came into the room and struck her several times on the head with a metal poker. Barker heard the screams and went into the kitchen where he found Wildy lying on the floor, covered in blood. Barker also saw Harvey run out of the back door.

When Mrs Weller came home she found Wildy on the floor and her father in a state of nervous tremor. Mrs Weller called for the police and a doctor to attend. The police attended and a search was conducted. In the rear yard someone noticed Harvey's hat near the well. An examination of the well found Harvey's body in the water. The body was lifted out, and police discovered a bucket containing several bricks attached to his neck.

On Friday 25 July an inquest was held at the Goodwood Park Hotel. Evidence was given that Wildy and Harvey had been going out, and that Wildy had ended the relationship owing to Harvey's temper and a fear that they could not be happy together. About four weeks prior to the murder, Harvey had asked Wildy if he could make up with her, but Wildy said that she only wanted to be friends.

At the completion of the inquest, the jury found Harvey guilty of Wildy's murder.

On Sunday 27 July, Harvey was buried. About 200 people attended and several clergymen were asked to officiate, but they declined and no service was performed.

Date	*Victim*	*Accused*
2 September 1879	John Golding	George White
Cause of death:	Assault	
Outcome:	Acquitted	
Location:	Waterloo Bay	

John Golding was a 15-year-old farmhand who worked for John Giddings at Waterloo Bay, 130 miles from Port Lincoln. On 2 September 1879, Giddings sent Golding on an errand that required him to pass the home of George White. Some time before this, White's wife had accused Golding of killing a pet lamb that belonged to her. Golding denied killing it and had called her a liar. When White saw Golding drive past in the cart, he went to the road, jumped up on the cart and punched Golding on the side of the head, causing his head and face to bleed.

Golding returned to Giddings' farm where he showed Giddings his injuries. Giddings went to White's house and spoke to him about striking a defenceless boy. White replied, 'Oh yes, a very innocent boy. I did not give him half enough.'

Port Lincoln Hospital, approximately 1900.
State Library of South Australia, B 33375

Golding complained of a headache and over the next few days he became ill. Giddings took Golding to the Port Lincoln Hospital where he was admitted. The treating doctors thought that Golding's outlook did not look so good, so a dying declaration was taken. Golding's condition worsened before he died on 11 September.

Dr Alfred Parker, who was in charge of the Port Lincoln Hospital, conducted a post-mortem examination. On removing the scalp he found severe injuries from the bone behind the ear to the bridge of the nose. There was no fracture and the brain was slightly congested but otherwise healthy. The right lung was completely collapsed by fluid and the left was in a state of acute inflammation. Dr Parker gave a cause of death as pleura pneumonia accelerated by extensive build-up of pus on the left side of the head.

On Friday 12 September, an inquest was held at the Port Lincoln Courthouse where further evidence was received from Dr Parker. At the completion of the evidence, the jury found that Golding died from pleuro-pneumonia accelerated by a blow by White. White was committed for trial and bail was refused.

On Tuesday 7 October, George White, who was described as an elderly man, appeared before the Supreme Court charged with manslaughter. After the medical evidence was heard in the trial, the crown solicitor stated that he could not proceed further with the case, and the jury, by the direction of His Honour, returned a verdict of not guilty.

Date	Victim	Accused
4 January 1880	**Robert Salomon**	**Ellen Salomon**
Cause of death:	Neglect	
Outcome:	Case dismissed (*nolle prosequi*)	
Location:	Chapel Street, Norwood	

Ellen (also known as Helen) Salomon lived in Chapel Street in Norwood with her husband and children, including Robert, her newborn baby. Ellen took care of her whole family, but around Christmas Day 1879 she started to drink, and was consistently drunk for the next two weeks. During this time, Ellen stopped caring for Robert, who was constantly crying. Peter Johnson, a labourer, lived close to the Salomon family and he and his wife had noticed Robert was being neglected. On Saturday 3 January, Ellen came to their house very drunk. Peter told her to go home and look after her children, but she replied, 'No, I'll be like the German niggers [*sic*], and not take care of the baby'.

On Sunday 4 January, Mr Salomon called Dr F Baily to see Robert. Baily was told that Dr Gaze had been attending to the child, but that his wife had insulted him and he had refused to come anymore. Dr Baily examined Robert and found him in a state of collapse. Robert was suffering from syphilis and Baily told Mr Salomon that it was almost past hope. Baily prescribed some medication for Robert and left. Later that afternoon, Mr Salomon went to Dr Baily's house and told him that Robert had died. Baily gave him a death certificate, which stated gave the primary cause of death as syphilis. Mr Salomon said that he was told that Robert was suffering from thrush and that they did not consider Robert to be seriously ill.

On Monday 5 January 1880, an inquest was held on the body of Robert Salomon at the Alma Hotel in Norwood. Evidence was given by George Gooden, a sanitary inspector of the Kensington and Norwood local board of health, who stated that on 2 January he went to the Salomon home and found it to be in a dirty state. Mrs Salomon was not at home and the baby was lying on the bed crying. When Ellen did come home, Godden told her to send for a doctor and to clean up the house. Ellen got 'very excited' and threatened to 'whack' him over the head with the baby. Godden left and returned the following day with Corporal Burchell and during a conversation with Mrs Salomon she said that she 'wished the little German nigger [*sic*] would die'.

Dr Gaze performed a post-mortem examination, where he found that Robert had died from exhaustion brought on by the syphilitic eruption and want of proper nursing and care of its mother. At the conclusion of the inquest, the jury found that Robert had died from exhaustion accelerated by Ellen's neglect. The coroner committed Ellen to trial.

On Wednesday 25 February, Ellen Salomon appeared before the Supreme Court on a charge of killing her infant child. The crown solicitor entered a *nolle prosequi* and Ellen was discharged.

Date	*Victim*	*Accused*
25 January 1880	Margaret O'Brien	John O'Brien
Cause of death:	Assault	
Outcome:	Found not guilty	
Location:	Thebarton	

On Saturday 24 January 1880, Margaret O'Brien and her 48-year-old husband John were at home with their niece, Mary Roach. Around midday, Maher, a friend of John's, came to the house, and everybody sat in the kitchen. Margaret got Maher a drink of water and Maher produced a bottle of rum. Margaret and Maher both drank some rum before Maher sent Margaret to the hotel to get some beer, which they began drinking on her return. After a while, Roach thought that there was a row brewing, so she decided to leave. Roach went into the bedroom and found Margaret on the floor going to sleep. John went into the bedroom and dragged Margaret by the shoulders along the floor and then placed her roughly onto the bed. Roach left the house along with Maher and John, leaving Margaret home alone.

John and Maher visited several pubs and had four or five glasses of beer. They purchased three bottles of beer and started heading back to John's house. They were separated until around nine pm that evening, when Maher arrived at John's house and found him drunk on the floor. John got up and lit a candle and Maher saw a lot of broken tumblers and bottles lying on the floor. He also saw several spots and a pool of blood on the floor. They both drank the beer and eventually fell asleep. Maher woke up about midnight and heard John saying, 'You drunken old [not printed], I've a good mind to kick the guts out of you'. Maher thought that John was speaking to Margaret. In the morning, John cleaned up the mess and mopped up the blood. Maher noticed that John had blood on his trousers and on his waistcoat. Maher also saw John burn something, but he could not see what it was. Maher heard Margaret groaning and moaning so he went out for a while before returning at around one pm. He saw Margaret sitting by the front door. She did not appear well and had a large cut on her lip, and could not answer any questions. Later that day, John and Maher left Margaret at home to go to a friend's house and tell them that Margaret was ill and was dying. Margaret died later that day.

Dr Corbin conducted a post-mortem examination and found that Margaret had injuries consistent with being kicked and jumped on.

An inquest was held on 26 January and 4 February at the Wheatsheaf Inn at Thebarton. Evidence was given by Richard McMahon, who went to the O'Brien's house on Sunday morning to fetch Margaret to milk his cow, as she usually did. Margaret told McMahon that she was very bad and that her husband had nearly killed her the night before. McMahon left and returned about two hours later when he saw Margaret running away from John who was close to her and hitting her on the head with his fists. Margaret managed to get inside the house and McMahon could hear John yelling at her.

At the completion of the inquest, the jury found John O'Brien guilty of killing Margaret with malice aforethought. The jury added a rider censuring Maher for his conduct in supplying the O'Briens with beer in the way he did. John O'Brien, who was committed to trial, said, 'I've nothing to say. I don't know whether I'm guilty or not'.

John appeared before the Supreme Court on Tuesday 2 March. At the conclusion of the evidence, the judge pointed out that there was no eyewitness to the assault, and also that the injuries Mrs O'Brien had could have been caused by her falling out of bed when drunk, as she was a 'heavy woman'. His Honour then directed the jury to find John not guilty, which they did.

Date	*Victim*	*Accused*
31 January 1880	**Thomas Whitlock**	**Thomas Quinn (Heard/ Scotty) and George Odey**
Cause of death	Assault (whip handle)	
Outcome:	Thomas Quinn murdered before inquest (see 1 February 1880) George Odey acquitted	
Location:	Rosina Street, Adelaide	

On Saturday 31 January 1880, Thomas Whitlock, a 24-year-old farmer from Burnside, went with his friend Francis Foster to the Galatea Hotel in Hindley Street. They arrived at around eight pm and had a few drinks before going for a walk in Hindley Street. They returned to the Galatea between nine and ten pm and ordered a drink. George Odey, who was with a girl, was also at the Galatea around the same time. The girl went to Foster and asked him to shout, so he purchased her a nobbler of brandy. Odey called the girl back to him and struck her in the face with his open hand when she was close enough. The girl left the hotel and Odey followed her. Whitlock and Foster finished their drinks and stayed another five minutes. They left the hotel and walked along Hindley Street, turning into Rosina Street. About halfway up Rosina Street, Whitlock and Foster were approached by 23-year-old Thomas Quinn and Odey. Quinn, who was very tall, went up to Whitlock and said, 'You're the chaps that's following us'. Whitlock denied following them but Quinn kept inisting that they were. Quinn got closer to Whitlock and said, 'I'll strike you', and Whitlock replied, 'If you strike me I'll give you a charge'. Whitlock held up a whip he had, and then lowered it to his side. Quinn grabbed the whip from Whitlock and struck him in the head with it. Foster ran off and Odey ran after him. Whitlock also ran off, but Quinn, who had dropped the whip, followed Whitlock and punched him several times in the head, then walked away towards Hindley Street.

Whitlock managed to get away and was later assisted by a resident of Rosina Street to see a doctor on North Terrace. Whitlock was sent to the Adelaide Hospital where his condition deteriorated. While at the hospital the treating doctors thought that due to the hot weather and Whitlock's condition, a dying declaration should be obtained. Police Constable Davidson attended and a statement was taken in his presence. Whitlock died from his injuries on Thursday 5 February.

The city coroner held an inquest on Friday 6 February at the Adelaide Hospital. Evidence was heard from several witnesses to the assault. Odey was present during the inquest, but Quinn had been killed prior to the inquest (see 1 February 1880). When the dying declaration was read, the solicitor representing Odey objected as it was taken without the suspect being present. Dr John Wilson and Dr William Baily both testified that at the time of giving the dying declaration, Whitlock was too delirious to make a reliable statement and no value should be attached to it. As a result the declaration was not accepted.

At the conclusion of the inquest, the coroner said that there could be little doubt that Quinn, who was now also dead, had killed Whitlock. The primary question for the jury was for them to consider if Odey aided or abetted in the killing. The jury retired and after a brief deliberation returned with the verdict that Quinn was indeed responsible for Whitlock's death, and that there was insufficient evidence to connect Odey to the murder. Odey was then detained in custody by the police who intended to bring him up at the police court on a charge of aiding and abetting in the assault.

Date	*Victim*	*Accused*
1 February 1880	**Thomas Quinn**	**James Viant**
	(Heard/ Scotty)	
Cause of death:	Assault	
Outcome:	Found guilty of manslaughter	
	Sentenced to three months imprisonment	
Location:	Victoria Bridge (Morphett Street Bridge), Adelaide	

Twenty-three-year-old Thomas Quinn (also known as Heard or Scotty) had been in South Australia for about 18 months. He was a man whose reputation did not stand very high in the city, as he had been keeping very bad company. On Sunday 1 February 1880, Quinn, who had been drinking, was at the Willows, a place near the southern side of the Victoria Bridge (now known as the Morphett Street Bridge). The Willows was '… a very celebrated resort for idling loafers and other disreputable characters'. Also at the Willows was Frederick Acourt, who was talking to two prostitutes called Emma Willis (Big Emma) and Sophia Thomas. Quinn went to the group and started talking to Thomas. Soon after, some other men joined the group, including James Viant. Viant called the girls to come over to him. Thomas replied, 'We ain't doing no harm'. Viant went to the group, where Quinn was sitting on the ground. Viant was leaning against the fence with his hands in his pockets and said to Quinn, 'Scotty, you can take it up if you like'. Quinn stood up and said, 'What did you say Jim?' Before Viant could reply, or get his hands from his pockets, Quinn punched Viant twice in the face. A fight then occurred between Quinn and Viant, which lasted about two to three minutes. The fight ended when they both fell onto the ground, with Viant landing on top of Quinn. Viant got up but Quinn said he could not move so some of those nearby carried Quinn and placed him underneath the bridge. One person got some water in Quinn's hat and gave him a drink.

Around six pm that evening, Constable Ryan was on duty when he was approached by a young boy who told him about a man who had fallen down at the bridge. Ryan went to the bridge and found Quinn lying on the ground. Quinn, who was quite sensible, said that he was in a bad way, that he had been drinking for the past fortnight, and that he had only been in town for the past few days. Quinn said that he was unable to move his arms and complained of a pain at the back of his neck, but never reported that he was in a fight. Quinn was taken to the Adelaide Hospital and died later that day.

Victoria Bridge, approximately 1875 looking north.
State Library of South Australia, B 58537

An inquest was held on 5 February before Mr T Ward, the city coroner. At the conclusion of the inquest, Ward stated that he 'was almost ashamed of the class of witnesses that had been called, some of them being of the lowest stamp that the colony possessed'. He explained to the jury that when two men were fighting and one was killed that it was undoubtedly a case of manslaughter, unless it was proved that the two men were in a confined place where for either to escape would be impossible. The jury retired and returned with a verdict of manslaughter, under provocation. Viant was committed to trial.

On Wednesday 3 March, Viant appeared before the Supreme Court charged with killing Thomas Quinn. At the conclusion of the trial, the jury returned a guilty verdict, with strong recommendation to mercy. His Honour Justice Boucaut agreed with the jury, and sentenced Viant to three months imprisonment without hard labour.

Date	*Victim*	*Accused*
2 June 1880	James Ford	John Dignum, William Norgrove, Margaret Dignum, and Bridget McNamara
Cause of death:	Assault	
Outcome:	John Dignum found guilty of manslaughter	
	Sentenced to 10 years imprisonment with hard labour	
	William Norgrove and Margaret Dignum acquitted	
	Bridget McNamara discharged (*nolle prosequi*)	
Location:	Thebarton	

During the evening of 2 June 1880, James Ford went to the City Hotel in Hindley Street, where he paid for a bed for himself and a friend. Ford went to the bar in the hotel, where John and Margaret Dignum were drinking. Ford struck up a conversation with Margaret and he treated her to a drink. Ford asked William Fairlie, the landlord of the hotel, for a bottle of rum, and paid with a £1 note. Fairlie gave Ford the rum and 16 shillings change in silver. After a short time, Ford left the hotel with the Dignums and went to the Adelaide Hotel where they met with William Norgrove and Bridget McNamara. All five ended up going to the Dignum's house at Thebarton with a small quantity of alcohol.

While at the house, an argument between John Dignum and Ford developed into a fight. Ford tried to kick Dignum, but he moved and knocked Ford down on the brick floor. While Ford was on the floor, Dignum kicked him in the head. When the fight settled, Dignum covered Ford, who was still breathing, with a blanket and they all went to sleep. Early the next morning, Dignum and Norgrove dragged Ford out of the house to the other side of the road and left him there.

A passerby located Ford and called for the police, who followed the drag marks back to the Dignum house. Ford was still alive and was taken to the Adelaide Hospital. Detective Constable George Farquhar visited the Dignums, where he cautioned them and charged them with assaulting Ford. The Dignums both stated that Ford was never in their house and that they had located him on their doorstep in the morning and dragged him to the roadway. John Dignum was searched and 16 shillings was located in his pocket. On the following Friday, the Dignums, Norgrove and McNamara were placed in the police yard where Ford identified them as the people who assaulted and robbed him.

On 11 June, Ford died from his injuries in the Adelaide Hospital. A post-mortem examination revealed that he died from a large clot of blood, which covered the left side of the brain. A coroner's inquest was held at the Adelaide Hospital on 12 June, where Dr Ward, who had conducted the post-mortem, gave evidence. Ward stated that when Ford was admitted to hospital he was insensible, with both his eyes blackened and a large cut on his lip. When he was conscious he complained of a pain in his head, after which his condition worsened until he died a week later.

The coroner stated that there was a presumption that there had been an understanding between the four prisoners, and that they had decoyed Ford to their house, which had previously been the resort of prostitutes and thieves, for the purpose of robbing him. At the completion of the inquest, the jury, after a retirement of 20 minutes, returned the verdict that 'John Dignum and William Norgrove are guilty of manslaughter of a most aggravated description, and that Margaret Dignum and Bridget McNamara are accessories to the crime'. All four prisoners were committed to the Supreme Court.

On Tuesday 10 August, the four appeared before the Supreme Court charged with the murder of James Ford. A *nolle prosequi* was entered against McNamara, who was discharged. At the completion of the trial, the jury found Margaret Dignum and William Norgrove not guilty, and John Dignum guilty of manslaughter. His Honour severely reprimanded Norgrove for his 'cowardly conduct' and sentenced Dignum to 10 years imprisonment with hard labour.

Date	*Victim*	*Accused*
12 September 1880	**Clark child**	**Louisa Clark**
Cause of death:	Strangulation	
Outcome:	Acquitted	
Location:	Riverton	

Louisa Clark, a 30-year-old widow, lived in a three-roomed cottage at Riverton with her two children, aged seven and five. Ellen Slough, 15, lived with the family and slept in the front room. On 27 September 1880, Clark told Slough that she was ill and remained in bed. Slough completed some chores and then went out to Sunday school and chapel. When she left there was a fire going in the fireplace of the front room.

Around eight pm that evening, Sarah Tyrell was walking past Clark's house when she noticed a light coming from Clark's room. Tyrell had a closer look and saw that the room was on fire. She notified the nearest neighbours, John and Louisa Ware, and raised the alarm. Louisa Ware and others went into the burning house and put the fire out. Louisa and Mr Gray went to Clark's bedroom, where they found her on the floor. Clark was only wearing stockings and was burnt. She was wrapped in a blanket and taken to another house where a doctor was called. An examination of the house found clothes, blankets and pillows spread about the floor. A number of dishes and other items were broken and there was some blood on the floor. The fire had reached the kitchen, but the fireplace there showed no signs of having a fire in it. A fire shovel was on top of the stove, in which the remains of a newborn infant were found. Mounted Police Constable Bertram and Dr Haywood attended the scene.

Riverton approximately 1880.
State Library of South Australia, B 15176

Dr Haywood examined Clark and found that she had recently given birth. He conducted an examination on the remains of the child and found that it was a male child who had been very much charred. He found a piece of a handkerchief tied tightly around the neck. Under the handkerchief the skin was smooth and untouched by the fire. Dr Haywood gave a cause of death as strangulation, but at a later Supreme Court trial, he stated that he did not give this opinion as a medical man, rather that it was his belief judging from the circumstantial evidence.

Constable Bertram later arrested Clark and charged her with child murder. A coroner's inquest was held, where Clark was found guilty of manslaughter and committed to trial.

On Wednesday 12 October, Clark appeared before the Supreme Court charged with the murder of her newborn child. During the trial Dr Haywood stated that 'It was very common for the mother to mistake the right time (of delivery) and consequently be taken unawares. Medical authority affirmed that women in these circumstances might, from pain and anxiety, become deprived of all judgement and destroy their offspring without being aware of what they are doing'. He also stated that 'it was possible for a woman to put a ligature round the child's neck to assist the delivery'.

At the conclusion of the trial, Clark was acquitted and released.

Date	*Victim*	*Accused*
31 October 1880	**William Bell**	**William Walsh**
Cause of death:	Knife wounds	
Outcome:	Found guilty of manslaughter	
	Sentenced to 12 years imprisonment with hard labour	
Location:	17th mile camp, Belair	

William Walsh and William Bell both worked as gangers on the construction of the Adelaide to Nairne railway. On 30 October 1880, 50-year-old Walsh and another ganger called McKay were at the Crafers Inn together. They slept at the inn and left together at around one pm to go to the 17th mile camp. When they arrived in the late afternoon, they went to McKay's tent. Later that evening, 35-year-old William Bell joined them in the tent. All the men were drinking and heavily intoxicated, with McKay being the most drunk. During the evening an argument started between Bell and Walsh about religion. Bell asked Walsh if he was a Roman Catholic, with Walsh responding that he was a Protestant and an Orange-man. Bell called Walsh a 'bloody turncoat', and Walsh told Bell that he was a 'bloody liar'. Bell struck Walsh three times as Walsh tried to get away from him. Walsh managed to grab hold of a butcher's knife from McKay's tent, and stabbed Bell several times. Bell was taken to a nearby tent and the police were called.

View of the partially completed viaduct over steep gullies. Its work team
(whose tents are pitched in the gully below) can just be made out in the centre
of the viaduct, posing for the photographer.
On back of photograph:
Viaduct on the railway to Nairne during construction c. 1882.
State Library of South Australia, B 5096

Police Constable James Watts, from Belair, arrived at the camp and spoke to Walsh. Watts took Walsh into the tent where Bell was and asked him if he recognised Walsh. Bell replied, 'I do, he stabbed me four times last night'. Watts asked Bell what he had been stabbed with, and Bell told him it was a butcher's knife. Watts arrested Walsh who said, 'I am sorry for it. I would not hurt a child. If I did do it I did it in self-defence'. Bell later died from his injuries.

On Friday 10 December, Walsh appeared before the Supreme Court charged with the murder of William Bell. The defence solicitor, in his closing argument, told the jury that:

> If two men fight upon a sudden quarrel, and one of them after a while endeavour to avoid any further struggle and retreat as far as he can, until at length no means of escaping remain to him, and he then turn around and kill his antagonist in order to avoid destruction, this homicide is excusable as being committed in self-defence. This was laid down in Roscoe, p. 686.

He also said, 'If the parties at the commencement of a quarrel attack each other upon equal terms, and afterwards in the course of the fight one of them in this passion snatch up a deadly weapon and kill the other with it, this would be manslaughter only. This was laid down in 1 East, PC 242'.

At the conclusion of the trial, the jury retired for about half an hour and returned with a verdict of manslaughter. Walsh was sentenced to 12 years imprisonment with hard labour.

Date	*Victim*	*Accused*
7 November 1880	Mary Ann Hartigan	Barbara Hartigan and Jeremiah Hartigan
Cause of death:	Assault, neglect	
Outcome:	Barbara discharged (*nolle prosequi*)	
	No record of Jeremiah appearing	
Location:	Wright Street, Adelaide	

Mary Hartigan, who was 13 years old, lived with her younger brother, father and stepmother in a boarding house in Wright Street. Mary had always suffered from fits and had spent some time in a convent at Kensington when she was five, but had to return home as her parents could not afford to keep her there anymore. Mary's father, Jeremiah, married Barbara when Mary was around five years old, and from that time Barbara began to mistreat Mary.

Ellen Reid lived next door to the Hartigans and often witnessed Barbara mistreating Mary. On one occasion, Barbara left Mary home alone to do the washing. When she retuned, she decided that the washing was not done to her satisfaction so she beat Mary with a broomstick. Mary was never properly clothed and was always dirty. Another neighbour, Mary O'Donnell, saw Barbara hit Mary with a strap or clothes-stick until Mary fell down. She also saw Jeremiah beat Mary, but not as often as Barbara did.

On Sunday 7 November 1880, Mary fetched some water and put it in the boiler over the fire. As she turned around she fell and struck her head on the doorframe. Jeremiah picked Mary up and put her into her bed. He thought that Mary was fine, but about three hours later he saw that she was about to die so he fetched the local doctor.

Dr Hartley Dixon arrived at the house and found Mary dead. He later conducted a post-mortem examination and, on opening the head, found that there was an amount of blood between the brain and the outer membrane. He believed that the extravasation (effusion) of blood on the brain might have been caused by a rupture of an aneurism or of an artery, and might have been caused by blows inflicted months or even years ago. The primary cause of death was given as apoplexy. Dr Dixon also thought that the mistreatment of Mary could have accelerated her death.

On Tuesday 9 November, an inquest was held at the Flagstaff Hotel, Franklin Street, where a number of witnesses gave evidence as to the treatment of Mary by her father and stepmother. At the completion of the evidence, the coroner told the jury that any person who was guilty of accelerating the death of any person was guilty of manslaughter. The jury returned the verdict that 'Mary Ann Hartigan died of apoplexy, that she had from infancy been subject to fits, but we wish strongly and distinctly to state that we think her death has been greatly accelerated by the ill treatment and neglect she had received from her stepmother and her father'. Jeremiah and Barbara Hartigan were committed for trial for manslaughter at the next sittings of the Criminal Court, and bail was allowed at £50 each.

On Tuesday 22 February 1881, Barbara Hartigan appeared before the Supreme Court where the crown solicitor, after communicating with the doctor and looking at the evidence of the depositions, said that he was convinced that there was no chance of a conviction, and he therefore entered a *nolle prosequi*. There is no mention of Jeremiah attending court.

Date	*Victim*	*Accused*
10 November 1880	**Ford child**	**Mary Ann Ford**
Cause of death:	Neglect	
Outcome:	Found guilty of concealment of birth	
	Sentenced to six months imprisonment	
Location:	Kapunda	

Mary Ann Ford was an 18-year-old servant to Maria and James Kester in Kapunda. On 10 November 1880, Ford told Maria that she was ill and was suffering from a bad cold. Ford had only been in the Kester's service for a short time, and the day after she started, Maria was told that Ford was pregnant. Maria asked Ford about her pregnancy, but she denied it. Ford left the employment of Maria suddenly on 10 November and went to see Fanny Reed, an elderly single woman who lived in the front part of Mr Grabert's house. Ford told Reed that she was very ill and was let in. Reed and Ford went to bed, and in the morning Ford again said that she was very ill and could not get up. Reed told Lucy Grabert, who got some food for Ford. Neither Reed nor Grabert knew that Ford was pregnant and had just given birth.

Ford remained in bed for several days, and Grabert said that she was going to call for the doctor. Ford objected, saying that she would be better soon.

Kapunda approximately 1880.
State Library of South Australia B5580

On Sunday 14 November, the body of a newborn child was found lying at the bottom of an old shaft in the Kapunda Mine. A coronial inquest was held that day in the Kapunda Court House where Dr James Hamilton, who had made a post-mortem examination of the female child, gave evidence that she had had a separate existence from her mother. Dr Hamilton's opinion was that the child had died from want of due care and attention, and from the umbilical cord not being tied, rather than from exposure. The jury returned a verdict that 'the body of the female infant, name unknown, found dead at the bottom of an old shaft on the Kapunda Mine, on Sunday, the 14th of November, was deposited there by some person or persons unknown, but whether death was wilful or negligently caused there is not sufficient evidence to determine'.

On Monday 15 November, acting on information he had received, Mounted Constable O'Mahoney visited Mrs Grabert's house and asked to speak to Ford. Grabert and O'Mahoney went into Ford's bedroom where they found Ford sitting on the bed crying. Ford said, 'Mr O'Mahoney, I am the mother of the child that was found'. O'Mahoney arrested Ford for the murder of her infant child. Ford said, 'I fainted, and when I woke up it was 10.30 and the child was born. I took it up to give it the breast, but found it was cold'. On Wednesday 17 November, a hearing was held at the Kapunda Police Court. Dr Hamilton testified that he had examined Mary and found that she had recently given birth. At the completion of the evidence, Mary was committed to trial for manslaughter at the Supreme Court.

On Thursday 9 December, Ford appeared before the Supreme Court where she pleaded not guilty of a charge of murdering her female child, but guilty to concealment of birth. The crown solicitor accepted the lesser plea and Mr Stock, who appeared with Mr Muirhead on Ford's behalf, appealed for clemency of the court in consideration of the mitigating circumstances of the case. His Honour passed a sentence of six months imprisonment.

Date	*Victim*	*Accused*
26 January 1881	**Mary Kubale**	**Johann Kubale**
Cause of death:	Assault (with a bottle)	
Outcome:	Found guilty of manslaughter	
	Sentenced to four years imprisonment with hard labour	
Location:	Edithburgh	

Sixteen-year-old Mary Kubale lived with her 55-year-old father Johann and her brothers on a farm near Edithburgh. On the evening of Wednesday 26 January 1881, Johann went to Edithburgh and returned around 10 pm. Mary went to bed at around 11 pm, in the same room her father and 11-year-old brother slept in. In the morning, Johann woke up and saw that Mary had a bleeding wound on her forehead. Johann told his son and he washed the blood away with a cloth. Johann sent his son Frederick to a neighbour's house for help. Frederick went to the house of Samuel Molkentine, which was about two miles away. Molkentine rode to the Kubale house and when he arrived he saw Johann and his two other sons, Charles and William, standing next to the bed where Mary lay. Mary was insensible and breathing heavily. She had a severe wound above her left eye, which was bleeding. Mary died about 10 minutes later. Molkentine told Johann that Mary must have been attacked, and Johann replied that she must have fallen. Molkentine said that it was not a fall, but a blow to the head. Molkentine noticed a nearly full bottle of wine on a table in the room. Johann left the room then returned with a stick to measure Mary for a coffin. The police arrived and took Johann into custody.

An inquest into the death occurred over two days. The coroner, in summing up, pointed out that from the principle evidence there was no doubt that murder had been committed, and that it was a very suspicious case. Johann refused to make any statement. The jury returned a verdict of wilful murder against some person or persons unknown, upon which the coroner said that he had no alternative but to discharge the prisoner. The public showed great indignation at Johann's release.

Mary's funeral took place on Friday 28 January in the presence of a large gathering. On his return from the funeral Johann was arrested on a charge of murder, as additional evidence had been located.

Johann again made no statement when arrested for Mary's murder. On Saturday 5 February, Johann sent for Mr Gottschalk, JP, and made the following statement:

> I hereby confess that I am not guilty of murder, but that on the night from 25 to 26 January, 1881, I must have struck my daughter Mary on the head, thus causing her death. I was under the influence of drink on coming home from Edithburgh on the evening of January 25. On arriving home I partook freely of colonial wine, and after my

sons left for Hennechke's I fell asleep on the sofa of the sitting-room. On awaking, according to my estimation at about 1 or 2 o'clock on Wednesday morning, I must have dealt the fatal blow. I am unable to account what caused me to strike my child. I have no recollection whether any words fell between the deceased and myself, and cannot say what instrument I used to deal the blow with. I had no intention to kill my child at the time, but under the influence of drink and stupidity caused by the mixture of colonial beer and colonial wine I must have been mad, and committed the deed.

Johann appeared before the Supreme Court on Tuesday 12 April charged with murdering Mary Kubale. He pleaded not guilty. A large amount of evidence was given that day and the trial was adjourned until the next day.

The trial resumed and Dr Hood gave evidence stating that Mary had died from a head injury, which could not have been caused by a fall. He later examined Johann and found fingernail scratches on his back, which he could not have done himself. The scratches could not have been made through a shirt. Dr Hood also stated that Mary was a virgin. At the completion of the trial, the jury retired and returned with a verdict of manslaughter. His Honour, in passing sentence, said that he supposed the jury had brought in that verdict because they thought that the prisoner did not know what he was doing when he committed the crime. He was inclined to agree, and as the prisoner had lost his daughter by this act he would be more lenient with him than otherwise. Johann was sentenced to four years imprisonment with hard labour.

Date	*Victim*	*Accused*
15 February 1881	**Patrick Brady**	**James Henry Martin**
Cause of death:	Assault	
Outcome:	Found guilty of manslaughter	
	Sentenced to six months imprisonment	
Location:	Stirling	

James Henry Martin, who was married with eight children all under the age of nine, was a teamster at Stirling. At about eight pm on Tuesday 15 February 1881, Martin and some of his men were carrying the horse feed inside, when he was approached by Patrick Brady. Brady asked Martin if it was his wagon inside the fence, and Martin replied that all of the wagons were his. Brady asked Martin if he had seen a handkerchief inside a wagon with some grapes in it. Martin said that he hadn't. Brady, who could not find the grapes, told Martin that he and his men were a mean lot, and if they wanted some of the grapes he would have shared them with him. Martin told Brady that he had probably eaten them himself, but Brady said that he wanted them for a party he was going to. Martin and Brady went to the wagon and found the handkerchief and another parcel that belonged to Brady, but the grapes were not there. Brady was continually talking to Martin, who thought that Brady was being cheeky to him, so he hit him once and Brady fell to the ground. Brady said, 'Do not strike a man when he is down', and got up and asked for his hat, which Martin gave to him. Brady started to run away and as he did Martin kicked him with the side of his boot and struck a heavy blow on his back. Brady continued on for about six to seven yards and fell to the ground.

Martin and some of the other men lifted Brady up and splashed some water on his forehead. Brady was carried away and was laid on a tarpaulin. One of the men, Henry Winship, told Martin that Brady had had a heavy fall and he thought Brady was going to die, so Martin rode his horse to Port Augusta to fetch the police.

Martin arrived at the Port Augusta Police Station and told Mounted Constable William Whitters what had happened. Whitters asked Martin if he thought Brady was dead, and Martin said yes. Whitters went to Dr Markham's house to tell him what had happened, and asked him to go to Stirling. Dr Markham said he did not think it was necessary for him to go and advised Whitters to bring the body back to the deadhouse. Whitters then went to Dr Cotter and asked him to go, but Dr Cotter also said he saw no necessity to go to Stirling to see a dead man. Dr Cotter said that if Whitters arrived to find the man was still alive, he should be sent for then.

Whitters went to Stirling and found that Brady had died. Whitters had the body removed to the North Stirling Hotel for the purpose of a coroner's inquest. The inquest was held on 16 February before Mr J Goodair, who acted as coroner. Dr Cotter performed a post-mortem examination, and found a large quantity of coagulated blood at the base of the head, which was quite sufficient to cause death. He thought that the collection of the coagulated blood would be likely to be caused by a blow at the back of the neck. At the completion of the inquest the jury returned a verdict of

North Stirling Hotel, approximately 1880.
State Library of South Australia, B 34900

manslaughter against Martin, who was committed to the Supreme Court.

Martin appeared before Mr Justice Andrews at the Supreme Court on Wednesday 6 April. At the completion of the trial, the jury retired for a quarter of an hour, before returning with a verdict of manslaughter, with a strong recommendation for mercy. Martin was sentenced to six months imprisonment.

Date	*Victim*	*Accused*
17 March 1881	**Eliza Beveridge**	**James Beveridge**
Cause of death:	Assault (with a broomstick)	
Outcome:	Found guilty of manslaughter	
	Sentenced to six years imprisonment with hard labour	
Location:	Regent Street, Adelaide	

James Beveridge, a 49-year-old carpenter, and his wife Eliza lived in Regent Street, Adelaide. Eliza moved out of home some time before March 1881, but returned home on 17 March. Upon her return James hit her several times with a broomstick. On 29 March, Eliza was still suffering from the injuries caused by the assault, so she went to see Dr William Gardner, who thought Eliza was close to death. Eliza provided a dying declaration:

> I believe I am going to die. My husband hit me with a broomstick last Thursday week, the 17 March [*sic*], just on the back. It hurt very much. I was in bed at the time. I have felt it ever since. He hit me because the little boy was outside when he came in. I have felt worse ever since. It was the head of the broomstick he hit me with. The broomstick produced is the one he hit me with. The marks on my back are those from the broomstick head. I was lying in bed very ill. I was sober at the time.

Eliza died from her injuries on 30 March. On Thursday 31 March, an inquest was held at the Earl of Aberdeen Hotel. During the inquest, James and Eliza's daughter, Margaret, gave evidence. Margaret stated that she did not see the assault as she no longer lived at home, but her mother had told her what had happened. Mr Whittell, who represented James, objected to the evidence as being mere hearsay, and wanted the coroner to take note of his objection. The coroner replied that he could not comply with Mr Whittell's request as so far as his knowledge went it was unusual to take notes of objections in the Coroner's Court.

The coroner, in summing up, laid down the law of manslaughter. He thought that there could not be clearer evidence of manslaughter than they had in this case. The jury returned a verdict that the death of the deceased was the result of natural causes, accelerated by the mistreatment by her husband. The coroner said that verdict amounted to finding the husband guilty of manslaughter, but it was pointed out by several jurors that it was not their wish to commit the man for trial for manslaughter. The coroner said that if twelve of the jury agreed to the verdict in that form, he would accept it. There was only one juror who disagreed, so the coroner fully committed James for trial for manslaughter.

On Thursday 21 April, James appeared before the Supreme Court charged with feloniously and wilfully killing Eliza Beveridge. He pleaded not guilty. Dr Gardner, who examined Eliza on 29 March, stated that Eliza was suffering from contraction of the liver, and that there was an enormous quantity of fluid in the abdomen. Dr Gardner conducted a post-mortem examination and discovered a bruise four inches wide extending across the shoulders, which may have been caused by a broomstick. Gardner stated that Eliza died from failure of the heart's action from the pressure of the dropsical fluid, which acted on the heart in every direction, and the effect of the blow from the broomstick would be 'to weaken the action of the already feebly acting heart', and therefore accelerate death. Eliza had been a very heavy drinker, and Dr Gardner found her system saturated with alcohol. In cross-examination, Dr Gardner said the primary cause of death was chronic alcoholic poisoning.

The jury retired, then returned with a verdict of manslaughter. James was sentenced to six years imprisonment with hard labour.

Just four years later, on Tuesday 4 August 1885, James appeared once more before the Supreme Court, but this time he was charged with forging and uttering an order for the payment of £7, with intent to defraud. Beveridge pleaded guilty and was imprisoned for six years.

Date	*Victim*	*Accused*
22 March 1881	**William Cuffe**	**Honora Dunn**
Cause of death:	Assault	
Outcome:	Found guilty of manslaughter	
	Sentenced to five years imprisonment with hard labour	
Location:	George Street, Norwood	

In April 1880, Mary Rowe gave birth to her illegitimate child, naming him William Cuffe. On 20 February 1881, Rowe placed William, who was 10 months old, with 40-year-old Honora Dunn for nine shillings a week. Dunn, who lived in George Street, Norwood, agreed to take good care of him. William was 'peevish from teething', but otherwise in good health. A week later Rowe visited William and saw that he was thinner. Rowe visited after another two or three days and noticed that both of William's cheeks were black with bruises. Rowe asked Dunn what had happened, and Dunn replied that she could not account for the bruises, suggesting that they were from William rolling about in the cradle. Dunn told Rowe that she was always very good to children, but she believed in giving them a good slap, because a child could not be brought up properly unless it was beaten when it did wrong. Rowe took William, who seemed to be in great agony, to see Dr Ward at the hospital who examined William and found him to be suffering from exhaustion, following diarrhoea. Dr Ward saw bruises on each cheek, which he thought must have been caused by violence of some sort. Dr Ward prescribed medicine for William and told Rowe to go to the Destitute Asylum. Rowe took William there, but he died within an hour.

An inquest was held at the Destitute Asylum over two days before the city coroner. Evidence was received from witnesses who stated that they had seen Dunn strike other children in her care. At the completion of the inquest, the jury found that William had come to his death from the injuries inflicted by Dunn, who was committed to trial.

Dunn appeared before the Supreme Court on Friday 8 April where she pleaded not guilty to feloniously killing William Cuffe. After receiving all of the evidence, the jury retired for an hour and forty minutes before they returned, stating that there was no chance of them agreeing on a verdict. The jury was discharged and, on application from the crown, Dunn was remanded to the next sitting of the Supreme Court.

On Thursday 9 June, Dunn appeared once again before the Supreme Court where she pleaded not guilty. At the conclusion of the trial, the jury retired before returning a guilty verdict. His Honour, Mr Justice Andrews, stated that the depositions had shown that Dunn had treated other children in a 'horrible and brutal' way, and that Dunn had killed William after he knocked over some milk that Rowe had paid extra for. Andrews said that he would only be wasting the time of the court by saying more, and sentenced Dunn to five years imprisonment with hard labour. He also told Dunn that he trusted that at the end of that time she would not return to the miserable business that she had been carrying on.

Date	Victim	Accused
April 1881	Aboriginal person	Aboriginal person
Cause of death:	Unknown	
Outcome:	Unknown	
Location:	Koppermanna Mission Station, near Marree	

On Saturday 18 February 1882, the following article appeared on page three of the *South Australian Advertiser*, under the heading 'Koppermanna Mission Station':

The following report on the condition of the Koppermanna Mission Station has been forwarded to the Protector of Aborigines by Mr C. A. Meyer: – Sir, I have the Honour to forward to you my report for the year 1881. I am pleased to state that during the past year the health of the natives, on the whole, has been very good, no births nor deaths have occurred. One unfortunate fellow has, however, been murdered by the natives in the month of April in consequence of their tribal feuds. A pretty large number of Aborigines [*sic*] have been living on this station during the past year, except for the months of August and September when the rations ran out. This was caused by the rations, on their way from Adelaide, being delayed owing to the dry nature of the country ...

There is no further information regarding this matter.

Date	*Victim*	*Accused*
18 April 1881	**Richard Dyer**	**William Giles**
Cause of death:	Assault	
Outcome:	Found guilty of manslaughter	
	Sentenced to six months imprisonment with hard labour	
Location:	Lewis Arms, Port Willunga	

On 18 April 1881, Richard Dyer, a shoemaker, and his friend Polkinghorne went to the Lewis Arms at Port Willunga. William Giles, the 44-year-old landlord of the hotel, was serving behind the bar when Dyer and Polkinghorne arrived. While there Dyer said to Giles, 'How about the boots?' Giles replied, 'You promised to make them for me, and you did not do it'. Dyer called Giles a 'bloody liar', and Giles threatened to hit him if he said it again. Dyer repeated that Giles was a liar, and struck Giles with a severe blow to the eyes and nose, knocking him backwards. Giles recovered and moved to the front of the bar and struck Dyer in the face, knocking Dyer back onto the corner of the bar, where there were some boxes and a stool. Dyer got up for a moment but then sat down again.

Giles got some water and washed the blood from Dyer's face but Dyer was not moving. Giles and Polkinghorne carried Dyer to Polkinghorne's trap, but as they were putting Dyer on the back they saw that Dyer was dead.

Sea View Hotel, Port Willunga, 1882.
The Lewis Arms Hotel changed its name to the Sea View Hotel.
State Library of South Australia, B 7814

A post-mortem was carried out by Dr McGowan, who found that Dyer had died from effusion of blood onto the base of the brain. The marks on the face from the punch had nothing to do with the effusion, and McGowan thought that they were caused when Dyer struck his head against the wall when falling.

On Friday 10 June, Giles appeared before the Supreme Court charged with manslaughter. After the evidence was given, many character references were called for Giles who was described as a decent, respectable and quiet man. After deliberation, the jury returned a guilty verdict with a strong recommendation to mercy on account of the provocation. His Honour sentenced Dyer to six months imprisonment with hard labour.

Date	*Victim*	*Accused*
16 May 1881	**Harry Edmond Pearce**	**Robert Johnston**
Cause of death:	Knife wounds	
Outcome:	Found guilty of murder	
	Sentenced to death, executed 18 November 1881	
Location:	Kingston SE	

The following article appeared on page three of the *Border Watch* on Saturday 21 May 1881, regarding the murder of Mounted Constable Harry Pearce, the son of The Honourable James Pearce:

This morning the Court House was crowded to hear the charge against William Johnston, alias Edward Higgins, for feloniously assaulting with intent to kill Constable Pearce. His case was heard before Messrs. G. W. Marshall and C. Gall, J.P.'s.

Sergeant Morris, sworn, said – I received a telegram from Meningie to arrest prisoner on a charge of supplying drink to Aboriginals, and yesterday morning dispatched Mounted-Constable Pearce for that purpose. Pearce left the station at 4.15 am. About a quarter past eleven he received information from Mr. Dungey that Constable Pearce had been stabbed, and was lying about five miles from Kingston. As soon as possible I proceeded to him, and leaving him in the care of friends, went in pursuit of prisoner, taking with me one Peter Anderson. First found his tracks at Hutchison's fence, and followed them up to the Naracoorte road. Kept on them till about half-passed [*sic*] two pm, when I arrested prisoner about two miles beyond Bowaka. Charged him with the offence, and cautioned him in the usual manner. He said I had made a grand mistake. Arrived at Kingston 5.15 pm, and took prisoner into the presence of Constable Pearce, who identified him as the man who stabbed him. Prisoner had three horses in his possession when arrested. On searching prisoner I found a sheath knife, which was identified by Pearce as the weapon with which the wounds were inflicted. (Knife produced in Court.) On arresting prisoner he had strapped on his saddle a large blue swag, and was dressed as he then appeared in Court.

At the conclusion of Sergeant Morris's evidence the Bench asked the prisoner if he had any questions to ask witness, to which he answered 'No'.

On the application of Sergeant Morris the prisoner was then formally remanded till Thursday morning at 10 o'clock.

On enquiry this morning there appears but little hope of Pearce's recovery. The poor fellow is frightfully cut about, there being at least 14 stabs and slashes.

It appears that the first arrest was quietly affected by Trooper Pearce, and the two proceeded several miles along the road, when the prisoner requested to be allowed to dismount. On preparing to start again the prisoner stabbed the constable in the back, following it up by a most determined attempt on his life. Pearce was found about an hour after the attack by W Dungey some distance from the road, having evidently been dragged along and partially hidden in the long grass. Pearce stated he was unable to use his revolver, (which was found some yards from him with all the chambers empty), as almost at the first attack he was disabled by prisoner drawing his knife across his hands. Before leaving the prisoner told Pearce that he left him there to die.

There is nothing very desperate-looking about the prisoner. He appears about 45 years of age, and of no great strength, but he, no doubt, disabled the trooper by the first attack and the cutting of the hands. A desperate struggle probably took place judging by the number of stabs and cuts which are all over the body.

May 19.

… Trooper Pearce … is rapidly sinking, and is not expected to last through the night. This morning, by the *Euro*, arrived his father, mother, sister, and brother, accompanied by Dr. Wigg, from Adelaide. Throughout his terrible suffering Pearce has retained consciousness, and is well aware of his approaching end. At the present time he is quite without pain. … The public strongly expressed their praise at Sergeant Morris' prompt capture of the prisoner. A large crowd

MPC Harry Edmond Pearce.
South Australia Police Historical Society, 1081

410

assembled to see him brought in, and freely expressed their detestation of the horrid and brutal deed.

May 19 (evening).

Police-Trooper Pearce died last night of his wounds. An inquest was held this afternoon on his body. The jury, which was composed of sixteen, unanimously found, 'That the deceased, Harry Edmond Pearce, died from wounds wilfully and maliciously inflicted by the prisoner at the bar, Robert Johnston.' Pearce's family will take the body with them to Adelaide by the *Euro* tomorrow. There was great excitement in the court-house, which was crowded.

On 22 May, Pearce was interred in the Walkerville Cemetery.

On 21 October, Johnston appeared before the Naracoorte Circuit Court charged with the murder of Trooper Pearce. The courthouse was crammed and the trial, which started at 10 am, was not concluded until 5 pm. Mr Nicholson appeared for Johnston and, in his defence, stated the theory was that Johnston dismounted to light his pipe without the permission of Pearce, who became angry and threatened to shoot him if Johnston did not submit to being handcuffed. A struggle then broke out, during which Pearce received his injuries. Nicholson also urged that, as Pearce did not have a warrant with him, the arrest was illegal, and that the prisoner had a right to resist. His Honour Mr Andrews said that the arrest was legal and summed up the evidence. The jury retired for a few minutes and returned a guilty verdict. Johnston was sentenced to death. On Friday 18 November, Johnston, who was also known as William Nugent and Edward Higgins, was executed at the Mount Gambier Gaol.

Date	*Victim*	*Accused*
26 May 1881	**Annie Marovitch**	**John Marovitch**
Cause of death:	Knife wounds	
Outcome:	Found guilty of murder	
	Sentenced to death, commuted to life imprisonment	
	with hard labour	
Location:	Port Augusta railyard	

Around October or November 1880, a German named Louis Thompson deserted from the barque *Alfred Hawley* and made his way to Port Pirie where he met 20-year-old Annie Marovitch, the wife of John Marovitch of Austria. Annie and John had married three years before when Annie was 17 and John was 27. They had a child together but their relationship was not strong. Annie took her child and ran off with Thompson and went to Port Augusta where they lived in a tent at the railway yard. John found out where they were living and paid them a visit where he threatened them with death. John took their child from Annie and gave it to a friend to look after.

Around eight pm on Thursday 26 May 1881, John went back to the railway yard where he saw Thompson near a wood heap. John charged at him and stabbed him from behind. The knife glanced from the left shoulder blade and caused a 'terrible' wound. Thomas started to run away and John fired at him with a revolver. John went to the tent where Annie was and stabbed her in the breast and abdomen, before running off. Thompson ran for the doctor who attended to Annie. The police also arrived and Annie was taken to the local hospital.

Two pistol shots were later heard near the sleepers in the railway yard and a pool of blood was found there. It was thought that John had attempted to take his own life. A search was conducted but John could not be found.

Annie died at seven am the following morning at the hospital. Thomas was also taken to the hospital in a very weak condition. An inquest into the death of Annie Marovitch was held that day before Mr Donaldson, SM, at the hospital. At the conclusion of the inquest, the jury brought in a verdict that John had murdered Annie.

On Saturday 28 May, during the evening, a young man named Kite met a man covered with blood about five miles out of Port Augusta. The man, who had 'a wild look' asked Kite to be directed to water, as he had not had a drink in two days. Kite told him to go to Port Augusta or to Chinaman's Dam. The man replied that he could not go to Port Augusta. Kite carried on to Port Augusta and found that the man he had spoken to matched the description of the person wanted for a murder.

Kite gave the information to Sergeant Leahy who, along with Kite, Mounted Constable Whitters, and an Aboriginal tracker, went to where Marovitch was last seen. Kite pointed out the tracks to the tracker, and the party followed them. When they were about a mile and a half from Chinaman's Dam they saw John in the distance. They rode towards John who started to run away, but he was too weak. Leahy and the others caught up with him and drew their revolvers and swords. John, who still had a revolver in his belt, gave up his escape.

John refused to say anything about the murder, except that his wife was faithless. John had a serious wound under the left side of his jaw and stated that he had no intention of shooting himself and explained that as he was running away, he tripped and fell to the ground and the revolver went off and inflicted the wound. John was in a weak state from loss of blood and was taken to Port Augusta.

Studio photograph of three mounted policeman, left: Sergeant Leahy; centre back: Mounted Constable Newton; seated right: Mounted Constable Whitters, 1881.
State Library of South Australia, B 34709

On 1 June, at Port Augusta, John was committed for trial for murder and wounding with intent to murder.

On Wednesday 10 August, John Marovitch appeared in the Supreme Court before the chief justice on a charge of murder. Marovitch pleaded not guilty and a trial commenced. At the conclusion of the trial, the jury retired for a period of 10 minutes before returning a guilty verdict, with a recommendation to mercy on account of Annie's adultery and Thompson's provocation. His Honour sentenced Marovitch to death, which was later commuted to life imprisonment with hard labour.

Date	Victim	Accused
24 June 1881	Emma Trye	Henry Trye
Cause of death:	Neglect	
Outcome:	Case withdrawn	
Location:	Payneham	

Henry Trye, a wheelwright, and his wife, 34-year-old Emma Trye, had five children together, the oldest being thirteen. They lived in Port Augusta before moving to Adelaide, where they lived in St Helena Place and then Halifax Street. They eventually settled in Payneham. Emma told her brother, Henry Thomas, that her husband had abused her and that he threatened to cut her throat and break her heart, and that he did not care if he swung on the gallows for it. On Saturday 18 June 1881, Emma was taken ill. She had a miscarriage and needed medical help. Emma told her brother that she went down on her knees and asked her husband to send for someone, and that she had to scream out before he would go. Emma complained that she was never given enough food and that she had to pawn her children's boots to buy bread. Emma's condition became worse before she died on 24 June.

An inquest has held into the circumstances of Emma's death at the Duke of Wellington Hotel at Payneham on Tuesday 28 June. The Trye's neighbours gave evidence that they had heard many arguments between the pair. On one occasion, Henry was seen to kick at Emma. Emma had told friends that she was never given enough money to get food for the family. Bertha Trye, the eldest daughter of Emma and Henry, said that there was always plenty of meat and bread in the house and that she had never seen her father strike her mother.

Duke of Wellington Hotel, approximately 1890.
State Library of South Australia, B 33723

The coroner, in summing up, pointed out to the jury the contradictory nature of some of the evidence heard. He recommended they take into account how improbable it was that the respectable and apparently reliable witnesses, such as the relatives of the deceased, should have fabricated any deathbed statement of the deceased of the cruelty and threats of her husband. The doctor had reported to the court the cause of death by explaining the effect of insufficient nourishment or continued cruelty to a woman, such as Emma, in delicate health. The jury retired for more than an hour, and returned a verdict that the death of Emma Trye was caused by peritonitis, brought on by miscarriage, and that 'such miscarriage was accelerated by gross neglect and cruelty of her husband'. Henry Trye was committed to the Supreme Court on a charge of manslaughter.

On Thursday 11 August, a certificate of no case was presented to the Court before the chief justice, and Henry Trye was released.

Date	*Victim*	*Accused*
1 July 1881	John Holmes	John Wilson
Cause of death:	Assault (with a rifle)	
Outcome:	Found guilty of manslaughter	
	Sentenced to three months imprisonment with hard labour	
Location:	Kulpara	

On Friday 1 July 1881, 30-year-old John Holmes and his friend John Wilson went out together for a day's shooting. They both went to the Travellers' Rest Hotel at Kulpara, where they had dinner and some drink. They began to quarrel about a dog and were separated by the landlord. After having another drink, they both left the hotel, appearing to be friendly to each other. After about an hour they were seen to pass the hotel again, going in the direction of the Hummocks, towards their home. When they were a short distance from the hotel, Holmes was seen to strike Wilson two or three times with his fist. Wilson pointed his rifle at Holmes and pulled the trigger, but the gun failed to fire. Holmes pushed Wilson and they both fell to the ground. After getting up, Wilson struck Holmes once or twice with either the butt or barrel of the gun. Holmes fell to the ground and the landlord, who had run from the hotel, picked up Holmes and accused Wilson of killing him. Wilson replied, 'If I have, I have done in self-defence'. The district constable arrived and took Wilson into custody. Holmes later died from his injuries.

An inquest was held at the Kulpara Hotel where Dr Wrigley gave evidence of his post-mortem examination. Wrigley found on opening the skull where the brain was 'much congested', especially in the area where Wilson had struck him. Wrigley believed the cause of death was concussion produced by rupture of the blood vessels of the brain and believed that the blow to the head from the barrel of the gun had caused the rupture. The coroner summed up the evidence at length before the jury returned the verdict that Wilson was guilty of manslaughter under great provocation. Wilson was committed to trial.

Wilson appeared before the Supreme Court on Friday 5 August where he was found guilty of manslaughter and sentenced to three months imprisonment with hard labour.

Date	*Victim*	*Accused*
19 July 1881	**Female child**	**Unknown**
Cause of death:	Suffocation	
Outcome:	Offender not located	
Location:	Adelaide	

On Wednesday 20 July 1881, some children were playing in the parklands in the plantation at North Terrace West when they found a parcel under a tree. One of the children, 13-year-old Edith Wilson, opened the parcel and found that it contained the body of a newborn female child. Wilson told a young man who was passing at the time, who in turn advised the police. Wilson did not see anyone else around at the time.

Residence of Dr William Talbot Clindening on North Terrace, 1880.
State Library of South Australia, B 2495

Dr W Clindening examined the child, and conducted a post-mortem. Clindening found that the child had recently been born alive and was full term. There were no marks of violence except round the face, the back of the neck and the chin. Those were marks of pressure, which appeared to have been made by a black cotton stocking, which was wrapped around the face of the child and had caused the child to suffocate. There was also a calico bandage wrapped around the face and neck.

Detective Hammill made enquiries as to the mother of the child, but he was unable to locate anyone. An inquest was held at the Destitute Asylum on Monday 25 July, where the jury found that the deceased had been wilfully murdered by some person or persons unknown.

Date	Victims	Accused
21 September 1881	William Clark and Charles Clark	Joseph Clark
Cause of death:	Unknown; suspected gunshot wounds	
Outcome:	Joseph Clark committed suicide	
Location:	Green Hills, near Millicent	

Joseph Clark lived with his wife and two children, eight-year-old William and six-year-old Charles at Green Hills, about five miles from Millicent towards Hatherleigh. The family had arrived from England around 1878. In 1880, Clark's wife died, leaving him to care for the two children. When Joseph talked to his neighbours, he would often cry when he spoke of his wife. Clark became more and more despondent and started to have troubles with money.

Clark spoke to Walter Day, the storekeeper in Millicent, on 20 September 1881. Clark seemed downhearted and alluded to his wife's death. Day offered to help him with his crop and Clark seemed more cheerful. Clark always told Day that he had difficulty in looking after his children without his wife. A neighbour saw Clark on his farm the next day, but he was not seen alive again.

On 10 October, John Wells was walking on the boundary fence of Clark's farm when he went to Clark's hut to see if he was at home. On approaching the hut he noticed a very bad smell. Wells looked through a window to see if anyone was home. Wells saw one of the boys lying on a bed. Wells was shocked at the appearance of the boy, as he had been dead for several weeks. Wells entered the house and saw that Clark and the other child were also dead. Wells left and went to Millicent where he notified the police.

Mounted Constable Patrick Shiels attended the hut and found Clark and his two children were in their beds. A five-shot revolver was on the bed next to Clark's body. Shiels noted that three of the chambers had been fired and two were still loaded. In the same room was a tin containing further cartridges. From the bloodstains on the floor and on clothing in the room, it was thought that Clark shot his sons while they were in their beds, then lay down and shot himself. There was evidence that Clark shot himself in the head, but no evidence could be found of where the boys were shot, as their bodies were too decomposed for an examination.

An inquest was held the following day where the jury found that Joseph Clark had committed suicide 'while labouring under temporary insanity', but that there was no evidence to show how the children had died.

Date	*Victim*	*Accused*
10 January 1882	**John Thompson**	**Morris (Maurice) Ewens**
Cause of death:	Assault	
Outcome:	Found guilty of manslaughter	
	Sentenced to three months imprisonment	
Location:	Morphett Street Bridge	

During the evening of Monday 9 January 1882, John Thompson and 21-year-old Morris Ewens were in the Theatre Royal bar on Hindley Street. They had not gone there together and both were with their own friends. As Thompson was leaving the bar, he bumped into Ewens, who told him to mind what he was doing. Thompson pushed Ewens away and Ewens said, 'If you push me again, I'll hit you'. Thompson kept saying to Ewens, 'You wouldn't hit me, would you?' After a short time, Thompson struck Ewens in the mouth with the back of his hand. There was a short fight in the bar before Ewens and Thompson went out to Hindley Street, followed by a crowd of onlookers.

Ewens walked west on Hindley Street when he saw Thompson in the lane next to the White Hart Hotel. Ewens went to Thompson and said, 'We had a bit of a row in the bar just now, and if you like to come on to the parklands, we'll have it out'. Thompson agreed and they shook hands and both walked off. Ewens and his friends walked to the Trinity Church on North Terrace where he was later joined by Thompson and his friends. The group moved to the northern side of the Morphett Street Bridge.

In the early hours of Tuesday morning the fight began. The fight lasted about 20 rounds and both Ewens and Thompson had a second, who was picking them up and assisting them between rounds. Thompson fought the best during the first two or three rounds, and Ewens was knocked insensible for a few minutes. Thompson's second, James Charles, said, 'That'll do Jack, no more of it', but Thompson refused and said he would turn on anyone

White Hart Hotel, south side of Hindley Street
on the east corner of Peel Street, approximately 1878.
State Library of South Australia, B 10711

who tried to stop him. The fight continued and Thompson was severely beaten, eventually falling to the ground, unable to get up. The fight ended and Thompson was placed in a cab. Thompson was found deceased later that morning in his bed in Pirie Street.

Police Constable Alex Wallace arrested Ewens that evening and charged him with manslaughter. Ewens said, 'I am very sorry it happened, I would sooner be in his place that in the position I am placed in'.

A coronial inquest was held at the Destitute Asylum on Friday 13 January, where evidence was given that Thompson was the aggressor and was a person who would pick fights when intoxicated. Dr Clindening gave evidence that he had conducted the autopsy and found that Thompson had injuries consistent with being in a fight. He found injuries to the head that indicated that great violence had been used against the deceased. There were injuries to the face, eye and teeth. A blood clot was found in the head, which was the cause of death.

The coroner, in summing up, reminded the jury that fights were illegal and that if two men had arranged to fight and one was killed, the survivor would be guilty of manslaughter. The jury retired before returning a verdict of manslaughter against Ewens, further finding that the seconds Thomas Baxter and James Charles were guilty of aiding and abetting. All three were committed to trial.

On Tuesday 7 March, Ewens appeared before the Supreme Court charged with manslaughter. Baxter and Charles also appeared. At the conclusion of the trial, Ewens was found guilty of manslaughter and Baxter and Charles were found guilty of aiding and abetting. All three were sentenced to three months imprisonment without hard labour.

Date	*Victim*	*Accused*
20 January 1882	**Ellen Blake**	**Johanna Mullins**
Cause of death:	Phthisis (a wasting disease)	
Outcome:	Charged with manslaughter	
	Outcome unknown	
Location:	Sturt Street, Adelaide	

Ellen Blake, a single 38-year-old woman, lived with her mother in Sturt Street, Adelaide. Four months prior to her death, Blake contracted consumption, and was confined to her bed in the last two months of her life.

About five weeks prior to her death, a woman named Johanna Mullins, who resided next to the Blakes, began to annoy Ellen. This continued until she died. Mullins used to knock at the partition wall, call Blake a prostitute and other names, and ask Blake when she was going to die. For a short time in the five weeks, Mullins was in gaol and this gave Blake some rest. At one stage, the police were called, as Mullins was in a drunken state and making a racket. Mullins, who was standing on her own property, would make a loud noise by singing at the top of her voice while throwing water at the door of the Blakes' house. The police had no power to arrest Mullins as she was on private property. Just prior to her death, a priest attended at the Blakes' home, but he had been deterred by the noise from administering to the spiritual wants of Ellen, who died on Friday 20 January 1882.

The city coroner, Mr Ward, held an inquest at the Rose Inn on Saturday 21 January into the death of Ellen Blake. Evidence was heard from neighbours of the Blakes and Mullins who all testified that Mullins would cause disturbances in the street. Dr Clindening testified that he had lately visited Blake several times and on one occasion he found her greatly terrified. Blake was very much emaciated and was in the advanced stage of pulmonary disease. Dr Clindening was of the opinion that Mullins' conduct was sufficient to accelerate death. The coroner said that judging from Mullins' behaviour in court, she was capable of abusing anyone. The coroner told the jury that although there was no evidence of blows having been given, he thought that Blake's death had been accelerated by Mullins' conduct.

At the completion of the inquest, the jury found that Ellen Blake had died from phthisis, a wasting disease, and that her death had been accelerated by the actions of Johanna Mullins. The jury added a rider to their verdict desiring the coroner to call the attention of the Board of Health to the disgraceful state of the closet accommodation on the property where Blake died. Mullins was committed to trial on a charge of manslaughter.

Mullins appeared before the Supreme Court on Tuesday 21 February, charged with manslaughter. There is no record of the outcome of the trial. Johanna does not appear in the handwritten Supreme Court record of manslaughter convictions, so the charge was either dismissed, or Mullins was found not guilty.

Date	*Victim*	*Accused*
1 February 1882	**Papst child**	**Mina Papst**
Cause of death:	Strangulation	
Outcome:	Found guilty of concealment of birth	
	Sentenced to 12 months imprisonment with hard labour	
Location:	Criterion Hotel, Adelaide	

On 23 January 1882, Mrs Kirby, the landlady of the Criterion Hotel, engaged 24-year-old Mina Papst to work as a cook in the hotel. Papst told Mrs Kirby that she was a single woman. At about seven-thirty pm on 31 January, Kirby saw Papst lying on her bed, complaining of pains in the stomach. Kirby accused her of being pregnant, but Papst denied it, stating that the pain was cramps caused by eating plum pie for her dinner. Kirby checked on Papst around twenty-past nine that evening, when Papst said that she felt better and that she would be alright in the morning.

The next morning, one of the hotel's waitresses went to Kirby and said that Papst was not fit to be about the house, and if there were nothing wrong with her, then there soon would be. Kirby saw Papst coming up the stairs and Kirby told her to sit down as she was going to call for the constable. Papst begged her not to, saying it was all over. Constable Hughes arrived around seven am and was told by Kirby that she thought Papst had given birth. Hughes went to Papst's room and found evidence of a recent birth. He searched further and found the dead body of a newborn female child wrapped up in some clothes. Hughes noticed that a handkerchief was tied tightly around the child's neck. The body of the child was removed to the morgue and Papst was taken to the Destitute Asylum.

A coroner's inquest was held on Thursday 2 February at the Destitute Asylum, however it was adjourned, as Papst was not well enough to attend. The inquest resumed on Monday 13 February. Dr Dunlop, who had conducted a post-mortem examination, stated that the child had been born alive and had a separate existence from the mother. The cause of death was given as strangulation. At the completion of the inquest, the jury found Papst guilty of the suffocation of her child. The coroner committed Papst to trial, who burst into tears saying, 'I did not intend to kill my baby, I don't remember tying a handkerchief round its neck. The reason I did not tell them I was [pregnant] was I intended going to the country'.

Papst appeared before the Supreme Court on Friday 3 March, where she pleaded not guilty to the murder of her child. At the conclusion of the trial, the jury returned a verdict that she was not guilty of the murder, but guilty of concealment of birth. His Honour sentenced Papst to 12 months imprisonment with hard labour.

Date	*Victim*	*Accused*
9 February 1882	**Edward Lounder**	**Margaret Harris**
Cause of death:	Strangulated hernia	
Outcome:	Found guilty of manslaughter	
	Sentenced to five years imprisonment with hard labour	
Location:	Rosina Street, Adelaide	

Edward Lounder was born to Elizabeth Lounder, a brothel-keeper in Adelaide. When Edward was nearly 18 months old, Lounder found that she could not look after him due to the brothel she was keeping and because she was the mother of two other children. Lounder placed Edward with 26-year-old Margaret Harris, and paid her 10 shillings a week to look after him. Lounder had been told that Harris was kind with children, so she felt Edward would be cared for. Edward was with Harris for about a month, and during that time, Lounder visited him and saw that he was being looked after. Around that time, Lounder was imprisoned for two months for smashing windows.

Margaret Harris was a single woman with two children who lived with a man called Morris. Harris was constantly drunk and on one occasion a neighbour heard Edward screaming in the back yard. Harris was seen to smack Edward and her own two children, and she would leave the children alone in the house.

On 8 February, Susan Gallagher, a neighbour of Harris', heard a loud scream, so she ran to Harris' house and found her lying on the floor in a drunken state, squeezing Edward between her right arm and her side, trying to stop Edward from crying. The next day, Harris was out all day and had not returned by 11 pm. Gallagher could hear Edward screaming so she called for a policeman. When he arrived, the policeman said he would not dare open the door, even though they were not locked. Gallagher sent for another policeman who entered the house and found Edward on the floor gasping for air. Edward was taken to the Adelaide Hospital but died in under an hour.

At the inquest, a surgeon gave evidence, stating that Edward had a rupture to his right side and a bruise to the forehead. A post-mortem found that Edward had died from a strangulated hernia. The coroner, in summing up, referred in strong terms to the mistreatment suffered by Edward at the hands of Harris, and told the jury to consider whether or not his death was accelerated by her 'barbarous' treatment. The jury retired, then returned with the verdict that Edward had died from a strangulated hernia, 'brought about by the gross carelessness, cruelty, and negligence of Margaret Harris', and that Harris was guilty of manslaughter. The jury also recommended that the coroner make enquiries as to the negligence of the policeman first called to the house. Harris was committed for trial.

On Wednesday 8 March, Harris appeared before the Supreme Court charged with manslaughter. At the completion of the trial, the jury found her guilty. Harris was sentenced to five years imprisonment with hard labour.

Date	Victim	Accused
15 March 1882	Emma Wilkins	Margaret Wilkins and James Wilkins

Cause of death:	Neglect
Outcome:	James found not guilty
	No record of Margaret appearing
Location:	Stirling West

James and Margaret Wilkins lived in a small hut with their six children in Stirling West, not far from the police station. In March 1882, Police Trooper Donogan, acting on information from others in the neighbourhood, obtained a search warrant for the Wilkins' house. Donogan found the family living in a 'fearful state of destitution', as the children and Margaret had no underclothing and their outer clothing was so fine it was scarcely sufficient to hide their nudity. They slept on straw-filled sacks on the earth floor and used other sacks as blankets. The sacks were filled with maggots and filth. James, who was 37 years old, was found to have in his possession no less than £70, owned three horses and carried on a trade as a wood carter. James was charged with neglect of his wife and family in failing to supply them with sufficient food and clothing. He was committed to take trial in the Supreme Court.

When the house was searched, Margaret was holding Emma, her 9-month-old, child who appeared sickly and suffering from a lack of proper nourishment. Emma died on 15 March 1882, and a coronial inquest was held on 17 March. Dr Foster gave evidence and stated that gross neglect and want of proper nourishment had caused Emma's death. The jury returned the verdict that Emma had died from neglect and malnourishment caused by her parents. The coroner committed both to trial. Bail was allowed for both James and Margaret as it was hoped that during the interval between committal and trial, the children, who were all very young, might be better provided for and properly clad.

On Thursday 6 April, James Wilkins appeared in the Supreme Court before Mr Justice Boucaut where he entered a plea of not guilty to manslaughter. After a short time, His Honour pointed out that the evidence seemed to favour the prisoner, and that the depositions disclosed nothing against him. The crown solicitor, upon His Honour's suggestion, said he would withdraw any further evidence, and wondered how such a charge could have been brought.

The jury found James not guilty and he was discharged. There is no record of Margaret appearing before the court.

Date	Victim	Accused
April 1882	Male Child	Unknown
Cause of death:	Suffocation	
Outcome:	Offender not located	
Location:	Torrens Lake	

On 3 May 1882, William Allgood, an employee of the Railway Workshop, was out on the Torrens Lake in a boat when he noticed a black bag floating in the water on the west side of the Morphett Street Bridge, close to the north bank. Allgood recovered the bag and saw an infant's arm protruding from the opening. Allgood advised Mr Hannan, who opened the bag and found a body of a male infant wrapped in a sheet. The police arrived and took the bag and the child away.

Torrens Lake approximately 1880.
State Library of South Australia, B 9128

On Friday 5 May, an inquest was held at the Destitute Asylum where Allgood and Hannan gave evidence. The coroner adjourned the inquest so that the police could make further attempts to locate the parents of the child.

On Friday 19 May, the inquest resumed. Dr Dunlop gave evidence of conducting a post-mortem examination and stated that the infant was well-nourished and about five or six weeks old. He stated that the infant died from suffocation. Water Constable Brenner stated that he and Detective Burchell had made a thorough investigation into the parentage of the child, but were unable to find anyone. Brenner stated that the acting Police Commissioner had suggested that a further adjournment for a week be granted, so further investigations could be made. The coroner agreed and adjourned the inquest.

The inquest resumed on 29 May where Constable Hammill stated that since the last inquest the Government had offered a £50 reward for any information, but no further evidence had been found. The coroner summed up to the jury, stating that there was not the slightest doubt, if the evidence was to be believed, that the child had been murdered. The jury gave the verdict that they were 'of the opinion, in accordance with the medical evidence, that the male child, name unknown, found in the Torrens Lake on May 3, was murdered by suffocation'.

Date	*Victim*	*Accused*
19 June 1882	Coonah (Mary)	Jenniebutta Monyah (Jerry)
Cause of death:	Spear wound	
Outcome:	Found guilty of manslaughter	
	Sentenced to 12 months imprisonment with hard labour	
Location:	Near Lake Everard	

On 19 June 1882, James McKean was camped with others near Lake Everard. McKean left the camp and went in the direction of an Aboriginal encampment situated half a mile away. While he was walking there, he found Coonah, who was also known as Mary, lying face down on a rock. McKean turned her over to discover that she was still alive and had a spear wound to her chest. With the assistance of another man, McKean carried her to his tent, where she later died.

Suspicion fell on 35-year-old Jenniebutta Monyah, who was also known as Jerry and was Coonah's husband. Jenniebutta Monyah was nowhere to be found, so the police were advised. Two months later, on 17 August, Jenniebutta Monyah was arrested near Streaky Bay and a made a confession to the police trooper, stating that he had stabbed Coonah with a spear, but he did not mean to kill her. His reason for attacking her was because she had refused to go away with him from the whites, with whom she had been cohabiting.

Jenniebutta Monyah was conveyed to Adelaide, where on 10 October 1882 he appeared before the Supreme Court charged with the wilful murder of Coonah, his lubra. Mr Downer, who represented Jenniebutta Monyah, contended that the evidence was of a most untrustworthy character, and that the jury should not find him guilty of murder. Downer contented that if the jury believed that Jenniebutta Monyah killed Coonah, he was guilty only of manslaughter. His Honour Mr Justice Boucaut carefully summed up the evidence and pointed out the difference between manslaughter and murder. The jury were also directed that they must try an Aboriginal person in the same way as they would a white person, and must not consider murder justified by any native custom. The jury, after a lengthy retirement, found Jenniebutta Monyah guilty of manslaughter. Jenniebutta Monyah was sentenced to 12 months imprisonment with hard labour.

Date	*Victim*	*Accused*
3 October 1882	Thomas Maloney	Arthur Saddler, William Chidley, and one other unknown male
Cause of death:	Assault	
Outcome:	Saddler and Chidley found not guilty	
	Unknown male never identified	
Location:	Waymouth Street, Adelaide	

Around nine pm on Monday 2 October 1882, 30-year-old Thomas Maloney and his friend John Capper were at the Exchange Hotel in Adelaide. They had a drink then went to the Wellington for two more. They then went to the Clarence Hotel on King William Street, where they each had another beer. They left the hotel at 11.30 pm and walked towards Grenfell Street where Capper left Maloney, who was heading home towards the Town Hall. Maloney turned off on Waymouth Street and spoke to a woman named Mrs Hewitt near the *Advertiser* office. While he was talking to her, 20-year-old Arthur Edward Saddler and 22-year-old William James Chidley drove past them in a cab. James Parker, the cabdriver, was told to pull over. Saddler got out of the cab and spoke to Maloney and Hewitt. After a short time, a fight started between Maloney and Saddler. Maloney knocked Saddler down, who then got up and ran to the cab and said, 'I was struck cowardly'. Chidley got out of the cab, and the pair approached Maloney. The three men fought again. Maloney was knocked to the ground and was kicked while he was still down. Maloney got up and another man who was passing joined in and started to punch Maloney while the other two looked on. All three men then left, leaving Maloney in a pool of blood on the roadway.

Constable Wardell found Maloney lying on the tramline and arranged for him to be taken to the hospital where Dr Poulton saw him. Maloney was conscious but was 'stupid' in manner. He had lacerated wounds to his head where the bone was visible. Maloney died 10 days later from the injuries he sustained during the fight.

An inquest was held at the hospital, but it was adjourned several times to enable the police to conduct further investigations. On 18 October, Police Trooper Gardner arrested Chidley and Saddler at the Bridgewater Hotel, and on Monday 23 October, both appeared at the inquest. At the completion of the inquest, the jury returned a verdict of manslaughter against Saddler, Chidley, and the unidentified third man. Saddler and Chidley were committed to trial and bail was refused.

Chidley and Saddler appeared before the Supreme Court on Thursday 7 December charged with wilfully killing and slaying Thomas Maloney. Evidence was given that as Saddler and Chidley turned into Waymouth Street, they heard Hewitt scream, so they stopped the cab and went to her. Hewitt stated that Maloney had accosted her, knocked her down, struck her and insulted her. Saddler approached Maloney and threatened to strike him if he further insulted Hewitt, but Maloney struck Saddler and knocked him down. Chidley and Saddler then fought with Maloney, who started throwing stones at them. Saddler and Chidley retreated to the cab and drove off, leaving Maloney in the middle of the street still throwing stones at the cab. Another unknown man then fought with Maloney, who was later found in a pool of blood and later died. At the completion of the trial, the jury returned a verdict of not guilty against Chidley and Saddler. The unknown man was never identified.

Date	Victim	Accused
9 November 1882	Alice Tree	Henry Page
Cause of death:	Assault	
Outcome:	Found not guilty	
Location:	Currie Street, Adelaide	

Alice Tree, a 25-year-old prostitute, lived in a small cottage in Currie Street with 21-year-old Henry Page, who was described as a half-caste man. In the evening of 9 November 1882, a quarrel was heard by neighbours between Page and Tree. A constable attended the scene and saw Tree sitting on a sofa with Page standing in front of her with one hand on her shoulder and the other in a 'striking attitude', saying to her, 'If you do not stop I will do for you'. The constable told them to desist and Tree said it was alright. The constable left. The next day, Page called for the police, saying that Tree was dying. The police arrived and found Tree lying on her sofa in a lifeless condition. She had a black eye and several dark bruises on her face and left shoulder. Page had gone for a doctor and was arrested on suspicion of causing Tree's death on his return.

When the police searched the house, several articles of clothing and towels stained with blood were found. The house was littered with broken crockery and pieces of an ornament. Two chairs were broken and the house was in a state of disorder. There was a large spot of blood where the constable had seen Page raising his hand to Tree.

A coroner's inquest was held on Monday 13 November. After performing a post-mortem examination, Dr Jay stated that the cause of death was due to compression of the brain caused by extravagated blood on the surface. He further said that a blow on a part of the body might cause such extravasation. At the end of the inquest, the jury found Page guilty of manslaughter. Page was committed to trial.

On Friday 15 December, Henry Page appeared before the Supreme Court where he pleaded not guilty to feloniously and wilfully killing Alice Tree. During the evidence, the judge said that the case was one of violent suspicion, but he asked what proof there was that the injuries inflicted by the prisoner caused the death of Tree. The crown solicitor thought there was a case to go to the jury, although it was not a strong one. His Honour said he would send the case to the jury, but he would reserve a point for the full court as to whether the evidence was sufficient. Page, who was undefended, stated that he did not inflict the injuries to Tree. The jury returned a verdict of not guilty, and the prisoner was discharged.

Date	*Victim*	*Accused*
12 November 1882	**Christian Renderup**	**Patrick McGree,**
		Elizabeth McGree,
		and Margaret McGree

Cause of death:	Knife wounds
Outcome:	Patrick and Elizabeth found guilty of murder
	Sentenced to death, later commuted to life imprisonment
	Margaret found not guilty
Location:	Hamley Bridge

Christian Renderup, a 38-year-old Swede who had been in the colony for about 18 years, was employed in the scrub around the township of Hamley Bridge. Renderup knew the McGree family, 47-year-old Patrick, his 42-year-old wife Elizabeth, and their children, including 14-year-old Margaret. The McGrees lived about half a mile north of the township, and Renderup was known to visit there frequently with a quantity of alcohol to drink with them. On Saturday 11 November 1882, Renderup went to the McGree's house during the evening to drink with them. Between three and four on Sunday morning, Margaret Cairns was woken by the sound of someone screaming. Cairns lived in a house to the rear of the McGree house. Cairns opened her window and heard Renderup say, 'Oh, don't McGree', several times. Renderup sounded in 'dreadful agony'. Cairns thought the sounds were coming from inside the house and shortly afterwards she heard McGree call out to his wife in the garden. She heard someone groaning in the yard, and heard McGree go inside, singing and laughing.

Susannah Chambers, who lived opposite the McGree house, was also woken up by the sounds of screaming. Chambers opened her front door and heard Mrs McGree shouting, 'I'll murder you', two or three times as she was beating someone on the ground. Chambers heard Mrs McGree say, 'Give me an axe and I'll chop him up'. Chambers also heard Margaret ask her brother where the axe was.

Mounted Constable Delaney, stationed at Hamley Bridge, was woken up at four am by a young girl who told him that Christy (Renderup) was either killing or beating her mother. Delaney attended at the McGree house where he found Renderup dead on the ground with severe head and chest injuries. Delaney removed the body to the police station and arrested Patrick McGree on suspicion of murder. Delaney searched the house and found a shoemaker's knife, three hammers, a tomahawk, a hammer handle, a smooth stone and a broken rung of a sofa all with blood on them.

A coroner's inquest was held, and Patrick, Elizabeth and Margaret gave evidence. Patrick stated that Renderup was at his house on Saturday evening, but left to go to town, and that he didn't see him again until the next morning when he was found dead. Elizabeth stated that she was asleep on Sunday morning when Renderup burst in and grabbed her around the throat. At the same time an unknown 'dark' man came into the house, grabbed Renderup, and dragged him outside. Elizabeth said she was too scared to open the door and waited for an hour then sent her younger daughter to fetch the police. Both denied assaulting Renderup.

Margaret stated that she was asleep when she was woken up by the sound of Renderup breaking into the house and assaulting her mother, then she saw a large dark man drag Renderup out.

Dr John Nickoll, of Gawler, conducted a post-mortem examination and found that Renderup had nine knife wounds to the body and seven head wounds, including two fractures, caused by a blunt instrument. Dr Nickoll stated that the knife wounds were on such an angle that the victim must have been lying on the ground when they were inflicted. The head wounds were not sufficient to cause immediate death, but any of the chest wounds would have caused immediate death.

The inquest was adjourned for further investigation and resumed the following day. Further evidence was given and at the completion of the inquest, the jury retired for nearly an hour before they returned with a verdict of wilful murder against Patrick and Elizabeth McGree, and found Margaret guilty of being an accessory. All were committed to trial.

On Wednesday 20 December, Patrick, Elizabeth and Margaret appeared before the Supreme Court charged with wilful murder. At 12.55 pm, at the completion of the evidence, the jury retired, taking with them the clothes of the deceased and the weapons found at the house. Almost three hours later, the jury returned with a verdict of wilful murder against Patrick and Elizabeth, and a not guilty verdict against Margaret. Patrick told the judge that he was not guilty, and Elizabeth said, 'Welcome be the will of God'. Mr Kingston, who represented Elizabeth, briefly counselled her, after which she told the judge that she was with child. His Honour pointed out to the crown solicitor that the sheriff would be required to enlist a jury of matrons to decide whether Elizabeth was truly pregnant. The crown solicitor said it was not necessary to be done that day. His Honour said that he did not want to sentence Elizabeth until she had been seen by the matrons, but after some discussion, it was decided that His Honour would pass sentence that day and the sheriff would empanel a jury of matrons to consider the allegations of the prisoner the following day. The judge then found both Patrick and Elizabeth guilty of murder, and sentenced them both to death.

On 21 December, a jury of matrons was empanelled to try the allegation of Elizabeth McGree that she was pregnant, and therefore entitled to a respite of the death sentence. The jury found that Elizabeth was in an advanced state of pregnancy, and the judge would accordingly advise the governor to postpone the execution.

On 6 January 1883, it was reported that the Executive Council had decided that the extreme penalty of law would not be carried into effect in the case of the McGrees. Their sentences were commuted to life imprisonment.

Date	*Victim*	*Accused*
17 December 1882	**Howard child**	**Mary Howard**
Cause of death:	Suffocation	
Outcome:	Found guilty of concealment of birth	
	Sentenced to two years imprisonment with hard labour	
Location:	North Adelaide	

Mary Howard and her sister Ellen Howard were both employed as servants of James Blyth at his house at North Adelaide. They had been in his employ for about a fortnight and shared a room together in the house. On 16 December 1882, they were both in bed when 30-year-old Mary left the room for a short time, then returned. Ellen woke up at around five am and Mary asked her if she could clean out the laundry and the closet. Ellen found there was blood in the laundry and closet, which she cleaned. Ellen took a glass of water to Mary, who said she had diarrhoea. Ellen saw that one of Mary's nightdresses had some bloodstains on it. Ellen did not know that Mary was pregnant.

Around eleven that morning, James Blyth noticed the body of a child in the closet, but he was not sure that it was a body. He also saw some bloodstains on the floor. He returned around three that afternoon and tried to recover the body from the closet with some wire, but he was unable to do so, so he called for the police.

Blyth visited Dr Nesbitt's house and told him what he had found. Nesbitt and Blyth returned to Blyth's house where they managed to recover the body of the child. Mary expressed a wish to see Dr Nesbitt and told him that she was unwell and had diarrhoea. Nesbitt thought that Mary had recently given birth, but Mary denied it. Nesbitt later examined Mary with her consent and found that she had given birth.

Corporal Burchell arrived at the house and took charge of the body, removing it to the Destitute Asylum where Dr Nesbitt conducted a post-mortem examination. Nesbitt found that the child was fully developed and had a separate existence from her mother. He found evidence of nightsoil from the closet in the mouth and gave the cause of death as suffocation by the nightsoil.

An inquest was held at the Dover Castle Hotel at North Adelaide on 27 December. At the conclusion of the inquest, the coroner mentioned that the evidence pointed to murder, not manslaughter, and that Mary Howard, who no doubt was the mother of the child, committed the act. The jury, after about an hour's retirement, returned the verdict that the child had died from suffocation in the closet, but there was no evidence how it had gotten there. The jury added as a rider that Mr Blyth showed great carelessness in not reporting the finding of the body until four or five hours after his original discovery.

On Wednesday 3 January 1883, Mary appeared before the Police Court in Adelaide charged with murdering her illegitimate child. The depositions taken at the inquest were read and confirmed. The magistrate committed Mary for trial.

Mary appeared before the Supreme Court on Tuesday 27 February where she pleaded not guilty to manslaughter. During the trial, the evidence in support of that charge was very weak, and at His Honour's suggestion, the Honourable C Mann QC, crown solicitor, said that he would be content with a verdict on the lesser charge of concealment of birth. Mr Kingston, who asked for leave to withdraw his client's plea of not guilty and substitute one of guilty of concealment. This was accepted and His Honour, Mr Justice Boucaut, sentenced Howard to two years imprisonment with hard labour, remarking that there were circumstances in this case that made the offence an aggravated one.

Date	*Victim*	*Accused*
25 December 1882	Marian Todd	**John Reid, Adolph Heise, James Ford, John Minnis, Samuel Mead, Henry Purvis, and William Baker**

Cause of death:	Trampled
Outcome:	Charges withdrawn against Reid and Purvis
	Heise, Ford, Minnis, Mead and Baker found not guilty
Location:	Semaphore

On Christmas Day 1882, Hannah Harvey, a nurse-girl, left her home around 11 am for Semaphore beach. Hannah had seven-year-old Marian Todd and two other children with her. During the afternoon, as the children were playing on the beach, some horses being ridden by John Reid, 17-year-old Adolph Heise, 24-year-old James Ford, 26-year-old John Minnis, 21-year-old Samuel Mead, William Baker and Henry Purvis trotted by them in the direction of the fort. After some time, Hannah saw the horses galloping back. Hannah called out to the children, 'The horses are coming, come out of their way'. As the horses got closer, Marian ran into the path of the horses towards Hannah, and was knocked down by one of them. Purvis returned and helped Hannah put Marian in a trap to be taken to the doctor at Port Adelaide. By the time Marian reached Dr Mitchell's house, she was dead.

A coronial inquest was held on 26 December where the jury found that the incident was an accident.

On Wednesday 3 January, Reid, Heise, Ford, Minnis, Mead, Baker and Purvis appeared before the Police Court at Port Adelaide charged with wilfully and feloniously killing and slaying Marian Todd. During the trial, the police prosecutor, Inspector Doyle, withdrew charges against Reid and Purvis as they were too far behind the group of horses that collided with Marian. Evidence was given that the horses were galloping 'carelessly, jauntily and dangerously, in sort of a double-shuffle', and that on the way to the beach, Corporal Shanahan had cautioned the riders against fast riding.

Mr Dempster acted for Heise and protested to the magistrate that there was no evidence against him, and that the charges should be withdrawn. The magistrate refused to do so, stating that in a case of manslaughter all present in the company of the one who committed the act were presumed to be engaged in it. At the completion of the hearing, Heise, Ford, Minnis, Baker and Mead were committed to trial for manslaughter.

On Friday 23 February 1883, Heise, Ford, Minnis, Baker and Mead appeared before the Supreme Court on the charge of manslaughter. At the completion of the trial, the jury found the prisoners not guilty, and they were discharged.

Date	Victim	Accused
10 February 1883	**John O'Brien**	**John Clymas**
Cause of death:	Assault	
Outcome:	Pleaded guilty to manslaughter	
	Sentenced to imprisonment for one month	
Location:	Parkside Hotel	

John O'Brien lived with his family at Unley Park. On Saturday 10 February 1883, 50-year-old O'Brien left his house at around six in the morning to go to work. His daughter, Elizabeth, saw him leave. Later that day, O'Brien went to the Parkside Hotel with a group of friends. John Clymas and Henry George, who was the coachman for the Chief Justice, were also at the hotel. Around four-thirty pm, Clymas heard O'Brien call George a 'damned rogue'. George said nothing but Clymas said, 'You ought not to call a man a rogue unless you know he is one'. Clymas told O'Brien that he would throw him out of the hotel. Clymas and George left the hotel but Clymas returned and shaped up to O'Brien. O'Brien would not shape up to him and started to leave. Clymas caught hold of O'Brien and threw him out of the door. O'Brien hit his head on the scraper of the door and fell onto the ground.

O'Brien was insensible and was assisted to a chair. Dr Collins of Parkside was called to the hotel where he examined O'Brien. Collins saw that O'Brien's pupils were dilated and were not responsive to touch, which indicated compression of the brain. O'Brien's pulse was very weak and he had a scalp wound which was bleeding. Collins thought that O'Brien was suffering from a fracture of the base of the skull and that he would not live long. O'Brien was taken to the hospital, where he died at a quarter to six that afternoon.

On Tuesday 13 February, an inquest was held at the hospital on the body of John O'Brien. At the conclusion of the evidence, the coroner briefly summed up, pointing out a few small differences in the evidence and stating that the fact that the deceased interfering would not warrant Clymas going to the extent he did. The jury, after a short retirement, returned a verdict of manslaughter against Clymas. Clymas was committed to trial and given bail.

On Thursday 1 March, Clymas appeared before Mr. Justice Boucaut in the Adelaide Supreme Court charged with manslaughter. After some portion of the evidence had been heard, Clymas, by the advice of his counsel Mr Pater, threw himself on the mercy of the court, withdrew his not guilty plea, and pleaded guilty to accidentally killing O'Brien. Mr Pater made an earnest appeal on behalf of his client. Clymas was sentenced to imprisonment for one month without hard labour.

Date	*Victim*	*Accused*
12 February 1883	**James Officer**	**Margaret Officer**
Cause of death:	Suffocation	
Outcome:	Charges withdrawn by the attorney-general	
Location:	Port Adelaide	

Margaret and Christopher Officer lived in Port Adelaide with their two children, the youngest being James, who was four weeks old. Margaret was a drunkard, and Christopher had warned the local publican not to supply her with alcohol. On Monday 12 February 1883, Christopher returned home around six pm. Margaret was drunk, so he undressed her and put her to bed. He then placed James on her breast for a feed. Christopher left the house around eight pm to go to a meeting at the Working Men's Hall. He returned around eleven pm and went into the bedroom where he saw that James was white and not moving. Christopher woke Margaret up and told her that James was dead, but Margaret would not believe him. The police were called, who called for Dr Gethering to attend on their arrival. Dr Gethering examined James and stated that he had been dead for some time.

A coroner's inquest was held the next day at the Port Adelaide Courthouse. Christopher gave evidence and first stated that Margaret did not drink, and that she had gone to bed early as she had an infected eye, but after examination by Inspector Doyle he admitted that she was usually drunk. During the evidence, it was revealed that two of Christopher and Margaret's children had died several years previously. Margaret stated that one died from consumption but she could not recall how the other died. Inspector Doyle, referring to his records, showed that at an inquest held for the first child, the jury had found that the child had died from suffocation.

Margaret then acknowledged that and gave her evidence reluctantly and stated that she had got up after Christopher had left then went back to bed with James next to her. The jury retired then returned, finding that James came to his death through the culpable negligence of Margaret lying on him while drunk. Margaret was committed to trial.

On Thursday 1 March, in the Supreme Court, the attorney-general presented a certificate to the court stating that there was no case against Margaret Officer, who was subsequently discharged.

Date	*Victim*	*Accused*
7 March 1883	**Male child**	**Unknown**
Cause of death:	Suffocation	
Outcome:	Offender not located	
Location:	Glanville	

On Saturday 17 March 1883, an inquest into the case of the death of an unknown male infant whose body was found by some boys on the flats at Glanville on March 7 was continued at the Port Admiral Hotel. Inspector Doyle said that every enquiry had been made in the whole district, but no further evidence was obtained. The jury returned a verdict that the child had a separate existence from its mother, and had been wilfully killed by suffocation by some person or persons unknown.

Date	*Victim*	*Accused*
1 May 1883	**Martha Scatcheard**	**James Oakley**
Cause of death:	Assault	
Outcome:	Found not guilty	
Location:	Portland Estate, Port Road	

Martha Scatcheard was a 58-year-old nurse who lived with her son and grandchildren in the Portland Estate. Scatcheard's daughter Henrietta, who was married to 37-year-old James Oakley, also lived in the Portland Estate. During the evening of Tuesday 1 May 1883, Scatcheard, Henrietta and two grandchildren, one being Ellen Moon, went to the Oakley house, as there were concerns for Henrietta's safety. There had been several arguments between James and Henrietta earlier that evening. Scatcheard, Henrietta and Moon went into the house where Henrietta put her children to bed. Scatcheard went out the back of the house, under the verandah, where James joined her and an argument started between them.

Mary Dunbar, who lived in the house at the rear of the Oakley house, had heard arguments between Henrietta and James before. She had heard James threaten to cut Henrietta's throat and had seen him chase her in the back yard with an axe. On the night when Scatcheard was at the house, Dunbar heard an argument between James and Scatcheard during which James was telling her to leave. James said, 'If you don't go I will kick you out', and Scatcheard replied, 'You can do what you like, I will not go. I have come to protect my daughter, because you said the night before you will take her life'. Henrietta joined them and told her mother not to go. Dunbar heard a scream, then heard a cry of 'murder'. Dunbar could not tell who screamed, so she went into the backyard and saw James standing near Scatcheard, who was lying on the ground. James was smoking and Dunbar called him a coward for fighting with women. Henrietta said to James, 'You brute, you have killed my mother'.

Dr Toll was called to the house and examined Scatcheard, finding her dead. Toll later performed a post-mortem examination and found that she had died from a fracture to the right side of her skull. Toll thought that the fracture was as a result of an assault more than a fall to the ground.

On Wednesday 2 May, an inquest was held at the Portland Estate Hotel where evidence was given by Scatcheard's granddaughter, Ellen Moon. The inquest was adjourned for further evidence and James Oakley was remanded. The inquest resumed on Friday 4 May where further evidence was given. At the conclusion of the inquest, the coroner invited James, under the Accused Persons' Oath Act, to give evidence under caution, but he had no wish to give evidence. The coroner stated that, 'An anxious, loving, and excellent mother had gone to Oakley's house in the interest of her child, and it might be said the deceased had no business there, but a parent was privileged to go wherever her child was in danger. The evidence showed that the daughter was in fear of her life, and the mother, a highly respectable woman, was entitled to be present for her protection'. The jury, after a brief retirement, returned a verdict of manslaughter against James. Oakley made no statement and was committed for trial.

Oakley appeared before the Supreme Court on Thursday 7 June, charged with manslaughter. Oakley stated that he had tried to get Scatcheard out of the house and that she refused to go. After a few attempts, a scuffle ensued when Scatcheard fell to the ground. Oakley stated that it was an accident. The jury found Oakley not guilty and he was discharged.

Date	*Victim*	*Accused*
10 August 1883	**Tommy Ah Fook**	**Mah Poo (Charlie Bow) and**
		Way Lee Yung (William)
Cause of death:	Gunshot wound	
Outcome:	Mah Poo found guilty of murder	
	Sentenced to death, executed 10 November 1883	
	Way Lee Yung discharged	
Location:	Hindley Street	

Tommy Ah Fook operated an eatery situated at the west end of Hindley Street, Adelaide, opposite Messrs McLean Brothers, Rigg and Co. He had purchased the property from You Ting Lee, a Chinese merchant of Hindley Street, around March 1882. Tommy was married to an English woman but she had left him around March that year and started to work for a man called Fung Sang. Ah Fook employed a 26-year-old cook called Mah Poo, who was also known as Charlie Bow, an undercook called Way Lee Yung, also known as William, and a young lad called William Coop who was employed as a scullery boy. Coop, who was a cottonspinner, arrived in the colony on 10 July 1883 as a stowaway on board the *Sara Bell* from Liverpool. All three slept in the premises. Ah Fook was in debt to Ting Lee and paid him regular amounts to cover the debt.

Around 10 am on Saturday 11 August 1883, Ting Lee went to Ah Fook's shop to get an instalment on the debt, but Ah Fook was not there. Ting Lee asked Mah Poo where Ah Fook was. Mah Poo told him that Ah Fook had gone out the previous evening and had not yet returned. Ting Lee tried to get what money the shop had taken that morning, but was only offered five shillings and eight pence, so he said he would take charge of the premises.

Ting Lee was owed 67 pounds, 15 shillings and 8 pence. Ting Lee searched the shop and adjoining rooms and cellar for Ah Fook but could not find him. He went to the watercloset and saw some blood on the wall and floor and looked into the pit, but noticed nothing. He only made a cursory examination due to the overpowering smell. Ting Lee went to the police station and reported that Ah Fook was missing and that he might have been killed or gone away as he owed people money. Ting Lee did not mention the blood in the watercloset as he thought it was from a nosebleed.

Around three in the morning on Tuesday 14 August, John Ryan, who was employed as a nightman, was with another man cleaning out the cesspit at the rear of Ah Fook's shop. After about five minutes they found that the bucket would not sink, so Ryan got a shovel and put it into the pit, where he felt an obstruction. Ryan pulled up the shovel and found a shirt on the end of it. Ryan and the other man pulled the shirt and ended up pulling out Ah Fook's body. Another man who was with them went for the police. The police attended, as did Dr Clindening, who identified the body as Ah Fook's. Clindening found that his skull was severely fractured and the wound appeared consistent with a gunshot wound. The body was removed to the deadhouse and Detective Burchell attended at the shop arresting Mah Poo, Way Lee Yung and Coop on suspicion of murder.

A coroner's inquest was held on Tuesday 14 August and was adjourned for further investigation. Mah Poo and Lee Yung were remanded and Coop was released. The inquest resumed the following Friday and evidence was given that Mah Poo had recently purchased a pistol from Peter Saunders, a pawnbroker who had a pawnshop on the corner of Rosina Street. Further evidence was given and the inquest was once again adjourned. The inquest concluded on Saturday 25 August. The coroner, in summing up, directed the attention of the jury to the medical evidence, which left no doubt that the cause of death was injuries being inflicted from a revolver or pistol similar to the one owned by Mah Poo. The coroner stated that the jury could come to no other conclusion that the deceased had been brutally murdered, and that the murderer or murderers had disposed of the body in a disgusting manner. He further stated that 'scarcely a line' of Mah Poo's evidence remained uncontradicted. The evidence regarding the participation of Lee Yung in the crime was very meagre. In conclusion, the coroner praised the energy and ability displayed by Detective Sergeant Upton and Detective Burchell in collecting the evidence.

The jury, after a short retirement, found Mah Poo guilty of wilful murder, and Lee Yung guilty of being an accessory after the fact. The coroner said that he thought the jury should alter their verdict by finding Lee Yung an accessory before the fact. The jurymen explained that the opinion was that Lee Yung had no hand in the actual committal of the murder, but that he had assisted, probably urged by the threats of Mah Poo, in the removal of the body. The coroner said he would accept the verdict, and both prisoners, who made no statement, were committed for trial.

On Tuesday 2 October, Lee Yung appeared before the Chief Justice in the Supreme Court when the attorney-general issued a certificate that there was no case to answer. Yung was discharged.

Mah Poo.
South Australia Police Historical Society, 2418

Mah Poo appeared before the Supreme Court on Tuesday 9 October. The trial continued over the next few days. On Thursday, as the judge took his seat, the Sheriff rose and said,

'Your Honour, since the adjournment, my attention has been called to the extraordinary conduct of one of the jurymen. The man I refer to was pacing wildly up and down last night. He appears to be deranged. I understand his name is William Lehmann'.

Lehmann: 'I want to go home.'

His Honour: 'What is that for?'

Lehmann: 'I feel so bad, I am not right,'

His Honour: 'Do any other gentlemen of the jury wish to make any representation?'

Mr Lather: 'Yes, your Honour. We can't hear what the witnesses have said owing to his wild conduct. He kept jumping up in the box during the whole of yesterday, and consequently our attention was distracted from what was going on.'

Another juror: 'He appears to be quite deranged.'

His Honour: 'Quite deranged?'

Juror: 'Yes.'

His Honour: (to Lehmann) 'What is your name, Sir?'

Lehmann: 'William Lehmann.'

His Honour: 'I understand, Mr Sheriff, that the jury complained of his extraordinary conduct?'

Sheriff: 'Yes. The police in charge of the jury on Wednesday night also complained of the same thing"

Mr Lather: 'We had to get a policeman last night to put him in another room because he kept jumping about so much'.

After further discussion, Lehmann jumped up and left the box, and began leaving the court. A constable stopped him and Lehmann shouted out, 'Leave me alone, will you? I am free, free, free'. His Honour ordered that Dr Clindening and Dr Henderson examine Lehmann. The doctors found that Lehmann was in an excited state and were of the opinion that Lehmann would seriously affect the other jurymen in their duty, and that Lehmann was not capable of forming proper opinion on the evidence. Dr Henderson thought that Lehmann was suffering from 'considerable artificial mania'. The judge then discharged the jury and arranged for another one to be empanelled. This was done and the trial started once more.

The trial ended on Saturday 13 October. It was found that Ah Fook was murdered for a few pounds he had in his pocket. After a retirement of 12 minutes, the jury returned a guilty verdict against Mah Poo. Mah Poo was sentenced to death, and on 10 November, he was executed at the Adelaide Gaol. Prior to his death, Mah Poo made a statement in which he confessed his guilt. He also implicated two Europeans but the police believed that his assertions were entirely without foundation.

Date	Victim	Accused
2 September 1883	Ellen Tench	William Tench
Cause of death:	Neglect	
Outcome:	No case	
Location:	Norwood	

William and Ellen Tench married around 1878 and lived in the Norwood area. They had no children and did not get on very well together. They had often fought and quarrelled. Once Ellen threw a bottle at William's head and he struck her in retaliation. Ellen had been in the habit of leaving William for two or three weeks at a time, and in the three months prior to her death, Ellen and William did not see much of each other.

Ellen had spent some time in the hospital suffering from lung and heart disease. Ellen returned home in early August and soon afterwards was laid up in bed due to her poor health. William would spend time at the Alma Hotel and was heard on many occasions saying that he wished his wife were dead, and that the government would have to pay for her burial.

While bedridden, 31-year-old Ellen was visited by some friends who would bring her food and other supplies. There was no furniture in the Tench house, as bailiffs had recently removed a sewing machine and all of the household furniture. Ellen lay on some wood shavings and straw covered with sacks. Dr James Mann visited Ellen and prescribed medicine for her. He gave her two shillings for some necessities and told William to visit the Destitute Asylum for assistance, but he never did. William was drunk when Dr Mann visited, and Ellen had been drinking also.

Just prior to her death, Ellen made a dying declaration in which she stated:

Some four or five months ago my husband, William Tench, used to knock me around. I came out of the hospital about three months ago. He has not knocked me about since then, but he has been drinking these last three months, but not all the time. He has said when he had drink in him he wished I was dead. He is very kind when he is out of drink. Have been married to him five years. He has been a cruel man to me.

Ellen died on Sunday 2 September 1883. Dr Mann examined Ellen and found no marks of violence. He gave a cause of death of lung and heart disease. An inquest was held at the Alma Hotel on Tuesday 4 September. In summing up the evidence, the coroner stated that he thought a verdict ought to be returned in accordance with the medical testimony. Although he detested Tench's brutal way of speaking of his wife, he did not think there was sufficient evidence to warrant a verdict of manslaughter. It was up to the jury to decide if Tench's neglectful habits had accelerated his wife's death, for although she might not have lived much longer, anything William might have done to accelerate her death would be manslaughter.

Dr James Mann, approximately 1882, medical officer to the Destitute Asylum. State Library of South Australia, B 3575.

The jury retired then returned with the verdict that 'Ellen Tench came to her death according to the doctor's evidence, but accelerated by the husband's wilful neglect'. The jury were asked to reconsider their verdict, but made no alteration. The coroner ruled the jury's decision as a verdict of manslaughter against Tench, who was committed for trial. Bail was allowed in one personal surety (insurance that he would return to court) of £50 and two others at £25 each. When the sureties were received, Tench was released on bail.

On Tuesday 2 October, William Tench appeared before the Chief Justice in the Supreme Court when the attorney-general issued a certificate that there was no case to answer. Tench was discharged.

Date	*Victim*	*Accused*
January 1884	**Unknown child**	**Unknown**
Cause of death:	Unknown	
Outcome:	Open verdict	
Location:	River Torrens	

On Monday 28 January 1884, Henry Hannan, a boatman, was in his refreshment stall near the Morphett Street Bridge when he was told that there was a body of an infant on the western bank of the Torrens. Hannan found the body wrapped in a piece of black dress along with a brick. The package had been discovered when two young lads who were crayfishing in the lake had snagged it with a fishhook. The police attended the scene and took the body, which was badly decomposed, to the deadhouse.

The following day, the coroner, Mr Ward, held an inquest on the body at the Destitute Asylum. On opening the inquest, Ward remarked to the jury that the cases of infanticide were becoming 'lamentably and painfully numerous', and stated that the number of bodies found in similar circumstances where an inquiry was needed was a great expense to the government. The coroner stated that in another colony in Australia that there was some thought that the seducers of the young girls should be treated as felons and be punished accordingly After hearing evidence of the finding of the body, the coroner adjourned the inquest for further evidence to be obtained.

When the inquest resumed on Monday 4 February, Constable Rae gave evidence, testifying that he was unable to find the identity of the person or persons who put the child in the water. Dr Jay conducted a post-mortem examination and stated that the child had been in the water for two or three months. Jay was unable to determine if the child had breathed. The coroner instructed the jury to return an open verdict.

As Dr Jay was unable to determine if the child had breathed, this matter has not been recorded in the statistics.

Date	*Victim*	*Accused*
30 January 1884	**William Macklin (Ackland)**	**John Adams**
Cause of death:	Gunshot wounds	
Outcome:	Found guilty of manslaughter	
	Sentenced to imprisonment for one month	
Location:	Yalpara	

*1893 portrait of seven of the Ragless Brothers who had Yalpara station
(north east of Orroroo), and later, Witchelina Station.*
State Library of South Australia, B 7949

William Macklin, who was also known as William Ackland, worked with his 23-year-old friend John Adams at the Yalpara Head Station. On Thursday 30 January 1884, both men were at the station larking around. Lillian Ragless was standing on the station's porch watching Macklin and Adams. Ragless saw Adams with a gun in his hand, but took no notice of it as she thought he was going to show it to Ackland. Ragless turned around and walked into the kitchen when she suddenly heard a gunshot. She ran outside, as did Benjamin Ragless, who was in the dining room. Lillian heard Adams say, 'Oh, good God, it was loaded'. Lillian said, 'Oh, Mr Adams, you have shot Mr Macklin'.

Benjamin ran to Macklin who was stooped over, holding a wound in his abdomen. Benjamin and Lillian took Macklin inside where they bathed the wound and called for the doctor. Adams said to Macklin, 'Don't think I did it on purpose', to which Macklin replied, 'I know you did not'.

Dr William Clarke and Mounted Constable Cahill attended. Clarke examined Macklin and thought that the wounds were likely to be fatal as there were signs of internal bleeding. There were thirteen shots in his abdomen and groin and some had penetrated deeply. Macklin told Cahill that Adams was not at all out of temper at the time of the shooting. Cahill spoke to Adams who admitted that he had put a cap on the gun, which he did not know was loaded, in order to frighten Macklin. The following day, Macklin died from his injuries.

Mr Charles Price, JP, held an inquest at Yalpara Head Station on Saturday 2 February. At the conclusion of the inquest, the jury found that Macklin had been accidentally killed by a gunshot fired by Adams. The jury therefore found Adams guilty of manslaughter. Adams made no statement and was committed for trial at Gladstone.

On Thursday 20 March, Adams appeared before the Chief Justice at the Gladstone Circuit Court. At the conclusion of the trial, Adams was sentenced to one month imprisonment at the Gladstone Gaol.

Date	*Victim*	*Accused*
4 March 1884	**Andrew Kiddie**	**Mary Kiddie**
Cause of death:	Blade wound	
Outcome:	Found not guilty	
Location:	Market Buildings, Port Adelaide	

Andrew Kiddie was a tailor who lived with his wife, Mary, and their children at the Market Buildings in Port Adelaide. They had been married for about 20 years. Andrew had always been violent towards Mary and the children, and was often drunk.

Some time around eight am on 4 March 1884, Andrew went out for a walk but returned intoxicated. When he came back to the shop he approached Mary and verbally threatened her. Andrew grabbed hold of Mary's face and twisted it, inflicting several nasty bruises. Mary withdrew and threw a basin of water at Andrew, which maddened him further, and he again assaulted Mary. Mary picked up a pair of heavy scissors and threw them at Andrew, hitting him on the temple with the blade. Andrew fell onto a sofa, and as he did the scissors dropped out of his head, which was bleeding profusely.

Dr Toll arrived and dressed the wound. He stopped the bleeding and gave orders that Andrew keep quiet. Dr Toll visited Andrew over the next three days and found him to be healing. When Dr Toll visited the Kiddies on 12 March, Andrew mumbled his words slightly. Dr Toll noticed that Andrew's right eye was dilated and nonresponsive to light. Andrew gradually lapsed into a comatose state and he died at a quarter to 10 that night.

Dr Toll conducted a post-mortem examination and found that the wound on the right temple had penetrated the skull. He gave the cause of death as a fracture to the skull and wound of the brain. The end of the scissors matched the shape of the wound.

On Saturday 15 March, Mr Derrington, JP, held an inquest at the Port Admiral Hotel. At the completion of the evidence, the jury found that Andrew came to his death as a result of a wound inflicted by his wife in self-defence, 'after an experience of brutal ill-treatment'. The coroner remarked that he felt his position very keenly as it was the most solemn ceremony he had ever performed. When asked if she had anything to say, Mary said:

> If I had known I would have had a lawyer. I do not see how you could bring it in as a case of manslaughter, as I never meant to kill anyone, and have never hurt a soul in my life. Nobody but myself and children know what I have gone through during the last 22 years. I have always attended to his wants whether he has been drunk or sober, and I have always attended to his business for him. It seems so hard for you to take me away from my poor little ones, for when I'm gone whatever will become of them? I have always hidden my husband's wickedness from the world, and no one but myself and my children know how he has ill-treated us. It is only eight months ago that he got out of work, and I myself went to work and for a considerable time earned 16 shillings a week, so as to keep the public from knowing how poor we were. I have often had to take my little ones to sleep in closets, so as to get out of his road, and for you to bring in a case of manslaughter, it is bad.

Mary Kiddie was committed for trial and appeared before the Supreme Court on Wednesday 2 April charged with the manslaughter of her husband.

At the completion of the evidence, Mary explained to the jury how her husband had treated her at different times, and stated that during the last quarrel with him she picked up the shears and threw them at him, without intending to hurt him. The jury, after a short retirement, found Mary not guilty.

Date	Victim	Accused
10 June 1884	**Margaret Buxton**	**John Woodhead (Woods)**
Cause of death:	Suffocation	
Outcome:	Found not guilty	
Location:	Nairne	

Margaret Buxton was 65 years old and lived by herself at Nairne. On Tuesday 10 June 1884, Buxton went to the Miller's Arms Hotel at Nairne. While there, she met 28-year-old John Woodhead, also known as John Woods, who was a labourer working on the railway line. Woodhead and Buxton both sat at the bar. Robert Bulman, the landlord of the Miller's Arms, saw Woodhead speaking to Buxton. He also saw that Woodhead had one arm around her neck and was 'taking other liberties with her'. Between seven and eight that evening, Bulman thought that Buxton had had too much liquor, so he told her to go home. Woodhead left at the same time as Buxton.

Elijah Chapman saw Buxton and Woodhead walking from the hotel. Woodhead had hold of Buxton and was helping her walk as both were staggering along the road. Alexander Tullock also saw the pair, and as he walked by them, he heard Margaret say, 'Oh, no, no don't'. Tullock continued home.

Around nine that evening, Woodhead returned to the hotel. Bulman noticed that his eye was cut and bleeding and both sides of his face had scratches on them. Bulman asked how it happened and Woodhead said that he had fallen over near the water trough.

The next morning, as Tullock was going to breakfast, he saw the body of a woman lying in Mr Cook's garden. He noticed that her clothes were disarranged and that her hat, which looked broken and crushed, was lying underneath the fence close by. Trooper Charles Leiber attended and examined the area. He saw that Buxton's clothes were torn and there were signs of a struggle.

Dr Octavius Weld, of Mount Barker, conducted a post-mortem examination. Weld found a contusion of the right breast, two on the hip and another one of the lower portion of the right thigh. He concluded that Margaret died from suffocation. Weld also examined John's face and found that the injuries could not have been caused by a fall, but appeared to be scratches caused by fingernails.

An 1891 panoramic view of the township buildings of Nairne and surrounding fields which appear to be orchards or market gardens. The two-storey building with the verandah (in the centre of the view) is the Millers' Arms Hotel.
State Library of South Australia, B 394

David Chapman, JP, conducted an inquest into the death on Wednesday 11 June at the Miller's Arms Hotel. During the inquest, Woodhead stated that he might have been speaking to Buxton at the hotel, but he knew nothing about her death. Further witnesses were called, including Bulman and Tullock. At the conclusion of the inquest, the jury found that Buxton 'came to her death by foul play, and that the evidence points strongly to the witness Woodhead as being the perpetrator of the deed'. Woodhead was then committed to take his trial at the next Criminal Sittings.

Woodhead appeared before the Supreme Court on Thursday 7 and Friday 8 August, charged with the murder of Margaret Buxton. Dr Evan, who conducted an examination of Buxton, gave evidence. He found no external marks of violence and no signs of indecent assault. He found that the lungs were very congested and that this congestion may have been chronic. He suggested that through the inclement weather the congestion might have become acute and Buxton could have died suddenly. The lower parts of the lungs were black in appearance, which Evan attributed to either a disease, or suffocation. Evan also stated that he believed if Buxton had been lying on the ground for a considerable time that night, with the rain pouring down upon her, and considering her age and that she had not taken any food for some time, and the 'vitality of the system being low', she might have died. Woodhead did not give evidence.

At the conclusion of the trial, Mr Downer, for the defence, asked His Honour to say that there was no evidence at all that the deceased had come to her death through violence. His Honour disagreed and the trial continued.

The crown and defence summed up the evidence. His Honour then pointed out to the jury the law relating to murder, manslaughter and justifiable homicide. They must, he said, be satisfied first that the prisoner killed the woman, and secondly that under the circumstances it amounted to murder. If Woodhead was attempting to rape Buxton, and in carrying out his attempt caused her such injuries as to render her unable to go home, and in turn she died from exposure to the weather, the direction was that he was guilty of murder. If he was simply philandering with her, and in doing so she received injuries that rendered her unable to go home, he would not be guilty of murder. If the circumstances showed that the death was caused by using more force than necessary in persuading her to consent to his proposals, then he would be guilty of manslaughter. He was bound to say that in this case there was no evidence to justify Woodhead being found guilty of attempted rape.

The jury retired and after about three-quarters of an hour, returned a not guilty verdict. Woodhead was discharged.

Date	*Victim*	*Accused*
15 June 1884	**Gaskin child**	**Emma Gaskin**
Cause of death:	Suffocation	
Outcome:	Pleaded guilty to concealment of birth	
	Sentenced to three months imprisonment	
Location:	Portland Estate	

Emma Gaskin was a single woman who had a four-year-old child. She had a relationship with Frank Zornow and became pregnant. She told Zornow, who lived in Jerusalem at Port Adelaide, and he promised to be a father to the child and to marry her when he could afford it.

On 15 June 1884, Gaskin went to the home of Henry and Harriet Behncke at the Portland Estate. While there, Gaskin gave birth to a boy who she put into the watercloset before leaving. She did not tell anyone what had happened. Henry was later told by one of his children that there was a body of a child in the watercloset. Henry removed the body, put it into a bag and buried it in a hole near his house. Harriet told Constable Davidson from Queenstown, who sent for Henry to attend the police station.

The body of the child was recovered and examined by Dr Symonds, who found that the child was near full term and that it had a separate existence from the mother. There were no signs of violence and the cause of death was determined as suffocation. Dr Symonds thought that if the child had been recovered from the water closet just after being deposited there, it would have lived.

On Friday 4 July, an inquest was held at the Port Admiral Hotel into the death of the child. At the completion of the evidence, the coroner pointed out that the child had a separate existence from its mother, and he could not therefore direct the jury to any other verdict than one of manslaughter. The jury found Gaskin guilty of her son's death by negligence. The jury also added a rider to the effect that they disapproved of the conduct of Mr and Mrs Behncke in not reporting the matter earlier. Gaskin was committed to trial for manslaughter and the coroner severely censured Mr and Mrs Behncke for their neglect.

Gaskin appeared before the Supreme Court on Wednesday 6 August charged with concealment of birth. Gaskin pleaded guilty and was sentenced to three months imprisonment.

Date	*Victim*	*Accused*
3 August 1884	**Peter Conway**	**Patrick McGrath**
Cause of death:	Gunshot wound	
Outcome:	Acquitted	
Location:	Wellington	

Patrick Conway was a ganger who worked on the Millar Brothers' railway contract on the Overland Railway, near Tailem Bend. On Saturday 2 August 1884, Conway received his fortnight's pay from Harry Morris. Conway was paid seven pounds, three shillings, and six pence in notes and coin. Conway was a quiet person who lived with his wife in Salisbury. He was a healthy person of sober habits. While working on the railway line, Conway slept in a tent, where he was known to keep a pistol. Richard Rounder saw Conway heading towards his tent that night, which was about 200 yards from other tents, just before midnight.

Around twenty past seven on Sunday morning, John Chrisholm, a sheep farmer of Tailem Bend, noticed that Conway's tent was gone. Chrisholm went to where the tent was and found it completely burnt down, and a charred body on the ground. Lance Corporal Thomas Solly, stationed at Wellington, attended and inspected the area. No one heard anything during the night and it was thought that Conway, who used to read at night, died in the fire, which was not considered to be suspicious.

A coroner's inquest was held on Monday 4 August at Tailem Bend, where the jury returned a verdict that Conway was either suffocated by smoke or burnt to death in his tent on Sunday morning, but there was no evidence to show how the fire occurred.

The following day, the men who worked on the railway with Conway expressed dissatisfaction with the verdict, owing to the suspicion of foul play. Mr Millar, the railway contractor, communicated with the coroner and requested that the inquest be reopened. The coroner spoke to Dr Blue, of Strathalbyn, and ordered that a post-mortem examination be conducted.

Conway's body was exhumed and taken to Dr Blue, who conducted an external examination, which found a hole in the chest and the back. A post-mortem revealed that Conway had been shot at close range. A further inquest was held on Wednesday 6 August where the jury returned a verdict that Conway's death was caused by a gunshot wound to the chest, but there was no evidence to show by whom the shot was fired.

On Monday 11 August, the Commissioner of Police received a telegram from Wellington intimating that the detective despatched to inquire into the mysterious circumstances of the death of Patrick Conway had discovered an important clue, and he expected to be able to solve the mystery within a few days.

On Monday 3 September, Patrick McGrath was brought up before Mr Stephenson and Mr Richardson, charged with the murder of Patrick Conway. Inspector Hunt conducted the case for the police, and after preliminary evidence had been tendered, McGrath was remanded for 15 days in order to allow the production of further evidence.

McGrath appeared before Mr O'Halloran, SM, at Murray Bridge on 19 September, where 14 witnesses were examined for the prosecution, but although it was proved that Conway was murdered, and there were suspicious actions in McGrath's actions, there was not sufficient evidence to warrant a committal, so McGrath, who was undefended, was remanded once more for further evidence to be produced.

On Tuesday 14 October 1884, it was reported that McGrath had been acquitted, there being not the slightest evidence against him.

Benjamin Pickworth Hunt, who joined the South Australian Police Force in 1852, he served for 52 years and became a Senior Inspector, 1880.
State Library of South Australia, B 61904

Date	Victim	Accused
15 August 1884	**Martin Kenihan**	**James Kelly**
Cause of death:	Vehicle collision	
Outcome:	Found not guilty	
Location:	Hamley Bridge	

On Friday 15 August 1884, Martin Kenihan engaged 23-year-old James Kelly, the landlord of the Stockport Hotel, to drive him and his wife, Catherine Kenihan, from Stockport to Hamley Bridge, for the purpose of Kenihan attending the local court. On the return journey, both men were under the influence of drink. Kelly, who was driving, started off at a 'furious' rate. As the trap turned the corner at the end of the township, Kenihan was thrown out of the vehicle, and caught on the skid of the trap, where he was dragged for about 20 yards. A bystander named Patrick O'Dea stopped the horse with some difficulty, and Kenihan was removed from the skid. Dr Price, who was nearby, attended the accident and found that Kenihan was quite insensible. He was bleeding from the nose and head but had no broken bones. Kenihan returned to the township, but about an hour later he showed symptoms of concussion of the brain, so he was given an emetic, which brought up a large quantity of alcohol. Dr Price also put a mustard poultice on the heart and stomach for the purpose of inducing circulation. Kenihan died about five hours later. A post-mortem was conducted and the cause of death was given as concussion of the brain.

On 16 August, an inquest was held at Hamley Bridge, where the jury found that the death was caused by the 'furious' driving of James Kelly, who was then committed for trial on a charge of manslaughter. Bail was allowed.

Kelly appeared before the Supreme Court on Wednesday 8 October, where he pleaded not guilty. Evidence was given that Kenihan was a habitual drunkard who had had a lot to drink the day that he died, and that Kelly was a man of a very good character who had been drinking that day, but was not drunk. On the completion of the evidence, Mr Symon, for the defence, asked the judge whether he considered there was any case to go to the jury. His Honour replied that he certainly thought there was a case and that he intended to direct the jury on case law, which stated that if anyone took an intoxicated person into his trap, and through carelessness or neglect allowed the person to receive injuries from which death resulted, he would be guilty of manslaughter. His Honour then told the jury that the fact of the deceased being drunk did not absolve Kelly of blame. He said that if a person took a man into his trap drunk, knowing him to be drunk, he was not only bound to exercise reasonable care, but be more careful than if the man were sober. Therefore the question he would put to them was not whether the deceased was drunk, but whether reasonable care was exercised by Kelly, so that the man came to his death by his own act, and not by the culpable negligence of Kelly. The jury, after a short retirement, returned a verdict of not guilty, and Kelly was discharged.

Date	*Victim*	*Accused*
24 August 1884	**William Templer**	**John Templer**
Cause of death:	Drowned	
Outcome:	Found not guilty	
Location:	Gawler River	

John Templer lived with his wife and two children, 18-month-old William and a younger baby. The family lived at Mr Dawkins' farm, situated on the Gawler River, about five miles from Gawler. Mr Dawkins employed 34-year-old Templer as a farm manager. Templer was described as a man of sober and steady habits, who was exceedingly attached to his son William. Around the middle of August, Mrs Templer and William became ill, so Annie Ratcliffe stayed at the Templer's house to take care of them. Templer also looked after William, not leaving his side for 10 days. During that time Templer had little sleep and was disregarding his work. Dr Bickle attended their house on several occasions to treat Mrs Templer and William. Dr Bickle thought that Templer's attentions to William were a little too close, and urged Templer to let the women take care of William.

Around five am on Sunday 24 August 1884, Ratcliffe was woken up by Templer, who came screaming in to the room saying, 'Oh, I am out of my mind. I believe I am mad, for Willie and me have fallen into the water'. Templer was soaking wet and he was not wearing his hat. Ratcliffe looked for William, but he was not in the house. She went to Mr and Mrs Higgins' house, which was on the opposite side of the river, to get help.

Thomas Higgins, a farmer, attended at the Templer house and spoke to John. During the conversation, John said, 'Whatever shall I do, I went to drown myself, and I lost the child'. Higgins went to the river in company with Frederick Symes and Mr Wingate. Symes saw a hat on the bank near a log and reached into the water, which was about three feet deep, and found William's body. Symes took the body to the Templar house and the police later arrived.

On Sunday 21 August, an inquest was held where Dr Leonard Bickle gave evidence that William had died from asphyxia through drowning. Templer stated that he had been nursing William for ten days and he remembered William screaming early in the morning. He picked William up, as his wife had had no rest the night before. He could not remember anything else except coming home to the house wet and without William.

At the completion of the inquest, the jury returned the verdict that William had come to his death by drowning, but there was not sufficient evidence to show how he had gotten into the water. Templer was arrested and lodged in the Gawler police station.

On Thursday 8 October, Templer appeared before the Supreme Court charged with murder. At the completion of the prosecution case, Mr Symon, for the defence, asked the judge if he thought here was any case to go to the jury. His Honour replied that he was at a loss to see the motive for the graver offence of murder. Symons thought that the crown solicitor would say that there was no evidence of murder, and that it was a case of manslaughter. The crown solicitor replied that there was no doubt it was a very difficult case, and that the fact there was no perceptible motive strongly affected the case. He continued, pointing out the fact that Templer took the child out of bed and put it into the water. His Honour then said that there was no evidence that Templer had put William in the water, and asked if there was any evidence to show that he had done so. The crown solicitor said the inference would arise from the man's act. If a man chose to put a child into a waterhole, malice must be presumed and it was conclusive in his mind that Templer had put William in the water. His Honour said he preferred to let the case go to the jury.

The jury, after about half an hour's retirement, found Templer not guilty, and he was discharged.

Date	Victim	Accused
24 August 1884	**Male child**	**Unknown**
Cause of death:	Blade wound	
Outcome:	Offender not located	
Location:	Adelaide	

On Sunday 24 August, carpenter Thomas Turner was walking along Wakefield Street past the paddock adjoining St Francis Xavier's Cathedral, when he noticed a parcel covered with a piece of rag on the ground near the fence. Turner removed the rag and opened part of the parcel, finding the body of a child. Turner went to the police station and advised Constable Walker, who attended the scene and removed the parcel back to the police station where it was opened. The parcel contained the body of a male child that appeared to have its throat cut. The child was wrapped in newspapers from 21 and 22 August. Walker took the body to the city morgue.

Around the same time, Police Constable O'Donohoe found a parcel of bloodstained clothing wrapped in tissue paper on the doorstep of Mr Lorrimer's and Mr Rome's house on Waymouth Street. The blood on the cloth was wet and one of the pieces of clothing was stained with printer's ink. O'Donohoe later discovered a napkin with bloodstains in it below the grating to the windows of the *Advertiser* publishing department.

An inquest was held at the Destitute Asylum on Tuesday 26 August before the city coroner, Mr T Ward. The inquest was adjourned for further evidence to be located. The inquest resumed on Tuesday 2 September, but was again adjourned.

The inquest resumed on Tuesday 9 September where Detective Dunlevie stated that he had no more evidence to submit to the court, and that the police had nothing in view that was likely to reveal the circumstances connected with the child's death. The coroner, in summing up, stated that during his twenty years of experience he had never met with such an extraordinary case. No doubt the child was killed the same morning that the body was placed in the paddock, as the doctor had stated that decomposition had not set in. The jury, after a short retirement, returned a verdict of wilful murder against some person or persons unknown.

Date	Victim	Accused
15 September 1884	Marion (Mary) Kelly	William Bissett
Cause of death:	Assault	
Outcome:	Found not guilty	
Location:	Halifax Street, Adelaide	

During the evening of Monday 15 September 1884, Margaret Callighan was with her 60-year-old mother, Marion (Mary) Kelly, at her house on Halifax Street, Adelaide. Callighan left Kelly to go and post a letter. Around the same time, William Bissett, a jockey, and Edward Morrisey, an ironworker, were walking along Halifax Street. Both had been drinking. Kelly was standing in the middle of the footpath and as Bissett and Morrisey were walking past, Bissett knocked Kelly down. They both walked on further before stopping. Callighan returned home and saw her mother being assisted onto a chair, which someone had brought out onto the street for her. Bissett left the area and retuned wearing a different hat. Callighan spoke to her mother who pointed to Bissett and said, 'This young man knocked me down'. Bissett replied that someone else knocked her down, and Kelly replied, 'No, you are the man that did it'. Bissett started to light his pipe, and he and Morrisey were staggering as if they were intoxicated. Bissett called out to Morrisey before they both ran along Halifax Street in the direction of the racecourse, then turned up Tomsey Street to their house.

Dr O'Connell visited Kelly the following day. An order was signed for her admission to the Adelaide Hospital. An examination revealed that she had a fractured neck of the thighbone within the capsule of the joint. Kelly died in the Adelaide Hospital on 19 September. A post-mortem examination revealed that she was suffering from fatty degeneration of the heart and liver, and that she had a large stone in the gall bladder. The cause of death was the formation of blood clots in the arteries leading to the lungs. The condition of Kelly's organs was such that any shock, over-exertion, or stress put on the heart might have been expected to cause death.

Bissett and Morrisey gave evidence at an inquest held at the Adelaide Hospital. At the conclusion of the inquest, the coroner stated that the jury must consider if the fracture to Kelly's thighbone was a result of being pushed by Bissett, and whether or not it was a case of manslaughter. If Kelly was knocked down through carelessness, then it was manslaughter. Kelly was a strong person, and the evidence showed that Bissett had knocked her down. Neither of the witnesses Bissett or Morrisey had given their evidence satisfactorily. The coroner urged the jury to give the case their utmost consideration. The jury, after a short retirement, returned the verdict that Kelly had died after being knocked down by Bissett, and found Morrisey to be an accessory before the fact. The coroner committed Bissett and Morrisey to trial.

On Thursday 9 October, Bissett and Morrisey appeared before the Supreme Court. A certificate issued by the attorney-general was produced, which stated that there was no case against Morrisey, so he was discharged. Bissett pleaded not guilty to manslaughter and aggravated assault. During the trial, Bissett stated that he was lighting a pipe while walking along and did not intend to bump into Kelly. At the completion of the evidence, Mr Downer, for the defence, submitted there was no evidence to go to the jury. The crown solicitor held that if a man, while using the public highway, came 'lurching along' and knocked a person down, he would be guilty of assault. His Honour's opinion was contrary to the crown solicitor's, stating that the evidence was very unsatisfactory as far as it had gone. The crown solicitor stated that he did not wish to go on, so His Honour directed the jury that there was no evidence to support either of the charges. Bissett was found not guilty and discharged.

Date	*Victim*	*Accused*
3 November 1884	**William Howe**	**Johannes Larsen, Auguste Wehr, and Frank Tantow**

Cause of death:	Knife wounds
Outcome:	Larsen found guilty of manslaughter
	Sentenced to 12 months imprisonment
	Wehr found guilty of wounding with intent
	Sentenced to 10 years imprisonment with hard labour
	No case entered against Tantow
Location:	Commercial Wharf, Port Adelaide

William Howe was employed on the brigantine *Minnie*, which was moored at Port Adelaide. Also moored nearby was the German steamer *Catania*. Twenty-three-year-old Johann Larsen, 21-year-old Auguste Wehr and 24-year-old Frank Tantow were part of the *Catania's* crew. Between 11 pm and midnight on Monday 3 November 1884, Alexander Kyle, a boatswain onboard the *Bebington* was onboard the *Minnie* in company with Howe, Hugh McFarland and Henry Crowder. The four were having something to eat in the galley when a person called Abernethy called them on shore. Upon reaching the Commercial Wharf they saw four or five men standing there, including Larsen, Wehr and Tantow. For no reason, Larsen immediately struck Kyle on the head with his fist. Kyle noticed that both Larsen and Wehr had knives. Kyle picked up a length of wood from the ground and he heard someone shout, 'Look out for a knife, they are using them'. The group fought just next to the *Bebington*. Kyle saw Larsen stab Howe in the neck. Howe fell to the ground and died. Around the same time, Tantow attacked a man called Elliott with a knife with the intention of stabbing him, but the knife only cut Elliott's coat.

Commercial Wharf, Port Adelaide, 1885.
State Library of South Australia, B 10

William Monteith, a seaman of the *Bebington*, heard the fight and went onshore where he met Hugh McFarland, who said he was stabbed. Wehr replied, 'Me stab, me stab'. Monteith picked up a belaying pin and Larsen, Wehr and Tantow ran away. Monteith ran after the three and when he got close, Wehr turned around and rushed at him with a knife, so Monteith struck him with the belaying pin. Larson and Tantow started to throw stones at Monteith. The three ran off towards the *Catania* and Wehr and Larsen entered the bow of the vessel while Tantow entered the stern. Monteith called out to an officer on the hurricane deck of the *Catania* and asked him to watch the men while he went for the police, but the officer told him to go away.

Meanwhile, Kyle found a policeman on the wharf who accompanied him onboard the *Catania* where Larsen and Wehr were located and arrested. Kyle then went onboard the *Bebington* where McFarland and Abernethy were being treated for knife wounds they had received during the fight. Later that day, Kyle and the police again boarded the *Catania* where the crew were mustered. Kyle identified Tantow as being present at the fight and he was subsequently arrested. Kyle knew of no ill feeling between the crews of the *Catania*, *Minnie* or *Bebington*.

On Wednesday 5 November, the city coroner held an inquest on the body of Howe at the Port Hotel. The German Consul, Mr H Muecke, was present, with Mr Gustave Offelsmeyer acting as an interpreter. After receiving evidence during the day, the inquest was adjourned.

The inquest continued the following day. At the completion of the evidence, the coroner summed up the case, stating that some little disagreement arose between a number of sailors. It appeared that an English sailor had said that he was an Irishman, and in response, a German sailor had said, 'No you're not', and struck him down. The evidence showed that Wehr stabbed McFarland, Larsen stabbed Howe and Tantow stabbed at Elliott. The coroner stated that when three men went about with knives in their hands the law looked upon them with grave suspicion. He wanted to impress upon the minds of the jury the fact that the three prisoners all came from the same ship, were together at the time of the affray, and all went back to the same ship after the affray. The evidence showed that they had all used their knives in such a way as to lay them open to a charge of murder. After about half an hour's consideration, the jury found that Howe had been murdered, and that Wehr, Larsen and Tantow were all responsible. The coroner committed the three to trial.

On Wednesday 3 December, Larsen, Tantow and Wehr appeared before the Supreme Court charged with the murder of William Howe. The trial lasted for two days. At the completion of evidence, the judge told the jury that there was no evidence to show that the prisoners had drawn their knives for the purpose of killing others and there was no evidence of common design, and the case narrowed itself down to the prisoner Larsen, whom they could either convict of murder or manslaughter. His Honour explained that murder was the result of killing with malice aforethought, and manslaughter was killing without this operation of the mind. The judge further said, 'Where there is a sudden fight and in the excitement one used a deadly weapon and killed another, then the law regarded that as manslaughter, but in order to be entitled to that presumption the assailant must be acting in the excitement'. The jury, after half an hour's retirement, found Larsen guilty of manslaughter, with a recommendation for clemency on account of the 'irritation' of the wound he had received during the fight. The crown solicitor said that there was no further charge against Tantow and he could be discharged. Wehr was arraigned for trial for wounding McFarland with intent to murder.

On Saturday 13 December, Larsen and Wehr appeared before the Supreme Court for sentencing. Because of the disparity of the sentence, where Larsen received 12 months for manslaughter and Wehr received 10 years for wounding with intent, the sentencing remarks are reproduced in full.

His Honour:

Auguste Wehr, you have been convicted of wounding Hugh McFarland with intent to do grievous bodily harm. When this offence was committed there was an affray in which one man lost his life and two were stabbed, one dangerously. With respect to the latter you have been convicted practically on your own statement that it was your hand that inflicted the wound. Now, you know and God knows whether yours was the hand that stabbed the man that died. There was no evidence before the Court to prove that you were guilty of that offence, and it is not for me to express any opinion with respect to it. But, although in the sentence I am about to pass, I take into consideration the circumstance that there was a quarrel, in which it is at least debatable that the Englishmen who took part in it were as much the aggressors as the Germans, yet I quite agree with the view that was taken by the jury that the wound that you inflicted was not given in self-defence. I object to as untrue the statement that you were struck over the hands with a belaying-pin, and I accept the statement of MacFarland that he was doing you no harm. No doubt your blood was up in consequence of being engaged in this affray, but nothing would justify the striking of the cruel blow that almost cost Macfarland his life.

Now, whilst I am taking part in the administration of justice in this colony, I shall do all in my power to put down the use of the knife. It appears that some person on the other side used the knife in the affray, but it was not used upon you, and therefore I look upon it as a very cruel and unjustifiable act on your part, and one that should be severely punished. I could have taken an exceedingly different view of your case if it were shown that you were in any danger at the time you struck the blow. I am not inclined to disbelieve the evidence given before me in one of the other cases that yours was the hand that stabbed the carpenter (Howe) when he was on the ground. However, you are not convicted for that offence, and the sentence I have to pass is for the wound you inflicted upon Macfarland. You will be imprisoned and kept at hard labour for the term of ten years.

Larsen then stood up, and in reply to the usual question said he only wished again to declare his innocence. His Honour said:

Johannes Larsen, you have been convicted of the offence of manslaughter, but even upon the evidence that was brought before the jury, and altogether irrespective of the statement that you have made, I take a very different view of your case than of the case of the prisoner Wehr. One witness, and one only, speaks to your having had a knife in your hand, and to yours being the hand that struck the fatal blow. I think the jury were amply justified in the conclusion that they arrived at from the evidence, and if I had been sitting with them I should have come to precisely the same conclusions. But they recommended you, and rightly so in my opinion, to the merciful consideration of the Court. Within a few seconds, and almost immediately before, certainly within a very few minutes before, the unfortunate deceased came to his end, you had received a severe wound in the chest, a wound which was in a dangerous part, and which probably would have been fatal if it had not glanced off the bone.

Now, where a man's life is in danger and where he has been acting in self defence, when he is engaged in an encounter of that kind and the knife has already been used, it does appear to me that that the provocation in your case was immeasurably greater than anything that can be suggested on behalf of Wehr. Therefore, in the aspect of the affray that was laid before the jury, I think yours is a case in which I should be justified in passing a light sentence, and that view is not altered when I consider your character in the past. I find that you are at all events a brave man, and I have before me a certificate and medal from which I find that you received a silver medal and certificate and a sum of money from the authorities of the town of Hamburg for having assisted in rescuing the crews of two English vessels which were in peril in the North Sea so recently as last year. And in addition to that circumstance I have had the advantage of perusing the statement with respect to the facts which you have made. That statement was not before the jury. If it had been I am not prepared to say that it would not have made a difference in their verdict. At all events that statement is so important that I intend to submit it to His Excellency for consideration. But if in the meantime you can procure the evidence on board your ship in support of your statement that you had to borrow a knife from one of them for the purpose of removing the sperm from your arm, as you had no knife of your own at the time, that would be conclusive. That is from your own statement, and there must be some delay as the ship has sailed. I shall lay this statement before His Excellency for consideration, but in the meantime, I must deal with your case as it was laid before the jury, and in my view of the circumstances a light sentence should be passed. The sentence of the Court is that you be imprisoned in Her Majesty's Gaol at Adelaide for twelve calendar months.

The prisoners were removed and the court adjourned.

Date	Victim	Accused
20 December 1884	**Male child**	**Unknown**
Cause of death:	Blade wound	
Outcome:	Offender not located	
Location:	Kermode Street, North Adelaide	

On Friday 19 December 1884, a woman who was around 25 to 30 years old called into a shop on Kermode Street in North Adelaide and asked Ada Chickwidden, the shopkeeper, for the time. The woman was pregnant and appeared to be in great pain. At seven-thirty that evening, the same woman was seen in an empty house in Finniss Street. A neighbour saw her and went to her assistance. The neighbour went to ask her husband if the pregnant woman could come inside, and when she returned, the pregnant woman was gone. The neighbour went looking for her and found her near the junction of Kermode and Finniss Streets. The neighbour accompanied the woman as far as Pennington Terrace, where they parted company opposite Mr Downer's house. The pregnant woman walked in the direction of the oval. Early the next morning, Chickwidden heard the sound of a woman coaxing the watchdog into allowing her to enter the yard. In the morning, Chickwidden found blood on the brick floor of the back entrance. There was also brown paper missing and some children's napkins from the washing line.

Later that morning, David Fleming, an engine fitter, was walking to work through the Park Lands near the Children's Hospital. The area he was walking through was known as the Town Clerk's Avenue. As he was crossing a dry drain, he saw a brown paper parcel in the drain. Fleming examined the parcel and saw that it contained the body of a newborn male child. Fleming left the parcel there and walked to the City Watch House where he informed the police of his find. Fleming returned with the police who took charge of the package.

Dr Jay conducted a post-mortem examination, which revealed that the child was full-term and had a separate existence from his mother. The child's throat had been cut, and the wound was given as the cause of death. An inquest was held at the Destitute Asylum on Tuesday 23 December before Mr T Ward, the city coroner. The inquest was adjourned for further evidence to be obtained. Armed with the information from the shopkeeper from Kermode Street, the police offered a reward for information as to the unknown woman's identity. The inquest resumed on Tuesday 6 January and further evidence was given regarding sightings of the pregnant woman, whose identity was still unknown. Chickwidden stated that she saw the woman again on the beach at Largs Bay. She did not call for the police at the time, as she was not quite sure it was the same woman, but she later realised that it was. Other witnesses had seen the woman in Melbourne Street and other places around North Adelaide. Police Constable Rae, stationed at North Adelaide, found a knife in a yard at Pool Street, which was about 250 yards from where the body was found. Dr Jay thought that knife could have caused the injuries. The inquest was again adjourned.

The inquest resumed on Wednesday 14 January where the only evidence given was by Police Constable Carthy, who had examined the scene at the rear of the shop. The identity of the woman was never discovered and the jury returned the verdict of wilful murder against some person or persons unknown.

Date	*Victim*	*Accused*
24 December 1884	**Male child**	**Unknown**
Cause of death:	Asphyxiation	
Outcome:	Offender not located	
Location:	King William Road, Adelaide	

Around eight-thirty am on Thursday 25 December 1884, John Marsh, a blacksmith, was walking to work along King William Road towards North Adelaide. About 60 yards past the City Baths he noticed a brown paper parcel lying about three feet inside the fence. At the same time, a man named Edward Etherington, a greengrocer from Walkerville, was passing by in his cart, so Marsh called to him. They opened the parcel together and found the body of a newborn male child wrapped in some pieces of a dress and a boy's coat. Marsh asked Etherington to wait with the parcel while he fetched the police. Marsh returned with a police constable who took the body to the morgue.

An inquest was held the following day at the Destitute Asylum, which was adjourned until Wednesday 7 January for further evidence.

When the inquest resumed, Dr Melville Jay, who had made a post-mortem examination, reported that the child was fully developed and had a separate existence from his mother. The body showed signs of commencing putrefaction and appeared to have been dead over 24 hours. The cause of death was given as asphyxia, which he suggested occurred within a short time of the birth. The inquest was again adjourned for further evidence.

The inquest was resumed on Friday 16 January. Detective Dunlevie reported that the police had been unable to get any further evidence. The coroner informed the jury that there was very little use in further adjourning the inquest and that the police would continue their investigation after the close of the inquest. Without retiring the jury returned a verdict of wilful murder against some person or persons unknown.

Date	Victim	Accused
24 December 1884	**Lennox child**	**Emma Lennox**
Cause of death:	Drowned	
Outcome:	Emma found to have committed murder-suicide	
Location:	Wirrabara Forest, Ippinechil Creek	

Date	Victim	Accused
24 December 1884	**Emma Lennox**	**William Lennox**
Cause of death:	Drowned	
Outcome:	*Nolle prosequi* entered	
Location:	Wirrabara Forest, Ippinechil Creek	

Emma Lennox lived with her husband, William, and their children in a hut in the Wirrabara forest. Emma, who was 37 years old, had been married before and had two children from that marriage, Richard and Mary Murphy. Emma and William had children of their own, the youngest being a boy who was about a month old.

When William had been drinking, he became violent towards Emma, and was known to have assaulted her. During the evening of 23 December, William was drinking with a friend and was intoxicated. William was abusing Emma, who left the hut with her baby. Emma went to other huts in the area where she spoke to the occupants, telling them that she was frightened of what William would do to her. Emma ended up sleeping in a tent with her baby and Richard, who was 11 years old. William went to the tent and told Emma that if she did not come home he would burn the house down. Emma told him that she had removed all of the lucifers (friction matches) from the house, because she had feared he would burn it down. William told Emma that if she did not come home he would cut her throat. William went home and Emma remained in the tent. Sometime afterwards, Emma took her baby from the tent and Richard went to sleep.

Around five the next morning, William Dansie was by the creek when Mary called out to him and asked him to take her mother out of the water. Dansie approached the creek and found Emma lying in the water, which was about two and a half feet deep. The body of her child was tied to her with an apron. Dansie pulled Emma and the child out of the water and saw that they were both dead.

Dr T Hamilton arrived and examined the bodies on the bank of the creek. Emma and the baby appeared to have been dead for some hours. The cause of death was given as asphyxia from drowning.

An inquest was held that day, where William Lennox gave evidence. William stated that he had some drink the night before and could not recall much. He did recall Emma returning home during the night and that she woke him up, but he could not remember what she said or his reply as he was drunk. He also stated that Emma was always feeble in body and mind and she had attempted to take her life by taking laudanum about four years previous, when she was suffering from milk fever.

Dr Hamilton told the inquest that he was of the opinion that Emma took her own life, and the life of her child while in a temporary unsoundness of mind, which to some extent could have been in response to her husband's behaviour. Hamilton had known Emma for three or four years and had frequently noticed a peculiarity in her manner, but never thought she was of unsound mind. Hamilton was of the opinion that the treatment Emma received from William would tend to 'increase her desire to destroy herself'.

At the completion of the inquest, the jury returned a verdict that 'Emma Lennox destroyed her life and that of her male infant child whilst in an unsound state of mind, which was brought about by the bad treatment she received from her husband, William Lennox'. The coroner then committed William Lennox for trial at the Circuit Court, and he was taken to the Gladstone Gaol.

On Thursday 19 March, William Lennox appeared before the Chief Justice at Gladstone Circuit Court accused of accelerating the death of his wife and charged with manslaughter. The crown entered a *nolle prosequi* and Lennox was released.

Date	*Victim*	*Accused*
27 March 1885	**William August Hebberman**	**Mary Cotter**
Cause of death:	Neglect	
Outcome:	Acquitted	
Location:	Adelaide	

Mary Cotter was 26 years old and the single mother of an illegitimate son, William August Hebberman. When William was about six months old, Cotter was sentenced to six months imprisonment for loitering. Cotter kept her son with her while in custody, where she appeared to pay proper attention to William. Just prior to her being released, William became ill. Dr Paterson, the colonial surgeon, found that he was suffering from marasmus (severe malnutrition).

Cotter was released and stayed with a friend called Emma Raedel. While staying with Raedel, Cotter would spend her money on drink and not food for herself or for William. On one occasion, she threw William on the floor and neglected to take him to the doctor when he was sick. Cotter would go out at night, taking William with her, and would return home drunk. She would take William into the city with her where she was trying to obtain food. The nights were cold and raining and William's illness worsened. Cotter left William in the care of Raedel for three or four nights while she stayed at Ah Sing's in Hindley Street. On Friday 27 March Cotter was told that her son was very sick, so she took him to Dr Clindening who sent them to the Destitute Asylum. William died that night.

Dr Clindening conducted a post-mortem examination and found that one-year-old William was malnourished and in the last stage of emaciation. There were no signs of external violence, but there was ulceration of the arms. Further examination found that William was suffering from congestion of the lungs and congestion of the brain. The cause of death was given as pneumonia and congestion of the brain.

The city coroner, Mr T Ward, held an inquest at the Destitute Asylum on Monday 30 March. At the inquest, Dr Clindening stated that taking William out at night while he was unwell would accelerate death. In summing up, the coroner commented on the painful nature of the evidence, especially noting the allegations of Cotter loitering at night with the sick infant in her arms. The coroner said that 'one could hardly believe that any woman could so degrade herself as to walk the streets under such circumstances', and that Cotter was an 'object of pity'. The jury, after deliberating for about 10 minutes, returned a verdict to the effect that William's death was the result of wilful negligence by Cotter. The coroner said he presumed that this was a verdict of manslaughter, which the jury confirmed. Cotter was then committed for trial, and said, 'I am not guilty of neglecting my child about or ill-using it in any way in gaol or out of gaol'.

Cotter appeared before the Supreme Court on Wednesday 15 April, charged with manslaughter. At the conclusion of the evidence, His Honour Mr Justice Bundey stated that he should reserve a case for the Full Court on the whole question whether there was a case to go to the jury, because he felt it was very difficult to find any portion of the evidence that there had been wicked and wilful negligence on Cotter's part. Cotter had asserted that the woman who had given evidence against her had been prompted by vindictiveness. There were more witnesses who gave evidence that Cotter had treated her child with kindness. The jury subsequently acquitted Cotter.

Date	*Victim*	*Accused*
24 May 1885	**Charlotte Neiass**	**Albert Gurney**
Cause of death:	Medical procedure	
Outcome:	Discharged (certificate of no case to answer provided)	
Location:	Redhill	

Charlotte Neiass was a married woman who was pregnant with her third child. Towards the end of May, Neiass was in the last stages of pregnancy and was being attended to by Kathleen Bairnstow, a nurse who had previous experiences from over 250 pregnancies without having had the need for medical assistance. When Bairnstow saw Neiass, she thought that the case was a very bad one, so she recommended that Dr Albert Gurney (Gerny) should be sent for, as Bairnstow thought that he was a properly qualified man. Dr Gurney attended and said that there was nothing unusual in the case, and suggested that it would be better to call for another medical man. Dr Gurney remained and about two hours later, the child was found to be stillborn. During the delivery, Dr Gurney used instruments on Neiass. Bairnstow thought that the child had been deceased several days before Neiass gave birth.

After giving birth, Neiass became ill and was in great pain. On 24 May Neiass was seen by Dr Parkinson, who advised that she be removed to Crystal Brook for personal attendance. Neiass was taken to Crystal Brook and her condition improved, but she gradually worsened before she died on 1 June.

Dr Parkinson and Dr Hamilton, from Laura, conducted a post-mortem during which they found lacerations and other injuries to the vagina. An inquest into Neiass' death was held at Crystal Brook on Tuesday 2 June, where the jury found that Neiass died as a result of Gurney's unskilled use of instruments, and that Gurney was guilty of manslaughter. Gurney was committed for trial and taken to the Gladstone Gaol, where he was released on bail.

On Friday 24 July, Gurney faced a charge of manslaughter at the Gladstone Circuit Court, but a certificate filed by the crown stated that there was no case to answer. Gurney was discharged.

Date	Victim	Accused
12 June 1885	**Elizabeth Lines and Maurice O'Connor**	**Alfred Lines**
Cause of death:	Gunshot wounds	
Outcome:	Murder-suicide	
Location:	Stanley Street, North Adelaide	

On 3 September 1881, 19-year-old Elizabeth Stephens married 22-year-old Alfred Lines. By 1885 they had had two children, one being about two years old and the other an infant. The family lived at Mitchell Flats, in the neighbourhood of Kooringa. Alfred was said to be addicted to drink as he had appeared before the magistrate at Kooringa on charges of drunkenness and disorderly behaviour.

Maurice O'Connor, an 18-year-old labourer employed as a farm hand around Kooringa, resided about a hundred yards from the Lines household. In early 1885, Elizabeth and O'Connor had an affair. Alfred and Elizabeth's marriage became strained and on 17 March 1885 Alfred wrote and signed the following:

> I hereby give my handwriting stating that I am no longer the husband of Elizabeth Lines, she can go anywhere she likes, and can marry who ever she likes.

Alfred had begun an affair with his 16-year-old sister-in-law, Amelia Grow, who gave birth to his child in early June 1885. Around that time, Alfred told his family that he was going droving to Cooper's Creek and that he would be absent for about six weeks.

On Friday 5 June, O'Connor and Elizabeth met at the train station and took the train to Adelaide, posing as husband and wife. Before she left, Elizabeth sent a letter to Alfred, writing:

Good-by Alf. You must never trouble after me. All you have got to do is to look after the children. I could never live happy with you anymore. It seems you are stuck after Amelia, and she is putting all trust in you. She is determined to have you, and the best thing you can do is to go and get her to come and look after the children together. Here is your ring. So good-by for ever.

When O'Connor and Elizabeth arrived in Adelaide, they briefly stayed with relatives of O'Connor. On Tuesday 9 June, O'Connor and Elizabeth, again posing as a married couple, went to Mrs Wager's house in Stanley Street, North Adelaide, and asked if she could rent them a cottage in Stanley Street. The cottage was a three-roomed single-storey building in a block of other cottages, about 300 yards from the Congregational Church. On the following Thursday, furniture was delivered to the house and O'Connor and Elizabeth moved into the cottage the next day.

Meanwhile, Alfred returned home to Mitchell Flats and found Elizabeth's letter. Alfred travelled to Adelaide to find Elizabeth and visited the police station to enquire after her whereabouts. On Friday morning, Alfred went to the shop of Mr W Ekins, a gunsmith in King William Street, where he enquired about purchasing a revolver. Ekins showed Alfred two revolvers, warning that the cheaper one might misfire on the second chamber. Alfred purchased the more expensive British Bulldog five-chamber revolver for three pounds fifteen shillings, as well as a number of cartridges.

After purchasing the revolver, Alfred caught a cab from King William Street and was taken to the church on Stanley Street. Alfred was seen by some residents of Stanley Street looking into the windows of cottages with an 'anxious eager stare'.

Elizabeth and O'Connor had just finished lunch when Alfred burst into their cottage. Alfred shot Elizabeth in the chest at close range, killing her instantly. O'Connor ran towards the door and Alfred shot at him as he ran, with one bullet passing though his clothing and just grazing his flesh. O'Connor ran to the cottage next door and Alfred followed, firing at him as he ran. O'Connor managed to enter the back door of the cottage next door, but inside an internal door was locked. Alfred ran after him, and as O'Connor turned back at the locked door, Alfred fired twice, hitting O'Connor in the stomach and chest, hitting his heart.

Mrs Schutt was walking past the cottages at the time and heard screaming and the sound of gunshots. She walked to the right of way beside the cottages and saw Alfred coming towards her, noticing the smoking revolver in his hand. Alfred pointed at the cottage and said, 'That woman is my wife, and she is not the wife of that fellow. I have shot them both, and now I'm going to shoot myself'. Schutt, who had seen a man cut his throat before, put her hand up to her face in terror and begged Alfred not to shoot himself before her. Schutt turned around and ran out onto Stanley Street, followed by Alfred. Schutt turned around and saw Alfred stop running, deliberately place the revolver to his chest and pull the trigger. Alfred fell to the pavement and in a few moments he died.

Stanley Street, North Adelaide, south side, April 26th, 1924, showing the premises of J.W. Ells' Blacksmith and Wheelwright. This property was the scene of a double murder in July 1885.
State Library of South Australia, B 2215

Police Constables Wellington and Cruniten soon arrived at the scene, and a large crowd congregated in Stanley Street. As Wellington was examining Alfred, Schutt asked him to come and attend to Elizabeth and O'Connor, who she said had gone into the yard somewhere. Wellington entered the cottage and found Elizabeth dead on the floor. The bullet hole in the fabric of her dress was still smouldering, due to the shot being fired at close range. Schutt came in and told Wellington that the body of the other man was in her cottage.

Constable Wellington searched the bodies, and found the letter previously written by Alfred in Elizabeth's pocket. In Alfred's pocket, Wellington found a letter penned by Alfred, stating:

Adelaide, June 12. My dear Father and Mother, I have found Lizzie and Maurice. They are living together as man and wife. Mother and sister, I hope you may take my dear children for me. When you get this, I shall be dead, so be kind to my dear children. As for me to live knowing that they are living together I could not, so I have bought a revolver and am going to shoot both of them and then shoot myself. I hope God will forgive me for it, it is all her sister's doings. So good-by, Hammet, Tom, and my dear father and mother, from your dear son. Do not fret, my mother. I hope to meet you in heaven, but I could not live, I am broken-hearted. Bless you all. Please bury me at Burra whatever you do. (signed) Alfred Lines. I got about £3 on me. Do be kind to my dear children. Good-by. I hope God will forgive me for what I have done.

William John von Petterswald, Commissioner of Police for South Australia, 1882–1896.
State Library of South Australia, B 11122

The murders of Elizabeth and O'Connor and the suicide of Alfred caused a great sensation in Adelaide. Mr Ward, the coroner, was about to start an inquest into another matter but adjourned it, and attended Stanley Street with Mr Petterswald, the Police Commissioner. Dr Gorger, Dr Jay and Dr Campbell attended and examined the bodies. An inquest was organised for the following day.

The inquest began on Saturday 13 June, with the coroner and jury visiting the scene. Dr Jay examined the bodies, explaining each of the bullet wounds to the coroner. The inquest then moved to the Lord Melbourne Hotel where the only witness examined was Wellington.

The coroner found that Alfred had wilfully murdered Elizabeth and O'Connor, and then committed suicide.

The families of Alfred and O'Connor organised for their bodies to be transported to Burra, where they were buried. Elizabeth was interred at the West Terrace Cemetery, at the expense of the Destitute Board.

Date	Victim	Accused
16 June 1885	**Peter Demell**	**Sydney**
Cause of death:	Gunshot wound	
Outcome:	Unknown	
Location:	Three miles from Angipena Head Station, near Beltana	

On 16 June 1885, Peter Demell, a native of Southern India, and a group of Aboriginal people, including one named Sydney, were travelling by horse and cart to a nearby mine. On the Tuesday night they set up camp about three miles from the Angipena Station, where Demell and Sydney helped themselves to some liquor which was intended for the men at the mines. An argument broke out between Demell and Sydney, during which Sydney shot Demell with a fowling piece. The bullet entered Demell's right hip and penetrated upwards. Demell lay on the ground for some time and was eventually attended to by others from the travelling party.

Word of the shooting reached Mr Davis, the manager of Angipena Station, the following day. Davis rode to the scene and arrived just as Demell died. Sydney, in the meantime, had hidden in the bush, but gave himself up on the Thursday morning and was taken into custody.

An inquest was held at Beltana where the jury returned a verdict of wilful murder against Sydney, adding a rider that Aboriginal people should not be allowed to carry firearms, and that the Gun Act should be strictly enforced. Great praise was given to Trooper Hughes for Sydney's prompt arrest, and for conveying him to a place of safety.

No further information was found.

Date	Victim	Accused
17 June 1885	**Male child**	**Unknown**
Cause of death:	Strangulation	
Outcome:	Offender not located	
Location:	Magill Road, Stepney	

On Wednesday 17 June 1885, John Lynch was walking on Magill Road close to Osmond Terrace, when he saw a body of a child lying in Second Creek.

Lynch saw that there was some kind of cloth wrapped tightly around the neck and tied in a knot. Lynch reported the find to the police who removed the child to the Norwood Police Station, then to the Destitute Asylum.

Dr Heyward examined the child and found that he had had a separate existence from his mother. The afterbirth and umbilical cord were still attached, and there was a large bruise over the left temple, which was caused prior to death. Heyward found two pieces of calico tightly wrapped around the neck, which he believed were wrapped before death. The cause of death was determined to be strangulation.

An inquest was held the next day, but it was adjourned for further evidence. On Friday 26 June, the inquest continued at the Sir John Barleycorn Hotel where evidence was given by Lynch and Heyward. The inquest was once more adjourned.

The inquest resumed on Monday 6 July where the coroner informed the jury that the detectives had made diligent enquiry amid the 'class of people who might be suspected of committing such crime' without obtaining any clue that would lead to the discovery of the person who had placed the child in the creek. The coroner regretted that so often cases came before him where it 'appeared probable that young women were destroying their offspring, and displayed such cunning in the act as to avoid all fear of detection'. The jury, without retiring, found a verdict of wilful murder by strangulation against some person or persons unknown.

The foreman, on behalf of his co-jurors, asked the coroner to consider their claim to some further remuneration, that five shillings for an inquest that had broken into three working days was insufficient. The coroner, Mr Ward, told the foreman that he was only authorised to pay five shillings to each juror for every inquest, but he would bring their application under the notice of the attorney-general who might probably suggest that the clause in question should be altered.

Date	*Victim*	*Accused*
July 1885	**Female Child**	**Unknown**
Cause of death:	Strangulation	
Outcome:	Offender not located	
Location:	Murray Bridge	

On Saturday 11 July 1885, Walter Lock was walking near the River Murray looking for bait for his fishing when he saw the body of a dead child on the riverbank. Lock thought that the body was of a black child and that it was 'nothing in particular', so he did not report the find until the next day.

Dr Deane of Mount Barker conducted a post-mortem examination, finding that the body was that of a white female newborn. Deane thought that the child had been born alive and had been strangled by a handkerchief, which was still tied around the neck. The child had been deceased for some time. An inquest was held before Mr Clark, who adjourned the inquest for a week to enable the police to conduct an investigation.

The inquest resumed on Monday 20 July where Mary Ann Wooten was suspected of being the mother of the child. Wooten denied the allegations and no firm evidence was found against her. The jury returned a verdict of wilful murder against some person or persons unknown, and asked the coroner to censure the witness Lock for not reporting the finding of the body earlier than he did.

Date	*Victim*	*Accused*
11 August 1885	**Maria Carroll**	**Edward Carroll**
Cause of death:	Assault (with a fire bar)	
Outcome:	Found guilty of manslaughter	
	Sentenced to life imprisonment with hard labour	
Location:	Liverpool Street (now Myers Street), Adelaide	

Edward Henry Carroll was a 38-year-old plumber and galvanised ironworker, who was previously a teacher at the Pirie Street Wesleyan Sunday school. Edward married and had six children, but his wife died around the beginning of 1884. Later, Edward started seeing 39-year-old Maria.

Maria had known Edward for about 20 years, as they went to Sunday school together. Maria, whose maiden name was Stevens, married Richard Thomas and had children, including one called Edwin. Maria and Edwin ended up living with Maria's mother in Queen Street, Adelaide. Around January 1885, Maria and Edward married, and they lived with some of their children in Liverpool Street. The neighbours would frequently hear them argue and they were both known to drink to excess and become violent towards each other.

Between 11 and 12 in the morning of Tuesday 11 August 1885, Edward and Maria were seen quarrelling in the street before returning to the house.

Shortly afterwards, Mrs Andrews, a neighbour in Liverpool Street, saw Edward leaving his house with a gash to his throat. Edward was holding his throat and said to Andrews, 'See what she has done'. Andrews' daughter was sent for a policeman, finding Police Constable Daniel McKenzie in King William Street, who she brought back to the Carroll house. The front door was closed so he went into the rear yard where he found two young children crying. McKenzie tried to open the back door, but it was locked, so he entered the house through an open window.

McKenzie searched the house and found Maria lying dead on the floor of the kitchen. Maria had severe head injuries. A fire bar (a long iron pole) was found on the floor near the body.

Edward had walked directly to the Police Watch House where he asked to be locked up. The officer, who saw blood on Edward's clothing, asked what had happened, to which Edward replied 'I have had a dispute'. As Edward had injuries to his throat, he was taken by cab to the hospital. On the way the police officer asked Edward how he sustained his injuries. Edward told him that he was 'too inquisitive'. The injuries were treated at the hospital and assessed as superficial, but the doctor stated that Edwards should remain there for about a week for treatment.

That morning the city coroner, Mr Ward, held a preliminary enquiry at the Brecknock Arms on King William Street. A jury was formed and they visited the house and viewed the body in the kitchen. McKenzie then gave evidence regarding finding the body. Sergeant Detective Upton told the coroner that Edward had been taken to the hospital suffering from a wound in the throat, and that the medical officers said that he would not be able to attend the inquest for a week. The coroner adjourned the inquest to Tuesday 18 August.

When the inquest resumed, further evidence was given by Carroll's neighbours who confirmed the arguing between the couple. Dr Corbin, who conducted a post-mortem examination, gave evidence. Corbin found that Maria had seven separate wounds to her head, which were caused by the fire bar. Maria had been struck while she was standing or sitting, as well as when she was on the floor. Corbin stated that the cause of death was haemorrhaging due to the wounds on the skull.

In summing up, the coroner stated to the jury that having heard the evidence clearly given by Corbin, they could only arrive at the conclusion that a 'most diabolical and revolting murder had been committed upon a poor helpless woman', and that in all his experience he had never heard of or saw more shocking injuries to the skull.

The jury, after about twenty minutes deliberation, brought in a verdict of wilful murder. Edward, who throughout the enquiry had maintained a quiet demeanour but was keenly watching the proceedings, suggested that he would reserve his defence. He was committed to the Supreme Court.

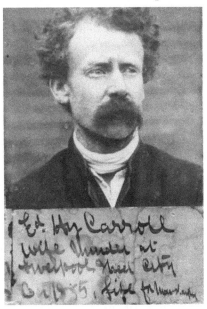

Edward Henry Carroll.
South Australia Police Historical Society, 2381

Edward appeared before the Supreme Court on Thursday 8 and Friday 9 October, charged with Maria's murder. The Honourable C Mann QC prosecuted with Mr C Kingston, with the assistance of Mr Hewitson acting as Edward's defense. Dr Lloyd, the junior house surgeon at the Adelaide Hospital, testified that he examined Edward when he arrived with the injuries to his throat, and he thought that the injuries were self-inflicted. At the completion of the prosecution case, Edward addressed the court, saying, 'I recollect seeing her take the bar and strike me, and I recollect nothing more. I believe I cut my own throat. She was a good wife but for drink'. The jury, after a retirement of two hours, found Edward guilty of manslaughter.

His Honour, Mr Justice Bundey, sentenced Carroll:

Edward Henry Carroll, you have been found guilty of the crime of manslaughter, after a most careful enquiry and a most earnest and able defence on the part of your learned counsel, Mr Kingston. Everything that could be urged on your behalf has been, and the jury from first to last have given your case the utmost consideration. The finding of the jury is, no, I won't say fortunate for you, because it must be a most miserable thing for you to remember that you have been guilty of the death of one whom you were bound to protect. The jury in their wisdom have found a verdict acquitting you of the more heinous crime of murder, and under the circumstances of the case I agree with their finding. The crime you have committed is a most revolting one, and but for the extenuating circumstances would undoubtedly have been regarded as a hideous murder. The circumstances have reduced your crime to that of manslaughter, but whatever may be urged on your behalf through the fountain of mercy in this colony, I, in the discharge of the sacred duty that devolves on me, must prevent you or any such as you who possess the dangerous impulses you have been shown to have from being at large. I don't want to say another word to add to the regret you, who have been shown to be a kind-hearted man, must necessarily feel at having given way to an uncontrollable impulse of temper. In the discharge of my duty I am compelled to lock you up for the term of your natural live. The sentence of the court is that you be imprisoned and kept to hard labour for the term of your natural life.

In March 1886, Edward became insane while in prison, and he was transferred to the Parkside Lunatic Asylum.

Date	*Victim*	*Accused*
3 December 1885	**William James**	**Reinhold (Bernard) Marquardt**
Cause of death:	Assault (with a broomstick)	
Outcome:	Found not guilty	
Location:	Wallaroo	

William James, a young lad employed as an ostler, and Reinhold (Bernard) Marquardt, a middle-aged saddler, worked together in the Government Stables at Wallaroo. Marquardt had been the victim of many practical jokes played by

James and another lad called John Mackey. On Thursday 3 December 1885 an argument developed between them about some red lead, and Marquardt called James a thief. James went into the room where Marquardt was and said something to him, after which Marquardt got off his chair, ran to James and pushed him under a harness. James got up and threw a box at Marquardt, which hit him in the face. Marquardt ran after James, who caught hold of a stable broom, which Marquardt grabbed and pulled from him. Marquardt struck James on the head with the broom, knocking him to the ground. Dr John Gosse attended the stables and examined James, finding him to be suffering from concussion of the brain. James was sent to the hospital where his symptoms worsened, dying shortly after arriving.

Gosse conducted a post-mortem examination and found that James had the thinnest skull he had ever seen on a boy of that age. Further examination found that there was a severe fracture of the skull and a large quantity of blood on the brain.

On Friday 4 December, an inquest was held on the body. At the completion of the evidence, the jury returned a verdict that James came to his death by a blow on the head, but the evidence was not reliable as to how the blow was inflicted. The coroner suggested that the verdict should be reconsidered, but the foreman, Mr Taylor, reported that that was the only verdict they could agree on.

The next day, Marquardt was arrested and committed to take his trial at the Supreme Court on a charge of manslaughter.

On Wednesday 17 February 1886, Marquardt appeared before the Supreme Court charged with killing James. In summing up, His Honour Mr Justice Bundey stated that Marquardt was deserving of great commiseration, but the jury must 'lay aside all sentiment' in judging the evidence. If Marquardt was engaged in a continuous assault upon the boys, he was committing an unlawful act, and would be guilty of manslaughter whether he gave the blow with the broom accidentally or not. If he merely sought to defend himself on being attacked with the broom by James, and the injury inflicted was accidental, then the jury might bring in a verdict of acquittal. The jury, after an absence of 15 minutes, returned a verdict of not guilty.

Date	*Victim*	*Accused*
9 December 1885	**Male child**	**Unknown**
Cause of death:	Strangulation	
Outcome:	Offender not located	
Location:	Port Adelaide	

On Thursday 10 December 1885 the body of a newborn male was found by Bridget Maloney, wrapped in a parcel on Leadehall Street in Port Adelaide. The body was taken to the Port Adelaide police station where enquiries were made as to the mother of the child, but no one was found.

Dr Curtis conducted a post-mortem examination and found that the child had a separate existence from his mother. Curtis thought that the cause of death was asphyxia from strangulation.

On Wednesday 16 December, the coroner, Mr Ward, held an inquest at the Port Admiral Hotel, where the jury returned a verdict of wilful murder against some person or persons unknown.

Date	*Victim*	*Accused*
December 1885	**John Reardon**	**John Flannagan**
Cause of death:	Assault	
Outcome:	Charges dismissed	
Location:	Petersburg (now called Peterborough)	

In December 1885, John Reardon and John Flannagan were in the hotel at Petersburg when they became engaged in a quarrel in the front of the hotel. Reardon was thrown to the floor, cutting his thumb when he landed. Reardon left, and over the following days, neglected the wound by covering it with dirty rags, tobacco juice and other non-medical remedies. Reardon's hand and arm became infected and rapidly worsened, and he was sent to the Burra Hospital. After a few days gangrene set in; an amputation was performed, but Reardon died.

On 10 December, an inquest was held but the jury were unable to decide how Reardon was originally injured. The police took the matter up, and arrested Flannagan on a charge of manslaughter. The case was adjourned until the following Wednesday for production of further evidence.

On 16 December, the court resumed before Mr Edmunds, SM, however, Dr Sangster of Burra telegraphed that he was unwell and unable to attend. The court severely commented on the doctor's actions, and felt inclined to issue a warrant for his arrest. Edmunds stated that a warrant would be issued if the doctor did not attend the following Saturday.

On Saturday 19 December, Flannagan appeared once again before the court charged with wilfully and maliciously killing Reardon. Sangster attended, and prior to giving evidence told the magistrate that threatening to issue a warrant for his arrest had done him harm, as he was too unwell to attend. Sangster also informed the magistrate that he had been provided with a doctor's certificate. The magistrate told Sangster that the dignity of the court must be maintained and that the government had been put to unnecessary and great expense through his disobeying the subpoena, and that his duty as a medical man was to try and assist the court. Sangster then gave evidence stating that death resulted from gangrene of the arm, though he was unable to state the primary cause. The magistrate dismissed the case against Flannagan, reminding him of his narrow escape from a serious charge.

Date	*Victim*	*Accused*
26 April 1886	**Albert Ossenton**	**James Forrest**
Cause of death:	Train collision	
Outcome:	Sentenced to six months imprisonment	
Location:	Nairne train line, near Belair	

Albert Ossenton, a 42-year-old train driver, was working on 26 April 1886, Easter Monday. As there were more passengers and trains than usual on the Nairne line where Ossenton was working, three extra signalmen were employed to work the 16-and-a-half-mile siding. One of those signalmen was 29-year-old James Forrest.

The signalmen's job was to see that the points were properly closed after each train had gone through. On that day, a train from Strathalbyn arrived at five-thirty pm, but Forrest was not at the points, and had not been there for about an hour and a half. The points were set wrong, and the train that Ossenton was driving was thrown down the siding. Ossenton was stuck under his train for about an hour before being taken to the Adelaide Hospital. An examination found that Ossenton had no broken bones, slight abrasions on both arms and hands and 'a good deal of nervous shock'. None of his injuries were considered fatal.

Two or three days later, Ossenton had severe shivering, although his symptoms subsided after receiving treatment. Three or four days after this, Ossenton's temperature rose, and his body was covered with a rash. The symptoms resembled scarlet fever, so he was moved into an isolation ward for a few days until it proved not to be scarlet fever. Ossenton complained of feeling unwell; he had severe shivering, a temperature, and was vomiting. After being in hospital for a month, Ossenton died from blood poisoning.

Forrest was charged with manslaughter and appeared before the Supreme Court on Tuesday 10 August. Mr H Downer, for the defence, told His Honour Mr Justice Bundy that there was no case for Forrest to answer, as Ossenton did not die from Forrest's actions. The judge said that he would not interfere at that stage, so the trial began. At the completion of the trial, Forrest was found guilty of manslaughter. The case was appealed to the Full Court, which heard the argument on 30 November. The verdict was upheld and Forrest was sent back to the Supreme Court to be sentenced.

Forrest appeared once again before Justice Bundy on Tuesday 14 December where he was sentenced to six months imprisonment with hard labour.

Date	*Victim*	*Accused*
27 April 1886	**Unknown child**	**Unknown**
Cause of death:	Suffocation	
Outcome:	Offender not located	
Location:	River Torrens	

On 28 April 1886, the body of a newborn was found wrapped up in a bundle in the River Torrens. The inquest into the death was held over several days, to enable the police to gather evidence. The inquest concluded on Tuesday 11 May, at the Sir John Barleycorn Hotel, where Dr Astles gave evidence of conducting a post-mortem examination. Astles stated that the child was born alive but was killed after about 12 hours, and that it had died from suffocation and not drowning. Detective Burchell stated that after making a diligent search for the mother of the child, he had not been able to find her. The jury returned a verdict of wilful murder by some person or persons unknown.

References

The History of South Australia

http://boundforsouthaustralia.net.au, accessed 4 December 2014

Charles Hill, The Proclamation of South Australia, 1836 (1856), Art Gallery of South Australia southaustralianhistory.com.au/proclamation.htm

June 1837, John Driscoll, Reppindjeri (Alick)

South Australian Gazette and Colonial Register, 29 July 1837, p. 3

South Australian Gazette and Colonial Register, 18 August 1838, p. 3

Southern Australian, 27 February 1839, p. 2

South Australian Gazette and Colonial Register 11 May, 1839, p. 4

South Australian Register, 30 December, 1889, p. 6

Photograph 9228 printed with permission from the Police Historical Society

Keeping a Trust, South Australia's Wyatt Benevolent Institution and its Founder Carol Fort, 2008

State Library of South Australian, B 464, Sir John Jeffcott

5 July 1837, Aboriginal Woman, Aboriginal Man

South Australian Gazette and Colonial Register, 8 July 1837, p. 3

8 March 1838, Enoch Pegler, William, George

South Australian Gazette and Colonial Register, Saturday 17 March 1838, p. 3

Early Experiences of Life in South Australia, and an Extended Colonial History, John Wrathall Bull, printed by E. S. Wigg and Son, Adelaide, South Australia, 1884

August 1838, Roach and Delve, Pilgarie

http://oceans1.customer.netspace.net.au/sa-wrecks.html

SA Govt Gazette, 10 September 1840

South Australian Gazette and Colonial Register, Saturday 25 August 1838, p. 3

21 April 1839, William Duffield, Yerr-i-cha, Monichi Yumbena, Parloobooka

South Australian Gazette and Colonial Register, Saturday 4 May 1839, p. 1

Southern Australian, Wednesday 29 May 1839, p. 1

Dying Declaration 'A man will not meet his maker with a lie in his mouth' a paper by Raghvendra Singh Raghuvanshi, February 2010

26 April 1839, James Thompson, Picta CulNaena, Wang Nucha, Tippa-Wair-i-Cha

South Australian Gazette and Colonial Register, 4 May 1839, p. 1

South Australian Gazette and Colonial Register, 25 May 1839, pp. 2–3

Southern Australian, 29 May 1839, p. 1

August 1839, Alexander Riches, John Dutton
South Australian Register, 31 August 1839, p. 4
South Australian Register, 9 November 1839, p. 6

November 1839, Thomas Young, Aboriginal people
South Australian Register, 16 November 1839, p. 4
South Australian Register, 30 November 1839, p. 5

11 May 1840, child of Mrs Sydney, Richard Manifold
South Australian Register, 30 May 1840, p. 7
South Australian Register, 18 July 1840, p. 8
The Register, Friday 1 January 1915, p. 5

16 June 1840, child of Eleonara Rau, Eleonara Rau
South Australian, 10 July 1840, p. 3
South Australian, 21 July 1840, p. 3
Southern Australian, 4 September 1840, p. 4

July 1840, Passengers and Crew, *Maria* shipwreck, Mongarawata, Pilgaru
http://www.abc.net.au/backyard/shipwrecks/sa/mariacreek.htm
http://en.wikipedia.org/wiki/Maria_%28brigantine%29

26 July 1840, John Gofton, Joseph Stagg
South Australian, Friday 19 June 1840, p. 3
Southern Australian, 28 July 1840, p. 3
Southern Australian, 31 July 1840, p. 4
Southern Australian, Friday 13 November 1840, p. 2
South Australian Register, Saturday 21 November 1840, p. 2
South Australian Register, 19 February 1874, p. 5

5 October 1840, Frank Hawson, Aboriginal people
Southern Australian, 23 October 1840, p. 4
Southern Australian, 3 November 1840, p. 3, *Advertiser*, 7 April 1911, p. 8

4 November 1840, Betty , Tom
South Australian Register, 14 November 1840, p. 4

2 August 1841, Kudnurtya (Worta), William Roach
Southern Australian, Friday 3 September 1841, p. 3
South Australian Register, 4 September 1841, p. 3
South Australian Register, 11 September 1841, p. 3
Southern Australian, 11 March 1842, p. 3

23 September 1841, John Williams, William Sturgess
Southern Australian, Friday 24 September 1841, p. 3

South Australian Register, 25 September 1841, p. 3

Southern Australian, Friday 5 November 1841, p. 3

2 March 1842, John Brown, Francis Lovelock, Aboriginal people

Southern Australian, 29 March 1842, p. 2

South Australian Register, 2 April 1842, p. 3

29 March 1842, Rolles Biddle, Mrs Stubbs, James Fastings, Nultia, Moullia, Ngarbi

South Australian Register, 16 April 1842, p. 2

Southern Australian, Tuesday 22 November 1842, p. 2

Southern Australian, Friday 10 March 1843, p. 2

Southern Australian 15 July 1842, p. 2

2 June 1842, George McGrath, Wira Maldera, Wekweki, Kooeykowminney

South Australian, 17 January 1845, p. 3

South Australian Register, Tuesday 21 January 1845, p. 3

South Australian Register, 12 March 1845, p. 3

South Australian Register, 22 March 1845, p. 3

South Australian, 10 June 1845, p. 2

South Australian, Friday 13 June 1845, p. 3

South Australian Register, Saturday 19 July, 1845, p. 1

The Register News – Pictorial, 7 February 1931, p. 9

http://www.wilmap.com.au/samaps/coorong.html

28 September 1842, George Jefferay, John Spicer

Southern Australian, 11 November 1842, p. 3

Southern Australian, 18 November 1842, p. 3

Southern Australian, 22 November 1842, p. 2

25 January 1843, Maria , George Gregory

Southern Australian, 24 March 1843, p. 3

18 March 1843, John Murdoch, Charles Hedditch

Southern Australian, 28 March 1843, p. 2

Southern Australian, 21 July 1843, p. 3

South Australian Register, 17 September 1856, p. 3

South Australian Register, 17 September 1865, p. 2

21 June 1843, Aboriginal, William Skelton

South Australian Register, Tuesday 18 July 1843, p. 3

Southern Australian, 28 July 1843, p. 2

Southern Australian, 10 November 1843, p. 2

June 1844, Ngunnirra Bourka, Maryann, Charles Spratt, Charles Pitt, William Smith

South Australian Register, 25 December 1844, p. 3

South Australian, 27 December 1844, p. 3

South Australian, Tuesday 11 March 1845, p. 2

South Australian, 18 March 1845, p. 3

12 June 1844, child of Rosa Hyrdess, Rosa Hyrdess

Southern Australian, 5 July 1844, p. 2

Southern Australian, 24 September 1844, p. 3

Southern Australian, 29 November 1844, p. 3

22 October 1844, John Charles Darke, Unknown natives

Southern Australian, 15 November 1844, p. 3

Advertiser, 12 February 1910, p. 12

8 February 1845, child of Sarah Lygoe, Sarah Lygoe, Thomas James

South Australian Register, 19 February 1845, p. 3

South Australian Register, Saturday 22 February 1845, p. 3

South Australian, 11 March 1845, p. 2

23 June 1845, Salteye, Terralia

South Australian, 21 November 1845, p. 3

South Australian Register, 3 December 1845, p. 2

South Australian Register, 17 December 1845, p. 3

1 July 1845, William Brown, Unknown natives

South Australian, 12 August 1845, p. 3

26 February 1846, Donald Scott, Charles Whitney, Nakhunda Bidden, Meiya Makarta

South Australian Register, 25 July, 1846, p. 2

South Australian, Friday 19 March 1847, p. 4

1 September 1846, Kingberri, Thomas Donelly

South Australian Register, 25 November 1846, p. 3

South Australian Register, Wednesday 17 March 1847, p. 3

South Australian Register, 31 March 1847, p. 2

3 November 1846, Ronkurri, Rallooloolyoo

South Australian, 10 November, 1846, p. 5

South Australian Register, 14 November 1846, p. 2

South Australian Register, 28 November 1846, p. 3

South Australian Register, 17 March 1847, p. 3

http://en.wikipedia.org/wiki/Bremer_River_(South_Australia)

11 November 1846, Richard Carney, Tatty Wambourneen

South Australian Register, 9 December 1846, p. 2

South Australian Register, 30 December 1846, p. 4

South Australian Register, Wednesday 10 March 1847, p. 2

South Australian, Friday 19 March 1847, p. 4

South Australian Register, Saturday 20 March 1847, p. 2

South Australian Register, Saturday 18 March 1848, p. 3

8 November 1846, Melicka, Manooka Bidea

South Australian Register, 21 November 1846, p. 2

South Australian, 24 November 1846, p. 6

South Australian, 14 September 1847, p. 3

South Australian Register, 27 October 1847, p. 3

17 October 1847, Mulianolo, Rambalta

South Australian, Friday 16 March 1849, p 4

South Australian Register, Saturday 26 June 1852, p. 3

22 March 1848, Mary, Milaitya (Bobbo)

South Australian, Tuesday 20 June 1848, p. 4

27 May1848, Edward Olliver, James Snow

South Australian, Tuesday 20 June 1848, p. 2

June 1848, Hart, Unknown native

South Australian, 25 July 1848, p. 2

South Australian Register 25 January 1850, p. 4

23 June 1848, John Hamp, Mingalta, Malgalta

South Australian, 21 July 1848, p. 3

South Australian, Friday 28 September 1849, p. 2

South Australian Register, Saturday 29 September 1849, p. 2

The Recorder, Wednesday 15 September 1937, p. 1

24 January 1849, John Lester, Michael Callaghan

South Australian, 9 February, 1849, p. 3

South Australian Register, 10 February, 1849, p. 4

South Australian, 13 March, 1849, p. 2

South Australian, 16 March, 1849, p. 4

March 1849, 9 Aboriginals, James Brown

South Australian, 20 March 1849, p. 2

South Australian, 30 March 1849, p. 2

South Australian Register, 16 June 1849, p. 3

April 1849, 5 x Aboriginals, Patrick Dwyer

South Australian Register, Saturday 20 October 1849, p. 4

South Australian, Tuesday 6 November 1849, p. 4

3 May 1849, James Beevor, Neentulta, Kulgulta, Yabmanna, Pullurunyu, Pakilti, Pullarpinye, Maltalta

South Australian Register, 9 June, 1849, p. 2

South Australian Register, 18 August, 1849, p. 3

South Australian Register, 12 September, 1849, p. 3

South Australian Register, 25 September, 1849, p. 1

South Australian Register, 26 September, 1849, p. 4

South Australian, Friday 28 September 1849, p. 2

South Australian Register, 19 January, 1849, p. 4

South Australian Register, Saturday 1 February 1851, p. 3

7 May 1849, Ann Easton, Malpita, Pakilta, Puturpynter

South Australian Register, 18 August, 1849, p. 3

South Australian, 11 September 1849, p. 2

South Australian Register, 26 September 1849, p. 4

South Australian Register, Wednesday 3 October 1849, p. 4

3 July 1849, Nantariltarra, George Field

South Australian, Tuesday 4 September 1849, p. 3

South Australian Register, 5 September 1849, p. 4

South Australian, 18 September 1849, p. 2

12 July 1849, Tom Armstrong, Thulta

South Australian Register, 14 July, 1849, p. 2

South Australian Register, 28 July, 1849, p. 2

South Australian, 18 September 1849, p. 2

South Australian, 27 November 1849, p. 3

2 August 1849, William Scott, Wilcumramalap, Thulta

South Australian Register, 15 August, 1849, p. 3

South Australian, 11 September 1849, p. 2

South Australian Register, Wednesday 28 November 1849, p. 4

South Australian Register, 20 April, 1850, p. 3

August 1849, James Stone, James Johnson

South Australian Register, 20 October 1849, p. 4

12 August 1849, Milartyappa, Harry Jones, Henry Morris

South Australian, 31 August, 1849, p. 3

South Australian Register, 1 September 1849, p. 3

South Australian, 18 September 1849, p. 2&3

South Australian Register, Wednesday 19 September 1849, p. 4

20 October, 1849, Thomas Keorby, Francis Flynn

South Australian Register, 27 October 1849, p. 3

South Australian, Tuesday 4 December 1849, p. 2

25 December 1849, John Smith, Carl Gottliet Keirnall

South Australian Register, 29 December, 1839, p. 3

South Australian Register, Thursday 14 March 1850, p. 3

South Australian, 15 March 1850, p. 2

5 January 1850, Amelia Fry, Robert Fry

South Australian, Friday 11 January 1850, p. 2

South Australian, 22 January 1850, p. 2

South Australian, 29 January 1850, p. 2

South Australian Register, 5 February 1850, p. 3

South Australian Register, 13 February 1850, p. 3

South Australian Register, 3 July, 1850, p. 3

22 May 1850, Alexander Wood, George Pyke

South Australian, Tuesday 25 June, 1850, p. 2

South Australian, Friday 5 July, 1850, p. 2

South Australian, Thursday 15 August, 1850, p. 4

27 May 1850, Thomas Roberts, Patrick O'Connor

South Australian Register, 10 June 1850, p. 3

South Australian, 22 August 1850, p. 2

15 June 1850, Male child, Unknown

South Australian, 21 June 1850, p. 3

18 June 1850, John Doyle, David Spears

South Australian Register, 6 July, 1850, p. 3

South Australian, 15 August, 1850, p. 3

24 July 1850, John Mansforth, John Yates

South Australian Register, Thursday 1 August, 1850, p. 3

South Australian Register, Tuesday 20 August, 1850, p. 2

South Australian, Monday 2 September, 1850, p. 2

South Australian Register, Friday 6 September 1850, p. 4

25 August 1850, child of Mary O'Brien, Mary O'Brien

South Australian Register, Tuesday 27 August 1850, p. 3

South Australian, Thursday 28 November 1850, p. 2

September 1850, Budlaroo, Kutromee
South Australian Register, 14 September 1850, p. 3
South Australian Register, 15 January 1851, p. 3
South Australian Register, 13 February 1851, p. 3

2 November 1850, Henry Baird, Pulgalta
South Australian, 28 November 1850, p. 2
South Australian, 23 May 1851, p. 3
http://en.wikipedia.org/wiki/Streaky_Bay,_South_Australia

1 February 1851, Hadgee, Dumah
South Australian Register, 18 February 1851, p. 3
South Australian Register, 19 May 1851, p. 4

11 February 1851, Maltalta, Tuk Karin, Ngalta Wikkanni, Konga Woilf
South Australian Register, 5 March 1851, p. 4
South Australian Register, 20 May 1851, p. 3

March 1851, Marponin (Salt Creek Paddy), Maramin, Weepin, Parrot, Penchungy
South Australian Register, 21 May 1851, p. 2

5 March 1851, Charles Crocker, John Shepherd, Kumbilti
South Australian Register, 24 June 1851, p. 2
South Australian Register, Monday 25 August 1851, p. 3
South Australian Register, 30 October 1851, p. 4

14 April 1851, George Jenks, Marialta, Ngamalta, Cooleltie
South Australian Register, 29 April 1851, p. 2
South Australian Register, 25 August 1851, p. 3
South Australian Register, Tuesday 19 May 1857, p. 3
South Australian Register, Tuesday 2 June 1857, p. 2
www.pioneerssa.org.au/files/24%20Tennant%20APPROVED.pdf

11 May 1851, Wartpu Purti , Charles Jacques, Jeremiah Nicholls
South Australian, 23 May 1851, p. 4
South Australian Register, 22 August 1851, p. 4

15 May 1851, William Bagnall, Murrepa
South Australian Register, 27 September 1851, p. 4
South Australian Register, 11 February 1852, p. 3

15 October 1851, Female child, Unknown
South Australian Register, 22 October 1851, p. 2

References

26 October 1851, John O'Dea, Sydney Glover, Charles Grosse
South Australian Register, 27 October 1851, p. 3
South Australian Register, 26 November 1851, p. 3
South Australian Register, Monday 1 December 1851, p. 3

14 March 1852, Robert Richardson, Billy and Jemmy
South Australian Register, 20 April 1852, p. 3
South Australian Register, Monday 22 November 1852, p. 3

26 June 1852, Jane McCaskill, Daniel Horgan
Adelaide Morning Chronicle, Monday 28 June 1852, p. 2
South Australian Register, Monday 28 June 1852, p. 3
Adelaide Morning Chronicle, Monday 16 August 1852, p. 3

9 July 1852, Warrin Yerriman (Jimmy), Crackingyounger, Ballycrack, Pot Pouch
South Australian Register, Saturday 14 August 1852, p. 3

30 September 1852, Mr Brown, Aboriginal people
South Australian Register, Monday 8 November 1852, p. 2s

9 December 1852, Henry Hiern, Dennis Wood Hiern, Henry Holloway, Thomas Davies
South Australian Register, Saturday 25 December 1852, p. 3

15 January 1853, Robert Head, William Wright
Adelaide Morning Chronicle, Monday 17 January 1853, p. 3
Adelaide Morning Chronicle, Monday 22 February 1853, p. 3

19 February 1853 , George Arnold, Thomas Whitham, Henry Hunt, Sarah Kelly, Ann Lynam
South Australian Register, 4 March 1853, p. 3
South Australian Register, 16 May 1853, p. 3
Adelaide Observer, Saturday 2 April 1853, p. 3

4 April 1853, Watte Watte, Kanadla
South Australian Register, 8 April 1853, p. 3
South Australian Register, 11 May 1853, p. 3
South Australian Register, 28 May 1853, p. 2

25 April 1853, Selina Thomas, Elijah Thomas
South Australian Register, Tuesday 26 April 1853, p. 3
South Australian Register, Thursday 12 May 1853, p. 3

1 May 1853, Female child of Fanny Port, Fanny Port
South Australian Register, Monday 6 June 1853. P3
South Australian Register, Wednesday 10 August 1853. P3

1 June 1853, Ngallabann, Worrungenna, Tengunnmoor, Tungkunnerramor, Crup-Crup Bonat
South Australian Register, Tuesday 6 September 1853, p. 3
South Australian Register, Monday 28 November 1853, p. 3
South Australian Register, Tuesday 13 December 1853, p. 3

22 June 1853, George Smith, James Searle
South Australian Register, Friday 1 July 1853, p. 3
South Australian Register, Thursday 11 August 1853, p. 3

12 October 1853, David Broadfoot, Alexander Stephens, John Crawford
South Australian Register, Friday 11 November 1853, p. 2
South Australian Register, Friday Saturday 18 February 1853, p. 3
South Australian Register, Saturday 29 April 1854, p. 3
The Advertiser, Friday 14 December 1945, p. 12

2 November 1853, Joseph Taylor, Peter Fagan, Catherine Morris
South Australian Register, Monday 7 November 1853, p. 3
South Australian Register, Thursday 8 December 1853, p. 3
South Australian Register, Tuesday 14 March 1853, p. 3

1 March 1854, Angus MacDonald, James Bryce, John Tippett
South Australian Register, Wednesday 8 March 1853, p. 3
South Australian Register, Saturday 11 March 1853, p. 3
South Australian Register, Saturday 29 April 1853, p. 3

30 July 1854, child of Mary Connell, Mary Connell
South Australian Register, Wednesday 2 August, 1854, p. 2
South Australian Register, Tuesday 8 August 1854, p. 2
South Australian Register, Wednesday 23 August 1854, p. 2

9 November 1854, Augusta Ulbrecht, William Bell
South Australian Register, Monday 13 November 1854, p. 2
South Australian Register, Friday 8 December 1854, p. 3
11 December 1854, Loorumumpoo, Poowoolupe, Marielara
South Australian Register, Tuesday 20 February 1855, p. 3
South Australian Register, Wednesday 30 May 1855, p. 3
South Australian Register, Tuesday 14 August 1855, p. 3

26 December 1854, Emily Bentley, Joseph Bentley
South Australian Register, Friday 19 January 1854, p. 3
South Australian Register, Saturday 10 February 1855, p. 3
South Australian Register, Wednesday 30 May 1855, p. 3

24 January 1855, William Thomas, John Smith

South Australian Register, Thursday 8 February 1855, p. 3

South Australian Register, Saturday 27 October 1855, p. 3

South Australian Register, Thursday 22 November 1855, p. 3

South Australian Register, Monday 11 February 1856, p. 3

South Australian Register, Wednesday 5 March 1856, p. 3

17 February 1855, Thomas Lee, John Walker

South Australian Register, Tuesday 20 February, 1855, p. 3

South Australian Register, Saturday 26 May, 1855, p. 3

1 June 1855, Peter Brown, Wadniltie, Wenpalta, Pankalta and Ilyelta

South Australian Register, Wednesday 5 December 1855, p. 4

South Australian Register, Saturday 8 December 1855, p. 3

South Australian Register, Monday 21 January 1856, p. 4

1 September 1855, Henry Nixon, Ogonoron

South Australian Register, Thursday 6 December 1885, p. 3

The Law Reform Commission of Hong Kong, Report on 'The Year And A Day Rule in Homicide' Ms Cathy Wan, Senior Crown Counsel, June 1997

AFP media release http://www.afp.gov.au/media-centre/news/afp/2008/September/state-police-look-to-canberra-to-honour-fallen-officers

Staunford, Les Plees del Coron (1557) F 2tv

*Chief Justice Coke's institute*s ((1809) Vol. 1 Part 111, p 47)

September 1855, Female Aboriginal, Male Aboriginal

South Australian Register, Friday 21 September 1855, p. 3

September 1855, Child of Jane Shepherd, Jane Shepherd

South Australian Register, Saturday 8 December 1855, p. 3

21 September 1855, Mary, Waren-boor-inem, Parich-boor-imen

South Australian Register, Friday 30 November 1855, p. 3

21 September 1855, James Spencer, Unknown

South Australian Register, Friday 28 September 1855, p. 2

2 February 1856, child of Marianne Hocking, Marianne Hocking, Martha Jones

South Australian Register, Friday 8 February 1856, p. 3

South Australian Register, Saturday 16 February 1856, p. 4

South Australian Register, Tuesday 19 February 1856, p. 3

18 March 1856, child of Bridget Hahn, Bridget Hahn

South Australian Register, Wednesday 26 March 1856, p. 3

South Australian Register, Saturday 17 May 1856, p. 4

September 1856, Powang, Karende
South Australian Register, Friday 14 November 1856, p. 1
South Australian Register, Friday 5 December 1856, p. 3

16 October 1856, Thomas Murriss, Gregory Jordan, John Christoff, Charles Forward
South Australian Register, Wednesday 22 October 1856, p. 2
South Australian Register, Wednesday 3 December 1856, p. 3

17 October 1856, James Mitchell, 3 Aboriginal people
South Australian Register, Monday 17 November 1856, p. 3
South Australian Register, Saturday 23 May 1857, p. 2

24 December 1856, John Carthew, Stephen Ryan
South Australian Register, Thursday 19 February 1857, p. 3

10 January 1857, Michael Macnamara, Henry Kochne
South Australian Register, Wednesday 18 February 1857, p. 3

15 May 1857, Richard Moon, George Hobbs
South Australian Register, Tuesday 18 August, 1857, p. 3
South Australian Register, Saturday 22 August 1857, p. 2

19 June 1857, Bullocky, Beerdea
South Australian Register, Tuesday 18 August 1857, p. 3

30 June 1857, Cooekin, Goodoognaybrie, Toorapennie, Tommy
South Australian Register, Wednesday 8 July 1857, p. 3
South Australian Register, Saturday 18 July 1857, p. 4
South Australian Register, Tuesday 18 August 1857, p. 3

11 August 1857, William Bereft, Charles Gray, John Date
South Australian Register, Thursday 26 November 1857, p. 3

October 1857, Wilddog, Warreah, Piulta, Goniah, Moniah
South Australian Register, Friday 12 February 1858, p. 3
South Australian Register, Friday 26 February 1858, p. 2

15 October 1857, Willamy Warriah, Warreah
South Australian Register, Friday 12 February 1858, p. 3
Observer, Saturday 14 October 1916, p. 35

30 November 1857, child of Honora Keating, Honora Keating
South Australian Register, Friday 12 February 1858, p. 3

8 December 1857, Coodnogee, Midluck, Tommy
South Australian Register, Wednesday 9 December 1857, p. 2
South Australian Register, Friday 12 February 1858, p. 3

May 1858, Johnny Come, 8 Aboriginal people
South Australian Register, Wednesday 9 May 1860, p. 3

15 September 1858, child of Winnifred Lennon, Winnifred Lennon
South Australian Advertiser, Saturday 18 September 1858, p. 3
South Australian Advertiser, Tuesday 23 November 1858, p. 3

October 1858, Aboriginal, Aboriginal
South Australian Register, Wednesday 3 November 1858, p. 3

2 December 1858, Unknown, Meenalta, Marguiltie, Coonguiltie
South Australian Register, Friday 18 February 1859, p. 3

16 January 1859, child of Bridget Kilmartin, Bridget Kilmartin
South Australian Register, Thursday 24 February, 1859, p. 3
South Australian Register, Tuesday 1 March, 1859, p. 3

4 March 1859, Baldanant, Wooloobully
South Australian Register, Wednesday 16 March 1859, p. 3
South Australian Advertiser, Tuesday 17 May 1859, p. 3

24 April 1859, Male child, Unknown
South Australian Advertiser, Tuesday 26 April, 1859, p. 3

27 July 1859, Ann Gillen, Anton Sokolowski
South Australian Register, Saturday 30 July 1859, p. 3
South Australian Register, Wednesday 3 August 1859, p. 3

August 1859, Pantwirri, Langarynga, Eyungaree
South Australian Advertiser, Saturday 20 August 1859, p. 3
State Library of South Australia, B 15276/32, Plate 32: Native dwellings

12 December 1859, William Rule, James Irvine
South Australian Advertiser, Friday 13 January 1860, p. 3
South Australian Weekly Chronicle, Saturday 14 January 1860, p. 7
South Australian Register, Friday 17 February 1860, p. 3

13 May 1860, John Jones, Manyalta, Kainmulta
South Australian Register, Tuesday 22 May 1860, p. 3
South Australian Advertiser, Saturday 18 August 1860, p. 3
South Australian Register, Tuesday 23 October 1860, p. 3
South Australian Advertiser, Friday 7 December, 1860, p. 3

4 September 1860, child of Mary McCombe, Mary McCombe
South Australian Register, Tuesday 27 November 1860, p. 3
South Australian Advertiser, Saturday 1 December 1860, p. 3

October 1860, Pinderrie, Popeltie, Padneltie
South Australian Register, Tuesday 23 October 1860, p. 3
South Australian Advertiser, Friday 7 December 1860, p. 3

11 January 1861, Thomas Gustava Bergeest, Nelgerie, Tilcherie
South Australian Register, Tuesday 23 April 1861, p. 3
South Australian Register, Monday 20 May 1861, p. 3
South Australian Register, Friday 16 August 1861, p. 3
South Australian Advertiser, Friday 20 September 1861, p. 3

28 January 1861, child of Anna Donk, Anna Donk
South Australian Register, Friday 15 February 1861, p. 3

11 March 1861, Mary Rainbird and her two Children, Emma and Robert, Warretya, Warretya, Moanaitya, Warretya, Tankawortya Pilti Miltinda
South Australian Advertiser, Saturday 18 May 1861, p. 3

2 May 1861, Margaret Impey, Mangeltie, Karabidue
South Australian Register, Monday 20 May 1861, p. 3
South Australian Register, Friday 16 August 1861, p. 3
South Australian Advertiser, Friday 20 September 1861, p. 3

10 May 1861, child of Rachael Williams, Rachel Williams
South Australian Register, Monday 20 May 1861, p. 3
South Australian Advertiser, Monday 1 July 1861, p. 3
State Library of South Australia, B 58365, early view of the Police Court, 1860

17 October 1861, Nicholas James, George Burkby
South Australian Register, Tuesday 10 December 1861, p. 3
South Australian Register, Friday 14 February 1862, p. 3

12 November 1861, William Lawless, Peter Stars
The *South Australian Register*, Saturday 16 November 1861, p. 3
South Australian Advertiser, Thursday 5 December 1861, p. 3
South Australian Advertiser, Friday 6 December 1861, p. 3

20 January 1862, child of Annie Hooper, Annie Hooper
South Australian Register, Tuesday 28 January 1862, p. 3
South Australian Register, Wednesday 12 February 1862, p. 3
South Australian Register, Thursday 20 February 1862, p. 3

4 February 1862, Richard Pettinger, John Seaver
South Australian Register, Tuesday 5 February 1862, p. 3
South Australian Register, Wednesday 19 February 1862, p. 3
State Library of South Australia, B 478, King William Street, 1863

References

4 February 1862, Jane Macmanamin, Malachi Martin, William Wilson
South Australian Advertiser, Wednesday 3 December 1862, p. 3
South Australian Advertiser, Thursday 4 December 1862, p. 3

24 February 1862, Robert French, John McMahon
South Australian Register, Saturday 1 March, 1982, p. 3
South Australian Advertiser, Thursday 15 May 1862, p. 3

9 March 1862, William Walker, Magnultie
South Australian Register, Monday 24 March 1862, p. 3
South Australian Advertiser, Tuesday 8 April 1862, p. 3
South Australian Advertiser, Friday 15 August 1862, p. 3

10 May 1862, Marianne Paulovitch, Eliza Paulovitch
South Australian Advertiser, Wednesday 14 May 1862, p. 3
South Australian Advertiser, Saturday 17 May 1862, p. 3
State Library of South Australia, B 2773, Botanic Gardens, Adelaide, 1860
4 August 1862, Yaditepunen, Yeppungen, KingPullen, Linikkerperrup
Border Watch, Friday 15 August 1862, p. 3
South Australian Weekly Chronicle, Saturday 23 August 1862, p. 7
South Australian Advertiser, Monday 25 August 1862, p. 3
South Australian Register, Saturday 30 August 1862, p. 3

17 September 1862, Anne Bean, James McEnhill
South Australian Weekly Chronicle, Saturday 20 September 1862, p. 7
South Australian Advertiser, Saturday 20 September 1862, p. 2
South Australian Register, Tuesday 25 November 1862, p. 3

22 September 1862, child of Winnifred Lennon, Winnifred Lennon, William Reylin
South Australian Register, Thursday 25 September 1862, p. 3
South Australian Advertiser, Friday 28 November 1862, p. 3
South Australian Advertiser, Friday 5 December 1862, p. 3

1 December 1862, Robert, Henry Hammond
South Australian Advertiser, Thursday 18 December 1862, p. 3
South Australian Register, Thursday 18 December 1862, p. 2
South Australian Register, Tuesday 17 February 1863, p. 2

13 December 1862, Joseph Ryder, Charles Harding
South Australian Advertiser, Tuesday 16 December 1862, p. 2
South Australian Advertiser, Saturday 14 February 1863, p. 2
South Australian Advertiser, Wednesday 18 February 1863, p. 3

27 January 1863, child of Margaret Casey, Margaret Casey
Border Watch, Friday 30 January 1863, p. 2
South Australian Register, Saturday 25 April 1863, p. 2

12 February 1863, Nanangaleen, Tarryaka, Warrangarina
South Australian Advertiser, Saturday 21 February 1863, p. 3
South Australian Register, Thursday 21 May 1863, p. 2

8 May 1863, William Maylor, Jane Adwin
Border Watch, Friday 20 May 1863, p. 2
Border Watch, Friday 30 October 1863, p. 2

September 1863, Cusak, Morculta, Niccaltie, Kacuppia, Poonbinga
South Australian Register, Friday 13 May 1864, p. 3

7 September 1863, child of Emily Robins, Emily Robins
South Australian Advertiser, Saturday 12 September 1863, p. 3
South Australian Register, Friday 4 December 1863, p. 3

27 October 1863, John Plunkett, John Smith, John Grant
South Australian Register, Friday 6 November 1863, p. 3
South Australian Advertiser, Saturday 28 November 1863, p. 2
South Australian Register, Saturday 28 November 1863, p. 3
South Australian Advertiser, Thursday 10 December 1863, p. 3

November 1863, Woolgaltie, Koongiltie
South Australian Advertiser, Friday 13 May 1863, p. 3
South Australian Register, Friday 13 May 1863, p. 3

December 1863, Meenulta, Russell Barton, Alexander Miller
South Australian Advertiser, Tuesday 16 August 1864, p. 3

8 January 1864, Pompey, Samuel Stuckey
South Australian Register, Thursday 25 February 1864, p. 6
South Australian Advertiser, Monday 14 March 1864, p. 3
South Australian Register, Wednesday 4 May 1864, p. 3

5 September 1864, child of Annie Webb, Annie Webb
South Australian Advertiser, Friday 18 November 1864, p. 4
South Australian Advertiser, Thursday 1 December 1864, p. 3

13 October 1864, Bridget Ashley, Charles Ashley
South Australian Register, Saturday 15 October 1864, p. 3
South Australian Advertiser, Saturday 10 December 1864, p. 3
South Australian Advertiser, Wednesday 22 July 1868, p. 2

References

10 November 1864, John Torpey, Frederick Stafford
South Australian Register, Saturday 7 January 1865, p. 1
South Australian Advertiser, Saturday 18 February 1865, p. 3
South Australian Register, Friday 24 February 1865, p. 2

February 1865, Oongiltie, Nielbury
South Australian Register, Thursday 17 August 1865, p. 3

13 April 1865, John Walter Jarrold, Parrallana Jacky
South Australian Register, Saturday 10 June 1865, p. 2
South Australian Register, Friday 30 June 1865, p. 3
South Australian Register, Monday 23 October 1865, p. 2

5 August 1865, child of Mary Kelly, Mary Kelly
South Australian Register, Wednesday 9 August 1865, p. 3
South Australian Advertiser, Thursday 24 August 1865, p. 3

23 October 1865, George Young, John Walker
South Australian Register, Tuesday 31 October 1865, p. 3
South Australian Advertiser, Saturday 9 December 1865, p. 3
South Australian Advertiser, Friday 15 December 1865, p. 3

24 October 1865, George Smith, Robert Sutcliffe
South Australian Advertiser, Wednesday 1 November 1865, p. 3
South Australian Register, Friday 8 December 1865, p. 3
South Australian Advertiser, Friday 15 December 1865, p. 3

8 December 1865, Carl Neumann, Moonabuckaneena, Freddy
South Australian Advertiser, Saturday 17 March 1866, p. 2
South Australian Register, Wednesday 5 September 1866, p. 4
South Australian Weekly Chronicle, Saturday 8 September 1866, p. 6

20 January 1866, Male child, Unknown
South Australian Register, Wednesday 24 January 1866, p. 2
South Australian Register, Friday 2 February 1866, p. 2

8 February 1866, William Forrester, Michael O'Donnell
South Australian Register, Saturday 10 February 1866, p. 2
South Australian Advertiser, Tuesday 13 February 1866, p. 3
Border Watch, Wednesday 19 September 1866, p. 2

29 March 1866, Harriet Stone, Jane Green
South Australian Register, Saturday 31 March 1866, p. 2
South Australian Advertiser, Thursday 5 April 1866, p. 2
South Australian Register, Tuesday 11 September 1866, p. 2

17 May 1866, child of Henrietta Bruder, Henrietta Bruder
South Australian Register, Monday 28 May 1866, p. 2
South Australian Advertiser, Wednesday 22 August 1866, p. 2
South Australian Weekly Chronicle, Saturday 15 September 1866, p. 6

2 January 1867, Cooelta, Pagulta
South Australian Register, Saturday 18 May 1867, p. 3

February 1867, Samuel Stubbs, Tommy Dutton
South Australian Advertiser, Saturday 25 May 1867, p. 3
South Australian Register, Friday 24 May 1867, p. 3

5 June 1867, child of Margaret Brown, Margaret Brown
South Australian Advertiser, Friday 7 June 1867, p. 2
South Australian Register, Saturday 17 August 1867, p. 3

22 September 1867, Eliza Goodridge, John Goodridge
South Australian Advertiser, Monday 30 September 1867, p. 3
South Australian Advertiser, Thursday 21 November 1867, p. 5

13 October 1867, child of Mary Stephens, Mary Stephens
South Australian Register, Saturday 26 October 1867, p. 2
South Australian Register, Wednesday 4 December 1867, p. 3

13 November 1867, Peter Franklin, Poolunta Yaria, Billybung
South Australian Advertiser, Friday 6 December 1867, p. 2
South Australian Register, Tuesday 8 September 1868, p. 2
South Australian Register, Saturday 28 November 1868, pp. 2, 4

7 December 1867, Unknown female child, Unknown
South Australian Register, Thursday 12 December 1867, p. 2

20 January 1868, child of Catherine Pope, Catherine Pope
South Australian Advertiser, Thursday 20 February 1868, p. 3
South Australian Register, Friday 28 February 1868, p. 3

30 January 1868, Jinny, Jacky
South Australian Advertiser, Thursday 21 May 1968, p. 3

5 August 1868, James Wade, Poolunta Yaria
South Australian Register, Thursday 20 August 1868, p. 2
South Australian Register, Tuesday 8 September 1868, p. 2
South Australian Register, Saturday 28 November 1868, pp. 2, 4
South Australian Register, Wednesday 2 December 1868, p. 4

3 November 1868, child of Mary Demschke, Mary Demschke
South Australian Register, Monday 9 November 1868, p. 2
South Australian Advertiser, Wednesday 2 December 1868, p. 3

5 December 1868, Frederick Jackson, George Tyrrell
South Australian Register, Tuesday 8 December 1868, p. 2
South Australian Advertiser, Friday 12 February 1869, p. 3

24 December 1868, Whycanning, Bookmark Jack
South Australian Advertiser, Saturday 13 February 1869, p. 3
South Australian Register, Saturday 20 February 1869, p. 3
South Australian Chronicle and Weekly Mail, Saturday 15 July 1871, p. 10

5 January 1869, child of Elizabeth Bottrill, Elizabeth Bottrill
South Australian Advertiser, Saturday 13 February 1869, p. 3

13 June 1869, Mount Remarkable Tommy, Jimmy Yates, Bullocky Tommy
South Australian Register, Thursday 8 July 1869, p. 2
South Australian Register, Thursday 29 July 1869, p. 2
South Australian Register, Saturday 21 August 1869, p. 3

28 September 1869, child of Sarah Scott, Sarah Scott
Border Watch, Saturday 2 October 1869, p. 2
Border Watch, Saturday 16 October 1869, p. 2

5 February 1870, Yaltilta, Bambenia
South Australian Advertiser, Tuesday 22 February 1870, p. 3
South Australian Register, Saturday 26 February 1870, p. 3
South Australian Advertiser, Tuesday 1 March 1870, p. 3

5 March 1870, Lionel Edwards, William Sedgley, James Dunn
The Northern Argus, Friday 18 March 1870, p. 2
South Australian Register, Saturday 21 May 1870, p. 3

21 March 1870, Mary Legge, William Legge
South Australian Register, Monday 21 March 1870, p. 5
South Australian Register, Tuesday 22 March 1870, p. 5
South Australian Advertiser, Wednesday 18 May 1870, p. 3

28 April 1870, Alexander Barre, William Pomroy
South Australian Advertiser, Wednesday 25 May 1870, p. 3
South Australian Register, Friday 12 August 1870, p. 3

17 June 1870, child of Fanny Dumbledon, Fanny Dumbledon
South Australian Register, Monday 11 July 1870, p. 3
South Australian Advertiser, Saturday 13 August 1870, p. 3

17 June 1870, child of Susannah O'Neil, Susannah O'Neil
South Australian Chronicle and Weekly Mail, Saturday 9 July 1870, p. 11
South Australian Register, Friday 2 December 1870, p. 3

5 August 1870, Edward Gasgoine, Theresa Clarke
South Australian Chronicle and Weekly Mail, Saturday 13 August 1870, p. 4
South Australian Register, Monday 15 August 1870, p. 3
South Australian Advertiser, Tuesday 23 August 1870, p. 3

1 October 1870, Poolpa, Mealie
South Australian Register, Thursday 20 October 1870, p. 5
South Australian Register, Saturday 3 December 1870, p. 3

11 October 1870, child of Mary Partington, Mary Partington
South Australian Advertiser, Thursday 3 November 1870, p. 3
South Australian Advertiser, Thursday 8 December 1870, p. 3
South Australian Register, Friday 9 December 1870, p. 3
South Australian Register, Tuesday 13 December 1870, p. 4

14 November 1870, Hugh Ward, John Edwards
South Australian Register, Friday 18 November 1870, p. 3
South Australian Register, Friday 9 December 1870, p. 3

16 November 1870, James Jeames, Richard Dewdney
South Australian Advertiser, Friday 24 February 1871, p. 3

26 December 1870, Adelaide Jemmy, Donald McPherson
Border Watch, Saturday 31 December 1870, p. 2
Border Watch, Wednesday 22 February 1871, p. 2

2 January 1871, James Smith, Daniel O'Leary
Border Watch, Saturday 22 April 1871, p. 2

30 April 1871, Eliza Douglas, Charles Douglas
South Australian Register, Monday 1 May 1871, p. 5
South Australian Advertiser, Tuesday 2 May, 1871, p. 3
South Australian Advertiser, Thursday 18 May 1871, p. 3
South Australian Advertiser, Friday 26 May 1871, p. 2
South Australian Chronicle and Weekly Mail, Saturday 23 March 1878, p. 18

9 May 1871, child of Elizabeth Little, Elizabeth Little
South Australian Advertiser, Friday 19 May 1871, p. 3
South Australian Advertiser, Wednesday 16 August 1871, p. 2

17 May 1871, George Chisman, John Ramsay
South Australian Register, Wednesday 7 June 1871, p. 6
South Australian Register, Thursday 17 August 1871, p. 3

5 June 1871, William Howard, Sarah Howard
South Australian Advertiser, Thursday 8 June 1871, p. 3
South Australian Advertiser, Friday 11 August 1871, p. 3

29 June 1871, Thomas Garraway, Carl Jung
Border Watch, Wednesday 5 July 1871, p. 3
Border Watch, Saturday 21 October 1871, p. 3
South Australian Register, Saturday 11 November 1871, p. 5

21 December 1871, John Guerin, Ernest Boehm
South Australian Register, Saturday 23 December 1871, p. 3
South Australian Register, Saturday 17 February 1872, p. 3

10 January 1872, child of Christina McGillivray, Christina McGillivray
Border Watch, Saturday 13 January 1872, p. 2
South Australian Register, Thursday 18 April 1872, p. 5
Border Watch, Saturday 20 April 1872, p. 2

6 April 1872, James Burke, Christopher Charlton
South Australian Advertiser, Monday 8 April 1872, p. 2
South Australian Advertiser, Wednesday 10 April 1872, p. 2
South Australian Register, Wednesday 29 May 1872, p. 3

6 April 1872, child of Mary Hayward, Mary Hayward
South Australian Advertiser, Tuesday 9 April 1872, p. 2
South Australian Register, Tuesday 9 April 1872, p. 6
South Australian Advertiser, Friday 17 May 1872, p. 3

30 April 1872, William Mason, James Edwards
South Australian Chronicle and Weekly Mail, Saturday 4 May 1872, p. 6
South Australian Register, Wednesday 29 May 1872, p. 3

7 July 1872, Cheepa, Morcutla
South Australian Advertiser, Tuesday 10 September 1872, p. 3
South Australian Chronicle and Weekly Mail, Saturday 30 November 1872, p. 10

24 July 1872, James McFarlane, John Tynan
South Australian Chronicle and Weekly Mail, Saturday 3 August 1872, p. 6
South Australian Register, Saturday 17 August 1872, p. 3

18 December 1872, Thomas Holyoake, John Hope
South Australian Advertiser, Monday 6 January 1873, p. 3
South Australian Register, Monday 17 February 1873, p. 3

28 December 1872, William Wyatt Jnr, James Slape
South Australian Advertiser, Monday 30 December 1872, p. 2
South Australian Register, Tuesday 31 December 1872, p. 5
South Australian Register, Wednesday 1 January 1873, p. 5

29 March 1873, Ellen Hunt (Laycock), Susan Appleby
South Australian Register, Thursday 10 April 1873, p. 7
South Australian Register, Thursday 22 May 1873, p. 3

15 May 1873, Mary, Narikonyary (Isaac)
South Australian Advertiser, Tuesday 20 May 1873, p. 3
South Australian Chronicle and Weekly Mail, Saturday 24 May 1873, p. 14
South Australian Register, Friday 17 October 1873, p. 3

5 June 1873, Frederick Burt, William Ridgway
South Australian Register, Thursday 21 August 1873, p. 5
South Australian Register, Monday 25 August 1873, p. 5
South Australian Register, Thursday 28 August 1873, p. 3
South Australian Register, Wednesday 10 December 1873, p. 3
South Australian Register, Friday 12 December 1873, p. 3
South Australian Advertiser, Friday 2 January 1874, p. 7

26 July 1873, Charles Withecombe, Joseph Adams, Thomas McLean, William Edgar, Benjamin Rebbeck
South Australian Register, Tuesday 29 July 1873, p. 6
South Australian Advertiser, Friday 15 August 1873, p. 2
South Australian Advertiser, Saturday 23 August 1873, p. 2
South Australian Advertiser, Monday 16 August 1880, p. 4

9 August 1873, Donnaller, Johnny, Dick, Billy
South Australian Advertiser, Tuesday 4 November 1873, p. 3
South Australian Register, Tuesday 18 November 1873, p. 5
Border Watch, Saturday 25 April 1874, p. 3
South Australian Advertiser, Thursday 9 July 1874, p. 2
Border Watch, Saturday 29 August 1874, p. 2

4 September 1873, Thomas Woolcock, Elizabeth Woolcock
South Australian Register, Monday 8 September 1873, p. 6
South Australian Advertiser, Wednesday 3 December 1873, p. 5
South Australian Register, Friday 5 December 1873, p. 4
South Australian Register, Wednesday 31 December 1873, p. 5

7 March 1874, Thomas Hanlin, William Niblock
Kapunda Herald and Northern Intelligencer, Tuesday 10 March 1874, p. 3
South Australian Advertiser, Thursday 18 June 1874, p. 1

19 March 1874, Susannah Moore, William Moore
South Australian Chronicle and Weekly Mail, Saturday 28 March 1874, p. 12
South Australian Advertiser, Saturday 13 June 1874, p. 3

19 May 1874, child of Mary Townsend, Mary A Townsend, Mary Townsend
South Australian Advertiser, Monday 8 June 1874, p. 3
South Australian Advertiser, Tuesday 9 June 1874, p. 3
South Australian Advertiser, Friday 19 June 1874, p. 3

7 June 1874, George Knight, James Cavendish, Joseph Wilson
South Australian Register, Tuesday 9 June 1874, p. 6
South Australian Register, Wednesday 17 June 1874, p. 2

4 July 1874, child of Isabella Stott, Isabella Stott
South Australian Register, Friday 11 September 1874, p. 3

31 August 1874, Bridget Eliza White, Bridget White
South Australian Register, Wednesday 2 September 1874, p. 3
South Australian Register, Friday 11 September 1874, p. 3

2 September 1874, child of Sarah Ballard, Sarah Ballard
South Australian Advertiser, Friday 13 November 1874, p. 3

16 November 1874, John Lewis, Evan Ellis
South Australian Register, Saturday 13 March 1875, p. 3

18 January 1875, Edward McMahon, James Reilley
South Australian Register, Tuesday 19 January 1875, p. 5
South Australian Register, Tuesday 23 March 1875, p. 3

20 January 1875, Timothy Maloney, Catherine Maloney, Charles Merritt, George Northover, Duncan Waddle
South Australian Advertiser, Wednesday 27 January 1875, p. 5
South Australian Advertiser, Thursday 18 March 1875, p. 3

1 February 1875, James Glassenbury, Mary Glassenbury
South Australian Advertiser, Friday 5 February 1875, p. 5
South Australian Register, Tuesday 23 March 1875, p. 3

6 February 1875, child of Caroline Klopp, Caroline Klopp
South Australian Register, Wednesday 10 February 1875, p. 4
South Australian Chronicle and Weekly Mail, Saturday 13 February 1875, p. 7
South Australian Advertiser, Friday 19 March 1875, p. 2
South Australian Register, Thursday 25 March 1875, p. 3

27 February 1875, Sylvia Howard Ellis, Eliza Ellis
South Australian Register, Monday 1 March 1875, p. 3
South Australian Register, Tuesday 2 March 1875, p. 3
South Australian Advertiser, Tuesday 23 March 1875, p. 3

10 March 1875, Harriet Sneyd, George Sneyd
South Australian Register, Tuesday 23 March 1875, p. 6
Border Watch, Saturday 10 April 1875, p. 2
South Australian Register, Friday 30 April 1875, p. 5
South Australian Register, Saturday 22 October 1881, p. 1

5 May 1875, Unknown child, Unknown
South Australian Register, Thursday 6 May 1875, p. 5
South Australian Register, Friday 7 May 1875, p. 5

11 July 1875, Mary Buchan, William Page
Southern Argus, Thursday 5 August 1875, p. 3
South Australian Register, Saturday 7 August 1875, p. 5
South Australian Register, Thursday 7 October 1875, p. 5
South Australian Register, Thursday 28 October 1875, p. 5

24 July 1875, Female child, Unknown
South Australian Advertiser, Wednesday 28 July 1875, p. 7

November 1875, Coolcawaninie, Milly Ingarlta, Coongulta, Wongie
South Australian Register, Thursday 23 December 1875, p. 5
South Australian Advertiser, Monday 21 February 1876, p. 4
South Australian Register, Friday 24 March 1876, p. 3

1 February 1876, Hanchie, Chelengie
South Australian Register, Friday 24 March 1876, p. 3

28 April 1876, child of Lavinia Cox, Lavinia Cox
South Australian Register, Thursday 4 May 1876, p. 6
South Australian Advertiser, Saturday 17 June 1876, p. 6
South Australian Register, Tuesday 20 June 1876, p. 3

22 June 1876, Mary James, John Harman
South Australian Advertiser, Saturday 24 June 1876, p. 6
South Australian Advertiser, Thursday 21 September 1876, p. 6
South Australian Advertiser, Thursday 28 September 1876, p. 7

10 September 1876, Ellen Benjamin, Benjamin
Southern Argus, Thursday 14 September 1876, p. 3
Border Watch, Saturday 16 September 1876, p. 3
Southern Argus, Thursday 21 September 1876, p. 3

17 November 1876, Lucy Capel, Alfred Dickinson
South Australian Register, Saturday 18 November 1876, p. 6
South Australian Advertiser, Wednesday 22 November 1876, p. 6
South Australian Register, Thursday 22 March 1877, p. 3

References

18 November 1876, James Grant Walsh, Felix O'Neill

South Australian Advertiser, Tuesday 21 November 1876, p. 5

South Australian Register, Thursday 5 April 1877, p. 3

South Australian Advertiser, Monday 9 April 1877, p. 3

14 December 1876, Frederick Went, William Hocking

South Australian Chronicle and Weekly Mail, Saturday 23 December 1876, p. 10

South Australian Register, Thursday 29 March 1877, p. 3

South Australian Advertiser, Friday 30 March 1877, p. 3

15 December 1876, William Knox, Winginia (Sambo)

South Australian Register, Wednesday 17 October 1877, p. 5

South Australian Register, Saturday 17 November 1877, pp. 3, 5

South Australian Advertiser, Wednesday 21 November 1877, p. 7

South Australian Register, Wednesday 21 November 1877, p. 3

25 December 1876, Gertrude Dudley, John Dudley

South Australian Advertiser, Thursday 4 January 1877, p. 5

South Australian Advertiser, Wednesday 28 March 1877, p. 3

South Australian Register, Thursday 5 April 1877, p. 3

South Australian Advertiser, Thursday 22 April 1880, p. 5

South Australian Register, Wednesday 11 December 1889, p. 7

6 January 1877, Robert Rogers, Thomas Gale

South Australian Register, Thursday 5 April 1877, p. 5

South Australian Register, Tuesday 19 June 1877, p. 3

25 February 1877, Unknown female infant, Unknown

South Australian Advertiser, Tuesday 27 February 1877, p. 5

April 1877, Mary Myles, William Myles

South Australian Advertiser, Wednesday 18 April 1877, p. 6

South Australian Register, Wednesday 13 June 1877. P5

State Library of South Australia, B 7006, Head and upper body portrait of William Edwards, 1851

18 April 1877, Robert Woodhead, Charles Streitman

South Australian Advertiser, Friday 20 April 1877, p. 6

South Australian Advertiser, Wednesday 27 June 1877, p. 6

South Australian Advertiser, Wednesday 25 July 1877, p. 6

19 April 1877, Margaret Hurley, Matthew Elsegood

South Australian Advertiser, Friday 27 April 1877, p. 7

South Australian Register, Wednesday 20 June 1877, p. 3

State Library of South Australia, B 32143, Sturt Road, Marion approximately 1880

August 1877, Henry Graham, Coochinna, Waragutty Pallina
South Australian Register, Saturday 8 February 1879, p. 5
South Australian Register, Saturday 12 April 1879, p. 6

20 October 1877, Hannah Morgan, Walter Bucke
South Australian Register, Friday 9 November 1877, p. 6
South Australian Register, Monday 26 November 1877, p. 5
South Australian Advertiser, Saturday 16 March 1878, p. 6

18 November 1877, Alexander Ness, James Day
South Australian Advertiser, Saturday 2 February 1878, p. 7

26 November 1877, Patrick Bannan, Hugh Fagan
South Australian Advertiser, Wednesday 28 November 1877, p. 5
South Australian Register, Wednesday 28 November 1877, p. 5
Southern Argus, Thursday 29 November 1877, p. 3
South Australian Register, Wednesday 20 March 1878, p. 1
South Australian Advertiser, Wednesday 17 April 1878, p. 6

December 1877, Chunkey, Woomatie, Koolma, Warpooka
The Wallaroo Times and Mining Journal, Saturday 15 December 1877, p. 3
South Australian Register, Thursday 21 March 1878, p. 1
South Australian Advertiser, Tuesday 9 April 1878, p. 5
http://www.burrahistory.info/BurraRedruthGaol.htm

8 December 1877, Marty Cullinan, John McGillicuddy, Michael Foley, James Richardson, Michael Cahill, George Culhane, Jeremiah Hannafin, Edward Staunton, William Richards, William McGowan
The *South Australian Register*, Saturday 29 December 1877, p. 4
South Australian Advertiser, Saturday 23 March 1878, p. 7
South Australian Register, Monday 25 March 1878, p. 3

25 December 1877, Michael Doyle, William Webb
The Australian Register, Monday 31 December 1877, p. 5
South Australian Advertiser, Saturday 16 March 1878, p. 6

12 March 1878, Mary Prest, Jonathan Prest
South Australian Advertiser, Wednesday 13 March 1878, p. 6
South Australian Register, Thursday 14 March 1878, p. 4
South Australian Chronicle and Weekly Mail, Saturday 22 June 1878, pp. 11, 12

18 March 1878, John Kennedy, John Sheehan
South Australian Register, Friday 22 March 1878, p. 5
South Australian Register, Friday 22 June 1878, p. 3
State Library of South Australia, PRG 1258/2/767, Bogan Hotel, Mannum 1877

References

27 March 1878, Cornelius Mulhall, Logic
South Australian Register, Thursday 25 November 1880, p. 5
South Australian Chronicle and Weekly Mail, Saturday 26 February 1881, p. 19
South Australian Advertiser, Saturday 17 October 1885, p. 4
The Naracoorte Herald, Friday 11 December 1885, p. 3

10 April 1878, Mount Brown Charley, Murrayon
South Australian Advertiser, Monday 15 April 1878, p. 7
South Australian Chronicle and Weekly Mail, Saturday 27 April 1878, p. 7
South Australian Advertiser, Wednesday 21 May 1879, p. 5
South Australian Advertiser, Saturday 9 August 1879, p. 6
Border Watch, Wednesday 3 September 1879, p. 3

1 July 1878, Female child, Unknown
South Australian Register, Wednesday 10 July 1878, p. 5

9 July 1878, Henry Farrell Mansell, Henry Burke
South Australian Advertiser, Friday 12 July 1878, p. 6
South Australian Advertiser, Monday 15 July 1878, p. 5
South Australian Chronicle and Weekly Mail, Saturday 20 July 1878, p. 8
South Australian Advertiser, Thursday 19 September 1878, p. 6

8 August 1878, child of Lucy McNeil, Lucy McNeill
South Australian Advertiser, Thursday 15 August 1878, p. 5
South Australian Register, Wednesday 21 August 1878, p. 4
South Australian Chronicle and Weekly Mail, Saturday 5 October 1878, p. 10

11 August 1878, Sarah Lowe, Thomas Bascombe, Mary Bascombe
South Australian Chronicle and Weekly Mail, Saturday 17 August 1878, p. 7
South Australian Chronicle and Weekly Mail, Saturday 17 August 1878, p. 21
South Australian Advertiser, Saturday 21 September 1878, p. 6

19 August 1878, John Pells, Thomas Harrop
The Wallaroo Times and Mining Journal, Wednesday 28 August 1878, p. 2
South Australian Register, Thursday 26 September 1878, p. 2

28 October 1878, Benedict Suck, David Smith
South Australian Register, Friday 1 November 1878, p. 6
South Australian Advertiser, Friday 1 November 1878, p. 6
South Australian Advertiser, Saturday 23 November 1878, p. 4
South Australian Chronicle and Weekly Mail, Saturday 30 November 1878, p. 11

7 November 1878, Walter Long Couzner, Catherine McCaffrey
South Australian Register, Saturday 9 November 1878, p. 3
South Australian Advertiser, Saturday 23 November 1878, p. 4

14 November 1878, James Crabb, W Bennets, Edward Quintrell, John Roberts
The Wallaroo Times and Mining Journal, Saturday 16 November 1878, p. 2
South Australian Register, Wednesday 19 March 1879, p. 1
South Australian Advertiser, Thursday 20 March 1879, p. 6

20 November 1878, William Murnane, William Wilkinson
South Australian Advertiser, Thursday 27 March 1879, p. 4
South Australian Chronicle and Weekly Mail, Saturday 29 March 1879, p. 11

12 December 1878, Sarah Fergusson, David Fergusson
South Australian Register, Saturday 1 February 1879, p. 6
South Australian Advertiser, Saturday 1 February 1879, p. 6
South Australian Advertiser, Saturday 29 March 1879, p. 6

12 June 1879, Mary Kain, Abigail Fitzgerald
South Australian Advertiser, Saturday 14 June 1879, p. 6
South Australian Register, Thursday 21 August 1879, p. 6

9 June 1879, Annie Statton, Unknown
Burra Record, Friday 20 June 1879, p. 3
South Australian Register, Friday 20 June 1879, p. 6
South Australian Chronicle and Weekly Mail, Saturday 21 June 1879, p. 11

21 June 1879, James O'Leary, Herman Stubing
South Australian Chronicle and Weekly Mail, Saturday 23 August 1879, p. 11

17 July 1879, child of Johanna Sullivan, Johanna Sullivan
South Australian Advertiser, Monday 28 July 1879, p. 5
South Australian Advertiser, Wednesday 20 August 1879, p. 6
Border Watch, Wednesday 3 September 1879, p. 3

24 July 1879, Emma Wildy, Charles Harvey
South Australian Advertiser, Friday 25 July 1879, p. 5
South Australian Register, Friday 25 July 1879, p. 6
South Australian Advertiser, Saturday 26 July 1879, p. 6
Border Watch, Wednesday 30 July 1879, p. 3

2 September 1879, John Golding, George White
South Australian Advertiser, Tuesday 16 September 1879, p. 7
South Australian Chronicle and Weekly Mail, Saturday 11 October 1879, p. 10

4 January 1880, Robert Salomon, Ellen Salomon
South Australian Chronicle and Weekly Mail, Saturday 10 January 1880, p. 10
South Australian Register, Thursday 26 February 1880, p. 1

References

25 January 1880, Margaret O'Brien, John O'Brien
South Australian Advertiser, Thursday 5 February 1880, p. 6
South Australian Register, Wednesday 3 March 1880, p. 1

31 January 1880, Thomas Whitlock, Thomas Quinn, George Odey
South Australian Advertiser, Saturday 7 February 1880, pp. 5, 6

1 February 1880, Thomas Quinn, James Viant
South Australian Register, Friday 6 February 1880, p. 6
South Australian Register, Thursday 4 March 1880, p. 1

2 June 1880, James Ford, John Dignum, William Norgrove, Margaret Dignum, Bridget McNamara
South Australian Advertiser, Wednesday 16 June 1880, p. 6
South Australian Advertiser, Wednesday 11 August 1880, p. 7

12 September 1880, child of Louisa Clark, Louisa Clark
South Australian Register, Thursday 14 October 1880, p. 6

31 October 1880, William Bell, William Walsh
South Australian Advertiser, Saturday 11 December 1880, p. 6

7 November 1880, Mary Ann Hartigan, Barbara Hartigan, Jeremiah Hartigan
South Australian Register, Wednesday 10 November 1880, p. 6
South Australian Advertiser, Wednesday 23 February 1881, p. 9
South Australian Register, Wednesday 23 February 1881, p. 1

10 November 1880, child of Mary Ann Ford, Mary Ann Ford
Kapunda Herald, Tuesday 16 November 1880, p. 4
South Australian Advertiser, Friday 19 November 1880, p. 6
South Australian Register, Saturday 20 November 1880, p. 6
South Australian Register, Friday 10 December 1880, p. 6

26 January 1881, Mary Kubale, Johann Kubale
South Australian Advertiser, Thursday 27 January 1881, p. 5
South Australian Register, Saturday 29 January 1881, p. 6
South Australian Advertiser, Tuesday 8 February 1881, p. 7
South Australian Register, Wednesday 13 April 1881, p. 7
South Australian Weekly Chronicle, Saturday 16 April 1881, p. 13

15 February 1881, Patrick Brady, James Martin
South Australian Advertiser, Monday 21 February 1881, p. 7
South Australian Chronicle and Weekly Mail, Saturday 9 April 1881, p. 13

17 March 1881, Eliza Beveridge, James Beveridge
South Australian Advertiser, Friday 1 April 1881, p. 6

South Australian Register, Friday 22 April 1881, p. 6
South Australian Advertiser, Wednesday 5 August 1885, p. 3

22 March 1881, William Cuffe, Honora Dunn

South Australian Register, Tuesday 22 March 1881, p. 6
South Australian Register, Saturday 9 April 1881, p. 1
South Australian Register, Friday 10 June 1881, p. 2

April 1881, Unknown Aboriginal, Aboriginal

South Australian Advertiser, Saturday 18 February 1882, p. 3

18 April 1881, Richard Dyer, William Giles

South Australian Register, Saturday 11 June 1881, p. 1
State Library of South Australia, B 7814, Sea View Hotel, Port Willunga, 1882

16 May 1881, Harry Edmond Pearce, Robert Johnston

Border Watch, Saturday 21 May 1881, p. 3
Border Watch, Saturday 22 October 1881, p. 3
South Australian Advertiser, Saturday 19 November 1881, p. 6

26 May 1881, Annie Marovitch, John Marovitch

South Australian Register, Saturday 28 May 1881, p. 6
South Australian Register, Monday 30 May 1881, p. 5
South Australian Advertiser, Tuesday 7 June 1881, p. 5
South Australian Register, Thursday 11 August 1881, p. 3

24 June 1881, Emma Trye, Henry Trye

South Australian Register, Wednesday 29 June 1881, p. 6
South Australian Register, Friday 12 August 1881, p. 2

1 July 1881, John Holmes, John Wilson

South Australian Advertiser, Monday 4 July 1881, p. 6
South Australian Register, Saturday 6 August 1881, p. 5

19 July 1881, Female child, Unknown

South Australian Register, Tuesday 2 August 1881, p. 1

21 September 1881, William Clark, Joseph Clark, Charles Clark

South Australian Register, Tuesday 11 October 1881, p. 5
Border Watch, Wednesday 12 October 1881, p. 3
South Australian Register, Thursday 13 October 1881, p. 6
South Australian Advertiser, Friday 14 October 1881, p. 2

10 January 1882, John Thompson, Morris Ewens

South Australian Register, Saturday 14 January 1882, p. 2

References

South Australian Advertiser, Saturday 14 January 1882, p. 6

South Australian Advertiser, Wednesday 8 March 1882, p. 7

20 January 1882, Ellen Blake, Johanna Mullins

South Australian Advertiser, Monday 23 January 1882, p. 6

South Australian Advertiser, Tuesday 21 February 1882, p. 4

South Australia Supreme Court records

1 February 1882, child of Mina Papst, Mina Papst

South Australian Register, Friday 3 February 1882, p. 7

South Australian Advertiser, Tuesday 14 February 1882, p. 6

South Australian Register, Tuesday 14 February 1882, p. 6

South Australian Advertiser, Saturday 4 March 1882, p. 7

9 February 1882, Edward Lounder, Margaret Harris

South Australian Register, Friday 17 February 1882, p. 6

South Australian Advertiser, Friday 17 February 1882, p. 6

South Australian Register, Thursday 9 March 1882, p. 6

15 March 1882, Emma Wilkins, Margaret Wilkins, James Wilkins

South Australian Weekly Chronicle, Saturday 25 March 1882, p. 13

South Australian Advertiser, Friday 7 April 1882, p. 7

April 1882, Male child, Unknown

South Australian Advertiser, Saturday 6 May 1882, p. 4

South Australian Register, Saturday 20 May 1882, p. 1

South Australian Register, Tuesday 30 May 1882, p. 7

19 June 1882, Coonah, Jenniebutta Monyah

South Australian Advertiser, Wednesday 11 October 1882, p. 2

South Australian Register, Wednesday 11 October 1882, p. 3

3 October 1882, Thomas Maloney, Arthur Saddler, William Chidley, Unknown male

South Australian Register, Tuesday 17 October 1882, p. 2

South Australian Register, Tuesday 24 October 1882, p. 2

South Australian Register, Friday 8 December 1882, p. 7

9 November 1882, Alice Tree, Henry Page

South Australian Register, Tuesday 14 November 1882, p. 2

South Australian Register, Saturday 16 December 1882, p. 2

12 November 1882, Christian Renderup, Patrick McGree, Elizabeth McGree, Margaret McGree

South Australian Register, Tuesday 14 November 1882, p. 2

South Australian Advertiser, Thursday 16 November 1882, p. 6

South Australian Advertiser, Thursday 21 December 1882, p. 6

Border Watch, Saturday 23 December 1882, p. 3

South Australian Register, Saturday 6 January 1883, p. 1

17 December 1882, child of Mary Howard, Mary Howard

South Australian Advertiser, Thursday 28 December 1882, p. 5

South Australian Advertiser, Thursday 4 January 1883, p. 6

South Australian Advertiser, Wednesday 28 February 1883, p. 6

25 December 1882, Marian Todd, John Reid, Adolph Heise, James Ford, John Minnis, Samuel Mead, Henry Purvis, William Baker

South Australian Register, Wednesday 27 December 1882, p. 6

South Australian Advertiser, Thursday 4 January 1883, p. 6

South Australian Register, Saturday 24 February 1883, p. 7

10 February 1883, John O'Brien, John Clymas

South Australian Register, Wednesday 14 February 1883, p. 7

South Australian Register, Friday 2 March 1883, p. 7

12 February 1883, James Officer, Margaret Officer

South Australian Register, Wednesday 14 February 1883, p. 7

South Australian Register, Friday 2 March 1883, p. 7

7 March 1883, Unknown child, Unknown

South Australian Register, Saturday 17 March 1883, p. 7

1 May 1883, Martha Scatcheard, James Oakley

South Australian Register, Thursday 3 May 1883, p. 7

South Australian Register, Saturday 5 May 1883, p. 6

South Australian Advertiser, Friday 8 June 1883, p. 3

10 August 1883, Tommy Ah Fook, Mah Poo, Way Lee Yung

South Australian Register, Wednesday 15 August 1883, p. 7

South Australian Advertiser, Saturday 18 August 1883, p. 9

South Australian Register, Monday 27 August 1883, p. 7

South Australian Advertiser, Wednesday 3 October 1883, p. 7

South Australian Register, Wednesday 10 October 1883, p. 2

South Australian Advertiser, Thursday 11 October 1883, p. 3

South Australian Register, Friday 12 October 1883, p. 7

South Australian Advertiser, Monday 15 October 1883, p. 1

South Australian Register, Monday 5 November 1883, p. 6

References

2 September 1883, Ellen Tench, William Tench
South Australian Advertiser, Wednesday 5 September 1883, p. 6
South Australian Advertiser, Wednesday 3 October 1883, p. 7

January 1884, Male Child, Unknown
South Australian Advertiser, Wednesday 30 January 1884, p. 7
South Australian Register, Wednesday 30 January 1884, p. 6

30 January 1884, William Macklin, John Adams
South Australian Register, Tuesday 5 February 1884, p. 7
South Australian Register, Friday 21 March 1884, p. 5
South Australian Register, Monday 24 March 1884, p. 1

4 March 1884, Andrew Kiddie, Mary Kiddie
South Australian Register, Monday 17 March 1884, p. 7
Wallaroo Times, Wednesday 19 March 1884, p. 2
South Australian Weekly Chronicle, Saturday 5 April 1884, p. 12

10 June 1884, Margaret Buxton, John Woodhead
South Australian Register, Saturday 14 June 1884, p. 7
South Australian Advertiser, Friday 8 August 1884, p. 4
South Australian Advertiser, Saturday 9 August 1994, p. 3

15 June 1884, child of Emma Gaskin, Emma Gaskin
South Australian Advertiser, Saturday 5 July 1884, p. 7
South Australian Advertiser, Thursday 7 July 1884, p. 5

3 August 1884, Peter Conway, Patrick McGrath
South Australian Register, Wednesday 6 August 1884, p. 6
South Australian Register, Tuesday 12 August 1884, p. 3
Border Watch, Wednesday 13 August 1884, p. 3
Southern Argus, Thursday 14 August 1884, p. 3
South Australian Advertiser, Thursday 4 September 1884, p. 6
South Australian Weekly Chronicle, Saturday 27 September 1884, p. 11
Northern Argus, Tuesday 14 October 1884, p. 3

15 August 1884, Martin Kenihan, James Kelly
South Australian Advertiser, Monday 18 August 1884, p. 6
South Australian Advertiser, Tuesday 19 August 1884, p. 6
South Australian Register, Thursday 9 October 1884, p. 7
South Australian Advertiser, Thursday 9 October 1884, p. 3

24 August 1884, William Templer, John Templer
South Australian Weekly Chronicle, Saturday 30 August 1884, p. 8
South Australian Advertiser, Friday 10 October 1884, p. 6

24 August 1884, Male child, Unknown
South Australian Advertiser, Wednesday 27 August 1884, p. 6
South Australian Register, Wednesday 3 September 1884, p. 6
South Australian Advertiser, Wednesday 10 September 1884, p. 6

15 September 1884, Marion Kelly, William Bissett
South Australian Advertiser, Wednesday 24 September 1884, p. 7
South Australian Register, Friday 10 October 1884, p. 3

3 November 1884, William Howe, Johannes Larsen, Auguste Wehr, Frank Tantow
South Australian Advertiser, Thursday 6 November 1884, p. 6
South Australian Advertiser, Friday 7 November 1884, p. 6
South Australian Advertiser, Friday 5 December 1884, p. 7
South Australian Register, Monday 15 December 1884, p. 7

20 December 1884, Male child, Unknown
South Australian Register, Wednesday 24 December 1884, p. 3
South Australian Advertiser, Saturday 27 December 1884, p. 5
South Australian Advertiser, Wednesday 7 January 1885, p. 6
South Australian Register, Thursday 15 January 1885, p. 7

24 December 1884, Male child, Unknown
South Australian Advertiser, Saturday 27 December 1884, p. 5
South Australian Register, Saturday 27 December 1884, p. 2
South Australian Register, Thursday 8 January 1885, p. 3
South Australian Register, Saturday 17 January 1885, p. 7

24 December 1884, child of Emma Lennox, Emma Lennox
South Australian Register, Saturday 27 December 1884, p. 2
South Australian Weekly Chronicle, Saturday 21 March 1885, p. 21

27 March 1885, William August Hebberman, Mary Cotter
South Australian Register, Tuesday 31 March 1885, p. 3
South Australian Advertiser, Tuesday 31 March 1885, p. 6
South Australian Register, Thursday 16 April 1885, p. 3

24 May 1885, Charlotte Neiass, Albert Gurney
South Australian Weekly Chronicle, Saturday 13 June 1885, p. 5
Northern Argus, Tuesday 28 July 1885, p. 2

12 June 1885, Elizabeth Lines, Alfred Lines, Maurice O'Connor
Burra Record, Tuesday 16 June 1885, p. 3

16 June 1885, Peter Demell, Sydney
South Australian Register, Tuesday 23 June 1885, p. 5

References

17 June 1885, Male child, Unknown

South Australian Advertiser, Saturday 27 June 1885, p. 6

South Australian Advertiser, Tuesday 7 July 1885, p. 7

July 1885, Female Child, Unknown

South Australian Weekly Chronicle, Saturday 18 July 1885, p. 10

South Australian Advertiser, Thursday 23 July 1885, p. 4

11 August 1885, Maria Carroll, Edward Carroll

South Australian Register, Wednesday 12 August 1885, p. 7

South Australian Register, Wednesday 19 August 1885, p. 7

South Australian Advertiser, Friday 9 October 1885, p. 6

South Australian Weekly Chronicle, Saturday 10 October 1885, p. 22

South Australian Advertiser, Friday 26 March 1886, p. 5

3 December 1885, William James, Reinhold Marquardt

South Australian Advertiser, Saturday 5 December 1885, p. 5

South Australian Advertiser, Monday 7 December 1885, p. 5

South Australian Register, Thursday 18 February 1886, p. 3

9 December 1885, Male child, Unknown

South Australian Register, Thursday 17 December 1885, p. 6

December 1885, John Reardon, John Flannagan

South Australian Advertiser, Saturday 12 December 1885, p. 5

South Australian Register, Thursday 17 December 1885, p. 5

South Australian Register, Monday 21 December 1885, p. 6

26 April 1886, Albert Ossedton, James Forrest

The Express and Telegraph, Wednesday 11 August 1886, p. 3

Evening Journal, Wednesday 11 August 1886, p. 4

South Australian Register, Wednesday 1 December 1886, p. 4

Evening Journal, Tuesday 14 December 1886, p. 2

27 April 1886, Unknown child, Unknown

South Australian Advertiser, Wednesday 12 May 1886, p. 5

Statistics

Rate of murder per 100,000

Population data from Australian Bureau of Statistics

Year	Estimated Population	Rate of murders per 100,000	Solved	Unsolved	Total
1836	546	0	0	0	0
1837	3273	61.1	0	2	2
1838	6000	50	2	1	3
1839	10315	38.8	3	1	4
1840	14630	205.1	28	2	30
1841	15485	12.9	2	0	2
1842	16340	42.8	5	2	7
1843	17196	17.4	3	0	3
1844	18999	21.1	3	1	4
1845	22460	13.4	2	1	3
1846	25893	23.2	6	0	6
1847	31153	3.2	1	0	1
1848	38666	10.3	4	0	4
1849	52904	45.4	19	5	24
1850	63700	14.1	8	1	9
1851	66538	13.5	8	1	9
1852	68663	10.2	6	1	7
1853	78944	11.4	9	0	9
1854	92545	5.4	5	0	5
1855	97387	7.2	5	2	7
1856	107886	5.6	6	0	6
1857	109917	7.3	8	0	8
1858	118665	3.4	3	1	4
1859	122735	4.9	5	1	6
1860	125582	2.4	3	0	3
1861	130812	6.9	9	0	9

1862	136562	8.1	11	0	11
1863	142784	4.9	7	0	7
1864	150754	2.7	4	0	4
1865	161477	3.7	6	0	6
1866	168907	2.4	3	1	4
1867	172875	4.0	6	1	7
1868	176568	3.4	6	0	6
1869	181607	1.7	3	0	3
1870	184546	6.0	11	0	11
1871	188644	3.7	7	0	7
1872	191828	4.2	8	0	8
1873	197685	3.0	6	0	6
1874	204246	3.9	8	0	8
1875	210076	4.8	8	2	10
1876	224560	4.0	9	0	9
1877	238155	8.4	17	3	20
1878	252099	6.3	15	1	16
1879	265055	2.3	5	1	6
1880	276393	3.3	9	0	9
1881	285971	4.5	11	2	13
1882	292092	4.1	11	1	12
1883	301907	2.0	5	1	6
1884	308947	4.5	11	3	14
1885	309313	3.6	8	3	11
1886*	306710	0.7	1	1	2
			Solved	**Unsolved**	
			89.3%	**10.7%**	

Average murders per year = 7.8
*Only six months of data (to 30 June) available for 1886

Number of victims, 1836–1886*

Adult victims	275
Child victims (excluding newborns)	48
Newborn victims	68
Total child victims	116

Only six months of data (to 30 June) available for 1886

Relationship between accused and child victim

Mother	57
Newborn; parent not located	19
Stranger	19
Offender known to child	8
Carer of child	5
Father	4
Partner of child	2
Step-parent	1
Procedure during birth	1
	116

Cause of death

Assault, no weapon	67
Assault with weapon	65
Spear wound/s	65
Gunshot wound/s	36
Strangluation/ Asphyxiation/ Hanging	33
Neglect	33
Knife/ blade wound/s	35
Unknown	18
Drowning	17
Poisoning	9
Vehicle collision	5
Medical procedure	4
Explosion	3
Fire	1

Relationship between accused and victim

Accused	Male Victim	Female Victim	Unknown Gender	Total
Offender stranger to victim	98	28	6	132
Friends/ acquaintances/ workmates	105	8	0	113
Mother of victim/ parent not found	39	34	3	76
Father of victim	3	1	0	4
Married, defacto or intimate relationship	3	35	0	38
Unknown	12	3	0	15
Carer	4	1	0	5
Healthcare provider (doctor/ nurse/ other)	2	1	0	3
Daughter or Son in-law	0	2	0	2
Mother or Father in-law	1	1	0	2
Step-parent	0	1	0	1

Age and gender of victim and accused

	Female Victim	Male Victim	Unknown gender Victim	Female Accused	Male Accused
Unknown age	36	153	5	56	245
Under 1	39	40	2	0	0
1 to 4	5	4	0	0	0
5 to 9	3	5	0	0	0
10 to 14	2	8	0	2	1
15 to 17	4	2	0	6	2
18 to 24	8	20	0	21	29
25 to 29	1	4	0	9	20
30 to 34	6	7	0	4	17
35 to 39	4	7	0	0	0
40 to 44	0	3	0	3	8
45 to 49	3	7	0	0	0
50 to 54	1	1	0	0	2
55 to 59	2	0	0	0	4
60 to 64	2	4	0	0	2
65 to 69	2	0	0	0	0
70 to 74	1	0	0	0	1
75 to 79	0	0	0	0	0
80 +	0	0	0	0	0
Subtotal	119	265	7	101	331
	Total Victims	391		Total Accused	432

Ethnicity relationship between victims and suspects or accused

270 Europeans were accused or suspected of murdering 237 Europeans

19 Europeans were accused or suspected of murdering 31 Aboriginal people

91 Aboriginal people were accused or suspected of murdering 46 Aboriginal people

79 Aboriginal people were accused or suspected of murdering 73 Europeans

1 Aboriginal person was accused of murdering 1 Indian person

2 Chinese people were accused of murdering 1 Chinese person

1 Lascar was accused of murdering 1 Europeans

1 Malayan person was accused of murdering 1 Malayan person

Individual accused results

Acquitted/ discharged, not insane	174
Guilty of manslaughter	95
Guilty of murder, executed	40
Guilty of murder, sentence commuted	26
Guilty of concealment of birth	21
Charges withdrawn	11
Unknown outcome	11
Found guilty of other offence	9
Known offender not located	9
Offender committed suicide before trial	7
Offender died before trial	5
Found insane	6
Nolle prosequi entered	6
Offender escaped custody, not located	4
Case dismissed	3
Criminal neglect	1

Names of People

Key

(A) = Accused or Suspect

(V) = Victim

(O) = Other

(P) = Police

(Dr) = Doctor

A

C

D

E

H

K

L

M

N

S

V

W

Place of Crime

N

P

Cause of Death

A

H

K

M

N

P

R

S

Domestic Violence

Key

(A) = Accused

(V) = Victim

Ashton's Hotel
The journal of William Baker Ashton, first governor of the Adelaide Gaol

Rhondda Harris

South Australia was meant to be the perfect colony: free settlers, no crime, and no mental illness. But good intentions go awry. Within three years plans for a permanent gaol were well established, along with a governor to oversee it: William Baker Ashton.

Researcher Rhondda Harris came upon Ashton's long-lost journal by happy accident, and was soon absorbed by 'The Governor's' handwritten pages. They told a hidden story of early Adelaide and its underbelly, of crashes and crises and crims. 'Ashton's Hotel', the colonists called their prison. His kindness of spirit, under nigh-impossible circumstances, shines through in this first published edition of his journal, expertly contextualised and introduced by Rhondda Harris.

'A great strength of the book is the editorial work of Rhondda Harris, who has added to the journal some insightful background on both the document and its times, and moreover inserts linking narratives between sections of entries and perceptive commentaries on the gaol, its governor, and its interesting times.'

– Peter Monteath, *Journal of the Historical Society of South Australia*

Out of the Silence
The history and memory of
South Australia's frontier wars

Robert Foster and Amanda Nettelbeck

When South Australia was founded in 1836, the British government was pursuing a new approach to the treatment of Aboriginal people, hoping to avoid the violence that marked earlier Australian settlement. The colony's founding Proclamation declared that as British subjects, Aboriginal people would be as much 'under the safeguard of the law as the Colonists themselves, and equally entitled to the privileges of British subjects'. But could colonial governments provide the protection that was promised?

Out of the Silence explores the nature and extent of violence on South Australia's frontiers in light of the foundational promise to provide Aboriginal people with the protection of the law, and the resonances of that history in social memory. What do we find when we compare the history of the frontier with the patterns of how it is remembered and forgotten? And what might this reveal about our understanding of the nation's history and its legacies in the present?

'*Out of the Silence* is a comprehensive examination of the nature and extent of violence between Aboriginal people and colonists on the South Australian and Northern Territory frontiers.'

– Nic Klaassen, *Flinders Ranges Research*

Wakefield Press is an independent publishing and
distribution company based in Adelaide, South Australia.
We love good stories and publish beautiful books.
To see our full range of books, please visit our website at
www.wakefieldpress.com.au
where all titles are available for purchase.
To keep up with our latest releases, news and events,
subscribe to our monthly newsletter.

Find us!

Facebook: www.facebook.com/wakefield.press
Twitter: www.twitter.com/wakefieldpress
Instagram: www.instagram.com/wakefieldpress